BEYOND
TRAINING

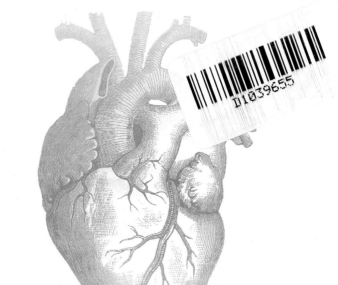

MASTERING ENDURANCE,
HEALTH, AND LIFE

BEN
GREENFIELD

Victory Belt Publishing, Inc.
Las Vegas

This book is for every high achiever, exercise enthusiast, weekend warrior, gym junkie, biohacker, and health nut who wants to achieve amazing feats of physical, mental, and lifestyle performance without destroying their body, mind, and life.

ACKNOWLEDGMENTS

The inspiration for this book came from the readers and listeners of BenGreenfieldFitness.com. Every day, your honest questions, creative feedback, and committed engagement helped me realize that all of you have amazing physical goals that you want achieve—and, to your credit, you really don't want to destroy your bodies, your families, and your lives in the process. You are the reason I do what I do.

Thanks also to my wife, Jessa, who is an amazing woman, superhero mother, pillar of support, and warm body for me to hug when I'm stressed out about chapter deadlines or writer's block. I am not sure if I should thank her for cooking, because I probably would have written this book much sooner if I hadn't been pulled away to the dinner table by her nightly presentations of aromatic cuisine.

Thanks to my twin boys, River and Terran, who are fully responsible for any typos you may find in this book, as finding the proper letter on a keyboard is more difficult when being attacked by two armed and caped villains who want to engage you in brutal wrestling matches.

Thanks to my parents, who taught me how to read, write, and spell (literally—I was homeschooled) and also served as chaperones and sponsors for tennis, soccer, basketball, running, bicycling, weight lifting, and any other sport I begged to do.

Thanks to Brock Armstrong, my sidekick on the podcast and trusted go-to man for strange tasks; to Eleanor Pell, who helped me with research and citations, which I'm notoriously bad at; to Trevor Parks, my Facebook and social media ninja; to Marge Aberasturi, my right-hand personal assistant; to Jake Perrin, my awesome web dude; and to the team at Victory Belt for making this book beautiful.

Thanks to all the mentors, coaches, and teachers who have taught me about fitness, nutrition, and healthy living—Rafael Escamilla, Kathy Browder, PZ Pearce, Roby Mitchell, David Minkoff, Todd Schlapfer, Nora Gedgaudas, Phil Maffetone, Dave Asprey, Peter Attia, Mark Sisson, Robb Wolf, Roger Drummer, Jeffrey Spencer, Tim Noakes—this list could go on and on. Please never underestimate the power of sharing your knowledge—it certainly made a difference in my life.

And, of course, thanks once again to you. You inspire many, many people when you decide to achieve your dream. And I'm one of them.

TABLE OF CONTENTS

Part 3. NUTRITION

Part 4. LIFESTYLE

Part 5. THE BRAIN

FOREWORD

I've had a huge passion for fitness and endurance ever since I was a young boy. As a fifteen-year-old, I could tell you all about the brutality of the Kona lava fields, where the legendary Ironman Hawaii takes place. I knew about the freezing cold waters of San Francisco Bay faced by the athletes in the Escape from Alcatraz triathlon. I could look you in the eye and tell you with absolute conviction that Ironman Europe in Roth, Germany, was the toughest Ironman to win because the Europeans raced so well at home.

I knew all the winners of the famous Wildflower Triathlon in California, the bike-record times on the Chicago course, and the fact that the "big four" really should have been the "big five," with the inclusion of the great Mike Pigg. There was nothing about this sport I didn't know, and I had a thirst for information like nothing else. I was not only a fitness fanatic, but also a triathlon geek, and no sport in the world meant more to me.

I still have that same thirst for knowledge. From the time I became a pro triathlete and began winning the races in all those cities I read about as a boy, I've spent countless hours with the best physiologists and sports scientists in the world, in Australian heat chambers and on the toughest racecourses you can imagine, learning and soaking up the most cutting-edge information I could find.

And through that process I've discovered that what happens in the lab does not always correlate with the realities of what happens out in the field. Many things look great on paper (or on a computer screen), but keeping an open mind, adapting, and spending time on the ground (or in the water!) have led me to a path of success that has often not been supported or accepted by the sports and nutrition powers that be.

Now, I don't have anything against science. It's a great place to start. But science does not offer one-size-fits-all solutions. That's why practical application matters. Unfortunately, many people put all their faith in lab numbers, but the on-the-battlefield results and trial-and-error experiences are far more accurate, and you need to dial the science in for each individual. Endurance racing and extreme fitness are relatively new ventures for humankind, and we are learning amazing things about the body and mind every day. So it takes more than stale numbers, heart rates, and thresholds to determine performance. It also takes paying attention to your own body, experimentation, and the willingness to think beyond commonly accepted training or nutrition or lifestyle practices.

Perhaps this is why, in twenty-five years of racing, I have never had an injury. This is unheard of at the professional Ironman triathlete level. Not a knee problem, a stress fracture, or a pulled muscle. Nada. People have diagnosed this as good genetics, but I suspect otherwise. I think it's because I have focused on understanding my body, on building a solid foundation of functional muscle, on perfecting fitness first, on not neglecting nutrition, and then building backward into all the swimming, bicycling, and running once my body was ready for it.

It's this kind of unorthodox, outside-the-box thinking that got me excited about Ben Greenfield's new book, *Beyond Training.* I've known Ben for a while, and for the past year he's been the nutrition and strength-training expert of our triathlon team at MaccaX. So I've always respected his opinion and loved the crucial training concepts he contributes to the field of health, fitness, nutrition, and endurance.

But I have to admit that this book you're holding in your hands takes practical, real-world, time-in-the-trenches thinking to a whole other level—above and beyond anything I've ever read on websites or in magazines, manuals, and training plans. It's not often I come across a training manual that teaches you how to eliminate chronic pain, balance your hormones, detox your body, maximize fat-burning efficiency, and even hack your brain waves. Most of the time, the focus is just on performance and beating up the body—and not on all the different components of true, whole-body fitness that Ben ties together using simple language.

And there's something else, too. See, as I've grown older, I've realized that there are critical aspects of health that are often ignored in training literature—like taking care of your digestive system, considering the antiaging capabilities of your skin so you don't wind up looking like an elephant from spending so much time in the sun, figuring out which personal-care products aren't harmful, and even tweaking your workouts so you're more efficient and can spend quality time on family, friends, your career, or other hobbies. I was excited to see that Ben takes these critical aspects of whole-body health into consideration, too.

Ultimately, as the tagline of *Beyond Training* says, this truly is the last book you'll ever need in order to master endurance, health, and life. You're about to take a huge step forward in learning how to achieve amazing feats of physical performance without destroying your body. I hope you enjoy this epic read as much as I did.

Cheers, and be healthy,
Chris "Macca" McCormack
BeyondTrainingBook.com/MaccaX

As a professional Ironman triathlete and the author of the book I'm Here to Win, *Chris has won more than 200 races around the world since 1993, including twelve Ironman triathlon victories, more than any other male athlete. He is a five-time International Triathlete of the Year, a four-time Competitor of the Year, and has been named the World's Fittest Man by ESPN.*

Is Exercise Unhealthy?

Athletes are unhealthy.

I'm just sayin'.

Sure, on the outside we exercise enthusiasts and gym junkies may look like pristine, spandex-clad Greek gods and goddesses dominating Ironman events, CrossFit Games, Spartan Races, and ultramarathons, but on the inside we've got depleted hormones, overstressed hearts, and damaged guts from our physically demanding lifestyle.

I first began to realize how damaging exercise—especially voluminous exercise and endurance exercise—can be when I attended a lecture by Dr. James O'Keefe, Jr., a cardiologist from the Mid America Heart Institute at Saint Luke's Hospital in Kansas City, Missouri, at a 2012 event called the Ancestral Health Symposium. O'Keefe reported on findings that exercise can be harmful, especially long, exhausting cardio efforts, such as racing in extreme endurance events like an Ironman. (These findings, along with many other resources for this preface, can be found in the link provided at the end of this preface.)

During his talk, O'Keefe reviewed many studies of physically active people, including those who trained for, and raced in, endurance sports, such as marathons, triathlons, ultramarathons, and long cycling events. Not surprisingly, the people who exercised regularly experienced significant benefits, including living seven years longer than those who weren't physically active.

But when the data of extreme endurance athletes was isolated, it was found that the health benefits of regular physical activity were less pronounced and that significant heart damage resulted.

Specifically, the completion of an event like an Ironman (or even just a marathon) was shown to cause structural heart changes and elevations of "cardiac inflammatory biomarkers." These markers are a pretty dang good indication that your heart has caught fire.

The heart generally returns to normal within a week after completing a tough endurance workout or race. But for those who frequently compete in such events (as most triathletes, runners, and endurance athletes do), the result can be repetitive cardiac injury over days, months, even years. This can lead to serious heart issues, such as atrial fibrosis (thickening and scarring of the heart's connective tissue), interventricular septum (holes in the heart), increased susceptibility to atrial and ventricular arrhythmias (abnormal heartbeat), and calcium buildup in the arteries (which increases the potential for plaque formation and subsequent heart attack).

The distance-running legend Micah True—better known as Caballo Blanco in the book *Born to Run*—died on a trail run, apparently from cardiomyopathy. True is just one of many seasoned endurance athletes who have suffered sudden cardiac events during exercise. Marathoner Ryan Shay and Ironman Steve Larsen are in that group, and Ironman Torbjorn Sindballe was recently forced into early retirement because of premature wearing of his bicuspid valve. Want more examples? They abound.

- **Eddy Merckx,** "the greatest cyclist of all time," had a nonobstructive hypertrophic cardiomyopathy—a genetic condition in which the heart muscle thickens abnormally, causing shortness of breath, chest pain, palpitations, light-headedness, fatigue, and fainting. This condition is actually the leading cause of sudden death in young athletes.

- **Hamish Carter,** the 2004 Olympic gold medalist in triathlon, suffered atrial fibrillation (rapid heart rate) due to heart scarring.

- **Emma Carney,** a former professional triathlete and two-time Triathlon World Champion, experienced cardiac arrest in 2004, was diagnosed with ventricular tachycardia (electrical abnormality in the heart), and has a pacemaker.

- **Samantha Warriner,** a professional triathlete, developed ventricular tachycardia, but, thanks to electrical ablation therapy (which destroys small areas in the heart that are causing trouble), she is still racing.

- **Greg Welch,** a multiple Triathlon World Champion, developed ventricular tachycardia and underwent nine open-heart surgeries between 2001 and 2003.

- **Hayden Roulston,** a professional cyclist, was diagnosed with a potentially fatal heart arrhythmia, but he's still racing.

- **Normann Stadler,** a two-time Ironman World Champion, experienced heart-valve failure and had an aortic aneurysm (in which the main artery from the heart balloons and "explodes").

Based on the data collected by O'Keefe, it appears that the cardiac remodeling induced by excessive exercise can lead to heart-rhythm abnormalities and, especially in extreme endurance sports, has been associated with as much as a fivefold increase in serious heart problems.

In a 2013 article published in the journal of the British Medical Association, O'Keefe proclaimed:

> Evidence is accumulating to indicate that exercise routines that are best for conferring cardiovascular (CV) health and longevity are not identical to the fitness regimens that are best for developing maximal endurance and peak CV fitness. The potential for CV damage secondary to extreme endurance exercise appears to increase in middle age and beyond. Thus, it would seem particularly important to avoid chronic excessive exercise doses after age 45 or 50 years.

That's right—it's not just professional athletes who need to be careful with this stuff. It's you and me, too. It's anybody who wants to check an impressive feat of physical endurance off his or her bucket list without kicking that bucket prematurely.

In O'Keefe's article, the term *cardiac overuse injury* was used to describe the heart issues, which basically consist of fibrosis and scarring of the myocardium (heart muscle), disruptions of the heart's electrical rhythms, and accelerated coronary atherosclerosis (a constellation of abnormalities dubbed "Pheidippides cardiomyopathy" by medical scientists). A more recent article in the *Canadian Journal of Cardiology* entitled "Transient Myocardial Tissue and Function Changes During a Marathon in Less Fit Marathon Runners" outlines that this issue is especially serious and potentially fatal for people who jump into a tough event with inadequate preparation. For those of us wanting to be around to see our grandkids, this is important information to consider. But it's also important if you simply want your skin to look good, you want to sleep better, or you don't want to get fat.

Now, in all fairness, any kind of exercise can damage your heart if you overdo it, and there are many good refutations of O'Keefe's findings, including the excellent series "Can Cardio Cause Heart Disease?" at evidencemag.com.

Regardless of how serious we should take the suggestions that too much exercise may be bad for your heart, one conclusion we can draw is that endurance exercise, especially extreme or ultra-endurance exercise such as a marathon or an Ironman, does not have all the cardio-protective effects we once thought it did, especially for those with preexisting heart ailments. I've personally undergone nuclear stress testing and a stress electrocardiogram, and you can see the results at BeyondTrainingBook.com. You'll be surprised by what a decade of extreme exercise did to my body. Ultimately, exercising for more than ninety minutes a day is where the law of diminishing returns seems to kick in. After that point, you're not gaining any additional benefits; instead, you are risking heart stress, and it simply doesn't make sense unless you're a professional athlete or bodybuilder or you really, really enjoy spending lots of time in a gym.

But the damage from excessive or improper training can go beyond your heart.

For example, in my job as a WellnessFX consultant and triathlon coach, I spend lots of time looking at biomarkers of very physically active people, talking to endurance athletes by phone and Skype, and conversing with athletes from my teams, clubs, and gyms. Their typical frustrations include:

- Low testosterone (especially in men) combined with low libido; bedroom "difficulties"; constant tiredness during the day; and a lack of motivation, competitiveness, and drive.

- Low luteinizing hormone and progesterone (especially in women), combined with brain fog, food cravings (especially at night), and a seeming inability to shed fat despite lots of training.

- Embarrassing bloating and gas after meals, despite eating seemingly healthy foods, and a constant feeling that something just "doesn't seem right" with digestive function, bathroom trips, and overall gut health.

- Trouble getting to sleep at night, or waking up multiple times during the night, often despite being tired during the day.

- Constantly sore joints, nagging injuries that won't go away, missed workouts from sickness or constant sniffles, and occasional "ghost" symptoms, like random headaches, heart flutters, or tingling and numbness.

Strangely, many of these serious problems are accepted as normal—or, even worse, are kept hidden because of embarrassment.

But when it comes to enhancing your body and building endurance, there's a better way to do things. And while I've talked about how you can avoid chronic-cardio self-destruction and still get extremely fit, there are a ton of nitty-gritty details that simply get left out of endurance training and nutrition manuals.

It's time things changed because, let's face it:

Being the best you can be is a challenge when you're dealing with brain fog, body fat, an irritated gut, depleted hormones, or constantly sore joints, so most of us endurance athletes live our lives at just a fraction of our peak capacity, completely powerless to tap into our full potential or achieve our goals as quickly as we should.

That's why I have written this book, and it's very unlike books I have written in the past.

See, my previous books were based on something called the "long tail." What do I mean by that?

While you can really get the gist of the long tail by reading Chris Anderson's book *The Long Tail*, the basic idea is this:

In all my previous health, fitness, endurance, and nutrition books, I focused with laserlike specificity on niche topics, such as getting rid of pain on the outside of the knee or lifting weights for triathlon. Those would be considered "long tail" solutions.

But within these pages, I've created a comprehensive compendium of everything you need to know so you can perform to your maximum physical ability without destroying your body—including precise training protocols, nutrition blueprints, supplementation details, detoxing instructions, blood-testing walk-throughs, lifestyle tips, travel and time-management tricks, self-quantification knowledge, antiaging strategies, and more. I'm going to teach you how smart healthy living, combined with the informed application of exercise and nutrition science, can promote enhanced performance with minimal training time and maximum longevity.

In other words, whether you're a triathlete, marathoner, CrossFitter, adventure racer, swimmer, cyclist, runner, or ultrarunner, this is the last book on endurance, health, and lifestyle you will ever need.

Don't worry—I'm not going to ask you to lower your expectations. You can definitely achieve all the feats of extreme physicality and endurance your heart desires—you just have to train properly. Most exercise fanatics suspect that they are motivated by more than a desire to improve their health. After all, research has shown that as little as fifteen minutes a day of exercise is all you really need to increase health and longevity.

The reality is that most folks do not scale mountains, skydive, do triathlons, or race motorcycles and cars at high speeds around a track for the health of it. They do it for the exhilaration, for the thrill of competition, to "escape" from the everyday routine, for a sense of accomplishment, or for the adrenaline rush.

From an ancestral viewpoint, our hunger for extreme exercise may also simply be a hardwired propensity to want to hunt, fight, or conquer. It may also be a natural, self-perpetuating mechanism to want to emulate heroes, leaders, or champions—so our brains convince us that running a marathon or competing in the CrossFit Games may be a way to become more of a leader or an important member of our "tribe."

Regardless of your motivation, if you want to climb your own personal Mount Everest and are concerned about maximizing your longevity and health, you definitely need to wear your helmet, so to speak. That, or significantly downgrade your physical performance dreams, which just isn't a fun or exciting option for many of us, right?

So here's what you're going to get in this book:

- A training section jam-packed with precise instructions, plans, foods, and bio-hacks on how to do as little damage as possible to your body while getting the maximum possible benefit with the minimally effective dose of exercise.

- A recovery section unlike anything you've ever seen before, with a deep dive down the rabbit hole of every highly effective recovery technique on the face of the planet—exactly what you need to bounce back with lightning speed.

- A nutrition section that shows you exactly how to fuel your body with the thousands of calories necessary to sustain high levels of physical activity—without destroying your gut and metabolism—along with instructions for special populations like aging athletes, vegans, and kids.

- A lifestyle section that teaches you all the little things you tend to forget about during your pursuit of a better body or higher performance—such as how to protect your body from hidden killers in your home and how to get more done in less time so you have more time for family, friends, career, and other hobbies.

- A brain section that reveals the secrets to eliminating brain fog, enhancing IQ, increasing focus, building motivation, and developing the fortitude to get you through even the toughest workout.

- A conclusion that ties everything together with training plans, nutrition plans, walk-throughs, examples, and ten simple rules that will jump-start your life-changing experience.

- A helpful link at the end of every chapter that leads you to a web page jam-packed with references, links (in addition to the links you'll find throughout the book), bonus materials and content, and lots of other extras. The nerds out there will love the extensive lists of complete scientific references for each chapter that are also included on the web page. The actual references are marked with a number in parentheses after a study is referenced in any section of this book, like this—[5]. Just go to the web page and scroll down to the numbered source. You should definitely check out the web page for each chapter if you want to get maximum mileage and benefit out of this book.

Finally, if you visit BeyondTrainingBook.com/audio, you'll find the full audio version of this book for your listening pleasure: a convenient form of entertainment for your exercise, house-cleaning, commuting, or lawn-mowing sessions.

Sound good? Are you ready to change your body, mind, performance, health, and life forever? OK, here we go . . . .

Let's start the link fun with this Preface! Additional resources, helpful websites, scientific references, and surprise bonuses are available at BeyondTrainingBook.com/preface. Enjoy.

How I Went from Overtraining and Eating Bags of Thirty-Nine-Cent Hamburgers to Detoxing My Body and Doing Sub-Ten-Hour Ironmans with Less Than Ten Hours of Training a Week

"Four hamburgers, two cheeseburgers!"

"Six hamburgers!"

"Four cheeseburgers!"

Piled into the backseat of the family Suburban, my two brothers and I shouted orders to our mom as we idled at the drive-through window of McDonald's—thirty-nine-cent hamburger and forty-nine-cent cheeseburger day rolled around only once a week, and when it did, boy, were we ever prepared.

We'd typically drive away with not just a meal for the evening, but eight or ten extra grease-stained bags of burgers that we could dig into during the remainder of the week.

Of course, we never skipped the greens. As we wolfed down our burgers, there would always be salad on the table to accompany them—a vat of chopped iceberg lettuce and shredded carrots floating in a salty, creamy ocean of ranch dressing. *Mmm . . . veggies.*

When we weren't devouring burgers, the three of us boys plowed through Take 'n' Bake Pizzas, giant sub sandwiches, and bathtub-sized bowls of peanut butter Cap'n Crunch cereal. And milk. Lots and lots of healthy cow milk for our growing bodies.

By the time I was thirteen, I was guzzling nearly a gallon of 2 percent milk a day from a big, plastic supermarket jug—after all, I had to support my newfound joy of hoisting ten-pound dumbbells and swinging at tennis balls for several hours a day.

And when I'd drink that final glass of milk, go to bed every night with gas and bloating, wake up every morning with more oily acne, and have painful upset stomachs several times a month, I chalked it all up to normal growing pains and not to the fact that I was dumping indigestible dairy sludge into my body every day.

Things didn't change much from high school to university, where I played collegiate tennis. Nearly every day before our three-hour afternoon practice, I'd pull up to the familiar McDonald's drive-through window and order my prepractice ritual meal:

Big Mac. Fries. Root beer. Supersize me!

I was fast, I was strong, I was about to punish my body for hours, and this food was the high-octane fuel my body needed. Sure, I'd get a sprain or a strain every few weeks, have frequent attacks of brain fog during tennis matches, and lose focus or take naps during classes, and I still had weird gut issues, but this was all normal, right? I mean, all my teammates seemed to struggle with the same issues.

Aside from the prepractice fast-food binges, which I didn't feel at all guilty about because I was exercising like a fiend afterward, the rest of my college diet was, by my measure at the time, pretty healthy. It included:

- Peanut butter slathered on bananas (especially after tennis practice)
- Sautéed steak or chicken and vegetables (nearly nightly)
- Fat sandwiches with deli meat and lettuce (served on whole wheat, of course)
- Yogurt with the fruit on the bottom and crunchy cereal (I graduated from Cap'n Crunch to Kashi)
- Lots and lots of trail mix (or, in a pinch, handfuls of peanuts and Craisins)

Since I was an exercise science major, I'd already launched into my physiology and nutrition classes, and this was the eating regimen we were taught to use for fueling performance. But I'd only tapped the surface of diet science, because I was about to take a deep dive into one of the most geeked-out training and eating sports on the planet—bodybuilding.

When I began bodybuilding, I switched to a high-protein, low-fat diet. I did two hours of daily, very hard weight training, and no day was considered complete unless it included significant soreness and masochistic fatigue. My diet consisted of three or four canned protein shakes a day, along with low-fat, low-carb meals like:

- Two or three cans of tuna over mixed greens
- Fistfuls of 400-calorie high-protein bars
- Eight- to ten-egg omelets with two or three big sausages
- Gallons of cow milk
- Bags of cheap beef jerky

I weighed my food, counted calories with laser precision, and molded my body into an impressive 210 pounds of muscle with 3 percent body fat. Granted, most days, I had zero sex drive, felt like I was crapping out of a straw, was frequently sick and had sore joints, and experienced many signs and symptoms of protein toxicity (which you'll learn about later), but I sure looked damn good.

I also learned early on in this process that you can buy energy.

As a bodybuilder who practically lived at the gym, it made sense for me to moonlight as a personal trainer. During a rigorous 5 a.m.–to–9 p.m. day, jam-packed with studying, classes, and putting myself and my clients through workouts, I could easily guzzle three or four Red Bull, Monster, or Rockstar energy drinks larded with amino acids like taurine, megadoses of B vitamins, and, of course, caffeine. I was flying high. And low. And high. And low. . . .

But I figured that energy roller coasters were normal when you're training hard.

As if my body weren't being taken for a wild enough ride, I added cardio to my weight-training mix for an extra challenge. I bought a mountain bike and started riding to school, began teaching several spin classes a week, taught myself to swim so I could join the water polo team, and even started running the stairs in the football stadium.

I was an exercise machine, and with the cardio I could easily eat every calorie in sight and maintain incredibly low body fat. So I shrugged off my random episodes of moodiness, constant urges to sleep, significant daily fluctuations in resting heart rate, and legs that burned even when I climbed a normal flight of stairs. It was the necessary price of looking good.

Of course, the logical next step was the most exercise-crazed sport I could find: triathlon.

My switch from explosive sports to endurance sports began with the local university sprint triathlon on the back roads of Moscow, Idaho: I began drinking the endurance-athlete Kool-Aid almost immediately after crossing the finish line.

By this time, I had married Jessa, my girlfriend of two years and a lean, fast 1,500-meter runner from the University of Idaho, the same school I was attending. I had my bachelor's degree in exercise science and was pursuing a master's in exercise physiology and biomechanics. I was a member of the university's triathlon club. I had gone from a 210-pound, 3-percent-body-fat bodybuilder to a 175-pound skinny triathlete (there's a link in the chapter resources about how I pulled off that amount of catabolism), and as a newly baptized endurance zealot, I was now consuming every piece of endurance-training and nutrition literature I could find.

I learned that carbs are the lifeblood of any good endurance athlete, and I already knew that with my degree of activity I could eat as many as I wanted, so I switched to a traditional triathlete diet, which was 55 to 75 percent carbohydrates, primarily composed of:

- Sports drinks, energy gels, energy chews, recovery shakes, and recovery bars
- Huge bowls of oatmeal and whole-grain cereal drowned in newfound healthy milk alternatives: soy and rice milk
- Whole-wheat sandwiches and wraps, whole-wheat pasta, and any other whole-wheat products I could find
- Low-fat, whole-grain baked goods, including scones, muffins, cookies, and cakes
- Copious amounts of fruit, fruity yogurt, fruit roll-ups, fruit smoothies, and juice

While this was a nearly 180-degree shift from my low-carb bodybuilding diet, I was now heading out the door for daily hour-long runs, spending weekend mornings on an indoor bike trainer, and swimming until I was blue in the face. I'd committed to my first Ironman event, and I was convinced that I needed as much starch and sugar as I could get to fuel my long cardio sessions and otherwise insane amounts of exercise.

And that first Ironman was apparently a success.

Without really knowing what I was getting into, I crossed the finish line in 9:59 and, just as with my first sprint triathlon, was immediately hooked on the sport. Over the next few years I became a true long-distance triathlon junkie.

I was now an exercise physiologist for a local sports medicine facility, and I spent nearly every weekend of the spring, summer, and fall training hard for or traveling to race Ironmans; local sprint, Olympic, and Half Ironmans; as well as 5Ks, 10Ks, and half marathons.

I completed three more Ironmans.

Training was my life.

And then, in the throes of training for my first Ironman World Championship in Hawaii, we had twin baby boys.

Suddenly, life changed.

Time became a precious commodity. I began to experience a deep urge to provide for my growing family, to advance my career, and to spend time with my children. But I also experienced the pressure to be ready for Kona, and, as I knew from reading triathlon magazines and websites, like Ironman.com:

> Triathletes train an average of seven months for the Ford Ironman World Championship. The average hours per week devoted to training for the World Championship generally fall between 18 and 22. Average training distances for the three events:
>
> Miles per week swimming: 7
>
> Miles per week biking: 232
>
> Miles per week running: 48

Things got tough.

I was physically and emotionally drained from sitting in a bike saddle for five hours and running for three hours each weekend, swimming twenty thousand meters (about twelve-and-a-half miles) every week, and still desperately trying to carve out time for my wife, my babies, my career, and my hobbies while also having some semblance of a social life.

To make matters worse, I just felt run-down—whether because of years of overusing my body, twelve-hour workdays followed by marathonesque training sessions, or the stress of a new family. Every few months a new health problem seemed to pop up. IT band friction syndrome on the side of my knee. Rotator cuff pain on the front of my shoulder. Low-back pain on the bike. Sniffles. Sore throat. Low libido.

I was only twenty-seven, but I was already feeling like an old man.

There had to be a better way.

So over the next two years, I delved into the dozens of exercise physiology manuals littering the floor of my office; reams of training literature on periodization, intensity, and volume; and massive tomes on the biochemistry of muscular and cardiovascular adaptations. As I realized that with anaerobic training and interval training, the human body could still respond with significant aerobic adaptations, I slowly began to make some serious changes.

I quit riding my bike for four to six hours on the weekends, started doing short, interval-based sessions on the indoor bike trainer, and found that my power on the bike began to skyrocket.

I realized that running more than three times a week didn't make me any faster and that long runs kept getting me injured, so I cut my running down to two short twenty- to thirty-minute weekly sessions and one sixty- to ninety-minute weekend run, and I began setting PRs in my triathlon run splits.

I discovered that swimming long and slow makes you a time-crunched, slow swimmer. So rather than visiting the pool two or three times a week for an hour or more, I began doing short but frequent sessions of twenty to thirty minutes. I simply dropped by the pool when I happened to be driving or cycling by it, and suddenly I had way more time on my hands.

I found that my traditional "make-it-burn," old-school, bodybuilding style of weight lifting didn't make me as fast or strong as simply lifting heavy for a few reps with good form; in fact, just a few short lifts made me significantly stronger.

And boy, oh, boy, did I discover what a difference nutrition makes!

For the first time in my life, I seriously attempted to get to the root of my long history of gas, bloating, stomachaches, diarrhea, and a seemingly compromised immune system that resulted in frequent colds and flu.

I subscribed to every diet, nutrition, health, and longevity journal and blog I could find, inhaled half a dozen books a month, and roamed the Internet, reading about ancestral health, natural living, and a more primal approach to fueling and life.

I did poop tests, blood tests, urine tests, saliva tests, and every form of natural- and alternative-medicine poking, prodding, and self-quantification I could find. And I discovered some serious issues with my body and my diet:

- I had low testosterone, hormone imbalances, and bad cholesterol from my high-carb, low-fat diet.

- I was 100 percent lactose intolerant and had an immunoglobulin allergic reaction to most dairy proteins.

- The gluten in the bread, pasta, and other baked goods I was eating was literally tearing holes in my already irritated intestinal wall.

- My fasting blood sugar was skyrocketing, placing me at a high risk for developing type 2 diabetes.

- My amino acids and neurotransmitters were depleted from overtraining and a poor diet, which was severely affecting my focus, my sleep, my productivity, and my mood.

The list went on and on. As I continued to dig, I began to change my diet. I got rid of digestive irritants, such as whole-wheat bread, and enzyme inhibitors like soy milk. I cut out rancid vegetable oils and low-fat foods. I started paying attention to the origin of my food. I drastically lowered my sugar intake. I not only learned how to cook properly, but also how to soak, sprout, and ferment to make my food digestible, and how to give my body real fuel that wasn't wrapped, packaged, bottled, or crammed into a tub.

This training and nutrition paradigm switch was huge for me, and my body quickly began to morph as I connected the crucial dots between health, performance, and longevity.

Although I'd been seeing positive changes for a while, the proverbial lightbulb moment came in 2011 when I crossed the Ironman finish line in Hawaii in 9:36 after training only eight to ten hours a week—using the same strategies you'll learn in the training section of this book.

It turns out that the human body is naturally quite good at "going long," and that if you can just keep it healthy, it is capable of enormous endurance feats that don't eat up your precious time or make you feel like a hamster on a wheel.

After all, for thousands of years, we have hunted, gathered, and roamed the fields and plains, and in the process have developed an innate ability to engage in extended periods of sustained movement. As long as we don't inhibit our natural talents with copious amounts of training, sugar, fake foods, stress, lack of sleep, and a hectic life-style, our hardwired endurance can shine in a surprisingly strong way.

It took me years of destroying my body to realize that you can't just eat thirty-nine-cent hamburgers and train yourself fit.

You have to leave behind the exhausting pursuit of exercise for the sake of exercise and discover the beautiful balance between health and performance.

When you do, life becomes magically simple.

I wish this crucial information had existed within the pages of a single book when I first began my endurance journey, but I'm overjoyed to be able to bring it to you now so that you don't have to repeat my mistakes. You're about to discover everything you need to know to train right, eat right, and unlock your true endurance potential. You're going to get exact training protocols; nutrition blueprints; supplementation details; detoxing instructions; blood-testing walk-throughs; lifestyle, travel, and time-management strategies; self-quantification knowledge; practical antiaging secrets; and more. You're going to find that mastering endurance goes way beyond training.

Are you ready to learn how? Let's begin with a tale of two triathletes.

1

FITNESS

CHAPTER 1

A Tale of Two Triathletes:
Can Exercise Make You Age Faster?

Triathlon is a perfect example of a sport that includes lots of exercise. Let's see how two different approaches to training result in extremely different results, shall we?

Meet Chad. I'll bet you would be impressed with him.

Chad has been a triathlete for twenty-two years.

He is fifty-eight and has completed twelve Ironman events as well as handfuls of Sprint, Olympic, and Half Ironmans.

Like many of his triathlete peers, Chad is a type A and has lived a fast-paced life as an employee, manager, and now CFO of a Fortune 500 company. He travels at least one weekend a month for business, and endurance exercise is the one thing that keeps him sane and focused during his stressful workdays—plus he absolutely loves the endorphin high derived from training and racing. Oh, yeah: Chad is also married and is the father of three boys.

Chad's routine has been the same ever since he started doing triathlons. He swims for about an hour on Mondays, Wednesdays, and Fridays with a Masters swim group. When he gets closer to his big races, he sometimes throws in an extra pool or open-water swim on the weekends, swimming at a long, steady, aerobic pace for an hour or so.

He rides his bike twice a week for sixty to ninety minutes, sometimes on the trainer, sometimes outside—usually mixing it up with some tempo or interval training and occasionally a spin class. Most weekends, he goes out solo or joins a handful of friends for a three- to four-hour aerobic ride, which sometimes goes as long as five or six hours when an Ironman is approaching. Often, these long rides are followed up with a short- to mid-distance run of twenty to sixty minutes. Squeezing in these long rides gets a bit boring in the winter, since Chad is usually just spinning away on his indoor trainer while he watches movie after movie after movie. But these long training sessions are satisfying because they give him a sense of tough fitness.

Chad has never enjoyed running that much, but you can't do triathlons without it, so he generally runs three or four times a week for forty-five to sixty minutes in the morning or at lunchtime. These runs are usually done at a single, steady pace, without much interval training or speed work, which Chad cringes at trying to incorporate because he just wants to zone out and get the run done. Beginning several months out from an Ironman, Chad also does long weekend "death marches," typically slow runs that are two to three hours long and tend to leave him exhausted and drained, but mentally confident about being able to handle the marathon portion of an Ironman.

Chad hits the gym for cross-training occasionally, but without much structure. Sometimes he takes a Pilates or yoga class, occasionally he does some kind of core workout, sometimes he does just enough sets and reps using weight machines or dumbbells to make his muscles really burn, and occasionally he even throws in extra endurance work with an elliptical trainer or rowing machine. The goal is to just breathe hard and move stuff for a while.

Chad's diet is also pretty consistent. Most weekday mornings he has a multivitamin, a couple cups of much-needed coffee, a bowl of cereal or a few pieces of wholegrain toast with peanut butter, and a bottle of sports drink mix if he has a morning workout. Lunch is usually a sandwich or yogurt plus energy bar or protein bar and another cup of coffee or a diet soda. A piece of fruit or some trail mix is his afternoon snack, and dinner is fish, chicken, or steak with pasta or rice and probably beer or a glass of wine. After dinner, especially on weekends, Chad's appetite often spirals out of control, and he'll eat ice cream, some mini candy bars or chocolate, lots of nuts, or another energy bar or two. On the weekends, he throws in recovery shakes, smoothies, extra energy bars or gels, and salt pills to fuel his additional training—using the same kind of fuel and calorie intake he does during races.

For more than two decades, this has been Chad's life.

Eat, swim, bike, run.

Wash, rinse, repeat.

At first glance, you probably think Chad is pretty amazing to have the discipline to maintain this routine, to have achieved this level of fitness, to have the motivation and stick-to-it-ive-ness to compete in such a demanding sport. But you have no idea what's going on inside Chad's body.

Now, at fifty-eight, Chad definitely feels as if the training has taken its toll.

His joints often ache in the morning, and especially at night after long training sessions on the weekends—but it's usually nothing ibuprofen can't fix. Nonetheless, Chad has the ongoing frustration of dealing with seemingly one injury after another—sometimes pain on the outside of his knee that threatens to lock up his knees if he pushes too hard, sometimes plantar fasciitis, Achilles tendinitis, or some other kind of foot or ankle issue, and sometimes nagging pain on the front of his shoulder. Most of these issues clear up if he pops a pain pill, modifies his training, or skips a swim, bike, or run here and there, but he does get sharp pain in his hip almost every time he runs now, and this makes him a little nervous about whether he might need joint-replacement surgery soon. His hip even hurts sometimes when he's sleeping.

And that's another thing: sleeping.

It's more difficult now.

With his jam-packed life, Chad has never allowed himself more than six or seven hours a night, and sometimes less than that when he's in the throes of Ironman training. But now it seems to take longer and longer to fall asleep, and he often wakes up during the night or early in the morning and just feels tired and sluggish during the day, which often makes it hard for him to be productive at work or turns him into a grump around his family.

It's also been a while since Chad has had good sex. Most of the time, it doesn't really matter, because he hasn't had much libido in ages—and sex has always been a sore topic between him and his wife. Even when he does have sex, he has an increasingly difficult time maintaining an erection, and the thought that he has low testosterone or another hormone issue nags at him. However, his doctor does just a standard annual physical and doesn't test for that kind of stuff, so Chad doesn't know for sure. He's usually too tired by the end of the day to care much about sex anyway.

Finally, there are his stomach issues. It seems that more and more these days, Chad has to pop an antacid tablet with dinner to shut down the inevitable heartburn and acid reflux, especially at the end of a big training day that includes lots of fueling. And even though he has always had gas and bloating issues (sometimes to the extent that his long runs are hampered and he is haunted with worry during races), his digestive problems have gotten worse, and he now has occasional bouts of constipation or diarrhea. Something just doesn't seem quite right with his gut.

But at least Chad still has a nice body.

Aside from his dry, wrinkled skin (despite slathering on lots of sunscreen every time he goes out for a long ride or run), Chad is pretty proud of the way he looks. He's fit. He's trim. He has a low body fat percentage. Most guys his age are fat and dumpy and sit on the couch a lot, but Chad actually feels like he looks pretty damn good. Sometimes he wishes he could do more with his body, like play basketball, tennis, or golf or go skiing—but there really isn't enough time, especially when he's down to the wire with Ironman training.

Also, given that so much is on the line with his triathlons, why risk getting hurt with extra sports? This has been a concern of Chad's for a long time: He often feels a bit fragile. He's concerned that if he stepped the wrong way or played another sport that made him move too quickly, he'd strain or sprain something.

Chad often resents that he never really got into any other hobbies, like group sports, or cooking, or playing a musical instrument, or reading more books. But at the same time, he also takes pride in the triathlon medals, plaques, and finisher photos that line his office walls. The other guys don't have those kind of bragging rights.

And speaking of resentment, Chad also gets a gnawing feeling that he has never spent enough time with his kids, with whom he doesn't have a close relationship. Spending long hours swimming, biking, and running, while building a successful career, Chad was usually working or training during his children's formative years. But relationships have never been Chad's specialty—he has very few close friends and not a lot of time for social events anyway. Most of his socializing is done between swim sets in the pool or while pedaling down the road.

But despite his training buddies, Chad still sometimes feels lonely.

And despite his success, he still sometimes feels unfulfilled.

It will be a couple more years before Chad suffers his first "heart flutter" while out on a bike ride.

And it will be another year after that before Chad is forced to stop running because of the increasing pain in his hip that explodes into full-blown arthritis.

For several months, Chad will try to bike, swim, aqua-jog, get on the elliptical, and lift weights through the pain, until he gets extremely frustrated and begins to develop depression, insomnia, a "skinny-fat" look, and chronic fatigue that makes it hard for him even to get out of bed in the morning.

Unfortunately, Chad never got around to it, but if he had taken some blood and saliva tests or a gut panel, he would have discovered that he had:

- Hampered fat metabolism and a prediabetic condition from excessive sugar, starch, carbohydrate, and high-glycemic-index carbohydrate intake

- Chronically elevated cortisol levels, systemic inflammation, and blood vessel and nerve damage from oxidative stress and free radical production

- Skin, joint, and connective tissue breakdown from hormone depletion and high levels of inflammatory markers like hs-CRP, fibrinogen, and interleukins

- Rock-bottom vitamin D, depleted omega-3 fatty acids, and plummeting testosterone levels from a low-fat diet combined with exhaustion from overexercise

- A leaky intestinal wall, fungus overgrowth in the gastrointestinal tract, and severe neurotransmitter and sleep imbalances related to a damaged gut

- Low levels of elements crucial to the heart's electrical activity, such as magnesium and trace minerals, combined with excessive levels of oxidized cholesterol and plaque formation

For a long time, Chad stayed fit on the outside but was falling apart on the inside, and eventually it caught up with him. Within just a few years, Chad will barely be able to do any of the exercise that he relied on for so long to keep him sane and lean. Even simple movements will hurt.

And Chad will ultimately stop getting any enjoyment out of life.

Kirsten is also a triathlete.

Like Chad, she's been a big fan of triathlon for as long as she can remember. She does a handful of shorter races and usually an Ironman every year and, at fifty-three, just completed her fourteenth Ironman.

Kirsten owns her own graphic design firm and constantly juggles dozens of projects and hundreds of e-mails while managing her team of internationally based independent contractors and in-house employees. She has been married for thirty years and raised twin girls and a boy, who have all moved on to college.

Perhaps because of her college days as a rower, Kirsten has always enjoyed high-quality interval training. Her Ironman training routine consists of short dips into intense heart rate zones, followed by long periods of rest, recovery, and light physical activity at her standing desk, in her garden, walking the dog, or even riding her bike to the grocery store and library. She firmly believes that her ancestors didn't ramp up their heart rates significantly for several stressful hours each day "running from a lion" and that neither should she. Kirsten instead takes a hunter-gatherer approach to training—very low levels of exertion and light physical activity fueled primarily by stored fats, with occasional brief spurts of intense activity or heavy lifting.

In terms of swimming, Kirsten has always found Masters swim classes to be too long and exhausting. She opts to get into the water at least twice a week year-round for a quick "tune-up" bout of twenty to thirty minutes, and in the last couple months before an Ironman, she does a few "big" swim workouts, such as thirty 100-meter efforts at race pace. But these monster swim sessions are limited: She prefers to focus on simply maintaining swim efficiency, economy, and "feel for the water." She also combines her swim workouts with another activity at the gym, such as a strength-training session or a quick jaunt on the treadmill.

Kirsten does most of her biking commuting around town, and her once-a-week structured bike workouts are usually done indoors. She doesn't like wasting the extra time it takes to prepare for a road ride, especially when it involves meeting up with a group. And dealing with traffic and other road hazards significantly zaps the efficiency of her workouts. So to get the most bang out of her cycling buck, she does intense sixty- to ninety-minute interval workouts during her triathlon race season and just two or three long outdoor days during the last eight weeks before her Ironman. In the winter, when most of her triathlon friends are spending long Saturday mornings indoors on a trainer, she simply heads outdoors to ski, snowshoe, or just traipse around in the fresh air.

Just like Chad, Kirsten has never really enjoyed long runs, as they feel unnatural and always seem to entail a lot of recovery time. But unlike Chad, she stopped forcing herself to do weekly death-march runs or even hour-long lunchtime slogs ages ago. Instead, she simply hops on the treadmill twice a week or heads to the hill behind her house for brief, intense, twenty- to thirty-minute bouts of interval training. During race season, Kirsten works up to ninety-minute intervals at Ironman intensity, and she does just one eighteen-to-twenty-mile run about a month before her big race. Even this minimal amount of running beats her up more than anything else, so she tries to run only on soft surfaces like trails and treadmills and also uses foam rolling, ice baths, compression gear, and other little tricks to help her bounce back as quickly as possible. And she never pushes through a session if she's sore or her legs feel heavy: Kirsten listens to her body, and if something doesn't feel right, she does an easy swim, a little bit of yoga, or some light walking.

Finally, at least twice a week, Kirsten works all her muscle groups with dynamic strength-training sessions, in which she follows one simple rule: Lift heavy stuff. Avoiding light weights and machines, she challenges her body with barbells, dumbbells, and even kettlebells, which not only helps her maintain lean muscle mass and a nice body shape, but also makes her feel more powerful when she's riding a bike or running—plus, her physician always gives her a big thumbs-up when she gets bone density scans. This type of weight-bearing activity also helps to increase natural growth hormone production and insulin sensitivity, keeping her body lean and metabolically efficient. On Sundays, Kirsten takes a yoga class, which helps her maintain good mobility and keeps her stress levels down, and she incorporates some of that yoga into a short daily morning routine along with meditation and deep-breathing techniques.

Even though Kirsten has been an endurance athlete for many years, her whole life does not revolve around swimming, cycling, and running; in fact, structured triathlon training takes up only about eight to ten hours a week. Unlike many of her athlete friends, she is simply conscious of moving, engaging in moderate physical activity throughout the day—she doesn't try to "train away stress" with a hard workout after long, sedentary days stuck in an office chair.

Like her approach to physical activity, Kirsten has always made an effort to eat as naturally as possible. She has a small garden in her backyard where she spends time during the spring and summer planting and growing nutrient-rich vegetables and fruits like kale, spinach, raspberries, and watermelon and detoxifying herbs like parsley and cilantro. She buys most of her foods from local farms and the farmers' market and has always done her best to avoid bars and gels and sports drinks to fuel her workouts. Hormone-supporting, fatty-acid-rich foods like eggs, fish, olives, and avocados allow her to maintain her light levels of fat-burning physical activity during the day, and she keeps her distance from sugar and carbohydrates unless she's in the middle of a workout. Even then she keeps her fuel real rather than processed by eating dried fruits, sweet potatoes, yams, white rice, and other natural sources of carbohydrates.

Kirsten also gets tested for levels of crucial elements like magnesium, antioxidants, vitamin D, and hormones yearly, and rather than taking heaps of cheap multivitamins or trendy supplements, she takes supplements to target the specific nutrients in which she is deficient. While she'll be the first to admit that Ironman training does require extra help in terms of nutrition supplementation, she's very careful about what she puts into her body and relies on real, recognizable food for the majority of her nutrients.

Kirsten is toned and curvaceous, with glowing skin and a fantastic complexion. Because she has always controlled her sugar and carbohydrate intake, Kirsten's skin and hair haven't been affected by the breakdown of sugars, called glycation, that damages collagen, which keeps connective tissue smooth and firm. Keeping her stress levels down by not exercising excessively has also limited her inflammation, reducing spikes in cortisol and inflammatory damage, which can also accelerate the aging process. It has probably also helped that Kirsten has always been mindful about using harsh chemicals on her body or to clean her home, relying instead on natural beauty products and essential oils. And Kirsten's healthy habit of functional strength training a couple times a week and not doing "chronic cardio" has helped her maintain lean muscle mass, avoid a skinny-fat look as she ages, and support supple skin and natural curves.

Kirsten's sex life and libido are also good. Because she has always been careful to limit her exposure to excessive estrogens from diet, stress, and the environment, she never experienced hot flashes, sexual disinterest, or sexual discomfort during menopause. By consuming healthy fats and adequate protein, as well as keeping her sugar intake down and her training moderate (excesses of both sugar and exercise can deplete hormones), she has not turned to hormone-replacement therapy as many of her friends have.

Kirsten has happily led an active social life, as she's well aware that connections and relationships are key to aging well among every population on the planet. Even though most of her training sessions are solitary, because they are focused and intense, she has always had time left over to hang out with her friends, her children, and her husband—and she has no regrets about neglecting important relationships or fun social occasions. She has even had time to volunteer for local charities, play piano to keep her mind young, and witness the birth of her first grandchild.

In just a few years, at the ripe age of fifty-seven, Kirsten will qualify for Ironman Hawaii for the third time and head to Kona on the Big Island to race in the Ironman World Championship. That same year, she will be able to put in three solid months of driving on Saturday mornings for her local Meals on Wheels, teach her two grandchildren to play the piano, and even win an award for being a leading local businesswoman.

She continues to pay attention to her body and her health, and goes above and beyond a basic yearly physical to ensure that her preventive practice of eating healthfully, engaging in a broad range of physical activity, detoxing her diet and home, and living an active, stress-free life is continuing to pay off. And rather than revealing low bone density, depleted hormones, gut issues, or impending arthritis, her lab tests continues to show healthy numbers—far superior to those of even her healthiest peers.

Kirsten has a tough time imagining life without triathlon: Swimming, cycling, running, and racing are a part of her life, and one of the ways in which she defines herself. She'll be the first to admit that she is probably addicted to the endorphins and the other positive feelings she gets from exercising. But even though she is passionate about endurance sports, Kirsten has never let herself get stuck in a training rut or let her focus on fitness become so time-consuming or all-encompassing that it detracts from her health, her hobbies, her career, her family, or her friends.

For Kirsten, life is good.

Summary

As you can see, despite participating in the same sport, Chad's and Kirsten's very different approaches to training, eating, and living reaped shockingly different outcomes in their later years.

Chad beat up his body with excessive training in the "gray zone"—long tempo sessions consisting primarily of junk miles—while eating a standard endurance-athlete diet; deprioritizing sleep, recovery, and relaxation; and ignoring holistic-health concepts like hormone balance and gut integrity. While there certainly is a correct way to train twenty to thirty hours a week (and you'll learn about it in this book), Chad took the all-too-common approach of digging himself deeper and deeper into an overtraining hole from which he was never able to climb out.

By contrast, Kirsten went beyond training, implementing many of the concepts you'll find in this book, and found an optimal balance between her endurance, her health, and her life. She tested and listened to her body and engaged in smart exercise, nutrition, and healthy living.

Now it's your turn.

Additional resources, helpful links, scientific references, and surprise bonuses for this chapter are available at BeyondTrainingBook.com/Chapter1. Enjoy.

CHAPTER 2
Everything You Need to Know About Heart Rate Zones

In this chapter, you're going to learn everything you need to know about how heart rate zones work, and exactly what happens to your body, muscles, and energy systems as you train in these different zones.

But wait? Isn't this covered in every exercise physiology book and endurance-training manual on the planet?

Not exactly.

While many exercise manuals teach you about the different heart rate zones, the sad fact is that most references are rife with seriously flawed assumptions and myths about how to properly use these zones. This leads to lots of frustrated athletes, who are chained to their heart rate monitors or who simply toss their monitors in despair and train without any quantification at all—and get the same results year after year.

For example, one myth is that there's some kind of mysterious, junk-mile "gray zone" in which you should never, ever train. But I'll show you why training in this zone is absolutely crucial if you're ever going to actually *race*.

Another myth is that there is only one way to train properly—some kind of endurance-training-zone Holy Grail.

For some people, the Holy Grail of training is steady and slow aerobic training, often referred to as the Maffetone Method or Lydiard training and popularized by guys like Phil Maffetone, Arthur Lydiard, and Mark Allen. For others, the Holy Grail is the more new-school, high-intensity, go-till-you-puke method championed by organizations like CrossFit Endurance.

But in this chapter, you'll get the foundation to understand that there is more than one way to achieve things like mitochondrial density, stamina, VO_2 max, and lactate threshold, and then you'll be ready for the next chapter, in which you'll learn how to use both aerobic training and high-intensity intervals to achieve your goals as quickly as possible.

And while we're discussing myths, we'll delve into another myth—that each training intensity zone has some magical crossover point at which you smoothly transition to the next zone, shifting your utilization of fats versus carbohydrates as you go. If you, God forbid, somehow break the cardinal rule of venturing from one zone into the next, you're completely screwed. You're about to discover why this is completely bogus and how your body is a dynamic machine, not a zone-switching robot.

Ultimately, after reading this chapter, you're going to be smarter than 99 percent of the endurance-athlete population when it comes to understanding how your body, muscles, and energy systems truly operate when you're swimming, cycling, or running. You're about to cut through the nonsense of zone 1, zone 2, zone 3, zone 4, zone 5, zone 6a, zone 7x, zone 8abc, and every possibility that exists in the zone-training alphabet soup.

You're about to become a clear-thinking, exercise physiology ninja.

Humans Are Messy

Imagine, if you will, a car with three gas tanks.

At speeds below 15 miles per hour, the car relies on gas tank 1.

But once 15 mph is exceeded, the car abruptly switches to a new gas reservoir with a brand-new kind of fuel—tank 2. This new fuel works just fine until the car gets up to 60 miles per hour, at which point the car switches to the third tank, with an entirely new fuel.

Such a vehicle would create a variety of sticky situations for you. For instance, what if it ran out of fuel in just, say, tank 2, and then was unable to speed up enough to access tank 3? You might be stuck having to use the fuel in slow-speed tank 1 for the duration of a very long drive. Or perhaps it would be the inconvenience of having to fill three separate tanks every time you pulled into a gas station. This car doesn't seem like the most efficient of machines, does it?

Next, imagine a beast in the jungle. When ambling along at a lazy pace, this beast burns fuel only from seeds and nuts. But as soon as the beast breaks into a jog, it can no longer burn seeds and nuts for fuel and must rely on roots and tubers. Finally, should the beast need to full-out sprint, it could access fuel only from bananas. I have a hunch that this beast wouldn't survive too long—especially compared with an entirely different kind of beast that could make adaptations on the fly, perhaps by using any given mix of fuels for any given speed and even converting one fuel type into another.

A human is that different kind of beast.

We are each intelligently equipped to burn a messy and imprecise combination of phosphates, fatty acids, amino acids, and sugars—whether we are lying as still as a corpse in bed or riding a bicycle like a bat out of hell.

But despite the fact that we are not gas-tank-reservoir-switching machines, here's a typical scenario for a modern endurance athlete out on a run with his training buddy:

"Frank, we gotta slow down."

[Beep, beep, beep, beep.]

"Why, Ed? This pace feels great."

"Frank, dude, I'm in zone 4!"

[Beep, beep, beep, beep.]

"Zone what? And what's that beeping, Ed?"

"Zone 4, Frank! I'm burning up all my carbs. That's my watch beeping to tell me we need to slow down. I'm going to bonk."

[Beep, beep, beep, beep.]

Sound silly?

Not only is Ed likely to enjoy his training a bit less than Frank, but he also (falsely) believes that heart-rate-zone training or power-zone training or speed-zone training is the key to tapping into specific fuel sources and will make or break him as an athlete.

Don't get me wrong—knowing your approximate training zones is important for proper training and race pacing. It is also important for targeting the type of intensities you're going to use during the training year. But it is very important for you to understand that the human body is dynamic and flexible, and that zones should be used as guidelines, not as a means to shackle you to your training.

Fair enough?

OK, let's talk about why these zones exist in the first place.

Energy Systems 101

The human body produces energy by converting food into something called adenosine triphosphate (ATP), and then breaking ATP into adenosine diphosphate (ADP) and phosphate (P). As you produce energy, you have to replace your stores of ATP, and there are three ways to do so. These three ways are called energy systems. Pretty much all heart-rate-zone training systems are based on these three systems.

1. **The first energy system is your oxidative system, which predominates after two minutes of exercise. This is your aerobic energy system, also referred to as mitochondrial respiration.**

Basically, the aerobic (oxidative) energy system utilizes a combination of fats and carbohydrates to resynthesize ATP. Your body does this by combining glucose or fats with oxygen to form water, carbon dioxide, and energy. Once you've been exercising for more than about two or three hours, your body begins to throw protein into the mix as another fuel to be broken down into glucose and fed into this energy system.

But there's no "magic switchover" to fat or carbohydrates or protein as the preferred fuel source for your aerobic energy system. It's always a mix.

For example, depending on how good you are at using fat as a fuel, what you've been eating lately, and which hormones are circulating in your body, at rest about 70 percent of the ATP you produce is from fat and about 30 percent from carbohydrates. As you exercise with more intensity, you start to utilize more carbohydrates, but you're still burning fat. And as you exercise for longer than three hours, up to 18 percent of your energy can be derived from breaking down protein.

Figure 2-1 gives a great picture of exercise intensity combined with mixed-fuel utilization. As you check out Figure 2-1, think of plasma glucose as something you'd get from a gel or sports drink or bar (or from breaking down protein); plasma-free fatty acids as something you'd get from metabolizing your own fatty deposits or from nuts or avocado or the like; muscle triglycerides as stored fat in muscle (or perhaps

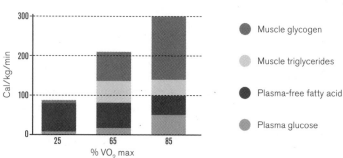

FIGURE 2-1: Relative Contributions of Macronutrients with Exercise

from an external source like coconut oil, if that's your fuel of choice, which you'll learn more about in the nutrition section of the book); and muscle glycogen as your body's stored carbohydrate.

2. The second energy system is your glycolytic energy system, which is often referred to as your anaerobic system.

The glycolytic system, as the name suggests, relies primarily on glycolysis (the breakdown of carbohydrates) from either glycogen stored in your muscles or liver or glucose delivered into the blood from food. This energy system predominates when you engage in intense exercise under two minutes, during which oxygen is in short supply. But it is also what you'll rely on quite heavily in the middle of an Ironman competition to pass someone on the bike, or for the final kick of a marathon, or to surge up to pack of swimmers in the open water. During glycolysis, your body converts carbohydrate sugar into pyruvate, which gets converted into energy (plus some lactic acid).

Interestingly, some of the pyruvate can also get shuttled back into the aerobic energy system, and some of the lactate can get converted back into glucose for use in more glycolysis, once again highlighting the fact that this is a fluid system without solid boundaries. Later you're going to learn how to take advantage of that fluidity to maximize your fuel utilization.

3. The final energy system is the phosphagen energy system, which kicks in when you exercise at maximum intensity for three to thirty seconds (depending on which physiology nerd you ask).

When your body creates ATP in this energy system, it breaks adenosine diphosphate (ADP) into adenosine monophosphate (AMP) and inorganic phosphate (Pi), and also combines Pi with the amino acid creatine to form creatine phosphate (CP), which can then be combined with ADP to form more ATP.

Most endurance coaches and athletes give short shrift to the phosphagen energy system, deeming it germane only for football players, sprinters, or bench-pressing, but the fact is that creating ATP using this energy system is one way your body can maintain glycolysis during tough efforts in a training session or race.

Traditionally, thirty seconds was thought to be the absolute maximum amount of time you could actually tap into your creatine phosphate system, but multiple studies have now shown that creatine can contribute to ATP production during exercise that lasts well beyond five minutes and up to nearly twenty minutes.

How can this be?

Being able to use creatine during longer efforts is a result of what is called the "size principle" of muscle. The size principle states that when smaller muscles fail to meet power demands, larger muscles are recruited. This progressive recruitment means that the creatine utilization from larger muscles won't be tapped into until you reach higher intensities of exercise.

So if you're doing, say, an Ironman, it's not as if you tap into your creatine system during the first ten to thirty seconds of the swim, and then that energy system is smoked and you move on to the next energy system. Instead, you may continue to tap into your larger muscle-fiber creatine stores when you surge to pass somebody during the bike leg of an Ironman or to run up a steep hill during a marathon.

The important takeaway is that athletes who have low creatine stores (for example, many vegan or vegetarian endurance athletes) or who haven't trained their high-intensity phosphagen energy system are setting themselves up to have less "kick," lower force production, and a reduced ability to surge during a race when it really matters—not just when lifting weights in the gym.

The Caveats

Of course, as I've already mentioned, the way these energy systems contribute to your training and racing is extremely complex and depends on myriad factors, which Tim Noakes, a professor of exercise and sports science at the University of Cape Town, in South Africa, elucidated in a good paper several years ago (you can find a link to it on the resource web page for this chapter).

For example, when it comes to dietary status, a high-carbohydrate diet is related to increased carbohydrate utilization during exercise, which means you would rely on a greater percentage of carbohydrates to fuel your aerobic system and might use a higher percentage of your glycolytic energy system. By contrast, a low-carbohydrate, high-fat diet would make you a "fat-adapted" athlete who would rely more on mitochondrial respiration and the burning of fatty acids for fuel. (In many cases, increasing fat availability immediately before exercise can actually increase endurance performance as well as enhance recovery. See Figure 2-2.)

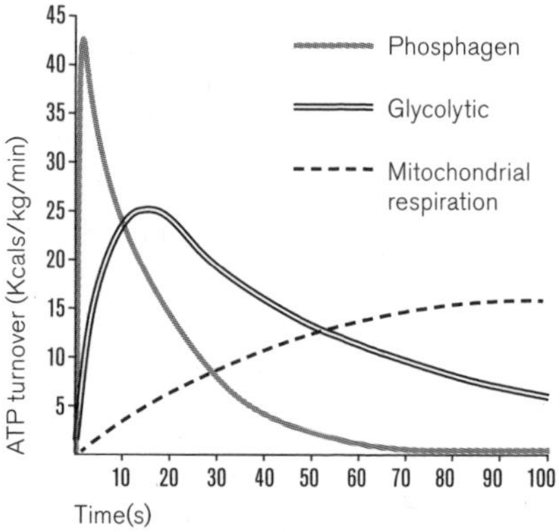

Training status can also influence what kind of fuel your energy systems use. For example, because of a higher density of mitochondria and more capillaries feeding into muscle, endurance athletes rely less on muscle glycogen and plasma glucose and more on fats for energy, whether resting or exercising, regardless of intensity.

Hormonal status also influences the type of energy you use. For example, high levels of circulating catecholamines, such as growth hormone, cortisol, epinephrine, and norepinephrine, can cause you to burn more carbohydrates as fuel, but endurance-trained athletes tend to produce fewer of these compounds during exercise.

FIGURE 2-2

You get the idea: Not only does your body use a cocktail of energy systems for any given intensity, but your individual diet, training, and hormonal status affect which energy system you use and which fuel you feed into that energy system.

As I said, humans are messy.

Why We Invented "Training Zones"

Now, don't worry—we're getting closer and closer to the practical, hands-on stuff. As you now know, a mix of energy systems are involved in any given intensity. So by quantifying and controlling the intensity, we can (to a certain extent) control which energy system predominates during training and racing, and we can therefore create intelligent training programs and get valuable feedback from our workouts. Hence the existence of training "zones" to quantify and control intensity.

Let's start simple.

As I'm writing this chapter at my standing workstation, I'm in a training zone—a very low one that uses lots of fat and a little carbohydrate as fuel, but because I'm standing and moving around just a bit, it's technically a training zone. It makes me feel good to think that at least a few of my mitochondria are respiring, anyway. Despite tapping away on a computer, I'm trying to stay in a "hunter-gatherer" mode as much as possible (another good reason to get a treadmill workstation).

And when I wander to my office doorway to do a few pull-ups and about thirty seconds of explosive jumping jacks or burpees (either of which I do as a rule every sixty minutes when I'm working), I'll shift into another zone, one that relies quite a bit on glucose and creatine phosphate.

Then, during my afternoon run later today, I'll shift from slightly higher intensity aerobic mitochondrial respiration as I warm up, into glycolysis and carbohydrate utilization as I surge into some intervals, then back into an aerobic state as I cool down.

If I wanted to plot this daily energy expenditure on a graph, the line would move from zone 1/2 to zone 5 to zone 3 to zone 4 and back to zone 1/2.

If I stayed in zone 1 all day, I probably wouldn't get very fit.

And if I stayed in zone 4 all day, I'd be overtrained and get injured.

Simple example, I know—but I really want to make sure that this whole physiology thing is clear. After all, I promised to turn you into an exercise physiology ninja.

How Many Zones Should You Use?

You're about to discover five different training zones, but depending on which coach, sport-governing body, or training system you reference, there may be more or fewer.

For example, the Norwegian Olympic Federation has a five-zone heart rate scale based on decades of testing lactic acid levels in cross-country skiers, biathletes, and rowers, while several other studies have used changes in oxygen utilization to categorize three training zones. On websites such as TrainingPeaks, the platform I use to coach my clients and athletes, you can choose and customize up to ten zones—enough to make you cross-eyed during training!

In reality, most of these zones overlap and achieve similar effects. For example, a five-zone scale and a three-zone scale are relatively superimposable, since the aerobic, fat-burning intensity defined in zone 3 of a five-zone system usually correlates with the aerobic zone 2 in a three-zone system and the aerobic zones 4, 5, and 6 in a ten-zone system.

So, for the purposes of this book, you're going to explain intensity and physiology using five zones, as noted in Table 2-1. After more than a decade of working with intensity scales, I've found that five is the perfect number of zones to allow for some complexity and a good explanation of exercise physiology.

I used to have a zone 6, but now I just refer to it as anything above zone 5, since I'm not an advocate of looking at your heart rate monitor while you're doing power cleans at the gym.

How to Find Your Personal Zones

Did you notice that my zones are based on a percentage of lactic acid threshold?

The reason I use a percentage of lactic acid threshold rather than a percentage of maximum heart rate is that testing lactic acid threshold doesn't require you to run or bike until you collapse (also known as a VO_2 max test). It's a safer and slightly more pleasant way to find your starting point to calculate your zones.

And, yes, you can use speed (pace) or power rather than LT heart rate if you'd rather track and train with those parameters. It's just that for the purposes of explaining the basic physiology behind these training zones, heart rate offers a great example. If we were going to use pace zones, I'd prefer the Jack Daniels method (no whiskey involved), and if we were going to use power zones, the Andy Coggan method. I offer links to websites with useful calculators for both of these methods on the resource web page for this chapter. There's also a fascinating and useful method that can even be combined with heart rate, power, or pace zones—breathing zones. (For more on breathing zones, check out *Running on Air,* by Budd Coates, and pay attention to the chapter on stress management later in this book.)

But for now, let's focus on heart rate zones, how to set them properly, and how to test your lactic acid threshold, or your "LT heart rate," so that you can set up your own heart rate zones.

The gold-standard way to determine your LT heart rate is with a lab test in which blood lactate levels are collected during a graded exercise session that becomes progressively more difficult every three to five minutes. But let's say you don't want to spend the money or take the time to venture to your local sports performance lab or university to have this test done.

Based on clear signals that occur in your body when you are at or very near LT, you can approximate your personal LT with what is called a "field test." Because of the varying muscular demands of each skill, your LT will change depending on whether you are cycling or running, so I recommend doing an LT test while both biking and running. Based on where your LT lies in each sport, you will be equipped with the information to train at your highest intensity (without overtraining) and to determine each of your training zones.

TABLE 2-1. ZONE TRAINING CHART

HEART RATE ZONE	% of Lactic Acid Threshold (LT)	DESCRIPTION
ZONE 1 Goal: Recovery Energy System: Oxidative	70-76%	After hard workouts or tough blocks of training, very easy workouts can accelerate recovery more than complete rest. Easy aerobic training stimulates blood circulation, which can help remove inflammation and increase tissue-healing response. The intensity in this zone is enough to increase blood circulation and trigger a growth hormone response, but not enough to cause muscle damage or significant energy or fluid depletion. Examples of a zone 1 workout include an easy yoga class, a light swim, and a walk with the dog.
ZONE 2 Goal: Endurance Energy System: Oxidative	77-85%	This zone will also feel very easy ("conversational" effort). Training at this intensity primarily uses slow-twitch muscle fibers. Since these fibers provide most of the mobility for events lasting two minutes or longer, workouts at this intensity should comprise the bulk of your training. Training above this intensity will not significantly overload your slow-twitch fibers, which you need to train to become more efficient at using fat and oxygen to produce energy while conserving carbohydrate stores. If you don't have a physically active job or aren't able to spend lots of time on your feet during the day, this intensity is important for training, especially if you compete in events lasting more than two hours. Although it will be difficult to keep your intensity low on these days, if you have lots of time on your hands and the type of training you want to do is primarily aerobic (as opposed to interval based), performing your endurance efforts at a higher intensity than zone 2 will reduce the effectiveness of your harder workouts on subsequent days by fatiguing muscles and depleting carbohydrate stores in fast-twitch muscle. This can lead to overtraining and injury. In other words, if you're going to use the "long, slow aerobic" method of training, you need to do most of it in zone 2, not zone 3.
ZONE 3 Goal: Muscular endurance Energy Systems: Oxidative, Glycolytic	86-95%	During an endurance workout, your intensity may reach this zone on slight hills or when you're beginning to push the pace on flats. Your body is still functioning primarily aerobically, conversation is possible, and burning in the legs and shortness of breath are minimal, but you're "working." A slight problem with this zone is that the intensity is too high for maximal stimulation of the slow-twitch muscle fibers and for fat burning. As intensity increases from zone 2 to zone 3, oxygen debt becomes greater, and since it takes more oxygen to burn one calorie from fat than from carbohydrate, more carbohydrate and less fat is burned. Because this zone is high enough to get the physiological "runner's high" and the satisfaction that you exercised with a slight amount of intensity, many athletes perform mile after mile in this zone, wear their bodies down, and never go much faster. On the flip side, this zone is, as you'll learn later, the "money" zone for many distances in endurance sports, as it allows you to go relatively fast without dipping too significantly into your carbohydrate stores. This is why long interval-training sessions or hill climbs in this zone can really help with race-pace training and race preparation. Good for eight- to twenty-minute intervals with short recovery periods in between.

HEART RATE ZONE	% of Lactic Acid Threshold (LT)	DESCRIPTION
ZONE 4 Goals: Muscular endurance, lactic acid tolerance, low-end speed Energy Systems: Oxidative, Glycolytic	96-103%	Lactate threshold (LT), or anaerobic threshold (AT), is the highest intensity at which your body can recycle lactic acid as quickly as it is produced. At this intensity, you are working very hard but can still maintain your maximum sustainable pace and relatively good form because lactic acid levels in the blood and muscles are steady, not increasing. Upping the intensity above or toward the high end of this zone can cause lactic acid to accumulate more rapidly and bring on premature fatigue and delayed recovery from acidic hydrogen ion buildup and more rapid carbohydrate depletion. Performing interval-training sessions near lactate threshold can teach your body to decrease the amount of lactic acid being produced and increase lactate removal at any given intensity. At this intensity, the fast-twitch fibers can be trained to produce less lactic acid, and the slow-twitch fibers can be trained to burn more lactic acid, both of which raise the lactic acid threshold and allow you to work harder at a higher intensity. Since you're not at an all-out, high-impact pace as you would be in higher, fast-twitch-muscle-utilizing zones, you can recover from zone 4 training faster than from other high-intensity training zones. From an interval-training standpoint, zone 4 gives you a lot of bang for your buck. When you experience "rubbery leg" syndrome, difficulty breathing, or an inability to maintain good form, you have reached the point where lactic acid is accumulating faster than it can be removed, which can severely lessen your ability to maintain a steady effort and to recover well. Do one- to seven-minute intervals in this zone with a work-rest ratio of about 2:1 or 3:1.
ZONE 5 Goals: Sustained speed, leg/arm turnover Energy Systems: Glycolytic, Phosphagen	104%-max	In this zone, intensity exceeds lactate threshold, and your body is relatively stressed in its ability to withstand high lactate levels and remove lactate. Lactic acid builds up quickly, so this intensity cannot be sustained for long periods, but it is useful for surges of as much as five minutes, as the aerobic energy system still helps out. Because muscle and joint impact and lactic acid levels become extremely high in this zone, this type of training requires longer recovery periods, especially for newbie athletes. In addition to increasing an athlete's speed, training at this intensity improves neuromuscular recruitment, economy, efficiency, and turnover, but tons of time in this zone is a common cause of overtraining. Typically, the only work done in this zone is interval training and hill repeats. It's good for two- to five-minute intervals with a work-rest ratio of 1:1 to 1:3.
Anything above ZONE 5 Goals: Explosive speed, power Energy System: Phosphagen	Max	This intensity primarily trains glycolytic- and phosphagen energy systems and may involve sets of five seconds up to a couple minutes in duration. Athletes who want to develop fast-twitch muscles, strength, or explosive power, or to improve cycling or running mechanics, should include training sessions at this intensity. These workouts are typified by short, explosive intervals followed by long recoveries in a work-rest ratio of 1:4 to 1:10, and include powerlifting, weight training, plyometrics, and other short bursts of energy.

There is no perfect LT field test, but here is an example for running, cycling, and swimming. You'll need a heart rate monitor or another accurate way to take your pulse for the running and cycling tests, and preferably some kind of swim pace or timing device like a FINIS Tempo Trainer for the swim test.

Running LT Test: Exercise for thirty minutes at the max effort you can sustain, monitoring your heart rate throughout. Your average heart rate during the final twenty minutes should correspond to your LT.

Sometimes people push too hard for this test. Follow this simple rule: Your pace should be the same at the end as at the beginning. If your legs start to go rubbery, leg turnover begins to slow down, your lungs begin to burn, and you start gasping for breath, you are going too hard! On a scale of 1 to 10, with 10 being the hardest, you want to be at about an 8.

Warm up easily for ten to fifteen minutes, then, on a treadmill, track, or flat outdoor course, begin a thirty-minute run and work up to your maximum sustainable intensity within the first ten minutes. Record your heart rate for the last twenty minutes and calculate the average: This is your estimated heart rate at lactate threshold.

If thirty minutes is daunting, you can perform three five-minute, hard, sustainable efforts with five minutes of rest between efforts, and simply monitor your average heart rate during each of those five-minute efforts.

Cycling LT Test: Warm up with ten to fifteen minutes of light cycling, then follow the protocol for the running test, but on the bike—preferably on an indoor trainer or a controlled course. An alternative method is this: Following the warm-up, cycle for eight minutes as steadily and fast as possible up a slight hill (2–3 percent incline), at an RMP (cadence) of 80 to 100. Record your average heart rate during the climb, then rest for three minutes (or descend). Repeat once and calculate the average of your two climbs: That's your LT heart rate for cycling.

Swimming CSS Test: Thanks to the guys at Swim Smooth (BeyondTrainingBook.com/swimsmooth) for inventing this one. I prefer this test to just getting in the water and swimming at your maximum sustainable pace for 1,000 meters, which is brutal. The Critical Swim Speed, or CSS, test involves two shorter swim efforts—400 meters and 200 meters. First do a good ten- to fifteen-minute swim warm-up. Do the 400-meter effort first: Simply swim a 400 at your maximum sustainable pace. Take four to eight minutes to recover completely. Then do 200 meters at your maximum sustainable pace. Try to pace the efforts as evenly as possible—don't start too fast and slow down. If you're not sure if you're pacing correctly, since it can be much harder to get a feel for pacing in the water compared to when you're cycling or running, you can get someone to take your 100-meter splits to see how much you are speeding up or slowing down. You can then use the calculator link on the resource web page for this chapter to calculate your CSS. Or, if you're a real nerd, you can simply do the math as CSS (m/sec) = (400 − 200) / (T400 − T200), where T400 and T200 are your 400- and 200-meter times in seconds. You then convert your speed from m/sec into time per 100 meters. On the web page for this chapter, there's a link to a page at SwimSmooth that does all these calculations for you.

Voilà!

You now know which energy systems and fuels you're tapping into at each exercise intensity and how to test yourself to set up your personal zones.

Feeling like an exercise physiology ninja yet?

Examples of Using Zones in Training

Once you know your zones, you (or your coach) can use them to build your training program more strategically. For example:

- Do you have a lot of endurance but get tired as soon as you begin producing lactic acid? Incorporate more zone 4 intervals.

- Can you do interval workouts easily, but fatigue after doing a long steady-state workout? Do more zone 2 efforts combined with quality, focused zone 3 intervals.

- Do you lack the power for the final kick in a 5K, marathon, triathlon, or the like? Do more zone 5 intervals.

- Do you need a recovery day? Do a zone 1 workout to increase blood flow and recovery speed.

See Table 2-2.

TABLE 2-2

ZONE	VO$_2$ (% Max)	EXAMPLES OF TRAINING SESSIONS	MANAGEABLE DURATION*
1	45–65	Continuous bouts	60–360 min
2	66–80	Continuous bouts	60–180 min
3	81–87	6 x 15 min, 2-min rec 2 x 25 min, 3-min rec 5 x 10 min, 2-min rec 8 x 8 min, 2-min rec LT 40–60 min 50 x 1 min, 20-sec rec	50–90 min
4	88–93	10 x 6 min, 2–3-min rec 8 x 5 min, 3-min rec 15 x 3 min, 1-min rec 40 x 1 min, 30-sec rec 10 x (5 x 40 sec, 20-sec rec), 2- to 3-min breaks 30-40 min steady state	30–60 min
5	94–100	6 x 5 min, 3–4-min rec 6 x 4 min, 4-min rec 8 x 3 min, 2-min rec 5 x (5 x 1 min, 30-sec rec), 2–3-min breaks	24–30 min

* Warm-up and rest periods in interval bouts are not included.   Source: sportsci.org
LT = lactate threshold (max steady state); rec = recoveries.

Example of Using Zones in Racing

Don't get me wrong: This book isn't meant to be strictly a triathlon training guide, but since it's a mix of three different sports, triathlon offers a perfect example of how training zones can be used in pacing and racing. Here's how:

Sprint: In a sprint triathlon, beginner triathletes should bike in zones 3 and 4, while more advanced athletes stay in zones 4 and 5 the entire time. During the run, both beginners and advanced triathletes should be mostly in zones 4 and 5; advanced triathletes primarily in zone 5 for the entire run. Even though it can be hard to quantify swim pace during a short race, swimmers of all levels should try to maintain a pace that's about five to ten seconds faster than their CSS pace for the swim.

Olympic: Olympic-distance triathlon is slightly less intense than sprint. While beginners should again be primarily in zones 3 and 4 on the bike, more advanced athletes may repeatedly surge into zone 5. For the run, beginners should stay primarily

zones 3 and 4 until just a mile or two before the end, at which point they can dip
o zones 4 and 5. Advanced athletes should start the run in zone 4 and gradually
ld up to zone 5 from the 5K mark to the finish. Beginners should be close to CSS
ring the swim, while intermediate to advanced athletes should swim about five to
seconds faster than their CSS pace.

Half Ironman: The bike intensity for beginners doing a Half Ironman should be
marily zone 3; the run should be in zone 3, gradually building to zone 4 by the
K mark, with the last 5K in zones 4 and 5. For more advanced athletes, the bike
ensity should be primarily in high zone 3 and low zone 4, with occasional surges
ove zone 4. On most courses, the run should gradually build from zone 3 to zone
y the 10K mark, zone 4 for the next 5K, and zone 5 for the final 5K. Beginner
letes should swim close to or slightly below their CSS, while intermediate to
vanced athletes should swim at or slightly faster than their CSS pace.

Ironman: For Ironman, the bike intensity should be primarily low to mid-zone
or all athletes, although advanced athletes may push toward the high end of zone
n hills or in crosswinds, and when passing may occasionally dip into zone 4.
cause of loss of blood volume from dehydration and central nervous system fa-
ue, heart rate and zones can be difficult to rely on during the marathon, so pace
perceived exertion is a better guide. Beginners should run near zone 3 until the
nty-mile mark; intensity can build to zones 4 and 5 for the final leg. For ad-
ced athletes, much of the run should be done near zone 3 pace, but they can start
reasing intensity to zones 4 and 5 as early as the half-marathon mark. Beginners
uld swim ten to fifteen seconds below their CSS, while intermediate to advanced
letes should swim about five seconds below their CSS pace.

n reality, most exercise enthusiasts don't really need a heart rate monitor or
ning zones to know what constitutes an all-out one-minute interval, an all-out
-minute interval, or an easy recovery interval. I'm personally a fan of spending
ne time, such as a year or two of training, really getting to know how your body
ls in each heart rate training zone and eventually getting to the point where you
simply unplug and intuitively "listen to your body" during training. But even
ou don't use them religiously, you now know what you need to know about how
rt rate zones work and the physiology behind what's going on as you train at a
iety of intensities.

Congratulations, ninja.

n the next chapter, you'll learn that there are two ways to use your knowledge
these zones to build fitness and succeed in a wide variety of sports and fitness
nts—a long, slow aerobic approach and a high-intensity-interval-training ap-
ach—both of which incorporate a concept called "polarized training."

Additional resources, helpful links, scientific references, and
surprise bonuses for this chapter are available at
BeyondTrainingBook.com/Chapter2. Enjoy.

CHAPTER 3
The Two Best Ways to Build Endurance as Fast as Possible (without Destroying Your Body)

The Black Hole

There's a big, big problem among exercise enthusiasts. It's a hole. A black hole. The black hole gets formed by:

- The runner who rolls out of bed three to five days a week to run for forty-five to sixty minutes at the same speed every single time.
- The triathlete who hops in the pool at lunchtime and swims for thirty minutes steady every single time.
- The cyclist who rides every weekend at a steady cadence and speed for two hours every single time.

Same speed. Same rpm. Same intensity.

Day after day, month after month, year after year.

Perhaps it's the thumb-sucking security we get from knowing exactly what our bodies are going to feel like during every training session. Perhaps it's the fear of going too slow or too hard and somehow messing up our training or our bodies. Or perhaps it's just not knowing exactly what to do and simply figuring that something is better than nothing.

Or perhaps exercise enthusiasts are just *lazy*.

That's right: Disguised by all our spandex, Speedos, expensive shoes, carbon bikes, and specialized training gadgets, we might just be lazy.

After all, compared with doing thirty minutes of hard, focused run intervals, it's easier to simply slog through a mind-numbing, two-hour death march.

Compared with doing a structured series of swim drills, it's easier to just dive into the water, turn the brain off, and stare at the black line for a while.

Compared with the laser focus of an intense set of hill climbs, it's easier to simply point the bike in one direction, hunch over the handlebars, and spin at what feels like a halfway decent pace.

Yes, you heard me correctly: We hard-charging, type-A, obsessive-compulsive exercisers could just be . . . lazy.

And regardless of whether it's sticking too close to the tried and true, fear of failure or injury, lack of training knowledge, or pure laziness, we athletes tend to accumulate the majority of training time at one single speed—the not-too-hard, not-too-easy, slightly-near-threshold zone that makes us feel like we're working pretty hard, but not too hard, and perhaps just hard enough to get us a little bit fit.

You could draw a parallel between this style of single-speed training and weight lifting or strength-training athletes who lift the same weight, do the same exercises, and load the body from the same joint angles every time they steps into a gym, with zero change-ups in sets, reps, weights, or exercises.

Sound familiar?

I call it black-hole training.

This problem has even been documented in studies[5]. (For this study, and all the others cited by a number in parentheses, see the corresponding number on the web page for the chapter in which it appears.) For example, despite what a coach's training plan may dictate, runners tend to go too hard on easy days and too easy on hard days: Workouts that are supposed to be long and slow become fast and short; workouts that are supposed to have variations in pace are done at a monotonous single speed. As a result, most workouts end up being performed at the identical intensity, session after session. So the athlete winds up racing at the same speed, season after season.

Whether you call it "junk miles," "single speed," or "no man's land" training, it'll dig you into a black hole. In chapter 2, I explained it as too much time in zone 3— going just hard enough to deplete energy stores and damage muscles, but not hard enough to elicit any significant training response.

In a *Bicycling* magazine article published back in the '90s, cycling journalist and coach Fred Matheny described it this way:

> NML (no man's land) workouts provide a kinesthetic sense of working hard but expose the rider to too much stress per unit gain. Instead, most base training should be guilt-producingly easy, and the top-end, high-intensity training should be very mentally hard, not sort of hard[13].

Stressing the same energy system over and over not only results in a single-speed athlete who can't go fast when it matters and never goes slow enough for recovery, but may also result in more rapid onset of overuse injury from repeated stress on the same joints.

For example, according to research, 10 to 15 percent of the population is predisposed to a condition called "femoroacetabular impingement," in which the hip bones are irregularly shaped, which can lead to arthritis in the hip when coupled with a sport such as triathlon from all the hip-jarring flexion during running and cycling[1].

Given that, who do you think is going to have a higher risk of hip replacement—a triathlete whose every training session is done at the same speed (often on the same course), using the same joints and energy systems time after time, or a triathlete who mixes things up with some trail running, some track work, some hill work, some lateral movement, some cross-training, and some recovery workouts?

Stressing the same energy system repeatedly also creates a huge negative energy balance (calorie deficit)—especially when the majority of the training is done at or near threshold—which, as you're about to find out, is not the case with most pro athletes but is the case with many recreational exercisers.

Studies have shown that this negative energy balance results in hormonal disruptions (such as testosterone deficiency and low libido in males, and estrogen deficiency and low bone density in females), a wildly out-of-balance secretion of appetite-disrupting hormones, and a host of other endocrine and chronic-disease-related health issues[6].

Yet another reason junk miles simply aren't worth it.

But wait! What about those stories of Kenyan marathoners and elite endurance athletes doing long, slow training sessions at a single speed? Isn't that black-hole training? Isn't that no man's-land-style junk miles performed at a single speed? If so, it certainly seems to be working for those guys, right?

The fact is, that type of training is actually not black-hole training—it's something completely different. And you're about to learn what that is and why it is one of the two best ways to build endurance, a skill that you're going to need whether you're a soccer player trying to build stamina, a CrossFitter who wants to branch out into triathlons or obstacle racing, a military athlete who needs to ruck for hours on end, or a tennis player who needs to sludge through a three-hour match. You get the idea.

The Pareto Principle

When you look at the training protocols of most elite endurance athletes, a group that typically performs ten to twelve workouts over fifteen to thirty hours a week, a distinct pattern emerges. Specifically, they spend about 80 percent of their training time below and about 20 percent above their lactate threshold (aka zone 4). See Figure 3-1.

This 80/20 pattern is so prevalent that exercise science has a special term to describe it: *polarized training.*

When you look at endurance athletes—from world-champion rowers to professional marathoners to elite cyclists and triathletes—nearly all the top athletes use a polarized-training protocol: a large amount of time spent at relatively easy aerobic intensities with occasional extremely hard bursts at a high intensity.

These athletes spend very, very little time in the black-hole region, in which you're training above an easy, aerobic pace but below any pace that becomes extremely uncomfortable.

You may already know this 80/20 concept as the "Pareto principle," which states that, for many events, approximately 80 percent of the effects come from 20 percent of the causes.

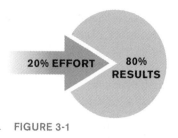

FIGURE 3-1

For example, one study[14] quantified the training-intensity distribution of professional swimmers over an entire season and found that about 77 percent of their swimming over the season was done at a purely aerobic intensity. Another study[3] investigated marathoners and found that during the twelve weeks leading up to the Olympic marathon trials, these athletes ran 78 percent of their miles below marathon speed, only 4 percent at marathon race pace, and 18 percent above lactate threshold.

And what about those Kenyan marathoners I alluded to? Another study found that elite male and female Kenyan runners do about 85 percent of their weekly volume completely below lactate threshold.

The evidence goes on and on.

For example, in one study[4], sub-elite distance runners were randomly assigned to one of two training groups:

- Group 1 performed 81 percent of their training in an easy zone 1, 12 percent in a moderate zone 2, and 8 percent in a high-intensity zone 3. (Note: They were using three zones to quantify training intensity rather than the five I delineated in chapter 2.)

- Group 2 did more lactate-threshold training, with 67 percent easy, 25 percent moderate, and 8 percent high intensity. In other words, group 2 did twice as much training at or near lactate threshold. Interestingly, the authors reported that the athletes were actually not able to spend more than about 8 percent of their time at high intensity—it was simply too hard. (That should give you a good idea of how hard high-intensity interval training is really supposed to be.)

The total training volume was identical between the two groups.

But guess what? After five months of this protocol, the running performance of group 1 was significantly better—despite the fact that they had been doing much lower intensity training than group 2.

Interesting.

But that wasn't an isolated study. In other research[9], a group of rowers were split into two training groups: one group (low intensity) who performed nearly 100 percent of their training below 75 percent VO_2 max (a relatively low intensity), while the other group (mixed intensity) performed 70 percent of their training at those same low intensities and the other 30 percent at a much higher intensity (above lactate threshold).

These two groups also performed nearly identical amounts of training.

And despite a significantly higher amount of training above LT, the mixed-intensity group didn't perform any better than the low-intensity group. Sure, after twelve weeks of their respective protocols, both groups had improved performance and achieved higher maximal oxygen consumption, but even though they spent significantly more time in the pain cave, the mixed-intensity group didn't see a significantly greater gain in performance.

Bummer for the mixed-intensity group.

So the takeaway so far is this: Across a wide variety of endurance sports, studies have shown that the best endurance athletes are naturally performing about 80 percent of their training volume at a low intensity and only about 20 percent at a high intensity[15], either through selectively choosing the proper intensities or being coached to do so.

And those high-intensity efforts are very, very high—with relatively little time spent in the no-man's-land training zones in which most recreational athletes train.

These athletes are doing enough low-intensity training to build big aerobic engines and ingrain correct motor patterns for improving movement efficiency and economy while incorporating just enough stress for significant cardiovascular and muscular adaptation.

So why, if lots of low-intensity training is good, wouldn't more be better? In other words, instead of 80/20, why not 90/10, 95/5, or even 100/0? It turns out that, especially in elite athletes, when mild doses of high-intensity interval training are added to a primarily aerobic training protocol, the results are always favorable—and not surprisingly always close to the 20 percent mark with HIIT (high-intensity interval training) dosing[10].

Stephen Seiler sums it all up quite nicely in a paper that appeared in the *International Journal of Sports Physiology and Performance:*

Numerous descriptive studies of the training characteristics of nationally or internationally competitive endurance athletes training 10 to 13 times per week seem to converge on a typical intensity distribution in which about 80% of training sessions are performed at low intensity (2 mM blood lactate), with about 20% dominated by periods of high-intensity work, such as interval training at approx. 90% VO_2 max. Endurance athletes appear to self-organize toward a high-volume training approach with careful application of high-intensity training incorporated throughout the training cycle. Training intensification studies performed on already well-trained athletes do not provide any convincing evidence that a greater emphasis on high-intensity interval training in this highly trained athlete population gives long-term performance gains. The predominance of low-intensity, long-duration training, in combination with fewer, highly intensive bouts may be complementary in terms of optimizing adaptive signalling and technical mastery at an acceptable level of stress[15].

So even though it feels very rewarding to roll up your sleeves and hammer at or near LT on your morning or lunchtime run, or to ride at a steady race-pace intensity for a few hours on the weekend, or swim lap after lap at your perceived racing intensity, *it's simply the wrong way to train.*

The Regression Problem

In all fairness, it is actually pretty darn difficult to go easy when you're supposed to go easy and go truly hard when you're supposed to go hard.

For example, the researchers I referenced above[4] tried to replicate the polarized training of successful elite endurance athletes with a program designed around more threshold training—but this time using the protocol on recreational runners.

The intended intensity distribution for the two training groups was supposed to be 77 percent low, 3 percent moderate, and 20 percent high intensity in a polarized training group, compared with 46 percent, 35 percent, and 19 percent in a lactate-threshold training group[7]. (Interestingly, the percentages in the lactate-threshold training group were based on American College of Sports Medicine–recommended training-intensity distributions.) But heart rate monitoring during the study revealed that the actual intensity distribution of the recreational runners was 65 percent, 21 percent, and 14 percent in the polarized group and 31 percent, 56 percent, and 13 percent in the lactate-threshold training group.

In other words, comparing the intended and achieved distributions in the study highlights the fact that most of us, when left to dialing in our own training intensities, tend to regress toward black-hole training—even if we're supposed to do otherwise.

But Wait—Shouldn't Exercise
"Break You Down" to "Build You Up"?

Hard exercise of any sort creates free radicals that cause some damage (called "oxidation") to your muscles, cells, and organs. As your body repairs this damage, you experience biochemical adaptations that make you more resistant to future oxidative damage from high-volume or high-intensity training. As you train more, your body simply increases its production of natural antioxidants to control the free radicals you're producing[2].

Based on this enhanced repair mechanism and surge in natural antioxidants that occurs in response to tough workouts, it would seem to follow that doing long sessions of black-hole-style training would make you fitter and faster.

However, although consistent oxidative stress is a critical component of fitness, a recovery period is necessary to allow the body to bounce back adequately. The key is to train in a manner that provides enough physical stimulus to increase fitness without overtraining or causing excessive oxidative stress. Rather than exposing your body to the same amount of stress and intensity day in and day out, you enhance its ability to fight free radicals by mixing it up with very hard days and very easy days.

My friend Armi Legge sums this up quite nicely in an article titled "The Truth about Extreme Exercise, Oxidative Stress, and Your Health" (evidencemag.com):

> Most evidence indicates that if you train in a progressive, intelligent manner, with adequate recovery between workouts, you can build up to extremely high training loads and still be protected against potentially dangerous levels of oxidative stress.

That's a Wrap?

Well, that should about wrap it up, right?

After all, it turns out that the whole Maffetone method[12] of (1) finding your easy aerobic "fat burning" zone and then (2) spending the great majority of your time training in this zone with (3) very brief forays into high-intensity work seems to work quite well. I guess Mark Allen was indeed onto something when he used this method to win those six Hawaii Ironman World Championship titles.

It would seem that we now know the ultimate way to build endurance. End of story.

Not so fast.

I don't know when the last time you peeked at the training log of an elite endurance athlete was, but:

- Professionals train at least ten to fifteen times a week. That's not *hours* per week—that's *times* per week. Do the math. Definitely more than one session per day, usually a multi-hour session.

- Most Ironman professional triathletes swim 20,000 to 30,000 meters per week. That's about six to eight hours.

- They're also cycling 150 to 250 miles a week. That's another eight to ten hours.

- They're running 25 to 40 miles a week. That's another four to six hours.

Not to mention the additional hours spent core training, weight training, recovery training, and, of course, preparing and eating the thousands of calories necessary to fuel these monster amounts of exercise.

And don't think that this amount of training is restricted to gonzo Ironman triathletes. Competitive marathoners, elite cyclists, top-level swimmers, and all other professional endurance athletes literally devote their lives to training.

Do you have twenty-five to forty hours a week to train and fit in everything else, too? And do you have the self-control necessary to hold back the reins and ensure that 80 percent of this training is done at a very easy aerobic intensity?

If so, then proceed with this polarized-training model and the 80/20 style of training, but proceed with the knowledge that the majority of these types of current training methods for endurance events like an Ironman are derived from the training schedules, race calendars, and lifestyles of professional endurance athletes who compete in the sport for a living and train for twenty-five to forty hours a week.

And know that this style of polarized training may mean that you have to neglect things like your job, family, friends, and other hobbies.

The way I see it, who cares if the training protocol works if it's bad for you or sucks time away from your career, friends, and family? Unless you're a professional endurance athlete and your sport is how you're supporting your family, your precious time may be better spent otherwise.

But you may have a different perspective.

Some recreational athletes do have enormous amounts of disposable income, careers that are on cruise control, and endless hours to devote to 80 percent low-intensity, 20 percent high-intensity polarized training a week.

Or perhaps you just love to spending endless hours alone training..

If so, then proceed, because polarized training is indeed one of the best ways to build endurance as fast as possible without destroying your body. But know that there is another way. . . .

Additional resources for the information you've read up to this point in the chapter are available at BeyondTrainingBook.com/Chapter3-Part1. Enjoy!

How Your Body Builds Endurance

Before we delve into how to build endurance without training for dozens of hours each week, you need to understand how your body builds endurance and what the primary determinants of cardiovascular and endurance performance actually are.

Your cardiovascular performance is based on three primary variables:

1. Heart rate (how many times your heart beats per minute)

2. Stroke volume (the amount of blood pumped per heartbeat)

3. Heart contractility (the forcefulness of each contraction of your heart muscle)

As each of these variables increases, the blood flow and oxygen supply to your exercising muscles also increase.

So at first glance it would seem that your heart is the primary thing you need to worry about when it comes to endurance training. Aerobic training has certainly proved to be one of the best ways to improve the above variables[18]. But there are important determinants of endurance success that go above and beyond the heart.

For example, when your muscles contract, they propel the flow of blood traveling through your veins and back to the heart, increasing the amount of blood filling your heart, which is called a "preload." This preload actually enhances the heart's stroke volume during exercise, making adequate contraction and strength of your skeletal muscles a major determinant of your endurance performance[12].

That's not all. Tiny powerhouses in your cells, called mitochondria, use oxygen to manufacture high levels of ATP via the breakdown of carbohydrates or fat. So if you increase your mitochondrial density, more energy becomes available to your working muscles, which allows you to produce greater amounts of force for longer periods.

In addition, your actual VO_2 max (the maximum amount of oxygen you can deliver to your muscles in a given amount of time) is a result of two variables:

1. How much blood your heart can send to your muscles (a combination of heart rate, stroke volume, and heart contractility)

2. How much of the oxygen sent to your muscles is actually extracted from the blood and used by the muscles before the blood heads back to your heart

The second variable above depends on oxygen delivery to active muscle fibers, and this is influenced by everything from blood-flow distribution to capillary density, arterial oxygen content, local enzymatic adaptations, and the number and density of mitochondria[18].

So the important question is this: If you want to optimize your heart's capacity to send blood to your muscles while increasing the number and the density of your mitochondria, raising your max, and strengthening your skeletal muscles for higher force production and better venous return to your heart, is there anything comparable to or superior to long, slow aerobic training?

The answer is an unequivocal yes. This is where HIIT enters the picture.

HIIT Your Mitochondria

I'll explain in just a bit what HIIT—high-intensity interval training—involves and how you can intelligently implement it into a training protocol without hurting yourself, but first I'll show you how HIIT can influence the components of endurance success just described[9].

Let's begin with your mitochondria.

For years, exercise scientists have been convinced that the only way to increase mitochondrial density is with aerobic endurance training, but recent studies have proved otherwise.

Not only is an increase in the size and number of mitochondria a proven adaptation to HIIT[8], but the mitochondrial benefit of HIIT goes way beyond size and number. For example, all your mitochondria contain oxidative enzymes, such as citrate synthase, malate dehydrogenase, and succinate dehydrogenase. These oxidative enzymes lead to improved metabolic function of your skeletal muscles—particularly by causing more effective fat and carbohydrate breakdown for fuel and also by accelerating energy formation from ATP.

So more oxidative enzymes means that you have a higher capacity for going longer and harder.

And it turns out that, according to an initial study[16] on the effect of HIIT on oxidative enzymes, there were enormous increases in skeletal muscle oxidative enzymes in seven weeks in subjects who did four to ten thirty-second maximal cycling sprints followed by four minutes of recovery just three days a week.

But what about HIIT as opposed to aerobic cardio?

Another six-week training study[5] compared the increase in oxidative enzymes that resulted from either:

1. Four to six thirty-second maximal-effort cycling sprints, each followed by four-and-a-half minutes of recovery, performed three days a week (classic HIIT training) or

2. Forty to sixty minutes of steady cycling at 65 percent VO_2 max (an easy aerobic intensity) five days a week

The levels of oxidative enzymes in the mitochondria in subjects who performed the HIIT program were significantly higher—even though they were training at a fraction of the volume of the aerobic group.

How could this favorable endurance adaptation happen with such short periods of exercise?

It turns out that the increased mitochondrial density and oxidative-enzyme activity from HIIT are caused by completely different message-signaling pathways than those created by traditional endurance training.

In the HIIT pathway, a "master switch" is activated that promotes the favorable endurance adaptation. This master switch is known as PGC-1-alpha, which stands for peroxisome proliferator-activated receptor gamma coactivator 1-alpha. PGC-1-alpha causes that favorable increase in mitochondrial density and oxidative-enzyme activity but can be activated by two completely separate signaling pathways—the calcium/calmodulin-dependent kinase (CaMK) pathway or the adenosine monophosphate-activated protein kinase (AMPK) pathway[15].

Continuous, voluminous endurance training seems to activate the master PGC-1-alpha switch via the CaMK pathway, while intense interval training activates it via a completely different pathway: the AMPK pathway. (See Figure 3-2.)

Conveniently, this increase in oxidative enzymes can actually change your metabolism, causing you to oxidize more fat during exercise. This may seem a bit confusing since you have so far learned that high-intensity interval training burns a higher percentage of carbohydrate for fuel while you're doing the intervals. But multiple studies[22,27] have proved that after just a few weeks of HIIT, fat burning increases significantly and carbohydrate burning decreases significantly.

So with HIIT you become a metabolically efficient, fat-burning machine in far less time than you could through long aerobic sessions[10].

But these benefits go above and beyond what you burn during your actual workout session. For example, many exercisers and athletes are also interested in weight loss (although we euphemistically say that we are trying to "improve our power-to-weight ratio" rather than "burn some fat off our ass").

The good news for those of us who want a better power-to-weight ratio is that, in addition to the body burning more fat during exercise, HIIT also increases excess postexercise oxygen consumption (EPOC). After a hard, interval-based workout, your oxygen consumption (and thus the total amount of calories you burn after the workout) remains elevated as physiological and metabolic factors in your cells are restored to their pre-exercise levels.

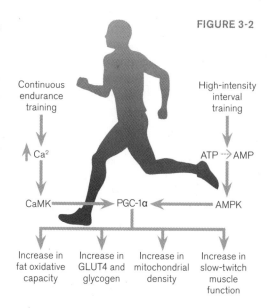

FIGURE 3-2

A review article of studies on HIIT[14] found significantly higher EPOC values with HIIT training than with continuous aerobic training—which translates into higher and longer calorie burning long after your workout is over.

Month after month, this "bonus" calorie burn can significantly add up.

HIIT Your VO$_2$ Max

Next, let's see how HIIT can affect your VO$_2$ max, your body's upper limit for consuming, distributing, and using oxygen for energy production.

In one study[9], four repetitions of four-minute runs at 90 to 95 percent of max heart rate followed by three minutes of active recovery, performed three days a week for eight weeks, resulted in a 10 percent greater improvement in stroke volume than long, slow distance training three days a week for eight weeks. Stroke volume is a key component of your body's ability to deliver maximum oxygen to working muscles.

Another study[24] showed that high-intensity intervals performed at 90 to 95 percent of VO$_2$ max increased left-ventricle heart mass by 12 percent and cardiac contractility by 13 percent—both of which are significant determinants of cardiovascular capacity and oxygen delivery during exercise.

Another study[6] measured the increase in VO$_2$ max among subjects who performed eight weeks of either a HIIT program or an aerobic-endurance-exercise program. As you can probably guess by now, the increase in VO$_2$ max was significantly higher in the HIIT subjects (15 percent) than in the aerobic-endurance subjects (9 percent).

Since improving cardiovascular function and increasing VO_2 max are two major ways to address cardiovascular disease, even cardiac rehab facilities are catching on to the idea of HIIT training and are beginning to prescribe it for heart disease patients. Even though traditional low-intensity, aerobic exercise can definitely improve heart disease risk factors, HIIT achieves the same results in less time, with fewer sessions[1].

HIIT Your Skeletal Muscle

And how about your skeletal muscle?

As you learned earlier, when your muscles contract, they propel blood back to the heart, which increases the amount of blood filling your heart and the heart's subsequent stroke volume. Within just a day or two of HIIT training, tiny blood vessel changes begin to take place in your skeletal muscle that improve the flow of oxygen in and out of the muscle and better "match" oxygen delivery to oxygen utilization[17]. These microvascular adaptations are accompanied by an increase in the strength of the skeletal muscle fibers themselves, which allows for even more forceful pumping potential.

In addition to improving the force and contractility of skeletal muscle, HIIT significantly lowers insulin resistance and results in a number of skeletal muscle adaptations that cause enhanced muscular fat oxidation and improved glucose tolerance[4]—yet another way HIIT can turn you into a fat-burning machine.

I've personally experienced skeletal muscle benefits from HIIT that go above and beyond what research studies have documented. For example, when I've exposed my body to "pain cave"–style workout sessions (such as forty-five minutes of hard cycling intervals), I'm not only able to dig deeper mentally, but I'm also less likely to experience protective muscles spasms or cramps.

This makes sense, since Tim Noakes, among other exercise scientists, has suggested that much of the cramping that athletes experience during an event may be a result of asking their bodies to do something during that event that their bodies simply haven't been exposed to during training. For example, if your quadriceps muscles have rarely produced 350 watts of power on the bike and you ask them to produce that amount of power when you attempt to pass someone or surge during a bicycle race or triathlon, they may rebel and go into a protective spasm.

As your quads curl up into a fetal position, you can throw back all the salt capsules you want, but they're not going to help if your cramping has nothing to do with your hydration status and everything to do with how you trained. (Caveat: Occasionally you can reverse the alpha motor neuron inhibition that holds your muscles in a cramped position with the mere taste of something very salty, such as pickle juice, mustard, or an electrolyte capsule broken open and dumped into the mouth. But if you've dug yourself deep enough into a hole to need to employ this strategy, there's an underlying training problem that probably needs to be addressed.)

The Problem with High-Intensity Interval Training

So it would seem that HIIT is the ultimate solution for people who can't put in the hours necessary for polarized training. But is HIIT the be all and end all?

No.

First, you get benefits from long endurance-training sessions that you simply can't get from HIIT. For example, researchers at the University of Western Ontario had twenty (untrained) volunteers train three times a week for six weeks[18]. Half ran steadily at an easy, aerobic intensity of 65 percent VO_2 max, starting at thirty minutes and building up to sixty minutes; the other half did thirty-second sprints with four-minute recoveries, starting with four repetitions and building up to six.

As expected from what we already know about HIIT, the subjects in the sprint group increased their endurance performance as much as or more than those in the aerobic group. All the subjects increased VO_2 max by about 12 percent, all increased their 2K time by about 5 percent, and all lost fat (although the HIIT group lost twice as much fat!).

But when researchers quantified maximal cardiac output (Qmax), which is a measurement of the largest amount of blood your heart can pump in a given amount of time, the aerobic group increased their Qmax by 9.5 percent, while the sprinters didn't increase their Qmax at all.

So what this study tells us is that if you want to get the most bang for the buck from your endurance training by maximizing not only how much blood your muscles can utilize (with HIIT) but also how much blood your heart can send to your muscles (with aerobic training), you must include some semblance of long, steady workouts in your training program. In other words, HIIT works more effectively on your peripheral muscle fitness, while endurance training works more effectively on your central, cardiovascular fitness.

There's also the argument, which is certainly a valid one, that by incorporating several longer endurance training or stamina sessions into your routine, you increase your tolerance to pain; mental focus; knowledge of how to use equipment such as chamois cream, packs, boots, or bicycling gear; opportunities to practice fueling strategies; and so on. But these types of "big" training sessions are often over-performed by overtraining athletes and are really just the icing on the cake that needs to be included only once or twice a month in a properly structured HIIT program. In other words, you don't need to do a two- to three-hour-long death march every weekend in order to be ready to run a marathon.

Should You Do CrossFit?

While I embrace HIIT as an ideal, time-effective way to build a big endurance engine, there is a definite limit to how much of it you can do before it takes its toll—beating up your joints with its excessive high impact and loading, depleting your hormones as you "sprint away from a lion" every day, and leaving you mentally frayed from having to repeatedly dip into the training pain cave.

In the same way that black-hole training can leave you exhausted, skinny-fat, or overtrained, too much top-end training can have a similar effect. And when it comes to HIIT, more is definitely not better.

Take CrossFit, for example. CrossFit is a high-intensity exercise program designed to improve core strength and functional fitness by employing Olympic weight lifting, kettlebells, gymnastics rings, pull-up bars, and a wide variety of bodyweight moves and calisthenics. A typical workout may include running, rowing, rope climbs, jumping up onto and off of boxes, flipping tractor tires, carrying heavy operational gear, or bouncing medicine balls against the floor or a wall. Typically, these workouts are done in a group setting with an instructor, and a great deal of emphasis is placed on outperforming your peers and pushing yourself to failure.

A daily CrossFit workout might look like this:

- Three rounds for time of:
  - 800-meter run with a 45-pound barbell
  - 15-foot rope climb x 3
  - 12 reps with a 135-pound thruster
- Plus, as many rounds as possible in twenty minutes of:
  - 10 pull-ups
  - 5 reps of 75-pound dumbbell deadlift
  - 8 reps of 135-pound push press
- Plus, five rounds for time of:
  - 9 reps of 135-pound deadlift
  - 6 reps of 135-pound hang power snatch
  - 3 reps of 135-pound overhead squat

CrossFit Endurance is a hybrid of CrossFit designed for endurance athletes. According to the CrossFit Endurance website, the target weekly schedule for triathletes includes four days of CrossFit, three strength-training days, and two days each of sport-specific training for swimming, biking, and running. (You can find a link for a sample twelve-week CrossFit Endurance program from *Competitor* magazine on the resource web page at the end of this chapter.) As you can see, the workouts of the day (WODs) in CrossFit Endurance are very similar to regular CrossFit, but with extra swimming, cycling, and running HIIT thrown in.

Don't get me wrong: *CrossFit can definitely get you fit, and has indeed been proved to increase VO$_2$ max.* As a matter of fact, a recent study found that ten weeks of CrossFit-based high-intensity power training significantly increased maximal aerobic fitness (VO$_2$ max) and body composition[25].

Granted, a whopping 16 percent of the subjects had to drop out of the study, citing overuse or injury—despite the fact that there was significant instruction in skill work for the improvement of Olympic lifts and gymnastics exercises. While peer-reviewed evidence of injury rates in these types of high-intensity training programs is sparse, there are emerging reports of increased rates of musculoskeletal injury and metabolic derangement[2].

I've done many CrossFit workouts and have my own suspicions about why injury and overtraining are rife with CrossFit, or any program that includes too much high-intensity interval training—especially when combined with hard weight-training sets.

First, Olympic weight lifting and many other moves in a workout such as CrossFit require proper technique and should ideally be performed with low repetitions (less than eight), good form, and energy to spare. This is simply not the case for many triathletes and endurance athletes, who combine high-repetition snatches or heavy clean-and-jerks with sprinting, tire flips, and rowing—especially for those new to such a program, who simply jump in and replicate what their peers are doing during the workout.

Second, having to complete a set number of reps "for time" forces many type-A athletes to push themselves to go harder than they might normally go, perhaps ignoring the body's warning signs to slow down or stop, especially if there are times or reps to beat written on a giant whiteboard in the gym. This often results in forcing the body through a particular motion, even if the supporting musculature is fatigued. It should come as no surprise that, after subjecting your shoulders to the strain of hammering in and out of a poorly performed overhead press or a swinging, ballistic pull-up when you're exhausted, they begin to grind and hurt during the next day's swim workout.

Third, in the majority of studies that show HIIT to be efficacious, without high-injury dropout rates, HIIT is incorporated in small and potent doses spread sparingly throughout the week—in contrast to the frequent, often daily CrossFit-style intense intervals combined with heavy weight training. For example, at the 2010 USA Triathlon Art and Science of Triathlon Coaching Symposium, an HIIT researcher named Stephen McGregor introduced an HIIT training routine that research has shown to lead to incredible increases in power output, peak power, and VO_2 max. It goes like this:

- Start with four thirty-second max sprints, with two to four minutes of rest after each sprint, just three times a week.

- Gradually increase to ten thirty-second max sprints with two-and-a-half minutes of rest, just three times a week.

- Do this for seven weeks, for a total of six-and-a-half to fifteen minutes of actual HIIT a week.

But instead of this minimalist, high-quality approach, many people incorporating HIIT into their training (including CrossFitters) are easily doing twice that volume —not just in a week, but in a single day!

Finally, your time in the gym should primarily be spent getting strong and developing clean and functional movement patterns that enhance balance, symmetry, and stability—not building your muscular and cardiovascular endurance or trying to compete for time or points while pushing through soreness and fatigue. I explore this concept extensively in my book *Weight Training for Triathlon: The Ultimate Guidebook*. Given the intensity of metabolic conditioning that comes with swimming, bicycling, or running, it can be very easy to pile on excessive metabolic stress in a gym setting. The short story: Use the gym for strength, and work on endurance elsewhere.

So, ultimately, here's the problem with CrossFit: If the highly anaerobic and power- or strength-demanding workouts are performed in a typical carbohydrate-depleted state by an endurance athlete who is simultaneously engaging in heavy bouts of aerobic training, the result could be (1) poor form and increased risk of injury during the actual CrossFit routine and (2) hormonal imbalances and faulty biomechanics from CrossFit-induced soreness or fatigue during any subsequent aerobic swim, bike, or run sessions.

In other words, endurance athletes bent on including big training sessions cannot have their CrossFit cake and eat it, too. I guarantee that if you're combining a "proper" CrossFit program with a "proper" triathlon or endurance-training program, there is absolutely no way that you are giving your testosterone-to-cortisol ratio or inflammatory response to exercise adequate time to recover, which will result in inhibiting your immune response, excessive loading of soft tissue and joints, and increased risk of overtraining syndrome.

As a practitioner for WellnessFX (BeyondTrainingBook.com/WellnessFX), I see the biomarker values of many, many CrossFitters each week—and they tend to be some of the most hormonally depleted folks I work with. If you don't want to suffer adrenal fatigue (see Figure 3-3), which is where hormonal depletion leads, my first piece of advice is typically to back off CrossFit and add in more recovery sessions, easy swims, yoga, sleep, rest, and calorie intake.

So can you do CrossFit and avoid adrenal fatigue? Absolutely.

There are fantastic CrossFit coaches who design workouts and training routines with good attention to form that allow for proper rest and recovery. They pay attention to tissue quality, mobility, technical proficiency, proper progression of workouts, and proper movement patterns. *Power, Speed, Endurance,* by Brian MacKenzie, is a very good book about doing CrossFit the right way, and as long as you're willing to avoid the temptation to "do extra," his CrossFit Endurance program can get you good results.

How to Do Polarized Training the Right Way

Now you know that if you have the time, you can build endurance effectively by performing 80 percent of your training in a very easy, aerobic zone and 20 percent in a very hard, anaerobic zone. This is called polarized training, and the biggest mistake most people make with this approach is not doing the 80 percent easily enough and not doing the 20 percent hard enough.

So what's the right way to do polarized training?

I'm not great at math, so let's work with a simple weekly training volume number—say, twenty hours. Begin by allocating sixteen hours a week (80 percent of the twenty hours) to easy aerobic training and the other four hours a week (20 percent) to HIIT. To find your aerobic training heart rate, go back to chapter 1 or use Phil Maffetone's easy two-step formula:

1. Subtract your age from 180.

2. Modify this number by selecting from the following categories the one that best matches your fitness and health profile:
   • If you have or are recovering from a major illness (heart disease, an operation or hospital stay, etc.) or are on any regular medication, subtract an additional 10.

FIGURE 3-3. Typical Adrenal Fatigue Progression

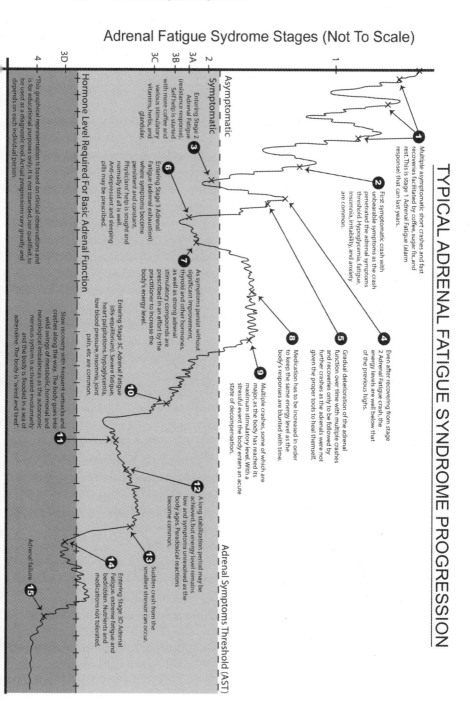

- If you are injured, have regressed in training or competition, get more than two colds or bouts of flu a year, have allergies or asthma, or have been inconsistent or are just getting back into training, subtract an additional 5.
- If you have been training consistently (at least four times a week) for up to two years without any of the previous issues, the number remains 180 minus your age.
- If you've been training for more than two years without any of the issues in the first two bullets and have made progress in competition without injury, add 5.

So, if you're a triathlete, four hours of HIIT leaves you enough time to perform one or two intense interval sessions each week for the swim, bike, and run. This might be two thirty-minute swim workouts comprising 25- to 200-meter repeats, a one-and-a-half- to two-hour bike workout with eight to ten short, steep, hard hill climbs followed by full recovery after climb, one track intervals running workout, and one hill repeats running workout. If you simply cannot do your HIIT sessions above your LT (or in a relatively anaerobic state), you're probably going too hard in your aerobic sessions.

Now this is all painting with a fairly broad brush. There is an entire branch of exercise training and science devoted to the concept of periodization, which dictates splitting your buildup to an event into periods of the year that have a specific training focus. In a traditional periodization model, based on polarized training, your training may be closer to 90 percent aerobic and 10 percent HIIT during the off-season and 70 percent aerobic and 30 percent HIIT as you get closer to a race. Or, from an even longer-term perspective, an athlete on a four-year development plan for the Olympics may do a higher percentage of aerobic training early in the process and gradually include more and more race-intensity intervals as the Olympics approach.

But this book is about how the average athlete can train for endurance while maintaining the delicate balance between health and performance, and that entails keeping things relatively simple. If you were to graph your training intensity for any given year, you'd come out very close to 80/20.

If this whole polarized training thing sounds like a lot of potentially exhausting exercise, you're right. So how on earth do professional endurance athletes do it for as much as twenty-five to thirty-five hours a week without crumbling from the stress? Mark Sisson provides some insight in his book *The Primal Connection,* in which he says that a major factor in the success of a pro endurance athlete is the absence of significant work stress—deadlines, office obligations, etc.

Here's how Mark puts it when describing his experiences coaching a team of world-ranked professional triathletes and comparing their lives to the life of an amateur triathlete:

The typical amateur triathlete was a type-A overachiever with a demanding career and a busy family life. Fitting in the requisite workouts was a constant juggling act between work and family obligations. The word "squeeze" was used repeatedly to describe scheduling efforts, starting with the morning alarm and an abrupt commencement of the day's first workout. Pacing seemed to be an obsession, not just for tracking workout speed, but minding the clock at all times in order to remain "on time" for every item on the packed daily agenda. The popular "quick lunchtime swim workout" referred more to the peripherals than the lap times—rushing out of the office, a presto change-o in the locker room, a one-minute postworkout shower, and then bursting back into the office an hour later with water beads still dripping from hair onto collar.

In contrast, the professional athletes—whose job was to simply race fast—lived lives centered around their workouts with minimal interference from real-life distractions or social obligations. While the pros conducted their workouts aggressively, the pace of their lives was leisurely. Lunchtime swim? Sure, but instead of toweling off, jerking the tie back into place, and rushing out to the parking lot, the postswim routine of the pros consisted of lingering in the poolside spa for nearly as long as the workout, shooting the breeze, stretching tight muscles, and generally decompressing from the intense effort in the water. Eventually, the pack moved from the spa into an easy lunch involving more shooting of the breeze. Eventually, they remounted their bikes for a couple more hours of pedaling, then took an afternoon nap, followed by a late-day run, followed by a stretching/icing session, followed by a quiet evening of television, reading, or lingering over a huge meal. As I spent more time in their world, I learned that the competitive advantage enjoyed by these professionals went beyond their impressive workouts. Embracing life both with purpose and at a more leisurely pace produces extraordinary results.

In a nutshell: Stress is stress—no matter whether it's from exercise or from lifestyle—and the more stress you're placing on yourself from your lifestyle, the less stress you'll be able to place on yourself from exercise.

How to Do HIIT the Right Way

What if you don't have time for polarized training, you don't want to waste your time with junk miles, but you also don't want to damage your body with excessive HIIT?

What I'm about to explain to you is exactly how I personally train for endurance. It's very similar to the method I use with most of my clients. I call it the "ancestral-athlete approach," and here's why.

If you look at our modern, sedentary lifestyles and our postindustrial diets, you can see that we have pushed ourselves far above and beyond what our bodies were designed for. Picture a typical day of sitting in an office surrounded by electromagnetic frequencies, deadlines, stress, and fake food.

Now contrast this day of "death by sitting" with the more natural life that our ancestors lived, which involved relatively high amounts of low-intensity physical activity—time spent hunting, gathering, farming, or gardening. These days of low-intensity (but hardly sedentary) activity were riddled with sudden bursts of high energy, such as when it became necessary to run from a lion, move a heavy rock or log, or engage in hand-to-hand combat.

Think of it this way: Until the recent industrial era, life was a constant physical challenge. We didn't have refrigerators, preservatives, microwaves, fast food, or pizza delivery to help us put dinner on the table. Rather than rushing to the grocery store with a credit card, we'd wander onto the plains with a weapon or go out to gather grasses, grains, fruits, and vegetables—and we'd expend extra energy properly preparing those natural foods. And while there were certainly drawbacks to this seemingly crude or uncomfortable mode of existence, there were powerful benefits in terms of physical fitness and endurance.

An ancestral approach to training is based on the theory that we are naturally designed to perform lots of low-level physical activity with occasional bursts of very high intensity, which builds endurance without significant physical and metabolic damage. Living and training in this manner means respecting our ancestors and critically considering how the environmental and training stresses we place on our bodies affect our health in positive or negative ways.

Of course, I'm all about the in-the-trenches application of these philosophies. After all, you can dream about hunter-gatherers all day long, but it doesn't help if you still head out the door every day at lunch to pound the pavement for an hour. So let's see what the ancestral-athlete approach would look like, using an Ironman training routine as an example.

A sample week of training (very similar to the training approach in my "Triathlon Dominator" and "Tri-Ripped" triathlon training programs) should be designed around one medium-to-long aerobic session per week for swimming, cycling, and running. Each of these sessions should be devoted to lots of time spent in zone 2, with focused zone 3, race-pace intervals. For an Ironman, this could be a two- to three-hour focused interval training session on the bike, a sixty- to ninety-minute high-quality run, and a forty-five- to sixty-minute swim that incorporates 400-meter to 1,000-meter intervals.

Here's the key to the ancestral-athlete approach: The remainder of your aerobic training should be accomplished simply by staying active throughout the day. Later in this book you'll learn about "biohacks" that allow you to incorporate this concept more easily into your everyday life, but here are some examples:

- Stand and walk as much as possible. (I stand six to eight hours a day while working and often conduct phone calls and consults while walking.)

- Never sit for longer than an hour without standing and doing fifty to a hundred jumping jacks, five doorway pull-ups, twenty push-ups or squats, or some other calisthenic movement.

- Spend as much time as possible outdoors in the fresh air, experiencing both hot and cold temperature fluctuations, without taking your phone and other electronic devices with you.

- Lift something heavy every day. (I usually flip a tire a few times or load up a barbell in the garage.)

- Commute whenever possible on a mountain bike or by foot, or even by new modes of movement, such as Parkour, MovNat, or fitness exploring.

- Begin every day with a cold shower to spark the metabolism, followed by deep breathing, calisthenics, and stretching.

- Visit a sauna one to five times a week to get all the cardiovascular and health benefits of heat training without any joint impact.

- Learn how to breathe, stand, and move properly so that your aerobic metabolism stays elevated throughout the day.

"AM I TOO OLD FOR HIIT?"

One concern that older athletes repeatedly express to me is the fear of tearing a muscle, getting a sprain or strain, or developing a stress fracture from the high intensities in a HIIT session. Yes, it can certainly be a bit more difficult to jump, sprint, and move as powerfully as you did in your younger years. Here are a few reasons:

1) Your metabolism decreases by about 10 percent from your thirties to your sixties, and another 10 percent from your sixties forward. This means that you may gain fat more easily.

2) Your maximum oxygen consumption decreases significantly. each decade from age twenty-five to sixty-five, and even more quickly from then on—which means intense cardiovascular efforts may be very difficult.

3) You grow less responsive to energy-stimulating hormones, called catecholamines (like epinephrine), and, as a result, your maximum heart rate decreases, which can also decrease the intensity of hard efforts.

4) Both the total amount of blood that your heart pumps per beat and the ability of your muscles to extract oxygen from that blood decrease, which can affect your cardiovascular capacity.

5) Your muscle strength peaks when you're about twenty-five, plateaus when you're thirty-five to forty, and then begins to decline quickly, with 25 percent loss of peak strength by the time you're sixty-five. This is because of a loss of muscle fibers.

6) Your tendon, ligament, and joint elasticity decreases as "cross-linkages" form between soft tissue fibers in these areas. This can cause a loss of two to four inches of lower-back and hip flexibility.

7) Your bone density decreases as you lose calcium and the matrix inside the bone begins to deteriorate, which can lead to increased risk of osteoporosis or fractures, especially in women.

But don't get depressed and let this information persuade you to stay away from heavy weights or a track: The HIIT approach can have a dramatic antiaging effect on many of the variables listed above.

For example, hard running intervals that involve heavy breathing and burning muscles can help boost a slowing metabolism, reduce the rate of VO_2 max decline, improve venous return back to the heart, and enhance flexibility and mobility better than a slow jog. When performed in moderation, the impact from hard running also has a potent bone-building effect.

To stave off loss of both bone density and muscle that occurs with aging, loading the bones and joints along the vertical axis is very effective. It can be achieved with strength exercises that will be discussed later, such as squats, overhead presses, chest presses, and lunges. These same exercises can build new neurons as your body and mind are challenged by movements that are generally more complex than simply spinning on a bicycle.

A study done by Ana Pereira at the University of Trás-os-Montes in Portugal found that a high-speed, power-based weight-training program can increase functional capacity of the muscles in the upper- and lower-body extremities in older people much more efficiently than a program of only slow and controlled weight training.

And both high-intensity intervals and weight training can cause catecholamine and hormonal responses that keep maximum heart rate high and maintain the body in a relatively anabolic state compared with pure, low-intensity cardio. Compared to a body-damaging catabolic state, an anabolic state is favorable to muscle building and a maximized release of good hormones like testosterone and growth hormone.

In other words, the hormone rush, mental stimulation, and thrill of lifting heavy stuff or sprinting will actually keep you young.

Or, in the words of eighty-three-year-old Ironman world record holder Lew Hollander: "Go anaerobic every day."

Once you program your main aerobic sessions into your week on the days that create the least stress for you (typically on the weekend for the average athlete) and naturally work light physical activity into your life, you can then inject brief bouts of high-quality intense workouts and structured weight-training sessions throughout the week—but only if you feel completely rested and able to do them with perfect form. Using these concepts, an Ironman training week would look like this:

- **Monday:** 30 minutes easy bicycling skills and drills; 20 minutes easy swim drills
- **Tuesday:** 20 minutes heavy barbell lifts; 30 minutes run HIIT workout
- **Wednesday:** 30 minutes bicycling HIIT workout; 30 minutes swim HIIT workout
- **Thursday:** 20 minutes heavy barbell lifts; 30 minutes easy run drills
- **Friday:** 60 minutes injury prevention (e.g., training weak links of your specific body) and core training, yoga, or an easy swim
- **Saturday:** 2.5 hours of 20 minutes on, 5 minutes off cycling intervals at race pace; 3 × 1,000-meter swim at race pace
- **Sunday:** 60 to 90 minutes of 9 minutes on, 3 minutes off running intervals at race pace

Although this snapshot of an ancestral-athlete approach to an Ironman training week may seem to merely scratch the surface, don't worry: In later chapters, I'll teach you about every biohack, healthy-living component, recovery protocol, nutrition blueprint, and other strategy you need to take the guesswork out of your training and prime your body for optimal health—because that's the only way this approach will work.

I quite frequently get asked about how to incorporate a HIIT-style training routine into your life if the goal is not to do some masochistic event like an Ironman, the CrossFit Games, or a Spartan race, but instead to simply maximize the ultimate combination of longevity and looking good naked. In other words, suppose you want to live as long as possible and look good doing it. Suppose you want to maximize your hormone balance, libido, fertility, strength, power, and cardiovascular capacity. Suppose you want to step back, investigate every shred of exercise science research, and inject only the most effective and proven strategies into your life, even if it's not for the primary sake of preparing for sufferfests like triathlons, marathons, obstacle races, or other feats of physical endurance, but rather because you simply want to maximize longevity, look good naked, or both.

Whether it's calorie intake, exercise, sunlight, carbohydrates, or work habits, we often think that we need much more than we actually do to get the results we want. Why crank out those extra reps or put in those extra few hours if you don't need to? Failing to heed the minimum effective dose can cost you money, time, and mental real estate. Sure, if you want to do an Ironman triathlon, you certainly need to put in the hours, but all those extra hours aren't necessarily good for you, and they certainly aren't necessary for being as fit as humanly possible while simultaneously maximizing your life span.

So what would an exercise program look like if you do just wanted to look good naked and live longer? Let's take a look.

Recently, the *New York Times* published an article entitled "The Right Dose of Exercise for a Longer Life." The article discusses the results of two new studies that investigated how much exercise we need to get longevity benefits. Before jumping into the results, it's important to note that rather than being controlled or randomized studies, this research relied on people's memory recall of their exercise habits. Similar to diet studies that rely on memory recall of meals, this data can be prone to human error, but it can still give us important clues.

The first study, "Leisure Time Physical Activity and Mortality," published in the June 2015 issue of the *Journal of the American Medical Association* (JAMA), found that people who did not exercise at all faced the highest risk of early death. Those who exercised a little (not meeting the current American Heart Association guidelines of 150 minutes per week, but at least doing something) lowered their risk of premature death by 20 percent. Those who met the guidelines of 150 minutes of moderate exercise per week enjoyed greater longevity benefits and a 31 percent lower risk of dying compared with those who never exercised.

But the greatest benefits came for those who tripled the recommended level of exercise and exercised moderately (mostly by walking) for 450 minutes per week (a little more than an hour per day). These people were 39 percent less likely to die prematurely than those who never exercised.

What's even more interesting is that after 450 minutes per week, the longevity benefits of exercise plateaued, but never significantly declined. Even the people engaging in ten times or more the recommended exercise dose gained about the same reduction in mortality risk as the people who simply met the 150-minutes-per-week guidelines. They didn't get any healthier, but (contrary to what many believe) their risk of dying young did not increase.

The second study, "Effect of Moderate to Vigorous Physical Activity on All-Cause Mortality in Middle-aged and Older Australians," also published in the June 2015 issue of *JAMA,* reached a similar conclusion, but focused more on exercise intensity and stands in stark contrast to other studies that have suggested that frequent, strenuous exercise might contribute to early mortality. This study found that meeting the exercise guidelines significantly reduced the risk of early death, even if that exercise was moderate in intensity (such as walking). No surprises there. But those who engaged in occasional vigorous and high-intensity exercise saw a significant additional reduction in mortality. Those people who spent up to 30 percent of their weekly exercise time in vigorous, intense activities were 9 percent less likely to die prematurely than those who exercised for the same amount of time but only at moderate intensity. People who spent more than 30 percent of their exercise time doing strenuous workouts gained an extra 13 percent reduction in early mortality, compared with those who never broke through that intensity barrier. Even among the few people in the study who were found to be completing the largest amounts of intense exercise, there was no increase in risk of death.

At this point, you may be wondering what qualifies as moderate and what qualifies as vigorous. Moderate-intensity aerobic exercise is when you're working hard enough to raise your heart rate and break into a sweat. Think of it this way: You're working at moderate intensity if you're able to talk but unable to sing the words to a song during the activity. Vigorous-intensity aerobic exercise is when you're breathing hard and fast, your muscles are burning, and your heart rate has increased significantly. If you're working at this level, you won't be able to say more than a few words without pausing for a breath.

So what's the ultimate takeaway from these two studies? Researcher Klaus Gebel, who led the second study, puts it like this: "Try to reach at least 150 minutes of physical activity per week and have around 20 to 30 minutes of that be vigorous activity." He also notes that a larger dose of exercise, for those who are so inclined, does not seem to be unsafe.

So it's clear from this data that you need at least about twenty minutes per day of structured exercise if you want to live a long time—and that is of course with the understanding that you're not spending the rest of the day sedentary or sitting. But it's one thing to live a long time and another thing entirely to look as good as possible doing it. Frankly, no matter what "looking good naked" means to you, you're going to need a bit more structured advice than a blanket recommendation to "try to reach at least 150 minutes of physical activity per week and have around 20 to 30 minutes of that be vigorous activity," right?

When it comes to having adequately low body fat to be cut and ripped but adequately high body fat to optimize hormones and fertility, high enough muscle mass to be strong and look good but low enough muscle mass to avoid being a short-lived, cancer-prone bodybuilder, and enough cardiovascular fitness to be venous and vibrant but not so much cardiovascular fitness that you're overtrained from excess volume, you need the minimum effective dose of cardiovascular fitness, muscle endurance, strength, mitochondrial density, metabolic efficiency, and stamina.

That's it. Check those boxes and you're going to hit every basic component of fitness and look really good doing it. So let's delve into exactly what a structured exercise program would look like if your goal was to check all those boxes to achieve the ideal combination of fitness, longevity, and a nice body. Ultimately, to be fit, live a long time, and look good naked, you need:

1. Maintenance of cardiovascular fitness.

Definition: Cardiovascular fitness is simply defined as the maximum amount of oxygen you can utilize, also known as VO_2 max.

How to do it: Based on the results of the July 2014 *Journal of Strength & Conditioning Research* study entitled "High-intensity interval training every second week maintains VO_2 max in soccer players during off-season," the minimum effective dose for cardiovascular fitness maintenance is five 4-minute high-intensity rounds at 87 to 97 percent of your maximum heart rate, with approximately four minutes after each round to allow you to recover sufficiently.

Summary: For the minimum effective dose of cardiovascular fitness, perform five 4-minute hard efforts with full recoveries once every two weeks. Got it?

2. Maximum muscle endurance and aerobic capacity.

Definition: The amount of work your muscles can endure and the amount of time you can "go to battle" while keeping your force output high.

How to do it: For improving muscle endurance while simultaneously increasing aerobic capacity, nothing beats Tabata sets. In one study (www.ncbi.nlm.nih.gov/pubmed/22994393), participants performed one 4-minute Tabata protocol (that's twenty seconds of all-out exercise followed by ten seconds of full rest) with a single exercise four times a week for four weeks. In this case, exercise choices included burpees, mountain climbers, jumping jacks, and squat thrusts, but for Tabatas, you could also use things like running, treadmill, indoor or outdoor cycling, rowing, or kettlebell swings. Compared to four steady-state thirty-minute treadmill exercise protocols per week in the control group, the Tabata group (which, if you do the math, was performing just sixteen total minutes of exercise per week) saw massive gains in both aerobic capacity and muscle endurance, and there's plenty more Tabata research to go around.

Summary: Most studies use two to four Tabata sessions per week. My recommendation is to aim for two Tabata sessions per week, especially if you're doing everything else included in this program.

3. Maintenance of ideal ratios of strength and muscle mass.

Definition: The maximum amount of strength you can muster in one tightly packed group of muscle fibers—in other words: hard, wiry strength. At PerfectHealthDiet. com, Paul Jaminet wrote an excellent article entitled "Are Bigger Muscles Better? Antioxidants and the Response to Exercise" outlining why this is a better approach than purely trying to pack on as much muscle fiber as possible.

How to do it: Sure, you can get strong and muscular doing CrossFit-esque workouts that require maximum deadlifts in two minutes or ungodly amounts of snatch reps or bodybuilding workouts that have you doing bicep curls until you're bleeding out the eyeballs, but none of that is sustainable when it comes to maximizing longevity. Remember, you want to be able to maintain strength and muscle when you're 20, 40, 60, and 80 years old. For this, I recommend two workouts per week:

1. A super-slow lifting protocol exactly as described by Doug McGuff in his book *Body by Science*—specifically twelve to twenty minutes of just a few choice multi-joint exercises with extremely slow, controlled lifting (thirty to sixty seconds per rep) and relatively high weights.

   - Super-slow upper body push (e.g. overhead press)
   - Super-slow upper body pull (e.g. pull-up)
   - Super-slow lower body push (e.g. squat)
   - Super-slow lower body pull (e.g. deadlift)

2. A high-intensity bodyweight circuit program exactly as described in the May 2013 issue of the ACSM *Health & Fitness Journal,* in which a pair of researchers designed a seven-minute workout to maintain strength and muscle in as little time as possible. Each of the following exercises is to be performed for thirty seconds, with ten seconds of rest between exercises.

   - Jumping jacks
   - Wall sits

- Push-ups
- Crunches
- Step-ups
- Squats
- Dips
- Planks
- Running in place with high knees
- Lunges
- Push-ups with rotation
- Side planks

Summary: Do two strength workouts per week—one with slow, controlled heavy lifting and one with high-intensity, light, bodyweight-esque movements.

4. Maximum mitochondrial density.

Definition: Mitochondria are the power plants of your cells, mitochondrial biogenesis is the creation of new mitochondria, and mitochondrial density is simply having as many mitochondria packed into your muscles as possible so that you can utilize more fat and glucose.

How to do it: One study has shown that a workout consisting of four 30-second all-out cycling sprints significantly activated mitochondrial biogenesis in the skeletal muscle of human subjects, and another study has shown three sets of five 4-second treadmill sprints with twenty seconds of rest between sprints, performed three times per week did the same thing. One other study showed that four to six 30-second bouts of all-out sprint cycling with four minutes of rest done three times a week also improved important components of mitochondrial health. As you can see, when it comes to maximizing mitochondrial density, it all comes down to short, intense sprints.

Summary: The Tabata sets I already mentioned will likely cover most of your mitochondrial bases, but if you have a bit more time to spare, then after either your strength workouts or your stamina workouts, perform a few brief sets of very intense sprints (for example, five 4- to 30-second sprints). Yes, you read that right: These sprints can be as short as four seconds. Consider this to be the icing on the cake, and squeeze it in when it's convenient. Alternatively, you could mark one spot on your calendar once every week or two to perform four to six 30-second bouts of all-out sprint cycling with four minutes of rest after each bout.

5. Optimized fat burning, metabolic efficiency, and blood sugar control.

Definition: Maximizing the body's ability to generate ketones and burn fatty acids as a primary source of fuel while avoiding frequent fluctuations in blood sugar.

How to do it: I have a comprehensive podcast at BenGreenfieldFitness.com entitled "Five Simple Steps to Turning Yourself into a Fat Burning Machine," and it basically comes down to this: (1) do a short aerobic workout as many mornings a week as possible, preferably in an overnight fasted state; (2) avoid frequent snacking; (3) save all your carb intake for the end of the day, and until that point eat high amounts of healthy fats with moderate amounts of protein; (4) stay mildly physically active all day long (use a standing workstation, take jumping jack breaks, etc.); and (5) stay anti-fragile by exposing your body to frequent fluctuations in temperature.

Summary: As you can see, this step is more lifestyle based. Start off each day, before eating, with ten to thirty minutes of very light activity (such as yoga, walking the dog, or doing yard work), take at least one cold shower each day, visit the sauna at least once per week, avoid non-nutrient-dense carbohydrates, and be as active as possible all day long. One research study showed that you can even get excellent blood-glucose-controlling results with something as simple as a fifteen-minute walk after your main meal of the day.

6. Stamina (optional, but highly recommended).

Definition: The ability to move at low to moderate intensity for ninety-plus minutes (it's at about the ninety-minute mark that glycogen levels become depleted and you must begin to rely significantly upon fat as a fuel).

How to do it: Stamina isn't entirely necessary for looking good naked or living a long time, but I like to know that, if necessary, I could hunt down an animal, ride my bicycle to a nearby city, hike over a mountain range, or survive for a significant amount of time in a zombie apocalypse. Contrary to popular belief among marathoners and triathletes, this does not require a two- to three-hour death march every weekend. The human body is actually quite good at going for long periods and requires only brief forays into stamina. So I recommend that once or twice per month, you go do something long, like a backpack hike, big bike ride, Bikram yoga session, or anything else that combines low- to moderate-intensity physical activity, endurance, and mental focus.

Summary: Again, unless you're signed up for something like an obstacle race, bicycling century, triathlon, or marathon, this last step isn't really necessary, but if you want to add the stamina feather to your cap, get out and do something that takes ninety-plus minutes at least once a month. If you really want to challenge yourself, you could even make that session something like "The Hardest Workout in the World," a Spartan race, or any other crazy fitness adventure, from rafting to rock climbing. The rest of your innate physical endurance will be built easily by simply ensuring that you keep your butt out of a chair all day long.

So that's it. Once you put it all together, it's actually not too daunting:

- To maintain cardiovascular fitness and VO_2 max, do five 4-minute intense intervals once every two weeks.
- To improve your aerobic capacity and muscle endurance, do two or three Tabata sets a week.
- To maintain the ultimate combination of strength and muscle mass, do one 12- to 20-minute super-slow strength session and one 7- to 14-minute high-intensity bodyweight workout per week.
- To maximize mitochondrial density, do a short series of sprint bursts one to three times per week (such as five 4-second all-out sprints with twenty seconds of rest between sprints).

- To increase fat burning and metabolic efficiency, include fasting, avoid snacking, avoid sitting, and figure out ways to engage in low-level physical activity all day long.
- To increase stamina, do something for ninety-plus minutes at low to moderate intensity once or twice per month.

When you do the math, you're really not spending more than thirty to sixty minutes per day on getting fit, looking good naked, and living a long time. And in my opinion, that's definitely doable.

As I mentioned, what I've described above is not designed to turn you into a super-athlete. It's designed to give you an amazing body and a long life.

A couple more things:

First, I designed a "Look-Good-Naked Longevity Plan" at BenGreenfieldFitness. com/longevity, in which all this is laid out for you on a weekly calendar that you can print and that syncs to your computer, phone, etc. In this eight-week program, I give you daily, step-by-step instructions for the exact muscle training, fat-burning, cardiovascular, and mobility protocols that research has proven to maximize every second you spend exercising. Pretty much everything you've just read, all conveniently spelled out for each week. Whether you want to look good naked or get massive gains in fitness (or, of course, both!), you can wash, rinse, and repeat this eight-week cycle throughout the entire year.

Next, if you're a complete geek and you want to quantitatively track this stuff, then you may want to check out the Greenfield Longevity Panels in the labs section at GreenfieldFitnessSystems.com. Working closely with WellnessFX, America's top laboratory for concierge blood testing and online access to all your blood-testing results, I developed the most comprehensive blood-testing package that money can buy. There is one package designed for men and one for women. I created it for health enthusiasts, biohackers, and antiaging individuals who want access to the same type of executive health panel and screening that would cost tens of thousands of dollars at a longevity institute. This panel covers virtually all hormones and all biomarkers. Yeah, it's still spendy, but if you want to test everything you can test, then this one is worth doing at least once in your lifetime. I personally do it once a year.

In the meantime, you're now equipped with everything you need to know to look good naked and live longer. I suggest you either use my prewritten program or sit down with your own calendar and map each of these sessions into your weekly routine.

Additional resources, helpful websites, scientific references, and surprise bonuses are available at BeyondTrainingBook.com/Chapter3. Enjoy.

CHAPTER 4

Underground Training Tactics for Enhancing Endurance

Now you are familiar with the two best ways to build endurance: polarized training with lots of hours (using the 80/20 approach) and HIIT with fewer hours (using the ancestral-athlete approach).

Regardless of which method you choose, you can implement a variety of "underground" tactics to enhance the effectiveness and efficiency of your training. These tactics come in especially handy if:

- Time management is important to you.

- You want to strengthen your cardiovascular, musculoskeletal, and nervous systems without doing significant damage to your joints, health, or metabolism.

In part 3 of this book, I'll show you additional strategies that you can use to encourage recovery, but right now we're going to focus on training strategies for enhancing endurance.

So let's jump right in!

Overspeed Training

Overspeed training is, exactly as it sounds, the practice of training your limbs to turn over at a speed beyond what feels comfortable or natural. Just envision the Road Runner from the old Looney Tunes cartoons.

Before getting into the how-tos of overspeed training, it's important to understand that by spinning your legs extremely fast on a bicycle, or running at an insanely high turnover, or swimming windmill-style, you're not necessarily replicating what you will do in a race.

For example, in the case of cycling, research has shown that lower cadences, such as 60 rpm, actually yield better efficiency and economy than a cadence of 80 or 100 rpm[2]. And the folks over at Swim Smooth have a fantastic stroke-rate chart showing that many swimmers actually do just fine with a relatively low stroke count.

But here's why overspeed training works: It is an effective way to recruit new muscle tissue, specifically by engaging more muscle motor units than by training at lower speeds. This is called a "neural adaptation," and you can consider it a form of training for your nervous system[3]. Through overspeed training, not only do your neurons literally learn how to fire faster and control your muscles more efficiently at higher speeds, but you also develop more powerful and quick muscle fiber contractions, which comes in handy for hard surges during a race or a tough workout.

Contrary to popular belief, you do not need fancy equipment for overspeed training. While there are antigravity treadmills that use differential air pressure to reduce your body weight to as low as 20 percent, and extremely fast treadmill belts with a harness that literally hangs you from the ceiling while you're running, you don't need these fancy machines. They certainly do allow for "extreme" assisted overspeed training in an underweighted or low-gravity environment, but you don't need to spend what a small automobile costs on a new treadmill.

Instead, here are some effective overspeed workouts you can easily do with equipment you probably already have, or at least with relatively inexpensive training gear.

Downhill overspeed running: Find a dry, nonbumpy area of grass where you can sprint about forty or fifty feet down a slope and then another forty or fifty feet once you reach the flat (to allow for the continuation of the overspeed effect without the assistance of gravity). Research indicates that a downhill grade of about 5 percent is ideal, but you don't need to go to the golf course with surveying equipment to find the best slope[3]. Just run down a relatively steep hill that isn't so steep that you fall on your face. If you really want to get fancy with overspeed running, you can grab a partner (or a pole) and an overspeed bungee for your repeats. The overspeed bungee actually pulls you along as you run, forcing you to turn over your feet very quickly. Follow the links on the resource web page at the end of this chapter to see how to use these types of devices.

Overspeed cycling efforts: A downhill slope or an indoor trainer works best for these efforts, although you can also do them on the flats. After a good warm-up, choose the gear with the least resistance that allows you to pedal extremely fast without bouncing in the saddle. Spin at the fastest possible cadence (preferably higher than 120 rpm) for a maximum of thirty seconds, and then recover completely before doing the next set, completing five to ten sets total.

Assisted swimming: For this workout, you need swim stretch cords. In a pinch, I've used a good set of fins to allow me to swim faster, but you'll get better results with less muscular and cardiovascular fatigue by using stretch cords. With the stretch cords attached to your waist, swim as far away from the wall as possible, then turn and let the cords pull you back as you swim, which will be much faster than if you were unassisted. If you do this correctly, you're going to find that your stroke turnover rate is incredibly difficult to maintain. You can add this kind of training to the beginning or end of one of your weekly swim sets.

Be aware that overspeed running can create significant eccentric muscular damage, caused by your brain attempting to "slow you down" just slightly with each step. The ensuing soreness can be pretty uncomfortable the day or two after an overspeed workout. To minimize this soreness, introduce overspeed training into your program only after you've got a solid six to eight weeks of weight training and plyometric training under your belt. Although swimming and cycling overspeed training don't cause significant muscle-tissue damage, your neuromuscular system does need plenty of time to recover and regenerate, so I don't recommend doing overspeed sessions more than once a week.

Underspeed Training

At the opposite end of the spectrum of overspeed training is underspeed training. You have a pretty good idea of what underspeed training involves if you've ever done a long, grinding bike ride up a hill, trekked up a stairmill at a gym, or done a resisted swim session dragging one of those ultrasexy drag suits.

Underspeed training is better for building strength and force-production capability. Similar to overspeed training, underspeed training can also help develop efficient movement patterns and muscle-fiber recruitment (but with a less-powerful neuromuscular "brain training" effect than moving your limbs wicked fast). When I did a podcast interview with Ironman champion Chris McCormack, I was surprised by the amount of underspeed ("grinding") sessions he does on the bike—sessions that he recommends specifically because they stave off fatigue late in a long race.

Underspeed training sessions also come in quite handy early in a race season, when building strength and developing proper movement patterns are crucial. Underspeed workouts include:

- Superslow training sessions similar to what Doug McGuff outlines in his book *Body by Science,* which involve extremely slow repetitions that last thirty to sixty seconds per repetition

- Steep 60 to 70 rpm hill climbs for five to fifteen minutes on a bike

- Running steep hills slowly

- Climbing a stairmill (with an optional weight vest or set of dumbbells)

- Performing intervals in the pool, dragging a parachute behind you or wearing a drag suit

Weight training could also technically be considered a form of underspeed training, but it is discussed more fully in the strength section of the next chapter.

EMS

You've no doubt seen it: the "as seen on TV" ad for the special electrodes you attach to your abs to magically get a six-pack.

Known as neuromuscular electrical stimulation (NMES), electrical stimulation (EMS), or electromyostimulation devices, these contraptions elicit a muscle contraction using electrical impulses that directly stimulate motor neurons (as opposed to a TENS unit, which is good for managing pain, especially in the low back, but stimulates only surface nerve endings, not motor neurons)[9].

The first few times you use an EMS device, it feels as though an invader has somehow taken over your muscles and caused them to contract without the help of your brain. These contractions can be quick and rapid, quick with longer pauses between contractions, or even as long as seconds and sometimes minutes at a time.

Normally, your brain sends electrical impulses through your central nervous system (CNS) to fire your muscles. But EMS circumvents the brain, allowing for deep, intense, and complete muscular contractions without taxing your CNS (or your joints and tendons), which is why it feels strange: Your body doesn't know the difference between a voluntary contraction and an electrically induced one—it just recognizes the stimulus.

To use EMS, you place the electrodes on your skin at each end of the muscle to be stimulated. The device usually has four channels with lead wires, and each wire is connected to two pads. Very small amounts of current run from one pad to the next and complete a circuit—using your muscle tissue as a conduit. The current runs at specific frequencies and pulse durations (microseconds), and the motor neurons within this circuit are stimulated. The muscle fibers innervated by the motor neurons then contract. And voilà—you start twitching. Which muscle fibers are stimulated depends on the frequency you use. Basically, three ranges of frequencies stimulate three different types of fiber. A slow-twitch muscle fiber will contract when stimulated by one set of frequencies, an intermediate-fast-twitch muscle fiber by a different set of frequencies, and a fast-twitch muscle fiber by the highest frequencies.

I personally own and use both a Compex Sport Elite device for EMS-based muscle training and a MarcPro for EMS-based recovery. I outline the difference between the two at BenGreenfieldFitness.com/marc. Although for several years I used EMS only for recovery, I now use it for strength- and explosive-strength-training sessions for my quads and hamstrings (while practicing deep diaphragmatic breathing at the same time), and even use EMS in places like an infrared sauna or a car or airplane. Interestingly, I've been able to get myself into a dripping-wet full-body sweat with these sessions, and, when performed before a bike ride or run, it is much easier for me to achieve both higher cadences and higher speeds. Multiple clinical studies back this up, and websites such as Hammer Nutrition's have entire libraries devoted to research and the proper use of EMS for muscle gain, lactic acid tolerance, and so on[1].

While an EMS device certainly isn't going to help you burn enough calories or fat to give you a Greek-sculpture six-pack, it can indeed result in a significant boost in cardiovascular and musculoskeletal fitness. For more tips on how to incorporate EMS into a training season, read my blog post "How to Use Electrical Muscle Stimulation to Enhance Performance, Build Power and VO$_2$ Max" (find the link on the resource web page for this chapter).

Finally, if you want to upgrade to a very expensive (and relatively teeth-grittingly intense) form of electrical muscle stimulation that can leave your muscles in a state of maximum contraction for minutes at a time and yield faster results than any other EMS device out there, check out the EVO Athlete program operated by Jay Schroeder in Arizona (evoultrafit.com). Jay uses an electrical-stimulation device called the ARPwave, which possesses characteristics not found in any conventional therapeutic neuromuscular electrical stimulator (specifically something called interferential, microcurrent, galvanic, Russian stim, iontophoresis). This wave is supposedly more compatible with the body's natural electrical wave production, and because it can pass more easily through skin and fatty tissue, the current can penetrate much deeper without nasty side effects like skin burning. It's like electrostimulation on steroids.

By combining movement patterns and the use of the ARPwave, Jay is able to achieve extremely fast injury-healing time. If you can combine this kind of electrostimulation training with heavy lifting or a type of training called "extreme isometrics," you can get amazing performance results in a very short period.

Hypoxic, Resisted, and Restricted Breathing

Pick up a straw. Breathe in and out through the straw. That's *resisted breathing*. Consider it to be weight training for your lungs.

Now go for a swim. Experience what happens when you breathe every five or seven strokes instead of every one or two strokes. That's *restricted breathing,* which sends a clear message to your body that oxygen molecules are few and far between. Finally, go climb a mountain or crawl into an altitude tent. That's *hypoxic training,* in which the air is truly thinner and you're actually pulling less oxygen into your body.

Resisted breathing enhances your endurance by strengthening your inspiratory and expiratory muscles, which increases your ventilatory capacity (lung capacity). Hypoxic training not only strengthens those same respiratory muscles but also results in:

- Improvements in oxygen uptake, transport, and utilization

- Production of neuroendocrine hormones that can have an anabolic-training effect

- Improvements in immune system strength

- Increased antioxidant-enzyme activity in the brain, liver, heart, and other organs (assuming that you don't overdo it, in which case you will actually suppress normal antioxidant processes)

- Increased red blood cell production, resulting in increased oxygen-carrying capacity in the blood

Finally, restricted breathing gives you benefits of both resisted breathing and hypoxic training[8].

Before I give you some practical ways to implement resisted breathing, restricted breathing, and hypoxic training, let's get something straight: Many resisted-breathing devices are marketed as hypoxic-training devices but do not simulate altitude at all and do not result in hypoxic adaptations.

Take, for example, altitude-training masks, which seem to have become rather popular of late. Most of them, which look like SWAT team gas masks or make you look like the Batman villain Bane, cannot (despite some manufacturers' claims) actually change the atmospheric pressure you're training in. They have to be designed as intermittent hypoxic training (IHT) devices to accomplish this, and most are not. The fact is that when you're charging down the treadmill sporting your scary-looking altitude-training mask, you're still breathing air that is approximately 21 percent oxygen, with the same partial oxygen pressure of whatever altitude you happen to be at. Most masks simply *restrict* your breathing by covering up your mouth and nose. These masks can certainly be effective for improving ventilatory capacity and for increasing your mental tolerance and stress resilience in situations where you have low oxygen or air availability, but they don't achieve the same physiological adaptations as true hypoxic training[5].

By contrast, real altitude training would require you to drive your car to the top of a high mountain, get out, and go for a run; to sleep in an altitude-training tent from a company such as Hypoxico; to use IHT sessions (inhaling low-oxygen air through a mask) to expose your body to periods of hypoxia (9 to 14 percent oxygen); or live and train in a place like Colorado.

It is in these true high-altitude, or high-altitude-simulating, situations that your body, deprived of oxygen, makes more hemoglobin to shuttle oxygen to your muscles and experiences many of the favorable hormone and immune system adaptations to hypoxia. Of course, simulating or training at high altitude can be a logistical nightmare and a time-suck if you don't already live in the mountains or have a significant other who finds sleeping in an altitude tent romantic. Probably the most practical method currently available is the home model of a true altitude mask made by Hypoxico, which you can wear on your face while exercising. At anywhere from $6,000 to $12,000, these units are pricey—but still cost less than moving to the top of a mountain.

However, from an economical and practical perspective, most of us are limited to resisted breathing or restricted breathing—both of which can yield great training benefits with less stress than altitude training. Here are some ways to implement these methods:

- Swim restricted-breathing sets: Instead of breathing every one or two strokes, breathe every three, five, or seven. Another favorite method of mine is to finish a swim workout by doing 10 × 25 sets of swimming from one end of the pool to the other without breathing[9].

- Swim resisted-breathing sets: Add a Cardio Cap to a front-mounted swim snorkel to restrict the amount of air you get. You can wear this cap during both long interval sets and short sprints.

- Wear an altitude-training mask (really a resisted-breathing device) during an interval run or cycling session[12].

- Keep a PowerLung resisted-breathing device in your car or at home and use it frequently throughout the week.

When combined with proper breathing patterns throughout your workday (such as habitual deep diaphragmatic breathing), these methods can be extremely efficient at improving your ventilatory capacity and efficiency of oxygen utilization[11].

Another useful form of breath training, often incorporated by freedivers, is O_2 and CO_2 interval training. Here's an example of a CO_2 static apnea table:

Round 1	Hold 1:00	Breathe 1:30
Round 2	Hold 1:00	Breathe 1:15
Round 3	Hold 1:00	Breathe 1:00
Round 4	Hold 1:00	Breathe 0:45
Round 5	Hold 1:00	Breathe 0:30
Round 6	Hold 1:00	Breathe 0:15

As you can see, the rest periods get shorter and shorter as the session progresses. During the rest period, it's important to breathe normally without hyperventilating. These types of sessions ideally would be done daily if you really wanted to increase your breath hold time or ability to "tolerate" CO_2.

While CO_2 tables train your body to deal with high levels of CO_2 in your system, O_2 tables train your lungs to store more oxygen, or your body to operate on lower levels of CO_2. With O_2 tables, your breath holds get longer while your rest periods stay the same. Here's an example of an O_2 table:

Round 1	Hold 1:00	Breathe 2:00
Round 2	Hold 1:15	Breathe 2:00
Round 3	Hold 1:30	Breathe 2:00
Round 4	Hold 1:45	Breathe 2:00
Round 5	Hold 2:00	Breathe 2:00
Round 6	Hold 2:15	Breathe 2:00

Cold Thermogenesis

I first discovered cold thermogenesis (CT) through Ray Cronise, a NASA materials engineer who appeared on my podcast along with Tim Ferriss, author of the *New York Times* bestseller *The 4-Hour Body,* in the episode "How to Manipulate Your Body's Temperature to Burn More Fat." Later, after experimenting extensively and successfully with CT, I interviewed neurosurgeon Jack Kruse, who specializes in the use of CT for weight loss, hormone stabilization, and performance, in the podcast episode "How You Can Use Cold Thermogenesis to Perform Like Lance Armstrong and Michael Phelps."

In short, a multitude of performance benefits are derived from frequent exposure to cold temperatures, cold-water immersion, cold showers, cold-hot-contrast showers, and the use of body-cooling gear, such as the vest from CoolFatBurner.com or compression gear from the company 110% Play Harder, including:

BAT Activation

Brown adipose tissue, or BAT, is found primarily around your collarbones, sternum, neck, and upper back. It is a unique kind of fat that can generate heat by burning the regular white fat (adipose tissue) found on your stomach, butt, hips, and legs[42].

In most cases, you'd need to exercise or engage in calorie restriction to first burn glucose (blood sugar) and then glycogen (stored liver and muscle sugar) before finally beginning to utilize fat as fuel. But BAT can immediately and directly burn calories (including calories from fat) to generate heat[14].

Although BAT is found in all mammals, anyone exposed to frequent bouts of cold temperature[22] tends to have more brown fat to generate heat and help keep warm[16]. And while exercise[13] and fasting[21] can also increase BAT, they can't hold a candle to CT.

To get your BAT to melt away stored fat, you can wear a Cool Fat Burner vest at the office or at home to keep the primary BAT areas on your collarbones and upper back activated.

Enhanced Immune System

CT enhances the immune system, primarily by increasing levels of immune system cells that help fight disease and infection[33].

Specifically, CT—probably because of its ability to stimulate norepinephrine release—can induce leukocytosis and granulocytosis, an increase in natural killer cell count and activity, and a rise in circulating levels of interleukin 6, all of which can significantly improve your immune system integrity[15].

Increased Cell Longevity

The protein mTOR is found in humans. Perhaps you've heard that worms, fruit flies, and mice live longer when exposed to calorie restriction[31], or that regular fasting may help extend life span. It is hypothesized that this is a result of downregulation of the mTOR pathway[21], which can also bring about cell autophagy. This is basically how your body cleans out metabolic "junk" within the cells—and it's the method that may allow cells to live longer and healthier lives.

CT affects cellular longevity by downgrading mTOR pathways the way calorie restriction and intermittent fasting do[32]. Basically, you can think of CT as a combination of increasing your cells' hardiness and health simultaneously.

Endothelial Nitric Oxide Upregulation

Endothelial nitric oxide is found in the lining of blood vessels. Nitric oxide aids in tissue recovery and regeneration[40], enhances blood flow, dissolves plaque, and dilates blood vessels, resulting in enhanced cardiovascular efficiency and blood delivery to tissue, which is very convenient for improving endurance performance.

An inadequate endothelial nitric oxide system and subsequent poor blood flow can rob the muscles and brain of blood, oxygen, and nutrients[33]. So both physical and mental function can be enhanced when nitric oxide is upregulated. Poor blood flow to the digestive tract is one cause of leaky gut and poor gut function, while high levels of nitric oxide can improve gut function.

Two protocols can significantly elevate endothelial nitric oxide: exercise[30] and CT.

Higher Metabolism and Lower Blood Sugar

CT can cause blood glucose to be burned rapidly as fuel to assist in heating your body or stored in muscles to enhance recovery or performance—before that blood sugar can potentially be converted into fat by the liver[37]. So while I'm not trying to give you an excuse to cheat on your diet and then use CT, it can come in handy should you slip up and eat too much ice cream (or too many sweet potatoes)[32].

In studies of human BAT metabolism, using a combination of measurements such as positron emission tomography and computed tomography, glucose uptake has increased twelvefold in BAT by exposure to cold temperatures[28], along with a significant increase in metabolism and energy expenditure.

In addition, cold thermogenesis results in adiponectin activation[22]. Adiponectin is a hormone released during cold exposure that breaks down fat and shuttles glucose into muscles (which can lower blood sugar). This not only has an anabolic, muscle-repairing effect but can also enhance recovery. Interestingly, low adiponectin levels have been associated with obesity, diabetes, and cardiovascular disease[35].

What all this boils down to is that cold thermogenesis can help keep you at a lean racing weight and also improve your cardiovascular efficiency, your immune system strength, your health and longevity, and your metabolic efficiency, thus enhancing your ability to burn more fat during endurance workouts or races.

Ready to start shivering? Here are some practical ways to begin implementing cold thermogenesis:

- Keep your home relatively cool (60 to 65°F)[28].

- While working at your computer or watching television, wear a Cool Fat Burner vest or compression gear that combines pressure and ice.

- Take a five-minute cold shower every morning, or alternate twenty seconds of cold water with ten seconds of hot water.

- Immerse your body in an ice bath or a cold lake or river for five to twenty minutes once or twice a week.

- Use body cooling gear that allows you to place ice or cold packs on specific areas of your body, like a CoolFatBurner vest or belt.

- When possible, swim in cold water. When the boiler at my local YMCA broke last year and I was stuck swimming in 55°F water for two weeks, I could eat practically anything in sight for the duration and was still losing fat at an unprecedented rate.

I'll return to a discussion of cold thermogenesis and icing in the recovery chapter of this book.

Heat

In the same way that cold thermogenesis can cause positive cardiovascular adaptations, heat enhances not only blood flow but also the ability to tolerate extremes of heat during workouts and races[44].

Gradual exposure to repetitive exercise and nonexercise heat stress produces several beneficial physiological adaptations, including improved heat transfer from core to skin, more efficient cardiovascular function, decreased heart rate during hot exercise, decreased skin and body temperature during hot exercise, increased blood volume, and less electrolyte loss via kidney filtration[43].

There are two ways to incorporate heat into your training: passively and actively. Because it is relatively less uncomfortable, I am a bigger fan of passive heat training. Passive heat training involves sitting or standing in dry-heat saunas or steam rooms and induces the same cardiovascular and sweat changes as active heat training, but without the recovery implications or discomfort that comes from, say, setting up your bike trainer or treadmill inside a sauna.

So what's better for passive heat acclimatization—a dry sauna or a steam room? Sweat evaporation and cooling efficiency appear to be more favorable in hot-wet conditions like a steam room, but both a sauna and a steam room will achieve favorable results, so it's your choice.

Positive adaptations can occur in as few as ten days of passive heat training. If you're doing passive heat training in preparation for a race, you should begin four to eight weeks before your event for optimal results. Start with ten to fifteen minutes and gradually work up to forty-five- to fifty-minute sessions every one to three days.

In contrast to passive heat training, active heat training is crucial for experiencing the physiological and psychological responses to hot-weather racing. Although more uncomfortable, it yields faster results than passive heat training. Active heat training, as the name implies, involves exercising in hot conditions.

This can be accomplished on a treadmill or bike in a dry-heat sauna or in a small room with a heater or humidifier under the bike or treadmill. You can use a steady-state exercise protocol or interval training. If you get too hot to exercise comfortably, you'll still get results if you stop exercising (or remove the heat), allow your body to cool, and then progress back into the exercise when you are ready. (The fancy name for this start-stop method is *controlled hyperthermia*.)

During active heat training, elevating both core and skin temperature is necessary for complete heat adaptation, but wearing too many extra layers of clothing during these sessions could actually be detrimental. Clothing is semipermeable to water, so the climate developed under your clothing can create a water-vapor pressure that prevents sweat evaporation and rapidly increases your discomfort and dehydration. So avoid the temptation to go Rocky Balboa and wear layers of cotton shirts or jogging pants during your heat-acclimatization sessions.

In a recent study published in the *European Physical Journal: Applied Physics,* elite rowers were put through a protocol of rowing for five days of heat exposure for ninety minutes a day. They were in a 104°F room with 60 percent humidity, and their effort wasn't too hard—but hard enough to overheat them slightly. The result was a 1.5 percent increase in their 2,000-meter rowing performance. This increase was attributed to a variety of effects, including higher blood volume (which is actually hard to achieve the more "elite" of an athlete you are; plasma volume increased 4.5 percent) and an enhanced ability to mentally handle slight dehydration. Ultimately, it tells us that heat stress, like cold stress, is beneficial.

If you're using active heat training to prepare for a race, its benefits require forty-five to sixty minutes of moderate-intensity exercise in the heat for seven to ten consecutive days, or four to five times a week for two to three weeks. This means that you adapt more quickly compared with passive heat training, but of course it's far more uncomfortable.

Here are some practical ways to implement passive and active heat training:

- Do short workouts in the sauna or steam room. For example, every week I do a thirty-minute injury-prevention routine that involves side raises, front raises, leg raises, and planks. I simply do it in the sauna.

- For passive heat training, multitask (and distract yourself) by listening to music on a waterproof MP3 player or by reading old books or magazines that you don't mind destroying with moisture and heat. You might as well learn something while you're sweating.

- If you're exercising indoors on a treadmill or bike trainer, get more bang for your buck by turning up the heat or putting a heater or humidifier nearby.

- During these sessions, you can use a product called Sweet Sweat (BeyondTrainingBook.com/SweetSweat), a topical combination of oils, waxes, and natural blood-flow enhancers, to increase circulation, sweating, and skin temperature and thus accelerate heat-training results.

Finally, you can lose the positive benefits of heat training in as few as seven days, so if you're using heat to acclimate for a race, continue heat training until just four to six days before your event, at which point you should begin staying away from the heat.

Infrared

I recently added an infrared sauna to my basement gym, and frankly, I'm addicted—in a very positive way. Knowing that I can venture downstairs and enter into a private chamber that gives my body myriad benefits makes a fifteen- to thirty-minute sauna sit a new daily must for me. I outline exactly how I biohacked this sauna at

BenGreenfieldFitness.com/hackedsauna, and I can think of ten reasons that make me quite glad I have access to it. In no particular order, here they are:

1. **Heart health and longevity.** A new report in *JAMA Internal Medicine* shows that regularly spending time in a sauna may help keep the heart healthy and extend life. Researchers from the University of Eastern Finland tracked 2,300 middle-aged men for an average of twenty years. The men spent an average of around fifteen minutes per sauna visit, and over the course of the study, 49 percent of the men who went to a sauna once a week died, compared with 38 percent of those who went two or three times a week and just 31 percent of those who went four to seven times a week. Frequent visits to a sauna were also associated with lower death rates from cardiovascular disease and stroke. This is likely due to the decrease in blood pressure and increase in blood vessel diameter that both infrared and heat exposure can provide.

2. **Detoxification of harmful chemicals and heavy metals.** The skin is a major detox organ, and sweating through the skin is a critical human detox function, yet most people don't sweat regularly or enough. The body is very effective at eliminating toxins via the skin, but it only works if we make the body sweat. Many of us sit in air-conditioned indoor environments all day, and even gyms with temperature control can make it tough to work up a serious sweat. In these environments, the skin stores toxins with little opportunity to eliminate them. To combat these effects, an infrared sauna helps purify your body from the inside out, eliminating compounds such as PCBs, metals, and toxins that are stored in fat cells, which can undergo lipolysis and release toxins upon exposure to infrared-based heat.

3. **Athletic recovery for pros and weekend warriors.** Growth hormone is crucial for repair and recovery of muscles, and research has shown that two 20-minute sauna sessions separated by a thirty-minute cooling period elevated growth hormone levels two-fold over baseline. Two 15-minute sauna sessions at an even warmer temperature separated by a thirty-minute cooling period resulted in a five-fold increase in growth hormone. Perhaps more amazing is that repeated exposure to whole-body, intermittent hyperthermia through sauna use boosts growth hormone immediately afterward, and two one-hour sauna sessions for seven days have been shown to increase growth hormone sixteen-fold! It is also important to note that when hyperthermia and exercise are combined, they induce a synergistic increase in growth hormone, which is why I do yoga, push-ups, and squats in my infrared sauna. For an additional recovery benefit, sauna use also increases blood flow to the skeletal muscles, which helps keep them fueled with glucose, amino acids, fatty acids, and oxygen while removing by-products of metabolic processes such as lactic acid and calcium ions.

4. **Arthritic and muscular pain relief.** In a report published in the *Annals of Clinical Research,* Volume 20, Dr. H. Isomäki discusses research results that show sauna use relieves pain and increases mobility. In the study, the pain relief induced by a sauna was attributed to an increase in the release of anti-inflammatory compounds such as noradrenaline, adrenaline, cortisol, and growth hormones, as well as an

increase in positive stress on the body, causing it to releases natural pain-killing endorphins. In the study, more than 50 percent of participants reported temporary relief of pain and an increase in mobility, most likely due to the fact that tissues comprised of collagen, such as tendons, fascia, and joint articular capsules, become more flexible when exposed to higher temperatures.

5. **Muscle gain and fat loss.** Sauna conditioning can promote muscle growth and fat loss by improving insulin sensitivity and decreasing muscle protein catabolism. Intermittent hyperthermia has been shown to reduce insulin resistance in obese mice; in this case insulin-resistant diabetic mice were subjected to thirty minutes of heat treatment, three times a week for twelve weeks. The results were a 31 percent decrease in insulin levels and a significant reduction in blood glucose levels, both of which can contribute to an increase in muscle growth and an increase in weight control and fat loss.

It has also been shown that a thirty-minute intermittent hyperthermic treatment can cause a significant expression of something called heat shock proteins in muscle, which correlates to 30 percent more muscle regrowth than a control group during the seven days subsequent to a week of immobilization. In other words, if you don't exercise but you do use a sauna, you can still maintain muscle!

6. **Immune system boost.** *The Journal of Human Kinetics* recently investigated the effect of sauna use on the immune system, specifically white blood cell profile, cortisol levels, and selected physiological indices in athletes and non-athletes. The subjects from both a sauna group and control group participated in fifteen-minute sauna sessions until their core temperature rose by 1.2°C. After the sauna session, an increased number of white blood cells, lymphocyte, neutrophil, and basophil counts was reported in the white blood cell profile, showing that sauna use stimulates the immune system. (Interestingly, a greater benefit to the immune system was shown in the athletes, indicating that exercise and sauna use is an excellent one-two combo for your immune system.) German sauna medical research also shows that saunas significantly reduce the incidences of colds and influenza, and both Finnish and German studies show that regular sauna bathing leads to a 30 percent less chance of getting colds and influenza.

7. **Skin rejuvenation.** When your body begins to produce sweat via the type of deep sweating that you experience in an infrared sauna, the rate at which dead skin cells are replaced can be increased. At the same time, heavy sweating helps remove bacteria from the epidermal layer of the skin and the sweat ducts. This cleansing of the pores also increases capillary circulation, which can give the skin a younger, softer-looking appearance. When you sweat, the movement of fluid to the skin delivers more nutrient- and mineral-rich fluids and helps fill spaces around the cells, increasing firmness and reducing the appearance of wrinkles. So by continually flushing waste through skin cells via the use of hyperthermia, you can increase skin health, tone, and color and cleanse pores.

8. **Improved sleep.** Researchers have found that sauna use can help provide a deeper, more relaxed sleep and relieve chronic tension and chronic fatigue issues, most

likely due to a release of endorphins. As endorphins are released into your body, they create a soothing, nearly tranquilizing effect that can not only help minimize chronic pain caused by arthritis and other muscle soreness, but also help with relaxation and sleep.

9. **Increased cardiovascular performance.** EPO is an illegal performance-enhancing drug made famous by professional cyclists in the Tour de France, but research has shown that thirty minutes of sauna treatment after exercise can cause an increase in oxygen consumption and red blood cell production that parallels the use of EPO! In the high temperatures of an infrared sauna, your skin heats up and your core body temperature rises. In response to these increased heat levels, the blood vessels near your skin dilate and cause an increase in cardiac output. Your heart rate can rise from 60 to 70 bpm (beats per minute) to over 150 bpm in a sauna. So with regular sauna use, you not only train your heart muscles and improve your cardiac output, but also help your body's regulatory system move blood around your body to areas that need cooling. You can enhance this cardiovascular conditioning even more by combining the sauna with alternating sessions in a cool shower or a quick dip in a cold pool or lake. Each time you rapidly change temperature (from hot to cold or vice versa), your heart rate increases by as much as 60 percent, which is comparable to the increase experienced during moderate exercise. This practice is known as "hot-cold contrast" conditioning.

10. **Increased stress resilience.** As mentioned earlier, multiple research studies have shown that hyperthermia conditioning via the use of a sauna can prevent protein degradation and muscle loss by triggering the production of heat shock proteins (HSPs), which your cells use to counteract potentially harmful stimuli, including environmental stress from pollutants, toxins, heat, cold, exercise stress, and more. Whenever a cell is exposed to an unfriendly environment, your DNA "separates" in specific regions and begins to read the genetic code to produce new stress proteins, including these HSPs. What this means is that exposure to sauna heat can induce a hormetic (protective stress) response, which promotes the production of HSPs that are crucial to stress resistance, prevention of free radical damage, support of cellular antioxidant capacity, and repair of damaged proteins.

Based on everything you've just read, I can truly say that my daily forays into my infrared sauna are just as important to me as sleep, exercise, and a healthy diet. If you haven't yet added sauna use to your protocol, I recommend that you do what I did to get started: Set a goal to squeeze ten sauna sessions into the next thirty days. Now go embrace the heat and sweat and enjoy the underground training benefits.

It's a Wrap

So that about wraps things up.

You may find it paradoxical that many of these "underground" training tactics for enhancing endurance involve equipment unavailable to our hunter-gatherer ancestors. But just as with the use of nutrition supplementation, there is a fine line between living ancestrally and neglecting to take advantage of better living through science.

For example, while I've seen plenty of evidence that pounding the pavement for hours each weekend can damage your body, deplete your hormones, and cause a metabolic catastrophe, I haven't seen the same kind of evidence when it comes to, for example, cold thermogenesis or overspeed training, so I'm willing to accept these training methods as being compatible with the thrust of this book: the ideal combination of health and performance.

Are you ready for more?

Additional resources, helpful links, scientific references, and surprise bonuses for everything you've read up to this point in the chapter are available at BeyondTrainingBook.com/Chapter4-Part1. Enjoy.

Isometrics and Superslow Training

Check out the video at BeyondTrainingBook.com/utubegrasp, in which narrator Jay Schroeder explains how to perform an "isoextreme" lunge. I discovered Jay in the winter of 2013, when I attended a biohacking conference in which he demonstrated the use of isometric exercise and superslow sets. He uses these techniques with many of the professional athletes he trains, often in combination with electrostimulation.

An isometric exercise (*isometric* comes from the Greek words *isos,* meaning "equal" or "same," and *metron,* meaning "distance" or "measure") involves a muscle contraction without any visible movement in the angle of the joint. This is in contrast to *isotonic* contractions, in which muscle length and joint angle change throughout the exercise.

If you've ever performed a wall squat, in which you simply sit in an imaginary chair with your back against a wall for as long as you can, then you're familiar with the high levels of lactic acid and intense muscle burn that isometric training can produce. The next time you're at the gym, lift your normal weight, but take ten seconds to lift it and ten seconds to lower—that'll give you the same effects.

If you really want to take isometrics to the next level, you can use a technique that Jay calls "extreme isometrics," in which you move, but very, very s-l-o-w-l-y. We're talking five to ten minutes per repetition. This technique takes intense focus. Go ahead and try to do a ten-minute push-up and see how your entire body responds.

Jay's clients also combine heavy weight training or isometric bodyweight exercises with electrostimulation (discussed earlier in this chapter). If you happen to own an electrostimulation device, you can recruit even more muscles and enhance the results of your isometric or superslow training.

So can this type of movement produce a cardiovascular training response that dramatically enhances muscular endurance or fitness? Yes, for four reasons:

1. Resistance enhances endurance because of increased cardiac output.

The cardiovascular response to resistance training is an idea I first encountered when I interviewed the author of the book *Body by Science,* a physician named Doug McGuff, in my BenGreenfieldFitness.com podcast episode "Does Weight Training Count as Cardio?"

As you already know, your cardiovascular system pumps oxygen and nutrient-rich blood to your body's tissues. *Cardio* refers to your heart, which is responsible for pumping the blood, and *vascular* refers to your blood vessels, which comprise an arterial system to transport blood from your heart to your tissues and a venous system to carry blood back from those tissues to your heart. The resistance that your heart has to pump against and the amount of blood your heart can pump out (your cardiac output) is directly influenced by the size of those blood vessels[20].

To increase your cardiac output, you can increase your heart rate.

- Increase your stroke volume (by having more blood like a doped-up Tour de France cyclist, or by filling the heart with more blood before each beat).

- Dilate your arteries, which decreases the resistance against which your heart pumps (called "peripheral vascular resistance").

- Increase the venous return of blood back to your heart.

As you learned in chapter 2, venous return of blood back to your heart is partly dependent on muscle contractions. In other words, forceful muscle contractions enhance cardiac return.

In addition, a release of chemicals called catecholamines occurs as a result of resistance exercise. Catecholamines stimulate vasodilation in the vessels, which further decreases peripheral resistance and also increases blood flow back to your heart. This decreased peripheral resistance, combined with enhanced venous return, fills your heart up with more blood and enhances your cardiac output.

An article in the June 1999 issue of the *American Journal of Cardiology*[9] discussed this very phenomenon. In the research, a catheter was used to measure pressure changes during a high-weight leg press exercise in patients with stable congestive heart failure. The participants experienced significantly increased heart rate and arterial blood pressure, but significantly decreased peripheral vascular resistance and increased cardiac output. (This is just one of many studies that Doug McGuff references in an excellent article he's written on cardiovascular adaptations to resistance training. A link is included on the reference web page you'll find at the end of this chapter.)

2. Resistance equals endurance because lactic acid gets cleared.

Lactic acid gets a bad rap, but the acidosis, or "burn," associated with muscle fatigue has very little to do with the formation of lactic acid[20].

The development of acidosis during intense exercise has traditionally been explained by the increased production of lactic acid—which causes the release of a hydrogen ion and the formation of an acidic salt called sodium lactate. This means that if the rate of lactate production is high enough, your body simply can't buffer those hydrogen ions fast enough, which results in a decrease in cellular pH and that dreaded burn.

Exercise scientists call this effect "lactic acidosis," and it has been a classic explanation of the biochemistry of muscle burn for more than eighty years. But it turns out that there is zero biochemical evidence that increased lactate production causes acidosis and muscle burn or muscle fatigue. As a matter of fact, as you'll learn shortly, lactate production can actually *decrease* acidosis.

So why do your muscles burn when you exercise? A more likely mechanism for the drop in pH or the increase in acidity during exercise is the breakdown of ATP energy.

It goes like this: Water (H_2O) is used to break down, or "hydrolyze," ATP to make energy. This results in one acidic positive hydrogen ion (from the water) plus ADP plus P (phosphate) plus energy for whatever you need energy for. (Go back to Energy Systems 101 in chapter 1 to review this topic.)

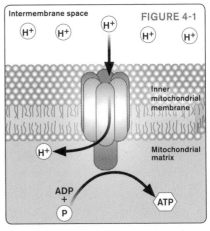

FIGURE 4-1

Intermembrane space

Inner mitochondrial membrane

Mitochondrial matrix

Every time ATP is broken down into ADP and P, a positive hydrogen ion (a proton) is released. When the energy and ATP demand of contracting muscles is met by mitochondrial respiration, there is no proton accumulation in the cell. How can this be? Because those same hydrogen ions are used by your mitochondria to recombine ADP and P, to regenerate ATP, and to maintain what is called the "proton gradient" in the intermembranous space of your muscle cells. You can see this in Figure 4-1.

So as long as your mitochondria are efficient at doing this (and that efficiency increases as you get fitter), the longer it takes for the buildup of hydrogen ions to create a burn. As soon as your mitochondria fail to supply ATP at the appropriate rate, because the number of the necessary transporters and enzymes is outmatched by your energy demands, you get that muscle burn and eventual muscle fatigue.

It is only when exercise intensity increases beyond steady state that there is more reliance on ATP regeneration from the rapid breakdown of blood, liver, and muscle sugar and the creatine phosphate system. This is why high-intensity exercise can result in a greater ability to generate ATP than easy aerobic exercise.

So why is lactic acid associated with muscle burn? Because as you break down more sugars at higher intensities, you need more of the molecule nicotinamide adenine dinucleotide, which can actually be supplied by increased lactate production. Thus, increased lactate production coincides with acidosis and is a good marker for cell conditions that induce metabolic acidosis. But if your muscles used sugars and phosphate to generate extra ATP and did not produce lactate as a by-product, then acidosis and muscle fatigue would occur more quickly because your mitochondrial activity would be outmatched by energy demands more quickly, and exercise performance would be severely impaired in the absence of lactic acid production.

While that may be enough to convince you that lactic acid is not the bad guy, just keep reading.

Ultimately, if you train your body at high intensities, you can become very efficient at shuttling lactic acid back to the liver and converting it into glucose, after which the lactic acid can be "recycled" and used as a concentrated energy source by your muscles. This is known as the Cori cycle.

So lactic acid can actually be a significant source of fuel! As you can probably guess, when you perform activities that produce a lot of lactic acid, such as HIIT or lots of resistance or isometric holds, you can teach your body how to do it more efficiently[13]. (See Figure 4-2.)

By the way, if you're doing isometrics and experiencing massive lactic acid buildup, you should know about something called "oxaloacetate."

Most chemical reactions in the body take place in a series of several steps. In chemistry, the rate (or velocity) of a reaction that has several steps is often determined by the slowest step, which is known as the rate-limiting step.

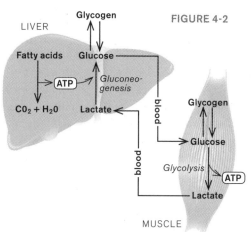

FIGURE 4-2

A significant rate-limiting step of converting lactic acid into glucose is the conversion of the molecule nicotinamide adenine dinucleotide (NAD) into nicotinamide adenine dinucleotide hydrogenase (NADH). So what does this have to do with oxaloacetate? In studies, acute oxaloacetate exposure enhances resistance to fatigue by increasing the conversion of NAD to NADH and allowing lactic acid to be recycled and converted to glucose at a much higher rate[16].

As a matter of fact, along with calorie restriction (which isn't much fun, really), enhancing your Cori cycle efficiency is also one of the ways in which you can significantly increase the enzyme AMPK, which, as you learned in chapter 3, can upregulate mitochondrial biogenesis and improve both carbohydrate and fuel utilization.

Basically, this means that you can become a complete lactic-acid-metabolizing endurance beast if you take about 100–200 milligrams of oxaloacetate in supplement form fifteen to thirty minutes before a workout that includes either high-intensity intervals, superslow training, or isometrics.

(That's just a glimpse of all the good stuff we'll cover in the nutrition and supplementation chapter, but I couldn't mention isometrics and lactic acid without cluing you in to that potent one-two combo.)

3. Resistance equals endurance because of better muscle utilization.

Whether you're running a marathon, shoveling snow, or lifting heavy furniture, if the wrong muscles are turned on for any given movement, you have poor technique, you increase your risk of injury, and you produce less-than-ideal force.

But your body can learn to utilize the correct muscles, and it's always easier to learn to use the right muscles when you train slow or hold a position, with an emphasis on maximally activating specific muscle groups[8]. When you use technologies like isometrics or superslow training, you are less apt to be distracted, and you spend more time under tension in any position you're focusing on, both of which lead to a better sense of which muscles are involved and how to activate them.

Take, for example, the lunge I cited in the video earlier. It roughly simulates the single-leg "landing" phase of a run. When you're able to use a superslow or isometric lunge to mentally focus on recruiting the correct muscles for that phase, you develop better body awareness (also known as "kinesthesia") and teach your body how to properly activate the hamstrings during that specific phase of running. In particular, you are learning how to actively pull yourself down instead of simply giving in to gravity and collapsing when your foot strikes the ground.

An added benefit of this improvement in muscle activation is that in addition to learning how to utilize the proper muscles for any given movement, you are training your joints to move through the full range of motion for that movement. As you move slowly through, or deeper into, a joint angle, the fascia, which is the layer of fibrous connective tissue that surrounds your muscles, is stretched considerably. As this stretching occurs, you can improve your dynamic range of motion and flexibility to a much great extent than you can by engaging in a static stretching protocol like yoga. For example, five-minute isometric doorway push-ups have significantly improved my shoulder range of motion while swimming.

So how can you utilize isometric or superslow protocols in your endurance training?

1. Do a weekly resistance-training session in which you incorporate at least one move or a series of moves performed very slowly. One short but highly effective strength-and-cardio session that I have many of my athletes do can easily be performed using weight machines, body weight, free weights, or a suspension trainer. Simply do one set of each of the following:

   • Upper-body pushing exercise (i.e., push-up, machine chest press, etc.), 5 to 10 reps of ten seconds up, ten seconds down
   • Upper-body pulling exercise (i.e., pull-up, seated row, etc.), 5 to 10 reps of ten seconds up, ten seconds down
   • Lower-body pushing exercise (i.e., leg press, squat, etc.), 5 to 10 reps of ten seconds up, ten seconds down
   • Lower-body pulling exercise (i.e., deadlift, leg curl, etc.), 5 to 10 reps of ten seconds up, ten seconds down

   This routine is adapted from the twelve-minute routine in Doug McGuff's book *Body by Science*.

2. Do an isometrics routine one to four times a month. Simply hold any or all of the following positions for two to seven minutes, depending on your level of fitness:

   • Push-up   • Dip   • Wall squat
   • Pull-up   • Lunge   • Standing hamstring

3. Incorporate isometric holds throughout your day. For example, twice a week after I finish playing tennis, I do a four-minute lunge hold for each leg followed by a four-minute wall squat in the sauna. And twice a week in my office doorway, I do a five-minute doorway push-up. Later in this chapter, you'll learn how this fits into the concept of "greasing the groove."

Or you can do isometrics as part of your current weight-training routine. For example, before doing a set of barbell squats, you can do a two- to five-minute isometric wall squat hold. This can have what is called a "potentiating effect." The exercise scientist Dr. Yuri Verkhoshansky has stated that this potentiation effect can cause an isometric exercise such as a squat hold to increase the force of a similar exercise you do after the hold (such as a barbell or dumbbell squat) by up to 20 percent!

4. Resistance equals endurance because of more muscle motor-unit recruitment.

It's important to understand that there's a big difference between muscle mass and muscle motor-unit recruitment (especially if you're nervous about bulking up too much). Muscle mass is not necessarily synonymous with strength and power. For example, top Tour de France cyclists appear to have toothpicks for legs compared with powerlifters and bodybuilders, yet they can produce nearly superhuman wattage on a bicycle. Champion swimmer Michael Phelps is one of the most powerful athletes in the sport of swimming, but he doesn't look as bulky as other top male athletes in the sport.

So how are such compact muscles able to produce strength and power? The answer lies in the relationship between the nerves, the muscle, and the motor unit. A motor unit is defined as a nerve and all the muscle fibers stimulated by that nerve. Muscle fibers are grouped together as motor units. If the signal from a nerve is too weak to stimulate the motor unit, then none of the muscle fibers in that motor unit will contract. But if the signal is strong enough, all the muscle fibers in the motor unit will contract. This is called the "all or none" principle.

It doesn't take much of a signal to recruit slow-twitch, or endurance, muscle fibers in a motor unit. It takes a stronger signal to recruit fast-twitch, or explosive, muscle fibers. However, the goal of weight training is not to increase the signal to the fibers, but rather to train the body to be able to recruit multiple motor units, whether those motor units comprise slow-twitch or fast-twitch muscle fibers[2]. Better athletes have the ability to recruit multiple motor units, which means that more fibers are firing. This increases force production.

So you can have a relatively small number of motor units, but with proper training you can recruit a significant number of them simultaneously. In that case, you don't need much muscle, just the ability to wholly recruit the muscles you have—and heavy resistance training or force production using techniques such as isometrics and superslow sets is how this is achieved.

The four reasons I've just discussed are not the only benefits of weight training for endurance athletes. More than twenty years of research have demonstrated lower injury rates for the shoulders, knees, hamstrings, low back, and ankles in athletes—including swimmers, cyclists, and runners—when weight training was used to strengthen the soft tissue surrounding and supporting the joints[21]. In some cases, injury prevention results from a correction of a muscular imbalance from targeted weight training; in other cases, injury prevention is a result of the increased ability of a joint to absorb impact.

Need even more proof that you can become a better endurance athlete by using resistance training?

Here you go: I've saved the big guns for last.

Check out the paper "Resistance Training to Momentary Muscular Failure Improves Cardiovascular Fitness in Humans: A Review of Acute Physiological Responses and Chronic Physiological Adaptations" in the *Journal of Exercise Physiology* online. Here is the abstract (the full text is freely available at http://ssudl.solent.ac.uk/2271):

Research demonstrates resistance training produces significant improvement in cardiovascular fitness (VO_2 max, economy of movement). To date no review article has considered the underlying physiological mechanisms that might support such improvements. This article is a comprehensive, systematic narrative review of the literature surrounding the area of resistance training, cardiovascular fitness and the acute responses and chronic adaptations it produces. The primary concern with existing research is the lack of clarity and inappropriate quantification of resistance training intensity. Thus, an important consideration of this review is the effect of intensity. The acute metabolic and molecular responses to resistance training to momentary muscular failure do not differ from that of traditional endurance training. Myocardial function appears to be maintained, perhaps enhanced, in acute response to high intensity resistance training, and contraction intensity appears to mediate the acute vascular response to resistance training. The results of chronic physiological adaptations demonstrate that resistance training to momentary muscular failure produces a number of physiological adaptations, which may facilitate the observed improvements in cardiovascular fitness. The adaptations may include an increase in mitochondrial enzymes, mitochondrial proliferation, phenotypic conversion from type IIx towards type IIa muscle fibers, and vascular remodeling (including capillarization). Resistance training to momentary muscular failure causes sufficient acute stimuli to produce chronic physiological adaptations that enhance cardiovascular fitness. This review appears to be the first to present this conclusion and, therefore, it may help stimulate a changing paradigm addressing the misnomer of "cardiovascular" exercise as being determined by modality.

In addition, you can find the most up-to-date research on strength training for endurance, and many more exercises that are designed for injury prevention, motor-unit recruitment, and other benefits for endurance athletes, along with a year-long periodized training program, in my book *Weight Training Guide for Triathlon: The Ultimate Guide,* at BenGreenfieldFitness.com/author.

If you're scratching your head about exactly what kind of workout to do for isometrics, here's a good place to start:

Wall Pushes: Get in a low lunge position and place your hands on a wall at about chest level. Lean into the wall and push with all your strength. If you slide backward, you may need to put on shoes with good grips. It's important to push as hard as you possibly can in order to fatigue the muscles. Complete two or three isometric repetitions, holding for 30 seconds or longer and resting for 45 to 60 seconds between reps.

Gun Show: Yep, this is just like flexing your biceps. Bring your arms to a 45-degree angle. Imagine your biceps getting tighter and tighter as you breathe in. After you complete that position, flex to a 90-degree angle. Tighten as much as you can, then relax. Finish with a third position just past 90 degrees with elbows even higher. Tighten as much as possible, then relax. Hold each position for one long inhale and move to the next as you exhale. Repeat two or three times, resting for 20 to 30 seconds between sets.

Wall Extensions: Stand with your back toward the wall. Bend at the waist and place the outer edges of your fists against the wall. Push against the wall with all your strength. Complete two or three repetitions, holding for 30 seconds or longer and resting for 45 to 60 seconds between reps.

Field Goal Pushes: Stand 1 to 2 inches away from the wall, facing outward. Raise your arms so they are parallel to the floor. Place your elbows at a 90-degree angle; your arms should look like goalposts. Push your elbows and forearms into the wall as hard as you can. You should feel this in the middle of your back—if you don't, try placing your arms perpendicular to the floor. Complete two or three repetitions, holding for 30 seconds or longer and resting for 45 to 60 seconds between reps.

Triangle: Imagine a triangle made by your floating ribs and the spot just beneath your navel. Sitting on the floor with your spine straight, exhale to draw the floating ribs toward your spine and activate your lower abdominals. As you inhale, maintain the activation of this triangle, keeping your shoulders down as your ribcage expands. Complete two or three repetitions, holding for 30 seconds or longer and resting for 45 to 60 seconds between reps. Try slowly extending the length of the hold over time, eventually working up to one repetition of 2 to 5 minutes.

Turtle Crunch: This isometric ab exercise is an extreme version of the triangle. Position yourself facedown on the floor in the fetal position. Cross your arms in front of you, resting against your knees and thighs. Use your abs to curl your upper body into your thighs while using your arms as a point of resistance. Push as hard as you can for 30 seconds or longer. Complete two or three repetitions, resting for 45 to 60 seconds between reps.

Plank: Place your hands under your shoulders and extend your legs behind you so you're flat like a board, with your shoulders, hips, knees, and ankles in one line. Now make it active, pressing back through your feet, reaching your chest forward, and engaging "the triangle." Don't hold your breath. Aim to hold for at least a minute. Repeat two or three times, resting for 45 to 60 seconds between reps.

Push-up Hold: From the plank position, exhale into a push-up, keeping your elbows in and your gaze forward. If you feel any discomfort in your lower back, you've lost your abdominal support and it's time to stop. Aim to hold for at least 30 seconds. Repeat two or three times, resting for 45 to 60 seconds between reps.

Wall Sit: Stand with your back against the wall, feet hip-width apart. Bend your knees, bringing your thighs parallel to the ground. Avoid leaning forward; instead, keep your core engaged and your sternum lifted. Press your heels into the ground and try to squeeze your feet together, engaging your inner thighs. Aim to hold for at least 30 seconds. Repeat two or three times, resting for 45 to 60 seconds between reps.

Here are a few quick tips for this isometric workout. First, engage each contraction as hard as possible. A 2002 study had two groups of subjects practice isometric exercises, one at 100 percent maximum voluntary isometric contractions and the other at 60 percent. While both groups saw significant gains in muscle volume, the 100 percent group saw much higher gains. In addition, if you're trying to build muscle mass, then longer contractions are better. Finally, breathe. Try to inhale and exhale evenly through your nose, letting the air rush through the back of your throat to create a sound like ocean waves.

I'll be delving into more specific strength-training recommendations in the next chapter, which shows you how to train the most neglected areas of endurance training, including strength, power, speed, balance, and range of motion.

Compression Gear

I can't remember the last time I went to a CrossFit workout, Spartan race, triathlon, or marathon and didn't see brightly colored compression socks nearly everywhere. As you'll learn in the recovery section of this book, compression gear can enhance circulation and help speed muscle recovery postexercise.

But despite extremely widespread use of compression gear by athletes, studies supporting its performance-enhancing abilities are sparse and relatively inconclusive. Some research indicates that wearing compression tights while doing impact-based exercise such as running may help decrease muscle vibrations (which could potentially cause muscle fatigue). Whether that results in better performance remains to be proved.

Most companies that make compression gear, however, don't dwell on its anti-vibratory effect but rather on how well it improves blood flow. But improving blood flow doesn't seem to significantly improve running endurance[6], and the one small study that found that compression gear improved circulation and running economy had a sample size of just six runners, with the actual results being self-reported by the subjects themselves[4].

Ultimately, thirty-seven compression gear studies have found that compression gear doesn't have a significant effect on exercise performance[22].

So why in the heck am I including compression gear as an underground training tactic?

Here's why: One big part of finding the balance between health and performance is treating your daily routine as an opportunity for physical activity in the hunter-gatherer way that I described in chapter 3. Remember that the entire reason behind this is to build endurance while you're working rather than sitting all day and then destroying your body with a monster exercise session.

And if you're following this recommendation, you're going to be standing. A lot. For example, you might:

• Work at a standing desk.

• Work at a treadmill desk.

• Walk or bike to work.

• Take frequent standing or walking breaks.

• Do fifty to a hundred jumping jacks for at least every hour that you sit.

• Stand up in meetings.

• Stand while waiting at the doctor's office, DMV, or airport.

Following my own advice, I find myself standing for nearly eight hours a day. And since I tend to do my workouts in the afternoon or early evening, my legs can feel extremely heavy and sluggish without compression gear to assist with venous blood flow during all those hours in the standing position. Just try it sometime, and you'll see what I mean.

So I don't wear compression gear because I believe that it directly impacts my workout, but because by the time I get to my actual workout, I'm able to push harder and feel better when my legs don't feel dead and swollen with blood (as a result of being on my feet all day).

And that's why I consider regularly sporting compression gear to be a training tactic for enhancing endurance. With the recovery implications you're going to learn about later in this book, you should add this to your protocol. I use a brand called 110% Play Harder because it has pockets for ice, so I can combine two of my underground training tactics: compression and ice. I also use a brand of space-age-looking compression boots called NormaTec boots that perform what is called "graduated compression" from your ankles up to your hips. They're spendy, but within twenty minutes they can make your legs feel light as a feather, even after a ninety-plus-minute run. You can check them out at GreenfieldFitnessSystems.com.

Music, Sound, and Frequencies

In 2010, British researchers had twelve men ride bikes while listening to music. During each twenty-five-minute session, the researchers increased or decreased the tempo of the music by 10 percent[26]. They found that speeding up the tempo increased the distance the participants rode and how hard and how fast they pedaled, and that slowing down the tempo had the opposite effect.

Interestingly, the study participants reported liking the music more when it was played at a faster tempo. A 2008 study that was performed on cyclists also found that it was far easier for the cyclists to pedal when they were in sync with the tempo of the music[29].

Furthermore, a 2009 study found that basketball players could shoot better free throws when they listened to catchy, upbeat music. Researchers have suggested that the same positive distraction that helped those basketball players shoot better can also distract us from fatigue or pain experienced during exercise[10].

Researchers have also observed that people who listened to music during exercise actually improved their mood, the speed of their decision-making, and even their verbal fluency. That means you'll not only be able to exercise harder when you listen to music, but you may actually get smarter, too, or perhaps have better focus.

So how does music motivate you to exercise? Although the mechanisms aren't entirely clear, it is known that there are two elements at play:

- The ability of music to distract your attention away from pain and fatigue, which could be described as the "psychological effect"[11].

- The ability of music to increase heart rate and breathing, which could be called the "physiological effect."

Together, the psychological and physiological effects of music make you exercise harder and hurt less[23].

So how can you take advantage of the power of music to enhance your endurance training?

1. **Do music intervals.** Being the technogeek that I am, I often load free Felix Cartal, Tiesto, or Planet Perfecto podcasts onto my MP3 player. These hour-long recordings have about four to seven minutes per track. I'll then do intervals that alternate hard to easy from one song to the next, or even play a song during my hard interval

and then switch to a podcast or silence during my recovery. I'm not a fan of carrying much electromagnetic pollution (which you'll learn about later) while I'm exercising, so I use the tiny iPod Shuffle and occasionally a SwiMP3 player for interval sets in the pool.

2. Use music sparingly. The tricky thing about music is that, just like caffeine, you can become desensitized to it if you use it too much to get motivated. For this reason, I don't recommend training with music all the time. For example, you can grab a podcast and listen to it for most of your workout, and then, when the going gets tough or during the last few minutes of the workout, play your music and finish up with a hard effort.

3. Use music for the warm-up. Imagine that you're driving home from work and you know you're supposed to hit the gym or hop on the bike. But sitting down on the couch with a glass of wine seems so much more appealing. Try this: Turn on your favorite motivational workout music and then pump up the volume. This can create just enough of a psychological and physiological effect to make you head for the gym!

You may have noticed that I also mentioned sounds and frequencies in the title of this section. Although I'll address them in the sections of the book devoted to mental performance and sleep, they should be included in any discussion of performance.

In my podcast episode "How You Can Use Sound and Music to Change Your Brain Waves with Laser Accuracy and Achieve Huge Focus and Performance Gains," I interviewed Dr. Jeffrey Thompson from the Center for Neuroacoustic Research. A link to that podcast episode is included on the resource web page for this chapter, or you can search for it at BenGreenfieldFitness.com.

During the interview, Dr. Thompson explained how the brain is made up of billions of cells called neurons, and how neurons (just like the rest of your body) use electricity to communicate with one another. As you can probably imagine, these billions of neurons sending signals all at once produce an enormous amount of electrical activity in your brain, and this can be detected using equipment like an electroencephalogram (EEG), which measures electricity levels over areas of your scalp[24].

When you graph the electrical activity of your brain using an EEG, you generate a brain-wave pattern, which is called a "wave" pattern because of its cyclical, wavelike nature. Brain-wave patterns are generally categorized as in Figure 4-3.

Most of us live the majority of our lives in a state where beta waves are primarily being produced—we're aroused, alert, concentrated, but also somewhat stressed. This is not a state you want to be exercising or racing in. There is too much stress to allow optimal focus.

In an alpha state, you can focus better, comprehend more, perform more elaborate tasks, learn languages, analyze complex situations, and even be in what sports psychologists call the "zone," which is a state of improved focus and performance, whether during a workout or a race. This is partly because the slightly decreased electrical activity in the brain can lead to significant increases in feel-good brain chemicals like endorphins, norepinephrine, and dopamine[7].

FIGURE 4-3. Brain-Wave Patterns

BETA: (12+ Hz)

At lower levels, increased concentration, arousal, alertness, and cognition. At higher or chronic levels, stress, anxiety, disease, feelings of separation, and "fight or flight" syndrome.

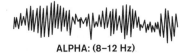

ALPHA: (8–12 Hz)

Relaxation, focus, increased serotonin production. "The zone" during exercise (i.e. runner's high). Presleep, prewaking drowsiness, mediation. Initial stages of access to unconscious mind.

THETA: (3–8 Hz)

Dreaming sleep (REM sleep). Increased production of catecholamines (important for learning and memory). Increased creativity, emotional experiences, behavioral changes, retention of learned material. Lucid dreaming, deep mediation, and access to subconscious.

DELTA: (0.1–3 Hz) "Sleep State"

Dreamless sleep during which human growth hormone is released. Deep, trancelike, nonphysical state with loss of body awareness. Access to subconscious mind.

For example, meditation brings you into an alpha state. You are focusing on *something*, whether it's a candle flame or your breath or a mantra or a prayer, and when you focus like that, the electrical patterns in your brain slow down and relax, and the amplitude of your brain waves generally stabilizes in the alpha-wave range.

But it turns out that you don't have to be an ordained monk or an expert meditator to achieve this state. Instead, you can achieve the same results through "brain-wave entrainment."

Brain-wave entrainment is any method that brings your brain-wave frequencies in sync with a specific frequency. It's based on the concept that the human brain has a tendency to shift its dominant EEG frequency toward the frequency of a dominant external stimulus (such as that of music or sound)[18].

The type of sound frequencies that are typically used in brain-wave entrainment are called "binaural" beats. The way these work is that two tones close in frequency generate a beat frequency equal to the difference between the frequencies.

It's not as complicated as it sounds. For example, a 495-hertz audio tone and a 505-hertz audio tone (whether overlaid in music or in a sound frequency) will produce a 10-hertz beat, which is roughly in the middle of the alpha-brain-wave range (see Figure 4-4).

A 2010 study showed that when it comes to enhancing EEG activity in the brain, and bringing your brain into an alpha-brain-wave state, 3 Hz is the "money zone" for the actual frequency of the music:

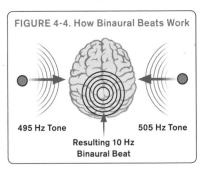

FIGURE 4-4. How Binaural Beats Work

495 Hz Tone   505 Hz Tone

Resulting 10 Hz
Binaural Beat

Results of this study give reason to speculate that a strong relationship exists between intrinsic and extrinsic oscillation patterns during exercise. A frequency of approximately 3-hertz seems to be dominant in different physiological systems and seems to be rated as pleasurable when choosing the appropriate music for exercising. This is in line with previous research showing that an adequate choice of music during exercise enhances performance output and mood[28].

Three hertz is three beats per second, which translates to 180 beats per minute—so if you really want to choose the right track for something like a run or a bike ride, head over to iTunes and download some of those 180 bpm tracks. If you want to dive deeper into the effects of sound and frequency, I recommend the articles "Methods for Stimulation of Brainwave Function Using Sound" and "Binaural Auditory Beats Affect Vigilance Performance and Mood." You'll find links to both of them on the resource web page for this chapter.

OK, so now we get to the cool, practical applications of sound and music to change your brain-wave frequencies to enhance endurance.

1. Pick up Dr. Thompson's CDs, which include tracks that train you for deep sleep, enhanced mental focus, and better athletic performance. You can play them before a workout or to enhance sleep or recovery.

2. Check out an app called SleepStream, which has binaural beats and soundtracks not only for focus and motivation, but also for power naps, sleep, and much more.

3. If you're a true sound and frequency geek, consider utilizing audiovisual entrainment, which takes the concept of sound one step further, combining it with flashing lights and pulsing tones to guide the brain into various states of brain-wave activity. Check out the Mind Alive devices at BenGreenfieldFitness.com/mindalive.

Links to these and other resources are available on the web page for this chapter. There are certainly other ways that sound can affect you, such as by amplifying the frequency of your heart's electrical signals, but we'll save that discussion for the recovery section of this book.

Mouthpiece

Yes, that's right: a *mouthpiece*.

I'll admit that I've caught some flak for mentioning strange devices like this before, but I wouldn't mention the mouthpiece if I didn't find it to be helpful for endurance training, especially if you're doing HIIT and gritting your teeth or clenching your jaw during workouts (and if you're going hard enough, you probably are).

I first introduced the mouthpiece in a podcast episode, based on some interesting research in the *Journal of the American Dental Association*. I have to admit that I was a bit skeptical about the idea that putting something in my mouth to clamp down on would somehow make my workout easier.

But a study conducted by Dr. Dena Garner, head of the Department of Health, Exercise, and Sports Science at the Citadel (whom I interview in the podcast episode "Can You Get a Better Workout by Chomping Down on a Leather Strap Like an

Ancient Viking Warrior?"), showed that participants wearing a mouthpiece during exercise experienced improvements in their ability to breathe—specifically taking in 29 percent more oxygen while expelling 21 percent more carbon dioxide than participants not wearing a mouthpiece. It also appeared that a mouthpiece could help lower cortisol levels.

So what does a fitness mouthpiece look like? You can see a video and a really good five-minute explanation at BeyondTrainingBook.com/bitetechvid.

It works like this: When you train or compete at high intensities, your natural reaction is to clench your jaw, which is part of your fight-or-flight hardwiring. By shoving a mouthpiece (or a leather strap) into your mouth, you maintain spacing between your teeth and counteract the negative effects of clenching.

CAT scans have displayed a dramatic increase in the airway opening with the use of a mouthpiece, which results in improved respiration. In addition, according to a study published in the *Journal of Strength & Conditioning Research* (October 2011), a mouthpiece can significantly lower your cortisol levels after one hour of intense exercise.

Back when I first decided to use a mouthpiece, I had to go to the dentist to have him take a chemical-filled mold of my mouth and then wait several weeks for my custom-fitted mouthpiece to arrive. But since then, things have gotten quite a bit easier, and you can now grab a training mouthpiece from an online retailer like Amazon.com. You can get the ArmourBite mouthpiece at BeyondTrainingBook.com/armour.

I do not recommend wearing a mouthpiece while swimming or during a race if eating and drinking quickly are paramount. But it can really come in handy during high-intensity interval training or resistance training.

Vibration Platforms

During a biohacking conference I attended a few years ago, I hopped on a vibration platform. Within a few minutes, another conference attendee got me to go into a single-leg yoga pose while the platform vibrated. This worked my nervous system to such an extent that my brain had an intense buzz after just a couple minutes.

Later that year, at a gym that had a vibration platform, I attempted several thirty- to sixty-second isometric squats on the platform, followed by two- to three-minute cycling intervals on a nearby stationary bike. And the next week, I repeated the same protocol with treadmill running. After both platform sessions, I not only experienced the same "brain buzz" but was able to push myself much harder during the cycling and running intervals.

Whole-body-vibration (WBV) therapy (basically, standing or moving on a vibration platform) is used by universities, professional sports teams, and medical facilities around the United States. WBV was invented by Russian cosmonauts in the 1960s and can:

- Detoxify and strengthen the immune system (by thoroughly moving fluids through the lymphatic system)[25].

- Help you regain muscle strength and bone density[1].

- Reduce recovery time[27].

- Stimulate healthier brain function[12].

WBV therapy can stimulate your hormonal, cardiovascular, lymphatic, and nervous systems simultaneously. You can use it to get the lymphatic and circulatory benefits of hours of walking, or you can exercise on it, or use it before more complex weight-training exercises or intervals.

A vibration platform's benefits include decreased time to fatigue, increased strength compared with resistance training alone, higher hormonal response to exercise, and much more. Of course, beyond just standing on a vibration platform, which quickly becomes easy (and, frankly, boring), you can do squats, push-ups, and any number of balance poses and yoga moves.

But can vibration training affect endurance performance?

A number of studies have used vibration therapy to improve anaerobic performance, longevity, recovery, and injury resistance in endurance athletes, including the following:

- A 2012 study investigated the effects of WBV training on aerobic and anaerobic cycling performance in nine road cyclists over a ten-week intervention period. The researchers tested lean body mass, cycling aerobic peak power, blood lactate accumulation (OBLA), VO_2 max, and Wingate anaerobic peak and mean power output[17]. The researchers divided the subjects into two groups, one that added in vibration training and one that didn't. The researchers had a challenge, as the subjects in the vibration-training group reduced their cycling training volume independent of the study design, which led to reductions in VO_2 max and other variables. However, the vibration-training group maintained cycling aerobic peak power and increased Wingate peak power by 6 percent, and Wingate mean power increased by 2 percent without an increase in lean body mass.

- Another 2012 study investigated the effects of eight weeks of WBV training on running economy and power performance in twenty-four male collegiate athletes[5]. The subjects were divided into two groups—one that performed half-squats on a vibration platform, and another that performed half-squats on solid ground. The researchers tested maximal isometric force and rate of force development (RFD) before and after the vibration training, as well as running economy at different velocities. They reported that maximal isometric plantar-flexion force, maximal isometric dorsiflexion force, RFD of 0 to 200 milliseconds during plantar flexion, and running economy were all significantly increased in the vibration-training group.

- Yet another recent study investigated the effects of ten weeks of WBV training on the bone density of fifteen well-trained road cyclists[19]. The cyclists were divided into two groups—one that performed vibration training in addition to normal cycling training and a control group that didn't. After the ten weeks, the vibration-training group displayed a significantly greater increase in hip bone mineral density, while the control group displayed no change.

A search of PubMed for whole-body vibration yields dozens more studies on the effects of vibration on hormones, strength, and power.

Vibration platforms, such as the Bulletproof Vibe (check out BeyondTrainingBook. com/vibe), are designed to transfer vibration energy to you, not to the floor. Although a unit like this doesn't quite give the enormous amplitude and frequency that I've experienced on the big commercial units in biomechanical labs and some fancy gyms, it is comparatively quieter, it stays in place, and at $1,495 it's several thousand dollars cheaper than a big commercial unit.

Here are some practical ways to use a vibration platform:

- Do a partial or full range-of-motion bodyweight squat on the platform for ten reps of thirty to sixty seconds immediately before a run or bike ride.

- Do a thirty-second to two-minute isometric squat on the platform in between two- to ten-minute intervals on an indoor bike trainer or treadmill.

- Do an entire yoga routine or a series of single-leg balances while standing on the platform.

- Put your hands on the vibration platform while doing push-ups, push-up variations, or mountain climbers.

- Simply stand on the platform for five to ten minutes each morning as you practice deep breathing, focus, and meditation.

So if you've got some cash to burn (or have access to a fancy gym) and want to get the lymph and blood flowing every morning or prime your nervous system before cycling or running intervals, add a vibration platform to your mix. For a slightly less effective but relatively potent and more affordable effect, you can use a mini-rebounder trampoline.

Greasing the Groove

The man who coined the phrase "grease the groove" is Pavel Tsatsouline, one of the world's top strength and conditioning coaches and a former trainer of the Russian special forces. I first encountered his unconventional training methods in his book *The Naked Warrior*, which I read when I decided I was "through" with bodybuilding and wanted to find a more natural, holistic approach to keeping my body strong.

What is "greasing the groove?" It's based on a simple equation designed by Pavel:

SPECIFICITY + FREQUENT PRACTICE = SUCCESS

When I was a bodybuilder, the prevailing belief was that strength was derived by simply building bigger muscles. As you've already learned in this chapter, that's not the case. A big part of strength (and power) is your ability to maximally recruit the muscle fibers you already have. Pavel's philosophy is that strength is not just size but also skill, and that you build a skill by doing what he calls "greasing the groove." Here's how it works.

Just like any other skill, the skill of strength can be practiced. For example, take the pull-up—a fantastic movement for improving posture in cyclists and runners and shoulder alignment in swimmers. I can do twenty-five perfect bodyweight pull-ups without an incredible amount of effort. But I rarely, if ever, do pull-ups during a workout. Instead, I had a pull-up bar installed in my office doorway, and every time I walk under that bar, I do three to five pull-ups. *With perfect form.* I'm not training to failure, and I'm not beating up my shoulders with excessive repetitions. I'm simply doing an extremely submaximal number of pull-ups (and yes, I started with just one). So I grease the groove daily with pull-ups, and by the end of the day, I'll usually have performed thirty to fifty.

This concept works because performing a movement frequently causes your neuromuscular system to become better at allowing your body, your nerves, and your muscles to work in sync to perform that movement more efficiently, and over time the movement becomes more natural and more economical to perform. When that happens, you're able to maintain better form and do more repetitions[3].

I use a similar strategy throughout the day with:

- Jumping jacks

- Short sprints to the mailbox, chasing my kids on their bicycles, or running into the store from the parking lot

- Push-ups

- Lunging hip flexor stretches

- Lifting a heavy weight in the garage

- Flipping a tire in a field near my house

- Doing short, intense commutes on my mountain bike to the grocery store, gym, bank, and the like

- Standing as much as possible (which you already learned about)

- Occasionally balancing on curbs, on fences, or on one foot while I'm preparing meals, brushing my teeth, and so on

I hope you now understand why greasing the groove is an endurance-training strategy. It's not because being able to do twenty-five consecutive pull-ups is going to somehow make you ride a bicycle faster (although it may keep your shoulders from getting injured after long periods in an aero position). It's not as though sprinkling push-ups or squats throughout the day is going to make you a faster runner per se.

But by the end of the day, you'll discover that you've actually been engaged in low-level, endurance-building physical activity throughout the entire day, without actually stepping foot into a gym or performing a structured workout.

By greasing the groove, you are indeed replicating the ancestral-athlete approach of moving constantly throughout the day—with brief spurts of intense physical activity. And when you combine this approach with high-intensity interval training workouts and small doses of longer aerobic efforts, along with the underground training tactics you've learned so far, you'll find that you will build both endurance and speed rapidly.

And you'll stay healthy, too.

It's a Wrap

Whew.

I'll admit that was a lot of information to digest. From overspeed, underspeed, EMS, cold thermogenesis, and heat to isometrics, superslow training, mouthpieces, compression gear, music, sounds, frequencies, and "greasing the groove," you now have many valuable tools in your endurance-training toolbox.

And remember: All this information is focused on efficiency. For example, you can do the superslow training routine that I described and get the cardiovascular-training effects of a one-hour run with just twelve minutes of weight training. But it's obviously not going to make you a more skilled runner. You still need to swim, bike, or run and use these tactics to enhance your results. You simply can't neglect sport-specific training, and I in no way condone ignoring training for your sport because you're convinced that doing isometrics while wearing a mouthpiece will get the job done.

But remember: The title of this book is *Beyond Training*.

So after just one more chapter devoted to training methods, we're going to begin delving into recovery, lifestyle, food, supplementation, detoxification, digestion, and much, much more.

Additional resources, helpful links, scientific references,
and surprise bonuses for this chapter are available at
BeyondTrainingBook.com/Chapter4-Part2. Enjoy.

CHAPTER 5
The Five Essential Elements of an Endurance-Training Program That Most Athletes Neglect

Why the Five Essential Elements Make Sense

If you look at the training methods of the best athletes and teams on the planet, you'll notice that they spend what seems to be an inordinate amount of time doing something other than their actual sport.

Take NFL players, for example. During a four-month internship at Duke University, I worked with the Kansas City Chiefs on training and rehab with some of their standout offensive linemen. On any given day, these players would spend an hour in the weight room, thirty to forty-five minutes performing mobility drills, twenty to thirty minutes engaged in recovery protocols, and then two to three hours of actual practice.

Or look at an elite swimmer. In one interview leading up the 2008 Olympics, forty-one-year-old swimmer Dara Torres described her day as follows:

> When I'm home in Florida, I get up at about 6:45 and walk my dog. Then I get my five-year-old daughter up and feed her, then head off to practice. I start swimming at eight. I'll swim anywhere from an hour to an hour and forty-five minutes. Then I'll do some weights and sometimes resistance work for a while, followed by lunch. After that I do about two hours of Ki-Hara stretching[8].

Before the 2012 Olympics, the *Huffington Post* interviewed U.S. Olympic Committee strength and conditioning coach Rob Schwartz, who trains athletes on Team USA. Here's what he had to say about a day in the life of an Olympian:

> A typical day for our athletes starts fairly early with breakfast between 6 and 7:15 a.m., as their first training or practice is at 7 or 8 a.m. It depends on the sport, but most practices are two hours per session and there are two sessions a day, five to six days a week. Their strength and conditioning session is usually one to one-and-a-half hours, with three to four sessions a week. The athletes also get "extra workouts," which are anywhere from fifteen to forty-five minutes, and focus on their individual needs, whether it's extra work in the weightroom or addressing a sport skill. Then they have sessions with sports medicine for rehab or recovery work. We spend a lot of time teaching the athletes that recovery doesn't just happen, they have to work at it. Proper nutrition/hydration and quality sleep have to come first and can't be overlooked. They have to make time for contrast baths, sauna, compression work with the NormaTec system and massage[7].

Perhaps you find this amusing. After all, most of us are not Olympic athletes prepared to devote our entire lives to training, eating, and recovering. We have to work, prepare meals, chauffeur kids, mow the lawn, and squeeze in everything else that life throws at us mere mortals. By the time we swim, bike, or run, is there really time left over for all this other stuff?

And let's face it: For a true endurance junkie, it's simply not glamorous or enticing to balance on one leg while lifting a heavy object overhead, to learn how to properly perform a lateral lunge, or to figure out what the heck a plyometric is.

To the first point of us not all being Olympic athletes with time to train, my advice is simply to keep reading, because I'm going to teach you how to easily implement each of the five essential elements into your life without becoming a gym rat or chaining yourself to a foam roller.

And to the second point of things like balance not being "fun," the unfortunate reality is that the mind-set that keeps you only swimming, only biking, or only running is the same mind-set of someone who:

- Drives a car (or bicycle) into the ground and never maintains his vehicle with so much as an oil change, then throws up his hands in despair when the engine starts smoking.

- Never visits the doctor, pays attention to her health, or does any preventive care, then gets frustrated and confused when she gets sick or has to shell out money for an emergency room visit.

- Expects home appliances like the washer, dryer, oven, and dishwasher to simply always work, and then is forced to spend an entire paycheck on an expensive repair or a replacement.

You get the idea.

When it comes to training for "fitness," it's easy to get caught up in an endless cycle of swimming, biking, running, rowing, hiking, and a host of other chronic repetitive-motion activities while neglecting to do the maintenance on our bodies that enables us to keep doing what we love to do. While you don't need to spend all your precious hours hoisting a barbell or jumping onto a box, you simply can't be a complete slacker when it comes to preparing your body for pounding the pavement or hammering the pedals.

STRENGTH

So that's why the essential elements make sense. And now let's jump into the first one: strength.

Essential Element 1: Strength

Strength is the ability of your musculoskeletal system to generate high amounts of force. Or, put more simply: Strength is the ability of your muscles to move stuff.

That stuff might be a barbell during a heavy squat, a bicycle that you're riding 140.6 miles, or your own body that you're running 26.2 miles. Regardless of the resistance, it takes a certain amount of muscle to move a barbell, a bike, or yourself. In the last two chapters, you learned why weight training is important, but strength is certainly one of its major benefits.

Want an example of how a lack of strength can hold you back?

PHOTO 5-1   PHOTO 5-2   PHOTO 5-3

Look at a Kenyan marathoner. There's a reason you don't see these men and women dominating a sport like the Ironman. Despite their aerobic superiority, they simply don't have the strength to generate the power necessary to move a bicycle 140.6 miles. For the same reason, professional Ironman triathletes tend to be slightly more muscular than their relatively slight, shorter-distance counterparts and marathoners, as you can see in photos 5-1 through 5-3.

If you're a triathlete and you tend to be a relatively strong runner but weak on the bicycle, a lack of muscle and strength may be an issue for you.

So how much strength or muscle do you actually need for endurance sports? Good question! Fortunately, this question has been studied by researchers[2] who looked at aerobic capacity (VO_2 max) per kilogram of muscle mass in subjects ranging from endurance athletes (marathon runners, cross-country skiers, rowers, etc.) to power athletes (shot-putters, football players, sumo wrestlers, etc.). In the endurance athletes, aerobic capacity peaked at approximately 180 milliliters of oxygen per kilogram of appendicular (arm and leg) muscle mass. Based on the data from the study, there appears to be a "ceiling" at which increases in muscle mass do not result in additional increases in VO_2 max.

Table 5-1 shows the findings of that study. (For more details on this study, go to the link on the resource web page at the end of this chapter.)

Take a marathoner, for example, who you can see from the table has a VO_2 max of 4.58 liters of oxygen per minute. If that marathoner wanted the maximum amount of muscle to get the most strength possible without sacrificing endurance, he'd want about 27.6 kilograms of skeletal muscle mass (pre-SMM).

Now I'm certainly not proposing that you rush out to buy a body fat scale so that you can measure the exact amount of lean muscle mass you need for ultimate success in endurance sports. But I am proposing that you not completely neglect the essential

Sport	Country	n	Height (cm)	Weight (kg)	% fat	FFM (kg)	Pre. SMM (kg)	VO$_2$ max L/min	VO$_2$ max ml/kg BM	VO$_2$ max ml/kg SMM	Method	Level	Reference
Sumo wrestling	Japan	8	176,6	117,0	24,0	88,9	48,2	3,60	31,1	74,8	CE	College	Present study
Untrained	Japan	8	171,5	56,1	13,3	48,4	20,6	2,50	44,6	121,4	CE	College	Present study
Judo	Canada	19	175,1	80,2	12,3	70,3	35,5	4,61	57,5	129,8	TM	National	Taylor and Brassard, 1981
Judo	Canada	22	174,2	75,4	9,3	68,4	34,2	4,49	59,2	131,2	TM	National	Thomas et al., 1989
Karate	Japan	7	172,9	66,3	10,7	59,2	28,0	3,81	57,5	136,4	TM	College	Thomas et al., 1998
Karate	Japan	9	169,5	60,1	12,6	52,5	23,4	3,44	57,2	146,9	TM	College	Thomas et al., 1998
Boxing	Italy	8	177,1	77,4	14,5	66,1	32,6	4,45	57,5	136,3	TM	Elite amateur	Guidetti et al., 2002
Wrestling	US	25	173,3	80,6	8,4	73,8	37,9	4,49	55,7	118,5	TM	Junior World	Silva et al., 1981
Wrestling	US	2	177,0	81,1	9,8	73,2	37,5	5,10	64,0	136,1	CE	NCAA champ	Fahey et al., 1975
Kendo	Japan	7	171,0	71,2	12,8	62,1	29,9	3,91	54,9	130,6	TM	College	Hayashi, 1994
Football (def. line)	US	32	192,4	117,0	17,9	96,0	53,0	5,30	45,3	100,0	TM	Professional	Wilmore et al., 1976
Discus throw	US	7	186,1	104,7	16,4	87,5	47,2	4,90	46,8	103,8	CE	World champ	Fahey et al., 1975
Shotput	US	5	188,2	113,0	16,8	94,0	51,6	4,80	42,5	93,0	CE	World champ	Fahey et al., 1975
Basketball	US	15	200,6	96,9	9,0	86,6	46,6	4,50	46,4	96,6	TM	Professional	Parr et al., 1978
Marathon	US	8	176,7	61,9	5,3	58,6	27,6	4,58	74,0	166,2	TM	Elite amateur	Pollock, 1977
Long dist. running	Finland	8	177,0	66,2	8,4	60,6	28,9	5,19	78,4	179,4	TM	National	Rusko et al., 1978
Rowing	Australia	9	189,7	88,7	7,3	82,2	43,6	5,51	62,5	126,3	TM	Olympic	Novak et al., 1978
CC skiing	Finland	17	174,0	69,3	10,2	62,2	30,0	5,42	78,3	180,6	TM	National	Rusko et al., 1978
MD running	Canada	7	176,7	67,0	7,8	61,8	29,7	5,09	76,0	171,3	TM	National	Ready, 1984

TABLE 5-1. Anatomic and fitness levels of sumo wrestlers vs. untrained controls compared with combat, aerobic, and power athletes from other studies.

Notes: n = number of participants, FFM = fat-free mass, Pre. SMM = predicted skeletal muscle mass. Country indicates nationality of the athletes. Method indicates modality of VO$_2$ max test. Level indicates the competitive status attained by the participants tested.

CE = cycle ergometer, TM = treadmill, CC = cross country, MD = middle distance.

element of strength if you are serious about everything from endurance performance to health, longevity, and (if this is important to you) looking good in a T-shirt and tight jeans.

Muscle Is Not Just Bulk

Some would argue that muscle is just extra bulk.

It is definitely not necessary for an endurance athlete to build rippling muscles capable of producing enormous amounts of force. Since muscle takes significant amounts of energy to cool and carry, there is without a doubt a point of diminishing returns when it comes to an aerobic athlete building muscle. Table 5-1 approximates those diminishing returns.

I personally experienced the disadvantage of muscle bulk when I began doing triathlon after being a bodybuilder, and some of my most painful memories of endurance competition come from the soreness, dehydration, overheating, and overall discomfort associated with packing more than twenty-five extra pounds of show muscle. But muscle mass does not necessarily equal strength. The reason lies in the relationship between the nerves, the muscle, and the motor unit, which, as you remember from the last chapter, is a nerve and all the muscle fibers stimulated by that nerve. Muscle fibers are grouped together as motor units. If the signal from a nerve is too weak to stimulate the motor unit, then none of the muscle fibers in that unit will contract. But if the signal is strong enough, then all the muscle fibers in the motor unit will contract. This is called the "all or none" principle[1].

It doesn't take much of a signal to recruit slow-twitch, or endurance, muscle fibers in a motor unit. It takes a stronger signal to recruit fast-twitch, or explosive, muscle fibers. However, the goal of weight training and strength building is not to increase the signal to the fibers, but rather to train the body to be able to recruit multiple motor units, whether those motor units comprise slow-twitch or fast-twitch muscle fibers[9]. The strongest athletes in any sport can recruit multiple motor units, which means that more fibers are firing. This increases force production and strength.

As an endurance athlete, you can have a relatively small number of motor units, but with proper training, you can gain the ability to recruit a significant number of those motor units simultaneously. If this is the case, you don't need much muscle— just the ability to wholly recruit the muscles you do have.

Of course, recruitment of multiple motor units is not the only benefit of strength training. Research conducted over more than twenty years has successfully demonstrated lower injury rates for the shoulders, knees, hamstrings, low back, and ankles in athletes, including swimmers, cyclists, and runners, when strength training was used to strengthen the soft tissue surrounding and supporting the joints[16]. In some cases, athletes prevent injury by correcting a muscular imbalance through targeted weight training; in other cases, they develop an increased ability for a joint to absorb impact (once again why Ironman triathletes tend to be bulkier than their shorter-distance counterparts).

Finally, the hormonal response to strength training is significantly different than the response to endurance exercise. For an endurance athlete, an increase in anabolic hormones, such as testosterone, may be beneficial for decreasing body fat, improving mood, having a better sex life, or increasing longevity. Studies have shown that endurance-trained men tend to have lower levels of testosterone than both sedentary and resistance-trained men. In a 2003 study titled "Effect of Training Status and Exercise Mode on Endogenous Steroid Hormones in Males"[20], the resistance-trained group had higher levels of luteinizing hormone, DHEA, cortisol, total and free testosterone, and hematocrit than the endurance-trained and sedentary groups.

The takeaway for endurance athletes is that a focus on aerobic training without any strength training may result in a less-than-ideal hormonal response to exercise, which may affect reproductive function, libido, and physical appearance.

So let's look at the exact sets/reps/rest and strategies necessary to build strength. If you want an entire book devoted to this subject (written by yours truly), check out *Weight Training for Triathlon: The Ultimate Guidebook.* The book is useful for athletes in any endurance sport and delves much deeper into the science of strength training.

Training Strategies for Increasing Strength

You should use three primary strategies for increasing strength: multijoint exercises, periodization, and proper timing. Here is an overview of each strategy.

Strength Strategy No. 1: Use Large, Multijoint Exercises

Strength-training experts and triathlon coaches always seem to highlight the injury-preventive and performance importance of tending to small, supportive muscles that are notoriously weak in endurance athletes, such as the rotator cuff, the gluteus medius, the small muscles along the shoulder blades, and the abdominal, hip, and low-back region, or core[15].

These are certainly weak areas that shouldn't be neglected, but for the average time-crunched endurance athlete, it simply doesn't make sense to spend several hours a week doing isolation exercises for these tiny, supportive muscles.

For example, a common rotator cuff exercise involves multiple sets and high repetitions of internal and external rotation with a piece of elastic tubing. If you have thirty minutes to spend at the gym on your lunch hour, do you really want to use ten of those minutes standing relatively motionless while a few small muscles in your arm and shoulder are firing?

Instead, you'll maximize your gym time by doing large, multijoint movements that incorporate the rotator cuff but also use many other major muscles, thus training coordination, motor-unit recruitment, and muscle strength[18] while strengthening the rotator cuff. Two examples would be barbell or dumbbell overhead presses and bodyweight or assisted pull-ups, both of which involve multiple large muscles and full upper-body coordination but also incorporate the smaller, stabilizing muscles of the rotator cuff.

Other examples of good full-body or multijoint movements include squats, cleans, and dead lifts. A video I created at BeyondTrainingBook.com/utubeweights demonstrates four key moves that incorporate multiple joints.

Strength Strategy No. 2: Periodize

In the same way that you shouldn't do the same swim, bike, and run workouts all year, you'll experience burnout and decreased performance if you use the same strength-training volume and intensity and the same sets, weight, and repetitions all year. So just as you should adjust your swimming, cycling, and running routine throughout the year, you should do the same with your weight-training routine[10].

For example, if you decrease sets, increase power, and incorporate more explosiveness as your high-priority races draw near, your strength-trained muscles will be at peak performance on race day.

This strength and performance peak is achieved through periodization. Most swim, cycle, and run programs use periodization. By following the simple rules below, you'll be able to effectively periodize your strength training.

- **Off-season:** If your goal is to develop muscle mass, tone muscles in a specific area, or build greater strength, this is the time to do it. There are generally few or no races in the off-season, and this is when athletes enjoy cross-training activities that go beyond their usual sport. Because endurance is de-emphasized, you don't have to worry about reducing muscle fatigue or soreness when strength training—which is great, because both are often the price you have to pay to increase muscle mass or strength. I call this off-season strength-training phase the "muscular enhancement" phase, and it generally consists of three to five sets of ten to fifteen reps for each exercise, at 65 to 75 percent intensity, with thirty to sixty seconds of rest between sets; optionally, you can do circuits (back-to-back exercises performed in sequence) with minimal rest.

- **Base or Foundation:** An endurance athlete's strength-training goal during the base or foundation part of the season (which typically follows the off-season) should be to develop strength and muscular coordination while taking into consideration the need for sport-specific training and thus the need for decreased soreness. Most endurance-training programs incorporate lots of volume during base training, so the number of strength-training workouts naturally decreases. Plyometrics and very explosive training should still be introduced, as explosive modalities do indeed increase risk of injury, so doing them all year can be risky. I call base training for strength the "foundation strength" phase. It should be done once or twice a week, using more weight than in the muscular-enhancement phase, and consist of three to five sets of eight to ten reps at 75 to 85 percent intensity, with sixty to ninety seconds of rest.

- **Build:** The build period of an endurance-training season typically increases in both intensity and volume in terms of endurance. While it may seem logical to simultaneously increase the intensity and the volume of strength training, doing so can detract from endurance sessions and increase risk of overtraining. So strength-training sessions should still be limited to once or twice a week—and it is totally OK to lift just once a week. I call this the "progressive strength" phase, and it usually consists of two to four sets of six to eight reps at 85 to 95 percent intensity, with ninety seconds to two minutes of rest. Typically at this point in the season, I also begin to include plyometrics.

- **Peak and Taper:** While strength and increased recruitment of muscle motor units can be built and maintained during the off-season, base, and build periods, the goal during the two- to four-week peak-and-taper period before a race is simply to maintain neuromuscular coordination and peak power. When these strength-training sessions are done properly, there is little to no soreness or muscle failure but tons of muscle-fiber stimulation. All lifts should be executed explosively, in most cases with a lighter weight than used in previous periods. I call this the "peak phase" and recommend just one to two sessions a week of one to three sets of four to six reps at a relatively light weight—just 40 to 60 percent—lifted quickly, with full, long rest periods of two to three minutes. Rather than simply standing around during these longer rest periods, it's OK to do movements such as foam rolling, leg swings, arm swings, or some of the mobility techniques you'll learn about later in this book.

- **Race:** While it is acceptable to strength-train up to seventy-two hours before a low-priority race, you don't want to tear up your muscles with that effort the week before a mid- to high-priority race. If you've got several high-priority races scheduled for consecutive weeks and weight training, strength, and power maintenance are in your plan for those weeks, then just do a single weight-training session no less than seventy-two hours after a race and no more than seventy-two hours before the next race. Use the same sets, reps, and load as during the peak-and-taper period—and occasionally simple bodyweight-training methods can be used to reduce joint load.

In case you didn't notice, all this contradicts the typical endurance-athlete strength-training advice to devote the off-season to strength training and then completely back off the heavy lifting and do basic core, bodyweight, and stability exercises during the entire race season. Considering that it takes just seven days for your muscles and strength to start melting away, following this advice is a surefire way to negate all the hard work you've been doing.

This is especially true if you're a longer-course endurance athlete, like an Ironman or ultrarunner. In these events, the closer you get to the end of the day, the less important the focus on your cardiovascular fitness becomes and the more important your sheer strength and ability to hold your body together until the finish line becomes. So ignoring strength training during the base or build periods leading up to your event can result in your losing much of the strength you may have gained over an off-season.

Strength Strategy No. 3: Use Proper Timing

Now that you have a basic idea of what a year of strength training looks like for an endurance athlete, you need to understand how to integrate strength training into a typical week. There are three basic timing rules:

- **Timing Rule 1:** Prioritize endurance training, such as swim, bike, and run workouts. If you're pressed for time, you must train as specifically as possible. So if your day calls for a swim, bike, or run and strength training, swim, bike or run first, then do the strength-training session immediately after or later in the day[14]. The first benefit is that you will engage in better biomechanics in your sport workout because your muscles will not be prefatigued by weight lifting. The second benefit is that, according to research, there's a higher calorie-burning response when strength training is preceded by cardio rather than vice versa. The only exception to this rule is the occasional need to train in a prefatigued state, in which case a short-tempo swim, bike, or run session could be done immediately after strength training.

- **Timing Rule 2:** Do strength-training workouts that target the same muscle groups at least forty-eight hours apart[12]. Muscles take at least that long to recover, so if, for example, one session includes barbell squats and the next one dumbbell lunges, both of which exercises train similar muscle groups, space these sessions out by at least forty-eight hours. You can, however, do strength training for different muscle groups on consecutive days.

- **Timing Rule 3:** Short and frequent or long and infrequent rules strength-training workouts. An example of short and frequent is two or three twenty- to forty-five-minute weight-training workouts a week[3]. Infrequent could be a fifty- to seventy-minute full-body session once a week. There is absolutely no need for an endurance athlete to lift more than three days a week, especially if you're following the ancestral-athlete model of doing HIIT and greasing the groove. But if you're weak and need to build strength, I recommend the basic three strength-training sessions a week and an additional one or two for maintenance.

Samples of Strength-Training Workouts

Table 5-2 gives you some workout options based on the number of days per week you can strength-train, along with the types of workouts you might choose. It is assumed that each of these workouts organically incorporates not just strength but also power, speed, balance, and mobility, which you'll learn about later in this chapter.

TABLE 5-2. Weight-Training Frequency/Mode

	1x/week	2x/week	3x/week
Option 1	Session 1: Full body	Session 1: Upper body Session 2: Lower body	Session 1: Upper body Session 2: Lower body Session 3: Weak areas/ trouble spots
Option 2		Session 1: Pushing exercises Session 2: Pulling exercises	Session 1: Full body Session 2: Core + weak areas/ trouble spots Session 3: Full body
Option 3		Session 1: Full body Session 2: Full body	Session 1: Core + weak areas/ trouble spots Session 2: Full body Session 1: Core + weak areas/ trouble spots
Option 4		Session 1: Upper body and lower body Session 2: Core + weak areas/ trouble spots	Session 1: Full body Session 2: Full body Session 3: Full body

Food for Strength

Later in this book, I'll go into more detail about diet for both vegans and omnivores, but in the meantime I'll provide some basic nutrition and supplement pointers as they relate to each of the five essential elements of endurance training. So here are basic food strategies for strength.

Eat a Testosterone-Supporting Diet

Zinc, cholesterol, B vitamins, and arachidonic acid all support testosterone, which is essential for strength building[4]. You get them from grass-fed beef, oysters, eggs, garlic, cold-water fish, and broccoli. I'll delve more deeply into testosterone support in both the recovery chapter and the supplements chapter.

Avoid Excessive Calorie Restriction and Excessive Alcohol, Soy, and Caffeine

Not eating enough, period, or consuming too much alcohol, soy, or caffeine can put a huge dent in your ability to build strength or add muscle[13]. In addition to being careful with alcohol (one drink a day max), soy (especially unfermented products like tofu, soy milk, soy nuts, etc.), and caffeine (one cup of coffee a day max), you should pay attention to your protein intake (more on that soon) and eat enough calories to sustain your metabolism (more on that in the nutrition section). And if you want to build serious muscle, you will need to eat 500 to 1,000 calories more!

Keep Blood Amino Acids and Glycogen Levels Topped Off

To build strength as quickly as possibly, the levels of amino acids circulating in your bloodstream (crucial for protein formation and muscle repair) and stored carbohydrate should be high when you hit the weights[17]. The best way to achieve this is by not working out when you're starving and by eating 20- to 25-gram portions of protein throughout day—focusing on highly bioavailable sources, such as goat-based or vegan protein powders without added sweeteners, soy, corn, and the like—taking 5 to 10 grams of essential amino acids before or during strength-training sessions, and consuming your biggest carbohydrate loads before strength-training sessions.

How Much Protein Do You Need for Strength?

Yes, you do need protein for strength building. When you eat protein, it gets broken down into amino acids, which are used for everything from repairing damaged muscle fibers to a host of other metabolic reactions[19]. But how much you need is generally blown way out of proportion—to the detriment of your liver and kidneys.

To determine how much protein you actually need, you have to get friendly with a term called "nitrogen balance." Here's how nitrogen balance works: Nitrogen enters your body when you consume protein from food or amino acid supplements, and nitrogen exits your body in your urine as ammonia, urea, and uric acid (breakdown products of protein). When the amount of protein you eat matches the amount of you use, you're in nitrogen balance.

As you can probably deduce, if you don't eat enough protein, you'll be in negative nitrogen balance, and your body probably won't be able to repair muscle after a workout (a "catabolic" state). If you consume too much protein, you'll be in positive nitrogen balance, and while you'll have what you need for muscle repair (an "anabolic" state), some health issues may arise when you've got excess nitrogen—since all that ammonia, urea, and uric acid have side effects (which I'll get to in a bit).

The current U.S. Recommended Dietary Allowance (RDA) is 0.36 grams of protein per pound of body weight per day, which allows for most people to be in nitrogen balance. While athletes and others who exercise a lot need more protein than this, bodybuilders, football players, weight lifters, and other big strength and power athletes frequently take it to the extreme and consume way more than the RDA (in some cases up to two grams of protein per pound of body weight!).

But studies such as the ones you'll find on the resource web page for this chapter suggest that even athletes don't need more than 0.55 grams per pound of body weight to maintain nitrogen balance[11]. If you're trying to exceed nitrogen balance to put on muscle, a study in the journal *Contemporary Issues in Protein Requirements and Consumption for Resistance Trained Athletes* indicates that your daily food consumption should not exceed 25 percent more than 0.54 grams per pound, which comes out to 0.68 grams per pound[22].

A spinach salad with fresh vegetables, hummus or flax seed crackers, and sardines is a go-to lunch for me. This meal has about thirty grams of protein.

Let's put those numbers into context. I weigh 175 pounds. If I don't want to gain muscle and just want to make sure I'm getting enough protein for muscle recovery and body repair, I should eat 0.55 × 175, or 96 grams of protein a day.

Rounded up to a nice, even 100 grams, that means I could have a couple scoops of an organic whey or vegan protein powder with my morning breakfast (which I do), a can of sardines with my salad at lunch, and four to six ounces of chicken with dinner. That's easily 100 grams, and it doesn't even count the protein I get from seeds, nuts, grains, legumes, and the like.

And if I wanted to gain muscle, I could eat 0.68 × 175, or about 120 grams. If I added a couple handfuls of almonds and a dollop of yogurt, I'd be good to go.

So what are the risks of eating too much protein or having a positive nitrogen balance?

First, consider that ammonia is toxic to the body. Once you get close to about 1,000 calories a day of protein (about 250 grams), you can no longer convert ammonia to urea, and this toxin begins to build up in your body. This is extremely stressful on your internal organs, especially your kidneys[21].

Next, excess protein can cause dehydration if you don't drink enough water, because your kidneys need water to convert ammonia into urea.

Most interesting to me, mammalian target of rapamycin (mTOR) is a gene that accelerates aging. Decreased activity in this gene is directly correlated to calorie restrictions and lower amino acid intake[6]. So excessive protein intake and a constantly positive nitrogen balance could actually shorten your life!

The takeaway: Eat as much protein as your body needs for repair and recovery, a little more if you want to put on muscle, and then take in the rest of your calories from healthy fats and vegetables, with limited fruits and carbohydrates for fueling intense bouts of physical activity.

I'll return to a discussion of protein in the nutrition section of this book.

Supplements for Strength

The following are my top recommendations for supplements to build strength as quickly as possible[5]. I've included links to the best sources at BeyondTrainingBook.com/Chapter5-1.

- **DEEP30 protein (goat whey) or LivingProtein (vegan blend):** 20- to 25-gram portions spread throughout day, at 0.7–0.8 grams per pound of body weight.

- **Creatine:** 0.66 grams per pound of body weight for five to seven days (this loading phase is optional but accelerates the rate at which the creatine kicks in) and 5 grams a day thereafter. As you have already learned, creatine's main job in the body is to store high-energy phosphate groups in the form of phosphocreatine. During strength-training sets, phosphocreatine releases this energy stored in phosphate groups to aid muscle contraction. This is how creatine increases strength, but creatine can benefit nearly every body system, including the brain, bones, muscles, and liver. Contrary to popular belief, there is no need to cycle on and off creatine. For powdered creatine, I recommend the highly absorbable form Creapure by EXOS, and for capsules, CRE-O2 by Millennium Sports.

- **Carnitine:** 750–2,000 milligrams a day, in two doses. Carnitine has been shown to be very effective at alleviating the side effects of aging, such as neurological decline and chronic fatigue, and also improving insulin sensitivity and blood vessel health. It helps repair neurons damaged by high blood sugar; can be used to increase alertness, mitochondrial capacity, and neuron activity in the brain; and increases fat burning and mitochondrial respiration. So you get a brain buzz and an energy boost when you take some before a strength workout. I recommend Citrulline by EXOS.

- **Citrulline:** 6–8 grams, thirty to sixty minutes before exercise. The amino acid citrulline helps detoxify ammonia. Ammonia is a by-product of muscle metabolism during exercise (from use of ATP); when it builds up it can impede calcium release and lower pH in muscles, thus decreasing the ability of muscles to contract. Citrulline reduces ammonia. It also increases ATP- and phosphocreatine-replenishment rates during workouts and delays time to exhaustion during weight-training sets. Try Citruvol by Millennium Sports.

- **Beta-alanine:** 2–5 grams, thirty to sixty minutes before exercise. Beta-alanine is a modified version of the amino acid alanine. When ingested, alanine turns into the molecule carnosine, which acts as a potent acid buffer in the body. Carnosine is stored in your cells and released in response to drops in pH (increases in acidity). Increasing your stores of carnosine can protect against diet-induced drops in pH (such as can occur from ketone production in a low-carbohydrate diet) and from exercise-induced lactic acid production. By buffering lactic acid, beta-alanine can enhance strength performance, and many people note being able to perform one or two additional strength reps when popping this stuff. I recommend the beta-alanine from EXOS.

- **Essential amino acids:** 5–10 grams before, and then every sixty to ninety minutes during, exercise. I have a comprehensive two-part series on the benefits of essential amino acids at BenGreenfieldFitness.com/aminoacids, and I highly recommend the brand NatureAminos.

- **Daily serving of concentrated greens (to balance pH and maintain alkalinity):** Greens brands vary widely. A few of my favorites are EnerPrime (capsule or powder), Athlytes or CapraGreens (low-calorie powders), and LivingFuel SuperGreens (meal-replacement powder).

I'm certainly not saying that all this stuff should be going into your body every day, 365 days a year, but if your goal is building strength as quickly as possible, or if muscle mass or strength is a limiter for you, I recommend taking advantage of most of these helpers on your strength-training days, especially if you are vegan or vegetarian, as most of the compounds listed above are found primarily in meat.

Gear for Strength

In addition to implementing some of the stealth training tactics you learned about in the last chapter, such as hanging a pull-up bar in your home for greasing the groove or doing isometrics daily, you definitely need to have heavy stuff around for building real strength. Among the gear you need:

- Free weights like barbells, dumbbells, and kettlebells

- Sandbags, tires, a strength sled, clubs, and battle ropes (see BenGreenfieldFitness. com/onnit to look into these ropes)

- Nautilus and Hammer Strength equipment, and other tools found in a gym that make strength-training movements easier to learn, especially for beginners

But you don't have to run to the gym or spend a lot of money. I have a small closet in my office into which I've managed to stuff an entire home gym, all for about $200. This allows me to do quick muscle-building or maintenance workouts at the drop of a hat. My closet gym contains:

- **Two dumbbells:** For presses, curls, squats, and deadlifts. Very useful and space-saving, adjustable dumbbells give you a range of five to fifty pounds for a single dumbbell. They are perfect for a small home gym, an office, or even a personal training studio with limited space. There's a link to some of my favorite brands on the web page for this chapter.

- **One Gymstick:** The portable, lightweight Gymstick comprises a fiberglass tube, a soft foam hand grip, a pair of latex rubber resistance tubes with durable fabric loops at both ends, and a rubber stopper at both ends of the stick for attaching the exercise band. They come in resistances of up to eighty pounds, which is enough for many folks to build good strength. Read more about the Gymstick at BenGreenfieldFitness.com/gymstick.

- **One PerFirmer set:** A pair of special handles that allow you to do some pretty tough variations of push-ups. Wheels and a revolving handle allow the base to use two functioning surfaces. One side of the base provides four-wheeled construction. The opposite side of the handle is a nonslip base. This unique revolving feature allows you to do a variety of advanced muscle-building exercises. These are also good for building balance and mobility. You can find them at PerFirmer.com.

- **One FIT10:** An easy-to-use fitness trainer that requires only a door, making it perfect for quick and highly effective home, office, or hotel workouts. With adjustable resistance levels for all fitness types, it can be used for upper-body, abdominal, and running/sprinting workouts as well as an unlimited number of other exercises. And because the FIT10 workout builds strength without compressing the spine or overstressing the joints, it is a very good option for people who need low-impact exercise. You can find it at GreenfieldFitnessSystems.com.

- **One Suspension Trainer:** An essential piece of travel equipment for me. The angle of your body changes the resistance for every inch you step forward or back, so you can increase or decrease your challenge, intensity, and the impact on your joints. If push-ups come easy to you, you can slip your feet in the straps and do a multijoint, core-challenging combo exercise. If you do not yet have the upper-body and core strength to do a traditional push-up, you can do a standing incline push-up, decreasing the pressure on your joints. As you get stronger, you can change your body angle for more challenge. Of course, you can also do single-leg squats, rows, curls, extensions, and more. I recommend the Mostfit Suspension Trainer at GreenfieldFitnessSystems.com.

- **One yoga mat:** So I don't drip sweat on my office floor, which is carpeted. I don't dig that gamey smell.

Sure, you could join a health club or have a custom gym built at your house, but having this simple and inexpensive equipment only a few feet away from your workstation vastly increases your chances of squeezing in a quick strength workout here and there when you don't have time to go to the gym.

Additional resources, helpful websites, scientific references, and surprise bonuses for everything up to this point in the chapter are available at BeyondTrainingBook. com/Chapter5-Part1.

POWER AND SPEED

Strength doesn't necessarily equate to muscle mass, huge shoulders, or rippling calves (unless that's a look you're going for). Instead, strength simply refers to your ability to recruit extra muscle fibers in times of need, such as when you're charging up a steep trail, surging to dust someone on your bike, or fighting an ocean swell. Of course, it also means that your joints, ligaments, soft tissue, and bones are strong and sturdy enough to withstand repetitive pounding.

But there are two other attributes that go hand in hand with strength (and are often mistaken for strength): power and speed.

Essential Element No. 2: Power

Power is the ability to generate lots of force in a short period. While strength refers to how much force your muscles can exert, power refers to how quickly that force can be exerted. If your muscles can't generate high amounts of force in short periods, then you're low on power and unable to use the muscle you do have to its full potential.

For example, if you're doing a strength-oriented task, it doesn't matter how long it takes you to complete it, whether it's lifting a weight, moving a couch, or climbing a flight of stairs. All that matters is that the task gets done; doing it slowly doesn't take away from the "success" of completing it.

But when the goal is power, speed counts. The speed with which you lift that weight, move that couch, or climb that flight of stairs dictates how successful you were at quickly recruiting your muscle—which is why power is often referred to as speed-strength.

So why is power important for, say, an endurance athlete, who seems to be moving relatively slowly across a course, especially compared with, say, a 100-meter sprinter?

It all comes down to the fact that training for power doesn't really train your muscles as much as it trains your nervous system. When you train for power, your central nervous system learns to control your muscles in a more efficient way, creating enhanced muscle utilization without the negative effects of too much muscle bulk. I like to think about it this way: Power simply allows you to fine-tune your strength (which you've hopefully been building, right?).

As a matter of fact, as long as you follow the power-training rules you're about to learn, such as keeping the number of repetitions low, lifting light weights fast, and moving quickly, power training will increase your ability to maximally utilize muscle without bulking you up (or tearing muscle fiber and subsequently making you sore).

The advantage of being able to more effectively recruit the muscle you already have, without necessarily increasing muscle mass, is that you'll need to recruit fewer muscle fibers for any given intensity. So power is like putting a faster engine in your car without increasing the size of the car or the weight of the engine itself. This results in lower energy costs, less muscular fatigue, and ultimately better endurance performance[7,12]. To summarize, power training for an endurance athlete promotes:

- The recruitment of more muscle fibers without additional muscle mass

- The ability to train for quick movements and high force potential without creating soreness

- Better economy and efficiency, even at relatively lower speeds

This is why I tend to favor more light-and-fast, power-based workouts and fewer heavy-and-slow, strength-based workouts as a race approaches. You've already put in the work, possibly gotten some extra muscle fibers, and built your brute-force capability in your off-season or early-season strength workouts. Now it's time to learn how to grab as many of those fibers as possible when it really counts.

Training Strategies for Increasing Power

There are three primary strategies for increasing power as fast as possible: plyometrics, speed-strength sets, and complex sets. Each of these strategies is based on the same concept: the "inhibition reflex."

You've probably heard this story: A small child is trapped under a burning car, and in a feat of superhuman strength, the child's mother rushes to the car and lifts the entire vehicle, rescuing the child from certain death.

You may have also heard that chimps and gorillas can be ten times stronger than humans, capable of bending steel bars, punching through walls, or throwing huge boulders.

FIGURE 5-1

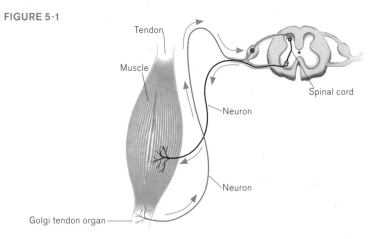

Tendon

Muscle

Neuron

Spinal cord

Neuron

Golgi tendon organ

Don't worry: Your training is not going to require you to lift cars or bend steel bars. But both the mother and the ape are relying on a complete rewiring of a special mechanism in the body that prevents a muscle from tearing from excessive force. This mechanism is the inhibition reflex, and here is how it works.

Built into every muscle is a special organ called a Golgi tendon organ (GTO). When your muscle contracts and generates a force, the GTO fires off nerve impulses to your spinal cord, and your spinal cord responds with an inhibition reflex[2], which tells your muscle fibers to limit force production when muscle tension increases (see Figure 5-1).

While this mechanism is certainly a good way to keep you from, say, tearing your biceps when lifting a couch, it can unfortunately inhibit your sports performance when you're trying to push the pedals hard or run up a hill. In the case of the mother saving her child from the burning car or a gorilla escaping from a zoo by bending steel bars, the brain has overpowered the inhibition reflex, resulting in a higher threshold of the GTO.

Now here's the good news: Just like the mom and the ape, you can increase the excitatory threshold of your GTO to improve your maximum power. In other words, you can "turn off" just a little bit of your body's natural protective inhibition. A poorly trained person always has a GTO that kicks in before much force can be produced, but with proper training, you can trick your muscles into contracting at a higher force and speed before the muscle-protecting inhibition kicks in.

Here's how: By teaching your body how to have a faster "stretch-shortening cycle," you can make your GTO less likely to send signals to limit force production when the muscle has increased tension. This allows for greater contraction force than you would normally be able to produce during a movement, during a strength or power exercise, or during endurance activities like swimming, cycling, and running[13].

The stretch-shortening cycle is simply the time it takes your muscle to transition from an "eccentric" phase, in which a muscle is lengthening (such as when your foot lands during running), to a "concentric" phase, in which the muscle is contracting (such as when your foot pushes back off the ground). This entire stretch-shortening cycle is trained through explosive, powerful movements, which are often referred to as plyometrics.

Now that you understand how to trick your muscles into power, it's time to learn the three main strategies that will let you get the job done. Each of the following strategies will train your GTO to absorb a force and then contract to produce a new force as quickly as possible, thus decreasing the time of your stretch-shortening cycle.

Power Strategy No. 1: Plyometrics

In the simplest terms, plyometric training can be described as any activity that involves the rapid stretching of a muscle (eccentric phase) immediately followed by a rapid shortening of that muscle (concentric phase). Hopping, skipping, bounding, jumping, and throwing are all examples of basic plyometric movements.

Each of these movements relies on the concept that when a muscle is rapidly stretched, elastic energy in the muscle's tendon is built up and briefly stored there, and when the muscle contracts, the stored energy in that tendon is released, thus contributing to the speed of a movement or contraction.

Plyometric exercises promote high movement speed, lots of muscle-fiber recruitment in a short period, and trained release of the powerful elastic energy stored in tendons. This means that when your foot strikes the ground, it spends less time in contact with the ground, leaves the ground more quickly, and moves you along faster.

When training with plyometrics (or any of the other power strategies you're about to discover), the delay between the stretching, eccentric phase and the shortening, concentric phase needs to be very short—no longer than about a quarter of a second. This is why all plyometric exercises need to be characterized by fast, powerful movements. (I have to say that most endurance athletes do plyometrics quite slowly and usually after they're already fatigued from a long run or the previous day's workout, so they're getting zero bang for their "plyometric" buck.) Do plyometrics explosively or don't do them at all.

Here are some of the best plyometric movements you can use in your endurance-training program:

1. **Depth jumps:** Jump off a raised platform or box, land on both feet, and immediately jump as high as possible. For this and all of the other leg exercises, minimize ground-contact time.

2. **Single-leg hops:** Hop up onto a slightly raised surface on one leg. Even jumping up onto a (nonmoving) treadmill belt is fine.

3. **Bounds:** Run, but with oversized strides and maximum time in the air. Every time your foot strikes the ground, push off as hard as possible to maximize stride length.

4. **Clap push-ups:** In a variation on the standard push-up, push up explosively, clap your hands, and land. You can do these from your knees if necessary.

5. **Medicine ball throws:** Take two to four steps and throw a medicine ball explosively from your chest as hard as possible toward a wall or training mat. Extend your arms fully when throwing.

6. **Medicine ball slams:** Hold a medicine ball overhead, then slam it onto the ground as hard as possible. Catch and repeat. As an alternative to medicine ball slams, you can do "muscle-ups" in the pool, pulling yourself up and over the pool wall.

7. **Power skips:** Skip playground-style, with your knees exploding toward your chest as high as possible. As with bounds, your goal is to maximize time spent in the air.

8. **Jump rope:** Perform double- or alternating-leg rope jumping, with a focus on minimizing ground-contact time and doing as many jumps as possible in the allotted period.

9. **Hurdle hops:** This side-to-side movement is included because lateral motion is missing from most endurance-training programs. Jump side to side over a line, tennis ball can, cone, or step bench as many times as possible in the allotted time. You can jump with one leg (more advanced) or both legs.

Here's a sample plyometric routine. During race season or the buildup to a big event, you need to do a plyometric workout like this only once a week to get results:

1. Depth jumps—10 from a 3- to 5-foot box

2. Clap push-ups—10

3. Single-leg hops—10

4. Medicine ball throws—8

5. Power skips—20 yards

6. Bounds—40 yards

7. Medicine ball slams—8

8. Hurdle hops—10 per side

9. Jump rope—20 seconds

You can go through this entire routine two to three times as a circuit. Unlike most circuits, you'll want full rest (typically sixty seconds to three minutes) between any sets that use similar muscles. For sets that don't use similar muscles, such as depth jumps to push-ups, you don't necessarily need to rest. I've included links to videos of these exercises on the web page for this chapter.

Power Strategy No. 2: Speed-Strength Sets

You've already learned how to strength-train by using multijoint moves, such as squats, cleans, overhead presses, and dead lifts. The only real difference between "strength" and "speed-strength" training is that for speed-strength, you perform the same multijoint, full-body lifts quickly and explosively, often using lighter weights so that you can indeed move a weight as fast as possible. Explosive training maximizes movement economy, motor-unit recruitment, and even lactate threshold[12].

When you throw Olympic lifting into your speed-strength mix, the added benefits include increased VO_2 max and decreased resting heart rate[15,6]. Olympic lifts involve very high power outputs, high rates of force production, and large amounts of muscular coordination, including the combination of ankle, knee, and hip extension. Traditional Olympic lifting (which typically involves tight leotards) is a standardized competition in which participants attempt the maximum lift of a barbell using either a snatch or a clean-and-jerk movement. When properly executed, the snatch and the clean-and-jerk are two of my favorite dynamic and explosive exercises for enhancing power in endurance athletes, but they do require a good bit of instruction to learn and can be associated with an increased risk of injury if performed improperly. If you already know how to do Olympic lifts, you should be doing them; if not, look to Dan John or find a qualified local weight-lifting coach to teach you correct form.

But you don't have to know the snatch and the clean-and-jerk to get the benefits of speed-strength training. Other ballistic, explosive exercises that don't involve as steep a learning curve include:

- Lunge jumps holding dumbbells
- Medicine ball throws
- Medicine ball slams
- Cannonballs
- Chest throws
- Power cleans

To get the most out of your speed-strength sets, you should generally perform three to five sets of just three to five reps for each exercise, using a weight that is 40

TABLE 5-3

Warm-up: Complete 3-5 min of aerobic exercise such as jogging, cycling, or elliptical trainer, then complete the following exercises.				
Exercise	Sets	Reps	Tempo	Weight
Hip Flexor Kickouts	1	8–10	Explosive	Body
Four-Step Hip Stretch	1	8–10	Fluent	Body
Foam Roller Quads	1	10–12	Fluent	Body
Foam Roller Hip Flexors	1	10–12	Fluent	Body
Foam Roller Hamstrings	1	10–12	Fluent	Body
Foam Roller IT Band High	1	10–12	Fluent	Body
Foam Roller IT Band Low	1	10–12	Fluent	Body
Foam Roller Lateral Calf	1	10–12	Fluent	Body
Foam Roller Low Back	1	10–12	Fluent	Body
Main Set: Complete the following exercises as single sets, 1-3x through, with 60-90 sec of rest after each set.				
Cleans	2–3	3–5	Explosive	40–60%
Overhead Press	2–3	3–5	Explosive	40–60%
Lunge Jumps	2–3	6–8/side	Explosive	body
Skates or Side-to-Side Hops	2–3	6–8/side	Explosive	body
Medicine Ball Slams	2–3	6–8	Explosive	40–60%
Cool-down: Hold each of the following exercises for 6-20 sec. If heart rate is high or breathing is difficult, complete 3-5 min of light aerobic activity prior to the stretches.				
Scorpion or Down Dog	1	1	Control	Body
Single-Leg Quadriceps	1	1	Control	Body
Calf	1	1	Control	Body
Standing, Seated, or Lying Hamstring	1	1	Control	Body
Seated or Standing Figure Four	1	1	Control	Body
Bridge (optional)	1	1	Control	Body

to 60 percent of the maximum weight you can lift as fast as you possibly can with good form. Recover fully between speed-strength sets (two to five minutes); when necessary, you can also use "intra-rep" recovery, meaning twenty to forty seconds of rest between each rep in a set. Yes, that may seem tough for the go-go mind-set of an endurance athlete, but you literally do a lift explosively with perfect form, set the bar down, walk away, come back, and do the lift again. If you're used to high-rep, medium-weight bodybuilding or CrossFit-style weight training, this may seem foreign to you, but it's what it takes to maximize power production.

Table 5-3 shows a sample power-training workout from my book *Weight Training for Triathlon: The Ultimate Guide*. Power workouts should begin to replace strength workouts the closer you get to your race (and you'll soon find out exactly how to properly time workouts throughout your season).

Power Strategy No. 3: Complex Training

You may have already been aware of the benefits of plyometric exercises and explosive weight lifting. But you might not have known that *combining* traditional strength and explosive exercises results in greater muscle-fiber recruitment and even faster improvements in power and the rate of force development[1].

"Complex training" is exactly that: a workout comprising a strength exercise followed by a plyometric or speed-strength exercise[9]. Examples of complex training include:

- Squats followed by squat jumps
- Lunges followed by lunge jumps
- Front squats followed by drop jumps
- Bench presses followed by medicine ball chest throws
- Overhead presses followed by overhead medicine ball throws
- Pull-ups followed by medicine ball slams

The science behind these pairs of exercises is that the strength half primes the central nervous system so that more muscle fibers are available for the subsequent explosive exercise. The difference between the type of strength sets in complex training and a traditional strength set is that repetitions are fewer and heavier in a complex set. For example, you go heavy on the first exercise, rest briefly, then progress to the next exercise, then finally rest long. (As I mentioned earlier, I'm a big fan of maximizing your time and doing the mobility work that I will be discussing later in this chapter during those rest periods.) For example:

- Front squat, heavy x 3, rest for 10 seconds, progress to drop jump x 6, rest for 2–3 minutes

- Overhead press, heavy x 3, rest for 10 seconds, then medicine ball throws x 6, rest for 2–3 minutes

Just like power workouts, complex training should be used more than traditional strength training as you get closer to your race.

Food for Power

Yes, you can build your nervous system by eating the right foods.

When it comes to power, the most important consideration from a food standpoint is supporting your nervous system, since the speed with which your nerves communicate influences the speed with which your brain can speak to your muscles and vice versa. The three best ways to accomplish this are with omega-3 fatty acid intake, amino acid intake, and B-complex vitamin intake.

Your nerves are.wrapped in myelin sheaths (see Figure 5-2), and a diet for power should be composed of the specific nutrients that support the formation of these sheaths, as well as the health of the nervous system as a whole. The reason I recommend omega-3 fatty acids (especially docosahexaenoic acid, or DHA) is that they are particularly important in building these sheaths around nerves[10].

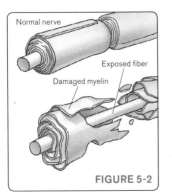

Normal nerve

Exposed fiber

Damaged myelin

FIGURE 5-2

Flax seeds and walnuts are excellent sources of omega-3 fatty acids, but the amount of DHA actually absorbed from seeds and nuts is relatively low. Very good sources of more readily available omega-3 fatty acids include salmon, sardines, cloves, grass-fed beef, halibut, shrimp, cod, tuna, kale, collard greens, and winter squash.

In addition, activity in your nerves is carried out with special messaging molecules called neurotransmitters—and in most cases, these neurotransmitters are amino acids or derivatives of amino acids[8]. For this reason, optimal protein intake, along with a balanced intake of amino acids from food or supplements, can also be very helpful in supporting your nervous system.

Some of the best high-amino-acid protein sources for your nervous system include grass-fed beef, wild salmon, eggs from pastured chickens, raw organic dairy, almonds and almond butter, quinoa, and spirulina and chlorella.

Finally, in order for the nervous system to synthesize and circulate these neurotransmitters, you need to have adequate B vitamins: B_6, B_{12}, and folate are especially important in nerve metabolism[14].

Excellent food sources of vitamin B_6 include bell peppers, turnip greens, and spinach; excellent sources of B_{12} include calf's liver and snapper; and excellent sources of folate include spinach, parsley, broccoli, beets, turnip and mustard greens, asparagus, romaine lettuce, calf's liver, and lentils.

Supplements for Power

The following are my top recommendations for supplements to build power as quickly as possible. Most support the nervous system the way the foods I recommended do.

- **Choline:** 250–500 milligrams, thirty to sixty minutes before a workout. As soon as you take it, choline makes its way to the brain and increases focus, muscle contractibility, and even memory (allowing you to form new neural circuits for learning complex activities such as multijoint lifts). Interestingly, when you take choline in lower doses throughout the day (which would be fine to do simply by including choline-rich foods, such as walnuts, fish, and eggs), it is used for methyl donation. This is enormously important for sustaining your metabolism throughout the day. Because of the one-two combo of this and the brain benefits, choline is one of the most highly recommended supplements to slow or reverse the neurological decline associated with aging[16]. In some studies, choline has been linked to increased endurance performance. I get my daily dose of choline from the Chinese adaptogenic-herb complex TianChi. Interestingly, many new smart drugs and nootropics also contain forms of choline, such as Alpha-GPC and phosphatidylcholine.

- **L-tyrosine:** 0.5–2 grams, thirty to sixty minutes before a workout. L-tyrosine, a naturally occurring amino acid, is the precursor to the neurotransmitter adrenaline (also known as epinephrine). So L-tyrosine not only is able to increase adrenaline levels in the body (quite handy before a power workout) but can also protect neurons from free-radical-based oxidation by embedding itself in cell membranes and acting as an antioxidant[4]. Brands vary.

- **Green tea extract:** 400–500 milligrams epigallocatechin-3-gallate (EGCG) equivalent per day. About 30 percent of green tea leaves by weight are flavonols, which are comprised mostly of compounds called catechins. Catechins are broken down into EGCG, epigallocatechin (EGC), epicatechin gallate (ECG), and epicatechin (EC). Although all these catechins share similar brain-boosting properties, EGCG appears to be the most potent in terms of elevated brain and neuronal activity[5]. Because of the massive quantities of green tea you'd have to drink before a workout to get the equivalent of 400–500 milligrams of EGCG (one cup of green tea contains only about 50 milligrams), I'm a fan of edible green tea, which you can simply grab out of a bag and munch on prior to a workout. You can check out this product at BenGreenfieldFitness.com/ediblegreentea. Research has shown that the efficacy of green tea is diminished when you consume it with food, so this one is best on an empty stomach.

- **Vitamin B complex:** Niacin (niacinamide) has been shown to help maintain normal nerve function. Vitamin B_6 (pyridoxine hydrochloride) is necessary for the production of the neurotransmitters dopamine, serotonin, noradrenaline, and adrenaline and plays an essential role in healthy nervous system function and energy production. Folate is essential for proper brain function. Vitamin B_{12} (cyanocobalamin) is the most potent B vitamin. It supports a healthy nervous system by helping to maintain the myelin sheath that insulates nerve fibers, and has been shown to help repair nerve damage. Finally, pantothenic acid (d-calcium pantothenate) plays a key role in helping maintain precise communication between the central nervous system and the brain, which is crucial to functions such as powerful muscle contractions and reaction speed. I recommend either a multivitamin from EXOS or the powder packet Life Shotz to get a wallop of B vitamins in one convenient serving (the latter is something I usually take before pool-based swim workouts because of the antioxidant protection it offers from chlorine).

As with my strength-supplement recommendations, I'm not saying that you need to take all this stuff every day, but if your goal is to build power as quickly as possible, if power is a limiter for you, or if you simply "do fast stuff slow," I suggest that you do. Incidentally, for a cool little self-test to determine whether or not a food or supplement is affecting your nervous system, get the CNS Tap Test app. This app measures how responsive your muscles are to signaling from your brain and spinal cord by how many times you can tap the screen in ten seconds, and allows you to easily log your progress. As you'll learn in just a bit, that's technically speed, not power, but it's a good app to own nonetheless. (See Figure 5-3.)

FIGURE 5-3. CNS Tap Test App

Gear for Power

If you're serious about building power, you'll also want to have the right gear for your plyometric and speed-strength training. Here are some of my top power-gear recommendations. (At many gyms this stuff is probably hiding in a dark corner just dying to be used.)

- **Power rack:** For Olympic weight lifting and many speed-strength exercises, so you can load up a barbell (more safely) with heavy weights. It's also useful to have rubber plates that you can drop from overhead or throw around more easily (and safely). You can usually snag power racks for a decent price off Craigslist—and if your gym doesn't have one, you should consider switching gyms.

- **Agility ladder:** There's nothing like a ladder for teaching your feet how to "touch 'n' go" quickly. Tennis players and soccer players, who rely on speed, quick movement, and the ability to change direction on a dime, are not the only athletes who can benefit from agility-ladder workouts and drills. Because agility ladders teach you to reduce ground-contact time and to increase your explosiveness from ground contact, endurance athletes can benefit from these, too. For agility ladder exercises, visit BeyondTrainingBook.com/ladder.

- **Stuff you can throw and swing without breaking,** such as medicine balls, kettlebells, and sandbags. Three of my favorite websites for fun fitness equipment like this are Onnit, Perform Better, and Rogue Fitness. There are also instructions for making your own sandbags at BeyondTrainingBook.com/sandbag.

- **Adjustable plyometric boxes:** For doing drop jumps or jumps up onto a box. You'll also need high surfaces in your house (can you say "kitchen counter"?) or gym to jump up onto and high ceilings so you don't smash your hands or head into the ceiling. You simply can't build much power without space to train and some elevated surfaces to jump on and off.

- **Weighted vest:** It should be snug but allow you to move freely. Start with five to ten pounds so you can move quickly and powerfully when jumping and sprinting; add weight slowly at a pace that allows you to continue to build power and speed. If the vest is too heavy, you'll slow your pace down too much, which will turn your weighted-vest workout into more of a strength or endurance session—and there are more efficient methods to build strength and endurance.

- **Power sled:** Or place a few weight plates on a towel and push them from one end of a hard surface (like a basketball court) to the other. Being able to accelerate more rapidly and apply more force with each step is a key to getting from point A to point B quickly, and a power sled that you can load with a light weight and push quickly teaches you to produce more force each time your foot touches the ground. As with a weight vest, you don't need a heavy load, but one that you can move quickly.

- **TNT Power Cable:** I'm a fan of elastic cables for easy, portable power training. The TNT brand is the most powerful resistance cable you can get, and you can change from one-cable resistance to three-cable resistance in just a few seconds. So, if you are using the lightest cable, you can go from 10 to 20 to 30 pounds of resistance in seconds, and from 100 to 210 pounds with the heaviest cables. These are good for resisted sprints and explosive upper-body work.

I consider this gear to be fun "extras" that can help with power development, but the most crucial power gear to use is free weights or your own body weight, and you must move that weight quickly and explosively.

Essential Element No. 3: Speed

Fortunately, now that you are aware of the training, food, supplement, and gear strategies for increasing power, you're 99 percent of the way to also being able to increase speed. So this section will go fast (pun intended!).

Speed is the ability to travel a set distance over as short a period as possible. Let's review the definition of power: Power is the ability to generate large amounts of force over a short period.

Get the difference?

Speed is independent of force. As long as you do something quickly, then congratulations—you're speedy. Even if that something was grabbing a feather off a tabletop or winning a game of spoons: You were able to move your hand over a set distance in a very short period.

A perfect example of a protocol for increasing speed is overspeed training, discussed in chapter 3: cycling, running, or swimming at an extremely high turnover rate, which recruits new muscle tissue, specifically by engaging more muscle motor units than training at lower speeds. This is called a "neural adaptation," and you can consider it as training for your nervous system.

Speed training teaches your brain to fire faster and control your muscles more efficiently at higher speeds and also develops quicker and more powerful muscle-fiber contractions. This comes in handy for hard surges during a race or a tough workout[3].

Ideally, by learning how to move your body parts quickly, you can move your entire body over a set distance in a very short period. And from a muscle-efficiency and recruitment standpoint, you know why this is important, even if you're a marathoner and not a 100-meter sprinter.

Training Strategies for Increasing Speed

Training to increase speed is like training to increase power, except that you need even less weight. In designing speed workouts, I typically restrict loads to no more than 10 percent of body weight. You simply get less benefit from adding external loads like heavy vests and heavy weights, as they diminish your ability to maintain a high turnover and to maximize neuromuscular recruitment.

In addition to keeping loads light enough that you can move your body or body parts as quickly as possible, the other crucial rules for speed training are:

1. **Do speed fresh.** Your neuromuscular system is very prone to fatigue, so doing a set of fast downhill overspeed runs at the end of a long marathon-training protocol is not a good idea (but doing them before your long run would be a perfect way to prime your nervous system for faster leg turnover). One of the biggest mistakes that most coaches make with speed training is the timing. Even for team sports like football, basketball, and soccer, speed work is often done at the end of the practice, when the neuromuscular system is already exhausted.

2. **Speed is not conditioning.** If you want to breathe hard, do metabolic work, or train your cardiovascular system, then swim, bike, run, row, or do another form of interval training. Speed simply requires brief doses of fast low-volume work. This is why, in a high-cadence overspeed cycling workout, you pedal at low, not high, resistance, and usually early in your workout. If you're exhausting yourself metabolically, it becomes very difficult to train your nervous system. This is also why speed training should include 100 percent recovery between sets, with zero muscle burn and zero hard breathing.

3. **Challenge your nerves, not just your muscles.** If you're not forced to think hard during a speed workout, it probably isn't challenging your nervous system. This is why overspeed training on a bike is not done at 80 or 90 rpm. It's a freakishly high 120 to 130+ rpm that makes your brain tired from trying to get your legs to turn over that fast.

For sample speed workouts, refer to the overspeed section on page 67.

Gear for Speed

The gear is the same for building speed as for building power—vest, sled, agility ladder, and the like. I'd just add stairs and water to the mix.

Stairs enhance speed building because they teach you to have "fast feet." Running up stairs is a fantastic speed-training workout. One of my favorite speed workouts is to head to the giant Kibbie Dome (the football stadium at my alma mater, the University of Idaho) and do fast-feet repeats up the stairs, fully recover at the top, and then slowly climb back down the stairs, for a total of ten to twenty overspeed uphill repeats.

If you are prone to shin splints, you need to be careful with stairs (and also read the recovery chapter of this book), but when used for speed workouts and not necessarily to beat yourself into a pulp, stairs are fantastic "gear" to utilize.

Water running is an extremely helpful, low-impact way to build speed and train neuromuscular turnover, especially if you're injured and can't ride a bike, run downhill, or do overspeed repeats on a treadmill. There are two different types of water running: (1) running in water so deep that you can't touch the bottom of the pool; (2) running in shallow water with your feet touching the bottom of the pool. Running in deep water is far superior for speed training.

To get the full benefits of water running, you need proper form and technique, ideally with a water-running belt to provide buoyancy (or, if you want to be a true water-running ninja, you can grab some of the other water-running gear that I discuss in the article "All About Aqua Jogging" at BenGreenfieldFitness.com/aqua). Most athletes use an upright running posture in the water. But for proper activation of hip extensors, you need to lean slightly forward and simply move your arms and legs as you would if you were running on land, exaggerating arm and knee drive and moving your limbs as fast as possible.

Using a fast cadence in deep water, a good water-running speed workout is ten to twenty repeats of just ten meters, with full "easy jogging" recovery or swimming after each repeat. This is also a great way to warm up for a swim workout. For more sample water running workouts, see the article I contributed to the USA Triathlon website at BeyondTrainingBook.com/usatri.

Finally, since speed is so dependent on nervous system optimization, the foods and supplements for increasing speed are the same as those for increasing power, so just flip back a few pages to review them.

Additional resources, helpful websites, scientific references, and surprise bonuses for everything you've read up to this point in the chapter are available at BeyondTrainingBook.com/Chapter5-Part2. Enjoy.

MOBILITY

This section addresses a key component that I've always observed to be sorely neglected (pun intended!) in the training of nearly every individual on the face of the planet. If you pay attention to what I'm about to tell you, you're going to change your life by changing the way your body feels 24/7, forever.

The topic we're digging into is mobility—namely the way your joints, tendons, ligaments, appendages, and body move.

After all, no matter how much strength, power, or speed you've acquired, your joints will slowly deteriorate, your body will fall apart, and you will move like an awkward stork unless you also optimize your mobility.

Why Mobility Matters

While I was working on this chapter, I did the Wildflower Triathlon in California. Not only is this one of the toughest courses out there, but it also includes brutal, joint-pounding, downhill stretches for the run that can leave your hips and low back locked up for days.

To earn my bona fides as a masochist, I actually signed up for the Wildflower Half Ironman on Saturday and the Olympic distance on Sunday. (You can read more about this brutal experiment and the body damage that ensued at BenGreenfieldFitness. com/bodydamage.) This meant I had less than twenty-four hours to recover between two very tough races.

But to my dismay, I woke up on Sunday morning with a completely immobile left hip and sharp pain deep in the hip joint with every step I took. No matter how much frantic stretching and leg swinging I did in the last precious hours leading up to that second race, the pain simply wouldn't diminish, and I limped about like a pirate with a peg leg as I prepared for the race, wondering if I'd even be able to finish.

Fortunately, an active-release therapist at the race expo dug her elbow into the side of my hip, did a few simple pressure-point and mobility tricks, and made me 100 percent mobile and pain-free. I had a fantastic race.

That's just one example of how mobility works.

Mobility is not necessarily all about stretching, flexibility, range of motion, or whether you can touch your elbow to your nose. It's time to learn exactly what it is.

Essential Element No. 4: Mobility

Mobility refers to your ability to move your body and limbs freely and painlessly through your desired movement.

And because we athletes tend to prioritize "conditioning" and ignore activities that don't make us breathe hard or feel the burn, mobility is perhaps the most neglected essential element in a training program, especially for a high-volume athlete such as an Ironman triathlete or marathoner.

Just think about it. Nearly all "chronic repetitive motion" training entails some kind of repetitive pattern that:

1. **Has limited joint range-of-motion,** such as sitting in a flexed position on a bike for hours, running at a relatively slow speed that never allows full hip extension or knee flexion, or swimming freestyle for a long time.

2. **Takes place in a single, front-to-back plane of motion**—with very little lateral movement aside from the occasional swerve to sidestep dog poo or roadkill.

3. **Involves forces applied in only one direction.** For example, a freestyle swimmer engages in repetitive internal rotation but very little external rotation of the shoulder. And a cyclist or runner engages in repetitive hip extension (a cyclist against the pedals and a runner against the ground), but, when it comes to hip flexion, tends to flex the hips against a relatively low resistance (lifting the leg up all by itself, without having to fight the force of the pedal or the ground).

So it's no surprise that weakness and tightness tend to be prevalent in active folks. Time and time again I have taught camps, clinics, and seminars during which athletes who could hammer like all get-out on a bike all day long or run stone-faced for hours on end simply couldn't do a full squat with both arms held overhead, or even a proper basic push-up.

As a result, despite decent fitness, these folks—and most of us exercise enthusiasts—are predisposed to all the disadvantages that accompany this lack of basic mobility, including:

- **Muscle tightness that creates ugly postural imbalances,** such as shoulders rolling forward, hips tilted back (to create that nice skinny-fat beer-belly look), and one side of the body being higher or lower than the other, which results in leg- and arm-length discrepancies, not to mention funny looks when you're wearing a swimsuit, tight clothing, or anything else that reveals your body asymmetries. Aesthetic annoyances aside, these are huge issues when it comes to injury risk. So you look weird and you get hurt easily. Not fun.

- **Soft-tissue, muscle, fascia, and tendon restrictions,** such as extremely tight IT bands, tight and immobile rotator cuffs, and restricted neck and upper-back muscles. Any of these restrictions can make even a young, spry marathoner move like an eighty-year-old couch potato when doing anything other than jogging. During triathlon clinics, I've seen triathletes lunge across a room with a medicine ball held overhead, and they suddenly looked a lot more like baby deer on ice than like athletes.

- **Joint-capsule restriction in the knees, hips, and shoulders.** Your joints are surrounded by a fibrous tissue sac called the joint capsule. This capsule is filled with synovial fluid, which lubricates the tissues and the space inside the capsule. When the joint capsule is immobile, fluid can build up in the joint and the tissue can't move properly, which predisposes you to premature cartilage breakdown in that joint, along with nasty meniscal tears, sharp pains, and "catches" in your joints, swelling, inflammation, and everything else that can't be permanently fixed with an ice pack, ibuprofen, and a session with your favorite massage therapist.

- **Muscular restrictions and faulty movement patterns.** It's not only your joints that get restricted. Since your muscles are composed of fiber and are surrounded by a spiderweblike sheath called fascia, immobility in this soft tissue can also cause some serious movement deficits. They include scapular and thoracic immobility that leads to shoulder pain while swimming, hip-extension immobility that leads to lower-back pain on the bike, and hip-flexor immobility that leads to calf pain and inner-thigh pain on the run.

- **Overworking of muscles.** When a joint is immobile, the joint above or below that immobile joint is forced to take up the slack or significantly assist with a motion it's really not suited for. Just picture a runner's or cyclist's knee doing weird sideways movements instead of hinging forward and backward. This happens because an immobile hip is stuck in constant external rotation, and as a result of the hip not being able to move properly, most of the hinging must be accomplished by either the knee joint or the sacrum, placing undue and unnatural strain on these areas.

An unsuspecting athlete might simply try fixing the knee or the low back without ever thinking to rescue the hip from its external-rotation misery.

- **Loss of movement economy and efficiency.** Many studies have found that when mobility decreases, so does economy. This makes perfect sense, especially if you've ever watched a swimmer with tight hips and limited shoulder mobility zigzag from one end of the pool to the other. For example, one study[11] found that when hip-flexion and hip-extension mobility were optimized in runners, there were noted improvements in running economy. Other studies[3,10,17] have found that when these same hip muscles are mobile, both economy and force production increase, especially over long running distances. Mobility may be even more important to economy in swimming than in running and cycling. For example, one study[16] found that shoulder mobility was responsible for nearly 30 percent of the performance variability in swimmers, and another study[24] found that ankle and trunk mobility were two of the most predictive variables in swimming performance. Here's the kicker: Mobility in these areas turned out to be even more important than threshold fitness and the body's ability to buffer lactic acid.

Let's face it: It's pretty frustrating to tough it out for months of solid training and build a huge cardiovascular and metabolic engine and an enormous number of well-firing muscle motor units only to arrive at the starting line with an inability to tap even halfway into your fitness because you simply can't move through the necessary range of motion.

My most painful memory of this was being forced to walk a six-hour marathon at Ironman Hawaii because I didn't pay proper attention to my hip mobility. A long death march down the lonely Queen K highway was the result.

But by working a few simple mobility drills into your weekly routine, you can avoid all this. Let's learn how.

Training Strategies for Increasing Mobility

So increasing mobility should be easy—you just need to stretch more, right?

Man, oh, man—I wish. Now, I do indeed stretch every morning for about ten minutes, combining basic yoga postures and deep diaphragmatic breathing. This kind of stretch-and-hold activity is called "static stretching."

But I don't do this because I think it's somehow going to make me more mobile—it's just a relaxing way to start my day. Static stretching actually slows down the body's sympathetic nervous system, your "fight-or-flight" response, which can lower blood pressure, control stress, help you focus better, and generally make you feel good.

Actually, static stretching really doesn't help much with mobility. Worse yet, when you're mixing it up with a workout or race, it can negatively impact your performance. For the intents and purposes of most endurance athletes, stretching is dead.

For example, a recent study[18] found that runners were on average thirteen seconds slower when they performed static stretching right before a one-mile uphill run. So much for those toe touches before you tackle hill repeats! In fact, several studies[2,14] have shown that static stretching can inhibit the amount of force a muscle can produce and limit physical performance in just about any jumping, running, or lifting activity after that stretching session. And further data[13] has shown that static stretching doesn't even reduce your risk of injury, which is one of the primary reasons you may have been led to believe that you should do static stretching before exercise. The *New York Times* recently reported on two new studies that likewise proved that static stretching preworkout is detrimental[9,22]. The first study showed strength impairments in people who did static stretching before lifting, compared with those who did the type of dynamic warm-ups you'll be introduced to shortly.

The second study looked at a total of 104 previous studies on stretching and athletic performance and found that in almost every study—regardless of age, sex, or fitness level—static stretching before a workout decreased performance. It all comes down to the fact that making muscles loose and tendons too stretchy before exercise prevents them from producing quick and powerful responses.

Think about it this way: When you're doing static stretching, you're doing the complete opposite of what you're trying to achieve through plyometrics—explosiveness! This is because stretching does not equate with mobility.

But that's not the only issue when it comes to stretching. If your body is already messed up or injured, stretching can actually create more problems than it fixes. For example, if you're genetically prone to hypermobility, too much stretching can make you—drumroll, please—too stretchy. This excessive joint laxity is a bigger issue in females and younger populations and, according to *Clinical Applications of Neuromuscular Techniques,* volume 1, is also more prevalent in people of African, Asian, and Arab origin. Joint hypermobility and the ability to hyperextend may make for cool party tricks, but they can mean less ability to produce force and increased risk of cartilage and bone injury.

Here's another drawback to static stretching: When you exercise frequently, your muscle fibers can easily get cross-linked, knotted, and stuck to one another in a pattern called an "adhesion." Think of your muscle as a rope with a knot in the middle. If you pull on both ends of the rope, what happens? The knot gets tighter and more difficult to untie. This is how static stretching can make things worse if you have poor mobility, adhesions, knots, and other "tissue issues."

I'll say it one more time: Stretching is not mobility. About the only times static stretching comes in handy for an endurance athlete are (1) to relax and assist with blood flow after a workout; (2) to decrease stress or increase focus at the beginning or end of the day (as with the yoga, meditation, and deep breathing I do); and (3) to relax muscles that tend to tighten and spasm during extended periods in a shortened position (doing a long stretch for your hip flexors before a hundred-mile bike ride, for example).

In contrast to static stretching and traditional flexibility exercises, true mobility addresses not just short and tight muscles, but also other soft tissues like tendons and ligaments, joint capsules, neuromuscular recruitment, movement dysfunction, and muscle-recruitment issues.

So how do you increase mobility?

Instead of static stretching, there are three primarily mobility-enhancing strategies that you can easily learn and incorporate: dynamic stretching, deep-tissue work, and traction.

Dynamic Stretching

I do some dynamic stretching before (or a few minutes into) any run. I also do about five to ten minutes after yoga each morning. Unlike static stretching, dynamic stretching, also known as "ballistic stretching," can prepare you for a workout session or improve mobility: studies have shown[22,23] that dynamic stretching can improve power, strength, and performance during a subsequent exercise session. Dynamic stretching does not involve just pulling on a specific muscle group, as static stretching does. Dynamic stretching incorporates posture control, stability, balance, and even ballistic and explosive movements, such as swings and kicks.

Try this: With your right hand on a wall, use your left hand to pull your left heel to your butt. This is a traditional static quadriceps stretch. Now, step away from the wall, take a giant lunging step forward with your right leg, use your left hand to pull your left heel to your buttock, release it, take a giant step forward with your left leg, and pull your right heel to your buttock. That's a dynamic version of the same quadriceps stretch—but suddenly you are quavering, balancing, focusing, and moving the muscle throughout the stretch. Because you're improving stability, balance, and mobility while actively contracting the muscles, this movement of a joint through a dynamic range of motion is a far superior way to stretch.

There are many, many ways to stretch dynamically, but a session typically incorporates basic movement-preparation patterns, such as lunges, squats, swings, and other movements of joints and muscles that prepare you for more advanced or loaded movements during your subsequent workout. Here are five good dynamic-stretch moves to get you started. Try these before your next workout or just after you've warmed up:

1. **Leg Swings.** Face a wall, press your hands against the wall (or hang onto a bar or anything else that offers support), then swing one leg out to the side and swing it back across your body in front of your other leg. Repeat ten times on each side.

2. **Frankenstein Walk.** Keeping your back and knees straight, walk forward and lift your legs straight out in front while flexing your feet. For a more advanced version, do this with a skip. Walk for ten to twenty yards.

3. **Walking Lunges.** Step forward using a long stride, keeping your front knee over or just behind your toes. Lower your body by dropping your back knee toward the ground. Then push off the back foot, take a giant step, and repeat with the opposite leg. To make this move even more effective, twist and look back toward the leg that is behind you once you're in the lunging position (for example, look over your left shoulder if your left leg is behind you).

4. **Bent-Torso Twists.** Stand with your feet wide apart, then extend your arms out to the sides and bend over, touching your right foot with your left hand, keeping your back straight and your shoulder blades reaching down your back. Then rotate your torso so your right hand touches your left foot. Keep both arms fully extended so that when one hand touches your foot, the other hand is pointing to the sky. Repeat twenty to thirty times.

5. Deep Bodyweight Squats. Stand with your feet shoulder-width apart and your arms straight out in front of you at shoulder height. Drop as low as you can, pushing your butt out behind you, keeping your knees behind your toes and swinging your arms behind you. Stand up, bringing your arms back to their starting posi-. tion. Do ten to fifteen reps.

Just like a rubber band, a muscle is always more pliable when it is warmer, so if you want to train your body to move through a greater range of motion during your dynamic stretching, do five to ten minutes of light cardio first. In other words, if you don't want to hear any snapping, don't get too enthusiastic if your muscles are cold rubber bands.

These five exercises are by no means comprehensive. In my own quest to constantly challenge my brain and body with new moves, I vary my dynamic stretching throughout the year based on what I stumble across on various websites and in magazines. Some fantastic resources on dynamic stretching include the article "The Dynamic Run Warm-up" on the TrainingPeaks site, which you can read at BeyondTrainingBook.com/tpstretch; "A Dynamic Routine" on the Runner's World site, which you can read at BeyondTrainingBook.com/rwdynamic; the DVD *Resistance Stretching,* with Olympic swimmer Dara Torres at BeyondTrainingBook. com/dara; and the many free stretch routines available at CorePerformance.com.

Deep-Tissue Work

"Deep-tissue work" is my umbrella term for any type of stimulation that gets deep into your muscles and connective tissue, such as the active-release therapy I resorted to when I could barely walk after my Wildflower triathlon. Deep-tissue work includes some of my other favorite mobility-enhancing techniques, including Rolfing, Muscle Activation Technique, Advanced Muscle Integrative Therapy, Graston Technique, Trigger Point Therapy, deep-tissue sports massage, foam rolling, and even simply using a tennis ball, lacrosse ball, or golf ball to dig into tight or sore spots.

When you have areas of chronic tightness or tension or a history of injury or overuse, adhesions (bands of painful, rigid tissue) usually form in the muscles, tendons, and ligaments there. These adhesions can block circulation and cause pain, inflammation, and limited mobility.

In sports medicine, this is known as the Cumulative Injury Cycle (see Figure 5-4).

In the Cumulative Injury Cycle, a repetitive effort (like riding a bicycle) causes muscles to tighten (such as your hip flexors). A tight muscle tends to weaken, and a weak muscle tends to tighten, which creates a vicious, well, cycle. As the muscle becomes tighter and tighter, the area of tension experiences more and more friction and pressure, which increases the potential for injury and inflammation.

This friction and pressure can occur even in the absence of an external force—that is, just by sitting all day—it doesn't necessarily require a myriad of barbell squats or long bike rides. As tightness in tissues increases, circulation decreases, resulting in even more swelling, a reduced flow of blood and lymph fluid to the area, and further pressure and tension. The lack of oxygen (cellular hypoxia) caused by restricted circulation can result in fibrosis (the thickening and scarring of connective tissue)

FIGURE 5-4. Cumulative Injury Cycle

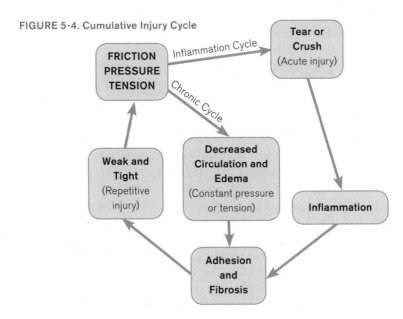

and adhesions in the tissues. Eventually, a tear or injury occurs, and this restarts the adhesion process.

This is where deep-tissue work—the act of physically breaking down these adhesions, usually by applying direct pressure or friction across the grain of the muscles—comes in[8,19]. As adhesions are broken down, blood and lymph flow to the affected area is enhanced.

When it comes to deep-tissue work, different strokes work for different folks (quite literally), but these are some of the more effective methods I've found for increasing mobility or reversing pain and injury in athletes:

- **Rolfing:** Unlike other deep-tissue methods, Rolfing focuses almost exclusively on fascia over a course of ten 60- to 90-minute sessions. During a typical session, you are guided through specific movements while your Rolfer manipulates your fascia, which, I have to tell you, can be pretty intense. I question whether the ten-session approach is more of a business model than a therapeutic necessity, but if fascial adhesions are your problem, then Rolfing is a great solution.

- **Advanced Muscle Integration Technique (AMIT):** In my BenGreenfieldFitness. com podcast episode "'Dr. Two Fingers' Reveals His Teeth-Gritting, Body-Healing Secrets," I interviewed the guy who invented AMIT. AMIT is based on the fact that all the tissue in your body is saturated with proprioceptors, sensors that monitor and control every aspect of body function. This complex system of receptors monitors tension, pressure, movement, stretch, temperature, energy fields, and compression. If you get injured or have lots of inflammation somewhere, these receptors become protective and shut off function or mobility in that area. Interestingly, sometimes a lack of mobility is due to a nearby muscle being injured (such as a quadriceps injury resulting in lack of mobility in the hamstring). AMIT restores proprioception by applying deep pressure on specific proprioceptive areas. As you might have guessed from the title of the podcast episode, it is (like Rolfing) a bit uncomfortable. But it's also an awesome technique to try if your lack of mobility is a result of injury.

- **Muscle Activation Technique (MAT):** MAT is based on the same concept as AMIT. But rather than improving mobility with pressure or kneading, MAT begins with range-of-motion (ROM) testing, followed by specific exercises (usually isometric) to address any deficient areas of ROM. For example, after years of riding a bike, you might find that your neck and head become stuck in a jutting-forward position. So an MAT therapist might fix that by having you look up and perform an isometric contraction with your head tilted back to try to bring your head back into proper alignment.

- **Graston Technique:** Graston employs six special stainless-steel tools to palpate your muscles and tendons. Although they look like they belong in a medieval torture chamber, the curved edges of the patented Graston instruments let them fit into the different contours of your body, allowing for ease of treatment, minimal stress to the therapist's hands, and maximum tissue penetration. Graston actually comes in quite handy if you're trying to break down scar tissue from injury or get rid of knots from muscle overuse—and although getting your IT bands "scraped" may sound painful, I've known many athletes who got a nearly instant cure from Graston.

- **Trigger Point Therapy (TPT):** Trigger points (aka muscle knots) are hyper-irritable areas in muscle that are tight, taut, or hard to the touch. TPT is based on the perception that pain frequently radiates from these points of tenderness to broader, sometimes more distant, areas (such as a trigger point in your armpit referring pain to the front of your shoulder). By applying pressure to the knots, you can alleviate the pain and restore mobility. There is actually a Trigger Point Therapy store where you can get instructions, along with special rollers and other devices for doing your own TPT, at BeyondTrainingBook.com/TPT.

- **Deep-Tissue Sports Massage:** In the podcast episode "How Quantum Physics Can Heal the Body and Enhance Performance," I interviewed my favorite deep-tissue sports massage therapist on the face of the planet—a guy named Herb Akers, from Sacramento, California. Herb runs the website Quantum Connective Healing at RulesOfTheMatrix.com and calls his special flavor of deep-tissue work quantum connective healing. It incorporates nutritional therapies, breathing, and deep-tissue massage. Deep-tissue massage is designed to relieve severe tension in the muscle and connective tissue, and, unlike Swedish massage and some types of relaxation massage, it focuses on the muscles that lie below—that is, deeper than—the superficial muscles. Pressure is applied to both the superficial and the deep layers of muscles, fascia, and other connective-tissue structures like tendons, and these sessions are way more intense than just about any other form of massage. (I usually cry like a baby when Herb works on me.) But despite the come-to-Jesus moments you'll experience during deep-tissue work, it is damn effective at restoring mobility.

Here's the best part about deep-tissue work: You can do much of it yourself[7]. I used to drive to a massage therapist every week until I learned how to do my own deep-tissue work with a golf ball; a RumbleRoller, which is a hard, ridged foam roller with which I have a love-hate relationship; a Myorope, which looks like several lacrosse balls strung together; and a rolling pin–like device called a Muscletrac. Now I need to see a therapist only when I run into a big mobility issue that I can't fix myself, which happens about 1 percent of the time.

If you're game to take charge of your own mobility, a fantastic "cookbook" for learning to do deep-tissue work on yourself (and a book that I highly recommend for every athlete looking to enhance mobility) is *Becoming a Supple Leopard,* by physical therapist Kelly Starrett, whose excellent website is MobilityWOD.com. In the book, Kelly goes into methods for self-deep-tissue work, like pressure waves, contract and relax, banded flossing, smash and floss, paper-clipping oscillation, voodoo flossing, flexion gapping, and a ton of other highly effective techniques that can literally keep you immune from injury and require little more than a lacrosse ball or a barbell.

You can get a taste of the mobility movements in *Becoming a Supple Leopard* by going to Kelly's website. You can also check out mobility WODs specifically designed for exercise enthusiasts at BeyondTrainingBook.com/10mobility, visit the mobility section at AllThingsGym.com, or read the article on self-myofascial release exercises for runners at BeyondTrainingBook.com/myofasc.

Let me remind you that deep-tissue massage is not a relaxing experience. Don't expect your session with a therapist skilled in any of the techniques I've just described to involve "hands of serenity" posters on the wall or ethereal music or a journey into la-la land. And the therapist probably will not use lotion or oil. You may want to bring a mouthpiece to keep from grinding your teeth into smithereens or bone up on breathing techniques for childbirth. I've been known to sob, even when it's just me, my immobile hip, and a seemingly innocent and harmless lacrosse ball.

You should also be prepared for the possibility of soreness after deep-tissue work, because as adhesions are broken up by friction, the same type of inflammation will accumulate in your tissues as when you lift weights or run downhill. Although this inflammation is temporary, it can cause some pressure and discomfort. I am proactive about potential soreness, so after a session I take a cold shower, flush my body by drinking generous amounts of water, and slather magnesium oil on the area that's been worked on.

Traction

The final training strategy for increasing mobility is traction. Traction is the application of force to the body in a way that separates and elongates the tissues surrounding a particular joint. Although chiropractors, osteopaths, or physical therapists are most often the ones applying traction, you can also traction yourself if you know what you're doing.

You can change the integrity of your fascia, muscle, and other connective tissue with deep-tissue work, and you can increase range of motion with dynamic and static stretching, but you will still have to deal with the bony, capsular area of the joint itself.

This is because your joints are constantly being compressed by the muscles, ligaments, and tendons that surround them. This brings the bones in that joint into closer proximity, especially when the surrounding muscles, ligaments, and tendons are tight—and tightness goes pretty much hand in hand with being active. Like tightening a knot in a rope, stretching a tight muscle just creates more tension in the joint, which brings the bones even closer together.

And if the bones in your joints are kissing close, it can completely rob that joint of mobility, limiting its ability to glide in a smooth and frictionless way. So even if the muscles, fascia, and connective tissue are mobile, the joint still can't move properly. Having muscles that move and joints that don't is a recipe for joint breakdown and osteoarthritis.

But traction is a great solution for this problem. Traction basically involves using some kind of bracing to apply force to your shoulders, hips, knees, and other joints, to pull apart, or "distract," that joint just slightly—and release any compressive forces causing limited mobility[5].

For example, say you get deep, aching pain in your hips after a long run or when you increase your running mileage. You can take a lacrosse ball to the side of your hips or do a bunch of side-to-side dynamic leg swings. But to restore mobility to the hip joint itself and get rid of your pain, you will need to do hip traction with a band (I use a Monster Band from Rogue Fitness) basically to pull apart your hip socket. And boy, does it feel good!

To perform hip traction, get on all fours with a long, straight spine. Loop one end of a giant elastic band around the top of your thigh, and the other end onto an immovable object, like a bedpost, couch, or rack at the gym. Move far enough away from that object so you feel tension in the band. Then rock your hips side to side and front to back, allowing your hip to move in the newly opened space created by the traction from the band. This movement under traction helps deliver small increases or movements in lubricating synovial fluid to the joint and also helps reduce cramps or spasms that have insinuated themselves into any overactive muscles surrounding the hip.

Traction may be tough to visualize, so you might want to check out videos of the "rubber band" stretch variations in the mobility section of allthingsgym.com. Many of them feature Kelly Starrett, whose book *Becoming a Supple Leopard* has detailed instructions on self-traction exercises.

Another traction tool I keep around is an inversion table. You can get one of these bad boys for $100 to $300 on Amazon.com, or you could probably find one on Craigslist that someone would practically pay you to take away. After a long day of work on my feet or a long bike ride or run, I hang from my inversion table for five to ten minutes. Not only does it apply potent traction to the knees, hips, neck, and back, but it also does a great job of helping to drain inflammation from exercised tissue. And yes, you can do the impressive upside-down sit-ups for extra inversion points.

That's about all you need for traction: an inversion table, a giant band, and some how-to resources.

Then toss in a golf ball, a gnarly foam roller, a lacrosse ball or Myorope, a Muscletrac, and the occasional tree stump, barbell, park bench, or anything else you can rub up against in a legal way, and you can pretty much skip the gear recommendation section because you'll have everything you'll ever need for mobility TLC.

A Metabolic Mobility Workout

I'm a big fan of frequent use of a foam roller to keep injuries at bay and keep the body mobile. Problem is, the twenty to forty-five minutes it takes to perform a full-body foam-rolling routine are twenty to forty-five minutes that I'm not able to spend "getting fit." So when I do my foam-rolling routine (which I perform two times per week), I put on a podcast or an audiobook, wear a resisted breath-training mask (aka "training mask"), and inject calisthenic exercises into my rolling so that I am able to achieve injury prevention, breath training, and cardiovascular exercise all at once. Here's how I do it:

Perform twenty to thirty "passes" with the foam roller on each muscle group outlined below. One pass means rolling up the muscle group and back down the muscle group one time. Complete each station once, progressing from one to the next with minimal rest.

- Station 1: 10 burpees. Foam roll Achilles and calf right side.
- Station 2: 10 burpees. Foam roll Achilles and calf left side.
- Station 3: Foam roll hamstring right side. 20 high leg swings right leg forward to backward.
- Station 4: Foam roll hamstring left side. 20 high leg swings left leg forward to backward.
- Station 5: 10 burpees. Foam roll right outside of hip.
- Station 6: 10 burpees. Foam roll left outside of hip.
- Station 7: Foam roll IT band right side. 20 side-to-side leg swings right leg.
- Station 8: Foam roll IT band left side. 20 side-to-side leg swings left leg.
- Station 9: 10 burpees. Foam roll right adductors/inside of thighs.
- Station 10: 10 burpees. Foam roll left adductors/inside of thighs.
- Station 11: 50 jumping jacks. Foam roll back bottom to top.
- Station 12: 50 jumping jacks. Foam roll entire right shoulder complex.
- Station 13: 50 jumping jacks. Foam roll entire left shoulder complex.
- Station 14: 10 burpees. Foam roll neck (back, left side, right side).
- Station 15: 10 burpees. Foam roll entire front of quads.

Because I've worked all the knots and fascial adhesions out of my tissues with this routine, I usually do five minutes of inversion table as a finisher. And yes, I get funny looks when the UPS driver rolls up to the house and I'm there hanging in my underwear, dripping with sweat and wearing a breath-training mask. But he'll survive.

In the meantime, if you need videos or demonstrations of any of these foam roller exercises, visit YouTube.com/BenGreenfieldFitness for a series of foam-rolling videos from yours truly. By the way, you get extra fitness points if you do this routine in a dry or infrared sauna.

Food for Mobility

As you've come to expect by now, no discussion about a neglected area of a training program would be complete without food and supplement tips. So it's time to put on my chef's hat and give you some culinary pointers for taking care of your joints and keeping your fascia nice and supple.

- **Bone broth:** Every week here in the Greenfield house, we make a big vat of bone broth that lasts all week. Typically, we use a whole chicken (although you can also use beef, pork, or other bones). Bone broth is a cinch to make and is a fantastic source of vitamins, minerals, amino acids, and fatty acids. Not only can a cup make your entire body feel like a million bucks, but the marrow that seeps into the broth can be one of the best things ever for your joints, joint pain, and joint mobility. If you don't have the time or desire to make bone broth, or you want to add even more joint-healing compounds to your diet, you can get some of the same benefits of bone broth by adding powdered gelatin to your smoothies. Gelatin powder is basically ground-up collagen; use an organic brand like Primal Peptides, Great Lakes, or Bernard Jensen. If you really want to geek out on all the benefits of bone broth, read "Why Broth Is Beautiful"[4] at BeyondTrainingBook.com/wpbbroth. I think that every person doing hard and heavy training would benefit from drinking a cup of bone broth every one to three days and adding one to two tablespoons of gelatin powder to smoothies. You can also get bone broth prepared for you and delivered to your home. There are two sources at GreenfieldFitnessSystems.com: The Brothery and Bone Broth Co.

- **Ginger:** Ginger extract has been shown to be just as effective at reducing joint pain as ibuprofen, but is, of course, far more natural[1]. You can simply slice up gingerroot, boil it for five to ten minutes, and eat four to six slices on hard workout days. You can also toss a large chunk of boiled or raw ginger into a smoothie or grate ginger into soups, stews, stir-fries, or whatever else you're eating. I always have a big chunk of raw gingerroot on the kitchen counter as a joint-supporting staple.

- **Fish:** Omega-3 fatty acids slow the progression of osteoarthritis[15]. Specifically, EPA and DHA inhibit the expression of various proteins that contribute to osteoarthritis, and decrease both the destruction and inflammatory aspects of cartilage-cell metabolism. In a study of 293 adults without osteoarthritis, some with and some without joint pain, higher intakes of monounsaturated fatty acids or omega-6 polyunsaturated fatty acids were associated with an increased risk of bone marrow lesions (abnormal areas of tissue change in bone marrow), so shifting the diet toward foods rich in omega-3 fatty acids (like fish) while decreasing consumption of omega-6 fatty acids (like vegetable oils, heated seeds and nuts, etc.) can be extremely helpful. Omega-3 fatty acids can help with stiff, tender, or swollen joints and joint pain and also with increasing blood flow to joints during exercise.

  I recommend eating several six- to eight-ounce servings of cold-water fish a week. Salmon, mackerel, trout, halibut, and white tuna contain more than 1,000 milligrams of fish oil per three- to four-ounce serving, and a British study found that regularly consuming this amount of fish oil is all it takes to stop cartilage-eating enzymes in their tracks (no megadoses of supplements required!).

Of course, you can also get fish oil in a capsule or liquid form, but be sure to buy a brand that's cold-processed and triglyceride-based and contains antioxidants: I think Pharmax, Barlean's, Carlson, and LivingFuel are the best. Cod liver oil has also been shown to be a great supporter of joint health. (I'd recommend a fermented form, which you can get from Green Pastures or via a GreenfieldFitnessSystems. com supplement called SuperEssentials.) I recommend consuming 4 to 6 grams of fish oil capsules or one to two tablespoons of cod liver oil any day you don't eat fish.

- **Antioxidants:** Vitamins B and C increase cell-wall elasticity and joint mobility and can be found in just about any dark-colored fruit, vegetable, or starch (such as acorn and butternut squash). Blueberries, raspberries, blackberries, purple grapes, pomegranates, currants, purple cabbage, kale, tomatoes, dark-orange carrots, sweet potatoes, yams, and taro contain the highest amounts of inflammation-reducing polyphenols and bioactive compounds (aka antioxidants) in the plant world. Any athlete's refrigerator or countertop should be chock-full of these gorgeous natural healers.

Supplements for Mobility

- **Proteolytic enzymes:** As the name implies, proteolytic enzymes (also known as proteases) "lyse," or break down, proteins. They include enzymes such as trypsin, chymotrypsin, papain, and bromelain. You could, for example, pop a few enzymes before eating a steak to help digest the proteins in the meat. But when used outside of meals, proteolytic enzymes can accelerate a multitude of healing processes. When they're not needed for digestion in the small intestine, these enzymes are free to roam through the bloodstream to break down hard protein, fibrin surfaces, scar tissue, granuloma, and tough cell coatings that can cause joint pain and lack of mobility[6]. In Europe and Japan, proteolytic enzymes are used quite extensively to speed healing from injury or surgery (although in Britain and the United States, they still fly under the radar).

  You'll get some proteolytic enzymes from eating papaya, pineapple, and meat, but for injuries and mobility you'll need more concentrated sources (unless you feel like eating a wheelbarrow's worth of pineapples a day). Dosages vary, but if you're really struggling with fascial adhesions and a lack of mobility from injury or scar tissue, I recommend the brands NatureFlex and Wobenzym.

- **Glucosamine-chondroitin:** Glucosamine is a sugar present in the protective exoskeleton of shellfish, and chondroitin sulfate is a major component of cartilage. Both are produced by your body. Glucosamine stimulates cartilage production in your joints, and chondroitin helps attract water to the tissue, which helps your cartilage retain its elasticity. Chondroitin may also block the action of enzymes that break down cartilage tissue[12]. Glucosamine sulfate is more effective at reducing joint pain and increasing mobility than glucosamine hydrochloride. You need to take at least 1,500 milligrams of glucosamine sulfate a day, and usually for at least three months, to notice any improvement in your condition.

I and the athletes I coach have tried many different brands of glucosamine-chondroitin and have found NatureFlex to be the most effective. It's not an everyday supplement, but one to use if you really need to see improvements in mobility, you're injured, or you need to nip nagging joint pain in the bud. In addition to glucosamine-chondroitin, it contains a cocktail of antioxidants and anti-inflammatories such as cherry juice, ginger, turmeric, white willow bark, feverfew, valerian, acerola cherry, and lemon powder. You can read more about it at GreenfieldFitnessSystems.com.

A Final Word on Mobility

Here's the final word on mobility: When you begin to use the techniques you've just been introduced to, you'll immediately notice changes in the way you move, the way your joints feel, and any nagging aches and pains. But these changes will be minuscule compared with how you're going to feel and move in six months to two years. Why will it take that long? Research on fascia (and the trusted word of Kelly Starrett) has shown that rewiring your fascia and completely changing your mobility and range of motion in a long-lasting way takes about six to twenty-four months.

So mobility is a game of patience. And it is totally worth it, even if means keeping a golf ball under your desk, a lacrosse ball in your underwear drawer, and a foam roller on your back porch for the next two years.

So what's next?

In case you haven't been counting, there is one more essential element of an endurance-training program that most athletes neglect: balance. And trust me, balance goes way above and beyond standing on one foot while you're brushing your teeth.

BALANCE

In this section, you're going to learn about the training element that allows you to run without looking like you just gave birth to a rhino, ride a bike without falling off, and swim without feeling like you're going to drown.

That element is balance. You're about to learn how to train your eyes, ears, and joints to turn you into a ninja. And because the training methods, foods, and supplements previously discussed for enhancing strength, power, mobility, and speed have excellent crossover applications in terms of improving your balance, you're not going to have to take in too much new information.

Essential Element No. 5: Balance

Let's start with an image. Picture in your mind, if you will, a runner. A really ugly runner. He doesn't necessarily have to have an ugly face—although you can imagine that if it helps—just a really ugly *gait*. A gait that only a mother could love.

This runner's hip collapses sideways when his foot strikes the ground, his foot flips awkwardly outward as his leg swings behind him, and he lands with a forceful, seemingly painful "oomph."

For four years, I managed an exercise physiology and biomechanics laboratory where runners and triathletes of all shapes and sizes came to get their gait analyzed with high-speed video cameras and treadmills. And I would bear witness to this same ghastly running pattern over and over again.

Economy, gone. Efficiency, gone. Just a slap, land, sway, kick, slap, land, sway, kick, over and over again. A surefire way to exhaust the body.

Interestingly, when I had the runners step off the treadmill and do simple balance drills like standing on one leg with their eyes open or closed, walking from one end of the room to the other, or jumping off one leg, the same movement deficits were in evidence. Why?

Surprisingly, the answer is not lack of strength, inability to produce power, or speed deficits. In many cases, it's not even a mobility issue. Instead, it's a pure and simple lack of balance[12].

So in this section, you're going to discover how to maximize your balance and learn about the training methods, lifestyle choices, foods, and supplements that support the three most important determinants of balance—your eyes, ears, and joints.

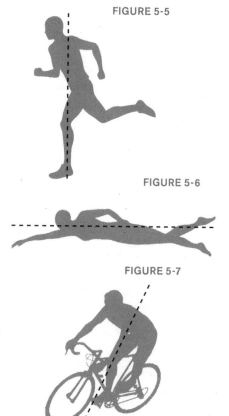

FIGURE 5-5

FIGURE 5-6

FIGURE 5-7

What Is Balance?

Balance is simply the ability to maintain a line of gravity (technically a vertical line from center of gravity) within a base of support with minimal postural sway or collapse[1].

Yes, that definition was a little geeky. So here's a clearer explanation: Balance is the ability to maintain the body's center of mass over its base of support.

Better? Need something even simpler? Here you go: Balance is being able to move around efficiently without falling on your ass.

If you're running, balance (and that line of gravity) can be pictured as in Figure 5-5.

If you're swimming, balance would look like the image in Figure 5-6.

And if you're riding a bicycle, balance—more specifically lack of balance—would look a bit like the image in Figure 5-7.

Maintaining balance requires the coordination of three sensory systems:

1. **Vestibular system**—the sense organs in your head, primarily your ears, which regulate equilibrium and give you directional information as it relates to your head position[6].

2. **Somatosensory system**—the nerves called proprioceptors in your joints, along with the pressure and vibratory sense information in both your skin and your joints[2].

3. **Visual system**—the ability of your eyes to figure out where your head and body are in space, and also where you are relative to other objects[5].

For you to be properly balanced, each of these components has to be optimized. In other words, you gotta have good eyes, good ears, and healthy joints (see Figure 5-8).

Training Strategies for Increasing Balance

Vestibular Balance

Let's start with your vestibular system. I promise not to delve too deeply into the science of your ears, but a quick overview will help you understand how you can optimize this system.

Sensory information about things like motion, equilibrium, and where your body is in space is provided by something called the vestibular apparatus, which is a part of your ear that includes the utricle, saccule, and three semicircular canals[7]. The utricle and saccule detect gravity and front-to-back or side-to-side movement. The semicircular canals detect rotational movement and are filled with a special fluid called endolymph.

When your head rotates in the direction sensed by one of those semicircular canals, the endolymphatic fluid in the canal lags behind because of inertia and exerts

FIGURE 5-8

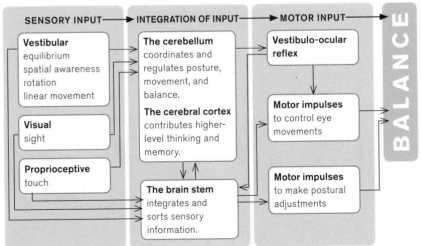

pressure against the canal's sensory receptor[10]. When this happens, the receptor sends impulses to your brain about what kind of movement is happening.

So how can you train and care for this precious vestibular apparatus? Two ways: You subject yourself to quick changes in linear or rotational movement, and you care for your valuable ear anatomy.

Here are my top tips for improving vestibular balance:

- **Avoid loud music, loud sounds, and cell phone radiation.** The first two probably make good sense to you. But the last one might be a bit of a head-scratcher. So go to a store that sells cell phones and check the label on any new phone package. It says not to bring the phone anywhere near your head. The electromagnetic field (EMF) from your phone is one of the best ways to fry the fragile outsides of your head and impair your hearing (see Figure 5-9). Later in this book, I'll dig into EMF and phone radiation a bit more, but for now, you can read the book *Zapped* by Anne Louise Gittleman, start digging into "The Biological Effects of Weak Electromagnetic Fields" at BeyondTrainingBook.com/weakelec, and grab yourself an air-tube headset for your phone. (I recommend something called an air-tube headset.) You can find a link to many of my favorite EMF mitigating tools in my book *How to Biohack the Ultimate Healthy Home,* available on Amazon and at GreenfieldFitnessSystems.com.

- **Go barefoot as much as possible, or use minimalist footwear.** Big, supportive, built-up shoes do all the balance work for you. If you have no feel for the ground because you're spending the day in overpriced moon boots designed to "control" your feet, then you're not letting all those micromotions that inform your vestibular system do their job. As you practice using minimal footwear, try to stand or walk on different areas of your foot—the outside, ball, and heel. This forces your vestibular system to microadjust to new linear and rotational movements.

- **Balance on one leg while keeping your gaze on something stationary.** Eventually, train yourself to look at objects farther away, then progress to closing your eyes completely. Finally, stand on an unstable surface with your eyes closed.

FIGURE 5-9. How Mobile Phone Radiation Penetrates the Brain

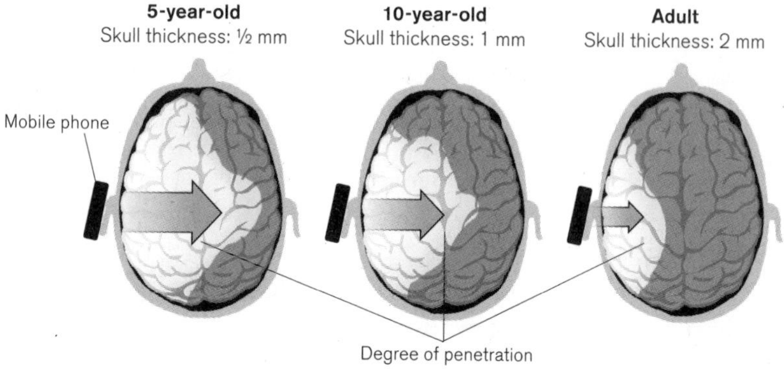

5-year-old	10-year-old	Adult
Skull thickness: ½ mm	Skull thickness: 1 mm	Skull thickness: 2 mm

Mobile phone

Degree of penetration

While this is a great way to train your visual and somatosensory balance systems, the small fluctuations in your balance when you're practicing this technique (especially with your eyes closed) also train your vestibular system. My rule of thumb is to do at least five single-leg squats on each leg, eyes closed, every morning, and I've recently started doing them on a half foam roller. When I first began, I couldn't even do one squat without my form falling to pieces, but now my single-leg stance is incredibly stable.

- **Look for things to stand on wherever you are.** Narrow ridges, sidewalks, posts, rails on fences, the back of a park bench. In my phone-app podcast episode with movement specialist Darryl Edwards, whose fantastic website is TheFitnessExplorer. com, I describe how I do a thirty-minute "fitness exploring" circuit once a week in a park near my house. It consists of running three giant laps around the park, with each lap including balancing on benches, single-leg hops on and off curbs, clambering up and walking across a wooden fence, and jumping onto picnic tables. This type of play, also known as Parkour or MovNat, is a fantastic way to build your vestibular system, especially if you keep the earbuds out of your ears.

Somatosensory Balance

Your skin, muscles, and joints all contain sensory receptors (proprioceptors) that are sensitive to stretching or pressure in the surrounding tissues[10]. For example, you feel increased pressure in the balls of your feet when you lean forward. The sensory receptors in your feet send impulses to your brain that help you recognize where your body is in space—even if your eyes are closed or your ears are plugged.

The sensory impulses in your neck and ankles are especially important. Proprioceptive cues from your neck tell your brain which direction your head is turned. Cues from your ankles indicate the body's movement relative to the specific characteristics of the surface you're standing on[8]—whether it's hard, soft, slippery, or uneven.

How can you maximize the quality of these cues? Here are my top tips for improving somatosensory balance:

- **Stand one-legged or two-legged on unstable surfaces,** such as wobble boards, thick balance mats, or balance disc pillows. By adjusting both the surface quality and the stability of what you're standing on, you stimulate greater proprioception. I'm a bit wary of advocating heavy overhead presses while wobbling around on a pink balance pillow at the gym or doing something dumb like a barbell squat on a stability ball. But consider other, safer things that you can do on an unbalanced or novel surface, such as talking on the phone or working on your computer. If you really want to take this to the extreme, do what I do and try walking on a slippery riverbed with tiny stones so your surface and its texture change with every step. That's proprioceptive training on steroids. Just remember to wear a helmet.

- **Use an unstable mat under your desk.** Companies like Topo and Kybun are producing special mats that force your body to shift and balance as you work at a standing workstation. I use the Kybun mat, which is patterned to simulate the texture of a rice paddy field. When the user stands on it, it forces the tiny hip and foot muscles to continually fire and adjust.

- **Do side or front leg kicks with a band or cable.** This is one of my favorite exercises for building knee stability and single-leg stability while improving proprioception. It can also help tremendously with eliminating knee pain that stems from poor tracking of the kneecap and weak quads. Simply attach one end of the cable or band to your ankle, attach the other end to a stationary object, stand on one leg, and kick either out to the front or to the side while trying not to use your arms or hands to support yourself.

- **Use a mini-trampoline or vibration platform.** Both trampolines and vibration platforms are fantastic unstable surfaces for practicing single-leg stances, with the trampoline having the added advantage of a jumping and landing component.

- **Stand on one leg on a raised height.** Elevated surfaces send an instant cue to your brain that you're in danger and can upregulate the quality and frequency of proprioceptive cues—hence the fence walking and park bench balancing that I do in my fitness exploring. If you're not into wandering around a city or park, inviting strange glances, you could concoct a home balance beam or simply stand on one leg on a slightly raised surface at the gym, like a step bench or box. Hip hikes are a great way to kill two birds with one stone, as they strengthen your outer glutes and simultaneously build balance on an elevated surface. You can find a video of me doing hip hikes at YouTube.com/BenGreenfieldFitness.

Visual Balance

Your visual balance system is composed of sensory receptors in your retina called rods and cones. When light strikes the rods and cones, they send impulses to the brain that provide visual cues about how your head, body, or limbs are oriented relative to other objects[5]. Most of us tend to rely too heavily on our visual balance, neglecting somatosensory and vestibular balance, but taking care of your visual system is nonetheless important. Here's how:

- **Use blue-light-blocking glasses when using the computer, and take breaks.** I wrote about glare and blue-light-blocking strategies quite extensively in a post on how to beat insomnia and get a better night's sleep. I've linked to that post on the reference web page for this chapter, and I talk more about it in this book's section on sleep. One of the best ways to destroy your visual system for life (in addition to extensively disrupting your sleep patterns) is to spend the day staring at a screen[3]. If you ever experience dizziness, headaches, light-headedness, or twitching around your eyes, you're probably straining your eyes too much. For the same reason, it's important to avoid small fonts and reading in rooms with low levels of light.

Fortunately, there are a number of apps—like Awareness, WorkRave, Time Out, and ProtectYourVision—that remind you to briefly stop working or to focus your eyes elsewhere. You can also follow the 20-20-20 rule, which says that for every 20 minutes you spend staring at the computer, you should spend 20 seconds looking at objects about 20 feet away.

- **Play a sport that requires eye tracking.** About the most complex visual exercise that endurance athletes get is looking around while riding a bike. But eye-tracking activities that actually build, train, or maintain eye muscle activity are few and far between. This is why cross-training sports such as soccer, golf, tennis, basketball, and even ping-pong are good not only for training the arm, leg, and core muscles that you don't use in your main sport, but also for keeping your eyes at the top of their game.

- **Sleep seven to eight hours a night.** Sleep is extremely anabolic for your entire body, but it's especially effective at relaxing your visual system and relieving strain on your eyes. If you've ever had a mysterious twitch in your eye that just wouldn't go away (a condition called myokymia), it was probably due to lack of sleep. Inadequate sleep can also lead to ischemic optic neuropathy, which is damage to the optic nerve from lack of blood supply. Glaucoma is another condition that can result from lack of sleep and can lead to complete loss of valuable peripheral vision, as well as blindness. You can find my best sleep-enhancing tips at BeyondTrainingBook.com/bgfinsomnia.

- **If your visual system is really impaired, you may want to try the Bates Method**[9]. It involves a series of exercises to strengthen the eye muscles as well as the mental connection between the brain and the eye. Many people with poor vision have found that glasses and contact lenses eventually become unnecessary.

- **Use the Vision Gym.** The good folks over at Z-Health (more details below) have developed an online program called the Vision Gym that teaches you simple ten-minute eye exercises to enhance advanced visual-acuity skills, such as depth perception, peripheral range, saccadic movement (how fast and accurately your eyes move when you read or scan), and color and contrast discrimination. It's basically a twenty-first-century version of the Bates Method, and it's the program I would follow before surrendering to glasses if my vision ever began to fail.

Z-Health

If you want to learn more about how each of these balance systems integrates with your nervous system as a whole, a good resource is Z-Health, which teaches the general public about the balance and nervous systems, certifies fitness professionals to specifically address these systems, and offers books and programs that teach you how to strengthen these systems.

Specifically, Z-Health is based on sensory-integration training, in which you train your nervous system to get accurate information from the visual, somatosensory, and vestibular systems so that you improve your ability to know where your body is in space, how fast it is moving, and what movement ranges are "safe." For more information, listen to the free interview I did with the folks at Z-Health at BeyondTrainingBook.com/zhealth.

Food and Strategies for Increasing Balance

This is easy: The foods and supplements for increasing mobility also strengthen your somatosensory system, while the foods and supplements for power and speed also enhance your visual system.

However, when it comes to your vestibular system specifically—and recommendations for better hearing, healthier ears, or better balance—folate is one nutrient that tends to fly under the radar. A study presented at the annual meeting of the American Academy of Otolaryngology–Head and Neck Surgery Foundation Annual Meeting in 2009 found that men over the age of sixty who consumed a lot of foods and supplements high in folate decreased their risk of developing hearing loss by 20 percent[11]. This is the largest study to examine the beneficial relationship between folate and hearing loss.

Be cautious, however: *Folate* is a general term for a group of water-soluble B vitamins found naturally in food, while *folic acid* refers to the potentially harmful, oxidized, synthetic compound commonly used in dietary supplements and food fortification. Because there are risks associated with folic acid in supplements, it's best to get your folate from food. The best sources of dietary folate are romaine lettuce, spinach, asparagus, turnip greens, mustard greens, parsley, collard greens, broccoli, cauliflower, and beets. If you soak them and prepare them properly, which you'll learn how to do later in this book, lentils are also a good source. And if you're feeling carnivorous, calf's liver and chicken liver are also excellent sources of folate.

Gear for Improving Balance

If you're using the gear suggested in the previous sections, you're already equipped to naturally stimulate your vestibular, somatosensory, and visual systems.

And, as I've already stated, you should try to add some balance tools and gear to your home gym equipment. You don't need everything, but a mini-trampoline or vibration platform, a wobble board, a thick balance mat, a stability ball, a balance disc pillow, and a half foam roller can all come in handy.

In addition to challenging your joints, make sure to protect your eyes and ears[3]. Use Gunnar glasses or other blue-light-blocking glasses when you're at your computer or spending lots of time staring at other screens.

Use an air-tube headset when talking on the phone, and keep your phone away from your head.

I believe that as science progresses, better methods will be developed for mitigating the effects of modern living on our delicate balance systems, but in the meantime, be sure to check out websites such as LessEMF.com and Lifehacker, both of which tend to have good health tips if technology such as computers and phones are a regular part of your life.

So that's balance.

When was the last time you tried standing on one leg while doing, say, an overhead press? Heck, when was the last time you tried standing on one leg while brushing your teeth or washing dishes? When was the last time you thought about taking care of your eyes? Your ears? Your joints?

Bottom line: You can do all the ChiRunning, Pose running, cycling on rollers, walking on balance beams, Total Immersion swimming, and every other endurance-balancing technique you want to, but until you begin taking care of the elements of your body responsible for keeping you in balance, you won't be maximizing your results.

And, worse yet, if you don't use the three systems you just learned about, they will deteriorate faster.

Strength, power, speed, balance, and mobility are essential if you want your body to last a long time—but most endurance athletes, weekend warriors, and recreational exercisers who may be able to pound the pavement for two hours at a time can't do even one single flawless one-legged squat, a Turkish get-up, or a lateral lunge. Can you? Remember: The ultimate goal is to be maximally equipped with the knowledge to build a body that expresses the ideal combination of health, longevity, and performance.

Additional resources, helpful websites, scientific references, and surprise bonuses are available at BeyondTrainingBook.com/Chapter5. Enjoy.

2

RECOVERY

CHAPTER 6
How the Underrecovery Monster Is Eating Up Your Precious Training Time

There's a paradoxical problem that you may have noticed. Up to this point, you've primarily learned about *training* techniques or ways to enhance a workout. And, as you may recall, the title of this book is *Beyond Training: Mastering Endurance, Health, and Life.*

So now it's time to truly move beyond training. Beyond lacing up the shoes and pounding the pavement, chalking up the hands and grabbing the bar, or cinching up the Speedo and diving into the water.

And I gotta admit, I freaking love the fringy, edgy stuff we're about to get into.

How about you? Are you ready to delve into what makes me all rabid and foaming at the mouth to talk about?

Good. I certainly am.

What Is the Underrecovery Monster, and Why Should You Care?

Boom—you roll out of bed, shake out your legs, and discover that they don't feel too bad. Your shoulders don't feel tight and restricted. Your eyes aren't overly droopy. So off to work out you go. You're recovered, right?

If you're anything like me, your simple definition of recovery goes something like this: "Recovery is when I'm not sore anymore." Or perhaps: "Recovery is when I can exercise again and feel pretty good when I'm doing it."

But neither of those are definitions of recovery. They're just statements about the way your body feels. Instead, recovery would be more appropriately defined like this: "Recovery is your body's ability to meet or exceed performance in a particular activity."

This is the definition of recovery that is used regularly in the scientific literature[7,14,16], and it makes sense. Let's say, for example, that you did a really hard bike workout. For some time afterward—specifically, until you're recovered—your ability to ride an all-out, personal-best, 40K time trial is going to be diminished.

So if you can speed up your rate of recovery and get your cells, muscles, joints, and nervous system to bounce back as quickly as possible, then you can train more, train harder, train happier, or just feel better when you get out of bed in the morning. More important, every time your body bounces back efficiently, you establish a new "ceiling" of performance capabilities.

Oh, yeah—one other thing: Because of the upregulation of oxidative enzymes, fat-burning hormones, and metabolic "bounce-back" you're going to learn about, you also avoid the dreaded skinny-fat syndrome.

The opposite of this happy scenario is what I call "underrecovery." And underrecovery is a real monster.

When you underrecover (which can be the same thing as overtraining), you end up completely wasting your training time. You're basically just training for the sake of training, with no change in performance or improvement. So in the same way that "black-hole" training results in stagnated performance, chronic underrecovering also results in your never getting faster, better, stronger, or happier with your results, year after year. When you're underrecovered, you're just a rat on a wheel—moving around lots but not getting anywhere.

The following graphs are from an article in the *Journal of Strength & Conditioning Research.*

Figure 6-1 represents the training and recovery curve for your average gymgoer or recreational exerciser, who trains at a fairly low level and easily recovers within a few hours after working out.

FIGURE 6-1.

Sub-elite/Recreational

The "0" point represents the individual's baseline training capacity.

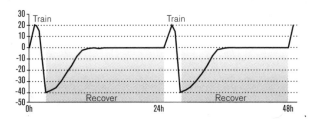

Figure 6-2 illustrates what happens to a more serious exerciser or an elite athlete, who puts in higher volume, higher intensity, or both (a triathlete, marathoner, CrossFitter, etc.). As you can see, recovery is barely complete between workouts, and every twenty-four-hour period is taken up by either (1) working out or (2) recovering. So there's no time left for any actual improvement, and the result is a performance plateau.

FIGURE 6-2.

Elite

The "0" point represents the individual's baseline training capacity.

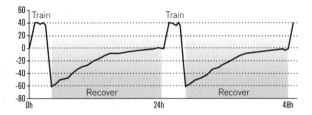

And then we get to Figure 6-3, which is where crap really hits the fan. Rather than simply achieving a disconcerting plateau, the individual is consistently overtraining, and the recovery between workouts is obviously incomplete. The exerciser begins every new workout in a slightly less recovered state than the workout before it, and eventually a state of complete fatigue and burnout is reached.

FIGURE 6-3.

Underrecovered

The "0" point represents the individual's baseline training capacity.

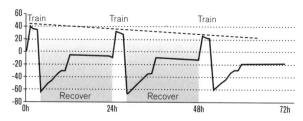

Finally, in Figure 6-4, you can see what happens when you speed up recovery using the methods I'm going to teach you. With more rapid recovery, every subsequent workout increases performance potential, and over weeks, months, and years, there is continuous improvement.

FIGURE 6-4

The "0" point represents the individual's baseline training capacity.

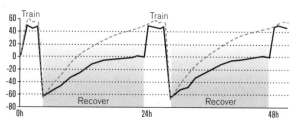

Of course, the key takeaway is that faster recovery cures performance plateaus and declines. So what's happening during that bounce-back period that magically allows you to raise the ceiling on your training?

Let's find out.

What Happens When You Recover the Right Way

Your Muscles

After you work out, your muscles look like scarred battlefields, especially after an impact-based workout or one that involved some deceleration, such as running or weight training. This is because straining your muscles causes trauma to the muscle fibers[7]—basically injuring yourself. *See, I told you extreme exercise can be a masochistic endeavor.*

But sometimes, this trauma can be good because of a phenomenon called "hormesis." Hormesis is a biological reaction in which a beneficial effect (improved health, stress tolerance, muscle growth, longevity, etc.) results from exposure to low doses of an agent that could be toxic or lethal at higher doses[6]. *So, sure, exercise could kill you if you did extreme amounts of it, but in low, moderate, or controlled doses, exercise can give you hormetic benefits, such as increased ability to fight free radicals, manage heavy loads, or be more resilient to environmental stressors.* Other examples of hormesis include fasting, calorie restriction, cold temperature, heat shock, low-level radiation, and even exposure to some natural bacteria and germs.

Here's why muscle injury is good in controlled amounts: Once a muscle fiber is injured, its organelles respond with inflammation and activate special "satellite cells"

FIGURE 6-5

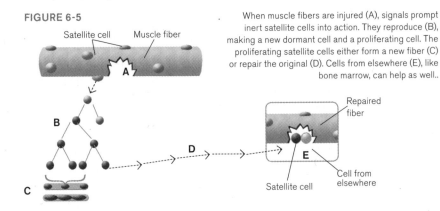

When muscle fibers are injured (A), signals prompt inert satellite cells into action. They reproduce (B), making a new dormant cell and a proliferating cell. The proliferating satellite cells either form a new fiber (C) or repair the original (D). Cells from elsewhere (E), like bone marrow, can help as well..

(see Figure 6-5), which are located outside, but very near, the muscle fibers[18]. A biological effort to repair or replace damaged muscle fibers begins with the satellite cells fusing to one another and to the muscle fibers. This not only repairs the muscle but can also increase muscle fiber in a cross-sectional area or even create new muscle protein strands, called myofibrils.

Some of these satellite cells even serve as a source of new nuclei, so you can synthesize more proteins and create even more contractile myofilaments—known as actin and myosin—in your muscle.

Interestingly, more satellite cells are found in slow-twitch (endurance) muscle fibers than in fast-twitch (power and strength) muscle fibers, since slow-twitch muscle fibers are constantly going through cell repair from daily activities like standing and climbing stairs[12]. So, as an endurance athlete, you've won the satellite-cell lottery, so to speak.

Unfortunately, especially for anyone restricting calories, eating a low-fat diet, or simply training too much, most of these repair adaptations are severely hampered because growth hormone or insulin-like growth factor levels are low, and both of these stimulate satellite cells to do their work. Insulin also stimulates muscle growth by enhancing protein synthesis and facilitating the entry of glucose into cells[18]. Your satellite cells actually use glucose as a fuel to promote their cell-growth activities. And glucose, of course, is also used for intramuscular energy needs.

Testosterone also affects muscle-fiber repair. This is because testosterone can stimulate growth hormone responses in the pituitary gland, and this increase in growth hormone then enhance cellular amino acid uptake and protein synthesis in muscle[10]. In addition, testosterone can increase the presence of neurotransmitters at the fiber site, which can also help activate tissue growth and interact with nuclear receptors in your DNA, resulting in protein synthesis. So low hormone levels, especially when it comes to growth hormone, testosterone, and insulin, mean that it's going to take you way longer to recover.

But let's say that your hormones are rocking. How long should muscle repair take? Researchers at McMaster University and the Washington University School of Medicine in St. Louis found that muscle protein synthesis increases by about 50 percent for four hours after a workout[3]—proof that muscles are repairing damage accrued from the workout and also building new material to make themselves stronger and more fatigue-resistant.

This repair process appears to peak about twenty-four hours after a workout, at which point the rate of muscle protein synthesis is up by a hefty 109 percent, according to the McMaster-Washington research. By about thirty-six hours postworkout, the whole process is pretty much complete. So every time you beat up and tear down muscle fibers, especially with running and weight training, you're looking at approximately thirty-six hours of recovery before another high-quality session is doable or efficacious. And if you jump in too soon, you're wasting precious training time by beating up your muscles in an underrecovered state.

Of course, a bigger problem is that underrecovery is not limited to your muscles. Your blood, bones, nerves, immune system, and hormones also need time to recover. Fortunately, they need about the same amount of time as your muscles, assuming we're talking about a relatively sane one- to two-hour bout of training.

Your Nerves

As you learned in Chapter 5, your central nervous system includes your brain and spinal cord and connects to your muscles through the peripheral nervous system. So when you need to contract a muscle, your brain sends a message via the spinal cord to individual muscle motor units through something called a neuromuscular junction. The muscle gets the message and fires.

But in the same way that training can take a toll on muscles, it can damage your nervous system[1]. This is called neural fatigue, and it can drain your central nervous system and the neuromuscular junctions. The main reason is that your body releases inflammatory cytokines (chemical messengers) in response to muscle damage from training. These inflammatory messengers dock on receptors in your central nervous system and thus hamper neural recovery. But unlike muscle damage, nerve fatigue can be a result of other nervous system stressors, such as lack of sleep, drugs, stimulants, alcohol, or lifestyle choices.

Since your nervous system is basically the "battery" that fires all your muscles, an underrecovered nervous system has a negative impact on the strength and function of your muscles. So your muscles could be primed and ready to rumble, but if your nervous system is underrecovered, you're not going anywhere. This is why you can still be theoretically overtrained or underrecovered even if you're not overdoing it at the gym, but are perhaps partying too much, working too much, or not sleeping enough.

And it's important to know that your central nervous system doesn't differentiate between muscle groups. If it's fatigued, it's fatigued. So if you do a hard run today, then head to the gym tomorrow, you may find that you can't press as much weight overhead: Unless you run on your hands and shoulders, that's not muscle fatigue, it's nervous system fatigue. Low-level, aerobic cardio doesn't really create as much neural fatigue as high-intensity cardio and sprints, which is why you should alternate aerobic and anaerobic sessions during the week if you want to allow for prime neural recovery[2].

How long does neural recovery actually take? In most cases, when your nervous system is drained from high-intensity efforts or too much stress, it needs forty-eight hours to fully recover. Any intense training within that recovery window just drains the nervous system even more. This is why you can't do hard-core workouts day after day, even if you're focusing on different muscle groups or on different activities (high-intensity bike one day, high-intensity run the next day, high-intensity swim the day after that). Eventually, your nervous system will poop out.

Of course, you can also drain those neuromuscular junctions. And it can take up to four days before they fully recover, which means that you may need to wait as long as four days after workouts that heavily stress the same muscle group to experience complete neural recovery.

This explains why you can have a crappy workout even if you're not sore—either your central nervous system or your neuromuscular junctions simply haven't recovered.

Your Blood

Angiogenesis is the process by which new blood vessels form from existing vessels. Increased muscle contractions increase angiogenesis, and during the recovery period after a hard workout, you actually produce new blood vessels and capillaries that feed into the working tissue[9]. Numerous studies have shown that capillary density, expressed as the number of capillaries per muscle fiber, does indeed increase in response to training and recovery.

Researchers have also found that reticulocyte counts (new red blood cells) increase during the tapering period after hard workout blocks, which suggests increased erythropoiesis (red blood cell production) during recovery[15].

Another interesting adaptation that takes place in your blood during recovery is an increase in eosinophils (white blood cell components that can detox inflammation-inducing substances and destroy allergen-antibody complexes) and lymphocytes (white blood cells that fight infection)[8]. This is one reason people who are underrecovered not only get sick more, but also tend to be more susceptible to food allergies and food intolerances.

So if you're sick a lot or short of breath often, your blood is probably underrecovered.

Your Bones

While overtraining or underrecovering can adversely affect connective tissue and decrease bone density, evidence suggests that habitual physical activity actually modifies connective tissue and allows for significant bone remodeling. Bone remodeling is a process whereby mature bone tissue is removed from the skeleton and new bone tissue is formed, which can lead to increased bone density.

Physical activity is one of the best ways to maintain bone-mineral density[5] because it stresses the bone. When you end your exercise bout, it activates bone cells called osteoblasts, which can help with bone remodeling and bone density. Unfortunately, the opposite is also true—repetitive stress without recovery results in bone deterioration and loss of bone density[17].

Repetitive stress in the absence of recovery also depletes essential bone-building minerals and vitamins. As long as you have adequate minerals onboard; don't consume much processed sugar; and your blood calcium, magnesium, and vitamin K levels are sufficient, your thyroid gland releases the hormone calcitonin, which inhibits the bone-destructive osteoclasts and activates the bone-building osteoblasts. But in a high-sugar-consuming, underrecovering athlete, it's the completely opposite story.

Did I hear someone say "stress fracture"? Yep, that's the underrecovery monster talking.

Your Metabolism

We gotta love McMaster University, because that institution is ground zero when it comes to churning out exercise research. One study there divided well-conditioned runners who averaged fifty miles of running a week into three groups[13]. The researchers then had these runners go into recovery mode for a bit. This study was focused more on tapering than on pure recovery, but it still shows some of the cool metabolic supercompensation adaptations that take place when the body is given a chance to rest.

During recovery mode, one group just chilled for a week, doing no running at all. The second group jogged easily for a total of eighteen miles over the course of a week. The third group ran six miles during the week, but almost all of it consisted of all-out 500-meter intervals on the track.

So every group got pretty good recovery time, but one group combined recovery with just a few intense doses of training. After a week, the group that chilled didn't improve at all, the eighteen-milers improved their time trial running performance by about 6 percent, and the interval runners' performance improved by 22 percent! What happened metabolically to bring about those results?

The researchers found that the runners in the last group had:

- Higher aerobic, oxidative enzymes in their legs
- More glycogen (stored carbohydrate) in their leg muscles
- More red blood cells
- More blood plasma

The boost in aerobic, oxidative enzymes should come as no surprise, because I talked about it in chapter 3, on building endurance. I just want to emphasize that you can't turn your body into a metabolically efficient, fat-burning machine through training alone. Recovery is a big part of the equation. That's why underrecovery can also make you skinny-fat.

Increased carbohydrate storage should also come as no surprise, since the runners were simply using less energy than they were before beginning the easy week of the test. But once again—if you're constantly depleting your liver and muscle glycogen stores by training without adequate recovery, you never allow this energy-storage supercompensation to take effect.

The appearance of more red blood cells and blood plasma was a little confusing at first, since red blood cell concentrations usually increase when blood plasma decreases and decrease as blood plasma increases; the two don't usually increase simultaneously. But it turns out that proper recovery stimulates the kidneys to produce more erythropoietin, which increases red blood cell formation and also hormone production to help retain blood plasma[11]. Interestingly, other studies have shown that higher blood plasma levels tend to be associated to a greater degree with high-intensity interval training than with easy aerobic work, and this is probably because high blood plasma allows for greater blood flow to the skin to promote cooling, as well as enhanced oxygen and nutrient delivery for working muscles to provide oxygen and energy.

In other words, if your exercise program includes high-intensity interval training combined with smart recovery, your red blood cell levels and blood plasma are both going to increase. Bonus double-whammy.

I could go on and on. Other juicy metabolic rewards inspired by taking your recovery seriously include:

- Increased peak-blood-lactate concentration and decreased or unchanged blood lactate at submaximal intensities, meaning less "burn" when you jump back into training

- Reduced blood-creatine-kinase concentrations, indicating less full-body inflammation and muscle damage—and, of course, less soreness

- Increased testosterone, decreased cortisol, increased plasma and urinary catecholamines, lower levels of sex-hormone-binding globulin, higher levels of growth hormone and insulin-like growth factor 1—all indicators of better hormone status, better recovery, and less propensity for skinny-fat syndrome

- Positive changes in single-muscle-fiber size and contractile properties, along with markedly increased muscular strength and power, often associated with performance gains at the muscular and whole-body level, which should come as no surprise

- Increased ATP and creatine-phosphate stores to rely on for high-intensity efforts and as substrates, which you can rely on even in the absence of glucose and carbohydrate

- Higher myoglobin content, which allows for oxygen transport and extraction within skeletal muscle

- Favorable changes in immune cells, immunoglobulins, and cytokines for enhanced overall immunological protection, meaning you get sick less often

- Higher natural antioxidant levels, less oxidative stress, increased lipid peroxidation (the ability to fight free radicals), and an overall upregulation of genetic repair mechanisms and enhancement of endogenous antioxidative systems—meaning that proper recovery is like eating vegetables, on steroids

- Less tension, depression, and anger, along with significant improvements in total mood disturbance and mental fatigue, as well as increased motivation, mental arousal, and psychological relaxation

Starting to get a pretty clear picture of the advantages of not going out and beating yourself up day after day, week after week, and month after month?

So when you're underrecovered, you have no chance of positively adapting to your training. And I don't know about you, but I want to feel and see results when I train. I don't want to waste my valuable time by running the same eight-minute mile ad infinitum or dead-lifting or squatting the same weight every freaking time I set foot in the gym. (See Figure 6-6.)

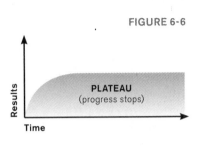

FIGURE 6-6

Sure, sometimes it's nice just to go out and get some fresh air, regardless of whether your body is "ready" for it. But if the majority of your training is not about getting faster, stronger, better, better-looking, or somehow improving your body or mind, you're wasting your precious time.

So are you ready to beat the underrecovery monster?

Good, because the next several chapters delve into some serious recovery hacking that teaches you how to maximize recovery and the effects of training on your muscles, nerves, bones, blood, hormones, and metabolism.

Additional resources, helpful links, scientific references, and surprise bonuses for this chapter are available at BeyondTrainingBook.com/Chapter6. Enjoy.

CHAPTER 7

Twenty-Five Ways to Know with Laserlike Accuracy if Your Body Is Truly Recovered and Ready to Train

In chapter 6, you learned about the difference between recovery and underrecovery and why it matters. You also learned about how training adaptations actually occur and about the amazing molecular and muscular bonuses that occur when you become a real recovery ninja. But how do you actually gauge recovery? How do you know if you're "ready" to ride, swim, lift, run, or race?

When I roll out of bed in the morning, I want to know with confidence whether my body is ready, rather than chancing it and winding up a few days later with the sniffles, a full-blown infection, a muscle strain, a season-ending injury, or just feeling like complete crap. Contrary to popular belief, that stuff is *not* normal and *not* anything you should have to deal with—end of story.

Knowing whether your body is truly recovered goes way beyond simply taking your morning resting heart rate, "listening" to your legs (whatever the heck that means), or stopping when you get too sore. Furthermore, you just can't be ideally recovered all the time. To get fit, you have to go outside your recovery comfort zone, but you also have to know how to identify exactly how far outside that comfort zone you've gone. This concept is called "supercompensation," and it goes hand in hand with two other important recovery concepts: overreaching and overtraining.

Believe it or not, you really do not need a crack team of coaches, physicians, and physical therapists following you around to figure this stuff out—just a little bit of knowledge and the simple tools you're about to be introduced to. From the color of your urine to your heart-rate-variability score, you're going to learn how to implement and interpret these tools for monitoring your body and your recovery.

Overreaching versus Overtraining

We are bombarded with stress every day—physical activity is just a drop in the bucket. Think about some of the other common stressors we face just by living:

- Death of a loved one
- Divorce or the end of a relationship
- Relationship or personality conflicts
- Sexual frustrations
- Change in residence or job relocation
- Overwork
- Loss of work
- Pregnancy
- New pets or children

- Financial challenges like mortgages, loans, and banking or credit issues
- Injury or chronic pain
- Academic pressure
- Toxins and pollutants from food and the environment
- Electrical pollution and electromagnetic fields (EMFs)
- Unhealthy municipal water
- Airborne pollen and other allergens
- Lack of encouragement
- Emotions such as boredom, anger, depression, fear, and anxiety

Then add the stressors that athletes of all stripes and people who travel are subjected to, often in greater amounts than the general population, such as:

- Excessive heat or cold
- Excessive or inadequate humidity
- Altitude changes
- Excessive ultraviolet radiation
- Poorly designed sports clothing
- Poorly designed training equipment
- Subpar training facilities
- Psyching oneself up too often
- Pressure to perform

For a nonathlete or a relatively sedentary person, these stressors are already a pretty big deal, but once you throw significant physical activity into the mix (note that exercise wasn't even mentioned in the stressors listed above), things can really get out of control in terms of the toll stress takes on the body and mind.

As a matter of fact, the most commonly referenced source of stress in an athlete is what's called "cumulative microtrauma," which is basically cellular damage from exercise that compounds over time. And when you combine the stress from cellular microtrauma with other stressors, the body eventually enters one of two states[7]:

1. **Overreaching:** An accumulation of training and/or nontraining stress that results in a short-term decrement in performance capacity with or without related physiological and psychological signs and symptoms of overtraining, in which restoration of performance capacity may take from several days to several weeks.

2. **Overtraining:** An accumulation of training and/or nontraining stress resulting in a long-term decrement in performance capacity with or without related physiological and psychological signs and symptoms of overtraining, in which restoration of performance capacity may take from several weeks to several months. True overtraining is also known as adrenal fatigue and manifests in stages.

Technically, there are two types of overreaching[15]: functional and nonfunctional. Functional overreaching is typically defined as a state of overreaching or excessive stress from which you can bounce back given about two weeks of appropriate recovery. Nonfunctional overreaching (what I like to call "stupid training") is when it takes anywhere from two to six weeks to bounce back. And of course, overtraining is at play if the drop in performance and symptoms of poor recovery last longer than six weeks.

So what does the word *decrement* actually mean? It varies. There are entire books and university courses devoted to the many signs and symptoms of overreaching or overtraining[2,7,25], but just a few include:

- Altered endocrine (hormonal) profiles
- Increased catecholamine (stress hormone) output
- Psychological profile changes
- Cardiovascular consequences (blood-chemistry alterations in things like iron status, protein status, and fluid and electrolyte balance)
- Reduction of pituitary hormones or changes in pituitary-hormonal-secretion patterns
- Changes in blood amino acid concentrations and effects on neurotransmitters like serotonin
- Musculoskeletal/orthopedic issues (joints, ligaments, muscle, bone, and other connective tissues)
- Immune suppression and accompanying illness rates (decrease in natural killer cell activity, neutrophil function, white blood cell response, and other measures of immunity)
- Appetite suppression and body mass changes

Until recently, most of this stuff simply couldn't be tracked by the average person and was best left to highly experienced medical sleuths. Frankly (and amazingly, based on the millions of dollars poured into sports), most athletes (even professionals) and many coaches still have no clue that most of these parameters can be tracked quite easily. And by the time they realize that they should be tracking them, it's typically too late. However, you'll get the lowdown on self-quantification techniques later in this chapter.

Recovery and Supercompensation

Before you learn how to track your recovery, you need to understand that your goal is not to avoid overreaching: If you can recover properly from cellular microtrauma and a state of overreaching, subsequent fitness gains will actually be greater than they would have been if you had played it safe and not pushed yourself to the edge[4].

This is basically a stairstep recovery effect (see Figure 7-1).

The problem is that many people overreach and then don't recover properly. So the graph looks like the one in Figure 7-2—with weeks and weeks of improper recovery eventually leading to overtraining and less fitness[16]. This is how most people live their lives, and the state most people are in when they get to the starting line of a triathlon or similar endurance event and scratch their head and wonder why they feel useless even though they trained so hard.

Aside from the very apparent opposite direction of the stairstepping effect, did you notice the primary difference between the two figures? Figure 7-1 indicates full recovery, while Figure 7-2 indicates only partial recovery—the notorious under-recovery monster rearing its head.

FIGURE 7-1.
Adaptation to
Repeated Training
Stimulus

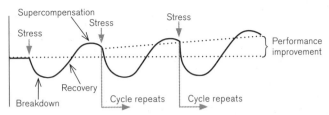

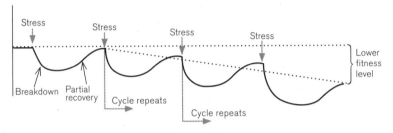

FIGURE 7-2. Overtraining Fitness Decreases

So the trick is to push yourself to the edge (overreach) and then achieve full recovery and a subsequent gain in fitness. The technical term for this is "supercompensation:" pushing yourself beyond your limits to the point of fatigue at least some of the time. All good training plans include some fatigue to induce supercompensation and a stairsteplike increase in performance over the course of training.

In a study published in *Medicine & Science in Sports & Exercise,* French researchers divided fit triathletes into two groups[40]. Both groups trained regularly for one week, but for the next three weeks one group continued training regularly while the other group ramped up training volume by 40 percent. Both groups then tapered for a final week before they were subjected to a performance test. The goal was to push the group of athletes who ramped up their training into a state of functional overreaching (that state in which you have decreased performance for a bit before bouncing back and getting fitter).

Interestingly, this particular study implemented measurements of heart rate and heart rate variability, two ways of tracking recovery status. In Figure 7-3, you can see the averaged weekly resting morning heart rate. The white squares represent the

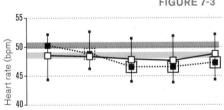

FIGURE 7-3

week before the overreaching period, the three overreaching weeks, and then the one taper week. The black squares are the overreaching group.

You can see that the control group had a resting morning heart rate that remained relatively constant, while the overreaching group's heart rate declined steadily during the overreaching period and then recovered slightly after the taper. While a decline in heart rate is considered a marker of improved fitness in the general population, in well-trained athletes who have already achieved low resting heart rates, significantly further declines can indicate overreaching. In this particular study, the same type of pattern was observed for heart rate during tempo efforts, heart rate variability, standing heart rate, and a number of other measurements.

Now here's where things get really interesting. Figure 7-4 shows the results of the run-to-exhaustion performance tests that each group performed at the end of each week. As you can see, the results of the control group did not change significantly, with only a slight boost after the taper. As expected, the performance of the overreaching group got steadily worse as the three weeks progressed—but then, after the taper, their fitness supercompensated and they had by far the best results of the study.

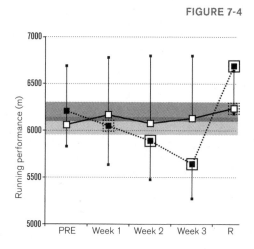

FIGURE 7-4

Hitting the Wall, Overtraining, and Adrenal Fatigue

No discussion of overreaching and overtraining would be complete without a warning about what happens when you dig yourself into an overreaching hole or repeatedly venture into an overtrained state.

Take me, for example. A few weeks ago, I had my cortisol levels tested. My cortisol levels were *through the roof.* This was a sign that my adrenal glands were churning out tons of fight-or-flight chemicals and that my body was ravaged and probably ready for a supercompensatory break.

So I was mildly concerned. But I actually would have been way more concerned if my cortisol levels had hit rock bottom, because this would have indicated that my body had been in a state of fatigue so many times that it couldn't even manage to be stressed out anymore. While I like to think of this condition as "pooped-out adrenals," the scientific term is *adrenal fatigue* or *hypoadrenia,* and it is completely synonymous with the term *overtraining*[1].

Think of your two little adrenal glands, which sit atop either kidney, as stress control central for the body. They produce adrenaline, DHEA, and cortisol. When chronically exposed to stressors, or in some cases to a complete lack of the building blocks necessary for hormone production (by starving the body of nutrients through calorie reduction), the adrenal glands eventually become exhausted and slow down production of these hormones. And that, in a nutshell, is adrenal fatigue and overtraining.

As I mentioned earlier, there are four stages before you reach complete adrenal exhaustion, with the symptoms becoming more severe with each stage: alarm, resistance, exhaustion, and failure.

Stage 1: The Alarm Reaction

This is the stage when your body, in response to stress, goes into overdrive, and the fight-or-flight response kicks in. Your adrenal glands churn out hormones like cortisol, but at this stage, no serious physical or psychological dysfunction is evident. Most athletes spend a lot of time in this stage. I like to think of first-stage adrenal exhaustion as a basic state of overreaching, as long as it is nipped in the bud.

Stage 2: Resistance Response

At this stage, stress levels are chronic and constant, and high levels of adrenal hormones have been sustained for weeks, months, or sometimes years. You can still exercise and go about your normal life, but a sense of fatigue (especially at the end of the day) is common, and recovery from workouts takes longer and longer. Weight gain and insomnia are also symptoms of this stage, and constantly elevated levels of cortisol can make the body resistant to thyroid hormone.

This is also usually the stage when you sense that something might be wrong and go to the doctor—and are, in most cases, prescribed some kind of pharmaceutical, like an antidepressant. But for obvious reasons, this fails to address the underlying cause, and unless you destress and rest, the problems grow worse as you move to the third stage.

Stage 3: Exhaustion

At this point, your body's ability to cope with stress has been depleted. Your adrenal glands are simply unable to produce enough cortisol in response to stress, and because cortisol is necessary for a base level of alertness and awakeness and for your liver to churn out sugar-based energy, you begin to suffer from constant exhaustion. Blood sugar levels plummet, which leads to further intolerance to stress, increasing mental, physical, and emotional exhaustion. Pretty much the only way for you to make it through the day is by consuming excessive amounts of caffeine-based stimulants, sweets, or sugary energy drinks, along with carbohydrate-rich starches and candy—all of which can cause a temporary spike in energy levels that "do the job" of cortisol.

Stage 4: Failure

At this point there is a total failure of your adrenal glands to respond to stress—and even trace levels of cortisol begin to disappear (see Figure 7-5). You basically just want to stay in bed all day. This is also the point at which extremely determined people who try to push through and somehow get themselves to work out have heart attacks while doing so.

This is serious stuff and can't be fixed with a few rest days or by

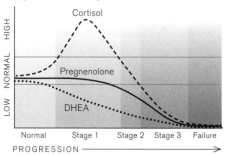

FIGURE 7-5.
Progression of Stages of Adrenal Exhaustion

eating a few extra calories. I've known athletes, including Ironman triathletes and bodybuilders, who have gotten themselves to that fourth stage and been forced to remain nearly bedridden or completely sedentary for three to six months to even begin to recover[13]. Even when using the recovery techniques you'll learn about in the next chapter, it can often take months or even years to completely recover from this stage of overtraining.

Eleven Ways to Know If Your Body Has Recovered

Now that you know why recovery is important, you need to know how to tell if your body has truly recovered. Granted, identifying some recovery parameters probably involves familiar practices, such as measuring your resting heart rate. But what you're about to learn goes way beyond simple heart rate measurements and is truly the cutting edge when it comes to recognizing recovery.

We're going to begin with the recovery measurements used by a company called RestWise, which is one of my favorite services for helping me track recovery, and then we'll move into some more advanced measurements, such as heart rate variability and laboratory biomarkers. I first mentioned RestWise in the blog post "How to Truly Know if You're Recovering from Your Workouts," and I later interviewed Dr. Vern Neville, a key researcher responsible for developing the recovery algorithm used by RestWise, in the podcast episode "The Top Eleven Most Important Factors for Recovery from Workouts." You can learn more about RestWise at BenGreenfieldFitness.com/restwise.

According to RestWise, the best way to consistently measure recovery on a day-to-day basis is to:

- Identify the research-based markers that relate to recovery and overtraining.
- Determine their relative importance.
- Build an algorithm that folds all the data together in such a way that the resulting calculation is meaningful.
- Wrap it in a web-based tool that doesn't require a doctorate to understand.
- Generate a score that tells you how prepared your body is for hard training.

The algorithm used by RestWise is based on eleven recovery variables, any of which you can measure on your own or by using the company's online tracking tools.

1. Resting Heart Rate

Sports scientists have confirmed the link between fluctuations in resting heart rate and overreaching or overtraining[10]. But this link is neither easily understood nor direct. The problem is that an elevated resting heart rate can indicate training stress, but it can also mean simply that you had a rough day at work or that you're dehydrated. To complicate matters, an elevated pulse may be a sign of sympathetic nervous system overtraining (too much intensity), while a dramatically lowered pulse may indicate parasympathetic stress (too much aerobic volume).

So, to be smart, you have to analyze variations in your resting heart rate within the context of other daily inputs. I'm a bigger fan of using the heart-rate-variability measurements you'll learn about later in this chapter than of using resting heart rate by itself. But measuring your heart rate is a good place to start. Resting heart rate should ideally be monitored while you're sleeping or first thing in the morning before you get out of bed. Day-to-day variations in resting heart rate of approximately 5 percent are common, but increases of more than 5 percent typically indicate a state of fatigue or overreaching from too much intensity, while decreases of more than 5 percent often indicate too much volume. In the case of an untrained individual, a decrease in resting heart rate could simply mean improved cardiac efficiency, which is another reason I'm not a big fan of using resting heart rate as an isolated measurement.

To get started, you can use a stopwatch and a fingertip measurement of your neck or wrist pulse to measure heart rate, or you can use a heart rate monitor.

2. Body Mass

A rapid drop in body weight indicates a compromised ability to recover from intense training. A rapid reduction in body mass occurs as a result of loss of fluid or storage carbohydrate or electrolytes, all of which can affect recovery and performance. An acute loss of 2 percent or more of your normal body weight (meaning that one day you weigh a lot less than you did the day before) can adversely affect cognitive and physical performance. So regular monitoring of prebreakfast body mass can help optimize fluid and energy balance, lead to more efficient recovery, and potentially improve performance.

But simply weighing yourself every morning isn't enough. Why? Because hydration status, the amount of carbs you eat, and your sodium intake can all influence your weight. Heck, even one hard day that increases cortisol levels can lead to excessive sodium retention and fluid-related weight gain. So, as with heart rate, you have to analyze changes in body mass within the context of other variables and trends.

3. Sleep

Having trouble getting to sleep at night, tossing and turning throughout the night, and waking up much earlier than usual (indicative of early adrenal fatigue stages) or much later than usual (indicative of later adrenal fatigue stages) can all be signs of inadequate recovery. As we all know, there is sleep . . . and there is sleep. A restless night can mean that you didn't eat enough after a workout, it's too hot in your room, or you have too much on your mind, but it can also mean that you've depleted the anabolic hormones important for muscle repair and recovery (such as growth hormone) or that your cortisol levels are too high.

Lack of sleep is a particularly vicious cycle, because when you don't sleep enough, immunity suffers and inflammation increases, resulting in further lack of recovery. A later chapter of this book is entirely devoted to sleep hacks, but for now you should at least be keeping track of how much you sleep. Although there is no consensus on what an optimal amount of sleep is, there is consensus on sleep being essential for repairing the damage that hard training inflicts, and most sleep specialists recommend seven to nine hours of sleep.

When an extremely physically active person regularly sleeps less than seven to nine hours a night, it is highly likely that recovery will suffer. Another common metric used to measure whether athletes are getting adequate sleep is whether they are getting five 90-minute sleep cycles per night or thirty-five 90-minute sleep cycles per week. Of course, it's important to realize that it's not just the duration of sleep that counts, but also sleep quality—the amount of time spent in deep sleep. Sleep-tracking gadgets appear and disappear from the market all the time, but I discuss the latest research on sleep lab technology and gadgets to track sleep in my articles and podcasts with Dr. Joe Zelk and Nick Littlehales at BenGreenfieldFitness.com.

4. Oxygen Saturation

Oxygen saturation is a measurement of how much oxygen the blood is carrying as a percentage of the maximum it could carry. Normal, healthy oxygen saturation values are between 96 percent and 99 percent at sea level (but tend to be lower for nonacclimatized athletes at higher altitudes). Oxygen saturation below 95 percent may indicate lack of recovery, although it may also occasionally signal anemia, especially when accompanied

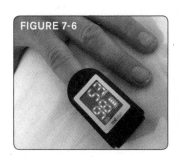

FIGURE 7-6

by chronic daily weakness, fatigue, and shortness of breath during exercise.

Although there is little evidence that blood oxygen saturation is a reliable way to detect overreaching, overtraining, or fatigue, it can be a helpful tool for detecting other training-related issues, such as altitude acclimatization, the possibility of presymptomatic bronchitis, the presence or risk of anemia, and the early stages of chronic overtraining. It is important to understand that it's normal and desirable for oxygen saturation to drop during training, but it should return to higher values after training and when rested.

RestWise has a pulse-oximetry tool (see Figure 7-6) to measure blood oxygen. I keep a finger-pulse oximeter like this beside my bed for occasional morning measurements. You can even find pulse oximeter tools on websites like Amazon.com that will measure your blood oxygen saturation levels all night long while you sleep.

5. Hydration

Since your cells rely on water for proper metabolism, dehydration can severely inhibit recovery. A good indicator of hydration is the color of your urine. If you're dehydrated while training—even just 2 percent—your cognitive functions and physical performance will be seriously impaired. If you're a quantification geek, you can also use urinalysis strips and a test called the specific gravity test to quantify your hydration levels using your urine. Urine-specific gravity is relatively straightforward. Using urine reagent test strips, which you'll learn more about momentarily, you can look at a marker called specific gravity (SG).

- A normal hydrated status is an SG of 1.005 to 1.015.
- An SG of 1.020 indicates that you're approximately 1 percent dehydrated of total body water volume.

• An SG of 1.025 means that you're probably approaching a point where physical and mental performance could be inhibited.

That's it. Easy, eh? Using this data, you can do things like identify activities that dehydrate you or choose when or when not to consume extra water and minerals. But the magic of studying your own pee doesn't stop there. For more, go to BenGreenfieldFitness.com and read "10 Things Your Pee Can Tell You About Your Body."

Dehydration can also have a negative impact on your immune status, body temperature, and cardiac output, all of which can undermine your efforts to recover from training. A "pee color chart" can be useful for checking your hydration status, but if you don't want to obsess over your morning pee, or if, like me, your significant other would forbid you from hanging such a poster on the bathroom wall, you can simply pay attention to your urine color: a pale to slightly yellow color is the goal (unless you've been taking a multivitamin, which tends to make your pee bright yellow).

6. Appetite

Your appetite typically decreases with underrecovery, high training load, and fatigue, which can create yet another vicious cycle—one that results in consistent energy depletion and subsequent amino acid, fatty acid, and hormone depletion. If you're not getting hungry anymore, it can mean that you're underrecovered. But once again, other recovery variables have to be taken into account, since, as you'll learn later in the nutrition section, loss of appetite can also mean simply that you're becoming more metabolically efficient and less reliant on constantly elevated blood sugar levels.

7. Muscle Soreness

One cause of delayed-onset muscle soreness (DOMS) is microscopic tearing of the muscle fibers, resulting in intramuscular inflammation and cellular microtrauma. DOMS is an absolutely normal reaction to high training intensity but can increase your risk of injury if you don't get adequate rest afterward, primarily because of the cumulative inflammatory cycle you learned about in the mobility chapter.

Persistent muscle soreness is one sign of overreaching and overtraining. Of course, the phrase "microscopic tearing of the muscle fibers" should alert you to the importance of monitoring this condition. While in some phases of training (initiating a resistance program, for example), you should expect some DOMS, it should not be a chronic condition.

8. Energy Level

The next few variables (energy levels, mood, and well-being) may seem a bit intangible, but by using surveys and scoresheets, tools like RestWise allow you to account for them in your overall recovery score. Take energy levels, for example. We've all had days when we didn't want to train but forced ourselves and ended up having a fantastic workout. We've also all had days when we didn't want to train, so we just took a nap, did some easy yoga or a recovery session, and felt much better afterward.

The trick is to be able to distinguish been low motivation derived from underrecovery and low motivation derived from nonphysical factors, such as laziness or mental stress after a tough day of work. You need to be able to distinguish between days when you are truly recovered but may just "feel tired" and days when your tiredness indicates a genuine need to rest.

A good way to gauge this is to start your workout, get through the warm-up, and then see how you feel. If you're still tired after the warm-up, you're probably underrecovered.

9. Mood State

Profile of Mood States (POMS) scores, like the one in Figure 7-7, were originally created to evaluate the efficacy of mental counseling and psychotherapy. In the sports world, POMS first gained favor among sports psychologists in the late 1970s to help athletes achieve peak performance. While RestWise does not explicitly use one of the POMS tests, its recovery algorithm does rely on an extensive body of research that supports it. More recently, researchers have used another medical model called the central nervous system score (CNS score) to quantify nonexercise-related stress.

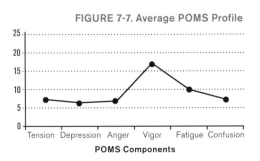

FIGURE 7-7. Average POMS Profile

POMS Components

With these two scores (POMS and CNS score), research confirms the link between mental and physical recovery and the impact that your mental state can have on recovery. This is why general apathy, mood swings, and depression or anxiety often signal fatigue, illness, or underrecovery or overtraining and are also commonly associated with periods of underperformance.

10. Well-Being

It's well known that sane and moderate levels of physical activity boost your immune system. But intense training that depletes the body of vital nutrients, vitamins, minerals, and hormones can do just the opposite, making you feel like you are always "about to get sick." Some athletes push their bodies so hard that they are more susceptible to sickness, often straddling the fine line between wellness and illness.

Well-being is simply tracking how you feel related to sickness. Qualitative variables, such as headaches, nausea, diarrhea, and sore throats, are common symptoms of excessive stress, fatigue, and illness. Symptoms of upper-respiratory-tract infections are another common manifestation of underrecovery and, if prolonged, can be a strong sign of overtraining. By tracking these symptoms and considering them in the context of the other signs of fatigue listed here, feelings of well-being become another significant way to gauge recovery.

11. Previous Day's Performance

For those of us who track GPS, speed, power, time to complete common courses, weights, sets, reps, and the like, it's no surprise that being able to do less than you could the day, week, or month before is a relatively valid indication of underrecovery. Of course, you can't set a personal record every time you pick up a barbell or clip into your pedals, and brief periods of underperformance should be expected in a properly constructed training plan. But prolonged underperformance means subpar recovery. Feeling overwhelmed? We're not done yet, but I'll admit that it can be pretty tough to keep a bead on all eleven variables and still have time to live, train, and enjoy life. Which is why I recommend that you use a tool like RestWise: It will gather, aggregate, and analyze all these variables for you, then generate a recovery score that you or a coach can use to inform your training. All you have to do is enter daily information online or by using an app, and RestWise generates a score, an explanation of what the score means, and a color-coded chart showing your score over time.

Although this is not an infomercial for a recovery-testing service, I can't help recommending RestWise because it is one of the best tools I've found for tracking recovery, especially from a qualitative standpoint. But let's say you want to do the dirty work yourself using your blood, saliva, and biomarkers. Figure 7-8 shows what a sample score looks like.

While there are literally hundreds of different blood, urine, and saliva measurements you could use to track recovery, and scientific advances are constantly making more and more test markers available, I'm going to share with you the best, most reliable indicators of proper recovery and the best tests for determining whether you're venturing into the land of overtraining.

FIGURE 7-8

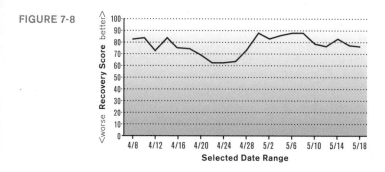

Selected Date Range

The Fourteen Best Biomarker Measurements for Recovery

You can easily get most of the tests you're going to discover here done through DirectLabs if you're comfortable interpreting the values yourself or hiring a guy like me to go over them with you. Just go to BenGreenfieldFitness.com/directlabs. You don't need a doctor's prescription for blood work. Just order the test(s) you want, and DirectLabs will send you a form to print and take to your local lab. (You can find a list of labs at BenGreenfieldFitness.com/benrecommends.)

If you want more hand-holding, a medical consultation to accompany your results, and a slick online dashboard for tracking and analyzing your results, I'd go with a company like WellnessFX (BeyondTrainingBook.com/wellnessfx). To see a sample WellnessFX result and all the variables you get to test, check out my article titled "What Kind of Damage Happens to Your Body After You Do a Hard Workout, Triathlon or Marathon?" at BenGreenfieldFitness.com/bodydamage.

At drugstores in California now and moving to other states very soon are tests from a company called Theranos. Many Theranos tests require only a few drops of blood and can be done while you're standing in a Walgreens or CVS. And all Theranos tests, including venous draws, require smaller samples than traditional lab tests, use much smaller needles (designed specifically for collecting venous draws from needle-phobes or children), and, by collecting a few drops with a finger stick or the smallest venous-draw sample possible, give you dozens of parameters. It's only a matter of time before FDA restrictions make this kind of data available from the comfort of your own home, using a blood stick and your smartphone, just like a home glucose test.

1. CRP (C-Reactive Protein)

CRP, or C-reactive protein, binds with something called phosphocholine on dead and dying cells and bacteria in order to remove those cells from the body. It's always in your bloodstream, but levels tend to spike when inflammation and cellular microtrauma get out of control[24]. During acute inflammation caused by an infection, for example, CRP can spike up to fifty-thousand-fold—peaking at about forty-eight hours and declining pretty quickly thereafter.

When it comes to CRP, think of exercise as a mini-infection. For example, check out what happened to my CRP levels when I had them measured after a Half Ironman (see Figure 7-9).

That's nearly a sevenfold rise in CRP-based inflammation. In other words, the intensity of this event created an inflammatory firestorm in my body.

But it's certainly no secret that doing a Half Ironman, a tough CrossFit workout, an endurance race, or a solid bout of weight training takes a physical toll. (You can go to BeyondTrainingBook.com/inf to read one of my favorite papers on the nitty-gritty of exercise and inflammation.)

I'm not saying that you should avoid damaging your body, or that postexercise inflammation and high CRP are bad. Research has repeatedly proved that extended exercise programs actually reduce markers of inflammation over the long term. This is because some degree of inflammation is necessary if you want to get any actual benefit from your workout.

FIGURE 7-9. CRP GENERAL INFORMATION MARKER

Risk Ranges mg/dL

	Jul 2012	Aug 2012	Sep 2012	Oct 2012	Nov 2012	Dec 2012	Jan 2013	Feb 2013	Mar 2013	Apr 2013	May 2013
High Risk ≥ 3											4,56
Moderate 1–3											
Low Risk < 1	0,31		0,7							0,63	

Muscle growth (hypertrophy), increased cardiovascular endurance, more strength, higher work capacity, and pretty much any other benefit of exercise result from your body's getting stronger and better able to handle the inflammatory response to a workout. The problem is that, in the absence of proper recovery, round after round of this acute inflammation can eventually become chronic inflammation, and that is when lack of blood flow to tissue, poor mobility, and risk of chronic disease or serious injury set in.

"Normal" CRP levels should be around 10 ml/L. Absent infection or acute stressors, such as a race, however, ideal CRP levels are well under 1 ml/L, and you want them to stay there. A level of 10 to 40 mg/L can indicate systemic inflammation and, if maintained, could bring on overtraining.

2. IL6 (Interleukin 6)

T cells are white blood cells that play a huge role in the immune response, and macrophages are cells that engulf and digest stray tissue and pathogens. Both of these cells secrete the gene IL6 as part of the inflammatory response, so elevated IL6 can indicate systemic inflammation.

Your blood IL6 levels are correlated with your CRP levels (when IL6 goes up, usually so does CRP). In a study of athletes before and after a race, IL6 levels were within the normal range in all athletes before the race (0.9 pg/ml), increased dramatically (by eight-thousand-fold!) at the end of the race, and returned to normal forty-eight hours after the race (0.7 pg/ml)[19].

Studies like this provide evidence that IL6 is elevated during prolonged exercise to levels seen only in major trauma, septic shock, systemic inflammation, or near-death states! One of the major functions of IL6 during inflammation is to generate symptoms of sickness syndrome, such as sleepiness and fatigue, which protect you from exhaustion and additional tissue damage, promote healing of the damaged tissues, and can inhibit the inflammatory response.

But if IL6 levels are constantly above 1 pg/ml, you're in a constant state of this "hyperactive" immune response and actually become more susceptible to sickness and overtraining.

3. Tissue Omega-3 Content

This is a direct measurement of the omega-3 in your tissues. It's not a widely available test, but you can find it and the omega-3 index score (see #4 on the next page) at a site like genestest.com. Your omega-3 fatty acids are primarily anti-inflammatory, while your omega-6 fatty acids play more of a role in the inflammation process. Both are required in certain amounts, but people with high omega-6 tissue levels tend to produce way too many inflammatory eicosanoids, which are signaling molecules associated with inflammation.

Meanwhile, studies show that people with the highest omega-3 tissue levels have less inflammation and suffer from fewer inflammation-related conditions, like coronary heart disease. Research suggests that when taking this test, omega-3 tissue concentrations of about 60 percent are ideal[9]. This is the equivalent of a score of about 12–15 on an omega-3 index test. Interestingly, if you're limiting your intake of inflammatory omega-6 fatty acids like heated vegetable oils or roasted seeds and nuts, you need only about 2 grams per day of an EPA/DHA mix such as cold-water fish oil to reach this number.

4. Omega-3 Index

The omega-3 index measures your levels of EPA and DHA, which are two important omega-3 fatty acids, as a percentage of total fatty acids in your red blood cells. Even though the omega-3 index doesn't measure blood omega-6 fatty acid content, if you have a low omega-3 index, you probably have excessive omega-6 in your red blood cells.

An omega-3 index above 8 percent is considered low risk; levels of 12 to 15 percent are ideal and correspond to 60 percent omega-3 tissue content. But 4 percent or below is considered a higher inflammation risk.

5. Systemic Inflammatory Response Syndrome Score

Systemic inflammatory response syndrome (SIRS) is an inflammatory state affecting the whole body. It may be an immune system response to infection, but it may also be related to excessive damaging exercise[20]. A systemic inflammatory response syndrome score is based on four criteria; if you have two or more of them at once, you've got SIRS.

The criteria for SIRS are:

- Body temperature lower than 96.8°F or higher than 100.4°F
- Resting heart rate above 90 beats per minute
- High respiratory rate (20 breaths per minute or more)
- White blood cell count lower than 4,000 cells/mm^3 or higher than 12,000 cells/mm^3

I've seen athletes in an overtrained state who definitely fall into the SIRS category, and this one biomarker alone can be extremely valuable. You don't even need a lab to measure three of the criteria.

6. TSH

Thyroid-stimulating hormone (TSH) is made by the pituitary gland in your brain and triggers the thyroid gland in your neck to produce hormones—triiodothyronine (T3) and thyroxine (T4)—that are crucial for your use of energy (aka your metabolism). See Figure 7-10.

Thyroid hormones give your brain feedback as to how much TSH to release. If, for some reason, your T3 isn't being converted into active T4 (poor liver function), or you have a lot of thyroid antibodies circulating in your bloodstream (poor diet), or your cell receptors aren't very responsive to thyroid hormones (high stress), your body just keeps churning out more and more TSH to no effect. Eventually, your thyroid "burns out," and you're stuck with hypothyroidism and a low metabolism for the rest of your life.

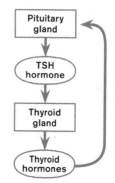

FIGURE 7-10

In athletes and active individuals, high TSH is usually due to three factors:

1. Through-the-roof cortisol levels, causing cell thyroid receptors to be insensitive

2. Small intestinal bacterial overgrowth from gut dysbiosis, usually because of excessive carbohydrate intake, psychological stress, or both

3. Excessive calorie restriction

It should be noted that many nutrition scientists believe that a low-carbohydrate diet depletes glucose, which is necessary for the conversion of T4 to T3 in the liver, and thus also causes high TSH. But because the body can make glucose from both protein and fats, this is unlikely. It is more likely that high TSH in the presence of a low-carb diet is due to the fact that eating calories elicits a release of insulin by the pancreas. This then spikes levels of the hormone leptin in the blood. Moderate, regular consumption of adequate calories spikes leptin frequently enough to help signal to the hypothalamus that the body is being fed. But without adequate leptin levels, the hypothalamus does not tell the pituitary to produce sex hormones or TSH.

In other words, in most athletes, low TSH is probably not due to low carbohydrate intake as much as to low overall calorie intake, and low calorie intake tends to be a real issue among body-conscious types like triathletes, cyclists, marathoners, and CrossFitters. For example, my normal weight when I eat when I'm hungry is 185 to 190 pounds. But for racing well in triathlons and improving my power-to-weight ratio, I keep myself at 170 to 175 pounds. And that means daily calorie restriction. I've found that this restriction has a deleterious effect on my thyroid—I get cold more easily and have dry skin and hair, brittle nails, and other signs of thyroid dysfunction[23], regardless of how many carbohydrates I'm eating. So calories are probably a bigger issue than carbs when it comes to thyroid.

Although modern medicine tends to find much higher TSH values acceptable, in healthy individuals, I recommend optimal TSH values between 0.6 and 2.0 mIU/L. There is also a very good ten-day test called the Broda Barnes Thyroid Titration Method in which you use a thermometer to check the potential health of your thyroid. I provide links to how to use this method on the resource web page that you'll find at the end of this chapter.

7. ApoB

Apolipoprotein B (apoB) is the primary protein that attaches to LDL cholesterol. Despite popular belief, LDL cholesterol is really not an issue in terms of risk for cardiovascular disease. Rather, it's high apoB, also known as high particle count, that is correlated with cardiovascular disease (see Figure 7-11).

ApoB on the surface of an LDL particle acts as a ligand for LDL receptors, meaning that apoB "unlocks" the doors to your cells and delivers cholesterol to them. Elevated apoB levels are present in nearly every athlete's blood panel that I see! A medical practitioner and health blogger named Chris Kresser elucidates the five

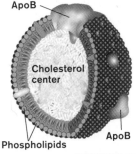

ApoB

Cholesterol center

Phospholipids

ApoB

FIGURE 7-11

reasons for elevated apoB in an article called "What Causes Elevated LDL Particle Number?" (see the link on the web page for this chapter):

- Elevated insulin with poor blood sugar control
- Poor thyroid function because of issues like high cortisol
- A leaky gut or an immune reaction to common food irritants, such as gluten
- Bacterial infection or bacterial imbalances in the digestive tract
- Genes

In most athletes, a combination of the first three probably results in their high apoB count, but that high count might also be due to increased delivery of cholesterol to tissues in response to inflammatory damage from exercise. Ideally, apoB levels should be under 60 ml/dl.

8. Insulin-Like Growth Factor (IGF 1)

Growth hormone (GH) is a potent antiaging and anabolic, muscle-building hormone. IGF 1 is stimulated by GH and is an easier way to measure GH activity than by measuring GH directly, which involves a more difficult and less accurate lab test. These are the main hormones responsible for cellular and muscle growth, and both support anabolic pathways that lead to enhanced repair and recovery[11], so if IGF 1 is suppressed, recovery is compromised.

You should be concerned about low IGF 1, specifically anything below about 115 ng/ml, which is usually a result of combined lifestyle stress, exercise stress, and calorie restriction or nutrient depletion.

9. BUN and Creatinine

BUN, or blood urea nitrogen, is a measurement of the amount of urea nitrogen in the blood. Nitrogen is formed when proteins from muscle or food break down into their amino acid building blocks and are metabolized in the liver[8]. Urea nitrogen tends to be elevated in people who exercise frequently (because of muscle breakdown) or who are dehydrated.

Similar to BUN, creatinine is a waste product formed when muscle cells break down. Your kidneys excrete creatinine, and therefore elevated creatinine can certainly be a sign of kidney dysfunction. But in athletes it is usually just a sign of everyday wear and tear.

Slightly elevated BUN and creatinine levels are common in people who exercise frequently, but if BUN is consistently above 21 ml/dl and creatinine is consistently above 1.2 ml/dl, your training could be putting a lot of undue stress on your kidneys.

10. Testosterone and Cortisol

By this point, you already know quite a bit about cortisol. It is released by your adrenal glands in response to physical and mental stress. (Athletes often ignore the latter form of stress, but I've personally tested my cortisol levels during relatively low levels of physical activity and still seen levels through the roof due to lifestyle stress.)

Levels can also be higher during times of starvation or calorie restriction—primarily because cortisol increases blood sugar for energy through the breakdown of muscle. Cortisol has also been shown to decrease fat breakdown, which can potentially increase fat storage. Excessive cortisol suppresses your immune system, making your body more susceptible to infection.

Of course, you're probably familiar with testosterone as a hormone (released by the adrenal glands and, in men, the testes) that does just about everything cortisol doesn't—it enhances libido, allows for muscle repair and recovery, increases competitive drive, protects your heart, and keeps you young.

High cortisol and low testosterone values typically result from academic-, family-, and work-based psychological stress combined with the daily physical stress of training and calorie restriction. This is a potent one-two combo common to many athletes, CEOs, and overachievers in general. The ratio between these hormones gives an indication of whether you're recovering well from exercise.

While a high testosterone-to-cortisol ratio correlates quite nicely with increases in physical performance[5], anything above a 30 percent drop in the ratio will have a negative effect on performance after recovery[4]. In the meantime, you also need a little increase in cortisol to stress your body enough for performance adaptations, and changes in the ratio of less that 10 percent are too small and lead to lesser performance improvements.

That may seem confusing, but think about it this way: Performance is optimal if your testosterone to cortisol ratio is between 10 percent and 30 percent about twenty-four to forty-eight hours after recovery from a tough workout. While you don't need to be rushing out and salivating into a tube to measure your values after every workout, you may want to consider testing testosterone and cortisol via a company such as DirectLabs after a few key hard workouts to check your values. I'm personally keeping my fingers crossed that an app and device will come to market soon that enables you to easily measure salivary testosterone and cortisol at the drop of a hat.

Either way, if you're geeky enough to measure your testosterone or cortisol levels yourself, the ballpark values in Figure 7-12 will help you with your ratios. First are approximate free-testosterone values (the best measurement of true, bioavailable testosterone) for both men and women.

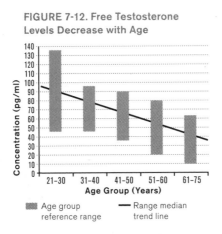

FIGURE 7-12. Free Testosterone Levels Decrease with Age

Things get a little more complex in women because of their monthly cycle, but Figure 7-13 is helpful, as is the excellent article "Female Salivary Testosterone: Measurement, Challenges and Applications," from which Figure 7-13 is derived[3].

Meanwhile, in both men and women, cortisol levels tend to fluctuate a lot throughout the day, but Figure 7-14 shows some rough values. There are four measurements, because salivary testing is the most accurate way to measure cortisol, and samples are collected four times throughout the day—upon rising, in the late morning, in the afternoon, and before bed.

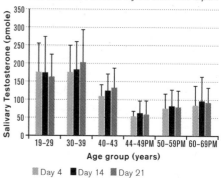

FIGURE 7-13. Salivary Testosterone Across the Female Cycle and Life Span

■ Day 4   ■ Day 14   ■ Day 21

FIGURE 7-14. Normal Diurnal Cortisol Range

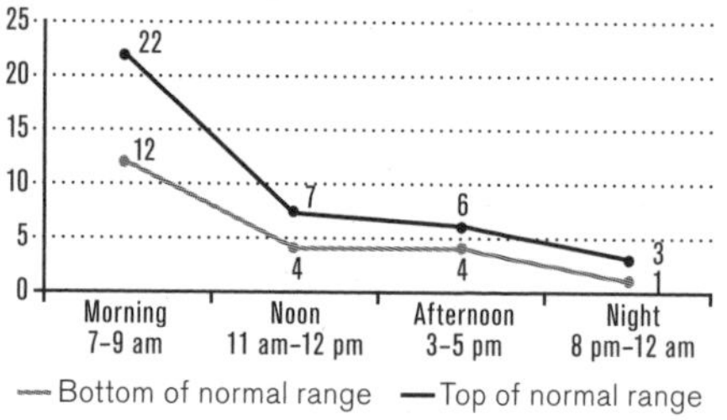

— Bottom of normal range   — Top of normal range

11. Adrenal Stress Index

In order to obtain a high-definition picture of the true human stress response, a company called Diagnos-Techs has come up with the Adrenal Stress Index (ASI) test. It looks at four different saliva samples at different points throughout the day and is very helpful in ascertaining whether you've reached a state of overtraining or adrenal fatigue. Here's what the ASI measures:

Cortisol levels: You measure cortisol four times a day to determine if you have a proper circadian hormonal pattern. Normally, your cortisol levels should be highest in the morning and then decrease throughout the day. This gives you the energy you need throughout the day, while lower cortisol levels at night allow you to rest and fall asleep.

If you're overtrained, cortisol levels are usually low in the morning and tend to be lower than normal throughout the day. As you know, though, it is common for cortisol levels to be high in the initial stages of overreaching, since this is the body's response to chronic stress. But over time, the adrenal glands grow weaker, which will eventually result in depressed morning cortisol levels.

DHEA: DHEA is manufactured by your adrenal glands and plays an important role in immunity and in the stress response. If you're dealing with chronic stress, chances are your DHEA levels will also be low.

17-OH progesterone: This steroid hormone is produced during the synthesis of glucocorticoids and sex steroids. It is produced mainly in the adrenal glands, and when your adrenals are weak, 17-OH progesterone levels are often low as well.

Gliadin AB: Antigliadin antibodies reflect your sensitivity to gluten, which is a common sensitivity, but may increase when your adrenal glands are fatigued or overstimulated. I don't think the Diagnos-Techs panel is the best way to identify a gluten sensitivity (Cyrex Labs has a better test), but high gliadin AB values, combined with some of the other ASI measurements, are a good indication of compromised adrenals.

Secretory IgA: This antibody, found in the saliva, plays an important role in immunity. Low values can indicate a problem with your immune system, which is common when adrenal glands are weakened. When this value is low, it also frequently indicates gastrointestinal tract problems, which often go hand in hand with adrenal fatigue and overtraining.

You can order an Adrenal Stress Index test through DirectLabs at BeyondTrainingBook.com/DirectLabs, and you can find an "Interpretive Guide for Adrenal Stress" at BeyondTrainingBook.com/adrenals. I recommend this test if you suspect that you may be overtrained or in any stage of adrenal fatigue.

12. Heart Rate Variability

An entire book could be devoted to the topic of heart rate variability (HRV), but I'm going to tell you everything you need to know so you can use it to track your training status. For more on HRV testing, check out my BenGreenfieldFitness.com podcast episode "What Is the Best Way to Track Your Heart Rate Variability" and my blog post "Everything You Need to Know about Heart Rate Variability Testing." I link to these and other excellent HRV resources on the web page for this chapter.

Your heartbeat originates in a node of your heart called the sinoatrial (SA) node. The SA node generates the electrical impulses that make your heart contract[17].

Generally, your SA node produces a certain number of these impulses per minute, which is how many times your heart beats per minute. Figure 7-15 shows how your SA node initiates the electrical impulse that causes a contraction to spread from the right atrium (RA) and the right ventricle (RV) to the left atrium (LA) and the left ventricle (LV) of your heart.

So where does HRV fit into this equation? Your SA node activity and heart rate and rhythm are largely under the control of your autonomic nervous system, which is split into the "rest-and-digest" parasympathetic nervous system and the "fight-or-flight" sympathetic nervous system.

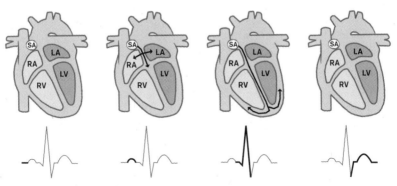

FIGURE 7-15

Your parasympathetic nervous system affects heart rate through the release of a compound called acetylcholine by your vagus nerve, which can inhibit activation of SA node activity and the variations in the amount of time between heartbeats, which would be decreased heart rate variability.

By contrast, your sympathetic nervous system affects heart rate by releasing epinephrine and norepinephrine and generally stimulates activation of the SA node and increases the variations in the amount of time spent between heartbeats, which would be increased heart rate variability.

If you're well rested, haven't been training excessively, and aren't in a state of overreaching, your parasympathetic nervous system interacts cooperatively with your sympathetic nervous system to produce finely tuned responses in your heart rate variability to respiration, temperature, blood pressure, stress, and the like[22]. As a result, you tend to have nice, consistent, and high HRV values, which are typically measured on a scale of 0 to 100. The higher the HRV, the better your score. A high HRV means that the amount of time between beats of your heart is changing slightly from beat to beat, which indicates that your heart's electrical activity is very responsive to the electrical signals sent to your heart by your nervous system.

But if you're not well rested (overreached or underrecovered), the normally healthy beat-to-beat variation in your heart rhythm begins to diminish. While normal variability indicates sympathetic and parasympathetic nervous system balance and proper regulation of your heartbeat by your nervous system, abnormal variability—such as consistently low HRV values (below sixty) or HRV values that tend to jump around a lot from day to day (seventy one day, ninety another day, sixty the next day)—can be a serious issue. In other words, this variability would indicate that your sympathetic and parasympathetic nervous systems are no longer maintaining their delicate balance.

In a strength or speed athlete or someone who is overdoing it in terms of intensity, there is typically more sympathetic nervous system overtraining and a highly variable HRV that bounces around from day to day.

By contrast, in endurance athletes or those who are overdoing the long, slow, chronic cardio, there is typically more parasympathetic nervous system overtraining and a consistently low HRV value[21].

In my own case, as I've neared the finish of my buildup to any big triathlon, I've noticed consistently low HRV scores, indicating that I am nearing an overreached status and that my aerobically trained parasympathetic nervous system is getting "overcooked." In the off-season, when I do more weight training and high-intensity cardio or sprint sports, I've noticed more of the highly variable HRV issues. In either case, a taxed nervous system can be fixed by training less, decreasing volume, or decreasing intensity—supercompensation, right?

But wait—HRV can get even more complex than a number between 0 and 100.

For example, when using an HRV tracking tool, you can also track your nervous system's LF (low frequency) and HF (high frequency) power levels. These levels are important for a couple reasons:

- Higher power in LF and HF represents greater flexibility and a robust nervous system.

- Sedentary people have numbers in the low 100s (100 to 300) or even lower; fit and active people have numbers from 900 to 1,800; and so on as fitness and health improve.

Tracking LF and HF together can really illustrate the balance in your nervous system. In general, you want the two numbers to be relatively close. When they are not, the body may be in a deeply rested state with too much parasympathetic nervous system activation (HF is high) or in a stressed state with too much sympathetic nervous system activation (LF is high). Are you as confused as I was when I first learned about this stuff? Then listen to the podcast interview I did with a heart-rate-variability testing company called NatureBeat at BenGreenfieldFitness.com/hr. There's also a follow-up, slightly more advanced podcast that covers power frequency and HRV at BenGreenfieldFitness.com/hr2.

So how the heck do you test HRV?

When it comes to self-quantification, there are a ton of devices for tracking HRV (and hours of sleep, heart rate, pulse oximetry, perspiration, respiration, calories burned, steps taken, distance traveled, and more). I give more resources for these tools at BeyondTrainingBook.com/Chapter7. For example, there is the emWave2, which seems to be the most popular heart-rate-variability tracking device among biohackers. Through biofeedback, the emWave2 trains you to change your heart-rhythm pattern to facilitate a state of coherence and enter "the zone."

Basically, in a few minutes a day, the emWave2 teaches you how to transform anger, anxiety, or frustration into peace and clarity. It comes with software that you run on your computer, but the device itself is kind of big; you certainly can't stick it discreetly in your pocket or take it with you on a run. However, there is an app called Inner Balance that is a bit more portable, albeit with less biofeedback potential.

Then there is the Tinke (see Figure 7-16).

A small, colored square with two round sensors, the Tinke, made by a company called Zensorium, is designed to measure heart rate, respiratory rate, blood oxygen level, and heart rate variability over time. When you take a measurement, it gives you your "Zen" score (how relaxed you are) and your "Vita" score (how alive or full of vitality you are) so that you can see how ready your body is for the rigors of training.

Just plug the Tinke into an iPhone (the only smartphone with which Tinke is currently compatible) and then place your thumb over the sensors so the Tinke can measure cardiorespiratory levels. The Tinke captures blood-volume changes from your fingertip using optical sensing and signal processing. It takes about sixty seconds to measure all the parameters you need, from your stress level to your breathing and more.

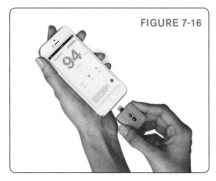

FIGURE 7-16

You can use the Tinke anytime, anywhere, and it's designed primarily to encourage deep-breathing exercises in order to promote relaxation and alleviate stress. While it's not a medical device, it can assist in stress relief and recovery, and I'll admit that as a self-proclaimed biohacker I am addicted to playing with my Tinke every morning (which sounds a bit perverted, I know).

Then there are simple apps that use your phone's camera lens to check your heart rate or heart rate variability, or even teach you how to breathe properly. Azumio's Stress Check app is a perfect example. It's not incredibly accurate, but it's inexpensive and a good way to start self-measuring.

There are also body-monitoring units that you wear throughout the day, such as the Jawbone UP and Fitbit, which measure sleep, movement, and calories but don't measure heart rate, pulse oximetry, or heart rate variability—so I don't consider them ideal recovery-monitoring devices. Finally, there are wristwatchlike units that are getting fancier, such as the Basis watch, which has multisensors to continuously measure motion, perspiration, skin temperature, and heart rate patterns—but once again, this device doesn't measure heart rate variability or pulse oximetry. One of the more promising devices to date is a ring called the Oura, which measures most of the variables I've mentioned so far except for pulse oximetry. It is a tiny finger device that, most important, does not emit a constant Bluetooth or Wi-Fi radiation signal like most other devices. For more on Oura, listen to the BenGreenfieldFitness.com podcast "Could This New Ring Be the Final Frontier in Self-Quantification, Biohacking, Sleep Tracking, HRV, Respiration & More?"

And while I've experimented with a variety of chest-strap-style measurement tools, including the BioForce and Omegawave, my top recommendation for measuring heart rate variability is the NatureBeat system, which I use every day for that purpose. The NatureBeat is easy to use, is intuitive, and allows you to track HRV in real time (like when you're out on a run or working at your desk). You can use it to test for food sensitivities by tracking your heart rate response to foods during meals. The full links appear on the resource web page for this chapter so you can decide which equipment you actually need for NatureBeat measuring, but it's pretty bare-bones.

Figures 7-17, 7-18, and 7-19 show sample charts of measurements and fluctuations taken during the time that both lifestyle and exercise stress increased significantly as I approached a big race. (For a more detailed explanation of these figures, read the blog post at BenGreenfieldFitness.com/bodydamage.)

FIGURE 7-17. LF vs. HF

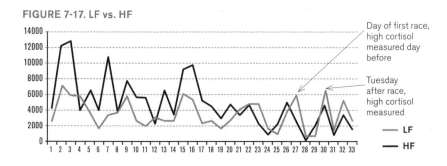

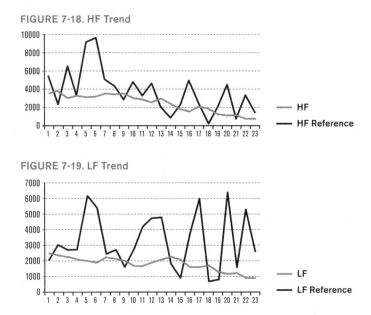

FIGURE 7-18. HF Trend

FIGURE 7-19. LF Trend

13. Adrenal Fatigue Measurements

Let's finish this discussion with some of the steps you can take if you suspect that you may have overtraining syndrome or adrenal fatigue, but you don't have the time or resources to get an Adrenal Stress Index measurement. Here are four good measurement techniques you can use if you suspect that you're suffering from adrenal fatigue:

1. **Dr. Wilson's Adrenal Fatigue Questionnaire:** Written by Dr. James Wilson, the author of the excellent book *Adrenal Fatigue: The 21st Century Stress Syndrome,* it's straightforward and should be pretty self-explanatory: adrenal-fatigue.org/take-the-adrenal-fatigue-quiz.

2. **Blood pressure:** Take and compare two blood pressure readings—one while lying down and one while standing. Lie down for five minutes before taking the first reading. Then stand up and immediately take your blood pressure again. If your blood pressure is lower after standing, you probably have reduced adrenal gland function—more specifically inadequate aldosterone, which is an adrenal hormone that regulates your blood pressure. The degree to which blood pressure drops while standing is often proportionate to the degree of aldosterone-related adrenal issues. If your adrenal function is normal, your body will elevate your blood pressure when you stand up in order to push blood to your brain. If adrenal function is not normal, your blood pressure does not elevate, and this is why overtrained athletes tend to get dizzy more often.

3. **Pupil test:** Go into a dark room with a mirror. From the side of your head (not the front), shine a bright light like a flashlight or penlight toward your pupils and hold the light there for one minute. Carefully observe your pupils. With healthy adrenals (and specifically healthy levels of aldosterone), your pupils

will constrict and remain constricted while the light is shining on them. In a state of adrenal fatigue, your pupils will constrict but will dilate again or flutter in an attempt to remain constricted after about thirty seconds. This happens because low aldosterone causes a lack of sodium and an abundance of potassium, and this electrolyte imbalance weakens and dilates the sphincter muscles of your eyes in response to light. Similarly, being overly sensitive to and uncomfortable with bright light can indicate adrenal fatigue, especially if accompanied by headaches.

4. **Temperature graph:** You can determine your adrenal (and thyroid) status by using the metabolic temperature graph developed by Dr. Bruce Rind. All you have to do is take your temperature three times a day (preferably with a mercury thermometer) for five days, starting three hours after you wake up and every three hours after that. Then average those temperatures each day. If your averaged temperature fluctuates by more than 0.2°F–0.3°F (with a lean toward 0.2°F) from day to day, you probably have adrenal fatigue. On his website, Dr. Rind gets a bit more specific and says, "If your temps are fluctuating but are low overall, you need more adrenal support and thyroid. If your temps are fluctuating but averaging 98.6°F, you just need adrenal support. If it is steady but low, you need more thyroid, and adrenals are likely fine."

Because it is more quantitative, I prefer the Adrenal Stress Index, but these simple tests can at least point you in the right direction.

14. Micronutrient Analysis

You may have noticed that the one variable missing from many of the tests I've mentioned so far is micronutrients—which includes everything from antioxidants to vitamins and minerals to a wide variety of fatty acids and amino acids. When you're trying to determine the tiny (or gaping) holes that may need to be filled from a nutrition or supplementation standpoint, this type of information can be extremely valuable.

For this reason, I recommend one test that gives an in-depth assessment of the full nutritional status of your body. Although it is pricey, you would need to do it just once (or on very rare occasions) if you wanted to ensure that your diet and body stores of micronutrients were 100 percent optimized.

The number-one, gold-standard test for this purpose is Metametrix's Ion Profile. You can order it from DirectLabs, and it tests specifically for:

- Functional deficiency markers for vitamins B_1, B_2, B_3, B_5, B_6, B_{12}, and folic acid
- Vitamins A and E, beta-carotene, and coenzyme Q10
- Amino acids
- Fatty acids
- Organic acids
- Lipid peroxides
- Homocysteine

Like many of the other tests that I recommend, it requires you to mail in a blood draw. It costs close to a thousand bucks, and insurance will probably cover it only if you have a medical diagnosis to justify it. Alas, my insurance company didn't think that "riding a bicycle faster" qualified as a medical necessity, but it was still well worth the one-time, full-spectrum picture of exactly what my body was deficient in.

Obviously, you could spend your entire day and waste all your precious time and financial resources tracking all your body's precious data. So, in the best of all possible worlds, what are most important recovery parameters to prioritize?

1. **Daily:** Use either RestWise or HRV measurements or both. I mostly do just NatureBeat HRV and encourage most of my athletes to do a combination so that I can keep an eye on them.

2. **Two to four times a year:** Comprehensive lab test for inflammation, hormones, and biomarkers. Either of the two particular performance tests I link to on the chapter resources page would cover most of your bases.

3. **If you suspect overtraining or adrenal fatigue:** Do an Adrenal Stress Index (ideally) or the self-tests listed above.

Easy, right?

Additional resources, helpful links, scientific references, websites, and surprise bonuses for this chapter are available at BeyondTrainingBook.com/Chapter7. Enjoy.

CHAPTER 8

Twenty-Six Top Ways to Recover from Workouts and Injuries with Lightning Speed

I'll admit it: I used to be pretty old-school and simple when it came to recovery. A postworkout shake. Maybe a little stretching or time with the foam roller. And if things got really bad, some ice massage or a cold bath.

Not that there's anything wrong with simplicity. After all, it's easy to get so carried away with new gadgets, toys, and recovery tools that you forget to take time to enjoy a glass of wine while taking in the sunset at the end of the day.

But I remember when I shared an office with a sports medicine doctor. All day long, marathoners, triathletes, cyclists, and weekend warriors came through the door complaining of chronic aches, pains, and injuries that they'd been fighting for weeks, months, and even years. With just a few of the recovery tips I'm about to share with you, those folks could have easily saved themselves a lot of pain and frustration, not to mention money on doctor's visits and operations.

So I would be remiss if I didn't equip you with every possible technique I know to keep your body in pristine shape, especially if you're laying down some serious damage by being more than a weekend warrior. Heck, as I write this chapter I am sitting on my couch after a tough bike ride, with an electrostimulation unit surrounded by a frozen ice pack driving topical magnesium into my knees. I want my joints to last longer, so I consider this type of recovery hack better living through science.

I'm about to give you the lowdown on my favorite twenty-six recovery techniques. Yes, I have mentioned some of these suggestions before, but here they are all assembled into one mighty chapter that will have you bouncing back from workouts, races, events, and injuries with, well, lightning speed.

The Best Recovery Techniques

1. Acupuncture

I'll admit that it may seem odd and a bit excessive to include acupuncture as a convenient recovery method, but as a coach and athlete I've found the occasional acupuncture session to be incredibly useful for everything from nagging aches and pains to full-blown adrenal fatigue. And it's not like you have to duck down back alleys to get treatment: You can find licensed acupuncturists operating out of pristine medical clinics throughout the United States through the National Certification Commission for Acupuncture and Oriental Medicine (NCCAOM).

Acupuncture, which is relatively painless, involves stimulating certain points on the body using a variety of techniques—the most common being penetrating the skin with superfine needles (which are then manipulated manually or electrically).

One of the oldest healing practices in the world, acupuncture has helped in recovery from muscular fatigue[19], recovery from overtraining and adrenal fatigue[39], management of muscle pain[12], and many of the common aches and pains experienced by physically active or overtrained people. I've used acupuncture to fix IT band friction syndrome and nagging hip pain. For more on acupuncture, and an interview with my personal acupuncturist, listen to my podcast episode "Exactly What to Expect if You Try Acupuncture" at BeyondTrainingBook.com/bgfep159.

But let's say you have an aversion to needles. Or you don't want to spend time driving to appointments. Later in this chapter, you'll learn about Pulsed Electromagnetic Field Therapy (PEMF), which is a noninvasive alternative to acupuncture and has been proven to work via a similar mechanism.

2. Stem-Cell Therapy

Yes, I'm hitting the fringe stuff early in this chapter: Stem-cell therapy certainly is a potent recovery method that flies under the radar. You'd want to reserve traditional, injectable stem-cell therapy as a last-ditch effort to, say, avoid a hip or knee replacement or to fix a joint before trading in running, lifting, or cycling for foosball.

But stem cells have incredible healing properties since they can be transformed into neurons, muscle, and several different types of connective tissue—allowing for rapid joint regeneration. In the United States, companies like ReCyte Therapeutics are on the cutting edge of developing injectable stem-cell treatments to do everything from regrowing spinal cord cells to eradicating cartilage pain.

If the idea of using stem cells doesn't jibe with your ethics, you'll be surprised to learn that stem cells can be harvested from sources other than human embryos, like body fat and bone marrow[16]. Clinics such as the Institute of Regenerative Medicine and Orthopedics in Tampa, Florida, inject nonembryonic stem cells into injury sites that need to heal fast or to permanently fix chronic aches and pains. In fact, at this point, you are have to head to Europe or Asia if you want to be injected with stem cells from actual embryos.

But if harvesting and reinjecting your own or someone else's stem cells isn't a logistical or financially feasible option for you, there are other ways to upregulate your own internal stem-cell activity. At his Lifeworks Wellness Center in Florida, Dr. David Minkoff (who has himself completed forty Ironman races) prescribes a supplement called Celergen, which is based on a "biological DNA extraction technology" and is therapeutically similar to stem-cell therapy. Celergen is composed of a cellular marine complex and peptide collagens—two very popular antiaging compounds that also enhance recovery in active individuals. (You'll increasingly find that what is old antiaging news is new news for recovering or injured athletes.)

Another cellular compound that acts like stem-cell therapy is marine phytoplankton, a gooey green liquid that you can suck sublingually from a dropper. Marine cells are said to contain the proper ratios of amino acids, enzymes, fatty acids, minerals, and pigments to enable your body to rapidly generate new stem cells. The jury is still out on phytoplankton, but I do have a couple bottles of a brand called Ocean Alive in my refrigerator (and it does taste like what you think liquid algae would taste like).

3. Cryotherapy

Cryotherapy is a recovery method that I use nearly every day (in the form of morning and evening cold showers and many, many cold soaks in a bathtub or river). In chapter 4, you learned about the advantages of cold thermogenesis. The benefits of all those forms of cryotherapy include an enhanced immune system, increased cell longevity, decreased level of inflammatory molecules such as interleukin 6, and, of course, an incredible tolerance for running outdoors and doing snow angels in your underwear[8].

But what about simply icing a sore muscle or joint?

The application of cold to an injured area is hardly breaking news. The Greek physician Hippocrates wrote about cold therapy to control pain and swelling in the fourth century BC, and the Roman physician Galen described the use of cold compresses for analgesia following soft-tissue injuries in the second century AD.

During the Middle Ages, ice was used for presurgical anesthesia, and ice therapy has been used extensively for the treatment of sports injuries for many years. But despite the seemingly widespread acceptance of tossing a bag of ice on an injured ankle or an aching shoulder, there seems to be some skepticism about its efficacy.

The argument goes something like this: When an injury occurs, your body creates inflammation as a healing response. So if inflammation is the body's natural way to heal an injury, why would you want to disrupt this process with ice?

Furthermore, it is claimed that icing may increase the permeability of lymphatic vessels (tubes that normally help carry excess tissue fluids back into the cardiovascular system). Once lymphatic permeability increases, there may be risk of large amounts of fluid backflowing into the injured area, causing more swelling than if ice hadn't been applied in the first place.

Several studies are commonly cited in the argument against icing. The first is "The Use of Cryotherapy in Sports Injuries"[22]. But if you look closely at it, the researchers simply concluded that "Cold can inhibit as well as enhance inflammation." It should be noted that when ligament injuries were induced in pigs, swelling was greater in ice-treated limbs. However, in this study (as well as in another study, "Cryotherapy Influence on Posttraumatic Limb Edema"[21]), animals were subjected to extended icing for up to an hour. You'd be hard-pressed to find any sports medicine professional recommending a full hour of icing.

In addition, in the first study cited, it was demonstrated that permeability of the lymphatic vessels indeed increased with ice application, but that within twenty-five minutes after icing, permeability of the lymph vessels returned to pretreatment levels. Finally, ice was used alone in both of these studies—without compression (pressure) or elevation—two other highly recommended injury protocols. The majority of studies in which ice is combined with compression and elevation do not show the same increase in permeability or resultant swelling with cold treatment. This is because pressure on an injured area reduces swelling by increasing the pressure in the interstitial spaces, which equalizes the osmotic pressure within the lymph vessels and prevents fluid from leaking out of them.

Another study, "Is Ice Right? Does Cryotherapy Improve Outcome for Acute Soft Tissue Injury?"[5], is often cited by anti-icing crusaders. This 2008 review was basically an analysis of ten studies. Of the ten, six were human trials, but four of those were thrown out because of poor research. Of the other two human trials, one supported cooling while the other lacked statistical significance to show icing's efficacy. The four animal trials showed reductions in swelling from ice application. The final two pieces of literature cited were systematic reviews—one being inconclusive and the other suggesting that ice may hasten recovery speed. None of these results justify tossing your ice bags, but they do suggest that when it comes to recovery, icing alone may not always work.

Then a 2010 study at the Neuroinflammation Research Center at the Cleveland Clinic was instantly heralded in the press as conclusively proving that "putting ice on injuries can slow healing"[40]. But—and you're not going to believe this—a closer look at the study reveals that *no ice or cold treatments were used*. Researchers simply studied two groups of mice: one group that was genetically altered so as not to form an inflammatory response to injury and a control group. The researchers then injected the mice with barium chloride to induce muscle injury and found that the mice that could not mount an inflammatory response did not repair their damaged muscle. So while this research demonstrated that the absence of inflammation will shut down the muscle-healing response—it did not investigate the effect of ice at all!

So the important question is this: Does ice—or any form of cryotherapy or cold thermogenesis—indeed interfere with inflammation and thus decrease the rate of soft-tissue repair by suppressing the body's natural healing response?

To answer that question, you have to look at reactions associated with the body's natural healing response. Take swelling, for example.

Ice does not in fact reduce normal swelling significantly. Pressure and elevation do it more effectively. But ice can prevent excessive swelling from developing for quite a while after the initial injury occurs[31]. Here's how: Swelling allows important healing components, such as white blood cells and other chemicals, to migrate into damaged tissues through increased vascular permeability. It also physically protects an injured area by decreasing its potential range of motion. So there is no physiological reason to allow swelling to progress freely for hours or days after an injury occurs.

In fact, keeping swelling down is important because fluid that escapes into the tissues from excessive swelling can create a low-oxygen (hypoxic) environment that can lead to more tissue damage and delay healing. In addition, swelling can cause distension in joint capsules and other tissues and excitation of nervous system components called mechanoreceptors—which can increase pain. Ice simply causes vasoconstriction around the injury.

But the benefits of icing don't stop with controlling excessive swelling. The cold temperature can slow nerve-conduction velocity and shut down activation or spasm in highly sensitive parts of the muscles called spindles, making it a highly effective pain reliever and muscle relaxant. If a muscle is less sore or experiencing less pain and is more relaxed, you end up with greater mobilization and range of motion, and a return to functional-training status can occur much more quickly, which can limit muscle atrophy and loss of fitness.

Ice also reduces metabolic activity in the tissues that are iced, making them better able to resist the damaging effects of oxygen loss from inflammatory-swelling pressure[2]. In other words, lower tissue temperatures from icing mean that those muscles require less oxygen to sustain their integrity.

Finally, as you learned earlier, ice causes vasoconstriction. But unless you're in extreme conditions and you must get blood to your brain and vital organs to survive, your body will prevent tissue death by not allowing the body part you're icing to cool excessively. Through a process called "reactive vasodilation" (also known as the hunter's response or the Lewis reaction), your vessels create negative pressure in the capillary system, which causes inflammatory and metabolic by-products to be pumped out of an injured area while allowing additional healing components, such as macrophages and white blood cells, to surge into the area. When combined with pressure and elevation, this "pumping" action of ice can be an extremely effective rehabilitation tool. To see what I mean, just jump into a cold lake for about twenty minutes and watch your skin slowly turn red as reactive vasodilation occurs.

So while there are certainly sophisticated recovery modalities in this chapter, the simple fact is that ice is inexpensive, readily available, and easy to apply.

To get the full benefits, ice therapy can (and should) be initiated as soon as possible after the onset of an injury, for twenty to thirty minutes, using frozen ice cups, an ice bath, crushed ice, frozen vegetables in a plastic bag, or—one of my latest finds—a convenient PeazPod. Just be careful not to leave any chemical-based frozen packs on the skin too long unless you want to experience frostbite.

Ultimately, my take on cryotherapy for active people is just to use cold thermogenesis (such as daily cold showers or cold soaks), and then turn to traditional icing therapy, combined with pressure and elevation, if you get injured. Cool? I thought so.

4. Prolotherapy

Prolotherapy fits into the same category as stem-cell therapy—it's something to consider when you need to "bring out the big guns" because a joint or muscle injury just won't go away.

Think of prolotherapy as "spot welding" for an ache or pain. It is the precise injection of a solution into areas where tendons and ligaments attach to bone, or into places where cartilage is worn or damaged[28]. When a prolotherapy solution—which can be anything from hyperosmolar dextrose (basically glorified sugar water) to glycerine, lidocaine, or even cod liver oil extract—is injected, it creates a localized, controlled inflammatory response that stimulates the body's own repair mechanisms to heal the damaged tissue.

Specifically, the inflammation from prolotherapy leads to the creation of collagen, the protein that makes up ligaments, tendons, and cartilage[14]. This causes targeted repair to occur at the exact site of an injury and can be especially useful in areas of poor blood flow, such as cartilage or ligaments.

Dr. David Minkoff is a huge fan of prolotherapy and offers it at his Lifeworks Wellness Center in Florida. You can also check out the American Osteopathic Association of Prolotherapy Regenerative Medicine's website (prolotherapycollege. org) to find a licensed practitioner near you.

Very similar to prolotherapy is the medical procedure Orthokine, in which blood is extracted and then reintroduced to the body. Known more popularly in the United

States as Regenokine, the process removes about 2 ounces of blood from a patient's arm and then incubates the blood at a slightly raised temperature. This liquid is then placed in a centrifuge until its constituent parts separate. The yellowish middle layer is dense with agents that are believed to stop an arthritic, inflammatory agent known as interleukin-1, which can cause degeneration of the joints and breakdown of cartilage. The resulting serum is injected into the affected area. Treatment generally lasts five days, with six shots of the serum into the affected area followed by annual injections to ease joint discomfort. Several pro athletes, MMA fighters, and notable personalities such as Joe Rogan swear by the Regenokine procedure.

5. Deloading

It may not be the sexiest of methods, but the simple act of deloading is an extremely underrated recovery technique.

A deload week is just a fancy word for an easy recovery week. In the training plans that I write, I typically add a deload week every four to eight weeks, depending on an athlete's volume, age (the older you are, the more deload weeks your hormones, joints, and ligaments need), and the training time of year (usually fewer deloads during race season, since an easy taper week leading up to a race is technically a deload). Exercise is just like any injury, wound, illness, or other stressor, and it's during the recovery period that you grow stronger[25]: This is the whole point of supercompensation, which you learned about in the last chapter. So when used properly, a deload week doesn't just leave you with the same fitness you had before you deloaded; it can make you even more fit than you were before the deload.

But a deload week doesn't mean that you get to loaf on the couch and eat bonbons. In most cases, I recommend continued mobility work, yoga, easy "injury prevention" workouts, skills and drills to work on efficiency and economy, or learning new exercises and movements, along with a general reduction in weights, sets, and reps, and a few aerobic, fasted workouts (the fasting for reasons you'll soon understand). Since it takes up to three weeks of inactivity for muscular atrophy to set in, you don't need to worry about significant strength loss during a deload week; one study actually found that deloading for up to three weeks doesn't cause a loss of even an ounce of strength or power.

The Best Recovery Gear

6. Vibration Platform

One of the underground training techniques that you have already been introduced to is whole-body-vibration (WBV) therapy, which involves standing or moving on a vibration platform.

The use of a vibration platform has been shown not only to increase strength, power, and speed, but also to generate a hormonal, immune system, and anti-inflammatory response that can speed recovery[26].

Because there is an element of friction when you are standing on a vibration platform, you need to be careful in the early stages of healing for any ankle, knee, or hip injuries that may be irritated by the rubbing of ligaments on bone from friction (such as IT band friction syndrome). (I experimented with vibration for recovery within hours after I had sustained a knee injury from stepping the wrong way during a trail run and unfortunately found that the vibration left me reeling in pain for several hours, which probably slowed my recovery.)

But in the later stages of healing, and for any injured body part not bothered by vibration (if it hurts, don't do it), a simple WBV platform can be a handy investment and training/recovery tool to keep in your home gym, garage, or office. You can just stand on one for a few minutes in the morning or evening or implement it into your actual workout routine. Check out BeyondTrainingBook.com/vibe for an example of a simple, easy-to-use vibration platform.

7. Compression

Studies have shown that when you wear compression gear during a hard workout, your performance in subsequent workouts may improve—possibly because the increased blood flow from compression helps restore muscle glycogen levels and clear metabolic waste. When you wear compression gear, you may also have less muscle damage from tissue "bouncing up and down" while you exercise. If you sleep, rest, or travel wearing compression gear, you'll find that the improved support and blood flow leave you less stiff and sore.

Although I used to find compression gear a bit annoying and time-consuming to put on for a workout or race, I do wear compression socks or tights while at my standing workstation, I sleep in compression gear after particularly tough workout days, and nearly every day I finish up my e-mails and writing while wearing a special style of graduated compression boots called NormaTec boots, which combine three massage techniques to speed the body's normal recovery process:

- **Pulsing:** Instead of using static compression (squeezing) to transport fluid out of the limbs, pulsing uses dynamic compression, which mimics the muscle pump of the legs and arms, enhancing the movement of fluid and metabolic waste out of the limbs after a workout.

- **Gradients:** Your veins and lymphatic vessels have one-way valves that prevent backflow of fluid. Using this same type of action, a gradient holds pressures to keep your body's fluids from being forced down toward your feet by the pulsing action in proximal zones of compression boots. Because of this enhancement, this form of compression can deliver maximum pressure throughout the entire limb, and the effectiveness of the pulsing action is not diminished near the top of the limb.

- **Distal release:** Because extended static pressure can be detrimental to the body's normal circulatory flow, sequential pulsing releases the hold pressures once they are no longer needed to prevent backflow. By distal releasing the hold pressure in each zone as soon as possible, each portion of the limb gains maximum rest time without a significant pause between compression cycles.

You can read more about NormaTec boots at GreenfieldFitnessSystems.com. I've also experimented with compression shirts to enhance posture and upper-body blood flow and recovery[29].

2XU, SKINS, and Under Armour are among the leading compression-gear manufacturers—but the tights and leggings from a company called 110% Play Harder have pockets for recovery-enhancing ice packs. This is a bonus considering what you now know about how combining compression with ice can limit the amount of fluid leaking out of lymph vessels. You can get these at 110PlayHarder.com and use 10 percent discount and free shipping code GREENFIELD if you want a bargain.

And if you have almost $5,000 in spare change or just like to treat yourself really well, the Game Ready can achieve a similar level of compression with icy-cold water, but has the added benefit of a pumping action similar to RecoveryPump boots or a NormaTec device.

8. Magnets

Although there is a relative lack of research on the therapeutic use of magnets to help in reducing pain or speeding recovery, there have been some promising studies on their use to improve nervous-tissue regeneration and wound healing. It has been theorized that magnets increase blood flow, change the migration of calcium ions, alter pH balance, and have a positive effect on hormone production and enzyme activity[29].

For example, if a magnetic field is strong enough to attract or repel ions, like sodium and chloride, in the blood, these ions may eventually encounter the walls of the blood vessels, move more rapidly, and cause an increase in tissue temperature or an increase in blood flow.

Companies such as Nikken, MagnaPower, and BodyGlove make thin, light, and flexible magnets that you can wrap around your body or easily apply with adhesive and wear while you are sleeping, exercising, or working. I must admit that aside from occasional experimentation with small adhesive magnets and magnetic wraps for tennis elbow and a sore knee, magnets have not been a huge part of my own recovery routine, but many folks swear by slapping them on an injured joint or wrapping sore muscles with a magnetic wrap—and I'm not going to argue with as much anecdotal evidence as I've seen.

9. Kinesiotape

If you've been to an Ironman event recently or watched the Olympics, you may have noticed brightly colored strips of tape on athletes' shoulders, hips, knees, or lower legs. Manufacturers of this tape, such as RockTape and SpiderTech, claim that, unlike traditional athletic tape, kinesiotape increases fluid drainage by creating special channels in the skin and may alter joint motion through the elastic tension applied to the tape[3]. It supposedly lifts the skin away from the muscle, which is supposed to increase blood flow and lymph drainage.

I've seen little quality evidence to support the use of kinesiotape over other types of traditional taping in the management or prevention of injuries, but one advantage of this type of tape is that it is more flexible and easier to apply. If you find that kinesiotape works for you, it's probably not from any mechanical influence on joint motion, but rather from a tactile stimulation of the skin that may make you more aware of how you're moving a body part so you can slightly override some pain sensations.

Similar to magnets, kinesiotape is one of those recovery tools that requires you to be your own guinea pig to see if you notice a difference. In my opinion, one of the best uses of kinesiotape is for postural cuing for something like time-trialing. (There are some really good examples of postural cuing on RockTape's website, and I link to some other good resources on the resource web page for this chapter.)

10. Foam Roller

As you learned in Chapter 5, deep-tissue massage and trigger-point therapy are the only true ways to remove knots from your muscles, and having a good foam roller around keeps you from having to schedule a massage after every workout. As you learned, stretching after a workout makes knots in your muscles tighter (in the same way that if you tie a knot in a rubber band and pull the ends of the rubber band, the knot gets tighter).

So save your stretching for after deep-tissue and mobility work with a foam roller (or lacrosse ball, tennis ball, golf ball, etc.), which actually encourages release of the muscle knots. Your workout recovery order should ideally be foam rolling, exercise, foam rolling, and stretching.

Or, if you're like me and don't have oodles of time to foam roll before and after a workout, you can spend ten to twenty minutes once or twice a week making sweet love to a foam roller. I recommend a very firm roller equipped with ridges that can dig into muscle tissue, and I am a big fan of something called the RumbleRoller for this purpose. I include a video of and give instructions for using a Rumble Roller on the resource web page for this chapter. Another newer foam roller called the Hyperice Vyper combines foam rolling with vibration and ice and, though expensive, can vastly enhance the effectiveness of a foam-rolling protocol. Another unique foam roller called the Battlestar combines a coil design with a material called urethane, which creates far more grip on the tissue and a lot more shearing force in the joint tissues.

11. Massage Stick

The problem with a foam roller is that it doesn't fit too well into a carry-on, a suitcase, or even a gym bag. This is why you need a portable deep-tissue massage device, such as the Muscletrac, Myorope, or Tiger Tail. You'll find links to all these and some of my other favorite massage devices at BeyondTrainingBook.com/Chapter8.

While it's difficult to get as deep with these sticks as you can when pressing your entire body weight into a foam roller, they can do the trick on calves, forearms, neck, and hips.

12. Electrical Muscle Stimulation (EMS)

While EMS devices, such as the Compex Sport Elite (BenGreenfieldFitness.com/compex), can help build strength, they can also keep a muscle fit when you are rehabbing from an injury: You can, say, do an electrostimulation strength set for your quads if you have injured your feet and can't do lower-body exercise, or for your pecs if you have injured your shoulders and can't press or do push-ups. EMS increases blood flow to the area of damaged muscle tissue. You simply place the electrodes over the area that needs enhanced blood flow, and the electrical current causes a muscle contraction that results in heat and blood flow. At BenGreenfieldFitness.com/marc, you can read about the MarcPro, a device that uses a specific waveform of electricity called square waveform, which "gradually" grabs muscle fibers in a very gentle way, making it ideal for recovery and injuries, compared with other EMS devices that are primarily best for maintaining fitness in a muscle or building strength, muscular endurance, or power.

I've found that for sore muscles, almost nothing beats electrostimulation combined with pressure and ice. This icy e-stim treat is pretty simple to do. You just attach the electrodes on the affected area, place an ice pack over them, and then flip the switch for twenty to thirty minutes. You can also apply a topical treatment such as magnesium and use the EMS to drive that ointment deeper into the tissue.

By the way, it's crucial to place the electrodes accurately, so make sure that you know your anatomy. Most EMS devices come with instructions.

13. Cold Laser

Low-level laser therapy (LLLT), also known as cold laser, is more common in Europe than in the States but is growing in popularity among physical therapists and alternative medical practitioners everywhere. This treatment uses a special kind of laser called a light-emitting diode to reduce pain related to inflammation. It is effective for tendinitis, arthritis, and both acute and chronic pain, and it can lower levels of pain-producing chemicals, such as prostaglandins and interleukin, while decreasing oxidative stress from free radicals, bruises, swelling, and bleeding[10].

While a good cold-laser device costs several thousand dollars and is typically available only at a professional clinic, you can achieve some benefit with a handheld wand that costs between $100 and $500. You simply hold or gently move the wand over the area of damaged tissue for five to twenty minutes.

I have a cold-laser wand in my office and occasionally use it when a muscle feels a little tight or constricted after a tough workout day, basically just shining it on a joint while I'm talking on the phone or teaching an online workshop. You can buy one from Vetrolaser (vetrolaser.com) and Cold Laser Therapies (coldlasertherapies.com). Just be careful not to shine the laser into your eyes. (It's probably not a good idea to expose your crotch to a laser, either!) Alternatively, you can achieve a similar warming and blood-flow effect with infrared wraps and infrared saunas (see below).

14. Far-Infrared

Far-infrared light is radiant and thermal, like the type of heat we get from sunlight or from cold-laser therapy. Radiant heat is a form of energy that heats objects directly through a process called conversion, without having to heat the air. Exposing the body to infrared light has been shown to raise white blood cell count and enhance immunity, and also to heat tissue and increase blood flow to injured or recovering muscles[15].

In an infrared sauna, ceramic or metallic elements are used to emit energy. Unlike in a regular sauna or steam room, this energy penetrates the skin and heats from the inside as well as outside the skin, so the heat penetrates deeper. One drawback to most home infrared saunas is that they can produce unhealthful electromagnetic fields (EMFs), which you'll learn more about in the lifestyle section of this book. But there is a type of infrared sauna that uses infrared heat lamps. These actually produce "near-infrared" energy, which penetrates the body even deeper than far-infrared without producing any detectable EMF. I built a low-EMF infrared sauna in my basement gym and use it nearly every day for heat acclimation, building blood volume and new red blood cells, recovery, and detoxification. You can find the exact instructions for how I designed this sauna at BenGreenfieldFitness.com/hackedsauna.

As with cold-laser wands, handheld infrared wands are available, but more sophisticated infrared devices are becoming more common. For example, I know several athletes who swear by sleeping or resting on a far-infrared mat, like the one from BioMat. A BioMat mattress will set you back several thousand dollars, but it beats the pants off a grounding or earthing mat for reasons you'll understand in just a moment. BioMat is the only company that makes these; you can check them out at BeyondTrainingBook.com/biomat.

15. Pulsed Electromagnetic Field Therapy (PEMF)

Anytime I travel, have had a very difficult training day, or am experiencing jet lag, I sleep with a PEMF device called an Earthpulse (BenGreenfieldFitness.com/earthpulse) under my mattress, and I can place the same device on areas where tissue or bone needs healing. You can feel PEMF almost immediately when you use it for anything from sleep enhancement to injury management.

PEMF uses electrical energy to direct a series of magnetic pulses through injured tissue. The tiny electrical signal from each pulse stimulates cellular repair by upregulating a tissue-repair protein called "heat-shock protein" and increases the uptake of oxygen and nutrients into tissue. Tons of studies have shown PEMF to be effective in healing soft-tissue wounds, reducing inflammation, decreasing pain, and increasing range of motion[33]. By stimulating ATP production through a process called myosin phosphorylation, PEMF can also decrease the amount of time it takes to replenish energy stores after a workout. PEMF may also accelerate bone repair, which can come in handy if you have a stress fracture or broken bone.

Several PEMF devices are available for consumer use. Like I mentioned, I use a small doughnut-shaped device from EarthPulse. Similar to cold-laser or far-infrared wands, PEMF can be held or moved slightly over an area of damaged tissue or healing bone for ten to thirty minutes. Interestingly, the magnetic signal released by a PEMF device is very similar to that released by grounding or earthing mats, which professional cycling teams have used during the Tour de France to enhance both sleep and recovery for more than a decade. But unlike these mats, a PEMF device does not need to use a three-pronged plug to be plugged into an outlet and grounded—so it actually exposes you to less electrical pollution. (For more on the dirty electrical pollution issue with grounding or earthing mats that you plug into a wall, listen to the podcast episode at BeyondTrainingBook.com/dirty.)

16. Inversion

Hanging upside down like a bat may not seem like a stress-relieving or relaxing activity, but, as I mentioned earlier, I hang from an inversion table in my garage for five to ten minutes several times a week, especially after a long bike ride or run, and the "drainage" effect is amazing. Heavy, swollen feet and legs almost instantly become lighter and less swollen—and it feels great to hang after a long day of standing at my workstation. Inversion has been shown to assist with lymphatic fluid circulation, back pain, blood flow and circulation, and spinal or hip misalignment from high-impact workouts[24], and the use of an inversion table actually lengthens the spine and mobilizes the hips. Although it can achieve some of the same results, sitting with your legs inverted against a wall or doing a yoga inversion pose just does not accomplish the same gravitational pull and full body traction as an inversion table.

You can usually find good deals on inversion tables on eBay or Craigslist because people discover that hanging upside down like a bat isn't the cure-all they thought it would be.

Of course, you don't have to have an inversion table to invert. For example, after a long run, you can just elevate your legs above your head by propping yourself against a wall—and keep those legs elevated for at least one minute for every mile you've run. Another option is yoga inversions like the plow pose, a supported shoulder stand, a supported headstand, or if you dare, the feathered peacock pose (Google any of these inversion poses to see what they look like).

The Best Recovery Nutrition

17. Fasting

While the majority of sports nutrition recommendations advise you to shove carbohydrates and protein down your gullet as soon as possible after you finish a workout (which has merit in some cases, as you'll learn in the section on nutrition), there is actually quite a bit of evidence that fasting can have a recovery effect. In a study on cyclists, three weeks of overnight-fasted workouts increased postworkout recovery capability while maintaining lean muscle mass, lower body fat, and performance[11]. Another study on endurance athletes suggested that fasted training may more quickly activate muscle protein translation, especially compared with athletes who ate carbohydrates before training[36].

There are also benefits to fasting for weight training. A 2009 study found that subjects who lifted weights in a fasted state had a greater anabolic response to a postworkout meal[7]. In this case, levels of p70S6 kinase, a muscle protein synthesis-signaling mechanism that acts as an indicator of muscle growth, doubled in the fasted group compared with the fed group. Martin Berkhan, a big proponent of fasting whose blog is *LeanGains* (leangains.com), has a good take on the possible mechanism behind fasted-training adaptations:

> Another way to think of it is that by providing nutrients to the body, exercise is experienced by the body as less of a stressor compared to fasted-state training. No need to adapt or compensate when all is provided for you. A similar phenomenon can be seen with antioxidant intake, where recent studies show that ingesting antioxidants from supplements weakens the body's own response to deal with free radicals created by training. We are making it easy for the body and that may be a suboptimal way to train.

I personally use fasting in two ways:

1. A daily overnight fast of thirteen to fifteen hours, from around eight or nine at night to nine or eleven in the morning, leaving me with a nine- to eleven-hour daily "feeding window."

2. A low-calorie-intake day on my main, zero-exercise recovery day of the week, during which I primarily consume only greens such as EnerPrime or algae such as ENERGYbits, an amino acid supplement such as NatureAminos or EXOS Aminos, and coffee or green tea.

A word of warning: For extremely lean individuals with low stores of essential body fat, people prone to eating disorders, and women who are dealing with adrenal fatigue or hormonal imbalances, the risks and stresses of fasting outweigh any benefits.

18. Anti-Inflammatory Diet

It is especially important for injured or recovering athletes to avoid inflammatory foods. One huge pet peeve of mine is an athlete who "pulls out all the stops" to fix an injury or who struggles with constant joint soreness while eating supersized sandwiches on whole-wheat bread, drinking sugary sports beverages, and gulping down several cups of coffee every morning.

Gluten, sugar, and caffeine can all aggravate inflammation, so trying to fix an injury without fixing your nutrition is like fighting a fire in your house with water on one side and gasoline on the other.

What makes a food inflammatory? There are at least two dozen factors, including the amounts and proportions of various fatty acids, the amounts of antioxidants and other nutrients, and a food's glycemic impact, or effect on blood sugar levels[32].

But it is not as clear-cut as it might sound. Some foods have both inflammation-producing and inflammation-reducing factors. An orange, for example, contains antioxidants that can fight inflammation but also contains natural sugars that can have a mild inflammatory effect. Beef is another good example. A nice cut of steak contains mildly inflammatory saturated fats but also has a lot of anti-inflammatory monounsaturated fats.

The website InflammationFactor.com can help you cut through the confusion. Its IF (inflammation factor) rating system allows you to see quickly if a specific food is going to have an inflammatory or anti-inflammatory effect, and from there you can determine the inflammatory potential of entire meals or recipes.

Some convenient anti-inflammatory foods include:

- **Pineapple:** Pineapple is rich in a proteolytic enzyme called bromelain, which produces substances that help fight pain and inflammation.

- **Blue, red, and purple fruits and vegetables:** All of these contain antioxidant flavonoids that limit inflammation, prevent tissue breakdown, improve circulation, and promote a strong collagen matrix.

- **Ginger:** Two studies from the University of Georgia show that two grams of ginger a day helps fight inflammation and reduce exercise-induced muscle pain: Just boil several slices of ginger, juice a golf-ball-sized chunk of ginger, or add ginger to a smoothie.

Other foods with very high IF ratings include garlic, peppers, parsley, dark leafy greens, onions, salmon, avocado, and apple cider vinegar. For more ideas on what to eat, you can download the free Superhuman Food Pyramid at SuperhumanCoach. com. This pyramid is organized into Eat, Moderate, and Avoid categories (more details later in this book). For a proper anti-inflammatory diet, especially if you're injured or trying to optimize recovery, you'd want to eat only foods in the first category.

19. Vitamin C

Back in the 1940s, physicians began routinely giving their surgical patients 1,000 milligrams of vitamin C daily for three days before surgery, followed by 100 milligrams daily of vitamin C during recovery. These doctors reported in the *British Journal of Surgery* that 76 percent of wounds treated this way healed properly, with a three- to sixfold increase in wound strength[1].

Russian researchers have shown that surgical patients who take vitamin C are discharged from the hospital one to two days earlier than patients who don't. This is because vitamin C plays a critical role in collagen formation, and collagen is the primary component of connective tissue.

Vitamin C also works as an antioxidant to limit free-radical damage to tissues and boosts the growth of fibroblast and chondrocyte cells, which produce connective-tissue fibers and cartilage[6]. I don't take vitamin C unless I'm injured, but rather make sure to get adequate daily doses from fruits, vegetables, and whole-food antioxidant powders. If you are injured and want to use vitamin C, do not use synthetic vitamin C capsules (which can actually increase the risk of brain stroke), but choose a whole-foods vitamin C source, which is usually present in powdered antioxidant supplements such as Life Shotz or LivingFuel SuperBerry. A company called American Nutraceuticals also makes a very well absorbed vitamin C powder.

20. Proteolytic Enzymes

Proteolytic enzymes, such as papain, bromelain, trypsin, and chymotrypsin, promote healing by supporting the production of cytokines, activating immune system proteins such as alpha-2-macroglobulins, breaking down fibrinogen, and slowing the clotting mechanism[30]. This is another strategy that (like vitamin C) can help heal wounds faster or help you bounce back more quickly from surgery.

My two favorite brands of proteolytic enzymes are Wobenzym and NatureFlex. But, as with vitamin C, I don't go out of my way to use anything other than natural food sources of proteolytic enzymes unless I'm injured or really beat up from a workout or race. The best food sources are pineapple, papaya, and red meat. If you decide to supplement with proteolytic enzymes, be sure to take them on an empty stomach, because proteolytic enzymes taken with food will digest the proteins in the food rather than break down the fibrinogen in your body.

21. Amino Acids

When used in daily doses (preferably during workouts) of three to ten grams per hour, branched-chain amino acids (BCAAs), such as leucine, isoleucine, and valine, can significantly enhance performance; improve physiological markers such as red blood cell count, hemoglobin, hematocrit, serum albumin, and fasting glucose; and decrease inflammatory markers, such as creatine phosphokinase while enhancing restoration of muscle glycogen. You can easily find BCAAs in capsule or powder form; I link to some of my favorites on the chapter web page.

Because they are a more complete source of amino acids, and because they keep your body from "cannibalizing" your own lean-muscle tissue during exercise, whole amino acids (also known as essential amino acids, or EAAs) are a better option than BCAAs but are relatively pricey, especially if you're popping them during or after every workout[4]. Why are they so much more expensive, and what's the difference between them and other proteins? At the low end of the amino acid spectrum, you'll find whey and soy protein powders—and only 17 percent of their content is utilized by the body, with the other 83 percent leaving the body as nitrogen-based waste. Foods like red meat, fish, and poultry fare a bit better, with 32 percent being absorbed and 68 percent being wasted. Eggs are the winners in the food stakes, with 48 percent being utilized with 52 percent wasted.

Compare those numbers with EAAs, which have a whopping 99 percent utilization, with only 1 percent waste. EAAs are also absorbed by the body within twenty-three minutes, compared with several hours for food or powder sources of whole protein. (And weight watchers will be happy to know that there are only 0.4 calories per gram/tablet/capsule.) The brand I use (and swear by) is NatureAminos. It's completely legal to use EAAs in sporting events, and because they have a potent fatigue-fighting and recovery-enhancing effect, they're one of my most highly recommended supplements for both performance and recovery. I recommend taking five to ten grams before a hard workout or race, and another five grams each hour during the event.

22. Fish Oil

While omega-6 fatty acids found in vegetable oils and heated seeds, nuts, and nut butters can produce eicosanoids, which are pro-inflammatory (especially when eaten in the quantity that many endurance athletes tend to eat them), omega-3 fatty acids in cold-water fish, algae, and fish oil are anti-inflammatory[35]—which is why you'll find them ranked so highly at InflammationFactor.com.

Fish oil supplements generally contain significantly more EPA than DHA (usually a 3:2 EPA-to-DHA ratio), but mounting research suggests that higher levels of DHA are optimal for recovery and anti-inflammation, so you should look for one with closer to a 1:1 EPA-to-DHA ratio, and make sure that it is in a natural triglyceride form and not the cheaper, less-well-absorbed ethyl-ester form. It should also preferably be packaged with antioxidants, such as astaxanthin and vitamin E, to keep the fatty acids from becoming rancid (and to keep your fish oil from doing more harm than good to your joints).

I take four to six grams a day of LivingFuel SuperEssentials. Other good brands include Pharmax, Barlean's, Carlson, and Green Pastures. I include links to these on the web page for this chapter.

23. Ferritin and Iron

Researchers at the Center for Sports Medicine in San Francisco examined 101 female high school runners over the course of a cross-country season and found that the runners who were injured had average ferritin levels that were about 40 percent lower than those of noninjured runners. The runners with the lowest ferritin numbers had twice as many injuries as the runners with the highest.

What the heck does this have to do with iron, and why should you care? Ferritin is basically your body's critical iron-storage protein. Since iron is a key component of hemoglobin, which carries oxygen to muscles and other tissues, it's possible that athletes with low ferritin have decreased oxygen delivery to tissues, become fatigued more easily during workouts and races, and end up with exhausted muscles that are less able to stabilize and support the knees and ankles, which were, incidentally, the two primary sites of injury in the San Francisco study[13].

Furthermore, research in the journal *Medicine & Science in Sports & Exercise* has suggested that low ferritin might also decrease the rate at which muscles and connective tissues are repaired, allowing minor injuries to mutate into major problems[38].

Since iron can be toxic, and high stores of iron are associated with heart disease, I recommend testing both your ferritin and iron levels before supplementing. I'd also recommend looking into using a ferritin pyrophosphate supplement or Floradix (a good, nonconstipating source of iron-boosting compounds) before taking an actual iron supplement. The two times that I have had my ferritin tested and found it to be low, I've been able to turn things around by simply using Floradix for a month or two. If you find your iron to be low and you do take an iron supplement, choose a nonconstipating, absorbable form called iron bisglycinate (the company EXOS makes a good product).

24. Glucosamine and Chondroitin

You learned a bit about glucosamine and chondroitin in Chapter 5. Glucosamine is a sugar present in the protective exoskeleton of shellfish, and chondroitin sulfate is a major component of cartilage. Glucosamine and chondroitin are also naturally produced by your body. Glucosamine stimulates cartilage production in your joints; chondroitin helps attract water to the tissue, which helps your cartilage maintain elasticity. Chondroitin may also inhibit the enzyme activity that breaks down cartilage[34].

For this supplement to effectively reduce joint pain, you need to look for one that contains the sulfate form of glucosamine (glucosamine sulfate), because it's more powerful than glucosamine hydrochloride. In addition, you need to take at least 1,500 milligrams a day, and usually for at least three months, to notice any improvement in stiffness, pain, or mobility.

The athletes I coach and I have tried many different brands of glucosamine chondroitin and have found the stuff I mentioned earlier (NatureFlex) to be the most effective. It's not an everyday supplement, but one to use if you really need to see improvements in mobility, you're injured, or you need to nip nagging joint pain in the bud. In addition to glucosamine chondroitin, NatureFlex contains a cocktail of antioxidants and anti-inflammatory herbs and agents such as cherry juice, ginger, turmeric, white willow bark, feverfew, valerian, acerola cherry, and lemon powder. If you find your iron to be low and you take an iron supplement, then choose a non-constipating, absorbable form of iron called iron bisglycinate (the company EXOS makes a good brand).

25. Curcumin

Curcumin is one of my favorite ingredients; I consume it nearly every day in some form. It is the principal compound in turmeric (which happens to be a member of the anti-inflammatory ginger family) and is a widely recognized herbal anti-inflammatory that has been proved to be as effective at reducing inflammation as injectable cortisone. Curcuminoids, which are extracted from turmeric, are the subparticles that make up curcumin and have been found to be very powerful inhibitors of inflammatory compounds called COX-2—without damaging the gut the way ibuprofen does.

To enhance its anti-inflammatory effect, curcumin can be combined with boswellia, an herb that can also inhibit COX-2 in the body but operates by a slightly different mechanism than curcuminoids. I highly recommend Phenocane as a quality source for the one-two punch of curcumin and boswellia. Phenocane works very well in conjunction with NatureFlex, and for that reason the Injury Pack at GreenfieldFitnessSystems.com is my go-to pain management cocktail for an athlete in distress. Another form of curcumin that has extremely high absorption is curcumin phytosome. EXOS curcumin is a perfect example; the capsules can even be broken open and dumped into coffee or tea for a potent anti-inflammatory beverage. Finally, at BenGreenfieldFitness.com/CBD, you can read about how turmeric and curcuminoids can be combined with cannabidiols from the hemp plant for a very effective one-two combo that both decreases inflammation and enhances sleep.

26. Magnesium

You've probably heard that Epsom salts baths decrease muscle soreness, enhance relaxation, and displace many of the calcium ions that can accumulate in muscle tissue during workouts. This is because Epsom salts contain magnesium sulfate, which is the active compound that actually produces these effects. But concentrated magnesium chloride is even more effective than Epsom salts.

Why is pure magnesium so effective for recovery?

As you read this, you have about two ounces of magnesium circulating throughout your body—mostly in muscle and bone tissue. This mineral is essential for more than three hundred reactions, including nerve and cardiac function, muscle contraction and relaxation, protein formation, and, perhaps most important for exercisers, synthesis of ATP-based energy[23]. A magnesium deficiency can result in muscle cramping, excessive soreness, inadequate force production, disrupted recovery and sleep, immune system depression, and even potentially fatal heart arrhythmias during intense exercise.

Several studies have shown magnesium to be effective for buffering lactic acid, enhancing peak oxygen uptake and total work output, reducing heart rate and carbon dioxide production during hard exercise, and improving cardiovascular efficiency. In addition, supplementing with magnesium can elevate testosterone levels and muscle strength by up to 30 percent.

While seeds, nuts, grains, and vegetables are good dietary sources of magnesium, active people who eat these foods can still be deficient in magnesium because of mineral use and subsequent mineral depletion from high activity levels.

Unfortunately, an oral magnesium supplement may not fully compensate for this deficiency, as oral magnesium in the amount needed for an athlete is not easily absorbed and at high doses creates diarrhea. So while the use of oral magnesium (such as magnesium citrate powder) is certainly helpful, a far better way to deliver the required doses of magnesium is with topical (also known as transdermal) magnesium.

The delivery of drugs transdermally (meaning "through the skin") is used in medicine to avoid the risk or inconvenience of intravenous therapy, to lower loss of absorption as a drug passes through the gastrointestinal tract, to decrease metabolism of the drug by the liver, and to provide a more targeted application (for example, in the form of a topical nonsteroidal anti-inflammatory drug patch). This same method can easily be used to deliver high doses of precisely targeted magnesium to your muscles pre- or postworkout for enhancing performance and recovery. As you learned earlier, this effect can be magnified when combined with electrical muscle stimulation.

There are many ways to deliver magnesium transdermally. While Epsom salts deliver magnesium sulfate, which can help with postworkout recovery, magnesium chloride is even more effective. You can dissolve one to three pounds of pure magnesium chloride flakes or crystals in a bath, giving you a dose of about 500 milligrams for an extremely relaxing and soreness-relieving soak. Alternatively, after a long run or ride, you can soak just your feet in a magnesium chloride bath for fifteen to twenty minutes.

Magnesium chloride is also available as a spray (and, for even more pampering, as a lotion). I use eight to ten shots of the spray or a large dab of the lotion on my shoulders, arms, and legs before and after a race or hard workout. In most cases, ten sprays deliver approximately 100 milligrams of magnesium. Make sure that your skin is dry before applying the spray, and lightly rub the magnesium in after application. Magnesium spray may cause a tingling or slightly annoying burning sensation. This is normal and usually subsides with repeated use.

If you get sports massages, you can give magnesium chloride spray or oil to your massage therapist for use during your session. A magnesium sports massage can assist with the body's natural recovery process and speed up healing from a workout or injury, as well as help prevent future injuries from sore and stiff muscles. Finally, if you have a strain or sprain, topical magnesium can be used to improve circulation or decrease pain. Simply spray the magnesium on the sore area and rub it in.

It's important to keep track of exactly how much magnesium you're taking in between oral and topical use, because anything above 500 to 1,000 milligrams can cause loose stools or gastrointestinal discomfort. So make sure you keep track of total magnesium exposure unless you want to spend a lot of time on the toilet.

What about NSAIDs for Injury and Recovery?

If you're injured or excessively sore, why not simply take nonsteroidal anti-inflammatory drugs (NSAIDs), such as ibuprofen?

Unfortunately, when you take NSAIDs, you prevent your body from manufacturing prostaglandins, which are natural substances involved in protecting your stomach lining, regulating blood pressure, and bringing inflammation to an area that has been injured (which can result in pain, redness, swelling, and discomfort as that natural inflammatory process takes place). Because prostaglandins have other functions besides causing inflammation, NSAIDs can cause stomach upset or gastrointestinal bleeding. While there is definitely a risk of stomach irritation or bleeding increases with long-term habitual use of NSAIDs, many people who exercise pop these pills only every now and again—for example, to reduce post- or preworkout soreness or to be able to "push through pain" to complete a competition. But even if you use NSAIDs only occasionally, doing so is not a good idea, and you're about to discover why.

Although studies published since 2005 have investigated the safety of NSAIDs before exercise, a recent study titled "Aggravation of Exercise-Induced Intestinal Injury by Ibuprofen in Athletes" revealed some pretty upsetting information[37]. Nine healthy athletes were studied on four different occasions: (1) taking a standard dose of 400 milligrams of ibuprofen twice in the hours leading up to a bike workout; (2) taking no ibuprofen before a bike workout; (3) taking 400 milligrams of ibuprofen twice at rest; and (4) resting without taking ibuprofen.

In each case, researchers measured small-intestinal damage by monitoring intestinal fatty acid binding proteins (I-FABPs). They also measured urinary excretion of special sugar probes, which can determine the amount of gastrointestinal permeability—a sign that the gut is becoming leaky.

And what they found was that while both ibuprofen use and working out resulted in increased I-FABP levels (reflecting small-intestinal injury), levels were higher after taking ibuprofen and working out than when working out without ibuprofen. Gut permeability (leakiness) also increased, especially after taking ibuprofen and working out—which reflected a loss of gut-barrier integrity. In addition, the amount of intestinal injury from ibuprofen and gut-barrier dysfunction were extremely well correlated. Thus it's clear that exercise irritates your small intestine slightly, and ibuprofen makes the irritation worse.

In fact, the researchers concluded that "NSAID consumption by athletes is not harmless and should be discouraged."

So what about the popular practice of taking NSAIDs before a long event like an Ironman or a marathon to "mask the pain"? It turns out that this has been researched, too.

One study found that taking 400 milligrams of ibuprofen four hours before exercise reduced soreness but didn't actually prevent muscle-cell injury—which is cause for concern because it means that ibuprofen may mask pain and therefore lead to increased risk of injury. In this study, researchers measured creatine kinase (CK), a protein released by muscle cells when they are injured[9].

Other studies have found that NSAID use during long events, such as a marathon or triathlon, actually decreases kidney function. This can lead to dangerous issues, including a decreased ability to regulate sodium and electrolyte status and hydration levels[27]. This lack of proper regulation becomes especially dangerous in the heat, when there is already a lot of stress on the kidneys; this extra stress may create a high risk of long-term kidney damage or kidney failure.

One of the most eye-opening studies on ibuprofen use during exercise was performed during the grueling Western States 100-Mile Endurance Run[38]. Runners were split into three groups: a group that didn't take ibuprofen, a group that took 600 milligrams one day before and on race day, and a group that took 1,200 milligrams one day before and on race day. (Having a group taking more ibuprofen allows researchers to see if there is a "dose response," or to see whether more ibuprofen produces a more pronounced effect.) In this study, both of the ibuprofen groups had significantly higher levels of markers for severe muscle damage, including C-reactive protein, plasma cytokine, and macrophage inflammatory protein, with higher levels of markers in the group taking more ibuprofen.

And get this: Taking ibuprofen did not affect race time, postworkout soreness, or rating of perceived exertion. This means that (1) ibuprofen did not help at all, and (2) ibuprofen caused significantly greater inflammation and muscle damage compared with not using it at all.

So as you can see, the jury isn't really out when it comes to using NSAIDs. Just don't use them. Period. With so many other healthy alternatives, this should be a no-brainer.

The Role of Biofeedback in Enhancing and Tracking Recovery

In the last chapter, I gave you everything you need to be able to quantify how well a specific recovery technique is working for you. Many of those tools are self-biofeedback devices that train you to change your heart-rhythm pattern to facilitate a state of coherence so you can enter "the zone."

Take the emWave2, for example. When you use it a few minutes a day, it can teach you how to transform anger, anxiety, and frustration into peace and clarity. This may sound a bit airy-fairy, but it actually can control stress and enhance recovery, and since biofeedback has also been proven to lower cortisol levels, it can be a valuable tool for tracking and enhancing recovery. If you want to use biofeedback to track your recovery, I encourage you to reread the previous chapter and buy one of the devices I suggest.

If you need or want to take things to the next level from a biofeedback standpoint, you can try neurofeedback, also known as brain-wave biofeedback, EEG biofeedback, neurobiofeedback, and neurotherapy. This is an extremely powerful yet noninvasive method of strengthening and regulating the central nervous system, as well as mediating psychological and neurological stress.

In a neurofeedback session, sensors (that is, electrodes) are attached to your scalp, and your brain waves are displayed on a computer screen, which is monitored by a technician. Those same brain waves are displayed on another computer screen in an interactive "game" format, similar to Pac-Man or Space Race. You then "play" the game by controlling your stress, thoughts, and attention. This process serves to condition your brain and nervous system into a more relaxed way of functioning. Neurofeedback training is usually done in thirty-minute sessions two or three times a week.

For more information on neurofeedback, links to research, and a database of practitioners, check out my friend Nora Gedgaudas's website, Northwest Neurofeedback (northwest-neurofeedback.com). Nora is a nutrition and brain expert, author, and neurofeedback practitioner.

What about Adrenal Fatigue?

I need to point out that in the case of adrenal fatigue, there are some additional recovery-enhancing protocols that need to be considered.

For example, a very beat-up, exhausted, and physically and mentally tired triathlete recently showed me the results of his saliva testing for hormones. Nearly all his hormones were at rock-bottom levels, even cortisol. Cortisol is the stress-release hormone that we churn out when exercising and living, and when it drops way down, it's a warning sign that you're so exhausted, overtrained, and underrecovered that your adrenal glands simply can't keep up with you anymore. And when your body is such a wreck that damage has gone beyond mere muscle-fiber tearing and joint impact and has progressed to hormonal depletion, recovery becomes a much different story.

Here's what I told this triathlete to do to take care of his body so that he could bounce back from overtraining and adrenal fatigue:

1. **Eat a ton of extremely nutrient-dense foods.** Some of my favorites (which you'll learn more about in the nutrition section of this book) are:
   - Eggs, with the yolk
   - Organ meats
   - Grass-fed beef
   - Bone broth
   - Cold-water fish
   - Shellfish
   - Sea vegetables, such as nori, kelp, dulse, algae, spirulina, and chlorella
   - Natto (fermented soybeans)
   - Dark fruits/vegetables
   - Fermented foods such as yogurt, kefir, kombucha, and sauerkraut
   - Turmeric/curries

Conveniently, many of these foods also have a high inflammation-factor rating, which means that they either do not contribute to or even decrease inflammation.

2. Get rid of foods and habits that tend to aggravate the adrenal glands and worsen fatigue, including:
   - Bananas, dried figs, raisins, dates, oranges, and grapefruit (high-potassium fruits)
   - Fruit and juice in the morning
   - Refined-flour products, such as pasta, white rice, bread, pastry, and baked goods
   - Large amounts of fructose from honey, syrups, and soft drinks, as well as dried fruits and concentrated fruit juice

- Adrenal stimulants, such as coffee, energy drinks, black tea, alcohol, colas, and chocolate
- Heated oils and fats, especially vegetable oils
- Rushed and hectic meals

3. No caloric depletion, fasted workouts, or intermittent fasting and going hungry during workouts. Instead, eat a big breakfast with lots of protein and fat, and keep your energy levels topped off during the day. Don't try to lose weight or control body fat, which can be stressful for your body during a state of overtraining or adrenal fatigue.

4. Do two to four weeks of easy, aerobic workouts only (no hard intervals or monster training sessions), along with some kind of yoga, meditation, or very relaxing movement each morning. Basically, you need to do deload weeks until you're fully recovered (unless you really dig yourself into an underrecovery, overtraining hole, in which case you may need to deload for months, and sometimes over a year).

5. Consider using the following adrenal-supporting supplements, all of which I provide the best links and learning resources for on the web page for this chapter:

- Chinese adaptogenic herbs, such as TianChi or InnerPeace, which can fine-tune your adrenals and help you begin producing cortisol and adrenaline.
- Electrolytes—lots of them—preferably with liquid trace minerals or Himalayan sea salt, both of which can restore precious minerals that your body tends to lose when you're low on cortisol.
- Vitamin D at a dose of 35 IU per pound of body weight and huge amounts of morning sun exposure to ensure that you produce the necessary building blocks to restore hormones. To avoid vitamin D toxicity, vitamin D must be combined with vitamin K. EXOS makes a vitamin D/vitamin K oil mixed with medium-chain triglyceride (MCT oil) that works very well for this purpose.
- 2,000–5,000 milligrams of a whole-foods vitamin C source each day (or basically as much vitamin C as you can take until you get loose bowels). Your adrenal glands are one of the best storage sources of vitamin C in your body, and vitamin C depletion is often associated with adrenal fatigue. When you're taking these high doses, it's important to split the vitamin C into multiple daily doses, since your bloodstream can absorb and carry only small amounts at any given time.
- 4–6 grams per day of a good fish oil that contains vitamin E with mixed tocopherols (I recommend SuperEssentials) to reduce inflammation and restore the health of your nervous system.
- A B-complex supplement that is high in B_6 and pantothenic acid (I recommend Life Shotz or the EXOS multivitamin), both of which tend to be severely depleted during adrenal fatigue.
- Approximately 6 grams per day of red ginseng, which stimulates the body to begin producing cortisol again.
- Licorice root extract at 200–400 milligrams a day, which reduces the half-life of cortisol and allows it to be broken down by the body at a slower rate.

All these methods can help tremendously with adrenal fatigue, but in truth, fully recovering from adrenal fatigue typically requires very careful and precise attention to recovery status, heart rate variability, hormones, and inflammatory markers, and if you are overtrained or adrenally fatigued, I would caution you against trying to manage this condition completely by yourself. Most athletes attempting to recover from adrenal fatigue get much better results from working with a coach, wellness consultant, or medical practitioner.

If implementing all these recovery tools seems like overkill (or insane) to you, then you're very perceptive. After all, you don't necessarily need to do everything in this chapter if you've just gone out for a nice sociable Saturday morning bike ride, or even a "typical" week of training. But if you are injured and have an important race coming up, or are really wiped out from a tough series of workouts, or are at a training camp, or are doing a big deload week, you may want to consider pulling out as many stops as possible and truly geeking out on recovery so that your body is 100 percent repaired.

But maybe your head is spinning from trying to take in vibration platforms and electric stim and lasers and proteo-something-or-other and you actually want to apply those tools to your own personal recovery plan without feeling as though you're either:

1. Spending all your precious time fretting over repairing your body and not enjoying training, or

2. Exposing your body to a constant state of underrecovery

So what would a typical recovery day, week, or month look like if you were uninjured and just trying to maximize the results of your training? Or injured and trying to heal your body and bounce back as fast as possible? Or overtrained and in a state of adrenal fatigue? Or in those last few precious weeks leading up to a race? Or in the throes of healing your body from something like an Ironman or a marathon?

Properly programming these recovery techniques can take some serious forethought and scientific application. The good news is that in the plans that accompany this book, I include an adrenal fatigue recovery plan based on what you've just learned—in the same way that I'm including full training plans based on the underground training techniques you learned about in earlier chapters.

In other words, if you're concerned about how to string all this training and recovery material together into a viable and effective program that doesn't leave you gasping for air during a race because you spent too much time hanging from an inversion table or electrocuting yourself, don't worry. I include that information for your training plans in the resources section at the end of this book.

Additional resources, helpful links, scientific references, websites, and surprise bonuses for this chapter are available at BeyondTrainingBook.com/Chapter8. Enjoy.

CHAPTER 9

The Seven Best Ways to Beat a Hidden Killer That Sabotages Your Recovery

Stress is the number-one saboteur of anyone's pursuit of better performance, recovery, or physique, but in this chapter you are going to discover what stress does to the mind-body connection, how that mind-body connection works, and exactly what you need to do to make your mind-body connection 100 percent bulletproof.

Let's begin with a story.

Back in chapter 3, I talked about Mark Sisson's excellent perspective on the conundrum of stress and endurance training in his book *The Primal Connection,* in which he describes how a major factor in the success of some pro endurance athletes is relatively lower amounts of work stress—deadlines, office obligations, and the like.

As you may recall, Mark observed that amateur triathletes tend to add the stress of working out to the stress of work and family life. By contrast, he found that professional athletes take a more leisurely approach to their workouts, incorporating time to kick back and decompress.

In my own experience as a coach, I have witnessed this same scenario time and time again. The busy CEO-type athlete who wants to achieve it all and be successful in work, life, and sports tends to struggle from the ramifications of constant stress. The overachievers tend to get sick more, get injured more, and have subpar results in their workouts and racing events. This may not seem fair, but it's simply the reality of everybody having a finite biological stress-coping mechanism.

The reason I want to share this with you is that if you're reading this book, you're probably a pretty physically active person—and unless you're living in a pristine Himalayan resort, you probably have to cope with significant amounts of lifestyle, relationship, emotional, and work stress on a daily basis.

Once you add your exercise stress to all those other stressors, you can easily overload your body's built-in physiological mechanisms to cope with stress. Heck, in America alone, basic everyday stress *without* the added stress of exercise drives tens of millions of people each year to the point of chronic illness, depression, and suicide[15].

This is why suicide has surpassed car crashes as the leading cause of death, why a full third of employees suffer chronic debilitating stress, and why more than half of all millennials (those born between the early 1980s and the early 2000s) experience a level of stress that keeps them awake at night with insomnia.

It's also a contributing factor in the growing number of people with ADHD, anxiety, depression, and bipolar disorder. New research shows that stress renders you susceptible to serious illness—especially cancer and heart disease.

It's why controversial, mood-altering psychiatric drugs like SSRI antidepressants (complete with the FDA's "suicidality" warning label) are overprescribed these days, along with Ritalin and other psychostimulants. It's why nearly 30 percent of

American adults have a drinking problem and why more than 22 million others use mood-altering drugs like marijuana, cocaine, heroin, hallucinogens, and inhalants—all in a desperate attempt to cope with stress.

And don't feel too smug if you don't live in America. One major study has concluded that nearly 40 percent of Europeans are plagued by stress-related mental illness—and the issues of substance abuse and chronic disease are just as big in other countries.

But wait—doesn't exercise *reduce* stress?

Can Exercise Reduce Stress?

It's true, to a certain extent, that exercise can help you cope with emotional stress.

In his book *Spark: The Revolutionary New Science of Exercise and the Brain,* John Ratey[10] describes in great detail how exercise grows brain cells, improves mental functioning, allows for better focus, and significantly reduces stress. Here are a few highlights from the book:

- Exercising women lower their risk of dementia by 50 percent.

- Exercise can be as effective as antidepressants.

- Kids who exercised before school versus those who exercised in the middle of the day had better test scores.

- Exercise has been shown in multiple studies to reduce stress and anxiety.

One of the reasons exercise has such a powerful effect on stress is its effect on neurotransmitters, the signaling molecules that your body uses to talk to your brain and vice versa. You have both "inhibitory" and "excitatory" neurotransmitters. The inhibitory neurotransmitters are serotonin and GABA: They primarily make you feel happy and destressed and can even help you sleep when present in adequate amounts. However, if these hormones are depleted as a result of a poor diet, lack of physical activity, or a lot of stress, then depression, insomnia, anger, and a vicious cycle of even more stress can result.

The excitatory neurotransmitters are glutamate, catecholamines, beta-phenylethylamine, and dopamine. In balanced amounts, they help keep you alert, sharp, focused, and destressed. But in high amounts, they can cause more stress, panic, anxiety, and poor sleep.

The simple process of staying physically active can help keep these excitatory and inhibitory neurotransmitters available in proper amounts. This is a smart biological strategy to directly decrease emotional and mental stress. A recent Penn State study reported that people are more likely to have feelings of excitement and enthusiasm on days when they are more physically active, in large part because of neurotransmitter balance[9].

But there's also a law of diminishing returns. You need far less exercise than you think to lower stress or risk of chronic disease.

How Much Exercise Is Too Much?

One relatively recent study compared three groups over a thirteen-week period[7]. One group consisted of people who exercised thirty minutes a day, another group included people who exercised sixty minutes a day, and the third group had people who didn't exercise at all.

The exercisers were allowed to choose their activity but had to work fairly hard (at about 70 percent maximum capacity) at least three times during their exercise session. The rest of the time they could go as hard or as easy as they chose.

What were the results? The thirty-minute group lost 4 percent body weight and 14 percent body fat, while the sixty-minute group lost 3 percent body weight and 13 percent body fat.

Metabolism actually increased slightly more in the sixty-minute group than in the thirty-minute group, but the maximum oxygen capacity of the thirty-minute group slightly exceeded that of the sixty-minute group. Interestingly, the thirty-minute exercisers tended to have a greater daily calorie deficit than the other exercisers, indicating less of a propensity to compensate calorically for their exercise sessions.

Ultimately, the group that exercised twice as much didn't see anywhere near twice the benefit, despite spending that much more time exercising.

Another study tracked more than 400,000 adults for eight years, surveying them about physical activity and their health. Participants indicated what types of exercise they did and how many minutes per week they did it, and then the researchers calculated a special number called a "hazard ratio" (HR) for each person for the eight years of participation in the study[19].

An HR of 1 was assigned to those who were completely inactive, reporting less than an hour a week of exercise. An HR lower than 1 means that you have an increased chance of avoiding early death.

Surprisingly, the researchers found that low-volume, moderate exercisers, who exercised just seventy-five minutes a week (that's just fifteen minutes a day), had significantly better HRs than inactive people. This result held up even after controlling for a number of other factors, like age, sex, smoking, drinking, and other health issues. A change in HR like this means that for a typical thirty-year-old, as little as fifteen minutes of exercise a day increases life expectancy by two-and-a-half to three years. The study also showed that the health benefits of exercise significantly tapered off after more than ninety minutes of exercise a day.

So it seems that fifteen minutes a day of exercise will keep you healthy, thirty minutes a day will keep you fit and lean, and more than ninety minutes a day won't give you any extra benefit.

What Happens When You Exercise Too Much

In chapter 7, you learned about the adrenal glands and the four stages of adrenal exhaustion. These stages were first identified back in the 1950s, when Dr. Hans Selye conducted experiments creating stress in rats. Basically, the poor rats were forced to tread water with their legs tied together until they became exhausted and died.

Dr. Selye removed the adrenal glands from the rats at various stages of drowning and discovered that the adrenal glands respond to stress in several distinct stages. In the initial stage, they enlarge and the blood supply to them increases, but as the stress continues, the glands begin to shrink. Eventually, as the stress continues, the glands reach a completely depleted stage of adrenal exhaustion[20].

This makes sense, because in a stressful situation, your adrenal glands are responsible for raising your blood pressure, transferring blood from your gut to your extremities, increasing your heart rate, suppressing your immune system, and increasing your blood-clotting ability. They work damn hard to allow you to survive.

But this response is supposed to be short-lived, not a constant "treading" day after day. For example, if one of our ancestors were walking through the forest and saw a wild animal, the adrenal glands would kick in. Her heart rate would increase, her pupils would dilate, the blood would go out of her digestive system into her arms and legs, her blood-clotting ability would improve, she would become more aware, and her blood pressure would rise. At that point she'd either pick up a weapon and try to fight the animal or run.

And if she survived the ordeal, chances are that it would be while before a similar strain was put on her adrenal glands, and she would have plenty of time to relax, eat, recover, and play.

Our adrenal glands still work the same way, but most of us do not give our bodies the luxury of a recovery period after overworking them. As a result, we suffer from the ravages of chronic stress. Stimulation of the adrenal glands causes a decrease in immune system function, so if you're under constant stress, you tend to catch colds and have other immune system imbalance problems, such as allergies or exercise-induced asthma. Blood flow to your digestive tract is decreased, so you're prone to irritable bowel syndrome, constipation, and diarrhea. The increase in blood-clotting ability from prolonged stress can also lead to the formation of arterial plaque and heart disease. The list of deleterious repercussions from stress goes on and on.

To effectively care for your adrenal glands, you must eliminate as much stress from your life as possible while maximizing your stress-fighting capabilities. Although emotional stress is what most people think of when stress is mentioned, there are many other forms of stress that you must manage, including thermal stress from exposure to temperature extremes; chemical stress from pollution; rapid changes in blood sugar or pH; ingestion of food additives, molds, or toxins; and, of course, physical stress from heavy physical work, exercise, poor posture, spinal and structural misalignments, and lack of sleep.

As you've just learned, while science hasn't yet been able to tell us the exact number of minutes of exercise necessary to push your adrenal glands "over the edge," we know that more than ninety minutes a day isn't doing us any extra good from a health standpoint. It's likely that the exact amount varies from person to person based on vitamin, nutrient, and mineral status; training history; genetics; exposure to lifestyle, thermal, chemical, and emotional stress; and even mental attitude.

The Mind-Body Connection

That's right: mental attitude. For example, studies have shown that:

- Heart surgery patients with strong spiritual and social support have a mortality rate that's one-seventh of those who do not.

FIGURE 9-1. Mind-Body Communication: How Emotions Affect the Body

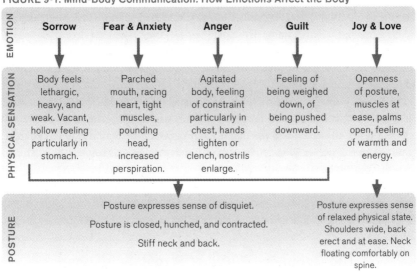

EMOTION	Sorrow	Fear & Anxiety	Anger	Guilt	Joy & Love
PHYSICAL SENSATION	Body feels lethargic, heavy, and weak. Vacant, hollow feeling particularly in stomach.	Parched mouth, racing heart, tight muscles, pounding head, increased perspiration.	Agitated body, feeling of constraint particularly in chest, hands tighten or clench, nostrils enlarge.	Feeling of being weighed down, of being pushed downward.	Openness of posture, muscles at ease, palms open, feeling of warmth and energy.
POSTURE	Posture expresses sense of disquiet. Posture is closed, hunched, and contracted. Stiff neck and back.				Posture expresses sense of relaxed physical state. Shoulders wide, back erect and at ease. Neck floating comfortably on spine.

- Meditating for just thirty minutes a day can be as effective as taking antidepressants.

- Elderly people with positive attitudes have a more than 20 percent reduction in risk of death from cardiovascular disease and a more than 50 percent lower risk of death from all other causes.

These results are all based on the mind-body connection, and it's why the stress-fighting weapons you're about to encounter actually work. Science has clearly demonstrated that a healthy mind-body connection and a positive mental attitude greatly affect your physical health and your adrenal response[14]. See Figure 9-1.

A healthy mind-body connection means that you can learn to use your thoughts and feelings to positively influence your body's physical response. For example, if you stop reading right now and recall a time when you were happy, grateful, or calm, your body and mind will automatically tend to relax. Go ahead, try it. Just think back to a wedding, a birth, a kiss, a snuggle, a hug, throwing up your arms as you cross the finish line of a race, or any other awesome event in your life, and you'll feel your body respond.

Similarly, if you recall an upsetting or frightening experience, you may feel your heart beating faster, you may begin to sweat, and your hands may become cold and clammy. You can try this, too. Close your eyes and imagine a time in your life when you were frightened, stressed, scared, under pressure, or overwhelmed.

Feel that? Your body responds. Your heart rate picks up a little, your breath quickens, and your hands clench slightly.

As these simple thought exercises show, if there are emotional, chemical, relationship, and other stressors constantly present in your mind or body, they can create a huge load on your natural biological stress response, and all these stressors acting together can be a serious deterrent to adrenal recovery. If your adrenals aren't recovering, the volume and intensity of the physical activity your body can handle before it goes on strike are severely limited.

But on the flip side, if you have very little daily stress (something most of us don't have the luxury of experiencing unless we quit our jobs and move to a mountaintop), or you're mentally and emotionally capable of handling a wide variety of stressors, you have superior ability to handle the stressful curveballs that life throws at you. You may even be able to handle a busy CEO lifestyle and still be immensely success-ful in sports, health, and life.

But before I bring out the weapons you'll need to handle all those stressors and make that success a reality, I'll repeat what I said way back in chapter 3:

Stress is stress—no matter whether it's from exercise or from lifestyle. The more stress you're placing on yourself from your lifestyle, the less stress you'll be able to place on yourself from exercise.

So now I'm going to give you seven of the best tools I've discovered for making your mind-body connection as bulletproof as possible and ensuring that your body is equipped to handle as much stress as you have to from lifestyle and exercise.

The Confusing World of Stress Solutions

Let's face it: Dr. Google can help you find millions of stress-fighting articles, web-sites, and books. I'm not going to pretend that I can, in a single chapter, comprehen-sively address every single stress-fighting method out there. After all, just check out the Wikipedia entry for stress-management techniques at BeyondTrainingBook.com/ wikistressmgt, and you'll find:

- Autogenic training
- Social activity
- Cognitive therapy
- Conflict resolution
- Exercise
- Getting a hobby
- Meditation
- Mindfulness (psychology)
- Deep breathing
- Yoga nidra
- Nootropics
- Reading novels
- Prayer
- Relaxation techniques
- Artistic expression
- Fractional relaxation
- Progressive relaxation
- Spas
- Somatics training
- Spending time in nature
- Stress balls
- Natural medicine
- Clinically validated alternative treatments
- Time management
- Planning and decision making
- Listening to relaxing music
- Spending quality time with pets

So, yes, to control stress you could certainly grab a paintbrush, adopt a kitten, and pipe some soothing music into your living room. But if I were you, I would go after the big wins—the stuff that I've found over and over again to work for hard-charging, physically active, stressed people like you and me to control stress as quickly and effectively as possible.

And that's what we're going to go after in this chapter. Ready? Here we go.

Breathing

Believe it or not, something you're doing right now (probably without even thinking about it) is a proven stress reliever: breathing.

And it turns out that deep breathing is not only relaxing, but it's been scientifically proven to positively affect your heart, brain, digestion, immune system, and possibly even your genes[4,13]. In his book *Relaxation Revolution: The Science and Genetics of Mind Body Healing,* Herbert Benson, a pioneer in mind-body medicine, discusses how breathing can literally change the expression of genes, and that by using your breath you can alter the basic activity of the cells in your brain.

This isn't really new information. In India, yogis have been using special breathing practices called pranayama (which means "control of the life force") to influence the mind-body connection for thousands of years.

Breathing can have an immediate effect on your physiology by altering the pH of your blood and by changing your blood pressure. Even more important, you can use breathing to train your body's reaction to stressful situations and to dampen the production of stress hormones. This makes sense, since rapid, shallow breathing is controlled by your (fight-or-flight) sympathetic nervous system, but slow, deep breathing stimulates the opposing parasympathetic system.

How do you know if you're breathing incorrectly? Here are seven warning signs:

1. **You inhale with your chest.** When you begin inhaling, you may notice that your chest is the first thing to move, typically going up or slightly forward. This indicates that you are engaging in shallow or upper-chest breathing.

2. **Your rib cage doesn't expand sideways.** If you place your hands on either side of your rib cage when you breathe, your hands should move outward about one-and-a-half to two inches as you inhale. If not, this is another sign of shallow breathing.

3. **You breathe with your mouth.** Do you find that even when you're not exercising, your mouth is open when you breathe? Unless you have a sinus infection or congestion that keeps you from breathing through your nose, your mouth should be closed as you breathe from deep within your nasal cavity.

4. **Your upper neck, chest, and shoulder muscles are tight.** Do you carry lots of tension in the muscles around and under your neck? If you get a massage or you reach back and feel those muscles, are they painful, tender, or tight? If so, your breathing may be stressed and shallow.

5. **You sigh or yawn frequently.** Do you find that every few minutes, you must take a deep breath, sigh, or yawn? This is a sign that your body isn't getting enough oxygen through normal breathing.

6. **You have a high resting breath rate.** A normal, relaxed, resting breath rate should be about ten to twelve breaths per minute. If you measure how many times you breathe each minute and it's more than twelve, it's a sign of quick and shallow breathing.

7. **You slouch forward.** Poor diaphragmatic control can cause specific muscles to become short and tight, typically in your chest and the front of your shoulders.

So if you find yourself slouching your head or shoulders forward, it can mean that you're not activating your diaphragm when you breathe.

If you experience any of these signs, there are lots of things you can do about it. Here are six ways to train yourself to breathe properly:

1. **Blow up balloons.** When you practice blowing up a balloon, it encourages you to contract your diaphragm and core muscles. You can enhance this effect by getting into a crunch or sit-up position on your back with your knees bent and your feet flat on the ground, then blowing up a balloon by inhaling through your nose and exhaling through your mouth. Try to keep your low back on the ground, not arched.

2. **Purse your lips.** Practice breathing through pursed lips by creating as small a hole as possible to breathe through. Pursed-lipped breathing helps keep you from breathing too fast. Take two to four seconds to breathe in through your nose, then four to eight seconds to breathe out through pursed lips. Do this once or twice a day for three to five minutes. Imagine you're blowing through a straw or trying to blow at a candle just hard enough to make it flicker but not extinguish it.

3. **Do planking exercises while deep breathing.** Planking exercises, like the front plank and side plank, are fantastic for strengthening your core and can also be used to teach you how to breathe properly. Simply get into a front or side plank position and take eight to twelve deep breaths, visualizing using the muscles around your bellybutton, breathing in through your nose and out through your mouth.

4. **Contract your abs as you breathe.** A simple activity that can teach you how to use your abdominal (core) muscles to breathe better is to place your hands around your waist and then try to push your hands slightly away and out to the side as you breathe out. You should feel your abdominal muscles moving your hands as you breathe.

5. **Apply resistance to your upper chest.** Lie on your back, place a hand on your upper chest, apply slight downward pressure to your sternum, and try to maintain that pressure while you inhale and exhale. This will force you to "bypass" your chest while breathing and instead breathe from deep within your belly.

6. **Limit shoulder movement.** Begin by sitting in a chair with your arms and elbows supported by the arms of the chair. As you inhale through your nose, push down on the arms of the chair, and as you exhale through pursed lips, release that pressure on the arms of the chair. The purpose of this exercise is to keep you from elevating your shoulders while breathing (which can cause upper-chest breathing).

Once you learn proper breathing technique, things begin to get interesting. You have a newfound power that not only vastly improves your training efficiency and focus but also controls how much cortisol your body releases during a workout by putting the brakes on your sympathetic nervous system while you exercise.

When combined with the five-step formula I'm about to teach you, proper deep breathing is one of the most useful and effective relaxation and stress-control tools I know of. I first talked about it in detail in a podcast interview with John Douillard, ayurvedic doctor and author of *Body, Mind, and Sport: The Mind-Body Guide to*

Lifelong Health, Fitness, and Your Personal Best. In the podcast episode titled "The Zen of 'the Zone'—How to Breathe the Right Way When You're Working Out" (at BeyondTrainingBook.com/bgfthezone), Dr. Douillard explains how the simple act of nasal breathing (rather than mouth breathing) keeps your body in relaxation mode while you're exercising, allowing for an intense feeling of relaxation similar to what you experience after a yoga or meditation session. You literally produce fewer stress hormones during a workout when you breathe the right way!

In addition, nasal breathing allows you to properly filter the air going into your lungs, warm the air to the ideal temperature (98.6°F) and humidity, and even increase the level of nitric oxide in the air that reaches your lungs. This nitric oxide is a powerful antioxidant that can help sterilize air and increase diffusion of oxygen into the bloodstream.

Since that podcast, I've combined Dr. Douillard's concepts with the rhythmic-breathing strategies outlined in Budd Coates's book *Runner's World Running on Air: The Revolutionary Way to Run Better by Breathing Smarter*[8]. While I recommend that you read both books for all the juicy details, I've come up with a five-step formula to lower stress during even the most extreme exercise sessions and races. (For entertainment, you can see me demonstrating this live on stage in my CreativeLive presentation at BeyondTrainingBook.com/CreativeLive.)

The Five-Step Formula to Turn Extreme Exercise into Relaxing Release

Think about the last time you took a series of deep, relaxing breaths. Or perhaps the last time you practiced yoga, took a walk in nature, or simply stopped your hectic workday for a brief moment of reflection. How did you feel afterward? Restored? Relaxed? Refreshed?

Next, compare that sensation with how you felt during your last workout. Perhaps your mouth was gaping wide open as you chest-panted while charging down a trail or pounding the pavement. Or maybe you were grunting and groaning as you struggled against a weight machine or barbell, or grimacing through a cardio kickboxing or spinning session.

But what if you could create the sense of relaxation you get from, say, walking in the woods when you're lifting a heavy barbell? What if exercise—even extreme exercise—did not send a catabolic-hormone-packed message to your body saying that you are running from a lion or fighting in a battle, but instead left you feeling completely restored afterward?

This challenges the paradigm of the way most of us think we should feel during or after a tough workout, but with a simple series of steps, you can transform extreme exercise into a relaxing release. You're about to discover exactly how to effect that transformation with the following five-step formula.

1. Begin with Yoga

You must prepare your body correctly for extreme exercise, such as a hard bike ride, weight-training session, run, or competitive event. Sure, you've heard that you must limber up, warm up, or perform dynamic stretches, but none of those activities prime your body for focused relaxation or allow for the reduction in cortisol or the activation of deep, diaphragmatic breathing patterns[3].

Instead, precede extreme exercise with a brief series of basic sun salutations. It doesn't take much—five minutes will suffice. If you don't know how to do basic sun salutations, simply watch the Howcast at BeyondTrainingBook.com/sunsalutation. Focus on deep nasal breathing from your belly during this session.

Your body is now primed for relaxation during your workout.

2. Continue Deep Nasal Breathing

Hopefully you were practicing deep nasal breathing from your belly while doing the pre-exercise yoga.

If you're like most people who have gotten used to going into fight-or-flight mode during extreme exercise, your natural reaction as soon as you start your workout is to begin getting precious oxygen through your mouth while engaging in shallow, stressful chest-breathing—which significantly bumps up stress and cortisol levels.

Resist that temptation.

Instead, continue the deep nasal breathing from the belly, which naturally relaxes your body and keeps perception of stress and cortisol release low. If you simply can't get enough oxygen, slow down until you get to the point where you can do your nasal breathing, then gradually speed up again to your higher intensity. As you back off and reapproach the higher intensities, you will get better and better at the deep nasal breathing. The more you practice this technique, the more natural it will become.

If you really struggle with nasal breathing and find yourself annoyingly congested or continually short of breath no matter what you do, try using a Breathe Right strip on your nose.

3. Breathe Rhythmically

Whether you're lifting weights, running, or cycling, rhythmic breathing is just as important as nasal breathing for keeping your body in a relaxed state no matter how hard you're going.

Learning to breathe rhythmically is difficult initially but becomes second nature within just a few days of practice. In a nutshell, when you're running or cycling, you want to inhale more than you exhale, and when you're lifting weights, your inhalation and exhalation are equal. Never let your breath get out of control or become nonrhythmic.

If you're running or cycling, simply take one deep nasal breath in for every three foot strikes or pedal strokes and one relaxed nasal breath out on the subsequent two foot strikes or pedal strokes. As you increase your intensity and go faster, you can continue this breathing pattern but speed things up by taking one deep breath in for two foot strikes or pedal strokes and one deep breath out on the subsequent foot strike or pedal stroke.

If you're lifting weights, release one deep nasal breath as you exert yourself and push or pull the weight, then take one deep nasal breath in as you return the weight to its starting position.

Those are the basics of rhythmic breathing. When combined with nasal breathing, this pattern allows for an intense feeling of relaxation and oxygenation after your workout, no matter how hard or heavy it is.

4. Unplug

If you work around computers, phones, or Wi-Fi routers or in any other "connected" environment, you've no doubt experienced the brain fog, eye strain, muscle tightness, and internal stress that constant exposure to electromagnetic fields (EMFs) can create. The effect of EMFs on your nerves, cells, heart, and brain is proven and substantial—and you'll learn about it later in this book.

But your body remains exposed to that same electrical stress if you are plugged in during your workouts, whether by carrying your smartphone on a trail run or venturing into a gym jam-packed with TVs and personal entertainment systems.

While there are some practical limitations to unplugging (for example, you need to carry your phone for emergencies, or the only place you can weight-train is a deluxe health club with state-of-the-art media all over the place), you should go out of your way to do your toughest workout sessions in as unplugged a state as possible.

No matter how much yoga you do before that extreme-exercise session, or how much nasal and rhythmic breathing you do during that session, you simply won't get the full removal-of-stress benefit or the complete avoidance of a fight-or-flight reaction unless you keep your distance from electrical pollution during your workout.

5. Finish with Dedication

This last step sounds New Agey and inconsequential, but it's crucial. Avoid finishing extreme exercise by jumping straight into the shower, flopping onto the couch, or checking e-mail. Instead, just as you would with yoga or a meditation session, finish with dedication and relaxation.

To do this correctly, you should gradually slow down toward the end of your workout while continuing to focus on your breath. When your breath is completely controlled and your heart is no longer pounding, simply stop.

Then close your eyes and dedicate the workout. You can dedicate it to yourself, to a loved one, to a teammate or workout buddy, or to whatever feels most important to you at the moment. Visualize that object of dedication in front of you, and acknowledge it respectfully. Take several deep nasal breaths in, fill your lungs, oxygenate your body, and finish with a full release of breath as you remove stress from your entire muscular and cardiovascular system.

You now have the knowledge to turn extreme exercise into relaxing release. When I first began practicing these concepts in my swim, bike, run, and lift sessions, they felt foreign and counterintuitive, but my body adapted within just a couple weeks. You'll be amazed at the feeling of pure relaxation that you can achieve even when you're pushing yourself to the absolute limit.

I realize that I've spent a lot of time talking about breathing. But breathing forms the foundation of most of the other stress-fighting weapons in this chapter, so you are now well equipped to sail through the rest of these concepts.

And remember to practice your deep, nasal breathing as you keep reading.

Mindfulness Meditation

If there's one thing you probably wouldn't associate with the stereotypical soldier, it would be sitting in a peaceful, Zenlike position while practicing deep, relaxing meditation. But the military has found the practice of mindfulness to be extremely helpful in overcoming stress[24].

And from Kobe Bryant to Joe Namath to Arthur Ashe, meditation has helped countless athletes manage stress, improve focus, and enhance performance[22].

The very best place to begin learning meditation is the simple act of mindfulness, which is how I learned to meditate and is how I now start every single day. I practice mindfulness before I even get out of bed in the morning, and usually pair it with heart-rate-variability readings from my NatureBeat tracker so that I can assess how mindfulness practice is influencing my stress levels. The results are pretty astounding. I can literally raise my HRV number by five to ten points with just a few minutes of morning mindfulness practice.

Mindfulness involves focusing your mind on the present. To be mindful is to be aware of your thoughts and actions in the moment, without judging yourself and without being distracted by stressful experiences from the past (for example, how crappy the day before was) or stressful anticipation of the future (for example, everything you need to get done that day).

Research has shown that mindfulness meditation can improve mood, decrease stress, and even boost immune function[16]. Here's how to start:

1. Find a quiet, comfortable place. I recommend that you sit in a chair or on the floor with your head, neck, and back straight but not stiff.

2. Try to put aside thoughts of the past and the future and stay "in the moment."

3. Become aware of your breathing, focusing on the sensation of air moving in and out of your body as you breathe using the techniques you've already learned in this chapter. Feel your belly rise and fall, and feel the air enter your nostrils and leave your mouth through pursed lips or leave your nostrils.

4. Watch every thought come and go, whether it is a worry, fear, anxiety, or hope. When thoughts come up, don't ignore or suppress them, but simply acknowledge them, remain calm, and use your breath as an anchor.

5. If you find yourself getting carried away by your thoughts, observe where your mind went (without judging yourself), and simply return to your breathing. Remember not to be hard on yourself if you become distracted—it's completely natural.

6. As the time comes to a close, sit for a minute or two, becoming aware of where you are. Then get up gradually.

Once you learn mindfulness-based meditation, you can easily start or end each day with it—a practice I highly recommend. One of my favorite free audio resources for walking you through a mindfulness session or a type of meditation called progressive relaxation can be found on the Buddhanet website (buddhanet.net/audio-meditation.htm).

Toss these tracks into your MP3 player and try them out. I especially like the "body scan." If using technology to help you meditate turns out to be something you like, you may want to check out two other apps: HeadSpace and Pranayama. I used to think that meditation was for hippies, but now I can't imagine not including meditation in my routine at least once per day.

Yoga

You probably don't need me to tell you that yoga is good for stress. Sure, you've already learned that practicing yoga right before any activity for which you need speed, strength, or power is not the best idea, and that it's also not the best way to improve flexibility, but when it comes to stress, yoga is one of my top stress-fighters[11], and I follow up my morning mindfulness meditation with a good five to fifteen minutes of yoga (in addition to beginning and/or ending workouts with sun salutations).

There are a ton of different styles, forms, and intensities of yoga, but hatha yoga is a good choice for stress management—particularly if you've perfected the rhythmic breathing and nasal breathing mentioned earlier in this chapter. Hatha is one of the most common styles of yoga, and most beginners appreciate its slower pace and easier movements.

By contrast, some yoga is actually quite stressful. Take Bikram yoga or hot yoga. Bikram, a hybrid form of hatha yoga done in a hot room, is really useful and effective if you're acclimating for a hot race or trying to build up your body to handle the heat; I like try to throw in four to eight weeks of weekly Bikram classes leading into Ironman Hawaii. Because you get so hot and sweaty, Bikram can also be good for detoxing and for strengthening your cardiovascular system when you're trying to avoid joint impact from something like running.

But Bikram is stressful. As your body shunts blood to your extremities in a rapid attempt to cool, your heart rate goes through the roof. For this reason, Bikram would definitely be considered one of the thermal stressors I referred to earlier.

Or take some of the more extreme forms of power yoga. I have a power yoga DVD called *Yoga for the Warrior,* starring TV's *Biggest Loser* personal trainer Bob Harper. From start to finish, it features rollicking rock music, teeth-gritting holds, and Bob screaming at you to make it even harder. Sure, it's a good workout, but it's not exactly stress-reducing. The same could be said for the Diamond Dallas Page DDP Yoga series: It's a great workout that I do occasionally when I want a video to walk me through a tough yoga routine, but I can't say that my cortisol levels are very low after finishing. So choose your yoga wisely.

Hatha yoga promotes physical relaxation by decreasing activity of the sympathetic nervous system, which decreases cortisol, lowers heart rate, and increases breath volume, so that's my personal recommendation. It's easy to learn, and once you've memorized some of the basic postures, you can easily take hatha yoga outside of a classroom or DVD setting and concoct your own stress-relieving routine on the spot, which is what I usually do since I rarely have the time to schedule and attend a class.

Tai Chi

Tai chi is a system of slow, graceful exercises that combine movement, meditation, and rhythmic breathing to improve the flow of chi (aka life force). Research has shown that tai chi can reduce stress, lower blood pressure, and help improve posture, balance, muscle tone, flexibility, and strength[2].

Tai chi is typically taught in groups in health centers, community centers, offices, and schools, but Amazon sells a variety of good DVDs and books; I own and use *Tai Chi for Beginners*.

I'm not sure if it's because tai chi is so slow and precise or because doing it makes me feel like some kind of ancient Chinese monk, but my stress levels hit rock bottom after a session. I do tai chi at least once a month; during easier recovery weeks I do one or two sessions a week.

Because of its stress-reducing efficacy, a weekly tai chi session is an integral and "nonoptional" part of the programs I oversee for individuals who are recovering from overtraining or adrenal fatigue. If you're not dealing with adrenal issues, you may get a bigger bang for your time buck with yoga and meditation—but because of the distinct correlation between chi, cortisol, and your adrenals and the variety of ancestral medical practitioners who recommend tai chi for curing overtraining adrenal fatigue, I'm a fan of learning this beautiful art form.

Coherence

Get ready to take a deep dive into hard-core heart and brain science for a quick moment. I promise it won't hurt too much.

Your heart is in a constant two-way dialogue with your brain—the so-called "heart-brain connection." Interestingly, your heart (and your entire cardiovascular system) sends far more signals to your brain than your brain sends to your heart[17].

These "afferent signals," or signals that flow to the brain, have a regulatory influence on many aspects of your nervous system, including most of your glands and organs. And these signals also have profound effects on your higher brain centers. Cardiovascular afferent signals have numerous connections to important brain centers like your thalamus, hypothalamus, and amygdala, and because of this, the signals from your heart play a direct role in determining your perceptions, thought processes, emotional experiences, and overall stress.

Research in the field of neurocardiology has firmly established that the heart is indeed a sensory organ and an information encoding and processing center—almost like a second brain. The heart's circuitry allows it to learn, remember, and make functional decisions independent of your cranial brain, which is mind-blowing. But the fact that the heart has an intrinsic nervous system and is itself a complex, self-organized system capable of forming new neural connections has been well demonstrated.

Figure 9-2 illustrates this heart-brain connection and shows the direct connection from your heart's neurons to organs such as your lungs, esophagus, skin, and arteries.

As you can probably imagine, this connection between the heart and the brain is a topic that could fill an entire book. Organizations like the Institute of HeartMath, which I link to on the resource web page for this chapter, have enormous archives of free research and articles on the topic. But the basic idea is that your heart is a primary generator of rhythm in your body, and that the heart can directly influence brain processes that control your nervous system, cognitive function, and emotions.

So when your heart rhythms are in a state of "coherence," which means that you have balanced feedback from your sympathetic and parasympathetic nervous systems, smoother brain function is facilitated. This not only decreases stress but also allows you more access to your innate intelligence, which enables you to improve your focus, creativity, intuition, and higher-level decision making. If you've ever felt in "the zone," then you've experienced ideal heart-rhythm coherence. Similarly, if you test your heart rate variability and it's high, it is also a good sign that you are in a state of coherence. As a result, you tend to feel confident, positive, focused, and calm yet energized.

Conveniently, you can create a coherent state in about one minute flat by using a strategy called Quick Coherence.

You can use this fast and powerful technique as soon as you begin feeling a stressful emotion—frustration, irritation, anxiety, anger, or the like. It's a technique that I use before situations that I know are going to be stressful, such as an important business meeting, a public-speaking engagement, a tennis match, or a triathlon.

Here's how to achieve coherence and optimize communication between your heart and your brain in three easy steps:

FIGURE 9-2. Heart-Brain Communication Pathways

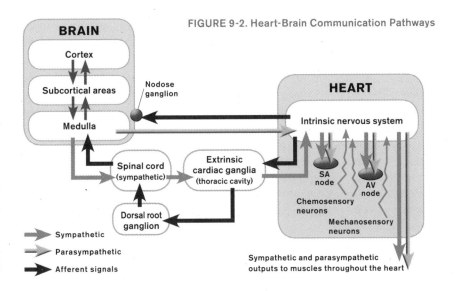

1. **Heart focus.** Focus your attention on the area around your heart, in the center of your chest. If you prefer, place your hand over your heart the first couple times you try it to help keep your attention there.

2. **Heart breathing.** Breathe deeply but normally, and imagine that your breath is coming in and going out through the area around your heart. Continue breathing with ease until you find a natural inner rhythm that feels good to you.

3. **Heart feeling.** As you maintain your heart focus and heart breathing, activate a positive feeling. Recall a positive memory, a time when you felt good inside, and try to reexperience that feeling. One of the easiest ways to generate a positive, heart-based feeling is to think of a special place that you've been to or the love you feel for a close friend, family member, or treasured pet. This is the most important step.

Using Quick Coherence at the onset of stress can keep the stress from escalating into a physiologically damaging or adrenal-draining situation. I've found this technique to be especially useful after an emotional blowup to get back into balance quickly.

The nice thing about Quick Coherence is that you can do it anytime, anywhere, and no one will know that you're doing it. But in less than a minute, it creates positive changes in the rhythms of your heart, which then sends powerful signals to the brain that directly affect your body via the mind-body connection.

You can check out the HeartMath Institute's resources at BenGreenfieldFitness. com/heartmath to learn even more about coherence and the research behind it. For useful, live biofeedback and watching your heart rhythm and heart rate variability in real time as you practice coherence (which can be extremely helpful, especially when you're first learning the technique), you'll need an emWave2 unit, the Inner Balance Sensor for your smartphone, or the NatureBeat app.

Learning

Earlier, I joked about grabbing a paintbrush or adopting a kitten to reduce stress. But I wasn't kidding.

Think about it: How many hard-core triathletes, marathoners, cyclists, and CrossFitters do you know whose lives pretty much consist entirely of working, exercising, and eating? Every single day, day in and day out, is the same: Eat a big breakfast, check off the WOD or workout, get through the workday, eat a big dinner, sleep, and maybe throw in a TV movie or book every now and again.

But whether it's music[5] or art[18] or journaling[6], having some kind of hobby[21] and engaging in regular learning has consistently been shown to lower stress. And let's face it: When you're on your deathbed, do you really want to lie there thinking about how good your marathon times were?

That's why I play guitar. I practice three times a week for twenty to thirty minutes. That's it. And considering that I played violin for thirteen years, practicing an hour every day, an hour a week of guitar is easy to find time for. Playing a musical instrument is especially good because it brings the added benefit of music's stress-relieving effects.

But that's not all.

Twice a week I cook. And I'm not talking scrambled eggs or a stir-fry. It has to be a new recipe that stimulates my brain, creates new neural pathways, and helps decrease stress. Last week it was vegan pad Thai one day and fried liver another. (Yes, I swing every which way when it comes to food.) You'd be surprised at how relaxing cooking is, especially compared with eating, which can actually be stressful for many people, especially body-conscious athletes.

And at least once a month, I try something new. This can mean going to a dance class with my wife, learning a kick serve for my tennis game, growing mint in my backyard, or dribbling a basketball between my legs. Teaching activates the same kind of stress-relieving neural pathways as learning, and if you have children, this can be a big bonus. For example, this month I'm teaching my twin sons how to dance, play chess, and speak Thai.

It doesn't really matter what you're teaching or learning, as long as you're doing something outside the daily routine of work, swimming, cycling, running, lifting, or eating.

Need some inspiration to get your creative wheels turning? Check out the blog post about forty sites for learning new stuff at BeyondTrainingBook.com/learn. Also, from cooking to music to cards, Tim Ferris's book *The 4-Hour Chef* is a fantastic resource for sparking your desire to learn and for ideas about what new things you might want to learn.

Sleep

Ah, yes, sleep.

Right up there with breathing, sleep is one of the most important stress-fighting weapons on the face of the planet[12,25]. As a matter of fact, not protecting and prioritizing sleep is one of the best ways to slowly destroy your nervous system and kill yourself.

Sleep is so important that I am going to devote the entire next chapter to enhancing deep sleep, napping, and preventing sleep-hacking, insomnia, and jet lag.

In the meantime, remember that just because you're adding all these stress-fighting weapons to your arsenal, it doesn't mean that you can pile on more exercise or lifestyle stress. No matter how many of these techniques you use, you still need to measure stress and exercise preparedness by using the recovery-tracking strategies you learned in chapter 7.

But as you implement breathing, meditation, tai chi, yoga, coherence, learning, and sleep into your daily routine, you're going to find yourself far better able to handle the stress that life throws at you and to recover from the stress that you throw at your body.

Additional resources, helpful links, websites, scientific references, and surprise bonuses for this chapter are available at BeyondTrainingBook.com/Chapter9. Enjoy.

CHAPTER 10

Everything You Need to Know to Sleep Better, Eliminate Insomnia, Conquer Jet Lag, and Master the Nap

I'm going to begin by answering a question I get quite often: How much do you sleep?

I sleep seven-and-a-half to nine hours every twenty-four hours, usually seven to eight hours at night plus a twenty- to sixty-minute nap during the day. When I hit this targeted amount of sleep, my workouts are better, my heart rate is awesome, my nerves are sharp, and my creativity and memory are at their peaks.

This may seem like a lot of sleep to you, but sleep is pretty darn important. And 99.99 percent of the time, if someone says that he needs "less sleep than the average person," he's lying to you or to himself—or both. Granted, not everyone responds the same way to sleep curtailment, and twin studies have uncovered genetic variations that may protect some people from sleep deprivation. The mutations that occur to the p.Tyr362His BHLHE41 gene appear to allow some people to tolerate shorter sleep durations and maintain normal alertness and limited signs of inflammation. Unfortunately, this genetic variation is extremely uncommon, and even successful celebrities and athletes who don't sleep very much—the "sleepless elite," like Barack Obama, Dean Karnazes, Martha Stewart, and Donald Trump, all of whom claim to sleep only four or five hours a night—are probably sacrificing something in some other part of their life to get such lowly amounts of shut-eye.

Somewhere in their life (for reasons that are about to become clear), creativity or memory is suffering.

Somewhere in their body, inflammation is running rampant.

Somewhere in a muscle or brain cell, regeneration is not occurring.

This is the kind of biological damage you invite when you don't sleep enough, especially when you combine lack of sleep with intense physical or mental activity.

In this chapter, I'm going to show you what a normal sleep rhythm looks like and how much sleep you really need. I'll also give you two reasons you'll die if you don't sleep, four biohacks to help you sleep better, nine supplements to help you sleep better, ten ways to master the nap, six ways to track your sleep, five strategies to eliminate insomnia, and eleven tips to beat jet lag.

Two Reasons You'll Die if You Don't Sleep

You heard right: If you don't sleep, you will die.

Or, as I believe I heard author Robb Wolf once put it: "If you want to kill someone quickly, take away their sleep."

OK, so this may be a slight exaggeration. After all, nearly everyone has pulled an all-nighter at least once. Although it can be an unpleasant experience, you can pretty much recover completely from it with one single night of a solid eight to nine hours of sleep.

But *cumulative* sleep loss is a different story altogether.

In one study, sleep researchers constructed a cruel contraption that woke up rats as soon as they fell asleep. Using this contraption, it took an average of three weeks to kill a rat by sleep deprivation. Other research[17] has shown demonstrable brain damage in sleep-deprived rats, primarily because of a severe lack of neurogenesis (regrowth or rebuilding of new brain neurons) from rampant levels of sleep-deprivation-induced cortisol.

While sleep deprivation is a well-known form of torture for rats, for ethical reasons researchers could not reproduce these studies in humans. But by looking at sleep disorders, we can get a pretty clear idea of what happens when people don't sleep enough.

For example, death occurs within a few months in humans who have fatal familial insomnia, a mutation that causes the affected person to suffer from a progressively worsening insomnia that ends in death within a few months[1]. Morvan's syndrome is another example of lack of sleep causing death: In this case the autoimmune disease destroys the brain's potassium channels, which leads to severe insomnia and death[12].

Because of their ability to cause high blood pressure and heart disease, sleep disorders add $16 billion to national health-care costs each year. And that does not include the cost of accidents and lost productivity at work, which in America alone amounts to $150 billion each year[21].

Remember the disaster at Three Mile Island? Chernobyl? The gas leak at Bhopal? The Zeebrugge ferry accident? The Exxon Valdez oil spill? If you do a little research, you'll find that these and many other major industrial disasters have been directly linked to sleep deprivation.

So why is sleep deprivation fatal? Primarily because depriving the body of sleep is like speeding up the aging process. There are two primary reasons:

1. The brain cleans up cellular garbage while you sleep.

2. The body repairs itself while you sleep.

Let's look at the first reason—the need to clean up cellular garbage.

One of the most important functions of sleep is the reorganization of neural networks in your brain. All day long—even on the most boring day possible—you are consciously or subconsciously learning new things, memorizing facts or task processes, acquiring skills, establishing new memories through creative associations, meeting new people, and the like. After a long day of these activities, your brain is full of myriad discrete pieces of information that have to be integrated with all the other things you have learned previously in your life.

If this reorganization isn't allowed to occur, your mind becomes a chaotic storehouse for cellular garbage, and you literally run out of space to store new memories. Once this happens, it affects nearly all functions of your body that are governed by your central nervous system, and your body begins to malfunction.

These malfunctions typically manifest as:

- Problems with heat or cold regulation

- A decline in immune function

- An increase in cortisol, catecholamines, and other stress hormones
- Imbalances in appetite- and blood-sugar-regulating hormones
- Increased levels of inflammatory hormones, such as interleukin and C-reactive protein

In later stages of sleep deprivation, you experience malnutrition, hallucinations, malfunctions of your autonomic nervous system (e.g., heart arrhythmias or kidney and liver dysfunction), changes in cell-adhesion and cell-clotting abilities, skin lesions, and DNA damage[13]. So that's the first reason you die a slow death if you don't sleep: Your body basically falls apart.

This is why it can be so freaking hard to do a run, bike, swim, WOD, or race when you're sleep deprived—much less make it through a day of mentally or physically demanding work. Your body is full of inflammation, hormone imbalances, and blood sugar dysregulation and is operating well below peak mental and physical capability. Unfortunately, many people live most of their adult lives in this state, thinking that it is completely normal to feel like a walking zombie.

It's very important for you to understand that the fix is not simply "an easy day" or a period of time spent putting your feet up. Unlike rest or conservation of energy, the mechanics of neural repair require your brain to be shut off entirely from environmental input. This means you must actually be sleeping for the repair magic to happen.

The second reason you'll die if you don't sleep is that sleep is the primary anabolic state of the human body.

During nighttime sleep, you experience an increase in growth hormone and testosterone—two crucial muscle-repairing hormones that also significantly affect your neural growth and the way you feel during the day. One study describes these nighttime hormonal surges as playing a "crucial role in consolidating and enhancing waking experience"[6]. And it's why you feel so damn good after a solid night of sleep. It's also why your body can take two to three times longer to repair and recover from physical exercise when you're not sleeping.

Not only do your muscles get a chance to fully repair and recover when you're sleeping, but the same can be said for the restoration of your adrenal glands, the detoxification of your body by your liver, and the rebuilding of your immune system. As a matter of fact, one of the leading causes of death in those rats that underwent sleep deprivation was opportunistic bacterial infections resulting from a decline in immune function.

So when you don't sleep enough, your body is in a continuous hormonally depleted, catabolic state and gets sicker and sicker.

And this is why I shake my head and laugh at people who brag about how little they sleep. They're shrinking their brains, shrinking their muscles, and making themselves sick.

Now I'm not saying you need to be like professional Ironman Andy Potts, who sleeps eleven hours a day (although he may indeed need that much sleep to compensate for the extent to which he beats up his body in training). But you likely need to prioritize sleep more than our overachieving, productivity-obsessed culture would have you believe.

How Much Sleep Do You Really Need?

This is a big can of worms. Because of age, genetics, environment, and individual differences in daily physical and mental strain, there can be huge variations in ideal sleep times.

The National Sleep Foundation has established some pretty good guidelines based on their up-to-date sleep research[10]. See Table 10-1.

If you're reading this book, you probably fall into the category of "Adults." And in most adults, sleeping fewer than seven hours a night is associated with decreased alertness and increased risk of chronic disease, while sleeping more than nine hours a night is associated with a shorter life and an increased risk of chronic disease.

TABLE 10-1.
How Much Sleep Do You Really Need?

Age	Sleep Needs
Newborns (0–2 months)	12–18 hours
Infants (3–11 months)	14–15 hours
Toddlers (1–3 years)	12–14 hours
Preschoolers (3–5 years)	11–13 hours
School-age children (5–10 years)	10–11 hours
Teens (10–17 years)	8.5–9.25 hours
Adults	7–9 hours

That's right: More sleep is not necessarily better.

However, if you're reading this book, you're probably not a 100 percent normal adult. That is, your level of physical activity is probably higher than normal, thanks to preparing for or completing triathlons, marathons, CrossFit workouts, cycling tours, ocean swims, or other feats of physical endurance.

Go ahead and check out the amazing infographic "Sleep to Be an All-Star" at BenGreenfieldFitness.com/sleepgraph. In case you don't have access to a computer right now, I'll highlight a few of the quotes:

Usain Bolt, the fastest sprinter on the planet: "Sleep is extremely important to me—I need to rest and recover in order for the training I do to be absorbed by my body."

Steve Nash, one of the world's best basketball point guards: "For me, sleeping well could mean the difference between putting up thirty points and living with fifteen."

Roger Federer, professional tennis player: "If I don't sleep eleven to twelve hours a day, it's not right."

Jarrod Shoemaker, professional triathlete: "Sleep is half my training."

Some of the stats from the infographic are quite interesting, too, including:

- Maximum bench press drops twenty pounds after four days of restricted sleep.
- With proper sleep, tennis players see a 42 percent increase in hitting accuracy.
- Sleep loss means an 11 percent reduction in time to exhaustion.
- Perceived exertion increases 17–19 percent after thirty hours of sleep deprivation.

Are you getting the idea that athletes and physically active people may need to sleep more? In my experience, professional athletes need ten to twelve hours of sleep per twenty-four-hour-day cycle, and the typical Ironman triathlete, hard-core CrossFitter, marathoner, cyclist, or exercise fanatic needs seven-and-a-half to nine hours of sleep per twenty-four-hour-day cycle[9].

What a Normal Sleep Cycle and Circadian Rhythm Should Look Like, and What Happens When It Gets Disrupted

If you don't want to die before your time and you want to optimize your performance, it's essential that you understand the basics of your circadian rhythm. Everything else I am going to tell you in this chapter will make much better sense if you have a basic understanding of what a typical twenty-four-hour cycle looks like.

On my Superhuman Coach website (SuperhumanCoach.com), you can find a free seven-part video series that reveals little-known tips and tricks to enhance your performance, fat loss, recovery, digestion, mental performance, hormonal balance, and sleep. There is a detailed video in that Superhuman series that explains what a normal circadian rhythm looks like and teaches you in even greater detail why some of the suggestions in this chapter work.

If you don't have the chance to watch the video right now, Figure 10-1 gives you an overview before you keep reading.

Starting at about 6 a.m., you get a surge of cortisol. This surge of morning cortisol is what turns on your brain and body. It also coincides with the release of the very important hormone vasoactive intestinal polypeptide, fittingly called VIP. VIP causes a variety of important wake-up actions, such as increased contractility in your heart, vasodilation (widening of your blood vessels), and liver glycogenolysis (breakdown of your liver's glycogen to naturally bring your blood sugar up)[20].

VIP relaxes the smooth muscle of your trachea, stomach, and gallbladder, which means that, within two hours of waking, it's a good time for a bowel movement. VIP also results in a natural surge of ghrelin, a hunger hormone, which can make you feel

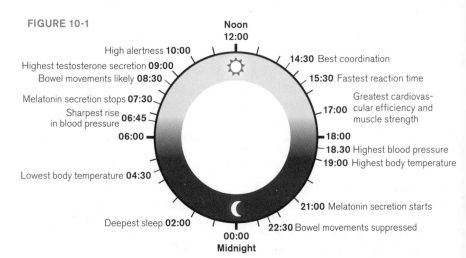

FIGURE 10-1

Noon
12:00

High alertness **10:00**
Highest testosterone secretion **09:00**
Bowel movements likely **08:30**
Melatonin secretion stops **07:30**
Sharpest rise **06:45**
in blood pressure
06:00
Lowest body temperature **04:30**
Deepest sleep **02:00**

14:30 Best coordination
15:30 Fastest reaction time
17:00 Greatest cardiovascular efficiency and muscle strength
18:00
18.30 Highest blood pressure
19:00 Highest body temperature
21:00 Melatonin secretion starts
22:30 Bowel movements suppressed

00:00
Midnight

like eating breakfast. If you happen to have hunger-hormone imbalances, which often manifest as cravings throughout the day, this is why it is very important to eat first thing in the morning—it resets your circadian clock and begins to get your hormones in rhythm. In other words, skipping breakfast or "defying morning hunger" by fasting is not a good idea if you have hormone imbalances.

Good exposure to morning sunlight helps maximize the effect of this cortisol release by giving your body a little kick start to get your circadian rhythm normalized. As you'll learn later in this chapter, that morning sun may help your cortisol levels naturally decline later at night, so if you miss the sun in the morning, it can be bad news for your sleep!

I step outside every morning to get at least five minutes of sunlight, but if you're not able to do so, you can still maximize this natural release of cortisol with small to moderate amounts of coffee, green tea, adaptogenic herbs, or even fancy blue light–producing devices such as the HumanCharger in-ear light device, The Re-Timer glasses, or a blue light box for your table. However, nothing is quite as effective as natural sunlight; this is why you may find that you need very little or no coffee in the summer, but you're a complete bear if you don't get your morning cup in the dark winter months.

At about 9 or 10 a.m., sex hormone secretion peaks. This is helpful information if you want to know the best time of day for a "quickie," or if your libido is flagging and you want to give it some help. Sex at this time of day may also help reset your circadian rhythm if you're having difficulty sleeping at night.

At about 2:30 p.m., you experience a peak in muscle coordination and reaction time. So this can be a good time to exercise or play sports.

However, at around 5 p.m., your cardiovascular efficiency, body temperature, muscle repair, protein synthesis, and workout-recovery capability peak, so this is an even better time of day to exercise, especially if your workout is intense. For this reason, whenever I have the luxury of choosing when I can work out, I usually start at around 4:30 and finish up sometime between 5 and 6 p.m. This means not only that I'm exercising hard when my body is most able to do so, but also that I'm eating my postexercise dinner during a time of peak protein synthesis and muscle repair. This is also why I encourage folks to do any easy, aerobic exercise earlier in the morning and harder interval training or weight training later in the day.

Next comes sunset, which is obviously going to depend on the time of year and where you're living. At this point, your blood pressure peaks. Interestingly, this is also a time when body temperature can peak again, which is why an early-evening cold shower or cold soak can help you get to sleep a bit better. Around sunset, the hormone leptin is released from your fat stores. If your circadian rhythm is in sync and leptin is able to do its job properly, leptin can actually shift your body into fatty-acid utilization, suppress your appetite, and control any late-night food cravings[2]. People who constantly eat too many calories, too many carbohydrates, or too many meals or who sleep improperly get into a vicious cycle of late-night food cravings because leptin isn't doing its job, but this can often be fixed by syncing the body back into proper circadian rhythm.

From sunset until bedtime, leptin continues to rise to control your appetite. Adiponectin, another hormone that can assist with fatty-acid metabolism, also tends to rise during this time. (Interestingly, taking 300–500 milligrams of magnesium before bed can enhance adiponectin release.) Unfortunately, high levels of insulin can hamper adiponectin production, so if you've consistently got high levels of insulin circulating from high carbohydrate or protein intake, your evening fatty-acid utilization is suppressed. This is why it's very important to limit snacking—especially on carbohydrates or protein-laden foods—in the evening. (Incidentally, some forms of calories, such as coconut oil and MCT oil, do not actually spike insulin and would be an acceptable evening calorie source.)

Assuming that you haven't been drowning in artificial light from televisions, movie screens, computer screens, smartphones, e-readers, and bright household lightbulbs, your body starts secreting melatonin at around 10 p.m. Melatonin lets your body sleep and recuperate, turns off waking brain activity to allow for neuronal repair, pulls oxygen and needed hormones away from muscle tissue and other cells, and generally makes it difficult to be physically active and easy to sleep. As you can imagine, if your body doesn't make melatonin, it becomes much harder to fall asleep[16].

The other thing that tends to happen at around 10 p.m. is that a protein called agouti peaks, which can stimulate your appetite the way ghrelin does—unless leptin is there to play bouncer, keeping the door shut on agouti protein. So you can see how you set yourself up for a vicious cycle of poor sleep, fat gain, and a nighttime explosion of cravings if you snack from sunset to bedtime, because snacking raises insulin levels, which causes a drop in leptin and leptin sensitivity and then suppression of leptin[5]. And that means leptin won't be around to counteract agouti protein, so you get massively hungry when you're supposed to be falling asleep!

Gastrointestinal activity begins to quiet down at around 11, and, as long as you've got the rest of your ducks in order, you should not need to use the bathroom until you wake up. Of course, this can be affected by consuming lots of water in the evening, but your brain-gut connection should be generally less active at this point.

At around midnight, melatonin peaks, and that's when leptin is able to enter an area of the brain called the hypothalamus. This is very important from a metabolic and weight-control or fat-loss standpoint, because when leptin enters your hypothalamus, your fat reserves are released and your thyroid gets a signal to upregulate thyroid function.

When leptin enters the hypothalamus, it also induces changes in your mitochondria to help them produce heat. When you are asleep, your core temperature falls, and your body has to maintain a set point of warmth, which can't be generated from running or lifting weights. In the same way that cold thermogenesis lets your brown adipose tissue produce heat from calories, a good sleep cycle lets your mitochondria produce heat from calories. So, in an ideal world, you mobilize and burn your fat stores while you sleep. Starting to get an idea of why obesity is linked to lack of sleep?

It is also around this point in the cycle that melatonin enters an area of the brain called the suprachiasmatic nucleus, and when it does, it decreases your neuron-firing rate[14]. Basically, melatonin slows down your brain and allows your neurons and nervous system to heal while cementing learning and memory and allowing you to feel a lot sharper when you wake up in the morning.

The other nice thing that happens when melatonin peaks at around midnight is that you get a release of prolactin, which is an incredibly important hormone. A deficiency in prolactin (often found in postmenopausal women) can cause a decline in brain activity, a propensity to gain weight, and high levels of inflammatory cytokine molecules associated with lack of recovery and chronic pain. Meanwhile, balanced prolactin levels increase the recycling of cells, the renewal of cells, and the creation of new cells. It also promotes the release of growth hormone.

If not much prolactin is released while you sleep, you tend to produce less growth hormone, which can cause low levels of DHEA, another very important hormone. Low levels of these hormones result in reduced cardiac function and reduced skeletal muscle function. You can now understand that, if melatonin doesn't enter the suprachiasmatic nucleus or leptin doesn't enter the hypothalamus, there will be some serious repercussions, especially for heart health, muscle repair, full-body recovery, and daily physical performance.

Interestingly, adequate levels of DHEA and growth hormone maintain a woman's reproductive cycle: Without adequate levels of them, women begin menopause earlier.

In menopause, the body no longer produces the corpus luteum, an endocrine structure that is essential to the female sexual reproductive function. The corpus luteum causes a monthly surge of progesterone, which is necessary to balance estrogen levels[15]. When estrogen is out of balance because progesterone is low from low levels of growth hormone and DHEA, women end up with issues like cognitive decline, loss of bone density, and weight gain. And a lot of women bring on these issues purely with a lack of sleep.

Between 2 a.m. and 6 a.m., your core temperature falls the most drastically, allowing for more neuron and nervous system repair, neuron growth, an upregulation of circulating T cells (the killer cells of your immune system), and a decrease in inflammation. If you can get solid sleep during this phase, you'll have a stronger immune system and less inflammation. But in order for your core temperature to drop like this, you need to have been asleep for up to six hours already. So if you're going to sleep at, say, midnight, your body is going to get less rebuilding and repair done between 2 a.m. and 6 a.m. While I realize that it may not be feasible for you to go to bed at 8 p.m., I would highly encourage you to try to be asleep by 10:30 p.m. I try to hit the sack by 10 p.m. whenever possible and often go to bed earlier than that in the winter because of the natural shortening of the day.

Interestingly, that drop in temperature signals your body to begin producing cortisol at about 6 a.m., which restarts the entire cycle. And so you wash, rinse, and repeat the cycle, healing your body, building new neurons, and strengthening your immune system along the way. Pretty cool, huh?

Are you convinced yet that sleep is important?

Now that you know why you'll die if you don't sleep, how much sleep you really need, and what a normal circadian rhythm looks like, let's talk about how to enhance your sleep, reset your circadian rhythm if it's out of whack, and fight stressors to a normal sleep cycle, such as jet lag and insomnia.

Four Biohacks for Better Sleep

1. Light

The ability of light to regulate your circadian rhythm or manage jet lag is pretty impressive. For example, for the one to three days before I travel from east to west across multiple time zones, I do several minutes of bright light exposure when it's morning where I'm going. So if I want to be wakeful at, say, 7 a.m. in the west, I'll use bright light at 10 a.m. in the east.

Then, when I'm in the west, I simply blast myself with light from sunlight, a Human-Charger, a Re-Timer, or a blue light box when I wake up or while I'm sitting drinking coffee and checking my e-mail. I even have special lights in my office called Awake & Alert Bulbs made by Lighting Science so I can bathe myself in light while working.

Next, I've had two races for which I've had to wake up one to two hours before my normal waking time. In both instances, I've instantly eliminated the typical grogginess from getting up earlier than usual simply by using bright light exposure with any of these devices as soon as I wake up in the morning.

You can also use blue light therapy on a sunless day, when afternoon sleepiness and mild amounts of seasonal affective disorder would normally set in. This often eliminates the need for a nap.

Occasionally, I've gotten into a pattern of waking up at about 5:30 a.m., when I'd rather sleep until 6:30 a.m. Each time, I've pulled myself out of that pattern by getting up at 5:30 a.m., avoiding sun exposure, and then, at 6:30 a.m. (the time I'd rather be waking up), putting myself through a ten- to thirty-minute light exposure protocol. So in this way, I can shift my circadian rhythm forward or backward.

You can also use light therapy if you've traveled to the west. Say you have a party, dinner, social event, conference, speech, or meeting at 7 p.m., which for you, if you come from the east, would be 10 p.m. You could use blue light beforehand for a quick blast of energy as an alternative to caffeine or some other stimulant. However, I avoid using it in a situation like this since I don't want to shift my circadian rhythm too far forward in the evening. I just like my sleep too much.

You already understand the importance of light in amplifying your morning cortisol levels. But you might live somewhere or have a life that doesn't allow for adequate morning sun exposure. In this case, you can use a special alarm clock that simulates sunrise, along with a light-therapy box that you can set on your desk or kitchen table in the morning.

Two light tools that I recommend are:

- NatureBright's SunTouch for morning-light therapy
- A sunrise alarm clock for waking

Sunrise alarm clocks are also great for waking children in a nondisruptive manner compared to a loud alarm. It should go without saying that you shouldn't use this kind of light therapy at night unless you're attempting to hack shift work by trying to convince your body that it's day when it's night and vice versa[3,8]. In that case, being exposed to light while working at night would be one way to mitigate the biological effects of shift work on your body.

2. Dark

You also now understand the importance of limiting artificial light at night, especially after sunset. In addition to keeping a TV out of your bedroom and keeping the laptop, tablet, and e-reader out of your bed or dimmed as low as possible, you can use the following tools to produce darkness:

- Dream Essentials or SleepNumber contoured face mask (both come with earplugs to enhance silence, or you can use wax earplugs, as I do). If you really want to go nuts with a sleep mask, look up SleepWithRemee.com, which has a sleep mask that induces lucid dreaming.
- Install f.lux (getflux.com) on your computer to dim the screen at night.
- Wear blue-light-blocking glasses, especially for evening computer use. I recommend Gunnar brand (because they actually look cool) or a custom-designed set of Irlen glasses (see BenGreenfieldFitness.com/vision).
- Use blackout curtains in your bedroom.
- Put a blue-light-blocker screen on your computer.
- If you really want to geek out, install low-blue lightbulbs in your home (or at least in your bedroom). I use the bulbs from Lighting Science.

If you want to argue that our ancestors slept under the stars and therefore these darkness-creating tools are necessary, I am totally willing to agree—as long as you go to sleep relatively close to sunset and wake at sunrise. I don't know about you, but I personally don't have that kind of discipline.

3. Sound

If you live in a noisy neighborhood or a train passes by your house at midnight, 2 a.m., and 5 a.m. (as it does by mine), then you may need some help blocking out noise. In this case, you can:

- Use a white noise app such as SleepStream (which "silences" barking dogs, crying kids, sirens, airplanes, and the like).
- Use the Dream Essentials or SleepNumber contoured face mask or sleep mask with earplugs to block light and sound.

But sounds can go way above and beyond simple white noise. If you understand how sound and music affect your brain waves, you can use this knowledge to alter your mental and physical performance states with laserlike accuracy. It sounds geeky, but I'm going to explain how.

At first glance, it can be a bit intimidating to try to understand how brain waves work. But here are the basics: Your brain is made up of billions of cells. These are your neurons, and they (like the rest of your body) use electricity to communicate with one another. As you can probably imagine, billions of neurons sending signals at the same time produces an enormous amount of electrical activity in your brain, which can be measured with electroencephalography (EEG)[4].

As discussed in chapter 4, when you graph the electrical activity of your brain using EEG, you generate a brain-wave pattern, which creates a "wave" pattern because of its cyclic nature[18]. (Refer to Figure 4-3 on page 91.)

Most of us spend most of our lives primarily in a beta-brain-wave state—aroused, alert, concentrated, but also somewhat stressed. But when we lower the brain-wave frequency to alpha, we put ourselves in an ideal state to learn new information, perform more elaborate tasks, learn languages, analyze complex situations, and even be in what sports psychologists call "the zone," which is a state of heightened focus and performance. This is partly because the slightly decreased electrical activity in the brain can lead to significant increases in feel-good brain chemicals like endorphins, norepinephrine, and dopamine.

You can also lull your brain into producing delta or theta waves. For example, when you meditate, you are focusing on something, whether it's a candle flame, your breath, a mantra, or a prayer. When you focus like that, the electrical patterns in your brain slow down, and the amplitude of your brain waves generally stabilizes into a relaxed range. But it turns out that you don't need to be a monk to achieve this state.

Instead, you can use what's called "brain-wave entrainment" to get the same effect. Brain-wave entrainment is any method that brings your brain-wave frequencies into step with a specific frequency. It's based on the concept that the human brain has a tendency to shift its dominant EEG frequency toward the frequency of a dominant external stimulus (such as that of music or other sound).

The type of sound frequencies that are typically used in brain-wave entrainment are called "binaural" beats. The way these work is that two tones close in frequency generate a beat frequency at the difference of the frequencies[22].

It's not as complicated as it sounds. For example, a 495-hertz audio tone and a 505-hertz audio tone (whether overlaid in music or in a sound frequency) produces a 10-hertz beat, which is roughly in the middle of the alpha-brain-wave range (see Figure 10-2).

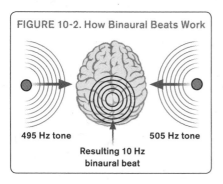

FIGURE 10-2. How Binaural Beats Work

495 Hz tone   505 Hz tone

Resulting 10 Hz
binaural beat

In my podcast episode "How You Can Use Sound and Music to Change Your Brain Waves with Laser Accuracy and Achieve Huge Focus and Performance Gains" at BenGreenfieldFitness.com, I interviewed Dr. Jeffrey Thompson from the Center for Neuroacoustic Research, and we discussed how you can use binaural beat-creating strategies like these:

- The pzizz iPhone app, which I've found works really well for short naps but not so well for long nights. You need to use it five to ten times in a row before your brain gets "trained."

- Dr. Thompson's *Delta Sleep System* CDs/MP3 downloads, which you can play as background music in your bedroom to lull you to sleep.

- The Superhuman Entrainer tracks, which are normally packaged with a grounding wristband but can also be purchased separately for about five bucks.

I also have a homemade sleep playlist, which has been very successful in helping me sleep, especially when I'm hyped up from work or on an airplane. It is designed to enhance delta-wave production, and to put it together all I did was:

- I spent 99 cents for a two-hour-long track called "3 Hz Binaural Pure Sine Delta Wave and Rain for Deep Sleep."
- Then I put four tracks from Superhuman Entrainer at SuperhumanEncoder.com (for a total of eight hours) on an iTunes playlist that begins with a free twenty-minute meditation and relaxation podcast called "ZZZZZZ . . . ," by Stin Hansen, that I downloaded from iTunes.

And that's it! This is the sound strategy that has worked best for me. Finally, if wearing headphones while you sleep is uncomfortable for you, try cozy SleepPhones. I put links to all these resources on the web page for this chapter, along with a link to SleepStream, my favorite sleep app of late, which allows you to create and mix your own sleep tracks.

4. Grounding

I spend about 90 percent of my time barefoot or wearing grounded shoes or sandals, sleeping with a grounding device under my mattress, and wearing a grounding wristband. This may seem strange, but grounding is one of the best sleep- and recovery-hacking strategies I know.

The idea behind grounding, or earthing, is that the surface of the Earth emits a natural magnetic frequency that assists with our circadian rhythm, hormonal cycles, and absorption of negatively charged free electrons (which can mitigate oxidation, stress, etc.)[7]. Dr. Jack Kruse, a brilliant neurosurgeon, wrote a really good blog post about grounding called "EMF—Does Your Rolex Work?" and has a wealth of other excellent resources on EMF in our free biohacking boot camp at www.JackKruse.com/BenGreenfieldFitness.

Since most of us spend a lot of time indoors wearing shoes, not touching the ground or grass, we are missing the benefit of the Earth's frequency. Using a mattress or mat wired to the Earth through an outlet is one way to tap into it and become "grounded."

Back in the early days of my website, when I was curious about how Tour de France cyclists make it through those grueling stages day after day, I interviewed Dr. Jeff Spencer, who said that professional cycling teams use grounding or earthing mats at the Tour to recover more quickly while they sleep. So if you live in or are traveling in Europe or Asia, I recommend that you use a grounding mat or grounding bedspread. I link to a few good brands on the web page for this chapter.

Another even more powerful way to ground is through devices that emit the same magnetic frequency as the Earth. The electromagnetic device under my mattress is an EarthPulse, and you can listen to a podcast I did about it at BenGreenfieldFitness.com/pulsepodcast.

I also wear a grounding device on my wrist 24/7 called the Superhuman Encoder (SuperhumanEncoder.com), which is embedded with a quartz crystal that releases that same 7.38-hertz frequency as the Earth. Dozens of users have said that enhanced sleep is consistently the most notable effect of wearing the wristband.

Then there's the BioMat mattress, which will set you back several thousand dollars but beats the pants off a grounding or earthing mat, for reasons you'll learn about in just a moment.

And what about those grounding shoes or sandals? I wear a brand called Pluggz and occasionally run in Earth Runners. Here's how grounding shoes work: Black plugs made from a carbon-and-rubber compound are placed in the soles under a weight-bearing part of the feet, ensuring electrical contact between the wearer and the Earth. The plugs, designed to conduct a flow of free electrons from the Earth to your body, allow you to become grounded when you walk on grass, sand, soil—or even concrete.

Finally, you can watch the amazing documentary *Grounded,* which tells the story of an entire town—Haines, Alaska—where lives were changed and health dramatically improved after people became grounded. I highly recommend that you add this film to your must-see list.

Dr. James Oschman, the scientist behind much of the research in the film, says that grounding is "probably the most important discovery since penicillin." You can watch the entire film for free at GroundedFilm.com.

Nine Supplements to Help You Sleep Better

A variety of supplements can be used to enhance sleep. They require some degree of self-experimentation, because certain ones work for some people and others don't. This is because light sleep, insomnia, or trouble getting to sleep can be dependent on a variety of factors—such as neurotransmitter balance, mineral deficiencies, leptin insensitivity, and melatonin secretion.

I've used way too many sleep supplements. From regular Valium use to the more natural, safe, and healthy methods I outline below, I've tried just about everything. This is probably partly because I'm knee-deep in the supplement industry and have been my own guinea pig, and partly because of my hard-charging lifestyle and occasional evenings spent staying up late, staring at a computer screen, and writing chapters like this.

So I tend to take advantage of "better living through science" for help getting to or enhancing sleep. These are my top nine sleep supplements and natural remedies—I provide links for all of them on the web page for this chapter, and I'm working on a sublingual spray that incorporates most of these ingredients (stay tuned to the Ben-GreenfieldFitness.com newsletter to find out when I finish that):

1. **NatureCBD.** Cannabidiol (CBD), the non-psychoactive, 100 percent legal ingredient from the hemp plant, activates the same adenosine receptors as caffeine, a stimulant. But when I heard that several patients with sleep issues reported that ingesting a CBD-rich tincture or extract a few hours before bedtime has a balancing effect that facilitates a good night's sleep, I tried it myself, and it worked amazingly well. Then I designed my own formulation that combines CBD with magnesium, lemon balm, and ashwaganda: all known relaxation, destressing, and sleep aids. You can learn more about these capsules at BenGreenfieldFitness.com/CBD.

2. **Sleep Cocktail.** Dr. Kirk Parsley's Sleep Cocktail is a sleep product designed to meet the needs of the world's most elite organization: the U.S. Navy SEALs. He designed the product to compensate for the toxic environment that SEALs frequently find themselves living in: high stress, heavily processed foods, and insufficient sleep. It is simply very small amounts of the nutrients involved in the production of melatonin, specifically L-tryptophan, 5-HTP, vitamin D_3, magnesium, and a very small dose of melatonin. Since an increase in brain GABA levels is also a normal player in the initiation of sleep, Dr. Parsley has included a small amount of a GABA that can cross into the brain, called phGABA. The quantities of each ingredient are intended to replenish normal levels of these nutrients to allow for the normal production of melatonin and to help initiate the cascade of events that lead to deep, natural sleep. If you use any supplement strategy at all and want to keep things simple, simply combine one or two packets of this stuff with two or three capsules of NatureCBD and you'll be out like a baby. Learn more at BenGreenfieldFitness.com/sleepcocktail.

3. **Potassium citrate, 400–500 milligrams.** Earlier, I mentioned Morvan's syndrome, an autoimmune disease that destroys the brain's potassium channels, which leads to severe insomnia and death[15]. Don't worry: If you need potassium citrate to get to sleep, it doesn't mean that you have a fatal autoimmune disease. But it may mean that you have a mineral imbalance, and potassium citrate can help address that and relax you. Potassium is most effective when balanced with magnesium, so you should combine it with 400–500 milligrams Natural Calm magnesium, taken about a half-hour to an hour before bed. Back off the dosage if you get loose stool. If the magnesium citrate in Natural Calm upsets your stomach, try magnesium glycinate or magnesium taurate. And if you want sleep along with a glorious morning bowel movement, use oxygenated magnesium in the form of $MagO_2$. I link to some good brands on the web page for this chapter.

4. **Two to three tablespoons MCT oil or coconut oil a half-hour to an hour before bed.** This works well if food cravings keep you awake, since it provides a slow-burning source of fat fuel and you won't get the insulin spike you'd get from carbohydrates or protein (if you recall from the explanation of circadian rhythm, this insulin spike can shut down leptin production). These oils works well if you're on a diet or have really turned up the volume on your physical activity; it's a strategy I use when I'm in the throes of Ironman training.

5. **Millennium Sport's Somnidren-GH.** Somnidren, a powder that you dissolve under your tongue, works really well at the end of a hard workout day as long as you haven't eaten within two hours of taking it—it doesn't work if your insulin levels are elevated. One of the most important hormones secreted by the pituitary gland while you sleep is growth hormone. Somnidren-GH supports growth hormone secretion by supporting GABA, dopamine, serotonin, and acetylcholine neurotransmitters while inhibiting a compound called somatostatin, which can inhibit some of this neurotransmitter action. If you use this stuff, you can build up tolerance relatively quickly, so you have to cycle it with a maximum of five days on and a minimum of two days off to maintain sensitivity to it.

6. **Hammer REM Caps.** A dose of Hammer REM caps contains three milligrams of melatonin, and I take one dose for two to three days upon arrival at my destination when I'm traveling and crossing several time zones. I'm OK with this dosage of melatonin when traveling, but I don't recommend it for long periods of time, because you don't want to inhibit your body's natural ability to produce melatonin[1]. As with any melatonin supplement, you should take these caps an hour before bed—because if a large, uncontrolled surge of melatonin hits your bloodstream while you're sleeping, it can actually wake you up. Hammer REM Caps also contain the natural relaxants valerian root and 5-HTP.

7. **Greenfield Fitness Systems Sleep Pack.** I custom-designed this supplement to balance hormones early in the day, then relax you in the evening. The Sleep Pack contains thirty packets of TianChi, a complex of Chinese adaptogenic herbs, and sixteen ounces of powdered Natural Calm magnesium citrate[3]. This is the only sleep supplement I use every day no matter what the time of year. Simply take one TianChi in the early or midmorning and then 400–500 milligrams (about a heaping tablespoon) of Natural Calm a half-hour to an hour before bed.

8. **Inner Peace.** Inner Peace is a potent adaptogenic-herb complex that is particularly useful if you need rest during or at the end of a very stressful day. The first time I took this stuff just before lunch, I curled up after eating and fell asleep for nearly three hours. After several repeats of Inner Peace, my adrenals stabilized, and the naps settled down to a saner forty to sixty minutes. Inner Peace is nearly identical to TianChi (and produced by the same manufacturer), but it contains no caffeine. This makes it especially useful for afternoon naps or for people who are suffering from adrenal fatigue and shouldn't go anywhere near a central nervous system stimulant like caffeine. I take Inner Peace before or after lunch three or four times week, usually on my more stressful workdays.

9. **Three thousand milligrams tyrosine plus 300 milligrams 5-HTP.** If your lack of sleep or trouble getting to sleep is due to neurotransmitter imbalances, the cause is probably a toxic lifestyle, overtraining, relationship stress, gut stress, or a poor diet[7]. These are all issues that eventually need to be addressed, but in the meantime, if you're struggling with depression and mood disorders along with a lack of sleep and you need a fix while you're addressing the other major issues, it can be very helpful to take three daily doses of 1,000 milligrams tyrosine and 100 milligrams 5-HTP. I don't use this combination personally, but I have several clients who have struggled with a combination of mood, emotional, and sleep disorders, and this strategy has helped them tremendously. In the brain section of this book, you'll find a list of supplements that are designed with the best ratios for specific neurotransmitters.

Ten Tips for Conquering the Nap

As I mentioned earlier, I nap for twenty to forty minutes nearly every day, usually by curling up with my twin boys in their tiny bed for a postlunch siesta. This nap makes a huge difference in my afternoon work productivity and quality.

Research on napping has shown that siestas tend to be very rich in non-rapid-eye-movement sleep, which you'll learn about shortly. A nap yields a significant increase in alertness, creativity, recall, and memory in the second half of the day. Naps also help reduce waking blood pressure and significantly improve cardiovascular health[16]. Well-timed napping can also significantly combat sleep deprivation. So when you miss a good night of sleep for one reason or another, napping can help you dig out of a sleep-deprivation hole. On the flip side, poorly timed naps (in the late afternoon or evening) can actually worsen insomnia and decrease alertness later in the day, which is why curling up for a nap before dinner is usually not a good idea.

What are some other napping dos and don'ts? Here are my top ten tips for conquering the nap:

1. **Don't use an alarm clock unless you absolutely have to.** Once you begin a healthy napping habit, your body will naturally wake in twenty to sixty minutes. Why shouldn't you use an alarm clock? I'm a fan of the disk and RAM metaphor used by SuperMemo (www.super-memory.com/articles/sleep.htm):

We can compare the brain and its NREM-REM sleep cycles to an ordinary PC. During the day, while learning and experiencing new things, you store your new data in RAM memory. During the night, while first in NREM, you write the data down to the hard disk. During REM, which follows NREM in the night, you do the disk defragmentation, i.e. you organize data, sort them, build new connections, etc. Overnight, you repeat the write-and-defragment cycle until all RAM data is neatly written to the disk (for long-term use), and your RAM is clear and ready for a new day of learning. Upon waking up, you reboot the computer. If you reboot early with the use of an alarm clock, you often leave your disk fragmented. Your data access is slow, and your thinking is confused. Even worse, some of the data may not even get written to the disk. It is as if you have never stored it in RAM in the first place. In conclusion, if you use an alarm clock, you endanger your data.

There are also biological implications from using an alarm clock. Just like a slap in the face or a bucket of cold water, an alarm clock quickly wakes you up and gives you an immediate, unnatural injection of stressful adrenaline and cortisol.
As an alarm clock alternative for both naps and nighttime sleep, I use an EarthPulse (the PEMF device I place under my mattress) to lull my brain into delta-wave production and then ease it back into alpha-wave production at about the point I want to wake up. If you must use an alarm clock, use the type that gradually wakes you up, such as the SunRise Alarm Clock, the Sleep Time by Azumio iPhone app, or the Sleep as Android app.

2. **Do time your nap.** You should ideally take your nap when you are the least alert, which is typically seven to eight hours after you wake. For example, I wake at 6 a.m. and generally have my best naps at around 1 p.m. Based on sleep lab research, two other very good times for a nap are 11 a.m. and 3 p.m.

3. **Don't drink coffee or caffeinated drinks before your nap.** It's a myth that if you drink these beverages before a nap, the caffeine will hit your bloodstream as you're waking up. Even tiny amounts of caffeine in your system can significantly

mess with sleep quality, especially if you are a "fast caffeine responder," which you can test with genetic testing via a company like 23andme.

4. **Do sleep more if you find yourself taking long naps.** If you nap for more than about an hour and a half, you probably are not getting enough sleep at night, or you have some adrenal fatigue that you need to address.

5. **Do avoid stress for an hour or two before napping.** I try to schedule my lowest-stress activities right before my nap. For me, this typically means office and household duties, like rearranging my desk or cleaning the garage, reading and writing, or eating lunch—definitely not doing phone consults or responding to e-mail.

6. **Don't exercise immediately before your nap.** Naps can assist with exercise recovery, but try to finish working out at least forty-five minutes before your nap.

7. **Do eat before your nap.** Don't go down for a nap hungry, as hypoglycemia can disrupt sleep. This is why a postlunch siesta can be so effective.

8. **Don't force it.** If you try for a month and you simply can't nap no matter what you do, don't force it or fret about it. Just go back to your regular routine, and pay attention to what you'll learn about free-running sleep below.

9. **Do have a napping ritual.** Whenever possible, nap at the same time of day, and focus on a similar pre-nap sequence each day (for example, work, exercise, shower, eat, nap).

10. **Don't use alcohol or sedatives to initiate a nap.** In other words, having a couple glasses of wine at lunchtime is not a good pre-nap idea; it can cause you to wake feeling very sluggish and fatigued.

Free-Running Sleep

I do not personally use "polyphasic" sleep (which I'll explain in a moment) or any fancy timed-sleep patterns that seem to be becoming common among biohackers. I've experimented with those techniques and sleep hacks and found them to be rigid and unnatural. Instead, I simply sleep when I am tired. For me, this means that I go to bed at around 10, wake up at around 6, and nap after lunch.

My personal sleep patterns are based on a concept called free-running sleep, and no discussion of sleeping and napping would be complete without mentioning it. Free-running sleep is simply sleep that is not artificially controlled to accommodate strict schedules and that does not require alarm clocks or sleeping pills. From an ancestral standpoint, free-running sleep is far more natural: Until the advent of electricity and rigid postindustrial work and school start times, humans were free to sleep when they were tired.

Although your lifestyle and work obligations may prevent you from experiencing 100 percent free-running sleep, the formula is fairly simple and is one you should adhere to whenever possible. For healthy and refreshing sleep during the day or night, go to sleep only when you are tired, not earlier or later, and wake naturally without an alarm clock. Of course, your sleep cycles and periods of tiredness, sleeping, and waking will vary with the seasons, travel, diet, and daily activity levels, so just listen to your body and sleep when you are tired.

If you combine free-running sleep with (1) eliminating artificial lighting after sunset and (2) avoiding excessive nighttime eating, 99 percent of your sleep problems could be eliminated.

And what about polyphasic sleep, a trendy concept that has cropped up in several blogs and books on biohacking? The idea behind polyphasic sleep (in contrast to biphasic sleep of twice per day or monophasic sleep of once per day) is that you can gain productive waking hours by sleeping a total of just three hours per twenty-four-hour daily cycle, split into six sleeping spurts interspersed throughout the day[2]. There are many other variants of polyphasic sleep, but with what you've already learned about the body's natural circadian rhythm, you can probably imagine how disruptive polyphasic sleep can be—especially because of the nearly complete loss of deep, healing, restorative REM (rapid eye movement) sleep.

So while I certainly agree that polyphasic sleep can help you get through a short period of sleep deprivation, such as finals week, a project deadline, temporary travel or relationship stress, or any other life equivalent of a Navy SEAL's Hell Week, the cons definitely outweigh the pros when it comes to making polyphasic sleep a consistent lifestyle choice.

If you want to learn more about the dangers of polyphasic sleep, I recommend the article at goo.gl/JIYj6.

Six Ways to Track Your Sleep

To see if you're actually sleeping as much as you think you might be (you'd be surprised at how little you might be sleeping, even if you're lying in bed for eight hours), or to see how the supplements and strategies listed so far are affecting your sleep, you can track your sleep cycle using a variety of different tools.

I'm not even going to pretend that I log my sleep cycles every night. I'm not that anal. I don't count my calories, either. But I did log my sleep cycles for one month to see what was happening, just as I counted my calories for one year to get an idea of how many calories are in the foods I eat. However, if you're anything like me, once you get a good idea of what is happening to your body based on the lifestyle choices you make, you don't have tons of precious time to spend testing and tracking. So think of tracking as a temporary educational tool.

But should you decide that you want an insider's glimpse into your sleep cycles, here are six recommendations for tracking your sleep. (Of course, if you use a phone next to or in your bed, be sure to leave it in airplane mode to reduce your exposure to wireless signals and ensure that phone calls and text messages don't disrupt your sleep.)

1. Sleep Time iPhone App by Azumio

Sleep Time by Azumio monitors and analyzes your sleep cycles to wake you during the lightest sleep phase, allowing you to feel more rested and relaxed when you awaken. Like many sleep monitors, it utilizes your iPhone's accelerometer to sense your movements and graph your sleep cycles through the night. For example, you can set a window of up to thirty minutes, and if the alarm is set for 7 a.m., the app will wake you between 6:30 and 7 a.m., ensuring that you don't wake quite as cranky as you might with a blaring alarm clock.

The app, which you place near you when you sleep (no additional equipment required),

FIGURE 10-3. Sleep Time iPhone App

also measures your sleep efficiency—which is an algorithm based on how much time you've spent in light sleep and deep sleep and how much time you were awake while you were in bed. You can see a sample screenshot in Figure 10-3.

2. Sleep by MotionX iPhone App

Sleep by MotionX is another sleep-cycle analyzer. You simply launch the app and attach your iPhone to your arm with an armband or set the phone next to you while you're sleeping. This app tracks your movements and uses that information to calculate the amount of time you spend in deep sleep, in light sleep, or awake. Like the Sleep Time app, it has an alarm that wakes you up at the right time in your sleep cycle. It also logs your sleep patterns so you can analyze how deeply you sleep. Compared with Azumio's app, MotionX's has more powerful graphing and visualization features, a heart-rate-monitoring log tool, and the ability to be used as a GPS during runs or bike rides.

3. SleepBot for Android

This app tracks your sleep, but it also tracks overnight movement and even auto-records sounds so you can hear whether you're snoring or having breathing problems overnight. Since sleep apnea is occasionally an issue in sleep disruption, and it can be hard to know whether you have snoring or breathing issues, this feature can come in handy—especially if you don't have a sleeping partner who will complain about your log-sawing. The app interface is packed with useful tips to help improve your sleep hygiene and help you fall asleep faster; there's a widget that lets you "clock in" and "clock out" when you go to bed; and, like the other comparable apps, it has a detailed sleep-analysis feature.

4. Sleep as Android

Sleep as Android was originally designed to wake you up when your sleep cycle says it's the best time for you to rise. But the app has evolved a bit and will now warn you if you're operating at a sleep deficit and you need to get back into a more optimal sleeping pattern. Similar to SleepBot, this app also pays attention to the sounds in your room to catch you snoring, record you talking in your sleep, or help you diagnose sleep apnea—and graph your sleep cycles.

5. Under-Mattress Sleep Tracking Devices

Many of the newer sleep devices that are even more accurate than apps or wearables simply attach to your pillow or slip under your mattress. For example, the Aura is a kit for those who regularly suffer from poor sleep. It works by tracking your sleep patterns and then waking you up during your lightest sleep phase. The visible part of the system is a strange-looking bedside lamp that monitors your sleeping environment (noise pollution and temperature) while soothing you with New Age sounds and gentle, slowly fluctuating light patterns. A thin sensor pad that you place under your mattress monitors your sleep patterns during the night and sends all the data that it collects (heart rate, motion, and respiration) to the bedside lamp device, which then calculates the most efficient time to gently rouse you.

Then there is the Beddit. Based on something called ballistocardiography (BCG), the Beddit's ultra-thin sensor tucks under the top sheet of your bed and gathers data on sleep quality, duration, heart rate, and respiration rate. It then automatically tracks your sleep without having to be told when you're in bed. The Beddit sensor uses Bluetooth to connect to your smartphone, which harvests the data.

Sense is a sleep tracker that clips onto your pillow. It detects the amount of movement you make during the night. It also gathers information about temperature, ambient light, and even noise to generate a profile of your nightly routine and the sources that might be affecting it.

6. Wearable Sleep-Tracking Devices (Oura, Fitbit, MyBasis, Jawbone, etc.)

These days people wear all sorts of bracelets and clips to keep track of how many steps they take over the course of a day, how active they are, how many calories they eat, and how much they sleep. In the case of a Fitbit, which costs $100, you place the clip on the wristband that comes with it and set it to sleep mode. It then tracks your movements overnight, telling you whether you get up and move around and whether you're awake but tossing and turning. You turn it off in the morning, sync it with the website or app, and get a complete report of how well you slept, along with how many times you woke up and when you were active. The Jawbone UP is similar but, at $197, more expensive. However, the battery lasts longer, and the app has more features. A host of other wearable devices are hitting the market (one very unique one is a ring called the Oura), and they make it easier than an app to remember to track your activity, diet, sleep, and so on.

If you want to quantify every aspect of your life, these devices are great—but if you simply want to get a few quick glances at your sleep cycle, an app is a far less expensive option. I also question the accuracy of these devices for very active people. I've found that wearables like Oura, MyBasis, Jawbone, and Fitbit seem to overestimate calories burned and are less GPS accurate than devices from Timex, Polar, and Garmin, among others.

Because of rapid advances in hardware and software technology, new sleep-tracking tools are always emerging; to stay abreast of the latest sleep-tracking technologies, you can follow a blog such as *Lifehacker* (lifehacker.com) or *Wareable* (wareable.com). And if you really want to geek out on sleep, you can get overnight sleep diagnostic testing, which is performed at sleep clinics and is considered the gold standard in sleep quantification and analysis. Go to BenGreenfieldFitness.com and listen to my interview with Dr. Joe Zelk or read the guest article he wrote. Many universities and hospitals have sleep clinics; Stanford's Sleep Disorders Clinic is recognized as one of the most advanced facilities in the world, and Dr. Zelk's company at SleepMedicineGroup. com will send similar sleep-lab sleep-tracking hardware to your home.

What Are the Stages of Sleep?

Many of the tracking devices I've described will give you feedback about your sleep stages. As more and more people are tracking their sleep patterns, I am getting more and more questions from athletes about what these stages mean and how long they should be in each stage. So here's a basic overview:

There are two main types of sleep:

- Non-rapid-eye-movement (NREM) sleep (also known as quiet sleep)

- Rapid-eye-movement (REM) sleep (also known as active sleep)

During the early phases of sleep, you are still relatively awake and alert. Your brain is producing small and fast beta waves, and as your brain begins to relax and slow down, you begin to produce more alpha waves. As you make that transition into alpha-wave production, you typically get what's known as a "myoclonic jerk," or an uncontrollable contraction of your limbs. You may also experience hypnagogic hallucinations, such as feeling like you are falling or hearing someone call your name[13]. And then you get into the first stage.

- **Stage 1** is a relatively light stage of sleep in which your brain produces high-amplitude theta waves, which are very slow brain waves. This period lasts only about five to ten minutes.

- **Stage 2** lasts for about twenty minutes. In this stage, your brain begins to produce bursts of rapid, rhythmic brain-wave activity known as sleep spindles. This is when your body temperature begins to decrease and your heart rate begins to slow.

- **Stage 3** is when slow delta brain waves begin to emerge and is a transitional period between light sleep and very deep sleep.

- **Stage 4** is often referred to as delta sleep because so many delta waves are produced during this stage. It is deep sleep that lasts for about thirty minutes.

- **Stage 5** is when most dreaming occurs; it is known REM sleep. REM sleep is characterized by rapid eye movement, increased respiration rate, and increased brain activity. This is when much of your nervous system repair and recovery takes place. During REM sleep, your brain and other body systems become more active, while your muscles become more relaxed and nearly paralyzed.

The important thing to know is that sleep does not progress through these stages in sequence. You begin in stage 1 and progress into stages 2, 3, and 4. After stage 4 sleep, you return to stage 3 and then stage 2 sleep before you gradually progress back into REM sleep. Once REM sleep is over, your body usually returns to stage 2 sleep.

FIGURE 10-4. Sleep Stages Through the Night

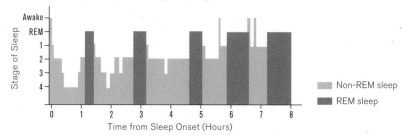

Depending on how long you sleep, you cycle through these stages about four or five times throughout the night (see Figure 10-4). An ideal night of sleep for most people is comprised of five cycles.

On average, you enter the REM stage about ninety minutes after falling asleep. You'll notice if you're tracking your sleep that the first cycle of REM sleep might last only briefly, but each cycle becomes progressively longer (especially if your body is in desperate need of repair and recovery), and REM sleep can often last up to an hour as the night progresses.

Five Ways to Eliminate Insomnia

If you follow all the instructions for sleep improvement I've given up to this point, it's highly likely that you're never going to have to deal with insomnia again. Once you've darkened your room, eliminated bright screens and electromagnetic frequencies, introduced smart sleep supplementation into your protocol, and given yourself license to engage in free-running sleep whenever possible, insomnia typically becomes a nonissue.

But let's say you are already using every imaginable sleep hack and you still can't get to sleep. In other words, for some reason you're still experiencing full-blown insomnia, which is driving you nuts and ruining your productivity, your relationships, and your life.

For that worst-case scenario of debilitating insomnia, I offer five strategies that will either free up the body's energy flow and unblock the meridians (energy pathways commonly used in Chinese medicine) that are interfering with sleep or eliminate hidden sleep stealers.

1. Eliminate Parasites

Prepare to be grossed out.

Intestinal parasites, which you can pick up from water, dirty food, or even public toilets, can affect your central nervous system and prevent your body from performing its normal bodily routines during sleep[4]. A parasite introduces toxins into your body that could cause restlessness and a shaky feeling, making it difficult to rest and sleep. And when you do finally get to sleep, a parasite can keep your liver from efficiently detoxing your body. When you combine this with the fact that most parasites are very active in your gut at night, normal deep sleep becomes very difficult.

I've had parasitic infections twice, probably from swimming in nasty water when I raced in triathlons overseas. In both cases, about every two weeks like clockwork, when the parasites were hatching, I had extremely restless nights. In both cases, I was able to identify the parasites using an at-home poop test, eliminated the parasites using an intestinal cleanse, and started sleeping like a baby again. To see how I did that, check out BenGreenfieldFitness.com/gutvideo.

Hey, I warned you about the gross-out factor!

2. Get Rid of Overtraining

As you learned in chapter 7, having trouble getting to sleep, tossing and turning throughout the night, and waking up much earlier than usual (early stages of over-training) or much later than usual (later stages of overtraining) can all be signs of inadequate recovery or adrenal fatigue.

In the early stages of overtraining, this type of insomnia is usually accompanied by a daily "tired but wired" feeling: You get really tired at night, but you simply can't fall asleep because it feels like your mind and body are racing. In the later stages of overtraining, insomnia becomes a nonissue, as you tend to simply fall asleep, stay asleep, sleep late, but never feel recovered no matter what you do because your body has been depleted of the building blocks necessary for nighttime repair.

The fix for overtraining was outlined at the end of chapter 8, so go back and read up!

3. Reduce Nighttime Stress

It's no secret that work and lifestyle stress can keep you awake at night. In the last chapter, you learned about many stress-control methods, but the very best insomnia-beating nighttime-stress-control strategy I've found is simply to have a "hard stop" at least sixty minutes before bed. This is when you completely stop responding to e-mail, thinking about work, paying bills, studying, or doing any task that is mentally demanding or even mildly stimulating. From this point until bedtime, you do can read for pleasure, play an instrument, have sex, watch something funny (with your blue-light-blocking glasses and screen dimmer, of course), or simply chill.

4. Try Acupuncture

It may not seem possible that poking fine needles into your body could somehow help you sleep better, but a 1999 study found that acupuncture improved sleep quality in normal people with insomnia[8]. A 2004 study found that acupuncture can increase evening melatonin production and total sleep time, and patients who received acupuncture in this study fell asleep faster, were less restless at night, and experienced less stress[14]. The researchers concluded that "acupuncture treatment may be of value for some categories of anxious patients with insomnia."

Another study found that acupuncture improves sleep quality in patients with HIV, a condition that can cause insomnia[9]. This makes sense, because an added benefit of acupuncture is relief from chronic pain, which is a common contributor to sleeplessness.

5. Address Mineral Imbalances

As you learned in chapter 8, correcting mineral imbalances can be a good way to fight adrenal fatigue. If your sleeplessness or insomnia is accompanied by a feeling of blood pounding in your ears as you try to fall asleep or by a rapid, annoying heart rate, it may be because you're in an early stage of adrenal fatigue, you have a mineral imbalance, or you've sweated out too many electrolytes in the day or week of training[6].

I've found that if I'm sleepless, getting out of bed and having one to two teaspoons (yes, that's three to six grams!) of an extremely mineral-rich sea salt can help tremendously.

My top three choices are:

- **Basic Himalayan sea salt:** You can order this online or find it at the grocery store. The sources of this salt can be iffy, and it's not as high quality as the other two options, but in a pinch (pun intended) the stuff is decent.

- **Himalayan salt:** The salt deposits from which this salt is mined were laid down long before the Earth became polluted with heavy metals, pesticides, and PCBs, so this is fairly pristine stuff. It can be pricey, but it's a better choice if you're concerned about quality.

- **Aztec sea salt:** Coarse, flavorful, natural, organically harvested, and artisanal Aztec sea salt is higher in minerals than the other two types. It is the gold standard of salt, and although it's expensive, I always keep some in my pantry.

- **Trace liquid minerals:** Plant-sourced trace liquid minerals are simply a purified-water extraction of soluble plant-derived minerals. The minerals are sourced from plant deposits called senonian vegetate, which are mineral-rich organic soils derived from plants and naturally protected from mineral depletion. This means you get a very high level of absorption and assimilation.

You can mix any of these salts or mineral sources into a glass of water before bed or postworkout. Fortunately, all of them are delicious on food, too. I link to my favorite brands at BeyondTrainingBook.com/Chapter10.

Eleven Ways to Beat Jet Lag

If you're a triathlete or marathoner or you travel a lot for business or for events and races where your body is expected to perform optimally, jet lag can be extremely annoying.

The symptoms include trouble falling asleep (especially if you're flying east); early waking (especially if you're flying west); interrupted sleep with multiple periods of wakefulness; trouble staying asleep; poor concentration and performance on mental tasks; increased fatigue, headaches, and irritability; and problems with digestion, including indigestion, constipation, and even reduced interest in and enjoyment of food.

Similar to the types of sleep problems caused by shift work, jet lag is a "chronobiological" issue that occurs when you travel across many time zones. Your body clock isn't in sync with the destination time because you've experienced daylight and darkness that are contrary to the rhythms to which you've grown accustomed. This upsets your body's natural rhythm, and the problem becomes compounded because the times for eating, sleeping, hormone regulation, and body-temperature variations no longer correspond to what you're used to[17].

So not much beats airplane travel for radiation exposure, full-body inflammation, production of free radicals, wrenches in your recovery process, and an inhibition of important biological processes, from muscle-building protein synthesis to muscle-repairing circadian rhythm.

It doesn't matter how fancy your compression socks are or how many bodyweight squats and calf raises you do in the back of the airplane. When you're on that plane, you're inside a tiny metal tube bombarded by solar radiation and completely disconnected from the Earth's natural magnetic field.

This is compounded by Wi-Fi signals bouncing around the cabin (which are often available during the entire flight), people talking on their phones and checking e-mail inside that metal tube (which happens for the entire gate-to-takeoff and landing-to-gate phases), dehydration from altitude, extremely dry filtered air, toxin-laden airplane food, bad water, germs and airborne pathogens in tight spaces, and—if you're traveling across multiple time zones—a disruption of your natural circadian rhythm.

I don't know about you, but when I'm traveling to races and have to perform at peak capabilities, often just hours after my flight touches down, I simply can't afford the loss of fitness, cellular oxidation, dehydration, and total body damage that can occur every time I hop on a flight to a race. So what can you do about it? Here are eleven ways that peak performers can beat jet lag.

Jet Lag Fix #1: Grounding/Earthing

Grounding (also known as earthing) involves exposing your body to the natural magnetic frequencies released by the Earth. At no time does grounding become a more effective destination strategy than when you're traveling in an airplane, since hurtling through space in a metal tube 40,000 feet above the planet is about as disconnected from the Earth as you can get.

The basic idea is that you aren't able to discharge all the positive ions that build up via cellular metabolism, you aren't able to absorb the negative ions you'd normally get if you were touching the ground, and this ion imbalance decreases the natural electrochemical gradient across your cell membranes, so you get disrupted cellular metabolism and inflammation.

So how do you actually earth or ground? As soon as I land at my destination, I make it a point to either (1) put on a pair of special shoes called Pluggz or sandals called Earth Runners, both of which have carbon plugs in them that allow for grounding without being barefoot or (2) go outside in my bare feet (yes, I'm the guy in spandex or a Speedo doing barefoot yoga in the grassy lot behind the hotel). I also use a device called Earthpulse, which can be placed underneath the mattress to "ground" a bed.

Jet Lag Fix #2: Exercise

Multiple studies have shown that exercise can regulate circadian rhythms. So as lousy and miserable as you may feel training after a long day of travel or a long few days of international travel, the sooner you can vigorously move after arriving at your final destination, the sooner you'll bounce back from jet lag and normalize your circadian rhythm and sleep.

But this doesn't mean you have to do a killer WOD or an epic run when you get to your destination. My top three choices if I'm feeling a bit blah after travel are walking (barefoot if possible) in the sunshine or on a beach, swimming (preferably in relatively cool water, as you'll learn about later), and, as mentioned in Fix #1, outdoor barefoot yoga. Finally, for each hour that I'm sedentary on an airplane, I do fifty air squats near the back of the plane or in any other open space I can find.

Jet Lag Fix #3: Avoid Caffeine

It's a relatively common recommendation for managing jet lag to discourage the consumption of caffeine, alcohol, and other stimulants, and because of their overstimulation of the central nervous system and their potential for disrupting circadian rhythm even more, I absolutely agree.

Aside from the trace amounts of caffeine in the TianChi or dark chocolate that I occasionally consume while traveling, I simply do not go near caffeine or any other central nervous system stimulant while en route to my final destination. Since coffee and adrenal stimulants in high amounts can also inhibit testosterone and other anabolic hormones, this is a very good way to fight against fitness loss from frequent airplane travel.

Jet Lag Fix #4: Melatonin

Because overuse of melatonin makes it possible to shut down the body's natural release of melatonin from the pineal gland, I do not use melatonin unless I'm traveling, in which case I take 1–3 milligrams of liquid melatonin or a use melatonin patch thirty to sixty minutes prior to bed. For a melatonin supplement, I used to use one that had valerian root in it (Hammer REM Caps), but I've switched to using slow-release patches. You can find some of my favorites at BenGreenfieldFitness.com/benrecommends.

This shouldn't be done while you're on a plane but can be useful for rebooting your circadian rhythm upon arrival at your final destination. Melatonin is also a natural anti-inflammatory, which will help decrease inflammation that builds up during air travel.

Jet Lag Fix #5: No-Jet-Lag Supplement

I discovered No-Jet-Lag at a Chinese herbal store in the Hong Kong airport when traveling home from a triathlon in Thailand. After inspecting the ingredient list to verify that there was nothing in it that would kill me, I tried it—following the instructions to take one tablet upon takeoff, one tablet every two to four hours while on the plane, and then one final tablet upon landing.

The stuff works wonderfully, both east-to-west and west-to-east. There are five homeopathic remedies listed as the active ingredients in No-Jet-Lag: arnica montana, bellis perennis, chamomilla, ipecacuanha, and lycopodium.

I'm no homeopathic expert, but my wife and I now use No-Jet-Lag when we are traveling internationally and have found it to be extremely effective in eliminating jet lag symptoms, especially when combined with the other strategies outlined in this section. Now that I'm here on the Onnit Academy, I'm going to give Alpha Brain or 180 a try as a substitute for No-Jet-Lag, since it may work quite similarly.

Jet Lag Fix #6: Water

You've no doubt heard that you lose more water due to the dehydration that occurs while flying in the dry air at altitude—so you obviously need to drink more water to stay hydrated and beat jet lag. But I've been going beyond the normal recommendations and experimenting with very high water intake—and finding that it helps out quite a bit compared with the standard disappointingly tiny cup of water handed to me by the flight attendant every couple of hours.

Instead, I've been drinking closer to 12–16 ounces of water (nearly a full bottle) each hour and feeling a distinct difference in sleep, mood, and energy upon landing. Just make sure to book an aisle seat or, if you're in a window seat, make sure that your aisle-based airline partner is spry and willing to move every time you need to pee—or just politely ask to switch spots.

Jet Lag Fix #7: Cold Showers

Cold showers decrease inflammatory cytokines, assist with the activation of brown adipose tissue for fat burning, and cause a rebound hormone response in the form of a release of adrenaline. I've been going so far as to actually go into an airline lounge in the airport for a ten- to fifteen-minute cold shower if I have a long layover. I also take a two- to five-minute cold shower in the hotel when I arrive at my final destination.

Splashing lots of cold water in your face is OK, but not quite as effective as cold water immersion or showering. Cold showers also have very good blood-vessel-expanding properties because they release more nitric oxide into your blood vessels, and the subsequent increase in glucose and oxygen uptake can dramatically reduce jet lag. For more on the benefits of cold, you can check out the article "Cool Temps for a Hot Body" on T-Nation.

Jet Lag Fix #8: Curcumin

Curcumin—which is found in turmeric and curries—is a powerful antioxidant that helps tremendously when taken on an empty stomach both before and after flying. Because of its ability to cross the blood-brain barrier and shut down inflammatory cytokines in neural tissue, it is a potent brain anti-inflammatory and may also boost testosterone and growth hormone.

I've used about 1,000 milligrams of curcumin from a highly absorbable source. I recommend a brand of highly absorbable curcumin phytosome called Rebound made by EXOS or NatureCBD, which is cannabidiol mixed with curcumin.

Jet Lag Fix #9: No Vegetable Oils

Although it can be difficult while navigating your way through airports full of "healthy" stir-fry and packaged crackers and health bars, you need to completely avoid vegetable oils if you want to avoid the inflammation that can occur during travel. Stay away from roasted or heated seeds and nuts, stir-fries, boxed foods, and just about anything else that contains canola oil, soybean oil, corn oil, sunflower oil, or safflower oil—as "healthy" as the food may be advertised to be.

While the 80/20 rule on vegetable oils may work much of the time, I follow the 100/0 rule when traveling—meaning that vegetable oils make up 0 percent of my diet. That usually means no airplane food for me, and instead lots of raw seeds, nuts, chlorella, spirulina, fresh fruit, avocados, nori, and other healthy, real foods.

Jet Lag Fix #10: Sulfur

Sulfur-containing foods are very good antioxidant precursors, especially for the type of inflammation that can occur when you're on an airplane. These include foods like broccoli, cauliflower, garlic, onions, and Brussels sprouts. Supplements containing glutathione, N-acetyl-cystine, MSM, or DMSO are also effective but can induce nausea, so be careful with them—I don't recommend more than a teaspoon.

Of course, if you opt for the preflight sautéed garlic and onions, you may need to brush your teeth afterward (unless you plan on creating enemies on the plane). But if you squeeze in a few meals containing these foods in the days leading up to the flight, you'll feel much better when you land.

Jet Lag Fix #11: Oxytocin

Finally, oxytocin is an extremely powerful hormone that acts to lift your mood and also acts as a potent antioxidant, antidepressant, and anti-inflammatory. Although it's most commonly known as a hormone that is released after sex in adults and during breastfeeding in babies, you can get your oxytocin hormone fix anywhere and at any time—including while you're traveling.

All you need to do is hug someone or (slightly less effective) warmly shake another person's hand. The simple act of bodily contact will cause your brain to release low levels of anti-inflammatory, mood-boosting oxytocin. So find the first person who's OK with it when you get to your destination and give her a big, loving bear hug. Or do some partner carries up the stairs at the hotel (incidentally, that's a great travel workout). Just brush your teeth first if you used the garlic trick.

Visit BenGreenfieldFitness.com/benrecommends for my latest tips on jet lag and new research that I discover.

I want to finish by giving you some of the best sleep resources I've ever found, because I've really only scratched the surface when it comes to getting better sleep—and I focused primarily on the practical strategies that you can implement right away. Heck, you may want to really geek out and become a true sleep expert.

My first recommendation is a gold mine of a website. I spent nearly a month poring over the information on it—and going deep into everything from advanced sleep hacks to timing naps strategically to perfecting free-running sleep. Although it's quite a lot of information, it will surely satisfy the sleep geek in you and fill in any holes in your understanding of the science of sleep. It's called SuperMemo, and you can go to http://supermemo.com/articles/sleep.htm to check it out now.

My second recommendation is an article on circadian biology by neurosurgeon Jack Kruse, a frequent podcast guest on BenGreenfieldFitness. This article is chock-full of information for geeks and also does an excellent job of delving into the link between hormones, your brain, and sleep. It goes into great detail about how our circadian rhythm is tied to our biology. You can access all of Jack's info at www. JackKruse.com/BenGreenfieldFitness.

My third recommendation is a slightly older book, but still an excellent read on the link between modern living, ancestral health, and sleep. It's called *Lights Out: Sleep, Sugar, and Survival,* by T. S. Wiley, whom I interviewed in a podcast episode on bioidentical hormone replacement (which is another potential sleep strategy). In the book, T. S. talks about how, if you are genetically adapted to cold weather and colder seasons (which defines many European populations) and you tend to eat a higher-carbohydrate diet and get a lot of artificial-light exposure, these things signal to your body that it's constantly summer. When your body thinks it's summer, the naturally higher leptin release that is supposed to occur in cold weather is impeded, as are fat loss, melatonin responsiveness, prolactin release, and DHEA and growth hormone release. Of course, you can put your body into constant-summer mode with something as simple as lots of nighttime Kindle reading while snacking on gluten-free crackers or dried fruit.

Finally, listen to the podcast "How to Sleep Better" at BenGreenfieldFitness.com/pulsepod, in which I interview Paul Becker, the inventor of the EarthPulse device. The guy is eccentric, but he delves into the sleep science of pulsed electromagnetic therapy quite well.

Additional resources, helpful links, scientific references, websites, and surprise bonuses for this chapter are available at BeyondTrainingBook.com/Chapter10. Enjoy.

3

NUTRITION

CHAPTER 11

Forty Easy Meals for Busy Athletes: How to Fuel Your Body with the Thousands of Calories Needed for Endurance and Extreme Exercise without Destroying Your Metabolism

I recently read a Boulder, Colorado, newspaper article titled "How Do Ironman Triathletes Eat?"

The main photo showcased healthy granola, Greek yogurt, and organic peanut butter—considered by many, many folks to be wonderful foods for fueling extreme physical activity. Nothing could be further from the truth. In this chapter, you're going to learn why and what you can do about it to ensure that your body and gut feel flawless when you're exercising.

I'm also going to give you a simple and comprehensive list of easy-to-prepare, quick, and nutrient-dense meals.

And I'm going to share a secret with you: Aside from occasional, lingering sit-down dinners, my personal diet is extremely quick and uncomplicated because I just don't have much time to cook.

As a coach, I scrutinize the diets of many endurance athletes, CrossFitters, weekend warriors, marathoners, cyclists, swimmers, runners, and triathletes. Many eat enough calories to support such an active lifestyle (although some do not—a problem we'll talk about in a bit), but in order to dump that amount of fuel into the body, several inflammatory, joint-aching, gut-disrupting, blood-sugar-spiking foods are dietary staples. These staples include:

- Coffee and a variety of baked goods from the morning swing by the coffee shop, including biscotti, scones, cinnamon rolls, and anything labeled "whole wheat," "whole grain," "fat-free," "healthy," and "energy," especially stamped with a "low-fat" or "healthy" label by the vendor.

- Cereal, including those that feature athletes on the box or claim to be loaded with muesli, whole grains, and added vitamins and minerals, which are usually designed to distract you from ingredients like genetically modified corn and soy or lots and lots of wheat.

- Bagels, including whole wheat, cinnamon raisin, and those with a guilt-free schmear of lite or fat-free cream cheese.

- Muffins, chewy and dense sources of carbohydrate-based energy, created with all the nutrition of a birthday cake.

- Granola, conveniently coated in vegetable oil and syrup or sugar and often washed down with a couple cups of milk or strawberry-banana yogurt.

- Bread—all types, shapes, and sizes, including whole wheat, whole grain, and fiber enriched.

- Energy bars, gummy sugar chews, and sugary sports supplements touted as organic or clean-burning energy sources.

- Cookies, whether the healthy energy kind or the traditional white sugar and trans fats variety.

- Deli meat, a dense and convenient source of 95+ percent fat-free protein.

- Commercial eggs, the fallback source of breakfast protein or a quick postworkout snack.

- Peanut butter and jelly sandwiches—peanut butter on everything, really.

- Pasta in all forms, shapes, sizes, regardless of what it's made of.

- Some type of sweetened dairy product, usually in the form of ice cream, a milkshake, or frozen yogurt, after a long day of training.

- Energy drinks, enhanced water, and anything in liquid bottled form that has added sweeteners and artificial flavorings and colors.

- Energy gels, sports drinks, and sports foods—for every training session, since you have to "practice" with them to get your gut ready for race day.

As a matter of fact, just this morning I was reading another article—this one off the front page of the Ironman website ("Master Your Morning with a Better Breakfast"), and the meal illustrating it was a Crunchy, Fruity Nut Butter Sandwich. The recipe instructed you to spread natural nut butter and chopped walnuts on one slice of whole-grain bread, spread 100 percent real fruit jam or jelly and a sprinkling of flax or chia seeds on another slice of whole-grain bread, layer strawberries, pears, bananas, or apples on top of both slices, and then enjoy your sandwich with a glass of milk or 1/2 cup yogurt.

Sure, this is a fast and cheap way to get calories down the hatch—and healthier than, say, an Egg McMuffin, but when you're truly trying to be healthy on the outside and on the inside, there is a much smarter way to do things.

Why Nutrient Density Is More Important Than Calorie Density

You definitely need to eat, and to avoid thyroid dysregulation, overtraining, and muscle wasting, many exercise enthusiasts and athletes need to eat more than they think, but a low-calorie diet means taking in not only fewer calories but also fewer micronutrients, which you need for health, performance, and recovery. Humans actually do quite well on a higher-calorie diet.

How high? According to a study that analyzed four popular diets, most diets would require you to eat, on average, 27,575 calories a day to supply your body with all the essential micronutrients you need—so you'd better pay close attention to the supplementation chapter of this book unless you plan on eating nearly 30,000 calories per day!

A recent study in the journal *Metabolism* also offered some pretty scary information. The study, titled "Neuroendocrine Alterations in the Exercising Human: Implications for Energy Homeostasis," highlighted the fact that we humans have complex mechanisms to defend against the adverse effects of negative energy balance (not eating enough calories). In contrast to people who have a sedentary or relatively less physically active lifestyle, for athletes training for endurance events and others with well above average or extreme amounts of physical activity in their life, too few calories is often more of a problem than too many calories.

Just a few of these responses to negative energy balance—most of which you've already learned about—include disruption of appetite-regulating hormones; decreases in crucial hormones like testosterone and thyroid and growth hormone; estrogen deficiencies; heightened cortisol levels and other effects that can cause cardiovascular problems; low bone density; and loss of reproductive function and libido; as well as muscle wasting, metabolic damage, and a host of other factors that are none too desirable.

So what's an active person to do? Simply eat more. Quit starving yourself and complaining about how little energy you have, and get some high-quality food into your gullet. Interestingly, not depriving yourself of food is all the more important when you are female—every calorie-restricting, intermittent-fasting goddess needs to read the article "Hormones, Homeostasis, and Why You (Probably) Need Carbs" at Stumptuous.com.

I'll summarize for you: By sending a signal to your body that its precious commodity of calories is not completely absent, you can stave off a lot of hormonal and metabolic downregulation.

As simple as it seems, this is sound advice. But the problem is that many of the foods lauded for their calorie density have inherent health drawbacks—many of which you'll learn more about in the gut-fixing chapter of this book. For example:

Peanuts and other legumes: Although loaded with calories, peanuts, peanut butter, and other legumes, like lentils (especially when unsoaked or cooked incompletely), are high in lectins, which can cause immune (allergic) reactions, gastrointestinal distress, and, ironically, nutritional deficiencies.

Nuts and nut butters: While almonds, cashews, walnuts, and other nuts, whether incorporated into trail mix or in the form of nut butter, tend to be healthy (and much healthier than most peanut butter), they are also very high in heated oils (which produce cell-damaging free radicals) and inflammatory omega-6 fatty acids—which tend to dump inflammation onto an already stressed-out athlete's body when overused (eaten by the handful and heaping tablespoonful). And while you could certainly eat raw nut and seed butters, many people just don't go out of their way for that expense.

Grains: You are probably well aware of the potential inflammatory and gut-disrupting effects of gluten. Unfortunately, however, cereals, granolas, designer breads, and other "healthy whole grains" are still considered staples in most endurance athletes' diets—and most of us do not make the effort to properly soak, ferment, or sprout these grains to make them digestible.

Dried fruits, trail mixes, and energy/meal-replacement bars and powders: These are touted as calorie-dense sources of energy, but upon inspection of the ingredients lists on most labels, you'll find added vegetable oils, sugars, preservatives, and chemicals—making these snacks more apt to produce a gut bomb or extra inflammation than lasting energy. And while there are more and more healthier bars, powders, and mixes on the market, and more nutrition companies making wise decisions to use natural ingredients, many triathletes are still stuffing themselves with fake, engineered "foods" from the grocery store bargain bin.

Perhaps you're stymied by what seems like a lot of limitations and thinking, "With this kind of nutrition Nazism, what's left to eat?" You're about to find out. But first you need to become familiar with the two missing keys in most fueling advice:

1. **Nutrient density:** Think of nutrient density as a ratio of actual nutrient content (vitamins, minerals, amino acids, and fatty acids) to total energy content (calories). Just because a food is energy-dense does not mean that it is nutrient-dense. For example, the notion that grains and legumes are among the healthiest foods comes from an analysis of them in their raw and inedible state. Once you look at their cooked values, they are among the worst from a nutrient-density standpoint.

2. **Digestibility:** The digestibility of a food refers to any propensity to resist being digested or to cause nutrient malabsorption because the food contains lectins, phytic acids, saponins, or other gut irritants or digestion inhibitors. For example, popular athletic fueling foods these days, such as quinoa, amaranth, millet, nuts, and seeds, are all relatively nutrient-dense, but unless you're willing to rinse, soak, and sprout them, they can't be digested, so you can forget about absorbing all those nutrients.

Now we know two things:

- Neuroendocrine alterations can be caused by low calorie intake combined with high levels of exercise.

- To combat this message of low energy, we must choose foods that satisfy the three criteria of being calorie-dense, nutrient-dense, and digestible.

So what are my favorite calorie-dense, nutrient-dense, and digestible foods for you to incorporate into your training diet? In no particular order, here are enough foods to keep your body satisfied all week long (and don't worry, those forty easy meals are coming soon).

1. Organic Eggs, with the Yolks

Eggs are easy to blend, cook, and scramble with other foods and are high in fat-soluble vitamins, choline, folate, selenium, lecithin, iodine, and omega-3 fatty acids. Get your eggs from a pastured, organic source, and don't skip the yolk. For full benefit, you need to eat fresh, whole eggs, not egg whites from a box. After a big workout, I love to scramble a few eggs with avocado, turmeric, sea salt, and a nice fatty fish like salmon or sardines, then wrap in a sheet of raw, organic nori.

2. Sea Vegetables

Nori, kelp, dulse, algae, spirulina, chlorella, and other ocean flora are incredibly high in iodine, magnesium, manganese, iron, and trace minerals. You can sprinkle kelp or dulse flakes on food, add dried kombu to soups and stews, add a side of seaweed salad when eating sushi out, and use sheets of nori as an alternative to bread or grain-based wraps. Another dense source of sea vegetables is ENERGYbits—chewable,

100 percent organic spirulina and chlorella tablets that are good to have around the house for nighttime cravings or to toss in a plastic bag for a workout. When purchasing sea vegetables, make sure that you purchase from sources that are low in heavy metals. NaturalNews.com has a great series of stories on this topic.

3. Organ Meats

Offal is really not all that awful. On most nutrient density charts, organ meats and oils such as cod liver oil blow any other food out of the water, and if you find it palatable, liver is a fantastic source of fat-soluble vitamins and nearly every nutrient on the face of the planet. Make sure that you get it from a reputable source, and then after a hard day's training, fry it up with butyric-acid-rich butter and quercetin-packed red onions and you'll feel like a million bucks the next day.

4. Bone Broth

As you learned in chapter 5, every weekend we make a big vat of bone broth that lasts all week—typically by putting a whole chicken in the slow cooker. Once you've learned how to make it, bone broth is easy to brew and is a fantastic source of vitamins, minerals, amino acids, and fatty acids. It can also heal your digestive system, assuage joint pain, and enhance sleep. If you don't have time to make your own broth, you can get some of the same benefits by purchasing and using gelatin regularly (Great Lakes, Bernard Jensen, and Natural Force Primal Peptides are good brands), or you can order bone broth from places like The Brothery and Bone Broth Co., both of which are available at GreenfieldFitnessSystems.com.

5. Shellfish

Oysters and mussels are extremely nutrient-dense, and just a few medium-sized oysters can supply more than 1,000 percent of your daily vitamin B_{12} needs, along with a huge dose of vitamin A, vitamin E, copper, selenium, zinc, and essential fatty acids. Mussels are a close second and are rich in the entire B-vitamin complex, along with selenium, zinc, protein, magnesium, and manganese. As with any meat or seafood source, it's important to choose a clean, fresh source of shellfish. Just one serving of shellfish a week can drastically improve your nutrient status.

6. Natto

This fermented soybean derivative is actually quite easy to make if you grab a starter portion from your local Asian market and then ferment with soybeans from any grocery store. Although the slimy texture takes some getting used to, natto has extremely high levels of one important bone- and blood-building vitamin that most people tend to be very deficient in: K_2. It can be eaten for breakfast with scrambled eggs and avocado or served solo, topped with sea salt and a generous drizzle of extra-virgin olive oil.

7. Any Dark-Colored Fruit, Vegetable, or Starch

This is perhaps a horse that has been kicked to death in nutrition advice columns, but the highest concentrations of polyphenols and bioactive compounds are found in fruits such as blueberries, raspberries, blackberries, purple grapes, pomegranates, and currants; vegetables such as purple cabbage, kale, organic tomatoes, and dark orange carrots; and starches such as sweet potatoes, yams, and taro.

8. Fermented Foods

Fermentation increases nutrient bioavailability and digestibility and renders many gut-irritating foods (such as dairy and soy) extremely digestible and nutrient-dense. Most cultures have a relationship with fermented foods. In Asia, there is natto, kimchi, and kefir; in the Middle East, pickles, yogurts, and torshi (pickled vegetables); in Europe, sauerkraut and rakfisk (fermented fish); and in the Pacific Islands, poi (fermented taro) and kanga pirau (fermented corn porridge). In America, we consume all of these as well as kombucha and dark chocolate. Include a variety of fermented foods in your diet to expose your digestive system to a wide range of friendly bacteria, and your gut flora and immune system will thank you.

As you can see, satisfying your crucial energy requirements in a healthy way goes above and beyond slathering peanut butter on a slice of whole-grain bread, downing a handful of trail mix, or gnawing on an energy bar or two. If you're serious about the ultimate combination of health, performance, and longevity, you should throw at least a few of these optimal foods into your daily fueling mix.

Finally, no discussion of nutrient density would be complete without pointing out the fact that modern human agriculture has led to a sadly serious loss in the nutrient value of the plants we eat most regularly. In her book *Eating on the Wild Side,* Jo Robinson points out that the micronutrients in antioxidant-rich foods begin to disappear soon after harvesting.

So when you eat extremely nutrient-dense vegetables that are exposed to large amounts of sunlight, such as artichokes, arugula, asparagus, broccoli, Brussels sprouts, kale, lettuce, parsley, mushrooms, and spinach, try to eat them when they're as fresh as possible—and avoid storing them in the refrigerator for long periods.

FORTY EASY MEALS FOR BUSY ATHLETES

So let's say you want to put everything you now know about nutrient density and digestibility to work in a meal plan that fuels your active lifestyle—without spending every spare second of your life in the kitchen. Well, I've done it for you, with forty meals that are easy to prepare. Bon appétit!

Sorry, there are no artistically styled photos or complicated instructions to make you feel like you're ready for an *Iron Chef* cook-off (although you can feel free to post your own photos of these recipes to Facebook.com/BGFitness), but you could easily go an entire year without eating or cooking anything except these meals. Hey, there's nothing wrong with keeping things simple and eating the same thing for breakfast, lunch, and dinner nearly every day, but you won't have to do that—unless you want to. (I do coach athletes who are perfectly happy drinking three or four smoothies a day.)

I am going to help you create your own personal meal plan based on calories, carbohydrates, proteins, and fats later on. But for now, quit worrying and start chowing!

Finally, you'll notice that I mention specific brands of some products. You'll find links and discount codes for all of them on the resource web page for this chapter at BeyondTrainingBook.com/Chapter11. Enjoy!

Breakfast Options

1. Eggs with Avocado and Vegetables

Because this is a lower-carbohydrate meal and takes longer to digest, it is best consumed when you are not going to work out within two to three hours afterward. Scramble, fry, poach, or steam two or three eggs from organically fed free-range hens.* Duck eggs are also OK. Cook on relatively low heat to avoid oxidation, and use butter from grass-fed cows, ghee, olive oil (not extra-virgin for cooking!), or coconut oil. (See Table 11-1.)

Cook a large serving of dark, leafy greens (bok choy, spinach, kale, Swiss chard, mustard greens, etc.) with the eggs or serve on the side. For an extra dose of healthy fats, add a handful of olives or a half or whole sliced avocado (or some pemmican or bacon). Add sea salt and pepper to taste and serve with fresh sliced tomato. You can also wrap this whole meal up in one or two sheets of nori.

For extra vitamin K and carbs, especially if this meal follows a morning workout, add a small side of natto (available at Asian markets). And for extra probiotics, add a side of kimchi. (You can learn how to make your own probiotics in the video posted at BeyondTrainingBook.com/ytprobiotics.)

TABLE 11-1

LOW-HEAT OILS			HIGH-HEAT OILS		
Oil	Smoke Point		Oil	Smoke Point	
Coconut oil	350°F	177°C	Almond oil	420°F	216°C
Flax seed oil	255°F	107°C	Avocado oil	400°F	204°C
Hemp oil	330°F	165°C	Canola oil	450°F	232°C
Extra-virgin olive oil	375°F	191°C	Cottonseed oil	420°F	232°C
Peanut oil	320°F	160°C	Grapeseed oil	420°F	216°C
Sesame oil	350°F	177°C	Hazelnut oil	430°F	221°C
Soybean oil	320°F	160°C	Mustard oil	489°F	254°C
Walnut oil	320°F	160°C	Palm oil	455°F	235°C

When I say organically fed and free-range, I mean it. If you're serious about wanting to look, feel, and perform better by limiting the amount of hormones, antibiotics, toxins, molds, and inflammatory omega-6 fatty acids that you consume, and you can't find "clean" versions of meat or other animal products, you're better off choosing a meatless meal. In chapter 16 I tell you more about why this matters and where you can go to find what you need locally or online. I also recommend that you read the excellent book Eat the Yolks by Liz Wolfe for more information on this topic.

2. SuperGreens or SuperBerry

This meal is easily digested up to an hour before a workout or can be used as a quick postworkout meal. Combine two to three large scoops LivingFuel SuperGreens or SuperBerry with four to six ounces full-fat, organic, BPA-free coconut milk (unsweetened; I use Native Forest brand and order by the case from Amazon), one to two tablespoons almond butter, one teaspoon cinnamon, and one tablespoon chia seeds or unsweetened coconut flakes. You can blend it, shake it in a mixer bottle, or simply stir it all together with a spoon. As an alternative to coconut milk, you can use organic yogurt or kefir. Most people who don't do well with unfermented forms of dairy find that they do just fine with these type of fermented dairy sources.

3. LivingProtein

This meal is OK up to an hour before a workout or as a postworkout meal. Combine two to three large scoops LivingFuel LivingProtein with four to six ounces full-fat coconut milk (unsweetened), one to two tablespoons almond butter, one teaspoon cinnamon, and one tablespoon chia seeds or unsweetened coconut flakes. You can blend it, shake it in a mixer bottle, or simply stir it all together with a spoon.

4. High-Fat Coffee (aka Bulletproof Coffee)

This meal is perfect as a "fasted" meal before a long, hard workout, and also on easier days when you need much less protein and carbohydrate than usual. Full credit goes to my friend and fellow health blogger Dave Asprey (the Bulletproof Executive) for this recipe. In a blender or shaker cup, combine eight to twelve ounces black coffee (preferably organic, mold-free Upgraded brand), one to two tablespoons MCT (medium-chain triglyceride) oil, one to two tablespoons Kerrygold butter (optional, for added calories), and a touch of vanilla powder and Upgraded Chocolate Powder to taste. I include links to all these products on the resource web page for this chapter.

Another high-fat coffee option that I've been enjoying quite a bit lately is turmeric tea. You follow the same recipe, but use a turmeric tea like Tumi turmeric instead of coffee. A final option that has quite a cranial kick is to add 3–5 grams curcumin to your high-fat coffee, which is an excellent strategy for fighting inflammation in the brain after a night of drinking or lost sleep.

5. Seeds and Nuts with Fruit

This is a good breakfast if you're in a hurry, and it's OK to eat up to an hour before a workout or postworkout. Simply eat one or two large handfuls of raw nuts or seeds (the best are almonds, macadamia nuts, walnuts, and pumpkin seeds; keep them in the freezer so they don't go rancid) along with a piece of fresh fruit, such as a pomegranate, grapefruit, or apple. It's best to soak your nuts and seeds first. Here's how: Place in a bowl with enough filtered water to cover completely, and add a heaping tablespoon of salt. The soaking times for some seeds and nuts can be found at BeyondTrainingBook.com/pacfitsoak.

6. Sweet Potatoes or Yams with Sea Salt and Honey

This higher-carbohydrate meal should be eaten only on the morning of a big training day, big workout, or race, or if you're "cycling carbs" on your higher-carb day. Bake or boil one or two sweet potatoes or yams, sprinkle with sea salt, and drizzle with one to two tablespoons local raw honey or organic maple syrup. For added calories (especially before a workout or race that's longer than two hours), you can add a dollop of organic grass-fed yogurt or kefir (if your gut tolerates it) and/or one to two tablespoons almond butter.

7. Breakfast Salad

Although a salad for breakfast may seem unconventional, to say the least, this is a perfect meal when you have a little more time to sit down for a morning meal and you're not going to be working out in the next two or three hours. Over a bed of spinach or kale, add two or three steamed or poached, pastured, organic eggs, one to two tablespoons olive oil, one sliced tomato, a half to a whole sliced avocado, a dollop of organic yogurt or kefir from grass-fed cows (if you tolerate it), and sea salt and pepper to taste.

8. Waffles or Pancakes (takes a little more prep time, but it's a great recipe)

Similar to the sweet potato recipe, this is a higher-carbohydrate meal that should be eaten only on the morning of a big training day or race. This is not for you if you are on a gut-healing diet (you'll learn about that later), because even though the grains are soaked and sprouted, they may still irritate a damaged gut. Begin by sprouting and fermenting the millet, quinoa, oats, or buckwheat.

To soak and ferment your grains:

- Rinse them four or five times and soak in enough filtered water to cover them overnight in a glass bowl covered with a plate.
- In the morning, rinse your grains thoroughly and cover with filtered water again. This time, add about one tablespoon whey or the juice of half a lemon to the water and cover again for twelve to twenty-four hours.
- Rinse and strain the grains. They are now ready to use.

To make waffles, place three cups of your sprouted, fermented grain, four organic, pastured eggs, three to four tablespoons butter from grass-fed cows (or coconut oil), two teaspoons baking soda, and one tablespoon vanilla in a food processor and process for at least five minutes or until nice and smooth. Cook the batter in your favorite waffle iron. This batter works for pancakes as well. Serve with grass-fed butter or almond butter, a dollop of organic, grass-fed yogurt or kefir from grass-fed cows (if your gut tolerates it), and a small amount of sliced bananas or berries of your choice.

9. Hot Power Cereal

This is another higher-carbohydrate meal that should be eaten only on the morning of a big training day or race. Like the waffles, it is not for you if you are on a gut-healing diet because the quinoa, despite being soaked and sprouted, may still irritate a damaged gut.

Soak and ferment quinoa using the instructions in the previous recipe.

Cook a serving for twenty minutes over medium heat, then remove from the heat and stir in two to three tablespoons almond butter, a pinch of sea salt, one tablespoon chia seeds or unsweetened coconut flakes, half a teaspoon vanilla, and one teaspoon cinnamon. For sweetness, you can add a touch of raw, organic honey if desired. If quinoa is new to you, you may want to grab the more specific instructions for cooking quinoa at BeyondTrainingBook.com/Chapter11.

10. High-Fat Smoothie

I often have this smoothie not just for breakfast, but several times during the day, especially when I'm super-busy. Hell, I sometimes have it for breakfast, lunch, and dinner on the same day. You'll need a powerful blender for this one, not a little As seen on TV portable one. I'm talking a big-engine, industrial-style blender that you see coffee shops and restaurants using, or the blender used by that guy who blends up things like smartphones on YouTube. Check GreenfieldFitnessSystems.com for some of my blender recommendations.

Here's what you need:

- A huge bunch of greens. I prefer kale, but spinach, bok choy, mustard greens, and the like also work.

- Some kind of herb. Cleansing herbs like parsley, cilantro, and thyme are nice. Get 'em fresh.

- Half an avocado, or a whole one if it's a high-calorie day.

- 4–6 ounces full-fat coconut milk.

The less coconut milk you use, the thicker your smoothie will be. I prefer an extremely thick smoothie that I have to eat with a spoon so that the digestive enzymes in my mouth can work on predigesting before the food even makes it to my gut. Like my mom always said, "Chew your liquids and drink your solids." Didn't you always wonder what that means?

- 2 teaspoons organic cacao powder.

- 2 teaspoons cinnamon.

- 1/2 to 1 teaspoon sea salt (I use the fancy Aztecan stuff).

- 1 tablespoon extra-virgin olive oil or coconut oil.

OK, stop there. Blend everything for about sixty seconds. You don't want to pulverize things like protein powder and collagen, and you don't want to pulverize the chunky chunks of goodness you're about to toss in. Now let's keep going. To your blended green goodness, add:

- 20–30 grams "clean" protein powder (check out my article about nasty ingredients in protein powders at BenGreenfieldFitness.com/2012/01/how-to-choose-protein-powder).

- Two teaspoons good organic collagen hydrolysate.

- Large handful unroasted, non-vegetable-oil coated walnuts or almonds.

Now blend again, quickly this time so you don't pulverize the chunks. About fifteen seconds will do. Finally, stir (don't blend) in the following ingredients:

- Small handful organic dark cacao nibs.

- Large handful organic unsweetened coconut flakes.

Boom. That's it. You're now ready to consume your smoothie, preferably with a spoon or spatula.

I recommend that you use a spatula to ensure that the entire contents of this relatively expensive smoothie make it into your container of choice. I use an enormous mug that I won in a triathlon, although I have been known to eat it straight out of the blender container when I'm in a hurry or I'm too lazy to make the transfer to a civilized cup.

11. Ketogenic Kale Shake or Green Smoothie

Here's another Dave Asprey–inspired meal. In a powerful blender, place one bunch steamed kale, two to four tablespoons butter, one to two tablespoons MCT oil, one teaspoon sea salt, two tablespoons high-quality protein powder, one to four teaspoons apple cider vinegar, full-fat coconut milk to the desired texture, and a handful of herbs (cilantro, parsley, oregano, etc.—great for cleansing the gut and liver). Blend and enjoy. There's a video of me making this shake at BeyondTrainingBook.com/ytkaleshake.

Alternatively, you can make a regular Green Smoothie. This one is way simpler (but less tasty and fat-filled) than the Ketogenic Kale Shake. Blend one-half to one cup spinach, one to one-and-a-half cups kale, a half to a whole banana, a small handful of almonds, three to five raw Brazil nuts, and one to two tablespoons cacao or carob powder. Use water, almond milk, rice milk, or (for added calories) coconut milk to achieve your desired texture.

12. Midmorning Snack Options (To maintain your metabolic, fat-burning efficiency, try to stick to beverages in the midmorning.)

- To one serving of TianChi or Life Shotz, add eight to twelve ounces water or unsweetened kombucha and one to two servings trace liquid minerals (I prefer the Natural Calm brand from GreenfieldFitnessSystems.com).
- Herbal tea of choice, including white, yerba mate, and green.
- Zevia all-natural soda.
- Coconut kefir, without added sugars (KeVita is good brand).
- Zukay kvass. Weird name; tasty stuff.
- Mushroom extracts such as cordyceps, reishi, and chaga. I'm a huge fan of drinking these solo or adding them to coffee. You can learn more about them at BeyondTrainingBook.com/shrooms.
- Soda water with essential oils like peppermint or lemon oil added.
- Sparkling or regular water with one GU Electrolyte Brew tablet, Nuun hydration tablet, or Hammer Endurolyte Fizz tablet.
- One cup bone broth.

Lunch Options

13. Caesar Salad

This recipe makes two servings, so halve the recipe if it's just for you. In a large bowl, mix two egg yolks, a quarter-cup olive oil, one teaspoon Thai fish sauce, two cloves garlic, the juice of one lemon, and two teaspoons Dijon mustard. If your stomach tolerates dairy, add several pinches of Parmesan or Pecorino Romano cheese. Add several pinches of sea salt and black pepper and a head of Romaine lettuce, torn into bite-sized pieces, or several large handfuls of mixed greens. Toss well and sprinkle with one to two handfuls of chopped walnuts.

14. Sardine Salad

To a bed of mixed greens or spinach, add a half to a whole sliced avocado, a half to a whole can of sardines (with oil), a half to a whole sliced tomato or a handful of cherry tomatoes, a squeeze of lemon juice, and any other chopped vegetables you like (for added crunch, use celery or carrots). Top with a handful of pumpkin seeds, and season with sea salt and black pepper to taste.

15. Grocery Store

If you're eating lunch on the go, simply venture into a grocery store and buy an avocado, a can of sardines or packet of tuna or salmon or (if good breath is important) a few ounces of raw nuts, grab a handful of salt and pepper packets and, if dairy is tolerated, a hard cheese, such as Parmigiano-Reggiano, Asiago, or Gruyère (preferably from Europe to ensure a higher likelihood of A2 cows and less growth hormone). Grab a plastic fork, a plastic knife, and a plate from the deli and make yourself an avocado, nuts, fish, and cheese plate. If you need more carbs for a preworkout meal, include a piece of fresh fruit.

16. Lunch Out

If you're not careful, lunch at a restaurant can be notoriously high-carb, full of grains, and laden with vegetable oils and other nasty stuff. The best bets are a salad with no cheese and dressing on the side (a Cobb salad always works) or an easy-to-digest protein such as wild-caught salmon served over a bed of mixed greens. Try to avoid grain-fed or hormone-larded meats. If you need additional carbs preworkout, you can include an order of mixed fruit on the side. Keep things simple: meat plus vegetables plus fruit.

17. Kale Wraps

In a large piece of kale (or Swiss chard, bok choy, or butter lettuce), wrap four to six ounces grass-fed beef, sardines, pastured chicken, or wild fish, a half to a whole sliced avocado, one to two handfuls sliced olives, and two to three tablespoons diced tomato. Add salt, pepper, turmeric, and fresh herbs such as parsley, thyme, or oregano to taste; you can also add a dollop of organic yogurt (if your stomach tolerates it) or homemade healthy mayo (recipe follows). If this is a preworkout meal or one of your higher-volume days, you can add sliced yam, sweet potato, or white rice to the wrap.

To make mayo: Place a whole egg, one tablespoon lemon juice, sea salt, and black pepper in a blender, and blend on a low setting while slowly adding one cup olive oil, macadamia nut oil, or avocado oil. If you don't have time for this, just buy olive oil mayo.

18. Chicken-Cashew Wraps

In a mixing bowl, add one diced pastured chicken breast, one tablespoon healthy mayo (see previous recipe), a half to a whole sliced avocado, a half to a whole diced tomato or several grape tomatoes, a handful of cashews, a small handful fresh arugula, and sea salt and black pepper to taste, and toss to combine well. Wrap in romaine or butter lettuce leaves. If this is a preworkout meal or a higher-volume day, you can add sliced yam, sweet potato, or white rice to the wraps.

19. Hors d'Oeuvres

I am not embarrassed to admit that my children and I have this for lunch all the time. It's a quick meal and can be eaten while working (not recommended, but sometimes you gotta do it). On a plate, arrange several rice crackers or flax seed crackers, a half to a whole sliced avocado, a half to a whole sliced tomato, one to two handfuls of olives, and, if your stomach tolerates dairy, three or four slices of a hard cheese, such as Parmigiano-Reggiano, Asiago, or Gruyère (preferably from Europe to ensure a higher likelihood of healthier A2 cows and less growth hormone).

For added protein and calories, you can add a can of sardines or a packet of tuna or salmon. Just scoop the ingredients onto crackers and eat.

20. Nori Rolls

OK, Nori Rolls isn't really so much a recipe as a grandiose way to explain my slightly barbaric habit of simply taking a sheet of nori (the seaweed used to make sushi) and using it as a means of delivering as many vegetables and as much olive oil as possible into my gaping maw. The procedure involves placing two to four sheets of nori on a plate, filling a bowl with vegetables, extra-virgin olive oil or avocado oil, and sea salt, shoveling as much of said bowl's contents onto a sheet of nori, wrapping it up, and then eating it as quickly as possible while olive oil dribbles down my face. (Don't worry, olive oil is good for your skin, too.)

21. Fast Avocado Soup

In a blender, purée one to two ripe avocados (pitted, peeled, and chopped), one to two cups coconut milk, and sea salt and cayenne to taste. Chill for one to six hours, and stir in two tablespoons lime or lemon juice before serving. You can garnish with chopped cherry tomatoes, sliced scallions, chopped mint, or a dollop of yogurt or a sprinkling of hard cheese. And you can add shrimp, chicken, beef, or fish for more protein if you like. For extra calories or carbs, you can serve the soup with a baked or boiled sweet potato or yam.

22. Sandwich

Miss your sandwiches with this whole "avoid bread" mantra? Good news: You can have a sandwich, but you just have to avoid modern grains and gut-irritating wheat. So why not just make your own bread, Betty Crocker style? It's easier than you think.

Preheat your oven to 375°F. Meanwhile, place 1/4 cup melted coconut oil, 1/8 cup almond flour, 1/4 cup protein powder, 5 pastured eggs, a teaspoon of sea salt, and a teaspoon of baking powder in a bowl and mix to combine.

Spread this mixture thinly on a greased baking sheet (brushing with olive oil is fine) and bake for 15 minutes.

Boom. Bread.

You can fill your sandwich with avocado; tomato; your healthy meat of choice; a hard cheese such as Parmesan, Asiago, or Gruyère; healthy mayo; and sea salt and black pepper to taste. To make mayo, see the recipe for Kale Wraps on page 263. Because of the added carbohydrate content from the bread, sandwiches should be consumed on higher-volume workout days only.

Quick Afternoon Snacks

23. Bar

In a pinch or for a fast preworkout pick-me-up, you can have one gluten-free, natural energy bar with as few ingredients as possible. I rarely eat bars, but when I do, my preferred brand is the bar I designed at GreenfieldFitnessSystems.com, whose ingredients include honey, almonds, unsweetened chocolate, gelatin, chia seeds, pea protein isolate, coconut, kaniwa, organic rice protein, sesame seeds, cocoa powder, cocoa butter, and sea salt. Other good bars: Hammer Whey or Vegan Recovery Bar, LaraBar, NoGii Bar, Quest Bar, Zing bar, and Health Warrior bar. On higher-calorie/higher-volume days or for a long bike ride, Bonk Breaker bars are also OK.

24. Algae and AAs

This snack is especially good for a lower-calorie or lower-carbohydrate day as a preworkout boost and is good for fasted workouts, too. It combines two of the most nutrient-dense foods on the planet: algae and amino acids. To pull off this meal, you simply swallow or chew twenty-five to fifty ENERGYbits and five to ten NatureAminos or EXOS Aminos capsules. Yes, I admit that this sounds super funky and strange, but try it and I guarantee that you'll feel amazing. You can read some of my articles about algae by going to BenGreenfieldFitness.com and doing a search for "algae."

25. Chia Slurry

Set three to four tablespoons chia seeds in a small bowl of water and place in the refrigerator for two to twenty-four hours. (The longer they soak, the more chia goodness your body will absorb from them.) Add lemon juice and stevia to taste, and eat it like Jell-O!

26. Pemmican or Jerky

Eat a half to a whole tube of organic, pastured pemmican from US Wellness Meats, a good source for this grass-fed, hormone-free, traditional Native American beef (as well as tallow) that is frozen and shipped straight to your door. Alternatively, you can learn to make your own beef jerky by watching the video of my wife Jessa making delicious beef jerky at BeyondTrainingBook.com/ytbeefjerky. You can also order jerky from US Wellness Meats at BeyondTrainingBook.com/meat. I posted a podcast interview with the owner of US Wellness Meats at BeyondTrainingBook. com/beef. That stuff is the real deal when it comes to "safe" meat. The company Onnit also makes a very good bison bar called the Warrior Bar with clean ingredients and minimal processing.

Dinner Options

27. Cobb Salad

A good choice as a low-carbohydrate meal on days when you are not going to work out in the afternoon or evening. For this salad, use two to three chopped, hard-boiled, pastured eggs, a half to a whole avocado, two to three strips cooked and crumbled bacon (organic and pastured), one small tomato, one scallion, a half tablespoon diced almonds or walnuts, half a red onion, and romaine or butter leaf lettuce. For more protein, add four to six ounces grass-fed beef, free-range chicken, or shrimp. Tear the lettuce into bite-sized pieces, add the other ingredients, and toss with olive oil, lemon juice, and sea salt and black pepper to taste.

28. Scrambled Eggs

Just the other night, I was joking with a group of friends about how often I depend on my old bachelor-days standby—scrambled eggs—when my wife's not home for dinner. Simply scramble two or three organic pastured eggs in coconut oil or butter while steaming four to five chopped vegetables of your choice (spinach, kale, carrots, mushrooms, and tomatoes). Serve the vegetables and a half to a whole sliced avocado over the eggs, and season with sea salt and black pepper to taste. Alternatively, you can plop the whole deal onto a sheet of nori and wrap into a cone shape. Or you could use kale, bok choy, Swiss chard, or butter lettuce for the wrap. Salsa is a good condiment for this meal.

29. Poached Salmon

This recipe calls for one pound of salmon, so it will be enough for two to three servings. Leftovers can be refrigerated for two to three days. You'll need:

* Sea salt and black pepper
* 1 pound wild salmon fillet
* 1 cup white wine
* 1 tablespoon white wine vinegar
* 1 bay leaf
* 1 clove garlic, sliced
* 2 springs fresh or 1/2 teaspoon dried dill
* 2 tablespoons butter
* Juice of 1/2 lemon

Salt and pepper the salmon and put it in a skillet. Add the wine, vinegar, bay leaf, garlic, and dill. Bring to a simmer over low heat, cover, and cook for six to eight minutes, or until the salmon flakes easily with a fork.

While the salmon is cooking, melt the butter in a saucepan, then add the lemon juice. When the salmon is ready, drizzle the butter sauce over it. Serve over cooked white rice and mixed greens or a salad, along with a sweet potato or yam or sweet potato fries. (I've got a sweet potato fry video at BeyondTrainingBook.com/bgfswtpotato. Because extra-virgin olive oil is unstable at high heat, I recommend using regular olive oil or coconut oil for your fries, even though I grabbed the extra-virgin oil when I made these!)

30. Steak

Choose a grass-fed cut of beef, bison, elk, or venison. Make a seasoning mix of one teaspoon garlic powder, two tablespoons paprika, one tablespoon thyme, one tablespoon oregano, one tablespoon cayenne (optional; avoid it if you're on a gut-healing protocol), one teaspoon black pepper, one teaspoon white pepper, and one teaspoon sea salt. Season the meat liberally and place the remainder of the powder in a plastic bag or another airtight container for future use. Heat ghee or butter in a cast-iron skillet, add the meat, and sauté, or grill (preferably on lower heat). Serve with roasted, steamed, or sautéed vegetables and, for additional carbohydrates if this is a postworkout meal or a high-volume day, a baked sweet potato, yam, or sweet potato fries.

31. Liver Pâté

You can spread pâté on anything, and this recipe might actually impress your friends. It uses a half-pound of liver, which is enough for two to three servings—and leftovers can be refrigerated for two to three days. I get my liver locally or order it from US Wellness Meats. Slice the liver into half-inch-thick pieces and soak for one to two hours in milk (preferably organic, from grass-fed cows). If you don't have milk or don't like milk, lemon juice is fine. Brown the liver slices in butter or ghee on low heat, cooking three to four minutes per side. Meanwhile, boil an egg. After the liver is browned or while the liver is cooking, sauté one diced onion for five to ten minutes in the same pan.

Put the liver, onion, cooking juices from the pan, boiled egg, two tablespoons coconut oil, and a handful of fresh chopped cilantro (or you could use kimchi) in a blender and purée.

Serve your pâté with rice crackers or flax seed crackers or wrapped in bok choy, Swiss chard, nori, or butter lettuce. Alternatively, serve it with a baked sweet potato or yam over a bed of mixed greens.

If this sounds like too much work, you can also try my super quick and tasty liver recipe. Simply soak the liver, then dip in a whisked egg, dredge with coconut or almond flour, and fry in butter for four to five minutes per side. This is fantastic with bacon and onions.

32. Easy Chicken Dinner

This recipe feeds three to four people.

- *3–4 chicken thighs or breasts*
- *5–6 heads broccoli, chopped into florets*
- *4–5 tablespoons regular olive oil*

- *2–3 tablespoons balsamic vinegar*
- *1 teaspoon garlic powder*
- *Sea salt and black pepper to taste*

Preheat the oven to 375°F. Place the chicken and broccoli in a 9-x-13-inch baking dish. Add the olive oil and vinegar, season with garlic powder, sea salt, and black pepper, and stir to make sure that the chicken and broccoli are well coated. Bake for 20–25 minutes, or until the chicken is cooked through. If this is a postworkout meal or a higher-volume day, serve with sweet potato, yam, or white rice. For a lower-volume day, serve with steamed carrots, cauliflower, parsnips, or beets in sea salt and olive oil.

33. Eating Out: Sushi

Eat at a sushi restaurant. Avoid soy, edamame, and fancy rolls with fried ingredients, and instead eat your choice of sashimi and seaweed salad if you're going low-carb, or indulge in sushi rolls if this is a postworkout meal or you're not worried about carbs. In most cases, you'll eat only nigiri or sushi roll—sources of starchy, white rice—if it's a high-volume day or a postworkout meal.

34. Eating Out: Meat and Veggies

Choose a meat-and-vegetable-based entrée at a restaurant, and remember these key rules:

- Always substitute roasted vegetables for bread or mashed potatoes, and turn down or avoid bread/chips if they're brought to the table.
- Acceptable starches: rice, quinoa, amaranth, millet, sweet potato, yam, squash, carrot, beet, or other non-gluten, non-GMO items.
- Acceptable proteins: anything from my Superhuman Food Pyramid (see page 285), but ask your server if, say, the fish is wild or farmed and whether the chicken is organic.
- Acceptable fats: coconut oil, butter, olive oil, flax seed oil, avocado oil, macadamia nut oil, and any fat that is 100 percent natural and not a vegetable oil. Avoid batter-fried foods. When it doubt, order creams, dressings, and sauces on the side and use small amounts.

Dessert or Evening Snacks
(Included by Popular Demand)

35. ENERGYbits

Notice that I said "dessert or evening snacks." This one definitely falls into the latter category, and it's especially good on a lower-calorie day or a day on which you're not exercising in the later afternoon or evening. Eat fifty to one hundred ENERGYbits (pop them like popcorn)—this is a fantastic way to quell your appetite in the evening. You can learn more about why these are so good at taming your evening cravings in my article "How to Eat Algae (The Ultimate Guide to Fueling with Spirulina and Chlorella)" at BenGreenfieldFitness.com/2015/09/how-to-eat-algae/.

36. Coconut-Chocolate-Chia Blend

You don't even need a blender for this one. In a small bowl, mix twenty-five to fifty ENERGYbits, 2 teaspoons carob or cocoa powder, four to six ounces full-fat coconut milk, and two to three tablespoons chia seeds or unsweetened coconut flakes. Stir, and chill in refrigerator for fifteen to twenty minutes. For added crunch, add some organic cacao nibs.

37. Sea Salt, Dark Chocolate, and Almonds

The title pretty much says it all. Sea salt is rich in adrenal-supporting electrolytes, almonds are chock-full of healthy fats, and dark chocolate is . . . well, dark chocolate. I keep a few bars of 80 percent or darker dark chocolate in the freezer, break up about a quarter bar, then toss it into a small bowl with a handful of raw almonds and two to three pinches of sea salt, preferably the mind-blowingly good Aztecan variety. I pop this snack like popcorn, often during a good flick. For added kick, use a pinch of cayenne.

38. Protein Parfait

Yes, protein can spike evening insulin levels, but in a postworkout scenario this isn't a big deal. Place one to two scoops organic whey or vegan protein powder in a bowl, add full-fat coconut milk to reach your desired texture, one to two teaspoons almond butter, a handful of unsweetened coconut flakes, and one teaspoon cinnamon. Stir to combine and eat with a spoon as you would ice cream or custard. And yes, I admit that I sometimes eat this for breakfast.

39. Healthy Chocolate Pudding

Place a half to a whole sliced avocado, one teaspoon cinnamon, one to two scoops organic whey or vegan protein powder, four to six ounces full-fat coconut milk, one to two teaspoons almond butter, one to two teaspoons carob or cocoa powder, and a dash of pure vanilla extract or vanilla powder in a blender and blend. Tell me this doesn't taste like the most decadent chocolate mousse, and I will call you crazy.

40. Dipped Dark Chocolate

You know those dark chocolate bars I keep in the freezer? For a quick dessert or preworkout snack, I sometimes grab half a bar and drizzle a tablespoon of raw almond or cashew butter over it, or (germophobes beware) simply dip the chocolate bar in the jar of raw nut butter. Careful with the calories on this one. It can get out of hand fast.

I experiment with many other "dessert-ish" recipes. Most of them include either full-fat yogurt or coconut milk, cacao powder and/or dark chocolate stevia, and something crunchy, like chlorella, coconut flakes, or chia seeds.

Resources

In chapter 16, I give you everything you might even think you'll need to fuel your endurance lifestyle, but meanwhile, here are some resources to get your creative cooking wheels spinning:

- **Cookbook:** *Nourishing Traditions,* by Sally Fallon (BeyondTrainingBook.com/amzn3909)

- **Grocery shopping guide:** *Rich Food Poor Food,* by Jayson Calton and Mira Calton (BeyondTrainingBook.com/amzn7503)

- **Science of proper fueling book:** *Perfect Health Diet,* by Paul Jaminet and Shou-Ching Jaminet (BeyondTrainingBook.com/amzn1929)

- **Food guide:** My Superhuman Food Pyramid (BeyondTrainingBook.com/bgfpyramid, or see page 285)

- **Meal plans:** Any of my wife Jessa's meal plans in Ben Greenfield Fitness Inner Circle (BenGreenfieldFitness.com/innercircle)

- **Website:** Chowstalker (stalkerville.net)

- **Blogs:** *The Domestic Man* (thedomesticman.com), *Francesca Eats* (francescaeats.blogspot.com), *Nutty Kitchen* (nuttykitchen.com), *tummyrumblr* (tummyrumblr.com), *The 10-Minute Meal* (10minutemeal.com)

As I mentioned earlier, I'm not going to leave you with your arms full of recipes and a refrigerator full of pastured eggs and bushels of greens and no way of knowing how much of what you should be eating. In the next chapter, I teach you exactly how to figure out how many calories, carbohydrates, proteins, and fats you should be eating. Later in this book, you'll get access to a meal plan that includes, among other helpful details, a plan for the off-season, recovery weeks, base building, the last few hard weeks leading up to an event, and the week of your race or event.

And what about leftovers from all this food? They're often best wrapped in nori, bok choy, butter lettuce, or Swiss chard. Avoid microwaving or excessive reheating, and to avoid mold, fungus, and toxins, try not to eat leftovers that are more than two or three days old. For extra probiotics, you can include a side of kimchi or sauerkraut.

Additional resources, helpful links, scientific references, websites, discounts on "special foods," and surprise bonuses for this chapter are available at BeyondTrainingBook.com/Chapter11. Enjoy.

CHAPTER 12

What Two Seven-Year-Old Boys Can Teach You About How to Track Calories and Log Your Diet the Right Way

I have seven-year-old twin boys. In just a moment, I'm going to share an important calorie-counting lesson that you can learn from these little guys.

But let's start here: I don't count calories.

As a matter of fact, I *hate* counting calories.

Sure, you've probably been brainwashed to believe that to maintain your energy levels, perform like a rock star, stay thin, and look younger than you are, you need to account for every bite of food that enters your mouth. But I think that counting calories sucks the enjoyment right out of eating, and when I make my morning smoothie, it's simply a handful of this and a pinch of that, with absolutely no measuring or weighing.

That's because I have the same attitude about counting calories as I do about blasting out of the house for a run wearing as much gear—a heart rate monitor, GPS device, foot pod, smartphone, and self-quantification wristband—as a Special Ops soldier. Sometimes you just need to unplug and go natural—paying attention to the way you look, feel, and perform rather than to what your vibrating smartphone is announcing. Sometimes you just need to soak in the beauty of nature rather than have your eyeballs locked onto a tiny screen on your wrist.

However, that being said, sometimes quantification is necessary. For example, if you want to become a better cyclist, knowing what it feels like to pedal at 300 watts is useful, and the only way you're going to know that is to spend a few sessions on a bike with a power meter. Pacing in swimming in crucial, and knowing the proper pace to swim a 1:30 100-meter speed for 1,500 meters requires you to watch the swim clock like a hawk for at least a handful of swim sessions. Maintaining a high cadence while running will vastly improve your economy and efficiency, but knowing what 90 steps per minute feels like when you're running requires you to wear a foot pod for a few runs.

And when it comes to maintaining ideal energy levels, performance, and weight, you have to have a decent idea of what you're putting into your body. You have to know that one large egg has 71 calories, 6 grams of protein, 5 grams of fat, and 0 carbs; that you eat 2,300 calories on an average Saturday and 1,750 calories on an average weekday; and that carbohydrates account for 55 percent of your daily caloric intake. That means you have to keep a food log for a little while.

But unless incessant counting, using a kitchen microscale, and being a data hound makes you jump with joy, you don't need to count calories or keep a food log for your entire life.

I've personally counted calories only three times in my life:

1. For six months, when I was a big, shiny, gold-flaked bodybuilder eating a high-protein, minimal-fat diet in an attempt to achieve a body fat percentage that would allow me to pose onstage in my underwear.

2. For one month, when I switched to a low-carbohydrate diet and wanted to eat less than 200 grams a day of carbs.

3. For one week, when I switched to a ketogenic diet and wanted to see if I could eat a diet that was 70 to 90 percent fat on a daily basis.

Why have I counted calories and logged my diet only three times in my life?

Because that's all it took for me to get a decent idea of the calorie, carbohydrate, protein, and fat content of my meal habits at those points in my diet journey. After that, I simply paid attention to the way I looked, felt, and performed. If I ever make another major dietary switch, I'll count again—even if it's just for a week to a month—to get an idea of the numbers behind what I'm eating. And then, just as I always have, I'll stop as soon as I've wrapped my head around them.

Logging your diet day after day, year after year, is not only overrated, it's boring as heck.

You'd be surprised by how much you can learn with just a little logging here and there. You'll be able to take a quick glance at a banana, a slice of watermelon, a handful of cashews, or a slice of pizza and size up its quantitative nutritional content. You'll also be able to know exactly how many daily carbohydrates you can eat before you'll notice some flab in your abs, or gas in your gut, or a hitch in your step. You'll know how much protein leaves you bloated and how much leaves you sore and underrecovered, and how many omega-6 fatty acids versus omega-3 fatty acids you're eating.

But you can become that kind of diet sleuth within just a few months—no need to log incessantly.

So here's what this all has to do with my twin boys: Have you ever seen a child count calories?

Absolutely not! Children happily rely on their built-in nutrition intuition.

For example, when my boys gear up to kickbox, go on a hike, build a fort, or ride their bikes up and down our cul-de-sac, they are blissfully ignorant of how many calories or grams of carbohydrates, protein, and fat they've eaten.

They're happy as clams simply wandering into the kitchen and eating real food when they're hungry. And guess what? They have all the fuel they need to expend the massive amounts of energy that their little lives demand. We have yet to find either of our boys passed out in the backyard from hypoglycemia because he didn't eat enough carbohydrates for the day, or experience extreme stunts in growth from inadequate protein, or slip into neural fatigue and loss of mental drive because he failed to consume enough fat for the week.

My boys just eat real food and enjoy it. And you should, too.

But somewhere between childhood and adulthood, we become convinced that to optimize our weight or performance, it is necessary to count and track every tiny morsel of food that slips between our lips. This is simply not true. In my experience, most of the people who stress about counting calories also struggle the most with eating disorders, weight issues, and hormone imbalances—a sad paradox.

The Five Best Ways to Track Your Diet

Now, as you've just learned, there is some value in terms of self-education to be had from keeping track of your food, even if it's just temporary. So what's the best way to log your diet, and which values should you pay attention to? Even though the world of diet-logging software and apps is constantly evolving, at the time of this writing, there are five tools for tracking your diet that I have personally used and recommend.

1. Meal Snap

Meal Snap is an iPhone app that allows you take pictures of the meals you eat and then magically tells you what food was in your meal and estimates how many calories you consumed. Its range is fairly broad (an egg, an orange, a banana, and a small container of yogurt yields a value of 269–404 calories), but the convenience of simply photographing your food is unparalleled. Even though you shouldn't be eating packaged foods, if you combine Meal Snap with the iPhone FoodScanner app, which spits out nutrition data based on barcodes, you've got a pretty decent one-two combo.

2. Flickr or Instagram

Many of the clients I privately coach simply start a private Instagram or Flickr account and then share that URL with me. When you take a photo and upload it to either of these sites, you can leave a short comment describing your meal. Although there is no quantitative analysis of calories, macronutrients, and so on, there is something very simple and elegant about this qualitative approach.

3. SuperTracker

The USDA recently launched SuperTracker, which allows you to compare your food intake with USDA recommendations—which is a rather ridiculous activity considering how useless those recommendations are. However, it is completely free, and it spits out some fairly impressive, detailed analyses of your vitamin, mineral, and nutrient intake. This is the software I had my wife, Jessa, use when she logged her diet for a week and had it analyzed for our Inner Circle members, and it actually identified a few holes in her nutrition, such as excessively low calcium, vitamin D, and potassium intake. This was valuable information that we wouldn't have been able to gather with other free software programs.

4. MyNetDiary

MyNetDiary is another free website for diet logging, but it also provides mobile calorie-counting apps for iPhone/iPod/iPad, Android phones and tablets, and BlackBerry devices. The mobile apps can sync to your website profile, and their 520,000-plus-item food catalog is one of the largest and most precise nutrition databases in the world, with hundreds of foods added by both members and MyNetDiary. There are also paid upgrades with options for Withings bodyweight scale and Fitbit linking, personal-health-data uploading, the ability to share data with your trainer and coach, and so on. You can view the nitty-gritty details of one of my recent logs from MyNetDiary at BeyondTrainingBook.com/bgfdietlog, from a day when I wanted to verify that I was eating about 100 grams of carbs to keep my body in ketosis. (Table 12-1 is an image of my daily fat/protein/carb intake from MyNetDiary.)

	Calories	Fat / g	Carbs / g	Protein / g	TABLE 12-1
Averages over the period	3570	295	101	153	
Calories percentage		72%	11%	17%	

5. Argus

I've always been a big fan of the Azumio body-tracking apps, and the new Argus Motion and Fitness tracker iPhone app is pretty amazing as a single, unified health-and-fitness data hub that allows you to track everything in one place, including hydration status, activity, sleep cycles, weight, workouts, and more. You can even take a photo of your meal and tag the food groups represented, and the app will spit out data about your eating habits—without your having to input portion size or specific ingredients.

Four Steps for Logging Your Diet the Right Way

Now that you know the five best tools for logging your diet, you need to know exactly what you should be looking for as you log. After all, it's great to sit back at the end of the day and see a beautiful analysis of everything you ate, but you need to know how to make use of the numbers you're getting. Here are four steps for logging your diet the right way:

1. Use your metabolic rate to figure out approximately how much you should be eating.

Most of the recommended diet-logging tools enable you to calculate your baseline calorie needs, but you can also use the free calculators at Get Fit Guy (getfitguy.com) to find out exactly how many calories your body burns at rest to maintain basic physical needs such as kidney, lung, brain, and heart function. This is called your basal metabolic rate, or BMR. The site has calculators that tell you how many calories you burn once you add in your daily activity levels, and approximately how much you should eat to lose fat or gain muscle.

Your personal metabolic rate will fluctuate based on several factors[4], including:

- **Genetics:** The one factor we can't directly change. Some people have fast metabolisms, and others have slow ones.
- **Gender:** Because of greater muscle mass and lower body fat percentage, men usually have a 10 to 15 percent faster BMR than women.
- **Age:** A younger person has a faster rate of cell division. Beginning at age twenty, your BMR drops about 2 percent every ten years.
- **Weight:** Because of increased body-tissue volume, an obese person actually has a faster metabolism than a thin person.
- **Height:** Tall, thin people have a higher BMR than short people of equal weight. If both are on the same diet, the short person will gain much more fat.

- **Body fat percentage:** A lower body fat percentage usually means a higher BMR because of metabolically active lean-muscle mass.

- **Diet:** A strict diet or severe calorie restriction can reduce BMR by up to 30 percent. This is one of the reasons people on a crash diet lose up to twenty pounds of water weight, then plateau as their metabolism slows.

- **Body temperature:** For every 0.5°C increase in internal body temperature, BMR increases approximately 7 percent. Physical activity significantly increases body temperature.

- **External temperature:** Prolonged exposure to extremely warm or cold environments increases BMR. People who live in these environments often have a BMR that is 5 to 20 percent higher than those who live in more temperate climates.

- **Endocrine function:** Thyroid glands that produce too much thyroxin can double BMR, while BMR can drop by 30 to 40 percent in individuals with hypothyroidism, or inadequate thyroxin production.

- **Exercise:** In addition to increasing body temperature, exercise increases lean muscle mass, which burns more calories than fat—even when you're not exercising.

The actual number of calories burned by BMR averages 2,000 to 2,100 a day for women and 2,700 to 2,900 a day for men, but the total day's energy expenditure can significantly increase this number, with very active people burning as much as 6,000 to 8,000 calories a day.

So how do you determine your personal BMR? While you can go to a lab to get your heat output or expired-gas exchange measured, you can also calculate BMR yourself with the old-school pen, paper, and calculator method. Although I stick to online calculators like the one at BeyondTrainingBook.com/gfgcalc, here are three formulas you can use if you want to do this yourself by hand or understand the method a bit more completely.

1. **Multiplication:** Multiply your body weight in pounds by 15 or 16 to get your BMR. If you want to lose weight, multiply by 12 or 13; if you want to gain weight, multiply by 18 or 19. This method is very simple but doesn't account for body fat percentage and overestimates caloric needs for someone who is obese (30 percent body fat or more).

2. **Harris-Benedict equation:** This formula uses height, weight, age, and sex factors to determine BMR. It is more accurate than the multiplication method but also does not account for body fat percentage and may also be prone to calorie overestimation for obese people. Remember, 1 kilogram is 2.2 pounds, and 1 inch is 2.54 centimeters.

Men:

$$BMR = 66 + (13.7 \times \text{weight in kilograms}) + (5 \times \text{height in centimeters}) - (6.8 \times \text{age in years})$$

Women:

$$BMR = 655 + (9.6 \times \text{weight in kilograms}) + (1.8 \times \text{height in centimeters}) - (4.7 \times \text{age in years})$$

3. **Katch-McArdle formula.** This is the most accurate method and accounts for body fat percentage. To find your lean mass in kilograms, multiply your weight in kilograms by your body fat percentage (which you can find via a body fat measuring tool such as a Withings scale or a quick measurement by a personal trainer at a gym).

Men and women: BMR = 370 + (21.6 x lean mass in kilograms)

It's important to realize that BMR does not take into account your activity level, and this is where heart rate monitors or body-tracking devices are useful for determining your total daily energy expenditure. You can also use basic activity multipliers:

- Sedentary = BMR x 1.2 (little or no exercise, a desk job)
- Lightly active = BMR x 1.375 (light exercise/sports 1–3 days a week)
- Moderately active = BMR x 1.55 (moderate exercise/sports 3–5 days a week)
- Very active = BMR x 1.725 (hard exercise/sports 6–7 days a week)
- Extremely active = BMR x 1.9 (hard daily exercise/sports and physical job or twice-a-day training)

If you really want to get an accurate BMR calculation, you can make an appointment at a sports medicine facility or university physiology lab to get your resting metabolic rate tested. Prepare for the time of your life: You'll have to fast for a minimum of four hours before, then lie motionless for at least twenty minutes while breathing through a mask. For a more in-depth analysis of using metabolic testing to determine both metabolic rate and exact energy expenditure during exercise, check out the article I wrote for *Triathlete* magazine at BeyondTrainingBook.com/metabolic.

2. Compare your calorie intake and how you actually look, feel, and perform.

Using any of the methods above to figure out how much you should be eating is just going to give you numbers. It's much more important for you to pay attention to your body (especially when you take into account what you're going to learn later in this chapter about how little calories actually matter).

For example, I know that, based on my calculated metabolic rate and activity, I should be eating about 3,200 calories a day to maintain my weight and energy levels. (I know that 3,200 calories is the exact number because I managed an exercise metabolic laboratory for three years and had the opportunity to undergo several tests.) I also know that my weight drops like a rock, my ribs begin to show, my cheeks get hollow, and I don't have enough energy when I consistently cheat myself of more than 500 calories a day. In active people, this 500-calorie-deficit-feeling-like-crap phenomenon is actually quite common. I also know that I begin to gain weight, I develop an increasingly thicker fold of waist fat, and I feel constant and excessive fullness when I consistently eat an extra 500 calories a day, which is also common among athletes. So with some very simple head math, I know that my daily target intake is 2,700 to 3,700 calories.

Should you step on a scale to help you in the initial phases of calorie counting? In most cases, no. Scales don't give you accurate body-fat-percentage measurements;

they notoriously fluctuate 5 to 10 percent based on your workouts, your blood volume, your plasma volume, and your hydration levels; and they simply preoccupy you with worry the same way that measuring your food and counting calories do. Just as the most successful athletes I coach rarely count calories, they also rarely weigh themselves—they just pay attention to the way they look, feel, and perform. As a matter of fact, since quitting bodybuilding (a sport for which I had to fall into a specific weight class), I have not owned a scale, and I never plan on owning one again.

3. Make microadjustments based on activity levels and goals.

If your activity levels fluctuate during the week (as they should), you'll rarely be eating the same number of calories every day. Continuing with the example above, if I have an easy rest day, I simply eat less, and if I have a very active day, I eat as much as I need to. As if by magic, if I were to lie in bed at the end of the day, close my eyes, and mentally add up calories, I would come very close to my target 2,700 to 3,000 on easy days and 3,000 to 3,300 on hard days—but this is all accomplished by the simple magic of following my appetite and intuition, not by counting calories or weighing every scoop of everything I put in my smoothie.

This microadjusting is easily accomplished by simply eating slightly larger or smaller portions at meals, adding or removing one or two snacks or small meals from the previous chapter, or eating during your workout on a long training day. For me, caloric intake is nearly all hunger driven: If I'm hungry after a long day of training, I eat, and on big training days, if hunger wakes me at 1 or 2 in the morning, I'll stumble to the refrigerator and guzzle a glass of coconut milk or suck on a spoonful of almond butter.

Amazingly, in many cases where athletes are struggling with low energy, a complex hormonal issue or micronutrient deficiency is not the cause; it's simply that they don't eat enough nutrient-dense fuel on big training days.

Aside from calorie intake, are there other microadjustments you should make?

Yes. If your goals include implementing the strategies you'll learn about later in this book—such as ketosis, carbohydrate cycling, or intermittent fasting—you'll certainly need to make macronutrient adjustments to your carbohydrate, protein, and fat intake, and initially you may indeed need to measure and log to ensure that your adjustments are accurate.

But even this seemingly more advanced process becomes simple and intuitive with practice, and the end goal should still be to learn to listen to your body. For example, when maintaining a state of ketosis, I measured my breath ketones for thirty days straight and got a good idea of how I felt and performed while I was in ketosis. Then I quit measuring and just listened to my body.

4. Quit logging.

Once you have a decent idea of how many calories you're eating a day and have dialed in your approximate percentage of carbohydrates, protein, and fat based on the recommendations you'll learn later in this chapter, then . . . quit logging . . . quit counting . . . quit fretting.

Simply start enjoying quality, real, nutrient-dense foods and meals and pay attention to the way you look, feel, and perform.

Eat an extra meal and eat during your workouts on big workout days, and eat less on the easy days. Keep things simple, beautiful, and clean. You'll be happier.

After all, calories really do matter less than you think, and you're going to discover why in the next chapter.

Is It OK to Be Hungry?

Athletes often ask me whether being hungry is a bad thing. When it comes to eating for endurance, I am reminded of the 1993 video replay of the Hawaii Ironman triathlon. A portion of that coverage was devoted to Chuckie V, the 1990s bad boy of triathlon who sported a Mohawk and actually was banned from Ironman Hawaii because of his controversial race antics. (You can watch a really entertaining video for an introduction to Chuckie at vimeo.com/11810691.)

Anyway, at one point during the Ironman coverage, Chuckie is standing on the road stuffing his face postworkout, and he jokes through mouthfuls, "The only thing that sucks about eating . . . is having to take the time to *breathe*."

How about you? Are you one of those extremely active people who are constantly hungry? Do you finish one meal and immediately begin thinking about or planning your next meal? And does being hungry all the time make you think that something is wrong with you or your physiology?

It's important to understand why you get hungry in the first place. When you eat, the fat cells in your body release leptin—a hormone that you've already learned about. Increased levels of leptin reduce your desire and motivation to continue to eat. Within a few hours after you've finished eating, your leptin levels drop, and this drop in leptin causes a release of a different hormone, ghrelin, which is released by your stomach and pancreas and makes you feel hungry[2].

One reason many people have a hard time controlling their appetite or stopping after they've eaten enough is that they're leptin resistant.

Leptin resistance can be a vicious cycle, because overeating over a long period (i.e., during those four years of college) causes chronic hyperleptinemia (high leptin levels), and then leptin eventually becomes less and less effective in controlling appetite.

So it's actually possible to eat yourself into having a chronically insatiable appetite. Interestingly, another pathway to leptin resistance is a habitually low calorie intake.

If leptin is doing its job, it triggers satiety signals in your hypothalamus, and you stop feeling hungry. Leptin can also inhibit hunger signals from the hypothalamus[6].

The other interesting part of this equation is that those chronically high leptin levels cause chronically low ghrelin levels. This makes your hypothalamus hypersensitive to ghrelin so that when small amounts of ghrelin are released, you get very hungry, very fast.

In addition to spending much of your life eating too much, other lifestyle choices that can cause a leptin-ghrelin imbalance include lack of sleep, too much stress, and—even if you're not overeating—eating "hyperpalatable foods," such as processed or packaged foods that are designed to be addictive (just one potato chip, anyone?).

Is leptin resistance the only thing that can make you hungry? Absolutely not. Other reasons you get hungry include:

- **Expecting to be hungry.** A 1998 study titled "What Causes Humans to Begin and End a Meal" showed that the memory of what you've eaten accounts for a significant portion of your hunger, and that being full is partly a matter of recalling whether you've eaten a meal appropriate for the occasion[5]. For the same reason that you might be reluctant to eat dinner foods like spaghetti or steak for breakfast, you may feel full after meals simply because you expect to be full, and you may get hungry simply because you expect to get hungry (which may be why frequent snackers have such a hard time switching to eating three times a day).

- **Changing your weight significantly.** An idea called "set point theory" suggests that your body has a specific weight range in which it is comfortable, usually somewhere around 10 percent of your body weight[4]. So if you weigh 200 pounds, you have a 20-pound range and can generally avoid intense hunger pangs if you're at 180 pounds or above. But whether because of genetics or because of an internal "Help! I'm starving!" signal, when you venture too far outside your set point, your body seeks homeostasis and begins adjusting your metabolism to maintain weight. And part of this adjustment can include craving food.

- **Burning lots of calories.** Let's face it: Whether because of a naturally high metabolism (I've been tested, and I burn 2,500 calories a day just lying on the ground) and/or because of extremely high activity levels (you're an Ironman triathlete), your body just needs more nutrients and more calories to keep from self-cannibalization[2].

- **Having a dopamine or serotonin deficiency.** Chronic use of antidepressants or selective serotonin reuptake inhibitors (SSRIs), in addition to a very low-fat diet, inadequate protein intake, or a high-stress lifestyle, can all cause disruptions in brain neurotransmitters that help control cravings or help you be more satisfied or happy with the foods you do eat[1].

- **Gut issues.** Parasites, yeast, fungus, and bacterial imbalances in your digestive tract can trigger hunger and cravings[7]—and you'll learn more about that in the upcoming gut-fixing chapter.

Finally, thanks to our innate survival instinct, just the sight or smell of food can make us hungry, even if there's no physiological need for calories or nutrients. That's why buffets can be like taking a walk on the wild side.

So is hunger a bad thing?

First, it's important to understand that, in a normal situation, the leptin-ghrelin interaction and the hunger it produces are necessary for survival. Starting from the time you were a baby, if you never got hungry, you'd have very little incentive to eat. Not eating would mean no nutrients or calories, which would severely limit your growth and survival.

But if there is no physiological need for hunger, and you have ample stored energy (from food or your own fat), there's probably something wrong if you're constantly hungry, and here's what I'd recommend you do:

1. **Resensitize yourself to leptin.** Try four to eight weeks of completely altering any lifestyle and eating patterns that may be contributing to leptin resistance. Here are the best ways to do that:

   - Avoid fructose: This sugar tends to be a real trigger for leptin resistance.

   - Exercise in moderation, avoiding chronic cardio and stressful marathonesque workouts, and instead do short HIIT sessions with full recovery.

   - Control stress and cortisol: Reread chapter 9.

   - Try cold thermogenesis: Cold exposure may help you overcome leptin sensitivity; there are practical tips in chapter 5.

2. **Avoid hunger triggers. Certain eating patterns and foods have been proved to be correlated with more hunger.** Here are some tips for controlling those triggers:

   - Keep sweets and snacks out of the house or hidden in opaque containers.

   - When you're eating, leave any extra food on the countertop (not the table), or put it away before you begin your meal.

   - Avoid higher-carbohydrate or high-glycemic-index foods, which cause a hunger response very soon after a meal.

   - Minimize your options by limiting the amount of food in your house—no bulk purchases from Costco or easy-to-grab single-serving cans, packages, and bags.

3. **Know what you ate. Review what you learned earlier in this chapter about food logging, and use those tools to create awareness, even if just for a short period.** Two additional strategies:

   - Don't snack too much. It's almost impossible to keep track of food and calories if you're snacking half a dozen times a day (as many nutritionists sadly suggest). Instead, eat just two or three square meals, and then, if you work out, eat either before or after the workout.

   - Make your own food. The less you eat out at restaurants, have other people prepare your food, or eat out of packages and containers, the easier it is to keep track of what you eat.

Finally, if you want one more reason not to fret about eating when you're hungry, then you should know that in active people, restricting energy and cutting calories actually make you fat.

That's right.

Chronic calorie reduction in active athletes like gymnasts and runners has been proved to increase body fat percentage. The combination of exercise stress and calorie restriction puts the body into starvation mode, which makes it more necessary to store fat than to build or maintain muscle. Don't believe that restricting calories can make you fat? In one study titled "Relationship between Energy Deficits and Body Composition in Elite Female Gymnasts and Runners," energy deficits of as little as 300 calories a day below what was required for meeting activity requirements decreased metabolism and increased body fat percentage in both runners and gymnasts[8].

Which is all to say that being hungry is not a bad thing if you are hungry because you have a biological need for more calories or nutrients. In this case, simply pay attention to your body and eat more if necessary.

But if you make calorie adjustments and you're still hungry, it usually indicates a hormonal imbalance, gut issue, or other biological trouble spot that may need to be addressed, in which case you should review the lab-testing methods discussed in chapter 7 and read the upcoming chapter on fixing your gut very closely.

Now you have a basic idea of how many calories you need to eat, what are the best tools for tracking your diet, how to log your diet the right way, and whether it's OK to be hungry.

In the next chapter, you're going to find out why calories don't matter that much and what you should be focusing on instead, in addition to learning exactly how much carbohydrate, protein, and fat you should be eating. When you finish that chapter, you'll know exactly what works for 99 percent of the endurance athletes and extreme exercisers I've worked with.

Additional resources, helpful links, scientific references, websites, and surprise bonuses for this chapter are available at BeyondTrainingBook.com/Chapter12. Enjoy.

CHAPTER 13

How Much Carbohydrate, Protein, and Fat You Need to Stay Lean, Stay Sexy, and Perform Like a Beast

In this chapter, I'm going to give you three reasons calories don't really matter. I'll tell you how much carbohydrate, protein, and fat you need to stay lean, stay sexy, and perform like a beast—and outline a sample week of eating to support ideal levels of performance, endurance, and exercise.

Three Reasons Calories Don't Really Matter

Earlier, you learned how to count your calories and log your diet. But it's important to realize that it's the nutrient density and quality of your food that truly matter—not the calorie content.

But wait—a calorie is a calorie, right? Not really.

In the most recent study of this issue[26], one group ate slow-sugar-release, low-glycemic-index foods (think raw nuts or beef jerky), and another group ate faster-release, high-glycemic-index foods (think white rice or wheat bread). But both groups ate identical amounts of calories.

Researchers then monitored the blood sugar levels and appetites of the subjects and found that those consuming the high-glycemic-index foods had a blood-sugar-level crash just a few hours after eating and were hungrier sooner than those who ate the slower-release foods. In other words, an identical amount of calories consumed from a sweeter food triggered symptoms of food addiction and hunger cravings.

If you want to read a great book about why calories matter much less than we think, I recommend *Good Calories, Bad Calories,* by Gary Taubes. But in case you don't have the time or inclination to read a whole book on the subject, I'll give you three quick reasons why your primary focus should not be on counting calories.

1. Humans Don't "Burn Calories"

Calories technically don't even exist. A calorie is just a unit of measurement used to describe the amount of heat produced when a nutrient is burned in a metal oven called a calorimeter. And your body is very different from a simple metal oven. The process of burning fat or turning nutrients into energy or stored matter is way more complex than counting fictitious calories—and as you learned from the study above, something as subtle as the difference in the speed of sugar release can result in significantly different hormonal and metabolic reactions to a food.

2. Calories Aren't Our Fuel for Exercise

Human motion is not fueled by calories; it's fueled by the nutrient-derived chemical adenosine triphosphate (ATP). The problem with counting calories—besides the nonexistence of calories—is that it somehow makes us believe that our bodies are using exactly what we ate before a workout for fuel. In reality, your own storage fat provides the most concentrated source of energy—and there are athletes (find them at RunKeto.com or on Jack Kruse's forum at www.JackKruse.com/ BenGreenfieldFitness) who exercise at a steady state for entire days without taking in any calories. Their bodies are producing ATP from fat stores.

3. Nutrients Are What Really Matter

In reality, nutrients matter far more than calories, and nowhere is this more true than in exercising individuals. When the focus is on calories, everything is about numbers rather than nutrition—and you can easily end up missing out on key vitamins and minerals.

For example, a highly processed (but relatively nutrient-empty) Taquitos snack pack advertised as just 100 calories seems like a real deal if you're counting calories. But in choosing the snack pack, you might pass on a calorically equivalent large apple that rings in at roughly the same number of calories. The apple delivers vitamin C, folate, fiber, potassium, vitamin B_6, thiamin, and riboflavin, while the chips deliver vegetable oils, preservatives, and starch.

So the apple beats the Taquitos. And incidentally, 100 calories of wild salmon beats the apple. And (although you may not like to hear this), 100 calories of organic, grass-fed liver beats the wild salmon.

Go back and reread chapter 11. That's where you'll find nutrient-dense foods that allow you to quit counting calories.

Where to Start

Great, Ben. I've got a bunch of nutrient-dense meals I can turn to now.
I'm following the rules.
I'm not incessantly counting calories.
I'm paying more attention to the way I look, feel, and perform than to scales and numbers.
I'm paying more attention to nutrients than to calories.
But how do I know how much carbohydrate, protein, and fat I should be eating to fuel my active lifestyle without destroying my body in the process?

Definitely don't start with the traditional food pyramid.

Since 1974, when the first food pyramid appeared in Sweden, triangular- or pyramid-shaped nutrition guides have been used worldwide. There is a great graphic on the *Huffington Post* (which I link to on the web page for this chapter) that depicts some of the more popular food pyramids from around the world. Although in 2011, the USDA Food Pyramid was replaced by the new MyPlate design (see ChooseMyPlate.gov), MyPlate is very similar to the old food pyramid in terms of nutrient percentages, and many countries still use a traditional food pyramid to dispense nutrition advice.

Interestingly, in food pyramids around the globe, from China's food pagoda to Greece's food pyramid, cereals, grains, bread, pasta, and other starchy carbohydrates consistently form the base of the diet—with fats near the top of the pyramid in a "use sparingly" category.

But this type of nutritional advice can lead to serious health problems. After all, dietary fat from healthy sources has actually been shown to help increase weight loss, reduce risk of heart disease, lower blood sugar, lower damaging forms of cholesterol, and maintain proper brain function, especially in children[34].

And if you listen to my interview "The Shocking Truth about Wheat" with Dr. William Davis or my interview with Paul Jaminet about his Perfect Health Diet (both available on my website), you will learn that consumption of carbohydrates can cause everything from weight gain to fuzzy thinking to heart disease.

But the issues don't stop with the predominantly high-carb, low-fat model endorsed by most food pyramids. Frequent consumption of recommended foods such as pasteurized whole milk and ground beef has been linked to heart disease, not to mention that:

- Dairy is extremely overemphasized—although calcium is important, many vegetable and meat sources contain plenty of calcium with fewer calories.

- There is no difference between "good proteins" and "bad proteins," "good carbs" and "bad carbs," or "good fats" and "bad fats."

- The minimum daily serving of fruits is two to four, and that much fruit is a great way to send your blood sugar levels on a roller-coaster ride all day long if you're not careful.

Furthermore, at least when it comes to the USDA food recommendations, we've barely acknowledged the lobbying and political power of Big Food and Big Agra to subsidize industries such as dairy, corn, and wheat and heavily promote their products. (A great book to read more about these shenanigans is *Food Politics,* by Marion Nestle.)

So what should a good food pyramid actually look like for an athlete?

Although I have yet to be convinced that a food pyramid is the best, most functional way to dynamically depict dietary recommendations, a couple years ago I acted on hundreds of requests from readers and listeners and created a "Ben Greenfield–endorsed" food pyramid that is rich in the best nutrient-dense foods to support an active lifestyle (see Figure 13-1).

I call this design the Superhuman Food Pyramid, and it address all the issues above, ties in my personal nutritional philosophies, and also gives you a spectrum of choices from "Eat" to "Moderate" to "Avoid" for each food group so you don't have to deal with, for example, "Fats" or "Proteins" lumped into just one category.

To make it easier to put the Superhuman Food Pyramid into practice, I've included several pages listing each food category and the "Eat," "Moderate," and "Avoid" foods within that category so you can print, grab, and go to the grocery store or farmers' market with your Superhuman Food list.

The Superhuman Food Pyramid is free (and you can listen to me expounding on why "Fat Is Good") at BenGreenfieldFitness.com/fatisgood.

FIGURE 13-1.

The Superhuman
Food Pyramid

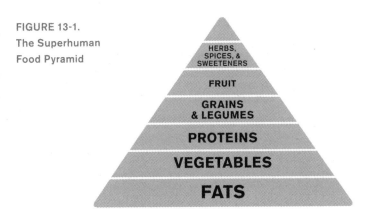

HERBS, SPICES, & SWEETENERS

FRUIT

GRAINS & LEGUMES

PROTEINS

VEGETABLES

FATS

HEALTHY FATS: 3–5 servings per day

EAT:

- Coconut oil
- Coconut meat
- Olive oil
- Macadamia nut oil
- Avocados
- Olives

- Organic grass-fed butter
- Organic yogurt (full-fat)
- Ghee
- Free-range eggs (with yolk)
- Grass-fed beef, bison, or lamb

- Sardines, anchovies, or haddock in water or olive oil
- Wild salmon, trout, tilapia, or flounder
- Triglyceride-based fish oil
- Pure cod liver oil

MODERATE:

- Raw nuts (except peanuts)
- Raw seeds
- Almond butter
- Palm oil

- Cold-press flax oil
- Bacon
- Mayonnaise
- Organic peanut butter

- Coconut ice cream
- Dark chocolate

AVOID:

- Roasted nuts
- Roasted seeds
- Regular peanut butter
- Regular butter

- Nonorganic meats
- Margarine
- "Spreadable" condiments
- Farmed fish

- Commercial salad dressings
- Safflower oil
- Sunflower oil
- Canola oil

- Cottonseed oil
- Commercial flax oil
- Soy ice cream
- Regular ice cream
- Milk chocolate

VEGETABLES: 3–5 servings per day

EAT:

- Sprouts
- Avocados
- Olives
- Asparagus
- Broccoli
- Cauliflower
- Cabbage
- Naturally fermented sauerkraut
- Naturally fermented pickles
- Bok choy
- Collards
- Swiss chard
- Kale
- Mustard greens
- Nori (seaweed)
- Organic greens powder or capsule

MODERATE:

- Sweet potatoes
- Yams
- Plantains
- Potatoes
- Corn
- Peas
- Carrots
- Celery
- Cucumber
- Squash
- Zucchini
- Romaine lettuce
- Red lettuce
- Iceberg lettuce
- Fennel
- Radishes

AVOID:

- Canned vegetables
- Nonorganic, unrinsed vegetables

Avoid these foods as well if you have an autoimmune disease or nightshade sensitivity:

- Potatoes
- Tomatoes
- Peppers
- Garlic
- Onions
- Eggplant

PROTEINS: 2–4 servings per day

EAT:

- Free-range eggs (with yolk)
- Grass-fed beef, bison, or lamb
- Pasture-raised, organic pork
- Sardines, anchovies, or haddock in water or olive oil
- Wild salmon, trout, tilapia, or flounder
- Organic whey/casein protein powder
- Organic rice/pea protein powder
- Organic hemp protein powder
- Organic yogurt (full-fat)

MODERATE:

- Yogurt cheese
- Raw cheese from grass-fed cows
- Organic cottage cheese
- Naturally preserved or dried meats
- Miso, tempeh, tamari, or natto
- Egg protein powder
- Soaked or sprouted beans and legumes
- Raw seeds and nuts
- Raw nut butter

AVOID:

- Nonorganic dairy products
- Processed cheeses
- Nonorganic, commercially processed meats
- Chemically preserved or dried meats
- Protein powders with artificial sweeteners
- Textured vegetable proteins
- Soy protein powder
- Tofu
- Roasted seeds and nuts
- Roasted nut butter
- Regular or canned beans and legumes

NON-VEGETABLE CARBOHYDRATES: 1–2 servings per day

EAT:

- Wild rice
- Brown or white rice
- Sprouted, organic quinoa, amaranth, or millet
- Sprouted legumes (beans and lentils)
- Gluten-free oats
- Organic full-fat yogurt

MODERATE:

- Soaked legumes (beans and lentils)
- Raw seeds and nuts
- Soaked, organic quinoa, amaranth, or millet
- Regular oats
- Fresh-milled kamut wheat
- Soaked and sprouted wheat products
- Non-GMO corn

AVOID:

- Canned legumes
- Regular wheat products
- GMO corn
- Roasted seeds and nuts
- Fava beans
- Soybeans
- Soy nuts
- Regular yogurt
- Cookies
- Biscotti
- Scones
- Crackers
- Bagels
- Bread
- Cereal

FRUIT: 1–2 servings per day

EAT:

- Apples
- Apricots
- Bananas
- Berries
- Cherries
- Cantaloupe
- Grapefruit
- Kiwi
- Mangoes
- Nectarines
- Oranges
- Papayas
- Peaches
- Pears
- Pineapple
- Plums
- Watermelon

MODERATE:

- Lemons
- Limes
- Grapes
- Strawberries
- Dates
- Figs
- Natural dried fruit
- Fruit juices

AVOID:

- Canned fruit
- Fruit in syrup
- Fruit candy
- Sugar-coated dried fruit
- Packaged dried fruit

HERBS, SPICES, & SWEETENERS: Use when needed

EAT:

- Cinnamon
- Cloves
- Allspice
- Stevia
- Xylitol
- Maltitol
- Turmeric
- Curry
- Cumin
- Fennel
- Star anise
- Garlic
- Ginger

MODERATE:

- Raw, pollinated honey
- Organic maple syrup
- Natural fruit sweeteners
- Blackstrap molasses
- Sucanat
- Truvia
- Regular table salt
- Red pepper
- Black pepper
- Fermented soy sauce
- Apple cider vinegar
- Brewer's yeast

AVOID:

- Processed sugar
- Candy
- High-fructose corn syrup
- Regular honey
- Agave syrup
- Aspartame
- Sucralose
- Acesulfame
- MSG

How Many Carbohydrates Should an Active Person Eat?

Now that you've got a supply of meals, a good way to choose nutrient-dense foods, and a handy grocery shopping list, it's time to dig into how many carbohydrates you should actually eat.

After all, isn't the answer to "How much carbohydrate?" the Holy Grail of fueling for athletes?

First, I'll readily admit it: I'm known as the low-carb, high-intensity guy. Based on what you've learned so far in this book, that's probably no surprise—train hard, eat healthy, don't stuff your face with too much sugar.

After living on a high-carb, junk-food diet and then switching to the high-protein, low-fat, low-carb diet that you read about the introduction to this book, I've followed the Paleo diet, a vegan diet, an Atkins diet, and even a ketogenic diet. The prevailing characteristic that defines how good or bad I feel is the amount of sugar and refined carbohydrates I eat, regardless of diet protocol.

My own experience with a low-carbohydrate diet began with an attempt to lose extra holiday pounds, followed by the stark realization that, contrary to my expectations and what I had been taught in traditional sports-nutrition classes, my performance, focus, and energy levels actually improved despite a lower carbohydrate intake. That was when I personally started digging into this stuff.

Turns out it's not just me.

Every month, I review dozens of clients' lab results, and the same pattern pops up over and over again: The higher the sugar and starch intake, the higher the blood triglycerides, the greater the inflammation, the worse the sleep, the more difficulty controlling body fat levels, and so on. Once the relatively nutrient-void carbohydrate sources—energy bars, whole-wheat bread, granola, cereal, muesli, pasta—are replaced with more nutrient-dense and healthy fats, proteins, and vegetables, biomarkers and performance quickly begin to take a turn for the good. Of course, there are other nutrient-empty foods that we cut, like vegetable oils, egg whites without the yolks, industrialized beef, and chicken and commercial dairy—but carbohydrates are the biggie, especially for athletes.

What I've discovered, and what you're about to learn, is that maintaining high blood sugar and constantly "topping off" storage carbohydrate levels to fuel your body for optimal performance may not actually be worth the health trade-off—especially if you can get the same results by eating less starch and sugar. There are proven health and longevity benefits to controlling high blood sugar, and I don't know about you, but if I can get those benefits and still maintain performance, I'm all in.

To understand the benefits, of controlling blood sugar roller-coaster rides—and the risks of having high blood sugar—see Figure 13-2[36-54] (and of course I'll include all study links at BeyondTrainingBook.com/Chapter13). I, for one, want to be around to see my grandkids, and considering that genetic testing has revealed that I have a higher risk for type 2 diabetes, I doubt that shoving more gooey gels and sugary sports drinks into my pie hole is going to do me any favors.

But (shocker!), I still do not recommend a low-carbohydrate diet for everyone. I usually do not recommend it blindly for:

FIGURE 13-2. Risks of High Blood Sugar

CANCER: Numerous studies have found that the risk for cancer increases with high blood sugar, which makes sense, since cancer cells feed primarily on glucose. This includes cancers of the endometrium, pancreas, and colon and colorectal tumors.

CARDIOVASCULAR DISEASE: High blood sugar has been shown to increase the risk for cardiovascular events, cardiovascular disease, and cardiovascular mortality—while lower glucose levels result in lower cardiovascular risk. Coronary artery disease risk has been shown to be twice as high in patients with impaired glucose tolerance, compared with patients with more normal glucose tolerance. The risk for stroke increases as fasting glucose levels rise above 83 mg/dL. In fact, every 18 mg/dL increase beyond 83 results in a 27 percent greater risk of dying from stroke. Incidentally, glucose can "stick" to cholesterol particles and render these particles extremely dangerous from a heart health standpoint, which is why it's all the more important to control blood sugar levels if you're eating a "high-fat diet."

COGNITIVE ISSUES: High blood sugar results in cognitive impairment and dementia.

KIDNEY DISEASE: Surges in blood sugar drive the production of fibrous kidney tissue and vascular complications in the kidneys, which can cause chronic kidney disease. There is a direct increase in chronic kidney disease as levels of hemoglobin A1c (a three-month "snapshot" of glucose control) rise.

PANCREATIC DYSFUNCTION: The beta cells in the pancreas that produce the insulin to help control blood sugar become dysfunctional with high blood glucose, raising the risk for type 2 diabetes. Researchers have discovered that beta cell issues are detectable in people whose glucose levels spike two hours after eating, despite those levels staying within the range considered normal and safe by the medical establishment.

DIABETIC RETINOPATHY: Diabetic retinopathy is damage to the retina that can lead to blindness—and it is highly aggravated by high blood sugar.

NERVOUS SYSTEM DAMAGE: It's been shown that patients with neuropathy whose after-meal glucose readings were above the diabetic threshold sustained damage to their large nerve fibers. Even neuropathy patients whose glucose readings remained well within the normal range showed damage to their small nerve fibers. Studies have shown that within any blood sugar range, the higher the glucose, the greater the damage to nerve fibers.

1. **Athletes in the heat of competition.** During, say, an Ironman triathlon or a Spartan Beast, you need a higher carbohydrate intake than on an easy training day. Duh. If you're going to go destroy yourself for nine to seventeen hours, you may need some extra glucose onboard. Interestingly, research suggests that this may be more because of a need to stave off neural fatigue than a direct carbohydrate need by the actual muscles[19]. In other words, even if you are eating a low-carbohydrate diet during your actual training, you will need to introduce a "slow bleed" of carbohydrates (along with some amino acids and fats) during longer training sessions or events that bring you past the point of glycogen depletion, which is typically sixty to ninety minutes of moderate- to high-intensity exercise or ninety minutes to two hours of low- to moderate-intensity exercise. I discuss the reasons for this in detail in the BenGreenfieldFitness.com podcast episode "Five Simple Steps to Turning Yourself into a Fat Burning Machine." But more on that in the chapter on a healthy race-day nutrition plan. For now, just realize that may you need extra carbs if you're going deep into the pain cave.

2. **Athletes doing an extremely heavy block of training that is higher load than they are accustomed to,** such as a triathlon camp that involves twenty-five to forty hours of hard work a week. In this case, you usually need more carbohydrates. I'm not saying that this volume of training and carbohydrate intake are healthy, but in some cases it can be a necessary sacrifice for building endurance in a big way. In other words, if you're going to ask your body to do a crap-ton of unnaturally heavy work, at least give it some sweet potato fries or an extra helping of white rice.

3. **Individuals with diseases or conditions that prevent them from properly metabolizing fats and proteins.** For example, if you've had your gallbladder removed, a high-fat diet full of Kerrygold butter, coconut oil, and bacon may not sit so well in your gut. Some of this can be managed with digestive enzymes that contain lipase and can assist with fat digestion, but ultimately, some folks simply can't handle extremely high amounts of fat combined with low amounts of carbohydrate. You might think that simply adding more protein would be the answer, but then you begin to play with issues related to protein toxicity and protein conversion to excess sugars.

However, if you're an average athlete putting in an average amount of training (that is, you are following the ancestral-athlete rules you learned about earlier), you need far fewer carbohydrates than what is widely recommended. There are three primary reasons for this:

1. **Eating fewer carbohydrates can help you get lean or stay lean.**

   A key component of weight loss is tapping into storage fat (adipose tissue) for energy. This access to fat cannot happen if the body is constantly drawing on carbohydrate reserves and blood glucose for energy[20]. In a moderate- to high-carbohydrate diet, not only does the utilization of fat for energy become far less crucial, but the body never becomes ideally efficient at using fat.

   There is a growing body of evidence proving that a high-fat, low-carbohydrate diet results in faster and more permanent weight loss than a low-fat diet. Furthermore, appetite satiety and dietary satisfaction significantly improve with a high-fat, low-carbohydrate diet that includes moderate protein. You can read about this research, as well as my own journey to becoming a fat-burning machine, in the two-part series entitled "How to Become a Fat Burning Machine" at BenGreenfieldFitness.com.

2. Eating fewer carbohydrates can increase health and longevity.
When glucose is used for energy, a lot of free radicals are produced. Free radicals are dangerous molecules that can damage normal cellular processes[9]. The burning of fat for energy does not create this same cellular damage. For an athlete who is already generating significant numbers of free radicals from exercise, further damage from high blood glucose levels is a double whammy.

In addition, the constantly elevated levels of circulating blood sugars that a moderate- to high-carbohydrate diet can cause are associated with nerve damage; small, dense cholesterol particles (the culprits in heart disease); high morbidity; bacterial infection; cancer progression; and Alzheimer's.

As you will learn later in this chapter, simply getting your energy from non-blood-glucose-based energy sources can directly improve your quality of life and ensure that you live longer and healthier.

3. Eating fewer carbohydrates can increase energy stability and eliminate gastrointestinal distress while training or racing.
Because of genetic predispositions, some athletes are much more sensitive to the fluctuations in blood sugar caused by carbohydrate intake[13]. Often, when these athletes consume a sports bar, drink, gel, or other carbohydrate source, this sensitivity prompts a sharp and drastic drop in energy after the short-lived initial increase in energy levels. But the calories from fats and proteins are utilized at a far steadier rate than carbohydrate sugar, resulting in more stable energy levels.

In addition, uncomfortable amounts of gas and bloating can be a result of the high bacterial activity caused by carbohydrate fermentation in the digestive tract. Many athletes experience an even greater degree of gastrointestinal distress from food allergies or intolerances to common carbohydrate sources, particularly wheat.

But Wait! Don't I Need Carbohydrates to Fuel Training?

Ah, the million-dollar question. Here's the thing: If you eat mostly carbs, your body will run mostly on carbs. If you eat mostly fat, your body will run mostly on fat.

But despite your very cool ability to change the fuel you burn depending on what you eat, carbohydrates are the darling of most modern sports-nutrition gurus. The standard recommendation to athletes engaging in regular training and racing, especially in endurance sports or extremely demanding exercise, is to consume seven to ten grams of carbohydrate per kilogram of body weight daily for optimal performance, and to consume large amounts of sugary drinks, gels, and bars during prolonged activity to keep blood glucose elevated. And many carbohydrate-loading protocols call for up to 85 percent carbohydrate intake in those last few days before a big workout or event. Talk about keeping cereal companies in business!

In other words, the Holy Grail seems to be to protect carbohydrate stores at all times. The general argument for carbohydrate consumption goes something like this:

- Fatigue during training and racing is thought to coincide with the carbohydrate fuel tank approaching empty (the infamous bonk, as is humorously demonstrated in the best cartoon I've ever seen on running at TheOatmeal.com/comics/running).

- Because it is thought that you can't burn fat as a primary fuel at training and racing intensities, all focus is on looking for ways to increase the size of the carbohydrate fuel tank (despite even the leanest of athletes having tens of thousands of calories of readily accessible storage fat).

- This entire process is driven partly by the cheapness of carbohydrate sources— hello, government subsidizing of grains and carbs!—and a mistaken belief that eating a lot of fat, no matter how healthy, may have deleterious health effects.

So, based on this advice, you roll out of bed and glance at your watch. You've got a twelve-mile run or some other big workout on tap for the day and limited time to get it in. Do you lace up and head out without grabbing a banana, a bagel, or a fistful of sports gels, or do you make sure that you have some valuable sugar to consume before and during your effort so you don't "bonk"? If you're a good little athlete who heeds popular nutrition "wisdom," you probably raised your hand and said, "Eat sugar!"

Now, there is absolutely no arguing with the fact that high carbohydrate intake before an endurance workout can postpone fatigue and improve performance. So there is some logic to the recommendation from most sports nutritionists to consume a diet that provides high carbohydrate availability before and during exercise.

But when it comes to finding the ideal combination of both performance and health, I have another question for you: How superior is high carbohydrate intake to its polar opposite—high fat, low carbohydrate intake?

Turns out that there is a lot about this stuff in the scientific literature.

- A study published in *Medicine & Science in Sports & Exercise* in 2010 suggested the answer to this question when the authors coined the phrase "train low, compete high" in response to results showing that untrained individuals achieved better training adaptations and aerobic capacity after ten weeks of training on a low-carbohydrate diet compared with subjects who had a high carbohydrate intake before and during exercise[21].

- A study in the *Journal of Applied Physiology* showed that trained individuals who performed twice-a-day sessions without eating for two hours after the first session (thus depleting carbohydrate stores with the first session) experienced a better ability to store carbohydrate, use carbohydrate as energy, and burn fat—with no loss in performance—compared with a group that trained only once a day and ate carbohydrates afterward[23].

- A study of trained cyclists doing high-intensity interval training with no carbohydrate intake showed improved fat utilization and an increase in the enzymes involved in energy metabolism—again with no loss of performance[28].

- Additional research shows that when carbohydrate stores are depleted by almost 50 percent, there is increased stimulus for enhanced enzyme activity in skeletal muscle—which is a good thing, since it means that you can more efficiently produce energy from fuel[32].

Want more?

I could fill an entire book. Literally. I actually did. It's called *Low Carbohydrate Diet for Athletes* (you can get it at BenGreenfieldFitness.com/author)—and it was written not just for triathletes, but for anyone who leads an extremely active life and wants to dig into the science, value, and practical hands-on application of a low-carbohydrate diet.

You can also read:

- *The Art and Science of Low Carbohydrate Performance,* by Jeff Volek and Stephen Phinney

- "High Fat Diets & Endurance Exercise Performance," a really good article by a Norwegian exercise scientist that I link to on the web page for this chapter

- An excellent series of articles called "High Fat Diet for Cyclists" by Jamie Scott at thatpaleoguy.com (don't worry, the articles are great for more than just cyclists)

Those last two resources dig quite thoroughly into how fitness is enhanced when you train with low levels of storage carbohydrate or low levels of carbohydrate intake during your workout. And because I just can't help myself from giving you a little extra lower-carbohydrate ammo, here's the CliffsNotes version for you:

- In trained individuals, a large amount of fat oxidation takes place at intensities well above 80 percent VO_2 max—giving an athlete the ability to get up to even very-high-intensity efforts without draining carbohydrate stores and also allowing an athlete engaged in steady-state exercise (for example, an Ironman triathlon) to tap into fat fuel stores even when going at a relatively fast pace. This also means that more carbohydrate stores will be available when you really need them, such as for an all-out effort.

- Incredible gains in metabolic efficiency and economy have been demonstrated when using fat as a primary source of fuel and doing high-intensity interval training, with this one-two combo causing potent 3–5 percent decreases in the oxygen cost of cycling, which is extremely significant. Translated into real-world numbers, this increased fat utilization from carbohydrate restriction and high-intensity interval training would allow you to pedal a bicycle at your lactic acid threshold of 315 watts, whereas a high-carbohydrate, aerobic-only program (the way most people train) would allow for only 300 watts. And 15 extra watts of power is huge in a sport like cycling.

- A high-fat diet trains your body to burn even more fat during exercise, even at high intensities. Fat is released faster and in greater amounts from your storage adipose tissue and transported more quickly into your muscles and mitochondria. In a fat-adapted individual, the muscles also store more energy as fat and use this fat-based fuel more efficiently and quickly. Even more interestingly, a high-fat diet can cause a shift in the gene expression that codes for specific proteins that increase fat metabolism and create very similar adaptations to exercise itself. So the mere act of shifting primary fuel intake from carbohydrates to fat begins to make you more "fit" even in the absence of exercise.

- Most studies that compare carbohydrate utilization with fat utilization fail to take into account the fact that full adaptation to gaining all the benefits of using fat as a fuel takes time—often more than four weeks. And since most studies comparing fat and carbohydrate utilization are short-term, we rarely see the benefits of fat adaptation fleshed out in research—and exercise intensity/fat oxidation graphs like the one in Figure 13-3 rely only on data from athletes eating a typical high-carbohydrate diet.

FIGURE 13-3. Exercise Intensity and Fat Oxidation

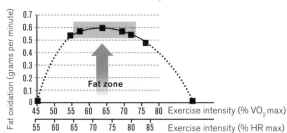

As I've just highlighted, figures such as the ones above are not based on data from fat-adapted athletes, for whom the fat-burning zone continues at higher intensities.

And guess what else? This one shocked me when I first realized it, but eating fewer carbohydrates during a workout can actually help you recover faster.

How? Without delving too deeply into the nitty-gritty of the science, it all comes down to the fact that the repair and recovery of skeletal muscle tissue is dependent on the "transcription" of certain components of your RNA. And a bout of endurance exercise combined with low muscle-carbohydrate stores can result in greater activation of this transcription. In other words, by training in a low-carbohydrate state, you train your body to recover faster.

So, sorry, Wheaties, but it's true: You don't have to be a carboholic to be a good athlete.

Despite the sports-gel-chamber-enhanced water bottles on those fancy new bikes and the tray for your sports gels on the gym's treadmill, as long as your workout is not performed in a carbohydrate-depleted state and does not exceed about two hours, there is zero evidence that not consuming carbohydrates during the session will reduce your performance. In fact, there is evidence to the contrary—that no loss of performance occurs!

Whether these benefits are due to decreased carbohydrate utilization or increased fat utilization is unclear, but there are obvious benefits to going low-carb before and during training. And if it isn't going to hurt your performance but is going to increase your quality of life, why not eat fewer carbohydrates?

So let's sum things up. If you moderately restrict carbohydrates before, during, and after training, you may:

1. Increase activity of the biological mechanisms responsible for building and repairing lean muscle tissue.

2. Increase your ability to preserve and ration valuable carbohydrate stores.

3. Increase your fat utilization during exercise.

4. Increase the activity of the enzymes responsible for metabolizing carbohydrates during high-intensity exercise, such as racing.

5. Increase your ability to recover fast.

6. Increase your health and longevity.

In just a moment, I'm going to dig into some of the common objections you may get from your pasta-pushing, Gatorade-guzzling friends when they find out that you're eating fewer carbohydrates. But first, please allow me to emphasize that I am *not* endorsing a zero-carbohydrate diet. I am not even encouraging the popular "fewer than fifty-grams-of-carbohydrate-a-day" diet. In most cases, when I say low-carbohydrate diet, I'm referring to about 100 to 200 grams a day, and I'll explain why in a moment. There is one special exception to this rule, called ketosis, which we'll get into in the next chapter, but most active people (and especially women) do not need to charge into the kitchen with a Sharpie and draw a skull and crossbones on their potatoes unless they want to invite some serious metabolic and hormonal damage.

In other words, just because fewer carbohydrates is good does not mean that trace amounts to none is even better. Read the excellent blog post "Carbohydrates for Fertility and Health" by my friend Stefani Ruper at paleoforwomen.com if you want more details on this.

Answering Objections

Once your training partners, family, or other friends learn that you're eating fewer carbohydrates—or once you begin skipping the obligatory pre-event pasta party—you're guaranteed to hear criticism and see raised eyebrows. Typically, the objections to a low-carbohydrate diet come in the form of three questions.

Objection #1: Aren't glucose and carbohydrate necessary for energy during exercise?

As mentioned earlier in this chapter, directly burning blood glucose for fuel causes a significant amount of free radical damage compared with burning storage carbohydrate, storage fats, or circulating fats in the bloodstream. This type of fuel utilization occurs in an athlete trained to eat a gel every twenty minutes during every single training session or to always have a sports drink on the edge of the pool and a bowl of pasta waiting at home to refuel after a workout.

While cells can certainly burn glucose for energy, fat is the preferred energy source of nearly every cell, especially mitochondria, which are the energy-creating organelles within most cells. Until extremely high exercise intensities are reached (rarely the case with endurance athletes) or until you have exercised continuously for two to three hours, fat is a completely usable energy source. Specifically, natural saturated fats, omega-3 fatty acids, and medium-chain triglycerides are extremely dense energy sources whose metabolizing produces very few damaging by-products. The specific parts of the body that do need glucose on daily basis are the brain, the nerves, special proteins called glycoproteins (which form compounds like mucus), and cells within the immune system, the gastrointestinal tract, and the kidneys. But the total daily amount of glucose calories required by these body parts is about 500 to 700 carbohydrate calories, not the 1,500 to 2,000 consumed by most athletes.

Objection #2: Doesn't fat lead to cholesterol-related heart disease as well as weight gain?

No! Not only does a high-fat, low-carbohydrate diet produce more weight loss than a low-fat, high-carbohydrate diet, but there is no evidence that the cholesterol particles derived from fat increase the risk of heart disease—unless fat consumption is paired with a moderate to high intake of starchy, sugary carbohydrate sources. It is at that point that cholesterol can become oxidized and increase risk of heart disease.

The entire idea that high cholesterol causes heart disease is flawed, and there are entire books that prove it. A very good place to start learning more about the positive and healthy properties of fats is the website Cholesterol-and-Health.com.

Objection #3: Don't you need to carbo-load before a race?

I'll dig into this a little more in the chapter on racing, but once you begin eating a low-carbohydrate diet, your body will, within about ten to fourteen days, begin to become more efficient at burning fat. Although it takes one to two years to adapt to a low-carbohydrate diet to the extent that you will be a fat-burning machine and can ride a bike for hours without eating anything (listen to my podcast episode "How to Live Like a Polar Bear and Eat Like a Great White Shark" with Jack Kruse at BenGreenfieldFitness.com/polarbear to learn why), your basic fat adaptations come more quickly than that. This means that you need relatively fewer carbohydrates during race week or the day before a race, since your body develops an enhanced ability to conserve storage carbohydrate and also an increased ability to utilize fat as a fuel, both during rest and on race day.

What this means is that an entire week of carbo-loading and high sugar intake—which, if your goal is weight loss, health, or longevity, may end up doing more harm than good—is not necessary. Since I shifted to a lower carbohydrate intake, I have found that the 85 to 90 percent carbohydrate diet I once ate during race week leaves me sick to my stomach and on blood sugar roller-coaster rides all week long.

The only adjustments in nutrition that you need to make during race week are: (1) a slightly more carbohydrate-dense breakfast the day before and the morning of the race; (2) moderate amounts of healthy starches with dinner, such as a sweet potato or white rice; and (3) carbohydrates during the actual race. This is still considered carbo-loading, but only relatively speaking, and not in the traditional sense of seven to ten days of high carbohydrate intake before an event. The simple fact is that the advice you'll find in infographics such as the one shown in Figure 13-4 is based on non-fat-adapted, high-carb-intake athletes. (There are more details on this study in an excellent article at BeyondTrainingBook.com/carbload.) Sure, this loading protocol boosts performance—but what are the health implications of eight cups of cooked pasta and half a liter of a sports drink for dinner?

More Low-Carb Resources

Just in case that's not enough ammo to enable you to fire back knowledgeably at your critics, and before I give you some specific carbohydrate, protein, and fat ratios, I want to share with you a ton more articles I wrote. Knock yourself out!

- "Can You Build Muscle on a Low-Carbohydrate Diet?" (BeyondTrainingBook. com/bgflowcarb)
- "Should You Eat Carbohydrates before Exercise?" (BeyondTrainingBook.com/ carbsnexercise)

FIGURE 13-4. HOW MUCH CAN YOU CARBO-LOAD?

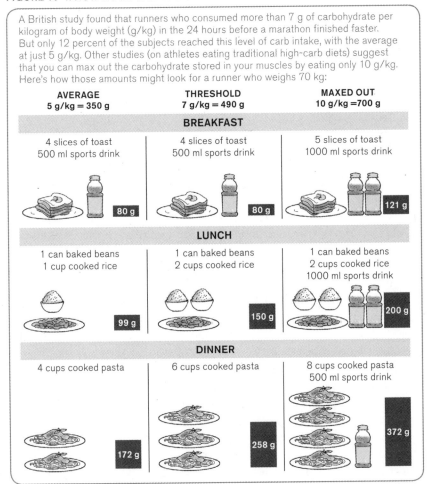

A British study found that runners who consumed more than 7 g of carbohydrate per kilogram of body weight (g/kg) in the 24 hours before a marathon finished faster. But only 12 percent of the subjects reached this level of carb intake, with the average at just 5 g/kg. Other studies (on athletes eating traditional high-carb diets) suggest that you can max out the carbohydrate stored in your muscles by eating only 10 g/kg. Here's how those amounts might look for a runner who weighs 70 kg:

AVERAGE 5 g/kg = 350 g	THRESHOLD 7 g/kg = 490 g	MAXED OUT 10 g/kg = 700 g
BREAKFAST		
4 slices of toast 500 ml sports drink	4 slices of toast 500 ml sports drink	5 slices of toast 1000 ml sports drink
80 g	80 g	121 g
LUNCH		
1 can baked beans 1 cup cooked rice	1 can baked beans 2 cups cooked rice	1 can baked beans 2 cups cooked rice 1000 ml sports drink
99 g	150 g	200 g
DINNER		
4 cups cooked pasta	6 cups cooked pasta	8 cups cooked pasta 500 ml sports drink
172 g	258 g	372 g

- "How I Ate a High-Fat Diet, Pooped Eight Pounds, and Then Won a Sprint Triathlon" (BeyondTrainingBook.com/bgfhifatdiet)
- "The Hidden Dangers of a Low-Carbohydrate Diet" (BeyondTrainingBook.com/bgflowcarbdanger)
- "Ten Ways to Do a Low-Carbohydrate Diet the Right Way" (BeyondTrainingBook.com/bgflowcarb10)
- "Five Ways to Get a Big Carbohydrate-Restricting Performance-Enhancing Advantage" (BeyondTrainingBook.com/bigcarb5)
- "Four Crucial Reasons to Think Twice about Eating Carbohydrates before a Workout" (BeyondTrainingBook.com/bgf4think2x)
- "Seven Supplements That Help You Perform Better on a Low-Carbohydrate Diet" (BeyondTrainingBook.com/bgfsupplmnts7)
- "How to Turn Yourself into a Fat Burning Machine by Fasting for Twenty-Four Hours Then Going Out and Do Monster Workouts Without Bonking" (BeyondTrainingBook.com/bgf24hfast)
- "Is It Possible to Be Extremely Active and Eat a Low-Carbohydrate Diet?" (BeyondTrainingBook.com/bgfextreme)
- "How to Become a Fat Burning Machine: Part 1" (BeyondTrainingBook.com/bgffatburn1)
- "How to Become a Fat Burning Machine: Part 2" (BeyondTrainingBook.com/bgffatburn2)

Give Me Some Numbers, Ben!

Yes, if you've been reading closely, you may have noticed that I haven't thrown any exact carbohydrate, protein, or fat percentages or ratios at you. Based on the way I feel about incessant calorie counting, and also the fact that these percentages tend to vary widely across daily activity levels, it will probably come as no surprise that I'm not too keen on having you obsess over your macronutrient ratios. But having a ballpark idea of what is healthy and optimal can be useful. So here we go.

I've got a secret for you: When it comes to the ideal ratio of carbohydrate, protein, and fat for the average human machine, the book has already been written.

The particular book to which I'm referring has been featured on my blog many times, particularly in the podcast episodes "Is There One Single Diet That Is Best?" (BenGreenfieldFitness.com/phd) and "If You Could Eat Fat All Day, Would You?" (BenGreenfieldFitness.com/phd2). It's called *Perfect Health Diet*. Written by Paul Jaminet, an astrophysicist, and Shou-Ching Jaminet, a molecular biologist, it bridges the gap between a natural ancestral-eating approach and hard data based on scientific evidence.

In a nutshell, the diet is based on the nutrient-rich foods you've already learned about, such as whole eggs, liver and other organ meats, bone broths, seafood, seaweed, dark green leafy vegetables, and fermented foods. It also includes a number of other meats, natural fats, healthy oils, and "safe" starches, such as white rice and sweet potato, to provide adequate protein and calories for the average person.

And, yes, it has actual numbers. The Perfect Health Diet is 20 percent carbs, 65 percent fat, and 15 percent protein.

To many people who eat or want to eat low-carb, 20 percent carbs may seem high. And to those eating the traditional athlete diet of 55 to 65 percent carbs, 20 percent may seem low. But 20 percent is based on what you've already learned about the body's need for glucose as a structural molecule, a brain and muscle fuel, and an immune booster. So in a 3,000-calorie-a-day diet, 600 of those calories, or 150 grams, would come from carbohydrate—and that would be enough to satisfy the body's basic energy needs (although there are specific instructions in the book about how to safely implement a very-low-carb, ketogenic diet with a carbohydrate intake as low as 50 grams a day).

The reason for 65 percent fat is the body's inherent need for fatty acids as a primary fuel source for the majority of our natural activities, and also the need for fatty acids as core structural components of the human body, especially the brain and nervous system. If you care to get into the nitty-gritty, the diet delves into percentage recommendations for omega-3 fatty acids, omega-6 fatty acids, saturated fats, monounsaturated fats, and the like.

Finally, 15 percent protein is based on the idea that the body needs enough amino acids for repair and recovery, but that excessive protein intake can cause ammonia waste from protein metabolism and toxins produced by gut bacteria that ferment protein.

Anyway, that's just a basic overview. If you want more details, go buy the book. (I highly recommend it as a companion to this book.) And if you really want to immerse yourself in the diet, check out the thirty-day Perfect Health Diet retreats in Austin, Texas—where a bunch of nutrition experts, including me, teach you how to implement the diet and tweak it to your specific needs.

But there is one problem with the Perfect Health Diet. The book wasn't written by a train-until-you-drop athlete. It was written by a brilliant yet mild-mannered astrophysicist and molecular biologist husband-and-wife team. They are not powerlifters, CrossFitters, or Ironman triathletes. So you may need to make some adjustments to the diet if you're doing extreme amounts of physical activity, specifically:

1. Some athletes need more than 15 percent protein intake on difficult, "eccentric," muscle-breakdown days, such as a day with hard weight training or running intervals. The same goes for athletes who want to put on lots of muscle quickly.

2. An intake of 20 percent carbohydrate sometimes needs to be "cycled" with a higher carbohydrate intake of up to 30 to 40 percent on longer, higher-volume training days, especially if your goal is not ketosis or 24/7 fat burning, which may have some health risks if you're not careful.

Once these two variables are taken into account, daily carbohydrate, protein, and fat intake tends to fluctuate quite a bit based on activity levels. So an easy training day might follow the Perfect Health Diet's 20:65:15 ratio exactly. But a long weekend workout, such as a hundred-mile bike ride, may demand a slightly higher carbohydrate and protein intake, more like a 30:50:20 ratio. A harder day of weight training or running may require more amino acids for repair and recovery and a 20:50:30 ratio. In the sample meal plan at the end of this chapter, you'll see how the ratios can vary slightly from day to day based on activity levels.

So I'd be lying if I gave you exact percentages of carbohydrates, protein, and fat that are "perfect" for the extremely high and variable activity levels of a very physically active individual. I'm sure you can guess that I don't pay much attention at all to my ratios. I just base every meal around fats and oils, add moderate amounts of healthy protein, and make sure I don't overeat carbs.

Conveniently, all the meals for athletes in chapter 11 fit a Perfect Health Diet model. And there are some great websites and blogs that post recipes compatible with the Perfect Health Diet, including:

- Tummyrumblr
- The Domestic Man
- Nutty Kitchen
- Francesca Eats

- Ancestral Chef
- Living in the Ice Age
- 10 Minute Meals
- Chowstalker

Finally, if you don't have time to read *Perfect Health Diet* but you have an hour, you can listen to a fascinating podcast interview with Dr. Barry Groves (at BeyondTrainingBook.com/groves) in which he delves into ancestral, biblical, mythological, and biological reasons to eat something very close to that 20:65:15 ratio. It is well worth your time and will give you a fantastic foundational understanding of why humans are so different from many other animals when it comes to our ideal nutritional ratios.

Now, before we get into a sample week of eating, there's one more important question to tackle. . . .

Are You Sure I'm Getting Enough Protein?

Now you understand the health importance of limiting carbohydrate intake. And now you know how important fat is for cells, the brain, and the nervous system. But when it comes to protein for athletes, you hear the same mantras over and over again:

"Athletes and exercisers need more protein."

"Protein is crucial for muscle repair and recovery."

"Eat more lean protein."

The problem is that while you certainly do need amino acids from protein for repair and recovery, neurotransmitter formation, and avoidance of self-cannibalization, the importance of protein is usually blown way out of proportion.

To determine how much protein you actually require, you need to become familiar with the term *nitrogen balance*. Here's how it works: Nitrogen enters your body when you consume protein from food or amino acid supplements, and it exits your body in your urine as ammonia, urea, and uric acid (all the breakdown products of protein). When the amount of protein you eat matches the amount you use, you're in nitrogen balance[3]. As you can probably deduce, if you don't eat enough protein, you'll be in negative nitrogen balance and quite unlikely to be able to repair muscle after a workout (a "catabolic" state). If you consume too much protein, you'll be in positive nitrogen balance, and while you'll definitely have what you need for muscle repair (an "anabolic" state), some health issues may arise because excessive nitrogen overfills your body with ammonia, urea, and uric acid, which have some nasty side effects that we'll get into in just a bit[32].

The US Recommended Dietary Allowance (RDA) is 0.36 grams of protein per pound of body weight per day. It was designed for most people to be in nitrogen balance—without protein deficit or excess. While athletes and frequent exercisers need more protein than this, bodybuilders, football players, weight lifters, and other big strength and power athletes frequently take it to the extreme and consume far more than the RDA (in some cases up to 2 grams per pound!).

But studies suggest that, even for athletes, there really isn't much additional benefit to be gained by exceeding 0.55 grams per pound of body weight to maintain nitrogen balance[23]. If you're trying to exceed nitrogen balance for the purpose of putting on muscle or recovering from extreme exercise sessions, studies also indicate that you don't need to eat more than 25 percent above that 0.55 grams per pound of body weight, which would be 0.55 × 1.25, or 0.68 grams per pound of body weight. For simplicity, I prefer to round that up to 0.7 grams[35].

Let's put those numbers into context. I weigh 175 pounds. If I don't want to gain muscle, and I just want to make sure I'm getting enough protein for muscle recovery and body repair, I should eat a minimum of 0.55 × 175, or 96 grams of protein a day.

Rounded up to a nice even 100 grams, that means I could have a couple scoops of protein powder for breakfast (which I do), a can of sardines on my salad at lunch, and four to six ounces of grass-fed beef with dinner. That's easily 100 grams, and it doesn't even count the other protein I get from seeds, nuts, grains, legumes, and the like. If I'm eating about 3,200 calories a day, which is typical for me, that puts my protein intake at about 13 percent.

Frankly, this is about exactly what I would eat on an easy exercise day. The rest of my diet is healthy fat (which keeps me smart, keeps my joints healthy, feeds my brain, and maintains high levels of hormones), along with large amounts of vegetables and small amounts of fruits.

If I wanted to gain muscle or I'm doing lots of muscle-damaging exercise such as a long, hard run, I would eat 0.7 × 175, or about 125 grams of protein. So I would basically just add a couple handfuls of raw almonds and a dollop of full-fat yogurt, or a couple extra scoops of protein powder, and I'd be good to go. This would come closer to about 16 percent of my daily calorie intake.

I've worked with some athletes who have trouble putting on muscle or recovering properly unless they eat 0.8 to 1.0 grams per pound of protein, which often puts them in the 15 to 25 percent protein range. While this does allow for optimal repair and recovery, these athletes are also at risk of ammonia toxicity, making rapid muscle gain a risky venture for precious organs such as the kidneys[5]. This is why I rarely exceed 150 grams of protein a day unless I happen to stumble upon a really, really good Korean barbecue joint.

This brings me to my next point. What are the actual risks of eating too much protein or having too much nitrogen in your system?

First, consider that ammonia is a toxic compound to the body. Once you get close to about 1,000 calories a day of protein (that's about 250 grams), you can no longer convert ammonia to urea, and this toxin begins to build up in your body. This is extremely stressful on your internal organs, especially your kidneys.

Next, excess protein can cause dehydration if you do not drink enough water, because your kidneys need more water to convert ammonia into urea.

Finally, mammalian target of rapamycin (mTOR) is a gene that is directly correlated to accelerated aging. Decreased activity in this gene can result from moderate calorie restrictions and slightly lower amino acid intake[14]. So excessive protein intake and a constantly positive nitrogen balance could actually shorten your life! Interestingly, the same can be said for being in a constant anabolic state via the use of substances such as growth hormone, hormone replacement therapy, and testosterone injections and creams.

The takeaway is this: Eat as much protein as your body needs for repair and recovery (about 0.55 grams per pound of body weight), eat a little more if you want to put on muscle (up to 0.7 grams per pound of body weight), and then consume the rest of your calories from healthy fats and vegetables, with limited amounts of fruits and safe starches for fueling intense bouts of physical activity.

A Sample Week of Eating

Now you know that for the ideal combination of performance and health, the ballpark values to shoot for on most days are 20 percent carbohydrates, 65 percent fat, and 15 percent protein.

Remember the sample Ironman training week from chapter 3? Let's revisit that week and take a look at how these nutrition concepts apply. The eating plan outlined on the following page is designed for a higher intake of healthy fat, carbohydrate "cycling" with slightly more carbs on more active days, and avoiding excessive protein. And it conveniently relies on many of the nutrient-dense meals from chapter 11.

Throughout the day, I recommend supplementing these meals and snacks with several servings of the liquid snacks from chapter 11, such as bone broth, green tea, kombucha, kvass, and coconut water.

You'll notice that meals—especially breakfasts and lunches—repeat quite frequently. I recommend this for several reasons: It allows you to stick to the tried-and-true so you know what your body's exact response will be; you can avoid wasting time preparing meals; and you don't have to worry about what to eat. In most cases, especially for busy athletes, the simpler the better.

Now that you have a basic idea of how many calories you need to eat, the best tools for tracking your diet, how to log your diet the right way, why calories don't matter much anyway, why your diet should be skewed toward a higher fat intake, how many carbohydrates you should be eating, how much protein is necessary, and whether it's OK to be hungry, you know exactly what works for 99 percent of the endurance athletes and extreme exercisers I've worked with.

But some of us are special cases. So in the next chapter, I'm going to discuss how to tweak your nutrition if you are, say:

- An aging athlete
- Female
- A child
- Vegan/vegetarian
- In ketosis
- Fasting

In the meantime, as usual, additional resources, helpful links, scientific references, websites, and surprise bonuses for this chapter are available at BeyondTrainingBook.com/Chapter13. Enjoy.

MONDAY:

30 minutes of easy bicycling skills and drills, 20 minutes of easy swim drills

Breakfast—High-fat green smoothie

Lunch—Sardine salad

Snack—Chia slurry

Dinner—Steak and roasted vegetables with butter from grass-fed cows

TUESDAY:

20 minutes of heavy barbell lifts, 30 minutes of running HIIT workout

Breakfast—High-fat green smoothie

Lunch—Leftovers wrapped in bok choy, Swiss chard, or kale

Snack—Protein powder in coconut milk or raw dairy

Dinner—Scrambled eggs

WEDNESDAY:

30 minutes of bicycling HIIT workout, 30 minutes of swimming HIIT workout

Breakfast—High-fat green smoothie

Lunch—Sardine salad

Snack—Pemmican or jerky

Dinner—Cobb salad

THURSDAY:

20 minutes of heavy barbell lifts, 30 minutes of easy running drills

Breakfast—High-fat green smoothie

Lunch—Leftovers wrapped in bok choy, Swiss chard, or kale

Snack—Protein powder in coconut milk or raw dairy

Dinner—Steak and salad

FRIDAY:

60 minutes of injury-prevention and core training, yoga, or an easy swim

Breakfast—Bulletproof Coffee or high-fat turmeric tea

Lunch—Nori wraps

Snack—Liver pâté with flax seed crackers

Dinner—Poached salmon and steamed vegetables

SATURDAY:

2.5 hours of 20 minutes on, 5 minutes off cycling intervals at race pace; 3 x 1,000-meter swim at race pace

Breakfast—Hot power cereal

Long-workout fueling—Raw seeds and nuts with dried fruit

Lunch—Grocery store

Snack—Pemmican or jerky

Dinner—Sushi restaurant sashimi and seaweed salad

Dessert—Coconut ice cream

SUNDAY:

60–90 minutes of 9 minutes on, 3 minutes off running intervals at race pace

Breakfast—Waffles or pancakes

Long-workout fueling—Chia slurry

Lunch—Mexican restaurant guacamole and beef; no tortillas

Snack—Protein powder in coconut milk or raw dairy

Dinner—Easy chicken dinner

Dessert—Dark chocolate and red wine

CHAPTER 14

The Zen of Customizing Your Diet to Your Unique Body and Goals

News flash: For some of us, nutrition isn't simple. We have dietary preferences. Our bodies change. Our internal biology fluctuates. We have stuff we always want to tweak, or tweaks we always want to test. We're unique snowflakes. We're crazy, biohacking guinea pigs. We spend thirty-seven minutes at the frozen yogurt store carefully analyzing which toppings to put on our tiny dab of gluten-free, animal-friendly, low-carb vanilla-kale yogurt.

Whichever category you happen to fall into, in this chapter you're going to discover exactly what to do if you have an extremely active lifestyle but are:

- Vegan or vegetarian

- Aging (that is, you fall into the masters category for your sport)

- Female (sorry, guys, but there are a few unique aspects of the female body that I suspect you're aware of)

- Young (nutrition is different for children and adolescents than it is for adults)

- Fasting (if periodic calorie restriction gets you excited)

- Ketotic (if you never met a carb you didn't hate and dig ketosis)

Ten Important Items to Include in a Vegan or Vegetarian Diet

As we thrash through the ocean chop, hammer our bike cranks for hours on end, repeatedly pound our flesh on hot pavement, and hoist large amounts of weight overhead, do we actually need meat, milk, and eggs to maintain and restore our amino acids, vitamins, and minerals? Or can we get all our performance and recovery needs from plants alone?

In my blog article "How to Be Extremely Active and Eat a Plant-Based Diet Without Destroying Your Body," I explore the omnivore-versus-herbivore debate, lay out the arguments of both sides, and reveal the plant-based diet regimens of a variety of athletes, from Ultraman Rich Roll to aging endurance athlete Dr. Bill Misner.

But my purpose here and now is not to argue for or against veganism, vegetarianism, or any other variation of a plant-based diet, since that's a can of worms. Instead, I just want to make sure that you get what you need nutritionwise if you eat a plant-based diet and are very physically active.

If you're not careful, there will be gaping nutritional holes in your plant-based diet. Common mistakes include not eating a wide variety of colors in whole plant foods, not eating enough calories, and not supplementing with vitamins, fatty acids, amino acids, minerals, and micronutrients that are notoriously missing from a plant-based diet.

The fact is, it is just as easy to eat poorly on a plant-based diet as it is on an omnivorous diet. Vegetarians can gorge on ice cream, Twinkies, Taco Bell, Domino's pizza, and McDonald's milkshakes all day long. And vegans can stuff their faces with crap like fast-food French fries, potato chips, and highly processed "meat" products made with soy and wheat gluten and still technically be eating a plant-based diet. Granted, omnivores can make many of these same bad choices, but it's harder to create deficiencies when you're eating meat, fish, and eggs.

Your top ten strategies if you're going plant-based are:

1. **Eat real food.** Avoid Frankenfoods, such as fake meats, textured vegetable proteins, and processed soy products. In addition to often being genetically modified, soy contains digestive irritants and digestive enzyme inhibitors, such as lectins, phytates, and protease inhibitors. Yes, most of these problematic compounds can be rendered generally harmless by fermenting soy and consuming it in forms such as miso, natto, and tempeh, but you should avoid processed foods such as soy milk and tofu. Soy also contains high levels of goitrogens, which are compounds that inhibit the thyroid's ability to utilize iodine correctly. Consuming a lot of soy could lead to hypothyroidism. Finally, soy contains plant estrogens in the form of isoflavones, which can raise estrogen levels and lower testosterone levels[3]. So women with estrogen dominance and men and women with testosterone deficiencies shouldn't be eating soy.

2. **Avoid a high intake of inflammatory omega-6 vegetable oils, such as soybean oil, corn oil, cottonseed oil, sunflower oil, peanut oil, and margarine.** Instead, use coconut oil, olive oil, avocado oil, and macadamia nut oil[9]. At the same time, increase omega-3 fatty acid intake from algae-based DHA supplements such as ENERGYbits (see the resource web page for this chapter) and get another essential fatty acid, alpha linolenic acid (ALA), from ground chia seeds, hemp seeds, or flax seeds.

3. **Supplement with vitamin K$_2$.** Vitamin K$_2$ is crucial for a healthy heart and skeletal system and is notoriously lacking in a plant-based diet[27]. I highly recommend about 100 micrograms of vitamin K$_2$ a day, along with generous amounts of natto (which incidentally goes well with avocado, sea salt, and extra-virgin olive oil for breakfast).

4. **Supplement with vitamin D$_3$.** If you want to keep your bones and teeth strong and give yourself adequate hormone and steroid precursors, I recommend thirty-five IU of vitamin D$_3$ per pound of body weight[8]. This could be tough if you're a strict vegan, because most supplemental vitamin D$_3$ is derived from lanolin, which comes from wool, and most vegan vitamin D comes in the form of D$_2$, which is a far less potent form. Garden of Life vitamin D$_3$ is one of the few vegan brands out there.

5. **Get vitamin A.** Vitamin A is crucial for healthy bone tissue, vision, and hormones, but plants contain only beta-carotene, which your body converts into vitamin A, but not very efficiently[29]. You need to focus on enhancing this absorption as much as possible by eating beta-carotene-rich foods with fat (that is, with olive

oil or avocado), attending to any of the gut issues that you'll read about later in this book, and getting adequate iron and zinc, which help convert beta-carotene into vitamin A. Cooking beta-carotene-rich foods also helps increase absorption. Beta-carotene can be found in concentrated amounts in sweet potatoes, carrots, kale, spinach, turnip greens, winter squash, collard greens, cilantro, fresh thyme, cantaloupe, romaine lettuce, and broccoli.

6. **Properly prepare grains, legumes, and nuts**. As you have learned, fermentation can make soy more digestible[28]. Similarly, you can neutralize many of the antinutrients and mineral-binding compounds in grains, legumes, and nuts by properly soaking and (if desired) sprouting and fermenting them. A useful soak-time chart for the most common grains, legumes, and nuts can be found at BeyondTrainingBook.com/pacfitsoak.

7. **Maximize iron absorption.** Nonheme iron is the form found in plant foods, and it's less bioavailable than the heme iron in meat[21]. But you can increase iron absorption from plant-based foods when you consume them with vitamin C (like eating beta-carotene-rich foods with fat). Combine foods such as Swiss chard, spinach, beet greens, lentils, beans, and quinoa with foods high in vitamin C, like tomatoes, bell peppers, lemon juice, strawberries, oranges, papaya, kiwis, pineapple, and grapefruit. You should also moderate tea and coffee consumption since both reduce iron absorption.

8. **Use iodine.** Plant-based diets are notoriously iodine deficient[25]. Sea vegetables, such as nori, kelp, and dulse, are the best natural sources of iodine. Check out Main Coast Sea Vegetables' nutritional analysis page at BeyondTrainingBook. com/seavegp15, where you'll find many more sources of iodine. Also consider taking a daily dose of six milligrams of liquid iodine.

9. **Take vitamin B_{12}.** Nearly every study conducted on vegans shows much higher rates of B_{12} deficiency than in omnivores, with elevated homocysteine as a result. (Homocysteine increases blood clotting and increases the risk of heart disease[21].) I recommend ten micrograms of a highly absorbable liposomal vitamin B_{12} per day (this is a form that you spray under your tongue).

10. **Supplement with taurine.** Taurine is an amino acid found only in animal foods, and it is crucial for brain development, healthy blood pressure, blood-glucose stability, fighting free radicals, and maintaining healthy vision[23]. Your body can make its own taurine from a combination of other amino acids, but this can be very hard for vegan athletes to pull off in adequate volume[20]. Now Foods makes a vegan taurine powder (trust me, it's a much healthier alternative than Red Bull), and I recommend one gram per day.

Those are the biggies.

If you want to go the extra mile, I recommend adding these performance-enhancing supplements: 2–5 grams of creatine (some research shows cognitive deficits in vegans related to creatine deficiency), 250–500 milligrams of L-carnitine (which enhances mitochondrial utilization of fat and is a common deficiency in a plant-based diet), and

1–2 grams of beta-alanine (a lactic acid buffer that can be helpful for non-meat-eating athletes) per day.

Besides the strategies above, what does "doing it right" actually look like? Here are sample food days in the lives of two successful endurance athletes.

Rich Roll, an ultrarunner and author whom I interviewed in the podcast episode "Some of the Craziest Superfoods You've Never Heard Of" (BenGreenfieldFitness. com/roll):

Preworkout morning smoothie: Kale, beets, chia seeds, hemp seeds, maca, orange, flax seeds, Vega Whole Food Optimizer

During workout: On bike—coconut water, Vega Sport, Hammer Nutrition Perpetuum; on run—coconut water, Vega Sport, Hammer Nutrition Heed

Postworkout: Coconut water; cold quinoa with coconut or almond milk, berries, Udo's Oil, and hemp seeds

Lunch: Salad with mixed veggies and vinaigrette or brown rice, beans, greens, and hemp seeds

Snack: Smoothie with brown rice, pea, or hemp protein; almond milk; cacao; almonds; and walnuts

Dinner: Lentils over brown rice with beet greens and avocado, arugula salad, and sweet potatoes

Dessert: Coconut milk ice cream or chia seed pudding

Bill Misner, PhD, a nutritionist, alternative-medicine practitioner, and top masters runner whom I interviewed in the podcast episode "Everything You Need to Know About How a Plant-Based Diet Affects Your Performance" (BenGreenfieldFitness. com/bill):

Breakfast: Oatmeal, ground flax, psyllium

Lunch/postworkout: Spinach, broccoli, Brussels sprouts, cabbage, carrots, sweet potatoes, and fruit (Bill eats a total of 200–300 grams of whole plant foods a day)

Dinner: Kale, black beans, asparagus, more fruit (Bill allows approximately three hours of "grazing" to eat a huge evening meal!)

Based on the success of plant-based endurance athletes like Rich Roll and Dr. Misner—and also Scott Jurek, Brendan Brazier, Hillary Biscay, and even UFC fighter James Wilks (whom I interviewed at BenGreenfieldFitness.com/wilks), it seems possible to eat a plant-based diet and avoid many of the potential deficiencies and health risks. But I do not eat a plant-based diet, nor do I endorse it.

As you learned in the previous chapter, I eat a high-fat diet, which is incredibly difficult to maintain primarily with plants. Unlike the gut of a gorilla or a ruminant such as a cow, the human gut is simply not large enough to turn vegetable matter into fatty acids at an adequate rate for ideal metabolic and nervous system health. This is one of the reasons most traditional cultures consume some sort of animal food, such as bone broths; fish and shellfish; land and water fowl; land and sea mammals; eggs, milk, and dairy products; reptiles; and even insects. In many cases, the whole animal is consumed, including muscle meat, organs, bones, and fat (with the organ meats and fats preferred). And the number of nutrients that can be gotten from animal foods is hard to replicate with a diet of kale and bananas, no matter how many vitamins and other supplements you take.

Finally, the extremely low cholesterol levels that I've seen in the blood labs and biomarkers of athletes on plant-based diets who have consulted with me give me a bad feeling about the potential for long-term health risks, especially with regard to the brain and nervous system. As *Primal Body, Primal Mind* author Nora Gedgaudas discussed at my Become Superhuman live event (SuperhumanCoach.com), those with total cholesterol under 200 do more poorly on cognitive tests than those with total cholesterol over 240, and this is perhaps why vegetarians and vegans have been shown in studies to have the smallest brains—even smaller than those eating the Standard American Diet. Low cholesterol also compromises immune function, increases overall risk of premature death, and increases the risk of stroke, cancer, depression, suicide, Alzheimer's, Parkinson's, kidney disease, and sickle cell anemia[13].

The takeaway: While I don't personally advise a 100 percent plant-based diet (especially if you're very physically active), you can at least mitigate its potential damage by going the extra mile to use methods such as soaking, sprouting, and fermentation when preparing your foods utilizing the strategies I've just outlined.

Two Essential Elements That Every Aging Athlete Needs

As you age, your body undergoes structural and functional changes that increase your need for specific nutrients. Inconveniently, at the same time, your ability to absorb and utilize specific nutrients begins to decline. And if you happen to be taking medication for health conditions brought on by age, that medication may interfere with nutrient absorption or deplete your body of precious nutrients. Because of this, your daily requirement for many nutrients increases as you age.

Two specific nutrient considerations to take into account as you age are:

1. Calcium

Bone density declines with age, especially if you're sweating out tons of minerals while burning through tons of calories—as is often the case with aging endurance athletes. As you age, you also secrete less stomach acid, which makes it harder for your body to absorb calcium[33]. This is why (at least in America) the recommended calcium intake for seniors is about 20 percent higher than it is for younger adults.

But I'm not a big fan of popping calcium pills, which have been shown to increase your risk of heart attack (probably because of calcium deposits in arteries)[5]. Instead, you should consume a wide variety of calcium-rich foods, such as full-fat raw dairy, sesame seeds, sardines, collard greens, and spinach. Supplement these foods with minerals and vitamins that assist with calcium absorption and improve bone density. Specifically, take magnesium (400–600 milligrams a day), vitamin K_2 (100 micrograms a day), and especially vitamin D_3 (2,000–4,000 IU a day for most aging adults), which tends to be more deficient in seniors.

For older athletes (and I'll describe in just a moment what I mean by "older") I also recommend one or two servings of liquid trace minerals per day and nine to twelve capsules of the bone-building, joint-protecting supplement NatureFlex on workout days.

2. Protein

Because of age-related muscle-mass loss (sarcopenia) and decreased hydrochloric acid production in the stomach, you need more protein as you age. Unfortunately, your ability to absorb protein is simultaneously decreasing[14]. For aging athletes, the 15 percent protein requirement discussed in the previous chapter may need to be adjusted to as much as 25 percent, preferably in conjunction with a good digestive enzyme combined with hydrochloric acid (such as a capsule that includes a full spectrum of digestive enzymes along with HCl and pepsin), consumed immediately before eating. As you get older, you need to eat more nutrient-densely, and since fatty foods are generally more nutrient-dense, I recommend eating more of them to increase protein intake at the sacrifice of carbohydrates.

Finally, I think that Bill Misner is onto something when he says that he takes several hours to eat dinner each night. The more you chew and the slower you eat, the more likely you are to absorb vital nutrients from your food. While I'm not necessarily saying that you have to devote your entire evening to eating dinner, you may find that you simply need to eat your meals more slowly as you age.

So what constitutes "aging"? I'll admit that it's hard to pin a definition on the term. If you're in the masters category for any sport, event, or competition, you probably qualify. If you find yourself losing muscle mass more quickly or your bone density decreasing, you probably also qualify. Heck, McDonald's will give you a senior discount if you're fifty or older. Ultimately, age is a slippery concept to define but is perhaps best left in the eye of the beholder.

Three Reasons Exercise Can Make Women Fat

In my podcast episode "Why Women Gain Weight When Training for Endurance, and What You Can Do about It" (BenGreenfieldFitness.com/219), I responded to a question from a woman named Lisa who wrote in and said:

I have a question about weight gain during marathon training. I'm a 28-year-old female training for my fourth marathon in June. I run anywhere from 50 to 70 miles/ week at the height of my training and I eat very clean. I also lift weights 2–3 times per week. I'm 5'6" and around 130 pounds. Whenever I train more intensely for marathons I end up gaining about 10 pounds. I don't think this is all muscle and I don't think it is due to overeating, since I track my food quite assiduously and usually end up about 700 calories in the hole every day. I've become concerned about this weight gain and was tested for hypothyroidism (which was negative). When I mention my weight to physicians, they seem dismissive, since I'm not overweight. Is there any way to explain this weight gain despite these steep calorie deficits? I ate a low-carb and high-fat diet for about a month in December when work prevented me from training at all, and I ended up losing 10 pounds in a month, then regaining it almost immediately once I resumed my training. I've been able to make massive time improvements despite this weight gain, but it leaves me feeling bloated and large in my "normal" clothes. I've heard of several others (mostly women) gaining weight during marathon training and I'm wondering what the explanation for this could be, especially when the person is OCD about calorie intake (as I have been).

Lisa is not alone. This is a huge problem among female athletes, especially those engaged in endurance exercise or a consistently high training volume combined with calorie depletion.

In my response to Lisa, I explained why many female athletes gain weight or become unhealthy. It is due to a combination of three factors:

1. **Excessive cortisol:** As the body churns out cortisol in response to repetitive training stress, it brings on sodium retention and subsequent fluid retention and bloating[22].

2. **Progesterone depletion[6]:** With excessive training stress, the body shuttles precious levels of the hormone precursor pregnenolone into cortisol production instead of progesterone production (the "pregnenolone steal," pictured in Figure 14-1). Since progesterone facilitates the utilization of storage fat for energy, this decreases the body's ability to tap into its own fat for fuel.

3. **Estrogen dominance[32]:** Estrogen is a hormone that promotes cell division, cell growth, and, in excessive amounts, formation of fat tissue. Estrogen dominance can be created by stress, poor sleep, and mineral imbalances (in addition to some of the other factors you'll learn about in the lifestyle section of this book). Of course, all three of these issues are magnified with huge amounts of training. In addition, since progesterone protects against the "pro-growth" effect of estrogen, the drop in progesterone and the concomitant rise in estrogen creates a weight-gain double-whammy.

FIGURE 14-1

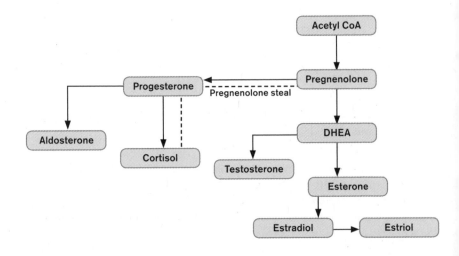

So if you're a female athlete training long, hard, or heavy, what can you do about this?

In addition to implementing every single one of the stress-control strategies you've already learned about, as well as eating a higher-fat diet to allow for adequate steroid and hormone production[16], you should follow these nutritional guidelines:

1. Limit your exposure to estrogen-raising factors in your diet, including excessive amounts of coffee (no more than two cups a day), unfermented soy sources such as tofu and soy milk, nonorganic meats, commercial dairy, sugars, and starches.

2. Help your liver deal with excess estrogen through natural detoxification. This can be accomplished by drinking two to three cups of green tea a day; eating lots of cruciferous vegetables, such as broccoli, cauliflower, and cabbage; and getting adequate fiber (a daily kale shake will do the trick).

3. Use a supplementation protocol that allows your liver to naturally detox high levels of estrogen. In addition to paying close attention to the gut-cleanse and detox chapter, I recommend that you:

   • Consider progesterone cream or sublingual progesterone under the supervision of a medical practitioner or someone well versed in the Wiley Protocol, which is a custom-tailored form of bioidentical hormone replacement.

   • Take a vitamin B and antioxidant complex (I recommend one packet of Life Shotz a day or daily use of the EXOS multivitamin).

   • Use a source of hops, such as Integrative Therapeutics AM/PM PeriMenopause Formula, which Dr. Sara Gottfried recommends in my podcast episode "The Cost of Being a Bad-Ass—How to Cure Your Hormones."

   • Use a natural anti-inflammatory high in curcumin, such as Phenocane or EXOS curcumin.

   • Take 200 milligrams a day of the detoxification compound diindolylmethane (DIM).

All the stress you're exposing your body to is actually training it to store fat, lower metabolism, and retain water, but the strategies I've just mentioned will at least help mitigate the damage.

Of course, female athletes can also experience a loss in body weight accompanied by a drop in bone density, loss of menstruation, and severe hormonal depletion.

This is an outcome I often see in women who have been living like Lisa for a long time and eventually hit the wall with adrenal fatigue and complete energy depletion. The low progesterone continues but is matched by an eventual drop in estrogen and cortisol and hormonal fatigue.

In this case, when chronic levels of training are combined with a low calorie intake, your liver and adrenals get "tired," you become insensitive to important hormones like leptin and insulin, your sleep suffers, your body weight drops, and you begin to have low-thyroid symptoms and menstrual dysregulation.

In other words, you become what is called "skinny-fat," a phenomenon in which you look thin but your entire body is covered in a layer of fat. You typically have sagging in your butt and a bit of a belly despite your skinny appearance. It's kinda like the female version of a skinny guy with the beer belly. Your rate of muscle loss and hormone depletion simply outmatches any rate of fat loss.

This may sound sexist or unfair, but women are simply less capable of "running from a lion" every day, day in and day out, the way men can. If you're going to go up against your biology and try to do so anyway, you'd better do an excellent job of eating adequate calories, detoxing your liver, and getting as much rest, recovery, and sleep as you can. By caring for your body with tons of nutrient-dense foods, getting lots of sleep, and implementing all the important recovery tips outlined in chapter 8, you can keep many of these issues at bay, but you must listen carefully to your body, because, as a woman, you are fighting an uphill battle.

Women can also take advantage of the significant gender differences in fuel selection during exercise[18]. For example, one of the most common methods to determine how much fat and carbohydrate you use for energy is a measurement called respiratory exchange ratio (RER), which measures the ratio of carbon dioxide produced to oxygen consumed. A lower RER means higher fat metabolism, and a higher RER means higher carbohydrate metabolism. Studies have shown that during low- to moderate-intensity exercise, women have a much lower RER (that is, they burn way more fat) than men.

This could be one of the reasons that as women exercise longer, their performance tends to parallel men's more and more. When corrected for distance, the time "gap" between a top female and male Ironman triathlon finisher is much smaller than the gap between a top female and male 100-meter sprinter. Apparently, because women are naturally better fat burners, they are good at going long.

Are there any practical fueling or training tips that can be fleshed out from this fact? While there's no research to back it up, I highly suspect that women will gain a great advantage in maintaining long-term training health by:

- Limiting the volume of extremely high-intensity, carbohydrate-utilizing, "exhausting" training sessions (such as CrossFit WODs, long track-sprint intervals, or tough workouts like Tabata sets) to two or three days a week maximum—especially if they're engaging in other longer, energy-depleting, stressful training sessions, such as triathlon or marathon training. Since women are even better than men at fat oxidation and endurance, their focus should primarily lie in strength, power, speed, mobility, and balance, with limited amounts of high-intensity metabolic conditioning and fat-fueled long aerobic sessions.

- Engaging in moderate amounts of low-volume movements throughout the day, including walking, using standing workstations, gardening, and easy aerobic sessions fueled by consuming lots of fat from coconut or MCT oil, nut butters, and the like.

- Eating enough carbohydrates to support normal fertility and health, without emphasis on fasting or constant ketogenesis. As I alluded to earlier, the article "Carbohydrates for Fertility and Health," by Stefani Ruper, will give you more details (see the link on the resource web page for this chapter).

To understand more about how where you are in your menstrual cycle relates to the way you feel and perform, I recommend reading *Running for Women,* by Jason Karp, who is also interviewed in an Endurance Planet podcast about fueling for female athletes (BeyondTrainingBook.com/karp). In the book (and in slightly less detail in the podcast), several topics are tackled that are relevant to all women, including:

- The impact of the menstrual cycle on hydration, body temperature, metabolism, and muscle function

- How and when to train during the menstrual cycle, pregnancy, and menopause

- How to avoid the risks of the female athlete triad—eating disorders, osteoporosis, and menstrual irregularities

- How to use gender differences to your advantage

Finally, ladies: Be cautious with fasting, and resist the temptation to focus on keeping your body in fat-burning mode by restricting calories for long periods. You'll learn more about fasting strategies for women later in this chapter.

Five Ways to Fuel Your Kids the Right Way

If you're reading this, you may have very active children, or perhaps you plan on having athletic kids in the future. When it comes to healthy fueling for kids, and especially what they should eat during exercise, quite a bit of confusion abounds.

The fact is, children are not just mini-adults, and growing children who are getting a lot of exercise have several defining physiological characteristics that make them different than the rest of us. There are five ways that nutrition should differ for active young individuals (up to age sixteen):

1. **Athletic girls can consume fewer carbohydrates than athletic boys.** This should make sense based on what you've already learned about the different nutritional needs of women in general. In large nutritional surveys on young athletes ranging in age from twelve to eighteen, the carb intake of female athletes tends to be on average three to four grams per kilogram of body weight lower than that of male athletes. What this means is that girls intuitively consume fewer carbs during training (which should not be taken as an instruction to eat fewer carbs than guys in general). Here's the rub, though: The current recommendation for carbohydrate intake is about four grams per kilogram for girls and seven grams per kilogram for boys. With 2.2 pounds in a kilogram, a 90-pound young female athlete should be eating about 165 grams of carbohydrates daily, or about 650 calories. Wowza. That's hardly low-carb or ancestral. I recommend that if you have a daughter who is an athlete or you are a young female athlete, you lean toward chia seeds, nut butters, and coconut oils for fuel rather than energy bars and gels.

2. **Fat is the preferred fuel for young athletes.** In most studies, exercising children have shown 10 to 40 percent higher fat oxidation rates than exercising adults[32]. As you've already learned, very well trained adults (such as Ironman triathletes) and fat-adapted athletes show these same high fat oxidation rates. I've always

wondered whether children's higher rates of fat oxidation are simply due to the fact that their metabolisms haven't had enough time to be messed up from years of chronic sugar consumption. Once again, I suspect that fueling children with avocados, coconuts, nuts, seeds, and other healthy fats may yield just as successful results as filling them up with candy and energy bars. So now you know that girls naturally burn fats better than boys, that children in general burn fat better than adults, and that female adults burn fat better than male adults.

3. **Physically active children burn less storage carbohydrate but more carbohydrate from food sources than physically active adults.** This is because children have lower levels of the enzymes that break down muscle carbohydrate to fuel, which is probably some type of mechanism to conserve storage carbohydrate for a child's growth and development. While you might think this means that you should make sure a child has some carbohydrates in addition to fat available during a training session or race, this may not actually be the case, as I point out below.

4. **During exercise that lasts seventy-five minutes or less, eating carbohydrates does not appear to give young athletes any performance advantages.** As you learned earlier, children burn fat more efficiently than adults, and it appears that during exercise this increased fat oxidation serves as a mechanism to keep blood glucose stable. Children's bodies can actually slow down the conversion of carbohydrates into energy during exercise. Interestingly, free fatty acids, which indicate available fats to burn during exercise, increase in children during exercise, meaning that children can readily mobilize fat stores for energy and possibly even use energy sources that have higher amounts of fat. Once again, this shows that, for those under the age of sixteen, it may be beneficial to choose fat-based energy sources rather than sugar, and that shoving Oreos into the face of a young soccer player may not do him or her any good. Incidentally, this also makes me wonder whether in a more natural setting—that is, without the corruption of the typically high-carbohydrate Western diet—these carbohydrate conservation and fatty acid utilization mechanisms might actually stick with us into adulthood.

5. **Regular adult sports drinks may not be emptied fast enough by a child's stomach during exercise.** In both children and adults, higher exercise intensities slow the rate at which fluids and fuels pass from the stomach into the intestine, which means that less fuel is absorbed and utilized. However, this occurs to an even greater extent in children, and the maximum amount of fluids (whether water or a sports beverage) that a child can absorb per hour in these conditions is approximately twenty to twenty-four ounces—the size of a standard water bottle. So don't overhydrate children during exercise if you don't want them to get a side ache.

Of course, everything I've just talked about refers to exercise-based fueling for kids. So what about the regular diet of a healthy child? Aside from slightly more snacking to support the extreme activity levels and screaming metabolism of a growing child, there's really no difference from the diet I recommend for adults. This is what the daily diet of our seven-year-old twin boys looks like:

Breakfast: Either eggs and bacon cooked in lard, butter, or coconut oil, or soaked quinoa cooked with chia seeds, coconut oil, raw honey, and walnuts

Snack: Raw nut butter on rice cakes

Lunch: Avocado, olives, and sprouts with protein, like a boiled egg or sardines

Afternoon snack: Fresh raw fruit or berries with soaked nuts

Dinner: Broiled fish with rice or sweet potatoes slathered with butter from grass-fed cows and a side of veggies

Before bed, our boys take a kid's liquid multivitamin from Organic Life, which includes omega-3 fatty acids, magnesium, a full vitamin spectrum, and DMAE (dimethylaminoethanol)—a substance naturally produced in small amounts in the brain that supports improved mental focus and neural growth (see Figure 14-2). Because the multivitamin that I personally use includes cortisol-lowering herbs such as magnolia and phellodendron, my kids take a different one.

What about parties and desserts? Don't worry—we don't completely deprive our young ones of sweets. I recommend that you surf over to my article "How to Create a No-Guilt Birthday Party Meal for Your Kids, or You" (BenGreenfieldFitness.com/bday) to see how your kids can have their cake and eat it, too.

Kids Calm Multi

Supplement Facts

Serving Size: 2 tbsp (1 fl oz/30 mL) Servings per Container: 30

Amount per Serving		% Daily Value
Calories	40	
Calories from fat	9	
Total Fat	1 g	1.5% †
Total Carbohydrates	2 g	< 1% †
Sugars	2 g	
Vitamin A (as retinyl palmitate, beta-carotene [50%])	5,000 IU	100
Vitamin C (as ascorbic acid)	200 mg	333
Vitamin D₃ (as cholecalciferol)	400 IU	100
Vitamin E (as d-alpha tocopheryl acetate)	30 IU	100
Thiamin (as thiamin HCl)	1.5 mg	100
Riboflavin (as riboflavin 5'-phosphate)	1.7 mg	100
Niacin (as niacinamide)	5 mg	25
Vitamin B₆ (as pyridoxal 5'-phosphate)	2 mg	100
Folic Acid	300 mcg	75
Vitamin B₁₂ (as methylcobalamin)	6 mcg	100
Biotin	50 mcg	15
Pantothenic Acid (as d-calcium pantothenate)	10 mg	100
Calcium (as calcium citrate)	200 mg	20
Magnesium (as magnesium citrate, Natural Calm®)	240 mg	60
Zinc (as zinc picolinate)	2 mg	13
Omega fish oil	1000 mg	*
Total Omega-3 (from fish oil)	180 mg	*
DHA and EPA (from fish oil)	150 mg	*
Proprietary Organic Kids' Fruit & Veggie Blend	200 mg	*
Banana, orange, pineapple, blackberry, tart cherry, raspberry, mango, cranberry, peas, strawberry, apple, blueberry, pumpkin, collard greens, spinach, tomato, beets, broccoli, kale, carrot, acai, noni, pomegranate, goji		
Proprietary Amino Acid Blend	50 mg	*
L-proline, L-glutamic acid, L-alanine, L-arginine, L-aspartic acid, L-glutamine, L-lysine, L-serine, L-leucine, L-valine, L-threonine, L-phenylalanine, L-tyrosine, L-methionine, L-isoleucine, L-histidine, L-cystine		
DMAE (as dimethylaminoethanol bitartrate)	35 mg	*
Mineral Complex (ConcenTrace® trace minerals)	30 mg	*
Choline (as choline bitartrate)	10 mg	*
Quercetin	10 mg	*

* Daily Value not established   † Percent Daily Values based on a 2,000-calorie diet

Other ingredients: purified water, glycerin (vegetable source), organic agave nectar, citric acid, organic flavors, organic stevia (leaf) extract, potassium sorbate, natural flavor extracts, xanthan gum. Contains fish (anchovy, sardine).

FIGURE 14-2

Six Steps to Fasting Properly

You already learned about the many benefits of fasting to support recovery in chapter 8. The fact is that, for our ancestors, food always had to be hunted and gathered and was never as readily available as it is today. The body is programmed to allow our digestive organs to take a much-needed rest—whether on a daily, weekly, or monthly basis.

Unfortunately, in an age of affluence and ubiquitous food, our digestive systems rarely get that break and are instead asked to work endlessly. No matter how healthy or nutrient-dense the diet, it can still be stressful for the digestive system to be constantly breaking down, digesting, absorbing, and assimilating a never-ending onslaught of food. In the same way that going without adequate sleep is stressful to our precious human bodies, so is eating ad infinitum.

In the rest of the animal kingdom, a snake will gulp down a mouse every few weeks and "fast" until its next meal. A dog will often laze around the house for an entire day without eating. But we humans are not so smart or self-controlled. Just think about what happens when you get sick. Say you have a fever. Your body often forces you to take a break from eating, which allows your body's energy to be directed toward "cleaning house"—producing mucus and beefing up immune system activity—rather than squandering energy on digestion.

The benefits of calorie restriction are often missed by type A athletes who rarely take a recovery day and are constantly fueling their bodies. On the one hand, you need to give your body enough nutrients to allow for adequate hormone formation and cellular repair and recovery, but on the other, you need to give your digestive system an occasional break to allow for the many health and life-extending benefits of calorie restriction[31].

So how should an athlete implement fasting without engaging in so much calorie restriction that it becomes unhealthy? While the goal of this chapter is not to present a thorough treatise on calorie restriction and fasting, I'm going to give you six recommendations to successfully incorporate calorie restriction without damaging your body. If you want more information on the subject, I recommend the most useful resource about fasting for athletes that I have ever read. Written by the brilliant Dr. John Berardi, it can be downloaded for free at Precision Nutrition (BeyondTrainingBook.com/interfast).

Recommendation #1: Twelve- to sixteen-hour daily fast. The most practical and effective fasting strategy used by both the athletes I coach and myself is a twelve- to sixteen-hour fast every twenty-four hours. You can, for example, eat dinner at 8 p.m. and then not eat again until breakfast or an early lunch sometime between 8 a.m. and noon the next day.

Recommendation #2: Skip the fast on high-volume days. On high-volume days, such as an Ironman training weekend that might involve several hours of exercise on both Saturday and Sunday, don't fast. Just eat when you're hungry. The risks of calorie restriction outweigh the benefits when a lot of exercise is part of the equation. This goes hand in hand with allowing yourself slightly more carbohydrates on big training days or big blocks of training days.

Recommendation #3: Don't do hard or long workouts fasted. An easy morning swim, run, bike ride, or bodyweight workout session after an overnight fast is fine. So is a ten- to sixty-minute, hard interval session, assuming that you listen to your body and you're able to maintain your goal intensity, recover well, and eat a big breakfast afterward. However, any workout that is (1) hard and longer than sixty minutes or (2) easy to moderate and longer than two hours should not be done in an overnight-fasted state. This is a quick path to overtraining and unhealthy levels of self-cannibalization.

Recommendation #4: Some foods are OK to eat when fasting. There are several foods that enable your body to maintain low levels of blood sugar and insulin but allow for adequate energy levels and even enhanced fatty acid utilization during a fast. By consuming these foods, you can also decrease the hormonal or metabolic stress you may experience when combining fasting with intense physical activity. These foods include MCT or coconut oil, essential amino acids or branched-chain amino acids, coffee (including Bulletproof Coffee), green tea, spirulina, chlorella, and greens powders or supplements.

Recommendation #5: Do a twenty-four-hour fast occasionally. At least every month or two, choose one day to take a break from exercising and clean out your body to allow for enhanced cellular autophagy (basically, eliminating your body's junk). This is especially important for athletes who are eating thousands of calories a day. This periodic day of complete rest for your muscles, adrenals, and digestive system can be incredibly therapeutic.

Recommendation #6: Be careful if you're female. Many women find that fasting causes sleeplessness, anxiety, and irregular periods, among myriad other symptoms of hormone dysregulation. Once again, this may seem sexist or unfair, but I can't help it if men are able to head off to the hills to hunt, gather, or fight in a fasted state while doing the same sends many women into a metabolic tailspin. There is a very good article about this titled "Shattering the Myth of Fasting for Women: A Review of Female-Specific Responses to Fasting in the Literature" (BeyondTrainingBook.com/pfwmyth), and I highly recommend reading it if you're a woman who wants to try fasting. I've found that, when it comes to maintaining health and hormonal status for the female clients I train, a twenty-four-hour fast is far more effective than daily intermittent fasting of twelve to sixteen hours. If you are female and simply cannot resist the idea of daily intermittent fasting, at least eat some of the foods in recommendation 4.

I'm often asked if I personally engage in intermittent fasting, and the answer is yes. I finish my workouts at around 6:30 p.m., eat dinner at around 7, have a snack like coconut milk with protein powder at around 8, and then generally don't eat breakfast until around 10 the next morning, at which point I usually make a high-fat kale shake or have some Bulletproof Coffee. This is my standard practice five days a week, and then on weekends, when my training volume is heavier, I generally just eat when I'm hungry.

Three Big Benefits of Ketosis

A lot of people are confused by the term *ketosis*.

You may have heard that ketosis is a dangerous state for the body to be in. But ketosis simply means that your body is using nearly 100 percent fat for energy. Ketones are molecules generated during fat metabolism—and that can be fat from the avocado you just ate or fat from the adipose tissue around your waist.

When your body is breaking down fat for energy, most of that fat gets converted into ATP energy. That process produces ketones[10]. When you eat fewer carbohydrates or dump lots of fats (such as coconut oil) into your body, your body turns to fat for its primary energy source and generates lots of ketones in the process.

Some of those ketones, including acetoacetate and beta-hydroxybutyrate, are used directly for energy. As a matter of fact, some of your body's organs, such as your heart muscle and your kidneys, actually prefer ketones to glucose. And most of the cells in your body, including your brain cells, are able to use ketones for much of their energy.

There are various definitions of what actual constitutes ketosis from a quantitative standpoint, but blood, urine, or breath ketone values above 1.0 millimoles per liter are generally considered to indicate a state of ketosis. (During exercise, I've seen my own body reach levels as high as 7.0 millimoles.)

So why do some people think that ketosis is a bad thing?

There are two reasons. One is the assumption that if your body is burning a lot of fat for energy, it must not be getting enough carbohydrates. You already learned in the previous chapter why this hypothesis is flawed and why the body can actually create lots of energy with relatively little carbohydrate intake.

The second reason is that a dangerous condition called ketoacidosis can develop in people with type 1 diabetes, and it is sometimes confused with normal ketosis[17]. People with type 1 diabetes are unable to produce insulin, which can result in extreme and uncontrolled ketosis, with such a severe accumulation of ketones that the pH of the blood decreases to the point at which normal metabolic function is no longer possible and serious health consequences ensue. But this is not a risk for you if you don't have type 1 diabetes.

As an athlete, why would you want to be in a state of ketosis? There are three primary reasons.

1. Metabolic Superiority of Using Fats as Fuel

Dr. Peter Attia is one of the world's leading experts on ketosis and exercise, and he gets into the metabolic superiority of ketosis in his excellent blog post "Ketosis—Advantaged or Misunderstood State?" (BeyondTrainingBook.com/ktosistate2). He explains how being in a ketogenic state vastly enhances lipolysis (fat-burning efficiency), aerobic capacity, and muscular endurance. This means that several groups of elite athletes (for example, Olympians) experience significant increases in aerobic power and efficiency across multiple physical tasks maximally stressing the aerobic system.

For these very reasons, the U.S. Defense Advanced Research Projects Agency (DARPA) has been investigating ketogenesis as a weapon for boosting soldiers' mental and physical performance in battlefield conditions[7]. Why? Because as a soldier's blood glucose drops, he becomes confused and sometimes ends up shooting at his own side. So they tested on rats a highly ketogenic fuel source (technically liquid ketones, which you can learn more about by listening to the fascinating podcast episode I did with Dr. Dominic D'Agostino at BenGreenfieldFitness.com/ketone) and found that it boosted physical and mental performance—and the rats became much healthier, lost body fat, and had lower levels of triglycerides (fatty acids) in their blood and lower blood sugar levels, with no harmful side effects. That same fuel is being developed for soldiers. However, it's not going to be as simple as giving them canteens full of MCT oil, since research has shown that consumption of MCT oil can result in significant gastrointestinal distress and diarrhea. Most successful athletes who use MCTs do so in combination with other foods, like whey protein, SuperStarch (made by UCAN), honey or some other glucose source, chia seed slurries, or amino acids (such as the Endurance Pack at GreenfieldFitnessSystems.com).

2. Mental Enhancement

Being in a state of ketosis is also a brain-hacking technique that goes way above and beyond smart drugs. Ketones are a potent source of fuel for your brain neurons. When you're ketogenic, you have higher levels of brain-derived neurotrophic factor and an enormous increase in brain neuron regeneration, focus, and mental acuity (once you get over the hump of the first ten to fourteen days of switching to using fatty acids as your primary energy source). If you want to learn more about why ketones are a high-power brain food, listen to the audio interview "Marvel of Ketone Science" at BeyondTrainingBook.com/ketone.

3. Health and Longevity Advantages of Controlling High Blood Sugar

In the previous chapter, you learned about the dangers of constantly elevated blood glucose levels. Ketosis simply takes high-fat dieting to a more extreme level. Rather than the 20 percent carbohydrate, 65 percent fat, 15 percent protein approach, a ketogenic diet brings carbohydrate calories down to 5 to 10 percent and fat calories up to 75 to 80 percent.

Many people experience all three of these advantages even when cycling in and out of ketosis, such as eating a 10:75:15 diet on weekdays and a higher carbohydrate intake of 20 to 30 percent on the weekends. I'm not aware of any evidence proving that (after the initial fat adaptation phase) cycling in and out of ketosis is harmful or somehow causes you to lose all the benefits of ketosis, but to reach a state of ideal ketone utilizing and fat-burning efficiency, it may be necessary to stay in a state of ketosis for months or even years on end.

In practical terms, what does a ketogenic diet actually look like?

For the "FASTER" study at the University of Connecticut, I followed a strict eight-month ketogenic diet, which I detail in the two-part series "How to Become a Fat Burning Machine" at BenGreenfieldFitness.com. For that protocol, my daily intake was 50 to 75 grams of carbs on an easy day, 75 to 100 grams of carbs on an average training day, and no more than 150 grams of carbs on a hard-and-heavy training day. I also consumed plenty of medium-chain triglycerides from coconut oil and MCT oil to keep my medium-chain triglyceride fat levels elevated so that my body relied primarily on those fats as fuel.

It's important to understand that, for most people, I do not recommend calorie-restricted ketosis—in which you simply cut calories to the point at which your body has no choice but to dip into its own fat for fuel. While this strategy can be useful for a sedentary person looking to lose weight, it can be especially stressful on an athlete's body. Instead, the example below is high-fat, high-calorie ketosis.

- **Breakfast:** High-fat kale shake prepared with MCT oil and butter from grass-fed cows or Bulletproof Coffee
- **Midmorning snack:** Tea, kombucha, decaf coffee, or sparkling water

- **Lunch:** Another high-fat kale shake or a large spinach salad prepared with extra-virgin olive oil, avocado, olives, walnuts, and sardines
- **Preworkout snack:** A cup of coconut milk or two to three ounces MCT oil. Depending on the length and intensity of the workout, small amounts of protein powder can be added, but since protein is readily converted into glucose via a process called gluconeogenesis, protein powder should be consumed in moderation only very close to the time of the workout.
- **Dinner:** Grass-fed beef, liver,* sweetbreads* (yes, that would be thyroid gland), wild salmon, or the like, with roasted vegetables. Depending on the volume of the day's workout, small amounts of carbohydrates or a glass of red wine may be included with dinner.
- **Late-night snack:** Two to three tablespoons coconut manna, which is a blend of coconut meat and coconut oil (see the link on the resource web page for this chapter).

---

*Why is it important to include organ meats in a low-carb, ketogenic diet? Here's an important excerpt from Weston A. Price's book *Nutrition and Physical Degeneration:*

> For the Indians of the far North this reinforcement [this refers specifically to reinforcement of ideal hormonal status for fertility and health] was accomplished by supplying special feedings of organs of animals. Among the Indians in the moose country near the Arctic circle a larger percentage of the children were born in June than in any other month. This was accomplished, I was told, by both parents eating liberally of the thyroid glands of the male moose as they came down from the high mountain areas for the mating season, at which time the large protuberances carrying the thyroids under the throat were greatly enlarged.

This makes good sense, since carbohydrates are necessary for proper thyroid activity (specifically the conversion of T3 to T4) and because high concentrations of free fatty acids can inhibit proper thyroid binding to its cell receptor. So while organ meats are good for everyone, it's even more important for people eating a very-low-carbohydrate ketogenic diet to eat organ meats such as liver and sweetbreads up to several times per week. That's because organ meats supply the thyroid hormones that your body isn't making in the absence of carbohydrates.

You can order organ meats from companies such as US Wellness Meats if you can't find, say, sweetbreads and liver from a local organic source. If you're not a fan of the taste or don't have time to prepare these foods, you can also use liver and thyroid supplements, but you need to be very careful with the source of desiccated liver and thymus gland. Standard Process thyroid complex is a decent option (take about two tablets a day), as is ThyroGold from NaturalThyroidSolutions.com; Argentinian organic desiccated-liver powder is also a good one. Take one rounded tablespoon of Now Foods desiccated liver powder per day. I link to all these resources on the web page for this chapter.

I eat sweetbreads once or twice a month. Once or twice a week I soak liver in lemon juice or milk, dredge it in pastured eggs and almond flour, and then fry it in butter. When served with onions and mushrooms sautéed in more butter and a touch of red wine, it makes for a fantastic meal that is incredibly therapeutic for a fat-fueled body!

While a ketogenic diet can certainly be successful for moderate levels of physical activity, the jury is still out on whether it can be successful for maintaining very high levels of performance in extreme endurance sports such as an Ironman triathlon. At BenGreenfieldFitness.com, I reported on the Great Ketogenic Ironman Experiment, in which I followed a 100 percent ketogenic diet during a twelve-week buildup to Ironman Canada and raced a 9:39 on a very difficult course there. All results and the follow-up story can be found at BenGreenfieldFitness.com. You can also watch a video of my 2013 ketogenic panel at the Ancestral Health Symposium with Mark Sisson, Robb Wolf, Jamie Scott, and Jimmy Moore at ancestralhealth.org.

Now that I am no longer following a strict ketogenic protocol (all for the sake of science, right?), I eat a macronutrient percentage of closer to 50 to 60 percent fat, 20 to 30 percent carbohydrate, and 20 to 30 percent protein, which eliminates many of the unhealthy food ingredients present in a higher-carbohydrate diet and introduces more stable energy levels, less inflammation, and better weight loss. While I find that the very low carbohydrate percentages on a strict ketogenic diet (5 to 10 percent carbs) will not sustain heavy bouts of high-intensity exercise or voluminous training, the slightly higher percentage of carbohydrates in the ratio described above allows sustenance of energy levels without completely emptying the carbohydrate tank.

Yes, you read right: The percentages listed above are not what you'll find in a strict "ketogenic" diet. Strict ketogenesis can be difficult and uncomfortable for most people, and it's not especially practical from a social eating perspective, either (such as when all your friends go out to an Italian restaurant and you're left eating roasted vegetables with olive oil while salivating over their fish and fettuccine). For a ketogenic diet, you'd be closer to 80 to 85 percent fat, 10 to 15 percent protein, and 5 to 10 percent carbohydrate. However, by saving the majority of your daily carbohydrate intake for the end of the day and preferably consuming them in a post-exercise scenario anywhere from one to three hours after your workout, you will indeed be in a state of ketosis the entire day leading up to that carbohydrate "feeding." Many nutritionists refer to this practice as "cyclic ketosis" or a "cycling low-carb diet."

This comes in quite handy, because if long-term carbohydrate deprivation and depletion of storage carbohydrate levels are accompanied by frequent bouts of training, then your immune system can eventually become depressed, physical performance and mood can decline, and risk of overtraining can increase. For this reason, storage carbohydrate should be "reloaded" once per week, preferably on a higher-volume training day when the increased carb intake will be less damaging to the body. This practice can be combined with the cyclic low-carb approach described earlier. The meal plan that I and many of my athletes follow is a six-day low-carbohydrate protocol, with one day of a moderate- to high-carbohydrate diet. That higher-carbohydrate-intake day should preferably be the hardest training day of the week, typically a Saturday or Sunday for most athletes. It's very important to note that if you aren't the type of exerciser or athlete who has a very-high-volume training day of the week, this extra carbohydrate reload day probably will not be necessary for you, especially if you're already doing the cyclic low-carb approach with mini carb refeeds at the end of each day. But if you find yourself bonking frequently, you'll definitely want to include this day.

Hopefully, you're now a little better equipped to make the right dietary decisions if you fall into any of the special categories in this chapter and still want to lead an extremely active lifestyle without sacrificing performance and health.

Of course, no matter which diet or nutrition strategies we choose, many of us first need to heal our digestive system and get a clean gut. In the next chapter, you're going learn everything you need to know about hitting the reboot button on your gut and detoxing your body.

Additional resources, helpful links, scientific references, websites, and surprise bonuses for this chapter are available at BeyondTrainingBook.com/Chapter14. Enjoy.

CHAPTER 15

Nine Bad Things That Happen When Digestion Goes Awry, How to Hit the Reboot Button on Your Gut, and the Best Way to Detox Your Body

As my toes dug into the Spanish sand, part of my body anticipated the blasting air horn that would start the 2012 Long Distance Triathlon World Championships and send me sprinting out into the water for a grueling 2.5-mile swim, 7-mile bike, and 19-mile run.

The other part of my body was messed up. My eyes were bloodshot from severe sleep deprivation; there was a deep, gnawing pain in my gut; and my usually spry pre-race muscles felt drained and empty.

No, this was not a result of a nasty Rioja wine-drinking binge, or too many Spanish café Largos the night before, or some kind of stomach bug.

It was simply me experiencing the same suboptimal state that has been described to me over and over again by athletes I coach, whether during a workout or right before an important race: that numb feeling of complete exhaustion and the inability to dig when it's time.

It had been so long since I've arrived at a triathlon starting line in that state that I had forgotten what it felt like to have a frustratingly unresponsive body, despite perfect training, a good taper, and very low emotional and lifestyle stress.

Six hours and thirty minutes later, I stumbled across the finish line after one of the most painful and uncomfortable races of my life, complete with gastrointestinal distress, vomiting, and, most important, the distinct frustration that accompanies these problems and is the bane of marathoners, cyclists, triathletes, and anyone else who needs to eat and perform simultaneously.

Some define these problems as "gut issues" and others "a weak stomach," but either way, my personal experience was a loud and clear reminder: Arriving at a starting line ready to race at 100 percent of your abilities means taking care of your gut, especially during race week.

Otherwise, by abusing or neglecting a section of your body that is even more exposed to external environments than your skin, you're setting yourself up for subpar performance that, unfortunately, is often accepted as part of the fueling perils of endurance events.

So what is it about the gut that invites this kind of dreaded pre-race or preworkout condition, and what can you do to avoid not feeling 100 percent when you need to?

Whether you want to spend less time on the toilet, not have to deal with embarrassing and uncomfortable gas and bloating, or get rid of cravings and mood issues that seem closely related to food, you're going to find out what you need to know in this chapter. But first, let's take a look at why it's such a big deal if your digestion goes awry.

What Happens When Digestion Goes Awry

You're not alone if you think of your gut as one long, twisting garden hose that extends from your mouth to your butt. Heck, even the classic *Gray's Anatomy*—a go-to manual for every aspiring medical student—describes the gut as:

A musculo-membranous tube, about thirty feet in length, extending from the mouth to the anus, and lined throughout its entire extent by mucous membrane.

But the gut is way more complex than that sentence makes it sound. For example, three-quarters of your immune system resides in your digestive tract. And that entire immune system is protected from the external environment by a thin, fragile lining only one cell thick. If that lining is damaged and the barrier that it creates is penetrated, crazy things happen. You become allergic to foods you normally would have been able to digest without a problem, you get sick much more easily, and your immune system becomes overactive, which results in your body becoming overrun by inflammation.

Your gut is very much alive and crawling with critters, too: Five hundred species and three pounds of bacteria in your digestive tract form a giant ecosystem that helps digest food, regulate hormones, excrete toxins, and produce vitamins and other healing compounds that keep your gut and your body healthy.

Your gut is intimately tied to your brain and mood, too. This is called the brain-gut connection (very similar the brain-heart connection that you learned about in chapter 7), and Dr. Jordan Rubin describes the relationship quite well in his book *Patient, Heal Thyself:*

Early in our embryogenesis, a collection of tissue called the "neural crest" appears and divides during fetal development. One part turns into the central nervous system, and the other migrates to become the enteric nervous system. Both "thinking machines" form simultaneously and independently of one another until a later stage of development. . . .

Then the two nervous systems link through a neural cable called the "vagus nerve," the longest of all cranial nerves. The vagus nerve "wanders" from the brain stem through the organs in the neck and thorax and finally terminates in the abdomen. This is your vital brain-gut connection.

This brain-gut connection is why:

- You get butterflies in your stomach before going onstage.

- You can get nervous or have stomach cramps before a hard workout or race.

- Antidepressants cause nausea and stomach upset, and stomach upset can depress you.

- Overeating when you're anxious helps your body produce extra "feel-good" chemicals.

- Stress makes you want to eat more.

- Food intolerances or gut inflammation can cause serious behavioral issues.

- An unhealthy gut can make you feel stupid or sluggish.

And then there's your liver, which is also part of your digestive system. Your gut has to somehow get rid of all the toxins that are metabolic by-products of digestion by transporting food components to your liver. If the liver or gut is not functioning properly, your body becomes toxic and your health suffers.

Your liver destroys old red blood cells; manufactures proteins, blood-clotting agents, and cholesterol; stores glycogen, fats, and proteins; converts fats and proteins to carbohydrates, and lactic acid to glucose; transforms galactose (milk sugar) into glucose; extracts ammonia from amino acids (proteins); converts ammonia to urea; produces bile; stores fat-soluble vitamins; converts adipose fat into ketone bodies; and neutralizes pharmaceuticals and alcohol[14].

So just imagine what happens if that important organ breaks down.

However, according to most sports nutrition manuals, gut issues, bloating, indigestion, and gas are simply due to excessive calorie consumption during exercise. *Yeah, that's right. You ate too much, cowboy. Next time, back off the Gatorade.*

And while it's true that feasting on gels, sports bars, and energy drinks during a workout can cause you to slow down and experience mild to severe stomach discomfort, gut issues cannot simply be explained away by "eating too much."

From the digestive glands in your mouth to your esophagus, gallbladder, stomach, small intestine, and colon, there are endless possibilities for what can go wrong inside your "giant garden hose."

As a matter of fact, there are huge manuals and websites devoted solely to gut issues. And one of my friends, Konstantin Monastyrsky, has what I consider to be the single most useful, non-run-of-the-mill, resourceful website on gut health that exists (gutsense.org).

You can dig more into specific gut anatomy and physiology on your own if you feel so inclined, but in this chapter I'm going to focus on the nine primary issues that I've observed to create problems for very physically active people and athletes—which is my wheelhouse. I'll tell you how to test for these issues and how to fix them. Sound good? Let's jump right in!

How to Identify and Fix the Nine Most Common Gut Issues

1. Gluten Intolerance

Let's begin by taking a look at the single most inflammatory substance you can find in modern food: gliadin. And now you're going to find out what happened to me in that race in Spain.

I have to admit that I was a bit hesitant to begin this section with gluten, simply because these days everybody and his dog seems to think he has a gluten allergy, when in fact—as you will soon learn—many people actually have a completely different problem.

Gliadin is a protein molecule found in most (but not all) gluten-containing foods—primarily the grains of wheat, rye, barley, kamut, spelt, teff, and couscous—with wheat being the biggest gliadin-containing culprit[1]. An inflammatory reaction to gliadin can take place in the small intestines of many people who do not have celiac disease or a full-blown gluten intolerance, but who instead have what is called a "subclinical" sensitivity to gliadin. This is often the case in those of Irish, English, Scottish, Scandinavian, and other Northern and Eastern European ancestries. (You can get your ancestry tested at 23andme.com.)

You might have this type of sensitivity if you experience a feeling of uneasiness in your gut after being exposed to gliadin. Its prevalence means that, in most cases, you don't need to be embarrassed to ask, "Is that gluten-free?" when you're ordering or being offered food—especially during a race or an important event week.

When gliadin is consumed, it causes an inflammatory reaction in the gastro-intestinal tract that involves heat, redness, swelling, and a change or interruption in the normal function of the small intestine. As your body attempts to fight off an indigestible foreign substance, blood vessels in the gut enlarge and become more permeable[13]. This brings more white blood cells and other immune system cells to the site of injury to provide protection.

In addition, fluids leak from these blood vessels into the surrounding tissues, bringing more white blood cells into those tissues for enhanced immune protection. A thin filament called fibrin (the same substance used for blood clotting) also forms at the site to aid in the intestinal wall's physical repair process.

Within twelve to fifteen hours after the gliadin-containing meal has hit the gut and the inflammatory response has occurred, the body's reaction diminishes and the gut is able to slowly heal, assuming that there is no further gluten exposure. But if you eat another gluten-containing food, the entire inflammatory response and damage to the intestinal wall is repeated. A vicious cycle sets in of never letting the gut heal before hammering it with more inflammation (see Figure 15-1).

And this can create some serious issues.

First, there may be a loss of nutrient absorption. Your small intestine is lined with tiny fingerlike projections called villi, which increase the surface area for absorption

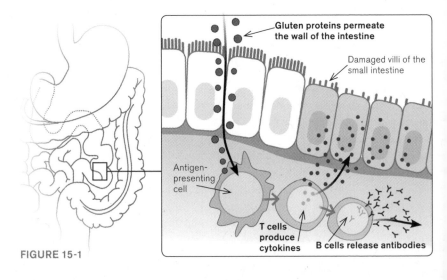

FIGURE 15-1

by up to a thousand times (which means that the absorptive area of your small intestine may be roughly the size of a basketball court!). These villi allow you to efficiently absorb massive quantities of nutrients from your food.

However, a substance like gliadin that irritates the lining of the small intestine can destroy the villi and significantly reduce the total area available for absorption. This not only affects your ability to absorb vital nutrients from food to support your training and racing, but also leads to indigestion, as food isn't properly absorbed in your intestine. Typically, this manifests as gut bloating, tiredness, a hyperactive bowel, and sizable or uncomfortable bowel movements—especially during exercise.

Next, there can be an increase in the permeability of your gut. Gut permeability already increases a bit as soon as you begin exercising, especially if you're exercising in the heat, but what we're talking about now goes way above and beyond that permeability. Your small intestine also has a mucosal lining—which is the same type of tissue that lines your sinus passages, your lungs, your urinary tract, your mouth, and your throat. The reason these areas are lined with a mucous membrane is to protect your body from infection. Under the chronic inflammatory stress that comes with repeated gliadin exposure, the mucosal tissue breaks down, and your gut becomes extremely permeable, resulting in an uncomfortable condition called leaky gut syndrome.

Leaky gut syndrome is like having a water filter installed in your house that has big holes in it. Stuff you don't want to be drinking ends up inside you because it hasn't been filtered out. In the case of a leaky gut, undigested food particles, particularly proteins, pass through the intestinal barrier and into the bloodstream, resulting in an immune response in the blood and an enormous amount of immune stress as your body tries to fight off these foreign invaders[8]. See Figure 15-2.

As I mentioned earlier, gut permeability is already increased with exposure to heat and during intense exercise. When they are combined with a leaky gut from gliadin exposure, your likelihood of getting sick, experiencing "brain fog," having a hard time sleeping, and feeling much less than adequate—just as I did when I arrived at the starting line of that race in Spain—is vastly increased.

But nutrient malabsorption and a leaky gut aren't the only issues brought on by gliadin. Regular consumption of gluten-containing foods may also cause fat malabsorption and lactose intolerance—even if you weren't prone to those annoying issues in the first place.

For example, in the tips of those villi are lacteals, which are responsible for breaking down fat into tiny, absorbable droplets[26]. When these lacteals are compromised, you can't properly absorb fat, which is crucial for forming hormones and building cell membranes. You also miss out on the absorption of fat-soluble vitamins, such as vitamins A and E, as well as essential fatty acids. And yes, this means you may not be getting any benefit from that expensive fish oil pill you pop every day.

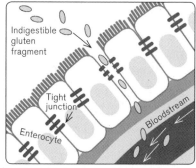

FIGURE 15-2

You've already learned about the importance of fat. As you can probably imagine, fat deficiencies can result in poor blood sugar control, inability to repair central nervous system damage, poor nerve cell function, low hormone production, low antioxidant levels, and many other issues.

Then there's lactose intolerance, which is also aggravated by gluten. As you probably know, milk products contain lactose sugars, which are normally digested by lactase, an enzyme that breaks down the milk sugars into a digestible and absorbable form. However, because a damaged intestinal wall cannot properly produce lactase enzymes, lactose intolerance often accompanies gluten intolerance—and people who normally can eat cheese, yogurt, and ice cream can't do so when they're consuming gliadin, which is why it is necessary to avoid milk products for several months after going gluten-free (it takes that long for the lining of your digestive tract to heal). On the bright side, many people find that they can comfortably eat ice cream after giving up bread.

So now you've learned that gliadin exposure from gluten-containing foods can cause inflammation, nutrient loss, a leaky gut, fat malabsorption, and lactose intolerance. You've also learned that the consequence of these problems can be gut discomfort, poor food absorption (especially while exercising in the heat), lots of bathroom stops, extreme tiredness, and trouble focusing or getting motivated.

With this understanding, we can come full circle to the reason many athletes—including me—experience frustrating gut issues, especially when traveling to a race. Let's use the race I described earlier as an example.

I am about 90 percent gluten-free in my day-to-day training and 100 percent gluten-free in the week of a race—and I never get gut pain or have trouble holding anything down during a race. However, just twice during that race week, I ate tapas (there's lots of wheat in even just a couple of these), nibbled bread at dinner (even small amounts pack a huge gliadin punch), and ate a few scoops of gelato in a gluten-based ice cream cone. These exposures may seem small or trite compared with a big bowl of pasta or an entire baguette, but when it comes to inflammation, even seemingly insignificant exposures are enough to set off a chain reaction in the gut for anyone with even mild gliadin sensitivities—and they left me sleepy, tired, bloated, and in subpar condition on race morning.

So what can you do about gliadin-related gut issues? What can you eat to eliminate these issues, and what should you avoid?

You can flip back to chapter 11 to review a bunch of gluten-free meals, but below is a basic list of easy-to-find foods that will give you ample calories (even giving you some carbohydrates that you can eat during something like a race week if you're not doing the whole ketogenic, low-carb thing) without bringing on the chain reaction of inflammation from gliadin:

- Beef, pork, lamb, bison
- Chicken, turkey, duck
- Tuna, salmon, trout, halibut, swordfish, shrimp, clams, mussels, crab, lobster
- Any vegetables
- Any beans except soybeans

- Corn, corn tortillas, corn chips
- Wild rice, basmati rice, brown rice, black rice, white rice, rice flour, rice bread, rice crackers
- Potatoes, sweet potatoes, yams
- Amaranth, buckwheat, chia, millet, quinoa, sorghum, kamut, einkorn, spelt, teff (these are sometimes called "ancient grains" because they were important food sources for ancient civilizations and either have no gliadin or are much lower in gliadin than genetically modified wheat crops bred for high yield)
- Wheatgrass and barley grass

If you want the "gold standard" test for gluten sensitivity and gluten intolerance, I highly recommend asking your physician to order you a test through Cyrex, which has the most thorough gluten-reactivity screening you'll find anywhere. In the BenGreenfieldFitness.com/333 podcast episode, I describe exactly why Cyrex is the screening method that I recommend for most forms of food allergies and intolerances and why so many of the other tests, such as ALCAT and ELISA, are inaccurate, give a host of false positives, or both.

Finally, if you are exposed to gluten, you can take peptidases (often sold as "gluten enzymes") to help break down the gliadin. To heal a broken gut lining or reduce gut permeability, you can also take marshmallow root, licorice extract, colostrum, L-glutamine, aloe vera juice, probiotics, and digestive enzymes.

My recommendation for these gut-healing compounds is one or two servings of bone broth or organic gelatin a day combined with daily use of the Gut Healing Pack that I designed at GreenfieldFitnessSystems.com, used as instructed on the package. It contains probiotics, digestive enzymes, colostrum, cleansing herbs, and oregano oil. Three other nourishing and healing compounds for the gut are chia seeds, L-glutamine, and bone broth[24].

When used in conjunction with a gliadin-free, dairy-free diet, these strategies will help give you that envied iron gut. And incidentally, even if gluten doesn't bother your stomach one bit, it can still cause some pretty serious brain inflammation and fuzzy thinking, which is discussed in detail in the excellent books *Why Isn't My Brain Working,* by Dr. Datis Kharrazian, and *Grain Brain,* by Dr. David Perlmutter.

2. FODMAPs

As prevalent as gluten issues can be, many people who think they're gluten-intolerant are not. This may be especially true if you eat healthy ancient grains.

A recent study found that people with self-reported gluten sensitivity actually had no bad gut effects from eating gluten and experienced complete elimination of their gut issues after reducing their consumption of fermentable, poorly absorbed, short-chain carbohydrates—also known as FODMAPs (fermentable oligo-di-monosaccharides and polyols). Specifically, the researchers reported that:

In all participants, gastrointestinal symptoms consistently and significantly improved during reduced FODMAP intake, but significantly worsened to a similar degree when their diets included gluten or whey protein[2].

In other words, it may not be gluten (or, incidentally, whey protein) that's upsetting your gut, but rather the combination of these foods with FODMAPs or the presence of FODMAPs all by themselves.

How could this happen? Let's back up for a moment and look into what FODMAPs really are. Many of the foods that we commonly eat, even in a healthy diet, are what are called "high-residue" foods. These particular foods, when being digested, leave behind a lot for bacteria to feed on. And when bacteria feed and proliferate, they ferment. When bacteria are fermenting in your gut, the result can be bloating, cramping, and gas.

What kinds of foods have a tendency to ferment more or ferment faster than others? FODMAPs.

Fermentable oligo-di-monosaccharides and polyols are sugars that you can't digest, so they end up feeding bacteria, creating fungal overgrowth in your digestive tract and throwing off the entire balance of your gut's ecosystem.

Sometimes, in addition to bloating, cramping, gas, constipation, or diarrhea, FODMAPs can create symptoms outside your gut, such as depression, fatigue, headache, or brain fog (which makes sense, since your body creates a significant amount of your neurotransmitters in your gut—it's that whole brain-gut thing you already learned about).

I list the foods that fall into the category of FODMAPs below. While I'm certainly not advocating that you cut these foods out of your diet completely, you may find that when you consume large amounts of them, especially at one meal or in one day, significant gut issues arise, and that when you eliminate these foods, you can eat gluten-containing foods without a problem.

- **Fruit, agave, and honey:** Fructose is fruit sugar and a monosaccharide. Fruits that are higher in fructose (like melons and tropical fruits such as mangoes) also fall into this category. Fruits high in polyols (sugar alcohols), such as apples, peaches, and pears, are also included. Many sweeteners, like high-fructose corn syrup, honey, and agave, also contain fructose. And of course, fructose is a major ingredient in most gels and sports drinks, so if sports gels make your digestive system go awry, fructose could be the reason.

- **Beans and lentils:** Oligosaccharides are short strands of simple sugars. All beans and lentils fall into this category. Maltodextrin, which is found in many sports gels, is also an oligosaccharide.

- **Wheat, onions, and cabbage:** Wheat is also an oligosaccharide and also contains sugar, called fructan. Wheat is found in many sports bars and energy chews. Fructans are also found in cruciferous vegetables such as cabbage and cauliflower, onions, scallions, and garlic.

- **Dairy:** Lactose, the sugar found in dairy (especially unfermented forms such as milk, as opposed to yogurt or kefir), is a disaccharide. You'll find large amounts of lactose in many postworkout recovery beverages.

- **Sugar alcohols:** Examples of sugar alcohols, which are ingredients in many packaged and processed foods, are xylitol, maltitol, and sorbitol. You commonly find these in sugar-free or so-called "health" foods, and also in items such as diabetic candy, toothpaste, and sugar-free chewing gum.

TABLE 15-1

	FOODS SUITABLE ON A LOW-FODMAP DIET	
fruit	banana, blueberry, boysenberry, cantaloupe, cranberry, durian, grape, grapefruit, honeydew melon, kiwifruit, lemon, lime, mandarin, orange, passionfruit, pawpaw, raspberry, rhubarb, rockmelon, star anise, strawberry, tangelo	
vegetables	alfalfa, bamboo shoots, bean shoots, bok choy, carrot, celery, choko, choy sum, endive, ginger, green beans, lettuce, olives, parsnip, potato, pumpkin, red capsicum (bell pepper), silver beet, spinach, squash, swede, sweet potato, taro, tomato, turnip, yam, zucchini	
herbs	basil, chili, coriander, ginger, lemongrass, marjoram, mint, oregano, parsley, rosemary, thyme	
grain foods	gluten-free bread or cereal products, 100% spelt bread, rice, oats, polenta **other** - arrowroot, millet, psyllium, quinoa, sorghum, tapioca	
milk products	**milk** - lactose-free milk*, oat milk*, rice milk*, soy milk* (*check for additives) **cheeses** - hard cheeses, Brie, and Camembert **yogurt** - lactose-free variations **ice cream substitutes** - gelato, sorbet **butter substitutes** - olive oil	
other	tofu, **sweeteners** - sugar* (sucrose), glucose, artificial sweeteners not ending in '-ol' **honey substitutes** - golden syrup*, maple syrup*, molasses, treacle (*small quantities)	
	ELIMINATE FOODS CONTAINING FODMAPS	
excess fructose	**fruit** - apple, mango, nashi, pear, canned fruit in natural juice, watermelon **sweeteners** - fructose, high-fructose corn syrup **large total fructose dose** - concentrated fruit sources, large servings of fruit, dried fruit, fruit juice **honey** - corn syrup, fruisana	
lactose	**milk** - milk from cows, goats, or sheep, custard ice cream, yogurt **cheeses** - soft unripened cheeses, e.g. cottage, cream, mascarpone, ricotta	
fructans	**vegetables** - artichoke, asparagus, beetroot, broccoli, Brussels sprouts, cabbage, eggplant, fennel, garlic, leek, okra, onions (all), shallots, spring onions **cereals** - wheat and rye in large amounts, e.g. bread, crackers, cookies, couscous, pasta **fruit** - custard apple, persimmon, watermelon **miscellaneous** - chicory, dandelion, inulin, pistachio	
galactans	**legumes** - baked beans, chickpeas, kidney beans, lentils, soybeans	
polyols	**fruit** - apple, apricot, avocado, blackberry, cherry, longon, lychee, nashi, pear, plum, prune, watermelon **vegetables** - cauliflower, green capsicum (bell pepper), mushroom, sweet corn **sweeteners** - sorbitol, mannitol, isomalt, maltitol, xylitol	

As you may already know from personal experience or pure common sense, eating an entire plate of sautéed onions is probably going to give you gas (because of the fructan content). You also probably wouldn't mow down a few bowls of beans and lentils or eat a smoothie made with four or five apples and not expect to experience some funky repercussions in your gut. But you can create a nuclear bomb in your gut by consuming 50 to 100 grams of fructose and maltodextrin per hour from sports gels during a triathlon or marathon, downing a wheat-filled energy bar every afternoon at work, or sucking down a lactose-laden recovery shake after a workout.

Unless you want to go out of your way to get a breath test from a source such as DirectLabs, there really isn't a good test for FODMAPs aside from simply eliminating the big fermentable triggers from your diet and observing how you feel—basically an "elimination diet" strategy. If you have gas, bloating, indigestion, or other gut problems, I highly suggest that you photocopy Table 15-1, stick it on your fridge, try a low-FODMAP diet for a week, and see what happens. Please note that some popular health foods, such as coconut milk, avocados, garlic, and onions, should be moderated or avoided on a low-FODMAP diet.

3. Insufficient Digestive Enzymes or Low Enzyme Activity

I often see this problem in people who stress their guts by eating large amounts of food and also eat before, during, or after exercise or in a stressed postworkout state. When you eat a meal, a bar, or an energy gel or sip a sports drink, your digestive system (primarily your pancreas and small intestine) secretes enzymes that break down proteins, carbohydrates, and fats into usable nutrients that can pass from your intestine to your bloodstream.

Meat, eggs, and beans consist of giant protein molecules that must be broken down by enzymes before they can be used to build and repair body tissues[15]. For example, pepsin, an enzyme found in the digestive juices of the stomach, starts the digestion of swallowed protein. Then, in the small intestine, several enzymes secreted by the pancreas and the lining of the intestine complete the breakdown of these protein molecules into even smaller molecules (amino acids).

These amino acids can then be absorbed through the small intestine into the blood and carried to all parts of the body to build the walls and other parts of cells.

But in many cases, the amount of food you eat can exceed the capacity of your digestive enzymes (very typical among high-calorie-consuming active individuals); or your pancreas or small intestine has a genetic inability to produce a certain enzyme (such as lactase); or your gut is ravaged from periods of poor eating, gliadin exposure, and the like and is simply unable to produce adequate enzymes; or enzymatic activity is decreased because of intense physical activity—such as when you try to down a protein shake a few minutes after walking in the door from a hard run.

For example, if pepsin isn't working properly or isn't present, then proteins are not completely digested, and undigested protein particles are more likely to make their way into the bloodstream through the intestinal wall with other nutrients. This results in the problematic phenomenon you already learned about called leaky gut syndrome.

So how do you know if you have a digestive enzyme insufficiency?

The best way to know is with a stool test, such as a three-day gut-testing protocol, which involves multiple stool collections that you send to a lab, which then measures for the presence of bacteria, parasites, yeast, fungus, and other compounds and measures how well you're digesting your food and how well your pancreas is producing digestive enzymes. Most doctors won't run these tests, and they may not be covered by insurance, but you can oversee the process yourself. The report you get with the test results is usually pretty self-explanatory.

You can also pay attention to symptoms. Symptoms that suggest you might have problems with digestive enzymes are:

- Gas and bloating after meals
- Feeling as if you have food sitting in your stomach after you eat
- Feeling full after eating just a few bites of food
- Seeing undigested food in your stool
- Frequent and consistent floating stool
- An "oil slick" in the toilet bowl (which indicates undigested fat)

The fix for digestive enzyme issues is pretty simple. First, clean up your diet using some of the strategies you've already learned about so that your gut is able to produce adequate digestive enzymes. Second, eat more slowly and avoid rushed, hectic meals. Next, jump-start the process of digestion by taking digestive enzymes before you eat. Before eating a large meal or downing a big steak, I pop two digestive enzyme capsules (especially before pre-race or big workout meals), and I'm good to go. Finally, as you'll learn in chapter 16 in the section on race-week protocols, I prefer to blend and juice most of my foods during race weeks and before big workouts. This seems to help tremendously. You can check GreenfieldFitnessSystems.com for some of my favorite gut tests and digestive enzymes.

4. Insufficient Gut Bacteria

A healthy human body has more than 100 trillion microorganisms in its intestines, which is ten times more than the total number of human cells in the body. The metabolic activities performed by these bacteria resemble those of an organ, and these microorganisms perform a host of useful functions, such as training the immune system, attacking foreign invaders (like food-poisoning compounds, toxins, and so on), preventing the growth of harmful pathogenic bacteria in your gut, regulating the development of the intestinal lining, producing vitamins such as biotin and vitamin K, and even producing hormones[10].

So how do your gut bacteria become insufficient?

In my article "The Art of Using Antibiotics: How to Limit the Damage" (BenGreenfieldFitness.com/anti)—which I highly recommend you read if you have ever been on antibiotics—I point out how pharmaceuticals can deprive your body of precious probiotics.

In addition, an extremely low-fiber diet can result in insufficient gut flora[20]. Prebiotics are fiber-based sugars that you get from fruits and vegetables, and they provide sustenance to the probiotics.

Insufficient intake of fermented foods rich in good bacteria can also be an issue, especially in a modern, Western diet. Unfortunately, most commercial probiotic foods have been pasteurized, are packaged improperly for keeping good bacteria alive, or have lots of added sugars to satisfy palates conditioned to sweet foods.

If you do have insufficient gut bacteria, you're likely to experience serious performance-inhibiting issues, including:

- Complete absence of gas (yes, you actually stop farting)
- Undigested fiber in stool, which appears as white or dark specks
- Constipation, with occasional periods of diarrhea or irritable bowel syndrome
- Frequent sickness and allergies
- Blood-clotting problems
- Neurological problems and brain fog

If you suspect that you have insufficient gut bacteria, I recommend the gut-testing kit that I mentioned earlier to test for the presence of bacteria. If you discover that you have a bacteria insufficiency or you have many of the symptoms described above, you have to repopulate your gut with good bacteria, get adequate amounts of prebiotics, and replace any bacteria that have been wiped out by an antibiotic protocol. I recommend this one-two-three combo:

1. Consume a wide variety of fermented foods with natural amounts of good bacteria. (For information on how to find fermented foods and prepare your own, you can read a comprehensive article I wrote at BeyondTrainingBook.com/wfxfermentation.)

2. Consume a full-spectrum probiotic, such as Caprobiotics, EXOS Probiotics, or PrescriptAssist. If you've ever been on antibiotics, also take *Saccharomyces boulardii* (Jarrow Formulas is good brand).

3. Consume lots of vegetables and moderate amounts of fiber from other sources, such as seeds and nuts to feed the probiotics, or include a greens supplement that is rich in prebiotics, such as LivingFuel SuperGreens or EnerPrime.

Finally, if your bacterial insufficiency includes a strange absence of gas accompanied by frequent constipation (which can happen if you've been on some big antibiotic regimens) and you want the shotgun, nuclear bomb, fix-everything-all-at-once approach, the best solution I've found (if you're not interested in the trendy new world of fecal transplants and "poop pills") is the Colorectal Recovery Program at BeyondTrainingBook.com/colo. It eliminates the issue by literally "infecting" or, as a microbiologist might say, "reinoculating" your large intestine with a bacterial strain. This formula has saved my ass (quite literally) after taking antibiotics and does not involve a messy process of fecal transplantation or the consumption of someone else's Number 2. Just Google "fecal transplants" if you want to learn more about that method.

5. Too Much Gut Bacteria

Small intestinal bacterial overgrowth, also known as SIBO, tends to fly under the radar, but it can be especially problematic in athletes who have been consuming a traditional high-carbohydrate diet because bacteria in the gut tend to readily feed on sugars and starches. As a matter of fact, I think SIBO is a hugely underdiagnosed issue.

Basically, SIBO is a chronic bacterial infection of the small intestine[3]. The actual infection comes from bacteria that would normally live in your gastrointestinal tract but have overgrown abnormally in a location that cannot sustain that many bacteria.

As you can see in Figure 15-3, these bacteria interfere with normal digestion and absorption of food and are associated with damage to the lining or membrane of the small intestine (leaky gut syndrome, which I prefer to call leaky SI in this case). This can be a serious issue because:

- The bacteria consume some of your food, which over time leads to deficiencies in bacteria's favorite nutrients such as iron and B_{12}, which can cause anemia.
- They consume food unable to be absorbed because of damage to the SI lining, which creates more bacterial overgrowth (a vicious cycle).
- After eating your food, they produce gas, which causes flatulence, abdominal bloating, abdominal pain, or constipation or diarrhea, or both.

FIGURE 15-3.
SIBO Pathophysiology

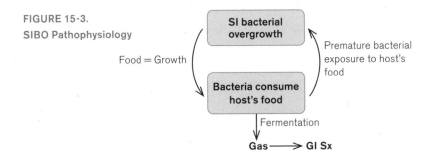

- Bacteria decrease proper fat absorption by "deconjugating" bile, which leads to deficiencies in vitamins A and D (and those lovely fatty stools).
- Through the damaged lining of the gut, larger food particles unable to be fully digested enter the body, and your immune system reacts to them, creating food allergies and sensitivities. (Leaky gut rears its ugly head once again.)
- Bacteria themselves can also enter the body and bloodstream. Your immune system reacts to these bacteria and their cell walls, which can produce something called endotoxemia, which causes chronic fatigue and stresses the liver.
- The bacteria excrete acids that in high amounts can cause neurological and cognitive symptoms.

How do you know if you have SIBO?

- In addition to experiencing many of the signs and symptoms listed above, you have a bad reaction when you consume fermented foods, such as kombucha and kefir. You can even get irritable bowel syndrome from consuming probiotics—which basically dump bacteria on top of bacteria. It may seem counterintuitive, but in this case fermented foods could actually be bad for you.
- You can order a simple at-home breath test that measures the amount of gas produced by bacteria. I recommend the QuinTron breath test at breathtests.com.

If you have SIBO, a combination of low carbohydrate intake, juicing, and herbal cleanses can eradicate the issue. This may be pretty difficult to do when you're in the throes of an intense exercise program, so you'll probably need to save it for the off-season unless you want to take thirty days off to take care of it. There are a variety of SIBO healing programs out there, but one basic protocol is this:

- Eat only nonfermentable carbohydrates, and limit carbohydrate intake in general. The Specific Carbohydrate Diet and a sample meal plan for SIBO can be found on the resource web page for this chapter.
- If you have a juicer, juice once or twice a day with fresh plantain leaves (you can often find them at local ethnic grocery stores—in my town, the Mexican one), a quarter of a medium cabbage, two small to medium beets, two carrots, two stalks of celery, and one piece of ginger.
- Use herbal antibiotics and tinctures daily, such as goldenseal extract, phellodendron, coptis, cordynopsis, garlic extract, and oil of oregano.

If you want to learn more about SIBO and how to fix it, check out the comprehensive and helpful SIBO website at siboinfo.com, and consider a SIBO breath test from BeyondTrainingBook.com/directlabs. At BeyondTrainingBook.com/torrent, you will find a bonus video and PDF to accompany this section of the book entitled "The Hidden Killer in Your Gut," which you can download for free.

6. Yeast, Fungus, or Parasites

This is nasty stuff to think about, but harmful bacteria are a fact of life—and I have been shocked at the number of seemingly healthy folks who have tested positive for parasites, yeast, and fungus. When these are allowed to take over and grow out of control, you get sick more often and end up with some serious gut issues.

A parasite is a microscopic organism that derives nourishment from its host without benefiting or killing the host. You can have parasitic fungi and parasitic yeast in your body. Intestinal parasites can lead to issues such as abnormal bowel movements, muscle aches and pains, chronic fatigue, insomnia, skin problems, and gut discomfort[4].

How do you get parasites?

They can be contracted in many ways, including from raw meat and fish (had sushi lately?), polluted water (like open-water triathlon swims), contaminated fruits and veggies (all over the place), contact with animals (yes, including your beloved cat or dog), insect bites, and contaminated water or food consumed during travel abroad.

For example, within three weeks of returning from a particularly long triathlon-training and racing trip to Thailand—which included elephant rides, open-water swims in stagnant human-made lagoons, liberal consumption of foods cooked in suspect ways, and many insect bites—I had some strange coughing, skin rashes, and seriously smelly poo. I tested with a home poop panel (the same gut test that I mentioned earlier) and, sure enough—I had a few nasty critters in my gut.

I opted to take a high-grade oil of oregano four times a day and a supplement called mastic gum twice a day, and I was good to go within a month. I probably got lucky, because many times, parasitic infections require more serious medication and long-term treatment. It all depends on the type of parasite you have.

How about yeast and fungus?

Yeasts are microscopic organisms categorized as fungi. The most common culprit for gut issues is *Candida albicans,* which is a normal inhabitant in your body but can wreak havoc if it grows out of control[5]. When that happens, you get chronic fatigue, can't lose weight, and have sugar and carbohydrate cravings, brain fog, and even food sensitivities or allergies to foods that were once OK for you to eat. This issue is very similar to SIBO in its consequences.

In my experience, women who eat lots of carbs are most susceptible—but guys can grow an overabundance of yeast, too. A low-carb diet combined with a cleansing protocol can eradicate the problem (see the SIBO recommendations beginning on page 334), but often you need an even more comprehensive protocol, including:

- Daily use of a sludgy drink comprised of 1/2 teaspoon diatomaceous earth and 1/2 teaspoon bentonite clay mixed into 16 ounces water.

- Yeast-eating probiotics such as *Saccharomyces boulardii* (a good brand is Orthomolecular), consumed separately from meals.

- An anti-fungal protocol that includes olive leaf extract, grapefruit seed extract, oregano, and other herbs (NatureCleanse is good brand).

- A diet that restricts sugar, refined carbohydrates, white rice, gluten, dairy, fried foods, fruit, fruit juices, foods made with yeast such as bread, pasta, and crackers, MSG, vinegar, fermented foods (yes, even sauerkraut, kimchi, kombucha, and yogurt), alcohol, moldy foods such as mushrooms, cheese, peanuts, and pistachios, and meats from animals that have been exposed to antibiotics.

So what can you eat? Your options include, but are not limited to, all vegetables, onions and garlic, healthy meats, eggs, gluten-free grains such as quinoa, amaranth, and millet, coconut milk, coconut butter, teas, olive oil, bone broth, nuts, and any beans except kidney beans, provided that the beans have been soaked. Throughout the course of a *Candida* cleansing protocol, which can take up to thirty days, you can test your progress by measuring your first morning urine and your second morning urine, looking for pH values of 6.8 to 7.2 to indicate that your body is recovering from a yeast infection.

Ultimately, I'm a big fan of a high-quality GI test for a full scan of exactly what is going on inside your gut. This is an at-home test that screens for *H. pylori* and pathogenic bacteria, *Candida albicans*, and fungus in addition to many types of protozoa and worms, including *C. difficile, Giardia, E. coli, Blastocystis hominis*, roundworm, *Toxoplasma, Trichinella spiralis* (from pork), and tapeworm.

All you have to do is collect a few stool samples and send them to the lab. Results go directly to the office of the service from which you order the test, and then you receive a personalized letter of test results and recommendations, which may include natural antiparasite herbal formulas, nutritional supplements, and diet or lifestyle changes. You can get a Comprehensive Stool Analysis from DirectLabs, and on the resource web page for this chapter, I've included a sample report so you can see what the analysis feedback looks like.

7. Insufficient Stomach Acid

It bugs the heck out of me when I learn that someone with indigestion or heartburn has been prescribed a proton pump inhibitor or some other medication that blocks stomach acid (hydrochloric acid, or HCl) production. If someone isn't digesting food properly, the last thing you want to do is further limit her ability to break down food in the stomach!

In many cases, the cause of heartburn, gastroesophageal reflux disorder, and the like is, paradoxically, inadequate HCl production (also known as hypochlorhydria)—often combined with bacterial overgrowth, lack of digestive enzymes, and too much carbohydrate. This is a pretty significant issue, since using HCl to sterilize food to destroy harmful microorganisms reduces your risk of being colonized by other harmful microorganisms (like parasites or fungus). Stomach acid also plays an important role in the digestion of proteins and the absorption of minerals and vitamins and signals the release of digestive enzymes and bicarbonate from your pancreas, which is crucial for digestion[19].

Insufficient stomach acid can cause the absorption of incompletely digested food molecules, which can lead to food intolerances or allergies. This happens because food particles that would normally be digested and absorbed in your upper intestines instead pass into your lower intestines and provide fuel for yeast or fungus, promote overgrowth of pathogens, and cause poor absorption of minerals, vitamins, and amino acids. Natural physician Dr. Carolyn Dean discusses this concept in detail in the post "Why Kill Your Stomach Acid" on my blog, which I link to on the web page for this chapter.

Low stomach acid levels can be genetic or acquired. The Heidelberg pH test is probably the most accurate way to gauge HCl insufficiency, but it is uncomfortable and invasive, and Heidelberg machines are not easy to find. A blood test through a company like WellnessFX can give you a decent indication of your HCl level, especially if your chloride value is less than 100 and your CO_2 level is greater than 27.

You can also simply pay attention to your symptoms: In most cases, if you're getting heartburn after a meal (especially a protein-containing meal), your HCl is probably low.

What can you do about insufficient stomach acid? A combination of the following can be very effective:

- Add raw, crushed garlic to your diet. It has the natural antimicrobial allicin, which can help lower levels of harmful bacteria and fungi, such as *Candida*.
- If you eat grains, legumes, seeds, and nuts, soak (and, in many cases, sprout) them to improve digestibility.
- Increase your fiber intake by adding a handful of dried prunes or ground flax or chia seeds to your diet to encourage healthy bowel movements.
- Add two to three tablespoons of extra-virgin coconut oil to your diet daily—it has great antimicrobial properties.
- Avoid simple or refined carbohydrates (white bread, pasta, cookies, cakes, crackers, and so on). Also avoid soda, alcohol, nightshade vegetables (tomatoes, eggplant, potatoes, and peppers of all kinds and colors), wheat and gluten, peanuts, shellfish, excessive caffeine, artificial sweeteners (aspartame, sucralose, etc.), nitrites (in processed foods like hot dogs, lunch meats, and bacon), MSG, hydrogenated or partially hydrogenated oils (trans fats) found in most processed foods, deep-fried foods, fast food, and junk food.
- Eat smaller, more frequent meals instead of fewer large, heavy meals—not because snacking a lot will magically boost your metabolism, but because it may be easier for you to digest small meals until you've fixed your HCl problem.
- Don't eat just before bed, and maintain an upright position for about forty-five minutes after eating to allow for easier digestion.
- Do not drink ice-cold water before, during, or after meals, as this can lower HCl production.
- Follow this supplementation protocol:
  - 1/2 capsule HCl with pepsin immediately before eating. If you experience no burning or indigestion, the next day take 1 tablet the same way. If you

still have no burning or indigestion, the next day take 2 tablets the same way. Continue until you experience burning, then back off.

- 1–2 servings of organic bitters immediately before a meal.
- 1–2 doses of NatureCleanse per day.
- 1–2 servings of bone broth or organic gelatin per day.

If you want to read more about the issues with heartburn medications and the methods you can use to fix insufficient HCl production and gastroesophageal reflux disorder (GERD), I highly recommend the heartburn/GERD section of Chris Kresser's website (chriskresser.com/heartburn), in which he expounds in great detail on Figure 15-4.

FIGURE 15-4

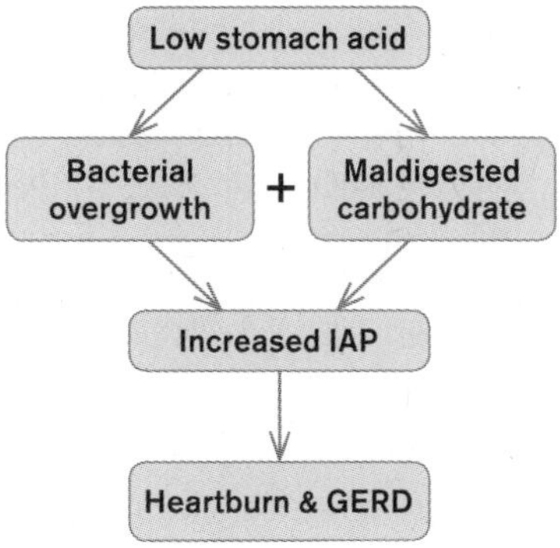

Low stomach acid

Bacterial overgrowth **+** Maldigested carbohydrate

Increased IAP

Heartburn & GERD

8. Other Food Intolerances or Sensitivities

Jane feels exactly the same way when she consumes foods containing fructose; however, unlike Joe, she has adequate liver enzymes but impaired fructose absorption from a deficiency of fructose carriers in the small intestine, which are responsible for carrying fructose across the gut barrier and into the bloodstream.

As you may have guessed, both Jane and Joe have an intolerance to fructose. Joe's is related more to a digestive enzyme deficiency, Jane's to a fructose carrier issue.

The term *food intolerance* (or *food sensitivity*) is widely used to refer to a variety of unpleasant responses to specific foods or compounds in foods. While you've already learned about gluten intolerance and lactose intolerance, a combination of the following six factors can also create intolerances[21]:

1. A deficiency, which is a lack of chemicals or enzymes necessary to digest a food.

2. Malabsorption, which is an inability of the digestive system to absorb specific nutrients.

3. A sensitivity, which is a hyperreaction to a normal amount of a substance, usually some type of pharmacological compound, like a food additive, preservative, or coloring.

4. An immune antibody response to food that is mediated by less-serious antibodies than a full-blown food allergy (for example, gluten intolerance).

5. A toxin present in food from either contamination or mold (for example, aflatoxin from peanuts).

6. A psychological reaction to food from an emotion associated with that food, such as being unable to eat chili without feeling nauseated because of that time you ate chili on a road trip and got carsick.

The most commonly known food intolerances—such as lactose and gluten, both of which have sparked entire industries of lactose-free and gluten-free foods—have already been discussed in detail. But some people have lesser-known intolerances to food additives, preservatives, artificial colors and flavors, fructose, and foods that contain high levels of salicylate, which is present in many fruits, juices, vegetables, spices, herbs, nuts, tea, wines, and coffee.

If you experience gas, bloating, frequent bathroom trips, or digestive cramping after a meal, it's very possible that you have an intolerance to one or several compounds in those foods. While moderate indigestion is normal from high carbohydrate and high calorie intake, especially during a long workout or race, it is not normal to have the excessive mucus, coughing, itching, rashes, sinus inflammation, or headaches that dozens of my clients have reported after a big workout or race. These are all potential signs of a food intolerance.

The good news is that by properly identifying specific intolerances, adjusting dietary intake, and choosing the right training and racing fuels, food intolerances can become a nonissue. However, testing for food intolerances is confusing, to say the least.

Options include breath testing, skin pinpricks, stomach gastroscopy, intestinal biopsy, stool analysis, skin sample analysis, electrical current testing, muscle testing methods, and more—and there is a lot of controversy in the medical and nutrition community about which test is best. Results go all the way from questionable to downright useless.

But if you suspect a specific intolerance, that hunch can help you choose the proper test. For example, a fructose intolerance is best identified by a breath test, which measures undigested fructose through hydrogen levels in the breath, whereas a lactose intolerance is better measured by analyzing the blood sugar response to lactose consumption. Meanwhile, an IgG and IgA test (not to be confused with an IgE test for a true food allergy) can measure immunoglobulin levels for specific protein-based food intolerances, such as those to chicken or eggs.

You can get food-sensitivity tests from companies like ALCAT and Metametrix. DirectLabs offers a test called an enzyme-linked immunosorbent assay (ELISA) methodology, which tests allergies and sensitivities to a variety of common allergens. You can also do an Antibody Assessment Panel, available from US BioTek, that tests for IgG and IgA. Figure 15-5 shows what my results looked like. (The light bars represent IgG and the dark bars represent IgA.)

It was very interesting to see that I apparently have food intolerances to:

- Dairy from cows (but not goats)
- Chicken eggs (not shown in the figure, but I tested sensitive to chicken eggs, but not to eggs from other fowl, such as ducks)

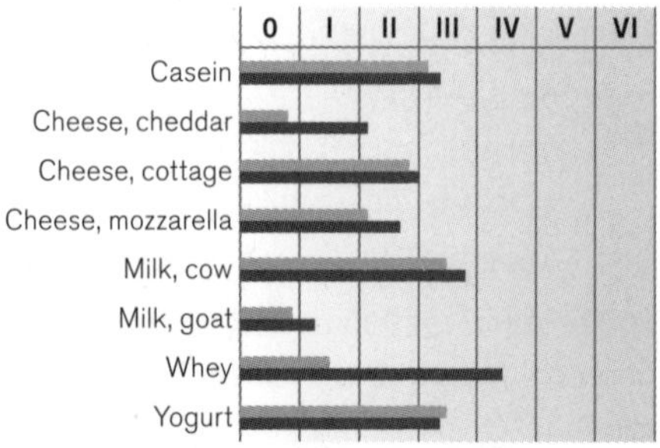

Considering the amount of omelets, raw-dairy yogurt, raw-dairy cheese, Greek yogurt, and even protein bars containing whey from grass-fed cows that I was consuming at the time, I'm

FIGURE 15-5. Dairy

not really sure which came first, the food sensitivities or the high levels of antibodies circulating in my bloodstream because I was eating those foods.

And herein lies the problem with blood-based food-intolerance testing: The presence of antibodies to certain foods does not necessarily mean that those foods are causing a harmful or inappropriate immune reaction. It more likely means that those are the foods you eat the most often or have eaten the most recently.

As a matter of fact, people who may have been allergic to milk or eggs as kids but eventually outgrew those allergies (which is fairly common) tend to have more antibodies to those foods. In other words, the presence of antibodies is linked to an increased tolerance to those foods, not a decreased tolerance. Yet when you test, you may receive a long and foreboding list of foods to avoid (often hundreds of them!) when that may not really be your problem. This is why, for the best accuracy, I recommend the Array 3, Array 4, and Array 10 tests from Cyrex Labs, which will give you plenty of information without producing any false positives or giving you a frustrating, extremely long list of foods that you can't eat. You can't order these tests yourself, but a physician can order them for you.

So I encourage you to simply keep a record of everything you eat for a few weeks and any symptoms that develop in response to specific foods. Doing so can help you narrow down the list of foods that may be causing you problems. The next step is a food-elimination diet, in which you avoid suspected triggers.

What do you do if you discover that you do indeed have a food intolerance?

The nature of the food intolerance will significantly affect the steps you take. For example, since a gluten intolerance is related to an antibody reaction and an immune system response to gluten, you have to switch to a gluten-free diet.

The same can be said for a fructose intolerance, which requires you to eliminate fructose and sucrose completely from your diet. In other cases, eliminating the food entirely isn't necessary. For example, if you have a lactose intolerance (as I do), taking a lactase enzyme pill immediately before eating any dairy or eating only raw, unpasteurized dairy, in which the natural lactase enzymes are fully intact and active, may do the trick.

Since having several food intolerances is quite common, you may need to adopt a diet that is free of the usual food culprits, especially if you are a triathlete who is chowing down thousands of calories a day. If you want an extremely clean "autoimmune diet" that eliminates just about every known food-sensitivity trigger, check out my four-week autoimmune diet (BenGreenfieldFitness.com/diet) or *The Autoimmune Paleo Cookbook* (BenGreenfieldFitness.com/immune).

9. Food Allergies

Compared with a food intolerance, a true food allergy is usually a much bigger deal.

A food allergy is often accompanied by serious, and sometimes even fatal, symptoms. It occurs when the body's immune system mistakenly identifies a protein—such as the protein in shellfish or peanuts—as harmful. Some proteins or fragments of proteins are resistant to digestion and are tagged by the antibody immunoglobulin E (IgE). These tags fool your immune system into thinking that the protein is an invader, and your immune system triggers an allergic reaction in defense[7].

These allergic responses can range from mild to severe and include hives, anaphylactic shock, a severe drop in blood pressure, dermatitis and other skin reactions, gastrointestinal and respiratory distress, and even life-threatening anaphylactic reactions, in which the throat swells and closes, requiring immediate emergency action.

Unlike a food intolerance, you usually know for sure when you have a food allergy, because the response is readily identifiable and usually very uncomfortable or severe. Allergic and other hypersensitivity reactions to foods are characterized by elevated allergen-specific antibody levels in you blood, and you can get IgE tests online from companies like DirectLabs. However, if you suspect that you have a food allergy, don't mess around: Consult with a licensed medical care provider who specializes in allergy treatments.

If you decide to go an alternative route, you can look into Nambudripad's Allergy Elimination Techniques (naet.com) or sublingual immunotherapy, in which drops of the substance you're allergic to are placed under your tongue in increasingly greater doses. An alternative medical practitioner can walk you through either of these methods. (I used the latter to successfully cure one of my twin boys of bee allergies and the other of peanut allergies.)

Perhaps your head was spinning as you read through the gut issues just described and thought, "I have that! No, wait—I have *that!*" Don't worry. It's typical for gut issues to be multifactorial—and often people have a nasty cocktail of bacterial imbalance, food intolerance or allergy, leaky gut, toxic liver, and so on.

The best way to begin figuring out what's going on in your gut is to:

- Test and pay attention to symptoms.
- Clean up your diet and use nutrition supplements wisely.
- Try to live stress-free, since stress significantly exacerbates gut issues.

If you want to learn more about the gut, I highly recommend the following resources. I've put links to all of them on the web page for this chapter.

- *Clean Gut: The Breakthrough Plan for Eliminating the Root Cause of Disease and Revolutionizing Your Health,* by Alejandro Junger
- *A New IBS Solution: Bacteria—The Missing Link in Treating Irritable Bowel Syndrome,* by Dr. Mark Pimentel
- *Gut and Psychology Syndrome: Natural Treatment for Autism, Dyspraxia, A.D.D., Dyslexia, A.D.H.D., Depression, Schizophrenia,* by Dr. Natasha Campbell-McBride
- *Specific Carbohydrate Diet (SCD) Lifestyle,* by Jordan Reasoner and Steven Wright
- Konstantin Monastyrsky's website, gutsense.org
- Dr. Allison Siebecker's website, siboinfo.com

So now that you've fixed your gut, are you ready to detox? Just keep reading.

The Best Way to Detox Your Body

Recently, I read an article in *The Guardian* entitled "You can't detox your body. It's a myth. So how do you get healthy?" In the article, author Dara Mohammadi said, "[D]etoxing—the idea that you can flush your system of impurities and leave your organs squeaky clean and raring to go—is a scam. It's a pseudo-medical concept designed to sell you things."

Is this true? Is detoxing just a scam?

To answer this question, it's important to begin with an understanding of what toxins actually are. No matter how "clean" you live your life, just about everybody shows some evidence of a buildup of toxins. When the Centers for Disease Control and Prevention (CDC) conducted the *Fourth National Report on Human Exposure to Environmental Chemicals*[27], it found some pretty shocking results.

On average, the CDC's report found 212 chemicals in people's blood or urine, 75 of which had never before been measured in the U.S. population. They included:

- **Acrylamide:** Formed when foods are baked or fried at high temperatures and as a by-product of cigarette smoke

- **Arsenic:** Found in many home-building products

- **Environmental phenols:** Including bisphenol A (found in plastics, food packaging, and epoxy resins) and triclosan (used as an antibacterial agent in personal-care products such as toothpaste and hand soap)

- **Perchlorate:** Used in airplane fuel, explosives, and fireworks

- **Perfluorinated chemicals:** Used to create nonstick cookware

- **Polybrominated diphenyl ethers:** Used in fire retardants found in consumer products, such as mattresses

- **Volatile organic compounds (VOCs):** Found in paints, air fresheners, cleaning products, cosmetics, upholstery fabrics, carpets, dry-cleaned clothing, wood preservatives, and paint strippers

When combined, these chemicals can present a toxic burden to the human body and, as the CDC has found, can accumulate in your blood, urine, and tissues. While your body does have detoxification organs that can process many of these chemicals and toxins (your liver and kidneys), exposure to these chemicals can potentially cause medical problems if your liver and kidneys are not functioning properly or are overburdened with a poor diet.

While the kidneys are indeed an important filtration mechanism for removing waste and excess water from the body, it's the liver that has the most crucial job when it comes to detoxification. Along with filtering your blood to remove toxins, your liver uses a two-phase process to break down chemicals and toxins[28]. During phase 1, toxins are neutralized and broken into smaller fragments. Then, in phase 2, they are bound to other molecules, creating new nontoxic molecules that can be excreted in your bile, urine, or stool.

But in order for this liver detoxification to work properly, your body must have adequate nutrients. If not, the phase 1 and phase 2 processes may not work properly[29], which can leave toxic substances to build up in your body. There are specific nutrients that support both pathways.

Phase 1:

- B vitamins (B_2, B_3, B_6, B_{12}, and folic acid)
- Flavonoids (found in fruits and vegetables)
- Foods rich in vitamins A, C, and E (carrots, oranges, wheat germ, and almonds)
- Glutathione (found in avocados, watermelon, asparagus, walnuts, fresh fruits and veggies, and the nutrients N-acetylcysteine, cysteine, and methionine)
- Branched chain amino acids (found in animal protein such as dairy products, red meat, and eggs)
- Phospholipids (found in eggs, lean meats, organ meats, fish, and soybeans)

Phase 2:

- Indole-3-carbinol (found in cabbage, broccoli, and Brussels sprouts)
- Limonene (found in oranges, tangerines, caraway seeds, and dill seeds)
- Glutathione (found in avocados, watermelon, asparagus, walnuts, and fresh fruits and veggies)
- Fish oil
- Amino acids from protein

Let's look into how these detoxing products actually work. The first claim in the *Guardian* article is based on a quote from Edzard Ernst, a professor of complementary medicine at Exeter University. He says:

"[T]here are two types of detox: one is respectable and the other isn't. The respectable one is the medical treatment of people with life-threatening drug addictions. The other is the word being hijacked by entrepreneurs, quacks and charlatans to sell a bogus treatment that allegedly detoxifies your body of toxins you're supposed to have accumulated."

The article goes on to explain that when it comes to products that range from dietary supplements to smoothies and shampoos, not one of the manufacturers can actually define what it means by detoxification or name the toxins that these products are supposed to remove.

However, just because a manufacturer of, say, spirulina powder can't say how it works doesn't mean that there isn't scientific evidence for its potential to remove toxins from the body.

For example, cyanobacteria is a specific type of bacteria found in spirulina that is an accumulator (also known as a "biosorbent") of heavy minerals[30]. It does this via a process called ion-exchange binding and can significantly reduce heavy metal toxicity in tissue[31]. In fact, 100 micrograms (a very small amount) of spirulina hexane extract has been shown to remove over 85 percent of arsenic in tissue[32]. At a dose of 250–500 milligrams per kilogram of body weight, spirulina has been shown to prevent metal toxicity in pregnant rats' offspring when the mothers were given fluoride[33], and it has been noted to reduce lead accumulation in brain tissue, protect against heavy metal cadmium buildup[34], and attenuate mercury accumulation in the testes[35].

Granted, spirulina is one of the few molecules in existence that actually has a large body of evidence to support its detoxifying activity, but other compounds such as dandelion extract[36], ginseng[37], and zinc[38] have also been clinically proven to reduce heavy metal buildup. And while heavy metals are only one form of toxin that can accumulate in your tissues, there is no doubt science has proven that these toxins can indeed be removed via the use of these specific detox compounds found in nature. So when the *Guardian* article guffaws at the idea of superfoods, such as spirulina, evidence suggests that there's more to the story.

Take milk thistle extract, another popular detox or cleansing supplement. While the *Guardian* article would have you believe that there is no value whatsoever in consuming this type of nutrient, studies show[39] that milk thistle actually protects and promotes the growth of liver cells, fights oxidation (a process that damages cells), and blocks toxins from entering the cell membrane.

Silymarins, a group of antioxidants extracted from the seeds of milk thistle, have antioxidant properties several times greater than those of vitamins C and E. In fact, silybin (a type of silymarin) has been shown to be especially effective in promoting liver health[40]. Milk thistle also helps enhance detoxification by preventing the depletion of glutathione[41], which is necessary for phase 2 liver detoxification.

We can look to farming for another example of detoxification of dangerous materials that have bioaccumulated in living organisms. Glyphosate, the active ingredient in herbicide used on crops around the world, has been shown to cause gut and genetic damage as it builds up in the bodies of animals[42]. Because of this, some farmers use activated charcoal and humic acid (a claylike substance extracted from soil) to detox their cattle after the animals have been exposed to glyphosate chemicals[43] while feeding.

As you can see from these examples, to claim that detox supplements and diets simply don't work is a gross oversimplification. While there isn't any evidence for the efficacy of the cayenne pepper, lemon, and maple syrup juice cleanse your coworker has been bragging about, evidence of other nutrients' detoxification capacity actually does exist.

The article's author, Dara Mohammadi, also writes: "[P]roponents will tell you that mischievous plaques of impacted poo can lurk in your colon for months or years and pump disease-causing toxins back into your system. Pay them a small fee, though, and they'll insert a hose up your bottom and wash them all away."

She goes on to say: "Some colon-cleansing tablets contain a polymerising agent that turns your faeces into something like a plastic, so that when a massive rubbery poo snake slithers into your toilet you can stare back at it and feel vindicated in your purchase."

When you think about it, the idea of toxins somehow being reabsorbed by your body as they sit in your colon actually makes some sense. After all, rectal suppositories are used to administer drugs rapidly—so if drugs can enter your bloodstream from your colon, it's certainly possible that toxins could be entering that way, too.

However, your colon is equipped with several natural mechanisms to keep toxins from building up. For example:

- Natural bacteria in the colon can detoxify food waste[44].
- Mucus membranes in the colon can keep unwanted substances from reentering the blood and tissues.
- The colon sheds old cells about every three days, preventing a buildup of harmful material and even allowing for the expulsion of parasites[45].

I suspect that if colon cleansing or enemas have any effect in making you feel like you have more energy or have been "cleansed," it is more likely to do with an activation of specific reflexes in your gut that cause your nervous system to relax[46], along with stimulation of bile production by the liver[47], which can indeed improve digestion, have a laxative effect, and relieve constipation.

Sure, this could potentially make you feel better by allowing you to better digest your food, or to even pass some feces that have built up over the past few days, but this is one point on which I completely agree with *The Guardian*. There is no evidence that waste can sit inside you for years, slowly rotting and toxifying your body.

Ultimately, as the *Guardian* article explains, your body has its own powerful methods of detoxification—and can activate these methods without the use of fancy diets or detox spa visits. These methods primarily come in the form of your liver and kidneys functioning normally.

For example, your liver prevents pathogens from passing into your bloodstream, processes environmental toxins for safe removal, and helps rid your body of excess nitrogen that builds up from the breakdown of proteins and amino acids.

Your kidneys filter blood, remove excess water, pass urea (which is a toxin that builds up as a by-product of protein breakdown), and send this all out of your body via your urine.

So if you eat foods that support your liver and kidneys or avoid foods that stress your liver and kidneys, you're already detoxing every day—and this is why I'm a fan of using things like herbal blends and colonic cleanses only sparingly and instead using natural detoxification protocols all year long.

For your liver, you can do things like avoid high amounts of omega-6 polyunsaturated fats from processed and packaged foods like canola oil and French fries. Instead, eat healthy fats from fish, meat, seeds, and nuts. You can avoid high amounts of fructose and sugar, limit alcohol, consume plenty of egg yolks (which contain choline that your liver uses to process fats), and eat organic liver every now and then.

Additionally, pay attention to the kinds of soaps, shampoos, and household cleaners you're using. Some contain toxins that can tax your body. You'll learn more about that in the upcoming lifestyle chapters.

For your kidneys, you can limit your intake of high-fructose corn syrup[48], drink plenty of water, limit alcohol, and—if you are predisposed to renal issues—limit excessive protein intake[49] (that is, eat no more than 200 grams per day).

As the *Guardian* article notes, many popular detox and cleansing diets probably seem beneficial because of what they eliminate and not because of any magical ingredients. All that lemon juice, cayenne pepper, maple syrup, and fancy water is probably not doing much when it comes to cleansing and detoxifying your body.

But all the processed fats, high-fructose corn syrup, alcohol, candy, soda, commercial meat, and snack foods you're eliminating while on a detox diet are giving your liver and kidneys a chance to step up and do their normal detoxification duties, since they're no longer overburdened with bad food and not enough micronutrients and minerals to support their normal function.

So, now that you know that detoxification is possible, what can you do to detox? Ultimately, you can fix your gut by using many of the methods you've learned about in this chapter. But if you have been exposed to overprocessed and refined foods, chemical additives, antibiotics and pharmaceuticals, pesticides, herbicides, chlorinated water, artificial sweeteners, or anything else that might be considered remotely "unnatural"—which means pretty much everyone!—you should think about doing a detoxification protocol (just don't overdo it, since, as you've just learned, your liver and kidneys do a pretty good job).

For example, have you:

- Drunk lots of diet soda?
- Eaten much nonorganic or non-farm-raised meat?
- Traveled extensively?
- Chomped on fruits and vegetables without washing them?
- Been sick and taken pharmaceuticals?
- Engaged in a few nights of excessive drinking?
- Been exposed to secondhand smoke?
- Spent much time inhaling the fumes of office or household cleaning supplies?

I don't about you, but my answer to many of the items listed above is "Yes!" So I detox my body at least once a year—typically in the off-season when my levels of physical activity and exercise are lower.

Think of a detox as spring cleaning for your body.

Heavy metals, toxins, pesticides, and other compounds that your body is unable to metabolize can accumulate in your tissues, cells, and digestive tract[16]. Perhaps not to the extent that some of the more extreme folks would have you believe (for example, you probably don't have pounds and pounds of plaque built up in your colon), but you certainly may have amassed enough toxins to affect the way your metabolism, brain, and other important organ systems function.

And when you detox, it really is true that you can feel a whole lot better, almost "reborn" in a way, especially if the detox remedies brain fog, gut distress, chronic fatigue, joint pain, and the like that are symptoms of toxic buildup.

The whole idea behind doing a detox, or cleanse, is to use herbal or medicinal components to induce peristalsis (contraction of smooth muscles that propel contents through the digestive tract) and more rapid and thorough clearing of compounds from your colon. Other herbal compounds can enhance the ability of the liver's two detoxification pathways (known as phase 1 and phase 2) to bind or excrete toxins. By restricting calories and doing light exercise while you're on the protocol, you can accelerate the rate at which fat tissues are metabolized by the body. Since your body stores many toxins in fat, this can also increase the rate at which your body detoxifies (see Figure 15-6).

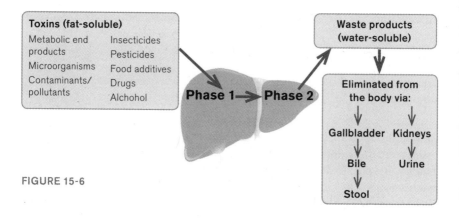

FIGURE 15-6

In a nutshell, you clean out your digestive tract, release toxins from your body, and accelerate fat burning. What's not to love?

Believe it or not, you don't need to sequester yourself in some exclusive spa on a mountaintop or spend the entire day on or near the toilet to do a detox or cleanse. You probably don't have time for that.

So here are four easy steps to a quick detox for active people. Simply do the following for one week to one month.

Detox Step 1: Go Easy

Switch your exercise routine to mostly light, aerobic exercise (such as an easy twenty- to thirty-minute walk each morning), with just a couple weight sessions a week. No hard sprints, intense intervals, or voluminous training sessions, as the impact, bouncing, jarring, and metabolic stress is not going to make a fiber-filled gut or a detoxing digestive system happy. Think low stress. If you want to maintain muscle and cardiovascular fitness while getting an added detoxification effect, consider a daily twenty- to thirty-minute sauna treatment. You can learn more about how to do this properly at BenGreenfieldFitness.com/hackedsauna.

Detox Step 2: Eat Clean

Completely eliminate all processed foods, like chips, crackers, cookies, and candy; cut out anything nonorganic, including meats, eggs, packaged foods, and the like; cut out central nervous system stimulants like caffeine and alcohol; and simply eat clean, real food. There are specific foods that enhance gut or liver detoxification pathways, including beets, cranberries, sea vegetables, dandelion leaves, broccoli, flax seed, lemons, garlic, artichokes, turmeric, and apples.

A sample day of eating might look like this:

Breakfast: Two free-range, omega-3-enriched eggs sprinkled with sea salt, black pepper, and turmeric, with a side of steamed spinach or kale, all wrapped up in a sheet of nori, and a large glass of water with lemon juice

Midmorning snack: Glass of 100 percent pure unsweetened cranberry juice, a handful of blueberries, or a pomegranate or another piece of raw fruit

Lunch: Kale smoothie with dandelion leaves, flax seed, and a couple cloves of garlic

Afternoon snack: Apple

Dinner: Mashed cauliflower, wild salmon topped with sautéed garlic and onions, and a side of steamed beets

For inspiration, some really good "clean gut" detox recipes are available as a free PDF from Dr. Alejandro Junger's website (BeyondTrainingBook.com/gutrecipe).

Detox Step 3: Relax

Get as much sleep as possible, limit stress and heavy workdays, and, if possible, get into a steam room or sauna or an easy hot yoga class, because sweat can also remove toxins.

Detox Step 4: Supplement

I highly recommend specific supplements for enhancing your detox and speeding up your body's ability to remove harmful compounds. Granted, there are a ton of detox supplements on the market, but most of them give you diarrhea or are chock-full of ingredients that you're already getting from eating clean food. The following supplements support a clean diet by binding toxins and metals, supporting liver detoxification pathways, clearing the gut, and enhancing the elimination of toxins through urine and stool—and they all come from high-quality sources:

- **Liposomal glutathione:** 2–3 sprays under the tongue; hold for 20–30 seconds. Once a day is fine.
- **Metal Free Heavy Metal Detoxification Formula:** Use several sprays sublingually in the morning and evening. See the best versions on the resource web page for this chapter.
- **Oral magnesium:** About 400–600 milligrams a day (or until you get a loose stool) before bedtime.
- **A high-quality greens supplement:** One with chlorella is best. I recommend RECOVERYbits (energybits.com). Eat 20–30 in the morning and evening, or put it into a daily smoothie.
- **Activated charcoal:** 2–3 capsules daily. (This stuff is great to have around anyway to take before meals that contain potential toxins, such as meat, animal products from unknown sources, and foods that tend to give you gas.)

In addition to these supplements, I recommend a daily detox drink that can certainly clean things up. You can view my recipe at https://youtu.be/4ZJgn8CTlDg.

Finally, as mentioned earlier in this chapter, rebuilding your gut lining is important and may complement a detox. So include one or two servings of bone broth or organic gelatin every day, combined with daily use of the Greenfield Fitness Systems Gut Healing Pack.

Because you'll be moving a lot of stuff through your digestive tract, expect to spend an extra twenty minutes or so on the toilet in the morning and possibly again in the evening—depending on how many toxins you need to eliminate. Incidentally, this is where a Squatty Potty, which raises your knees above hip level, can come in quite handy. (You can read more about why I recommend this exercise in my blog article "Why You Should Squat to Poop" at BenGreenfieldFitness.com).

You're going to find that detoxing your body goes hand in hand with detoxing your home and workplace, and in Chapter 18, you'll find out everything you need to know about how to detox your home. For now, check out my recommended Detox Gear at GreenfieldFitnessSystems.com.

Be warned that when you embark on a detox or cleanse using the four steps just described, you may experience gas, bloating, unpleasant body odor, rashes, hives, or other undesirable symptoms. If this happens, be sure to drink plenty of pure, filtered water, which will help you flush toxins and keep from reabsorbing them.

What about Alcohol Detox and Hangovers?

No discussion of clean eating or detoxing would be complete without some tips on how to mitigate the effects of alcohol. After all, we athletes do like to get our party on every now and again, right?

Most people think that hangovers are a result of dehydration. But if you've followed the sage advice to drink a glass of water for each alcoholic beverage consumed, you know that you can still wake up feeling less than stellar. Preventing a hangover is way more complicated than simply chasing your beer or margarita or glass of wine with a pitcher of water (or coconut water or Gatorade or Pedialyte).

Dehydration is just one factor in a hangover. Basically, your pituitary gland produces antidiuretic hormone (ADH), which increases your blood pressure by causing your body to retain water. When you drink alcohol, your pituitary churns out less ADH, so you stop retaining so much water. (That's one reason the bathroom line is so long at parties.) However, as soon as your buzz begins to wear off, ADH production increases once again, which causes a rebound of fluid retention, swollen hands and feet, puffiness in facial tissue, and a headache as blood pressure rises[11].

At the same time, your kidneys pump out more of the enzyme renin and the hormone aldosterone. This prompts the secretion of vasopressin. As the name suggests, vasopressin increases blood pressure by causing sodium retention and potassium loss. This is why people with heart problems are most prone to a heart attack when they have a hangover: The cardiovascular system goes into electrolyte roller-coaster hyperdrive trying to retain fluids.

And that's not all. Cortisol works with aldosterone to balance electrolyte levels—so when you're hungover, your body churns out more cortisol. This not only contributes to even more fluid retention but also raises blood sugar levels by converting amino acids into glucose in your liver (also known as gluconeogenesis). As blood sugar levels go up, the pancreas churns out more insulin, resulting in abnormal stress on both the pancreas and the liver. These chronically elevated levels of cortisol can also causes catabolism (decreased protein availability in skeletal muscles) as well as a redistribution of body fat from your legs and arms to your belly.

Oh yes, there's still more.

As you drink and force your body to metabolize alcohol, you're converting ethanol into acetaldehyde and acetate in your liver, which causes increased production of tiny blood vessel constrictors called thromboxanes. Thromboxanes also cause blood platelets to stick together (that is, form clots) and decrease levels of natural killer cells (crucial to the immune system). This surge in thromboxane creates symptoms very similar to those of a viral infection, including nausea, headache, and diarrhea[25].

Finally, most alcoholic beverages contain something called congeners, which significantly contribute to hangover symptoms. Congeners, which are found in especially high concentrations in dark-colored liquor like brandy, wine, dark tequila, and whiskey, contain free radicals and positively charged molecules that can significantly disrupt your acid-alkaline (pH) balance and increase your body's need to step up antioxidant activity to scavenge all those free radicals. As your body goes into fight mode to help you handle all those congeners from excess alcohol consumption, you get gastrointestinal issues, nausea, headaches, and sweatiness, clamminess, or chills.

And exercise the next day absolutely sucks. So what can you do about it? Here are my top three ways to detox your body from the effects of, say, a long night of postrace or postworkout partying.

1. Electrolyte Load

As you just learned, when you're in hangover mode your body is holding on to sodium and kicking out potassium. But by getting more potassium into your body before, during, and after drinking, you can control the propensity for fuzzy thinking and headaches from dehydration. I recommend not only drinking unsweetened coconut water all day leading into a big party, but also having it on hand for the next day. In addition, for every one or two alcoholic drinks you throw back, take an effervescent electrolyte tablet like Nuun's U Natural Hydration or GU Brew mixed into soda water or water.

What about bananas? Since they pack a fairly hefty dose of sugar, I'd leave them out of the equation. You're already getting enough sugar calories from the alcohol.

2. Use Cysteine

Cysteine is a primary ingredient in many of the hangover remedies at pharmacies and drugstores. Cysteine is an amino acid that helps the liver break down acetaldehyde from alcohol metabolism—so cysteine has a bit of a detox effect. You can get cysteine from poultry, oats, dairy, broccoli, red pepper, garlic, onions, Brussels sprouts, and wheat germ, but I recommend supplements that contain more potent doses to help your body metabolize acetaldehyde quickly. Many of these products also contain fumaric acid and succinic acid, which increase the effectiveness of cysteine.

So the faster you process acetaldehyde, the less severe your hangover.

One readily available, cysteine-based, antihangover remedy, which contains liver detox herbs like milk thistle, artichoke, goji berry, and ginger, is called Hangover Gone. Certain extracts derived from compounds like hybrid artichoke bud and the root of the sarsaparilla plant can be used as liver-regenerative and detoxification agents and as blood purifiers. This means they break down the toxins created when you consume alcohol and allow the liver to function more efficiently. A similar product is PreToxx, a time-release, antihangover tablet that contains prickly pear, milk thistle, and cysteine.

I use NatureCleanse (since I keep it around the house as a gut cleanse anyway), but it makes some people almost too regular the next day (if you know what I mean). For me, NatureCleanse works perfectly for liver detox, and because I tend to get constipated when I drink too much anyway, I take three caplets before drinking and three after. ,

If you opt to use Hangover Gone or PreToxx, just shake and drink one shot of Hangover Gone before or during partying (or up to every three or four drinks), or swallow three or four capsules of PreToxx both before and after drinking.

3. Use Pure Wine

If you're a wine connoisseur, you may want to take one more precaution, especially if you get headaches from the sulfites in wine. Preservatives have been used in wine for many decades, for three reasons:

1. To control undesirable microbial growth

2. To inhibit browning enzymes

3. To serve as an antioxidant (grape juice behaves like any other fruit in that it begins to deteriorate due to oxidation when exposed to air)

So to preserve the fresh, fruity flavor of the grape (and hence the wine), preservatives are added immediately after the grape skin is broken in the making of the wine, and used continuously throughout the winemaking process until the final bottling. The preservative is most commonly added either as a sulfur salt, such as potassium metabisulphite (which releases sulfur dioxide gas), or as sulfur dioxide gas itself, which is well known as an undesirable pollutant.

Exposure to sulfur dioxide gas is very unpleasant even at low concentrations; typical reactions include headaches, shortness of breath, sneezing, watery eyes, wheezing, sinus congestion, and dizziness. Asthmatics are particularly sensitive to sulfur dioxide, and the level of free sulfur dioxide in most wines at bottling is definitely high enough to trigger a reaction.

Because the use of preservatives (particularly sulfites) has been of concern to consumers for many years, many producers have stopped using them. But it is nearly impossible to produce high-quality wine without them.

Enter Pure Wine, which is available mostly in Australia but can be shipped anywhere. Adding five drops of Pure Wine to a glass of wine dramatically reduces sulfite levels, but the wine is kept fresh for up to twenty-four hours after opening. Pure Wine produces a blast of oxygen that eliminates sulfur dioxide gas without sacrificing the taste and quality of the wine.

So, to recap:

1. If you're headed out for a night of drinking or a post-race party and you plan on sticking to wine, pack some Pure Wine.

2. If you're venturing into the world of hard alcohol and beer, choose your cysteine-packed liver detox weapon of choice and take it both before or after drinking, and drink an electrolyte-laced glass of water for every alcoholic beverage.

Finally, if you forget to be proactive, or for some reason you wake up with a hangover, a headache, or an upset stomach anyway, here are a couple antidotes:

1. **For headaches:** Take 4–8 capsules of phenocane or EXOS curcumin as soon as you wake up. Curcumin contains potent natural painkilling compounds and can take the ache out of your headache. And it doesn't do a number on your liver as ibuprofen and other NSAIDs do.

2. **For stomach upset:** Drink a nice big cup of homemade bone broth or fresh ginger tea in the morning. Or if that's too much work for you, simply stir some Bernard Jensen or Great Lakes gelatin into hot or cold water, coconut water, or a smoothie. As you've already learned, gelatin can protect your stomach lining and limit gut damage, and you're going to notice its digestive benefits especially the day after drinking.

If you're serious about your performance and recovery, I don't recommend using these antidotes as license to engage in regular excessive drinking, but I do realize that athletes like to party once in a while. So when it's time to celebrate, make sure you've got the goods on hand to limit the damage.

Finally, you may want to check out BenGreenfieldFitness.com/hangovercure to read "Why You Get a Hangover, and How to Get Rid of a Hangover as Fast as Possible with the Best Natural Hangover Cures"; BenGreenfieldFitness.com/cocktails to read "Ultimate Guide to Making Healthy Cocktails"; BenGreenfieldFitness.com/partying to read "Three Semi-Healthy Drinks to Have if You're Partying"; and (especially if you're a wino) BenGreenfieldFitness.com/fitvinewine to read "Dark & Dirty Secrets of the Wine Industry, Four Ways to Make Wine Healthier, and What Kind of Wine Fit People Should Drink."

Congratulations! You now know everything you need to know about what to do when your digestive tract gets off track, how to hit the reboot button, and how to detox your body.

Additional resources, helpful links, scientific references, websites, and surprise bonuses for this chapter are available at BeyondTrainingBook.com/Chapter15. Enjoy.

CHAPTER 16

The Truth About Eating Before, During, and After Workouts and Races

From pastalicious parties to ginormous pizzas and bottles of red wine before; to just about every variety of gel, bar, drink, and supplement you can think of during; to ice cream, hydrolyzed goat protein powders, steaks, waxy maize starch, potatoes, and margaritas after—I have experimented with nearly every kind of food on the face of the planet when it comes eating before, during, and after workouts and races.

And the truth is, in the same way that there's more than one way to get fit fast and to build endurance quickly, there really is more than one way to fuel your body for working out.

By now, I hope you realize that your decisions about how you exercise and what you eat should be based not only on what works and what doesn't, but also on what enables you to achieve the ideal balance of performance and health. Unfortunately, most nutrition recommendations take into account only the former (performance at all costs) without considering the latter (long-term effects on your gut, heart, brain, and connective tissue).

After all, some of the best athletes known to humankind guzzle down chemical-laden Ensure before a race, eat stacks of PowerBars during a race, and recover with pizza and ice cream. But just because this seems to work for them doesn't mean that it's healthy.

For example, when choosing what to eat, do you think about what is local, fresh, and sustainable? Do you think about your body soaking up dense, precious, restor-ative, healing, and energetic nutrients or simply "fueling" it? Do you think about how you will feel immediately after your workout or race, or perhaps that night as you try to fall asleep, or even in the next few days because your gut and muscles will either be in agony or feeling fresh as a daisy?

These are all important questions that go above and beyond simply whether some-thing you eat makes you strong or fast in the short term. As triathlete Corey Steimel points out in a newspaper interview regarding the fact that more and more health-conscious athletes are throwing out sports drinks and turning to real fuel (a link to the full interview is on the web page for this chapter):

> You don't put crap fuel into a high-performance vehicle. . . . Just because a race car is burning through all that fuel doesn't mean you don't put high-quality fuel in it. Some people have the philosophy that they're training so hard and with so much intensity that it doesn't matter.

So in this chapter, you're going to discover which five things to eat and which five things to avoid before, during, and after your bouts of exercise; two good ways to fuel your long-distance events; how to use real food rather than Frankenfoods; when to eat solids and when to drink liquids; how to use water and electrolytes; why eating after a workout is much less important than you may think; and the exact nutrition protocol I use and recommend for Ironman triathlon.

Five Things to Avoid and Five Things to Eat Before Workouts and Races

There are some foods you simply shouldn't put in your body when you're about to ask it to perform at its highest level. Some of them directly decrease performance by creating bloating and gas or by drawing precious blood away from your muscles and into your gut for digestion. And some allow you to perform just fine but make you feel like crap after you're done—or that night, or the next day, or a decade later when your gut has been destroyed by years of cumulative unhealthy fueling.

Ultimately, there are five common dietary errors that athletes make before hitting it hard. So here's what to avoid:

1. FODMAPs Like Fructose and Maltodextrin

You learned all about FODMAPs in the last chapter—that they can be one of the leading causes of gut rot, GI distress, gas, bloating, diarrhea, and constipation if you eat a bunch of them before you exercise or race. The big three FODMAPs that a lot of athletes eat pre-race or -workout are wheat, dairy, and fermentable fruits like apples and pears. Many popular sports nutrition compounds also contain high amounts of fructose and/or maltodextrin. Not a good idea, especially if you have a sensitive stomach.

2. Large Amounts of Caffeine

As you'll learn later in this chapter, caffeine can enhance sports performance[2]. But that doesn't mean more is better—especially if you're concerned about your long-term adrenal health or overworking your central nervous system.

Most recommendations in the sports nutrition literature are to consume about 0.5–1.5 milligrams of caffeine per pound of body weight (that's about 1–3 milligrams per kilogram). For a 150-pound (68-kilogram) athlete, that's 70–210 milligrams of caffeine, which is the equivalent of one small and up to two large cups of coffee. But I recommend going for the least amount possible, because when caffeine intake gets too high or goes on for too long, there is an increase in side effects like jitteriness, nervousness, insomnia, headaches, dizziness, and gastrointestinal distress, all of which can impair your athletic performance or cause long-term adrenal issues.

3. Artificial Sweeteners and Chemical Cocktails

One common artificial sweetener in sports nutrition supplements is sugar alcohol—which is a FODMAP. Another common one is sucralose, which can damage the good bacteria in your GI tract. Many others, such as aspartame and acesulfame potassium, are neurotoxic and can cause brain fog while you're exercising. So I highly recommend avoiding all of them before exercise. Once you begin inspecting labels, you'll be surprised at how many sports fuels contain these nasty substances. Of course, it's not just artificial sweeteners you have to be concerned about in terms of chemical additives. Take Ensure, for example, a common pre-race meal for Ironman triathletes and marathoners. Its ingredients consist of the following:

Milk Protein Concentrate, Canola Oil, Soy Protein Concentrate, Corn Oil, Short-Chain Fructooligosaccharides, Whey Protein Concentrate, Magnesium Phosphate, Natural and Artificial Flavors, Potassium Citrate, Sodium Citrate, Soy Lecithin, Calcium Phosphate, Potassium Chloride, Salt (Sodium Chloride), Choline Chloride, Ascorbic Acid, Carrageenan, Ferrous Sulfate, dl-Alpha-Tocopheryl Acetate, Zinc Sulfate, Niacinamide, Manganese Sulfate, Calcium Pantothenate, Cupric Sulfate, Vitamin A Palmitate, Thiamine Chloride Hydrochloride, Pyridoxine Hydrochloride, Riboflavin, Folic Acid, Chromium Chloride, Biotin, Sodium Molybdate, Sodium Selenate, Potassium Iodide, Phylloquinone, Vitamin D3, and Cyanocobalamin.

If there are more than a dozen ingredients that you can barely pronounce, it's usually a pretty good sign that your body is going to have trouble digesting it during a workout, or that it might not be great for your long-term health. You can read more about my beef with Ensure and other so called "health foods" for athletes in the blog article at BenGreenfieldFitness.com/ensure, in which I talk about why these things are also a fast track for the average person to get fat.

4. Large Quantities of Fiber

Fiber is not only digested primarily in your colon, but it also significantly slows gastric emptying, so consuming too much fiber before a workout results in a lot of un-digested foodstuff in your stomach and intestines[16]. Big bowls of preworkout or pre-race fiber-enriched dry cereals, oatmeal, fruit smoothies, and kale shakes can cause serious issues, especially for long workouts—so be careful. Incidentally, I've found that I can pound the pavement hard as little as an hour after downing a well-blended kale smoothie, while the same amount of kale in a salad leaves me feeling like I want to crawl on the pavement. So blending (or juicing) can get you the phytonutrients without demanding as much work from your digestive system. More on that later.

5. Heavy, Nonportable Foods

If your goal is speed or aerodynamics, then massive sweet potatoes, bananas, water-filled fruits, and melted dark chocolate bars are not going to help in the moment. There are right ways to consume real food during a workout, but food that is big, bulky, and heavy (compared with a simple liquid that could be placed in a water bottle or flask) is potentially going to inhibit your performance via a loss of aerodynamics.

So what are my guidelines for eating before a workout or race? Assuming that we're talking about a glycogen-depleting effort of one-and-a-half hours or more (which is really the only time you'll get a significant performance-enhancing boost from eating beforehand), here are the top five foods to eat before a workout or race:

1. Blended and Juiced Foods

Blending or juicing helps predigest food so that your body doesn't have to work so hard to digest it. This takes a load off your digestive tract and frees up precious energy for you to devote to breathing, moving, and contracting muscles. Cell walls are broken down and nutrients are quickly released (especially from greens like kale or dark root vegetables like beets and carrots). You're essentially "chewing" your food much more thoroughly than you can with your teeth, and many foods that normally have given you digestive trouble—such as a bunch of carrots or a big spinach salad—will go through you just fine when blended or juiced. I recommend a quality high-speed blender, such as a Blendtec, Vitamix, or Omni Blender, an Omega masticating juicer, and a Magic Bullet for travel. Two of my go-to preworkout recipes are a kale smoothie blended with coconut water or coconut milk (usually with a touch of beet juice, cacao, or both) and a carrot-ginger-lemon juice (made in a juicer) with a touch of olive oil.

2. Small Amounts of Caffeine

As you learned earlier, caffeine can definitely help with sports performance. Popularly known as caffeine, 1, 3, 7-trimethylxanthine is the world's most consumed natural pharmacological agent[2]. It has been shown to improve endurance and time-trial performance in cyclists, increase endurance in runners, and improve performance times and boost power in rowers. It has also been shown to improve performance in cycling and running workouts lasting five minutes or more and to increase power output, speed, and strength in sprint and power events lasting less than ten seconds. (Incidentally, caffeine has been shown to have no effect, and may even be a negative factor, in sprint and power events lasting anywhere from fifteen seconds to three minutes.)

In tennis players, caffeine increases hitting accuracy, speed, agility, and overall success on the court. And players report feeling more energy late in their matches. Caffeine also reduces "rate of perceived exertion," or how hard you feel you're actually working—which essentially enables you to push harder and faster.

Unfortunately, most people average 238 milligrams of caffeine a day—the equivalent of two to three cups of coffee—and 20 to 30 percent of people consume a whopping 600 milligrams a day (about 71 percent of it coffee, 16 percent from tea, and 12 percent from soft drinks and energy drinks). When you shove high doses of caffeine into your system before a workout or race, it puts extra stress on the adrenal glands. Which is why my recommended effective dose of caffeine is about 0.5 milligrams per pound of body weight. For a 150-pound athlete, that's the equivalent of a small cup of coffee.

3. Easy-to-Digest Carbohydrates

White potato, sweet potato, yam, taro, and white rice are the five best-tolerated carbohydrate sources before hard workouts. But if you're adhering to the carbohydrate/fat/protein ratios recommended earlier, you know that you don't even need much of these. So how much do you need?

Let's say you wake up on race morning. You've primarily burned through your liver's glycogen stores while sleeping. The average human needs (at most) about 400 calories of carbohydrate to top off those stores. (Assuming that you haven't been starving yourself, your muscles are already full of glycogen and ready to rumble[4].)

So all you need to eat is 100 grams of any of the starch sources mentioned above—that's about two cups of cooked white rice or a couple large boiled or baked sweet potatoes or yams. Liberally add sea salt, throw in a few tablespoons of the healthy fats and proteins you'll learn about momentarily, and you have a perfect pre-obstacle race, pre-10K, pre-Ironman, or premarathon meal!

And as you may already know, 400 calories of carbohydrate is much less than the commonly recommended 600 to 1,500 calories.

If you're adhering to a ketogenic diet, you'll need even fewer carbohydrates. For your preworkout or pre-race meal, you can get away with the minimum amount of carbohydrate necessary to keep your brain's neurons firing so that you don't lose mental function, which is about 30 grams, or 120 calories. Because ketosis produces this state of fat-utilizing metabolic efficiency, most of the athletes I've worked with (including myself) who are following a ketogenic diet go into a big workout or race with a pre-event meal of Bulletproof Coffee, or a Ketogenic Kale Shake, or one to two servings of UCAN SuperStarch in coconut milk.

By the way, if you're exercising in a state of ketosis, you don't need to worry about neural fatigue from your brain running out of sugar. Once you begin exercising, your brain can draw upon lactic acid for energy[14] (your brain actually prefers to burn lactic acid and ketones rather than glucose!), along with fats, glucose derived from amino acids (gluconeogenesis), glucose derived from slow-release starches, and glucose derived from trace amounts of sports supplements—all of which you'll learn about later in this chapter. Interestingly, central nervous system and neural fatigue during exercise can be far more related to a low blood level of amino acids than to low levels of blood sugar. If you want to learn more about the minimum amount of carbohydrates your brain needs for fuel, I recommend that you read the blog post "Dear Mark: How Much Glucose Does Your Brain Really Need?" (BeyondTrainingBook.com/brainglucose)[15].

4. Easy-to-Digest Fats

In contrast to fats that take a long time to digest, such as those in eggs, bacon, cheese, and whole-milk yogurt, medium-chain triglycerides from sources like MCT oil, coconut oil, and coconut manna (a blend of coconut oil and coconut meat) bypass the normal digestion process and are absorbed directly into the liver—where they can be metabolized to provide quick energy. This makes MCTs a valuable addition to your "before" meal. For joint and heart health, you can also include small amounts of a concentrated source of anti-inflammatory omega-3 essential fatty acids from a cold-pressed, plant-based oil, such as Udo's Oil or PanaSeeda Five Oil Blend—just add to your smoothie or ladle over your favorite carbohydrate source. By healing a serious gut-malabsorption issue in former Olympian Andreas Wecker, the PanaSeeda blend actually resurrected him from near-death. You can read his story at BeyondTrainingBook.com/apventures and read more about PanaSeeda at BenGreenfieldFitness.com/pana.

5. Easy-to-Digest Proteins

Like many fats, proteins take a long time to digest and require lots of energy to break down—which is why a pre-race meal of steak and eggs is a recipe for gut disaster or subpar performance. But for efforts of longer than three hours, your body can get up to 15 percent of its energy requirements from protein. In addition, high blood levels of amino acid during exercise can lower your rate of perceived exertion and significantly decrease postexercise soreness.

For these reasons, I recommend that you include any or all of the following prior to a big workout or race:

- 20–30 grams of a hydrolyzed whey protein, which is a "predigested" protein that is more expensive but much easier to absorb and assimilate than regular whey protein (I recommend Mt. Capra's DEEP30 protein). Alternatively, you can use a vegan protein such as pea, rice, or hemp if it contains digestive enzymes, which have been shown to increase the absorption rate of plant-based proteins up to a level similar to an animal-based protein such as whey or casein protein powder (I recommend LivingFuel LivingProtein for this).

- 5–10 grams of essential amino acids, which have an extremely high absorption rate (I recommend NatureAminos).

- 10–20 grams of a hydrolyzed collagen protein source. I recommend either an organic, clean powder, such as Great Lakes or Bernard Jensen, or a cup of bone broth with your pre-race meal.

Compared with eating a steak, these protein sources put far less stress on your digestive system. Remember: You don't want to make your gut work any harder than it has to.

At the end of this chapter, you'll learn what to eat after your workout and why it's probably less important than you think. But first, let's address what may be the most common question I get: What should I eat during my race?

Three Reasons Not to Eat Concentrated Sugars When You're Racing

Let's begin with what I recommend you do *not* eat if you are serious about long-term health: large quantities of concentrated sugars.

At this point in the book, this should come as no surprise to you. Once again, it all depends on the lens through which you view your performance: Are you chasing performance at all costs, or are you willing to entertain the idea of thinking outside the box if it means that you can achieve similar levels of performance with better health?

There are three primary reasons I recommend that you do not consume large quantities of concentrated sugars during a sporting event, and they've all got great acronyms: FODMAPs, ROS, and AGEs.

1. FODMAPs

Are you sick of me talking about fermentable carbohydrates yet? Fructose and maltodextrin in their concentrated forms can be potent FODMAPs. They ferment in your gut, and while you may be able to get away with using them for a one-and-a-half- to three-hour event, if you keep imbibing them much longer than that, you're asking for gut trouble, especially if you have any of the fructose malabsorption or intolerance issues discussed in the previous chapter.

In addition, maltodextrin is a long chain of glucose molecules that breaks apart into individual glucose units by the time it hits your small intestine. This is called "high osmolality," and while it's theoretically supposed to be a great way to increase concentrated-energy-source delivery, it's actually a fast track to diarrhea and gut distress. In his book *Feed Zone Portables,* physiologist Dr. Allen Lim describes this scenario aptly when he discusses why he doesn't like the professional cyclists and triathletes he works with to use maltodextrin:

> To understand what that would feel like in your gut, imagine a completely full flight with 300 pregnant women, and midflight each of them giving birth to 20 screaming babies. That's a lot of little soldiers storming the intestinal wall.

2. ROS

ROS stands for "reactive oxygen species," and studies have shown the formation of these nasty little unstable oxygen molecules to be a central mechanism for glucose toxicity from chronic oxidative stress[9]. Your pancreas, which is one valuable organ, is especially sensitive to reactive oxygen species because of its low natural concentration of antioxidant enzymes. As a result, high-sugar diets can increase pancreatic cancer risk because of what is called "hyperglycemia-induced oxidative stress" and free radical damage to pancreatic cells. ROS also cause irreversible damage to the cell wall, cross-link collagen and elastin (a primary cause of wrinkles and premature aging), and lessen the skin's natural ability to repair itself. ROS together with AGEs (see below) is a potent one-two combo if you want to age much, much faster.

3. AGEs

Advanced glycation end products (AGEs) are a complex group of compounds formed when sugar reacts with amino acids. Their acronym is fitting because—along with ROS—they are one of the major molecular mechanisms by which cellular damage accrues in your body.

When sugar bonds with protein via glycation, it creates inflammation. As a result, your immune system's scavenger cells bind to the AGEs. Unfortunately, this defense process also causes its fair share of damage[10]. Inside your arteries, for example, the scar tissue created from this process is called plaque. AGEs also contribute to cross-linking of collagen protein fibers (more wrinkles), inflammation, inhibited skin-cell growth, and accelerated aging.

There is mounting evidence that AGEs are implicated in the development of chronic degenerative diseases, such as heart disease, Alzheimer's, and diabetes, and several studies have shown that restricting the consumption of AGEs can lead to an increased life span in animals[6]. Of all the molecules you can eat that are capable of inflicting AGE-related damage, sugar is the worst.

If those three reasons to avoid large quantities of concentrated sugars are not enough for you, you can review 141 additional ways that sugar destroys your health by going to BeyondTrainingBook.com/reasons141[1]. Ultimately, you *can* go fast on concentrated sugars—a combination of gels, energy chews, and sports drinks was all I used for five years until I discovered the information I just shared with you. But when I realized what I was doing to my gut, my heart, my skin, and my longevity, I switched things up drastically.

So if you aren't going to go the traditional route of concentrated sports drinks, gels, sugary bars, chomps, chews, bloks, and jelly beans, what are your alternatives?

TWO HEALTHY RACE-DAY FUELING STRATEGIES

Now you know that the typical sports nutrition foods, gels, and sugars are out if you're serious about your health.

The good news is that there are two great ways to fuel on race day that achieve an ideal balance of performance and health. Neither is 100 percent ancestral or what I would consider ideal from a healthy human-macronutrient-intake standpoint, but let's face it: Hammering on your bike for a hundred miles is not exactly ancestral, either. So the trick is either to gently nudge your body toward tapping primarily into its own fatty acids as fuel or to give your body as natural a fuel source as possible (whole foods such as white rice, bacon, eggs, and so on).

Healthy Race-Day Fueling Option 1: Eat moderate amounts of slow-release carbohydrates with small additions of easy-to-digest fats and amino acids

This first option is ideal if you want to maximize the use of your body's natural and preferred fuel stores (fatty acids) while minimizing the rate at which you deplete your storage carbohydrates (glycogen). It allows for extreme metabolic efficiency and fat burning with minimal gastric distress, and it is my preferred mode of fueling for myself and any athletes I work with who want to gain health and fat-burning benefits from lower carbohydrate intake or ketosis.

Here is what you need to pull it off:

1. Slow-Release Carbohydrate

An optimal carbohydrate source for athletes should have low osmolality (to keep those pregnant-mother carbohydrates from releasing all their babies midflight), with a slow time-release to avoid rapid fluctuations in glucose and blood sugar spikes or crashes[20]. To my knowledge, there is currently only one carbohydrate source that satisfies these criteria: SuperStarch, which is made by UCAN.

Contrary to popular belief among some athletes and coaches, SuperStarch is not a sugar or a fiber. Chemically, it is a complex carbohydrate or starch that is completely absorbed. It is an extremely large glucose chain with a molecular weight between 500,000 and 700,000 grams per mole.

What does it mean to have such a high molecular weight? Because molecular weight and osmolality are inversely correlated, SuperStarch exerts a very low osmotic pressure in the gastrointestinal tract. Because it is rapidly emptied from the stomach into the intestines, it is very gentle on your gut.

When it reaches the intestines, SuperStarch is semiresistant to digestion but eventually is absorbed into the bloodstream completely, which gives it a slow, time-released absorption profile. Because of this slow rate of release, your body taps into its own fatty acids for fuel, and you need about half as many carbohydrates—so if you usually consume three to four gels per hour, as I used to do when I raced the Ironman triathlon on pure sugar (gels are typically around 100 calories each), you would need only about one serving, or 100 calories, of SuperStarch per hour.

For some people, SuperStarch can cause fermentation, gas, and bloating due to its resistance to fast digestion. So try it in training before using it in a race! If you do have GI issues, I recommend a cleaner-burning carbohydrate that releases slightly faster but does not have high amounts of fructose or maltodextrin. Some of the better options include Infinit-E by Millennium Sports and Vitargo (both are potato-based starches) and a new carbohydrate blend made by EXOS, which you can find at GreenfieldFitnessSystems.com.

2. Easy-to-Digest Fats

Because the seed-based oils I mentioned previously are not very heat-stable, your top choices for fats are MCT oil or coconut oil—but you can certainly go overboard with either. Research shows that consuming more than about ten grams per hour over the course of a several-hour exercise session can lead to gastric distress. In the case of MCT oil, ten grams is the equivalent of about one tablespoon[22]. So you would add one tablespoon to one serving of SuperStarch per hour. Some larger male athletes can handle slightly more MCT oil and SuperStarch than this, but you need to experiment by starting with one tablespoon and one serving.

In terms of ease of absorption, chia seeds are unlike medium-chain triglycerides in that they take longer to digest and absorb. However, chia seeds soaked in water can give you a slow release of both amino acids and fatty acids. One example of a powdered fuel source that is based on this concept is Iskiate, made by NaturalForce. This fuel is a combination of coconut palm sugar, chia seeds, bee pollen, and royal jelly. One scoop contains 62 calories, and I have found that for voluminous endurance bouts, two to four scoops per hour offers a stable source of energy. At MyNaturalForce. com/#bengreenfield, code BEN10 will get you 10 percent off Iskiate. Another example of a liquid, easy-to-digest mix of fats and amino acids (along with plenty of minerals) is bone broth. To learn more about this strategy, visit BenGreenfieldFitness. com and listen to my bone broth podcast with chef Lance Roll.

3. Easy-to-Digest Amino Acids

To your bottle of SuperStarch and easy-to-digest fats, add either ten grams of hydrolyzed whey protein for each hour of exercise, five grams of essential amino acids, or ten grams of hydrolyzed collagen protein. (I crush essential amino acid tablets in a mortar and pestle and add them to my bottle.) If you really want to live on the edge, you can throw in an all-natural amino acid complex made by VESPA that's derived from the Asian Mandarin wasp and makes your muscles metabolize fat at a faster rate.

If you're a nerd like me, you can also add some compounds that allow your body to tap into fat stores more efficiently or maintain higher levels of ATP in the presence of low carbohydrate intake. This can include compounds such as a negative-glycemic-index sugar called D-ribose, disodium ATP, D-pinitol (which drives glucose into muscle tissue), and trace amounts of caffeine and glucose.

SuperStarch tends to clump and settle in the bottom of your bottle. To avoid this, it may be helpful to:

- Mix your brew at the last possible second, and stir and shake vigorously.
- Consider throwing everything in a blender and pouring it into a Floe bottle (which also allows you to add ice if you're racing in hot conditions). When I race, I often book condos or homes via AirBNB or VRBO because these options often have stocked kitchens with blenders.
- Put small amounts of electrolyte powder or electrolyte capsules (just break them open) in the bottle, which tends to reduce SuperStarch clumping.

Healthy Race-Day Fueling Option 2:
Eat small amounts of liquid fast-release carbohydrates and solid foods

There are a couple drawbacks to the first fueling option: It's pricey, and measuring and mixing all that stuff to prepare a bottle(s) is complicated and time-consuming. But frankly, you would need to do this only during races and every so often (about once a month) when training your gut for a race.

In every other situation, you can either exercise fasted with water only or just eat real food. If you flip back to chapter 11, you'll find real-food ideas, such as trail mixes and chia seed slurries. You'll even find low-carb, ketosis-friendly recipes for long workouts.

But if you're planning to race fast, at peak capacity, and you want to fuel with real food and want the best, most comprehensive resources for doing so, I highly recommend two books:

1. *Feed Zone Portables*

This cookbook, written by physiologist Allen Lim, has seventy-five recipes for cyclists, runners, triathletes, mountain bikers, climbers, hikers, and backpackers. Its recipes are easy to carry and are digested relatively quickly.

You can check out sample recipes on the book's website (BeyondTrainingBook.com/portasnacks), including Chocolate and Sea Salt Sticky Bites, Blueberry and Chocolate Coconut Rice Cakes, and Crispy Rice Omelets[18]. Lim even shows you a special wrapping technique that makes it easy to unwrap your real-food portables one-handed or in motion—on a bike ride, trail run, hike, etc.

2. *Real Food Basics: Endurance Planet's Recipes for Your Long Workouts*

Through recipes, anecdotes, and practical instruction, Elizabeth Ruiz teaches you the logistics of carrying and eating real food during training sessions, gives you portable recipes to fuel your long workouts, and makes sure that you know why eating the typical, fake, sugar-packed, engineered fuels damages your body.

Here's a sample real-food recipe that works well for many athletes: the mighty rice cake. Adapted from the books above, it's a savory bacon-and-egg rice cake. It's quick and easy to make and uses a simple-to-digest carbohydrate that is very low in toxins and digestive inhibitors—white rice:

In a bowl, mix 2–3 cups cooked sticky white rice, a few slices of crumbled cooked bacon, 2 scrambled eggs, and sea salt to taste. Press the mixture into a square baking dish, let cool in the refrigerator, and cut it into squares. Wrap individual rice cakes in wax paper, butcher paper, or plastic wrap. Grab and go.

Is your mouth watering yet? Here's another sample recipe:

Start with 2–3 cups cooked sticky white rice in a bowl. Add 1 cup coconut milk and the juice of 1 lemon, and stir. Let it cool, then spread half of it on a baking sheet. Sprinkle it with dark chocolate chips and blueberries, then press the remainder of the rice evenly over that. Let sit for 5 minutes, cut into squares, and wrap.

OK, one more—how about a ball instead of a square? If you can stomach these on a run (as you'll learn later, liquids digest better than solids while running), baked rice balls are easy to carry in plastic wrap:

Place 1 cubed cooked sweet potato, 1/4 cup crumbled cooked bacon, 1/2 teaspoon olive oil, 1 teaspoon sea salt, and 1 teaspoon ground cumin in a blender and blend. Add to a bowl with 3 cups cooked sticky white rice, and mix. Form into balls, then bake on an oiled baking sheet for 10–15 minutes at 350°F. Let cool, then wrap in plastic.

Pick up either of the books above for an inspirational assortment of additional recipes. Rice is high in calories but low in fiber, making it a perfect foundational carbohydrate. The books also include an array of gluten-free and healthy options for pancakes, waffles, pies, cookies, and brownies—all easy to carry in your pocket. Yes, you are still going to be consuming more carbohydrates than what I consider to be ancestral—which is why I personally tend to opt for fueling with chia seeds, raw nuts, and the like—but you will be consuming far less concentrated sugar than is found in typical energy gels, drinks, and bars.

And of course, the real-food options built around carbohydrates like rice actually do burn quite cleanly during a race (compared with, say, Brazil nuts). So what if you want to use rice cakes or rice balls during your race? In that case, your mantra would be: "Hydration in the bottle, fuel in the pocket."

I first explored this maxim with Dr. Stacy Sims, sports nutritionist and founder of Osmo Nutrition, in the podcast episode "Why Does a Guy Like Lance Armstrong Have Gastrointestinal Issues During a Triathlon?" (BenGreenfieldFitness.com/lance). During the interview, Stacy talked about how you should consume trace amounts of water, sugar, and electrolytes from a beverage and your primary calories from real food.

The beverage is the same type of fueling mix used by Allen Lim, who founded the nutrition company Skratch Labs based on a similar concept. The science behind both Skratch and Osmo is that the liquid beverage should not be a calorie source per se.

Although it does have seventy calories per sixteen ounces, the sugars and salts in the beverage provide just enough glucose, sucrose, and salts to allow your small intestine to maximize fluid uptake. You've already learned about the problem with too much osmolality, and these mixes avert that disaster with a carbohydrate concentration no higher than 4 percent. Then you simply get the rest of your calories from real food carried in your jersey pockets, a bike's top tube case, or wherever.

If you don't have the time to make real food, you can use the "safe" energy bars from chapter 11, such as the GreenfieldFitnessSystems.com Bar, Hammer Whey or Vegan Recovery Bar, LaraBar, NoGii Bar, Quest Bar, Zing bar, Bonk Breaker bar, or Health Warrior bar.

When it comes to the "fuel in the pocket, fluid in the bottle" strategy, the websites of Osmo Nutrition (osmonutrition.com) and Skratch Labs (skratchlabs.com) lay out the science behind this strategy much more thoroughly than I can in a single chapter, so I advise you to look at their helpful videos, FAQs, and PDFs if you want to learn more. The only reasons I don't personally follow this protocol is that I'm low-carb and race primarily in a state of fatty-acid utilization, and solid foods don't sit well with me when I'm running hard (more on that later).

Now, here's a caveat to everything you've just read: There are some situations in which using a liquid fueling scenario like the one I just described simply doesn't work, or some situations in which liquid fueling needs to be accompanied by other fuel sources. These situations include:

1. Liquids needs to be carried in either flasks or water bottles, and I've found that when doing races such as a Spartan or obstacle course event (in which you're often rolling or crawling on the ground), flasks and water bottles get smashed, leak, and can press up against your body in uncomfortable ways.

2. Sometimes you need a break from the texture of liquids. Especially during a long event such as an Ironman triathlon, you may find yourself wanting something to chew on or something that has more of a gel-like texture.

3. Premade gels require no forethought, planning, or mixing. You just put them in your pocket and go.

Fortunately, when it comes to venturing outside the realm of glucose, fructose, maltodextrin, honey, and other common sources of sugar that form the base of most gels, there are a variety of fat-based energy gel options. You can visit BenGreenfieldFitness.com/fatgels to read my article in which I review twelve fat-based alternatives to sickeningly sweet sugar-based sport gels.

If you don't care for the texture of gels and you don't have the time to make real food, you can also use "safe," gluten-free, soy- and lactose-free energy bars such as the CocoChia Bar, Hammer Recovery Bar, Hammer Vegan Recovery Bar, LaraBar, Nogii Bar, Quest Bar, Zing Bar, BonkBreaker Bar, and Health Warrior Bar. At the time this book is being written, I'm even developing my own high-fat, low-carb energy bar over at GreenfieldFitnessSystems.com, so be sure to check there, too!

Remember that the goal is not to use bottles full of dense energy or packets of gels or calorie-dense energy bars in all your training sessions. In most situations, you'll use the type of race-day fueling scenario that you've been reading about only during a race, or once every couple of weeks to "train your gut" during a training session. Otherwise, you can either exercise fasted with water only or simply eat real food, such as trail mixes, chia seed slurries, pemmican, jerky, spirulina or chlorella tablets, etc.

Liquids versus Solids?

But wait, isn't there an issue with using real-food-based solids during a race? After all, we've been taught that when the going gets tough in a workout or race, liquids beat solids hands down, right?

To see if this is true, let's break down a study published in the March 2010 *Journal of Medicine & Science in Sports & Exercise,* titled "Oxidation of Solid versus Liquid Carbohydrate Sources." Here's how the intro goes:

The ingestion of carbohydrate (CHO) solutions has been shown to increase CHO oxidation and improve endurance performance. However, the majority of studies have investigated CHO in solution and sporting practice includes ingestion of CHO in solid (e.g. energy bars) as well as liquid form. It remains unknown whether CHO in solid form is as effectively oxidized as compared to CHO solutions.

The researchers went on to study cyclists who did a three-hour aerobic workout. Here's what they found:

The present study demonstrates that a GLU+FRC (glucose + fructose) mix administered as a solid BAR during cycling can lead to high mean and peak exogenous CHO (carbohydrate) oxidation rates (>1g/min). The GLU+FRC mix ingested in the form of a solid BAR resulted in similar average and peak exogenous CHO oxidation rates and showed similar oxidation efficiencies as a DRINK. These findings suggest that CHO from a solid BAR is effectively oxidized during exercise and can be a practical form of supplementation alongside other forms of CHO.

Translation: The solid bars did just as well as the liquids, at least for cyclists.

Additional studies—along with lots of anecdotal evidence from professional cyclists—have backed up this idea[7]. So you can chomp away on real food when you're doing a nonjarring, nonimpact, non-weight-bearing exercise like cycling, but what about more stomach-sloshing activities, like running?

An interesting study on triathletes provides a good answer. In the study, scientists at Utrecht University in the Netherlands compared liquid versus solid carbohydrate intake before and during prolonged exercise in thirty-two triathletes who were training for at least a sprint triathlon. Study subjects did hard workouts consisting of two bouts of cycling lasting forty-five to fifty minutes at about 75 percent VO_2 max (85 percent of maximum heart rate) and two running workouts lasting forty-five minutes each, also at 75 percent VO_2 max[12].

First the athletes rode, and then they ran. Then, after a six-minute rest, they completed a maximal cycling test consisting of three minutes of pedaling at 175 watts and then three minutes of 100 percent all-out intensity.

Oh, and they weren't done yet.

After four minutes of rest, the athletes rode again, rested for six minutes, did a second maximal test on the bike, rested for four more minutes, ran again, rested for six minutes, and then completed a final cycling test.

If you were doing the math, that is more than three hours of exercise with an average heart rate at or above 85 percent of maximum heart rate.

As if that weren't enough, each participant had to do three sessions like that, each with a different fueling protocol: once with caloric liquids only, once with a mix of solids and liquids (white bread, marmalade, and bananas—yum), and once with a noncaloric liquid placebo that was basically just food coloring. Water intake was always the same.

So what worked best?

Half of the triathletes in the study were able to complete all three hours of hard exercise when they took in liquids only, but only nine could complete the same workout when solids were introduced. And those who couldn't complete the workout weren't able to go as hard as they could on liquids only.

In other words, once you introduce the stomach-sloshing of hard running (think a 10K to a marathon, not slow jogs or ultraruns), liquids beat solids, period.

The takeaway: Solids are just as good as liquids when you're riding a bike or doing a nonimpact activity, but once you start jarring your body and bouncing your stomach, try to stick to liquids (I would consider a gel to be just as good as a liquid, although there have been no studies that look at that in runners).

What about Water and Electrolytes?

There are two more topics to tackle before I lay out a sample race-day fueling protocol for you. One involves the confusing and myth-ridden world of water versus electrolytes; the other, postworkout fueling.

In the podcast interview "How You're Being Manipulated by the Sports Drink Industry and What You Can Do about It," with Dr. Tim Noakes (BenGreenfieldFitness. com/noakes), my paradigms shifted enormously when it came to electrolyte intake. In the interview, Dr. Noakes raises an argument against the worldwide brainwashing that has been done by the Gatorade Sports Science Institute—particularly the brainwashing that has caused exercise enthusiasts and athletes to rush out and guzzle electrolyte drinks, powders, and capsules during hot and humid exercise sessions.

For nearly a decade, I was one of those athletes.

But here's the deal: Your body is very, very good at regulating the electrolyte status of your blood and cells. If it was not good at this, then you would die or become severely ill if you were sweating without drinking water for a even a dozen minutes. And this just isn't what happens.

Instead, when you have too little sodium onboard, your body excretes less sodium from the kidneys, urine, and sweat, thus preventing losses. And when you have too little water, the body excretes more sodium from the kidneys and sweat so that you maintain a proper electrochemical gradient.

Furthermore, when you have too much sodium, the body excretes excess sodium in the kidneys, urine, and sweat. And therein lies the rub: People take a sports drink or a bunch of electrolytes to work out, find that they're sweating a lot or noticing white salt deposits on their skin, assume they're losing salt (oh, no!), and begin a vicious cycle of consuming even more electrolytes.

Noakes references several studies that have shown people going for days with no salt or electrolyte intake and doing just fine at exercise. In one study, a group of soldiers performed an extremely intense, daylong march in the heat and humidity. Although they lost liters of sweat, all they did was drink water. No electrolytes. And at the end of the march, their plasma sodium levels were the same as when they started. Their bodies simply held on to salt stores. But studies like this get suppressed by sports drink manufacturers.

In addition, we're taught that the body has finite salt stores of about 10,000 milligrams, so at normal salt losses of 1,000 to 2,000 milligrams per hour, you could go only between five and ten hours before you'd start to cramp. In reality, your salt stores are many, many times greater than 10,000 milligrams, which Dr. Noakes explained in detail during our interview.

So if a lack of electrolytes doesn't cause cramping, what does? In most cases, cramping is due to fascial adhesions and lack of mobility (revisit Chapter 5), neuromuscular fatigue from pushing your muscles harder than you've pushed them in previous races or workouts, areas of scar tissue from previous injuries, or very low hydration levels. To learn more about these reasons for cramping, visit BeyondTrainingBook.com/tritalk and listen to Tri Talk Episode #74, which is an extremely thorough discussion of mitigating muscle cramps. Or read the article at BenGreenfieldFitness.com/cramps.

Since I spoke with Noakes, I've competed in more than a dozen Half Ironman events, two Ironman triathlons, and several long training sessions in the heat with absolutely no electrolytes and did just fine, with no cramping. The only people who may need to worry about electrolyte intake during exercise are those who have been on a low-sodium or mineral-deficient diet for a long time or have medical conditions that can affect sodium retention and loss (such as hypothyroidism).

So here's the deal: Electrolytes aren't necessarily going to hurt you during exercise, but there are probably better places to spend your supplement or exercise dollars than on useless capsules.

As for how this jibes with the Osmo and Skratch approach, it's important to realize that the salts in those liquid formulations are there not to stop cramping but to create a proper concentration to drive water and carbohydrate absorption into the small intestine.

And water? It can be summed up in one simple sentence: Drink plain, clear water when you're thirsty.

I highly recommend reading *Waterlogged: The Serious Problem of Overhydration in Endurance Sports,* by Dr. Noakes, and checking out my interview with him that I linked to earlier if you want to delve into the science behind how much water to drink.

Ultimately, the takeaway is that electrolytes aren't going to hurt you, but they're not as crucial as you may think they are. And excessive water intake can definitely hurt you, so you should simply drink when you're thirsty. Experiment with any of this in training before you take it into a race. You'll be far more confident if you do.

The Postworkout-Fueling Myth

You may have noticed that I haven't talked much about what to eat after a workout—and there's a reason for that.

You've probably heard about a magical fueling window. From exercise physiology books to magazine articles to websites, nearly every resource on sports nutrition says that after you finish a workout, you have twenty to sixty minutes to replace precious energy by consuming a mix of carbohydrates and proteins.

Here's what they don't say:

In every study or experiment that has investigated the benefits of immediate postworkout nutrition replacement, subjects were fed after completing an exercise session that they had performed in a fasted or semistarved state.

Of course you're going to recover more quickly if you eat a meal after a workout in which you were completely depleted of energy and 100 percent fasted. But how many of us actually roll out of bed in the morning, hop on a bike, and ride hard for ninety minutes to two hours with absolutely no fuel?

So here's the deal: If you've had a preworkout meal, or had a meal in the not-too-distant past, there's no do-or-die need to eat after your workout—especially if you're still burping up that meal you ate before exercising. This is especially true if you have no other workouts planned for the day, because your body can completely replenish energy levels within just eight hours of normal hunger-driven, real-food eating. When you combine this information with what you learned about the health, recovery, and longevity benefits of fasting from chapter 8, you will realize that it doesn't make sense to fret as much about postworkout nutrition as most of us do.

But it does make sense to refuel within that twenty- to sixty-minute window if:

- You didn't eat anything before your workout and you're in a totally energy-depleted state (such as from a hard session before breakfast).
- You are going to work out again within the next eight hours.
- You're trying to pack on muscle as fast as possible (aka eat every piece of real food in sight and lift heavy stuff).

In any of these cases, within two hours after your workout ends, simply eat a big meal of real food in the form of a smoothie or any of the quick and easy-to-digest meals in chapter 11, and you'll be set. If you plan to work out within eight hours of the workout you've just finished, adjust that two-hour window to a twenty-minute window and consider a post-workout smoothie that includes a mix of carbohydrates and proteins (I must emphasize that this is necessary only if you are working out again within eight hours). Contrary to popular belief, the fat content of a real meal does not slow down amino acid or glucose absorption. Ideally, you can combine any post-workout meal with my comprehensive recovery tips in chapter 8.

Finally, if you want to geek out on the nitty-gritty science of postworkout nutrition, check out the Rock Star Triathlete Academy article "Putting the Pre- and Post-Workout Nutrition Debate into the Grave" (RockStarTriathlete.com).

A Sample Ironman Race-Day Fueling Protocol

Let's finish by applying everything you've just learned to a sample fueling protocol for one of the most nutritionally confusing events in all of sports: the Ironman triathlon. (You can use bits and pieces of this approach for a Half Ironman, marathon, etc.) I put links to all the resources you can use for this fueling approach on the web page for this chapter.

1. About two hours before the race, eat a meal of 600–900 calories. You'll need to experiment with the actual amount in training. If you're eating low-carb, it might be twelve to sixteen ounces of Bulletproof Coffee, a twelve- to sixteen-ounce Ketogenic Kale Shake, or one to two servings of SuperStarch in coconut milk. For a higher carbohydrate intake, eat a couple baked sweet potatoes or yams with sea salt or two cups cooked white rice. To either of these meals, add one to two tablespoons MCT oil or coconut oil and, for even more calories, one to two tablespoons cold-press plant-based oil, such as Udo's Oil or PanaSeeda Five Oil Blend. Also include twenty to thirty grams of hydrolyzed whey or vegan protein (like Mt. Capra's DEEP30 or LivingFuel LivingProtein), five to ten grams essential amino acids (like NatureAminos), or ten to twenty grams hydrolyzed collagen protein (like Great Lakes or Bernard Jensen).

2. Drink plain, clear water from breakfast until the swim start. If you want to include supplements, I recommend a potent cocktail of D-ribose, wild plant derivatives, Chinese adaptogenic herbs, and essential amino acids that is meant to be consumed thirty to forty-five minutes before the swim start. That's totally optional, but I consider it better living through science. My choice for this is a packet of powder called TianChi.

3. On the bike, mixed into a down-tube water bottle (more aerodynamic than your seat-tube water bottle), consume for each hour the following: one to two servings of SuperStarch (or your clean-burning carbohydrate of choice), one to two tablespoons of MCT oil, and five grams of essential amino acids. Optionally, you can include one more serving of TianChi and one serving of VESPA every two to three hours on the bike. If you're going to use electrolytes, mix them into this same bottle (breaking open capsules if necessary). You should have one bottle of this mixture for the first half of the bike ride in your bottle cage, and the other half waiting for you at the special-needs station for the race. Be sure to mix, stir, or even blend the bottle's contents well and give it a good shake before taking a slug, as most carbohydrate solutions tend to clump slightly. Drink plain water from a separate bottle when you're thirsty. Once you mix all this together, it forms a thick, gel-like substance in your water bottle.

4. On the run, do exactly as you did on the bike, but use a running flask or fuel belt. I prefer the Nathan Sports Vapor Shot flask, which is ergogenic and easy to hold. You can use one flask for the first half of the marathon and have another one waiting for you at the special-needs station for the second half. Continue to drink water when you're thirsty and, optionally, have five to ten grams of amino acids, one

serving of TianChi, and one of VESPA every two to three hours (have it waiting in the bike-to-run transition and in special needs for the run). If running with a fuel belt and flask annoys you or doesn't appeal to you, then read the fat-based energy gel article at BenGreenfieldFitness.com/fatgels and simply use a minimalist belt like a SpiBelt to hold your gels, then consume one "healthy" energy gel every twenty to thirty minutes, chased with four to six ounces of water from an aid station. With the gel scenario, you can still use amino acids, VESPA, and TianChi.

5. Then cross the finish line with a smile on your face, free of gut rot and much lower AGEs and ROS than if you'd been stuffing your face with simple sugars all day.

This is exactly the strategy I use, and it's what I recommend for the athletes I coach.

For details on the second strategy of real food plus light liquid, visit OsmoNutrition. com or SkratchLabs.com. Both websites lay out that scenario quite thoroughly, as does Allen Lim's book *Feed Zone Portables*.

Ultimately, by using the strategies outlined in this chapter, you're going to find the fueling protocol that works best for you and your unique body. When it comes to fueling your body for exercise, there is no single right way to do things. Not all athletes can function well eating the exact same foods and quantities because we are all as different on the inside as we are on the outside. The illustrations in the *Atlas of Human Anatomy* show that the human stomach alone has as many as nineteen different shapes!

Just remember: You have to think beyond what works well in the moment. Many athletes perform just fine on sugar, processed food, and chemicals, but that doesn't mean it's healthy.

If you strike the ideal balance between eating for health and eating for performance, your body will thank you for years to come. If you follow like a sheep and eat what everyone else is eating because that's what seems to make them fast, you may find yourself ruing those decisions later in life. Go back and read chapter 1 to see what I mean.

Additional resources, helpful links, scientific references, websites, and surprise bonuses for this chapter are available at BeyondTrainingBook.com/Chapter16. Enjoy.

CHAPTER 17

The Twenty-One Best Kitchen Tools, Grocery Shopping Guides, Cookbooks, Websites, and Local Resources for Fueling Your Active Lifestyle

In this chapter, you're going to find out which tools I rely on in the kitchen and which resources I turn to on a daily basis. These are crucial to the way my wife, Jessa, and I feed our boys and fuel our minds, and for keeping our kitchen as holistic and full of real food as possible.

Don't feel that you have to rush out and buy everything I mention right away. But do print this list, jot down notes as you read, or visit the resource web page at BeyondTrainingBook.com/Chapter17. And over the next year, make it your goal to gradually expand your arsenal of healthy nutrition options. If you like this kind of information and you'd like to take a sneak peek inside my own personal pantry, then head over to BeyondTrainingBook.com/pantryfoods, where I take you on a personal tour of the go-to foods that hold a special place in my pantry.

Kitchen Tools

1. Good Blender

I'm baffled by folks who buy a cheapo blender and then scratch their heads as to why their smoothies, pâtés, sauces, and other blended recipes seem so darn hard to make. A good blender has a big engine and sharp blades. It can handle a smoothie of several handfuls of kale and almonds, coconut milk, coconut oil, an avocado, protein powder, cinnamon, sea salt, spirulina, Brazil nuts, and anything else your fueling heart desires morning after morning without its engine blowing up or its blades breaking. A good blender also works for whipping up quick soups, stews, puddings, sauces, and dressings. Vitamix, Blendtec, and OmniBlender are a few of the brands I've found that do the trick and are reasonably affordable, with good warranties. The one drawback is that they're big blenders, so I travel with a small Magic Bullet blender.

2. Omega Masticating Juicer

A masticating juicer crushes and squeezes pieces of fruits and vegetables with an auger. Fruit and veggies go in the top of the tube, juice drains out the underside of the tube, and the pulp is ejected from the end of the tube. Because of the slower crushing and squeezing action, masticating juicers can process leafy greens like kale or smaller greens like wheatgrass, and the juice lasts much longer than juice made in a centrifugal juicer. Masticating juicers are pricier than centrifugal models, but they're worth it.

3. Cast-Iron Cookware

Convenient for athletes, you can actually boost your iron intake by eating food cooked in cast-iron cookware. But the benefits of using cast iron don't stop there. Replacing your nonstick or aluminum pots and pans with cast iron allows you to avoid the toxic fumes produced by most other cookware. Not only can you use a cast-iron pan on the stovetop, but you can also transfer it to the oven, at any temperature, and food cooks beautifully. Surprisingly, a preheated cast-iron skillet rivals the non-stick qualities of nonstick cookware as long as it is properly seasoned and cared for. It's sturdy, wears well, and is easy to clean, to boot. Cast iron lasts forever, so you can pass it on to your grandkids and find your own at secondhand stores. (We bought all our cast-iron cookware at our local Goodwill.)

4. Excalibur Dehydrator

Drying is a great way to preserve fruits, vegetables, and animal proteins and has been practiced since ancient times. A food dehydrator removes moisture from food through a combination of heat and air flow to aid in natural preservation. Removing moisture from food not only keeps bacteria from growing and spoiling food but also dramatically reduces the weight of the food. It's a fantastic way to create on-the-go items. We use an Excalibur dehydrator to make beef jerky, flax seed crackers, dried-fruit roll-ups, pancake mix out of leftover carrot pulp from the juicer, and much more.

5. SodaStream

Carbonated water is great for staving off cravings or for drinking something more entertaining than plain water. A SodaStream is a countertop machine that injects carbon dioxide into regular water, giving you natural sparkling water at about half the price of commercial cans and bottles. I often mix the juice of half a lemon (a fantastic digestive aid), chocolate stevia, or peppermint essential oil into a large glass of sparkling water and sip away while I'm working on my computer or before dinner. Soda water can also help you burp up any gas or bloating before heading out for a workout. And yes, it is a complete myth that carbonated water is somehow "acidic" or bad for digestion.

6. Good Kitchen Knife

When you're cooking with real, fresh food, prep will go much faster if you have a dependable blade. Thanks to Tim Ferriss's book *The 4-Hour Chef,* the Wüsthof Classic eight-inch cook's knife is my go-to blade. Treat yourself to a decent knife, and you won't be sorry. Bear in mind that a dull knife, even a Wüsthof Classic, takes much of the joy out of cooking, so make sure to keep it sharp. (I use a whetstone to sharpen my knives.)

7. Nutcracker

For thyroid and testosterone support, I shell and eat three to five Brazil nuts every day (preshelled, unfrozen Brazil nuts are notoriously rancid and laden with mold and toxins). Usually, I just throw them into my morning smoothie. I dare you to try shelling them without a nutcracker.

8. Canning·Jars

In the cookbooks and meal-preparation resources later in this chapter, there are a variety of tips for fermentation, lactofermentation, pickling, canning, and adopting many of the other natural food-preservation techniques our ancestors relied on. We use canning jars not only for these techniques, but also as containers for raw milk, water, soaked or sprouted seeds and nuts, dried beans, and just about anything else we don't want to be stored in nasty plastic containers (for reasons shared below).

9. Pyrex BPA-Free Glass Containers

Bisphenol A (BPA) is a hazardous chemical compound found in plastic products, including hard plastic baby bottles, water bottles, hard plastic microwavable cookware, some plastic storage bags and containers, and the linings of aluminum cans. If you want to avoid BPA, you can use Pyrex cooking dishes, which are more like glass, do not contain BPA, and have special flexible lids that are also BPA-free. You can use Pyrex cookware for food storage—and even though we don't use a microwave, it is safer to use Pyrex in a microwave than hard plastic microwavable cookware that contains BPA.

10. Cheesecloth

Cheesecloth is a loosely woven cotton cloth that closely resembles gauze. From draining blended almonds to making almond milk, draining yogurt, and making whey, cheesecloth comes in handy for draining solids (or straining liquids). You can reuse it many times—just make sure to wash it before each use, then let it air-dry. Alternatively, you can purchase more expensive nut-milk bags, or if you're on a budget, just use an old pair of nylons (wash them first, ladies).

11. Chest Freezer

Every few months, we do a bulk order from US Wellness Meats, and during hunting season I harvest at least one deer or elk. Each year, we also purchase half a grass-fed cow from our local farmer. When you hunt or you buy your meat in quantities like this, you save money and get good, fresh meat, but you need a place to store it, so a chest freezer—we actually have two, both purchased from Craigslist—is pretty much a necessity.

12. Slow Cooker

While writing this chapter, I wandered into the kitchen where my wife was hovering over the stove and asked her which one kitchen item she couldn't imagine not having. Without hesitation, she pointed to our trusty slow cooker, which we bought at Goodwill nearly two years ago and use every week. It's one of the best time-saving appliances we own. For making everything from bone broth to stews, roasts, curries, and casseroles, a slow cooker is a must-have—especially if you're feeding a family. Many of the recipes and meal plans that Jessa shares with the Ben Greenfield Fitness Inner Circle are based around our trusty slow cooker.

Books

13. *Nourishing Traditions: The Cookbook that Challenges Politically Correct Nutrition and the Diet Dictocrats,* **by Sally Fallon**

In this book, you'll learn how to soak, sprout, ferment, and do everything else you need to do to make just about every food you can imagine that is healthy for the human body. Fallon not only teaches you how to prepare real, healthy traditional foods but also educates you on important topics such as the health benefits of traditional fats and oils (including butter and coconut oil); the risks of vegetarianism; the problems with modern soy foods; the health benefits of sauces and gravies; the proper preparation of whole-grain products; the pros and cons of milk consumption; how to prepare enzyme-enriched condiments and beverages; and healthy diets for babies and children.

14. *Rich Food, Poor Food: The Ultimate Grocery Purchasing System (GPS),* **by Jayson Calton and Mira Calton**

Every healthy grocery shopper should have this book in his cart. This indispensable guide walks you from aisle to aisle, from produce to pasta, teaching you how to identify potentially problematic ingredients, including hormones, pesticides, and GMOs. It also shares tips on how to lock in a food's nutritional value during preservation and preparation. I recommend it to all my clients.

15. *Eating on the Wild Side: The Missing Link to Optimum Health,* **by Jo Robinson**

This new vegetable and fruit guide teaches you how to choose fruits and vegetables whose nutritional content comes closest to their wild ancestors'. It also shows you how to use simple, scientifically proven methods for storage and preparation that preserve and enhance the health benefits of plants, including:

- Putting fresh garlic through a garlic press and then setting it aside for ten minutes before cooking it to increase its natural immune-defense properties.
- Baking potatoes, refrigerating them overnight, and then reheating them before serving to lower their glycemic index and keep them from spiking blood sugar.
- Shredding lettuce the day before you eat it to double its antioxidant properties.
- Storing watermelon on the kitchen counter for up to a week to allow it to develop more lycopene.
- Eating broccoli the day you buy it to preserve its natural sugars and cancer-fighting compounds.

This book is a nutritional gold mine, and I highly recommend it.

Websites

You'll find links to each of these sites on the resource web page at the end of this chapter.

16. Local Harvest

When it comes to supporting your local economy and getting your food as fresh as possible, the best organic food is what's grown closest to you. You can use the Local Harvest website to find farmers' markets, family farms, and other sources of sustainably grown food in your area so you can buy produce, grass-fed meats, and many other real-food items that are nutrient-dense. The site has an easy-to-use search engine that allows you to quickly locate local farmers' markets, CSAs (community supported agriculture), co-ops, meat processors, wholesale food sources, and more.

17. Amazon Prime

Nothing beats supporting your local economy, but for items you simply can't find locally or need fast, regularly, or at good prices, you should definitely consider an Amazon Prime membership. For $99 a year, you get free two-day shipping on just about everything you need. We use it for everything from Native Forest organic, BPA-free coconut milk to Navitas Natural nori sheets and Wild Planet sardines to nearly all the personal-care products in my Detox Gear. As an alternative to Amazon Prime, there's a new website called Thrive Market that is like a combination of Whole Foods and Amazon Prime. Visit BeyondTrainingBook.com/thrive to learn more.

18. Mountain Rose Herbs

For bulk, certified-organic herbs and spices, culinary salts, peppercorns, seasoning blends, seaweeds, sprouting seeds, and other items that can be downright dangerous to order from questionable or low-quality sources, we use Mountain Rose Herbs, because it operates on the foundation of sustainable practices, toxin-free ingredients, and fresh products.

We also buy ingredients such as butters, waxes, and carrier oils from Mountain Rose Herbs to create our own personal-care products, as well as essential oils for the immune system (echinacea to astragalus) and to add fragrance (peppermint, lavender, chamomile) to household cleaning products, homemade soaps, and so on. Not all essential oils are created equal, and many are laden with synthetic oils, pesticides, and toxins, so we get most of our edible tinctures, extracts, and oils from this quality source.

19. Magnetic Clay Baths

They're not exactly traditional kitchen items, but for supplements, detoxing, and health-care products, such as nascent iodine, transdermal magnesium lotion, magnesium oil, magnesium bath flakes, and even the clay-based detox Edible Earth (which is especially interesting stuff based on a recent study associating clay treatments with increased fat loss), Magnetic Clay Baths is our go-to source. Though you won't be cooking with these items, you'll certainly want to order items from this site that are integral to detoxing your body.

20. Upgraded Self

Upgraded Self is our source for toxin-free, mold-free, slightly "fringe" items such as MCT oil, chocolate powder, vanilla powder, mold-free coffee, and supplements like oxaloacetate and glutathione. I trust the site's owner, Dave Asprey, as a well-educated biohacker who is devoted to hunting down clean, quality products to, well, upgrade your body.

21. Nutiva

For just about anything superfood and coconut related, Nutiva is a good bet. We get our coconut milk through Amazon Prime, but for high-quality extra-virgin coconut oil, Nutiva coconut manna (a wickedly tasty blend of coconut flesh and coconut oil), red palm oil, hemp oil, hemp proteins, chia seeds, and other fun superfoods, you should definitely bookmark Nutiva on your browser.

That's it. Walk into my house, and you'll find very few packaged, processed, or boxed items—mostly just real food that can be prepared with the resources I've just shared with you.

So, when it comes to the ideal marriage of health and performance, you should now have the nutrition part of things under your belt, so to speak.

Now, are you ready to learn how to detox the rest of your life—the stuff that goes beyond food? The daily enemies that your skin, hair, and lungs are exposed to that can make gradual but permanent dents in your energy levels and your longevity? The creepy critters that can hang out in your home and prevent you from achieving your goals?

The next section of this book focuses on lifestyle. You're going to learn about:

- Hidden environmental triggers that can decrease your performance and health, including EMF exposure, pollutants, toxins, molds, and water.

- How to live a clean life and mitigate the damage of post-industrial living, including how to detox your home, office, and workout environment; limit dirty electricity; use proper water-filtration methods; and implement the use of healthy personal-care and household cleaning products.

- How to stay healthy and perform at a high level when traveling.

In the meantime, additional resources, websites, helpful links, scientific references, and surprise bonuses for this chapter are available at BeyondTrainingBook.com/Chapter17. Enjoy.

4 LIFESTYLE

CHAPTER 18

How to Protect Your Body from the Ten Hidden Killers in Your Home

Home is where the heart is.

And, if you're anything like me, home is probably a place—aside from gyms, roads, and parks—where you spend a significant amount of time sweating and sculpting your body. Wouldn't it be a pity if you were turning your body into a chemical wasteland in the process?

You can't do much about inhaling diesel exhaust from trucks on the roads that you run or bike on, or the chemical-laden disinfectants sprayed on the treadmills and other equipment at the gym, or the pesticides and herbicides clinging to the grass at the park. But just as you have complete control over the kinds of foods and chemicals that you put into your body, you have control over how healthy—or unhealthy—your home is. You also have control over how well equipped your body is to handle potentially toxic environments, such as gyms, roads, and parks.

So now our journey takes us into the lifestyle section of the book. In addition to learning how to detox your home, over the next several chapters you'll also learn:

- How to equip your home so that you can remain naturally physically active throughout the day.

- Time-saving tips for combining a daily commute and training, managing training with kids and family obligations, and getting more done in less time.

- Other lifestyle hacks that can free up lots of time, including food-prep methods, combining workouts, and other cutting-edge productivity strategies such as utilizing virtual assistants, e-mail filters, to-do buckets and everything else that I personally do to free up as much time as possible during the day.

Why You Need to Protect Your Body

You've learned how to clean your gut and liver and how to detox your entire body, but how much consideration have you given to the toxins, pollutants, chemicals, heavy metals, and other hidden killers that are outside your body rather than inside? For example:

- When you're cranking out push-ups in your living room, have you ever thought about what kind of carpet you're shoving your nose into?

- When you're taking the cold thermogenesis showers that you learned about in chapter 4, have you ever considered what compounds your skin might be soaking up from the water?

- As you're sitting here reading this book, do you know how many spectrums of electromagnetic frequencies from smartphones, e-readers, and computers are bombarding and radiating your body?

The average home contains 500 to 1,000 chemicals, ten times more electrical pollution than forty years ago, and an untold number of molds, mites, fungi, spores, pollen, and other "bioaerosols." You can't see, smell, or taste most of them, but that doesn't mean they won't cause brain fog, an afternoon headache, a crappy night's sleep, or a horrible workout.

So let's learn what you can do about them. You'll find handy links to everything on the resource web page at the end of this chapter. In addition, at GreenfieldFitnessSystems.com you can find the book *Biohacking a Healthy Home,* which contains a series of amazing audio interviews, videos, and articles from some of the world's top experts on healthy homes.

1. Mold and Mycotoxins

Mycotoxins are toxic compounds produced by various species of mold. Among a variety of other health issues, they can cause asthma and breathing issues, cancer, cardiovascular disease, altered kidney and liver function, disrupted sleep, stunted muscle recovery, miscarriage, and a bad case of "fuzzy brain"[27]. At my Become Superhuman event (details and recordings at SuperhumanCoach.com), Dave Asprey revealed that a host of mycotoxins and molds are found in foods that are generally considered healthy and referred to mycotoxins.com as a fantastic place to find out whether a food you commonly eat is tainted with dead organic matter that could be compromising your health and performance.

The bottom line is that, unless you trust the source, I'd seriously reconsider including blue cheese and other "moldy" foods in your diet. Here are a few biggies: sour cream, buttermilk, and sour milk; cured, pickled, and smoked meats and fish; prepackaged meats, like lunch meats, salami, and some sardines; commercial pickles, olives, capers, salad dressings, and ketchup; vinegar and soy sauce; hotel room coffee packs; and, yes, even leftovers that have been in your refrigerator for several days. I'm not saying that you can completely abstain from these foods, but you should go out of your way to avoid them whenever possible.

But mycotoxins aren't just found in food. By having an Environmental Relative Moldiness Index test performed by a licensed contractor (I don't recommend it as a DIY project), you may discover that your house has toxic mold that produces bacteria that can be more deadly than the mold in your food. Within twenty-four to forty-eight hours after moisture seeps into an area of your house, mold can form, chomp down, and multiply on whatever it considers a food source, including dust, wood, paint, paper, cotton, oil, and building materials like drywall.

To prevent mold formation and exposure, I recommend that you:

- Keep house dust to a minimum. Mop floors at least once a week. Use a vacuum cleaner with a HEPA (high-efficiency particulate absorption) filter for your carpets. HEPA filters capture the widest range of particles and potential allergens. Also consider installing a HEPA air filter in your home and office.

- Use a dehumidifier to keep the humidity in mold-prone rooms, such as basement bathrooms, low.

- Operate an oscillating fan in the bathroom after showering, and fix or caulk any leaks as soon as possible.

- Regularly clean surfaces where mold usually grows—around showers and tubs and beneath sinks.

- Be conscious of toxins in carpeting, especially in products made from synthetic materials. Use natural-fiber wool and cotton rugs. If you want to take things to the next level, replace your wall-to-wall carpeting with hardwood floors, all-natural linoleum, or ceramic tiles, using nontoxic glues, adhesives, stains, and sealers for installation.

- Seal or replace walls, floors, and cabinets made of particleboard, which often contains formaldehyde and emits unhealthy fumes. Avoid synthetic, strong-smelling plywood, fiberglass, fiberboard, and paneling.

Let's say you want to know if you have been exposed to mold. In the United States, you can get tests from a company called EHAP LABS; similar tests are available in other countries. Or you can simply pay attention to symptoms. If you move into a new house or apartment and you don't change anything in your diet but you suddenly begin to experience allergylike symptoms, such as asthma and congestion, frequent sickness, headaches, joint pain, or brain fog, you should suspect mold[18].

FIGURE 18-1

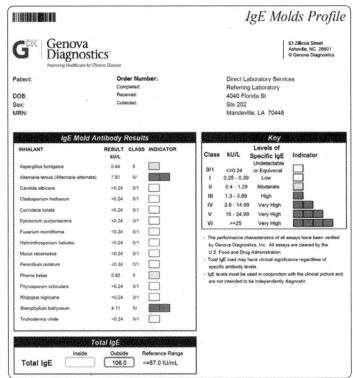

You can also get tested for mold allergies to everything from Candida to penicillin with a skin-prick test, which uses watered-down extracts of mold allergens to check your reactions. A little drop of allergen-containing liquid is applied to the skin of your arm or back and then pushed in with a little puncture or scratch. If a bump develops on any spot, it indicates a probable allergy to that substance.

Another, simpler DIY test is a blood-mold profile, which you can order from a company such as DirectLabs. You order the test and send your blood sample to the lab, where it's exposed to various mold allergens. Then your blood is checked for the presence of the antibody IgE, which is what your immune system produces in an allergic reaction. If it's there, you could be allergic to the mold you're being tested for. Figure 18-1 shows sample results of a blood-mold profile test.

If you are exposed to mold or suspect that you have a mold issue, or if a blood-mold test reveals high levels of mold allergens in your bloodstream, go back to chapter 15 and follow the detox instructions there. Two especially potent supplements for mold exposure are liposomal glutathione and oil of oregano.

Finally, if the laundry list of potentially mold-containing foods itself makes you feel like you've got asthma or brain fog, do a simple a Coca pulse test after you eat a suspect food that is a staple in your diet. I discuss this test in detail in a podcast on heart-rate-variability testing (BenGreenfieldFitness.com/hrv3), but it basically involves using an app, such as NatureBeat, to track what you're eating and record an increased heart rate of five or more beats in response to a food you've consumed that may be damaging to your nervous system. A positive test may signal an allergy or the presence of a potential mycotoxin in the food you've consumed. In simple terms, it indicates whether your body goes into fight-or-flight mode after eating—which is not a good sign!

Want to learn more about mycotoxins and how prevalent they are in our daily lives? Watch Dave Asprey's Become Superhuman talk at SuperhumanCoach.com/store and his equally shocking mycotoxin video at BeyondTrainingBook.com/mycotoxin. Listen to my podcast episode with Brett Bauer entitled "The Hidden Killer in Your Home and What You Can Do About It," which you can get at BenGreenfieldFitness.com/rainbow. Two good books for discovering how to "de-mold" your home are *My House Is Killing Me!* and *The Mold Survival Guide.* I've included links to these and other good books on this subject on the web page for this chapter.

2. EMF

There's a reason I unplug my wireless router before I go to bed or whenever I'm doing a home workout anywhere near my office. I never bring my cell phone near my ear, I don't use or touch a microwave, and I avoid heading out on long bike rides or runs with my phone in anything other than airplane mode.

The United States alone is wired with half a million miles of high-voltage power lines, and for wireless communication we depend on more than half a million microwave links. We also have tens of millions of broadcasting transmitters flooding our airwaves, use more than thirty-five million electromagnetic devices (increasing at an exponential rate), and plant ourselves in front of hundreds of millions of video and television screens.

EMF (electromagnetic field) radiation is the by-product of this profusion of electronic technology, and the radiation emitted by millions of household appliances, military installations, industrial machines, computers, broadcast and communications transmitters, and other electrically powered devices is a form of environmental pollution[28]. It can cause headaches, vision problems, anxiety, irritability, depression, nausea, fatigue, disturbed sleep, poor physical performance, and loss of libido.

Even worse, all metallic objects, including electrical circuits, telephone wiring, water and gas pipes, and even keys, watches, and jewelry, can act as antennae that collect and magnify these energy waves, creating a compounding effect that significantly alters the natural balance of the body's biochemical energy patterns.

When you're constantly bombarded by EMF waves in this manner, not only can it distort your internal cellular communications, but it can also "entrain" your body. Entrainment, also known as "sympathetic resonance," is the tendency of an object to vibrate at the same frequency as an external stimulus. That's why earthing or grounding, discussed in the recovery and stress-fighting chapters, works so well. Although the frequencies used in earthing or grounding take advantage of the natural frequencies of our planet, becoming entrained to any disruptive external frequency—such as the one emitted by your wireless router—may compromise the integrity of your intrinsic frequencies (that is, the natural vibration of your cells), which may erode physical and mental performance and lead to serious health issues[15].

I'll admit that a direct cause-and-effect relationship between electromagnetic radiation and illness has been difficult to prove, but the number of supportive studies continues to increase. To deepen your understanding of the seriousness of this issue, and for the nitty-gritty on protecting your home and body from the ravages of EMF, I recommend two books: *Zapped: Why Your Cell Phone Shouldn't Be Your Alarm Clock and 1,268 Ways to Outsmart the Hazards of Electronic Pollution,* by Anne Louise Gittleman, and *Disconnect: Truth about Cell Phone Radiation,* by Devra Davis.

In the meantime, here's a quick guide to jump-start your EMF radiation protection:

- Unplug your wireless router or switch off wireless mode when you're not using it. Better yet, purchase an electronic wall timer that automatically shuts off the router at night and then turns it on again in the morning.

- Limit artificial-light radiation by installing low-blue-light bulbs in your home, putting a blue-light-blocker screen on your computer, and using blue-light-blocking glasses, such as Gunnars.

- Invest in complete EMF protection for when you are sleeping. Don't cut corners here. Both are somewhat pricey, but I recommend either a BioMat sleep pad or an EarthPulse.

- Use a mattress that is free of springs. I give more details about the dust, EMF, mold, allergens, chemicals, and other health hazards in most mattresses in the article "Is Your Mattress Killing You?" at BeyondTrainingBook.com/mattress.

- Use dirty-electricity filters in the main rooms of your house. I use and recommend Greenwave filters.

- Use an air-tube headset when you're on the phone (I recommend the Envi air-tube), or use only the speaker setting.

- Keep your cell phone or laptop several inches away from your skin whenever possible, and put your cell phone on airplane mode if you need to put it in your pocket or near your head while sleeping or exercising.

- If you need to place an electronic device in your lap, use an EMF blocking pad, such as a HARApad, to block radiation.

- Avoid using your cell phone when the signal is weak (this amplifies EMF), and use an anti-EMF case, such as a Pong case, for your smartphone.

- Wear an Encoder wristband, which is designed to vibrate with the Earth's natural frequencies. You'll notice that you feel more "grounded" when you wear it while working with or around electrical equipment, such as your laptop or smartphone.

If you do everything listed above, you'll be well on your way to significant EMF protection, but if you really want to geek out on EMF protection or do a thorough test of EMF levels in your home, visit the website LessEMF.com, where you'll find a ton of additional equipment for EMF-proofing your home. Another excellent resource is Neuert Electromagnetic Services (emfcenter.com), which has consultants you can hire to help you "de-radiate" your home. I put a list of all these resources on the bonus page for this chapter.

3. Water

In my hometown (Spokane, Washington), they don't fluoridate the water, and boy, am I ever glad.

Fluoride is certainly a crucial compound . . . in pesticides. That's right: Sodium fluoride is a registered insecticide and rodenticide that is used in rat and roach poisons. It is a toxic waste by-product derived from the manufacture of phosphate fertilizers and from the aluminum-refining industry, which means that it also has a lot of lead as well as other toxic substances in it. But it's cheaper to simply dump fluoride into our water supply than to pay toxic-waste-disposal fees[1]. Unfortunately, fluoride can cause cancer, hip fractures, dental fluorosis, stained teeth, neurological impairment, lower IQ in children, and learning disorders.

Sure, fluoride has a good antidecay effect when applied directly to teeth—but you don't have to swallow the stuff. And when it comes to tooth decay, there is little to no difference between countries with fluoridated water and countries with unfluoridated water. If you really want to dig into this issue, listen to the podcast episode I did with Paul Connett (BenGreenfieldFitness.com/fluoride), author of the eye-opening book *The Case against Fluoride,* or read *The Fluoride Deception,* by Christopher Bryson.

Of course, fluoride isn't the only issue. Since 2004, testing by water utilities has consistently found thousands of pollutants in our tap water. More than half the chemicals detected are not subject to health or safety regulations and can legally be present in any amount. Unfortunately, at least in the United States, the federal government has not set a single new drinking water standard since 2001—and water utilities spend nineteen times more on water treatment chemicals every year than the federal government invests in protecting lakes and rivers from water pollution in the first place[2].

So what can you do to protect yourself from fluoride and other chemicals in your drinking water, shower water, bath water, and cooking water?

When it comes to filtering your water, there are a couple good options:

Water Filter Option #1: Install a reverse-osmosis (whole-house or under-counter) system. Make sure that it has one or more charcoal filters, which help remove unwanted substances like chlorine. Unfortunately, when you use a reverse-osmosis system, the good minerals, such as calcium, magnesium, and potassium, are filtered out along with the bad stuff, like fluoride. Demineralized water is also more acidic. So to make your filtered drinking water healthy with good minerals and to increase alkalinity, you can remineralize it with, or take a daily shot of, a trace liquid minerals supplement. Some of the better reverse-osmosis water filters also come with a remineralization feature. I link to some of my favorites on the web page for this chapter.

Water Filter Option #2: Install a whole-house structured-water system. You learned earlier about vibrational frequencies and how they can be either good or bad for your body. A structured-water system literally changes the frequency of the water, allowing it to envelop toxins and pollutants that will then pass through your body without harming you while retaining its mineral quality. I'll admit that when it comes to structured-water systems, the science is slightly farther out on a limb, but I have used the Greenfield Naturals water system for two years, have had urinary porphyrin tests and SpectraCell analysis for metals, chemicals, and other toxins, and have been perfectly clean. (Full disclosure: My father, Gary Greenfield, owns GreenfieldNaturals.com, a domestic and international distributor of structured-water filters that sells these systems to large agricultural enterprises to improve the health of their livestock.)

If you don't go the whole-house-filtration-system route, I highly recommend installing a KDF shower- or bath-head filter. This is important because your skin absorbs more chlorine, fluoride, and whatever other chemicals are in your water in a single twenty-minute shower than you'd get from five days' worth of your drinking water!

Finally, if you have been exposed to fluoride and unfiltered water for long periods and have been using fluoride toothpaste and other fluoride-filled products, such as Teflon pans; pesticides on produce; and even sodas, sports drinks, and beers, pay attention to what you'll learn in the next section on chlorine so that you can undo the damage and help your body recover and rebuild itself. David Getoff has an excellent presentation and other good resources on fluoride detoxification at BeyondTrainingBook.com/PPNF.

Even if you have a well, you aren't necessarily drinking clear, pristine water. For example, in testing the water in my own well, I've discovered bacterial iron and manganese, which are metals and minerals that I'd rather not have building up in my body. So I use a hydrogen peroxide filter for the iron, followed by a manganese filter, which passes through a whole-house water structuring unit to restructure the water before it finally winds up in my glass, sink, or shower. You can learn the details about elements such as iron, manganese, and copper in my interview with Dr. Wendy Myers at BeyondTrainingBook.com/watermetals.

4. Chlorine

Some of us don't just drink chlorine in our water—we also soak it up through our skin during workouts while we breathe in chloramines, the nasty by-products that form when chlorine reacts with organic matter such as dead skin cells.

I swim two to four times a week, and during the fall and winter it's not in the river or lake near my house, but in a chlorinated pool.

How much chlorine are you personally exposed to? If you're a swimmer or triathlete or hit the pool or hot tub at your gym regularly, probably quite a bit. If you're not a swimmer, you're still getting significant hits of chlorine just from showering or bathing if your water is municipal and unfiltered. Well water tends to be safer, although it may be laced with natural minerals (such as iron) that can be toxic in higher amounts—which is why most wells also need some type of filtration.

When I interviewed David Getoff on "How to Reduce the Risk from Swimming in Chlorinated Pools and Drinking Chlorinated Water" (BenGreenfieldFitness.com/chlorine), he talked about the cell wall damage and internal soft tissue damage that chlorine does, along with the autoimmune and allergy issues that are commonly aggravated by breathing and soaking in chlorinated water[19].

To mitigate the damage from chlorine (especially on days that you're in a chlorinated pool or hot tub), Getoff recommends taking the following daily:

1. **Vitamin C:** 2–5 grams
2. **Vitamin D:** 2,000–4,000 IU
3. **Vitamin E:** 10–20 IU of a natural source, such as d-alpha-tocopherol (I recommend LivingFuel's SuperEssentials fish oil)
4. **A serving of a full-spectrum antioxidant,** such as Life Shotz ·

Links to my preferred brands of all of the above are included on the web page for this chapter.

Unfortunately, most soaps and shampoos that are designed to strip chlorine from your skin and hair are laden with the endocrine disrupters and other dangerous personal-care-product chemicals that you'll learn about later in this chapter. One product called SwimSpray is a natural, vitamin C–based spray that removes chlorine odor, but it can't stop chlorine from being absorbed into your body. So the best thing you can do is to equip yourself internally to ensure that your body can handle the ravages of chlorine. If you need to test your antioxidant levels to see how well equipped your body is to deal with chlorine damage, I recommend getting an ION Panel Profile from DirectLabs.

Finally, if you have the luxury of a home pool or hot tub, add an ozone filter and then treat it with a healthy alternative to chlorine, such as those offered by Absolute Ozone, Grander Water, or NaturalSpas. These are typically mineral- or enzyme-based cleaners that require very little or no additional chlorine.

5. Household Cleaning Chemicals

From toilet bowl cleaners to laundry detergents, synthetic-chemical-based products are an enormous source of health issues and environmental pollution[8]. For example:

* Tide laundry detergent has high levels of 1,4-dioxane, a carcinogenic contaminant.
* Most fabric softeners contain synthetic fragrances that cause acute effects, such as respiratory irritation, headaches, and autoimmune reactions.
* All-purpose cleaners contain the sudsing agents diethanolamine and triethanolamine. When these substances come into contact with nitrites in the environment or your body and mouth, they react to form nitrosamine carcinogens.

But it doesn't have to be this way. Lemons, baking soda, and white vinegar are the foundation of the cleaning supplies in our house, from disinfectants to window cleaners. The Ben Greenfield Fitness Inner Circle (BenGreenfieldFitness.com/ InnerCircle) is chock-full of recipes to make your own cleaning supplies using these products. My wife and I also have an entire session of a show we did for CreativeLive in which we demonstrate how to make these products yourself. You can find it at BenGreenfieldFitness.com/creative.

And here's a list of inexpensive, easy-to-use, natural products that can be used alone or in combination for a variety of household cleaning applications:

* Baking soda cleans and deodorizes.
* Borax, despite its "scary" name, is simply sodium borate. It deodorizes, disinfects, softens water, and cleans wallpaper, painted walls, and floors.
* Lemons contain a natural acid that is effective against most household bacteria.
* Unscented natural soap in liquid, flake, powder, or bar form is biodegradable and will clean just about anything. We get soap from Mountain Rose Herbs.
* Washing soda, also known as sal soda, is sodium carbonate decahydrate, a natural mineral. It cuts grease, removes stains, softens water, and cleans walls, tiles, sinks, and tubs.
* White vinegar cuts grease and removes mildew, odors, some stains, and wax buildup.
* Cornstarch can be used to clean windows, polish furniture, and shampoo carpets and rugs.

But how, exactly, do you use these ingredients? Here are a few "recipes" to get you started. (And there are many thorough instructions for making planet- and home-friendly products at eartheasy.com.)

* **Carpet stains:** Mix equal parts white vinegar and water in a spray bottle. Spray directly on the stain, let it sit for several minutes, and clean the area with a brush or sponge using warm, soapy water.
* **Disinfectant:** Mix 2 teaspoons borax, 4 tablespoons white vinegar, and 3 cups hot water.
* **Laundry detergent:** Mix 1 cup Ivory soap (which is pure) with 1/2 cup washing soda and 1/2 cup borax.

Of course, you don't *have* to turn your kitchen into a cleaning-supplies factory. From kitty litter to diapers (those are technically a cleaning supply, right?), there are good, nontoxic commercial household cleaning products; I mention some in my blog post "How Safe Is Your House from Being a Chemical Wasteland?" Among them are:

- Here's the Scoop!—natural, unscented, clay clumping litter
- Bon Ami cleanser—no chlorine, perfume, or dye
- Seventh Generation free and clear natural dish liquid
- Seventh Generation chlorine-free diapers

You can find many other safe products at places like the Organic Consumers' website (organicconsumers.org). My wife and I have several webinars inside the Ben Greenfield Fitness Inner Circle that teach you how to make your own cleaning products. Another excellent resource is the Environmental Working Group's (EWG) searchable database. I walk you through the entire process of vetting your personal-care products and household cleaning chemicals via the EWG site in the podcast episode BenGreenfieldFitness. com/330. But you now have enough information to start cleaning cleanly.

No discussion of cleaning chemicals would be complete without warning you about carpets, furniture, mattresses, flooring, and other surfaces. When any of these items (especially carpets or area rugs) give off that "new carpet" smell, it means that they're "off-gassing."

Off-gassing is the evaporation of chemicals from any material[23]. Furniture, plastics, vinyl products, paint, new cars, clothing, cosmetics, water bottles, carpet, and mattresses do it. Off-gassing materials emit volatile organic compounds (VOCs) and small particulate substances throughout the entire life of the material—and carpet is a major offender.

Synthetic carpets are made from nylon fibers with a polypropylene backing. Of the chemicals released from carpet, most notable are styrene and 4-phenylcyclohexene (4-PCH), both of which come from the latex backing used on 95 percent of all carpets. So that "new carpet" smell is the odor of 4-PCH, which is an eye and respiratory tract irritant that can seriously mess up your central nervous system. If that wasn't bad enough, the adhesive used to attach the carpet to the floor typically contains benzene and toluene, some of the most harmful VOCs[29].

Ideally, new carpet should be aired out before installation, but if that's not possible, keep any carpeted room extremely well ventilated. Besides headaches, nausea, dizziness, and shortness of breath and other asthmatic reactions such as restricted airways, here's how to tells if carpet is giving off gas:

1. Take a clean, fragrance-free paper towel and fold it in half twice.
2. Place it on a section of the carpet and cover it with aluminum foil, secured with tape.
3. After twenty-four hours, fold the towel inside the foil quickly.
4. Then go outside and unwrap it just enough to take a whiff.
5. If it stinks, your carpet is giving off gas.

You should also avoid stain-guarded clothing, furniture, and carpets, and be conscious of toxins in carpeting and other flooring, especially anything made from synthetic materials. Buy natural-fiber wool and cotton carpets, rugs, and mattresses whenever possible, and if you really want to go whole hog, replace your wall-to-wall carpeting with hardwood floors, all-natural linoleum, or ceramic tiles—using non-toxic glues, adhesives, stains, and sealers for installation.

If you have been exposed to unhealthy flooring and furniture for a long time, I highly recommend that you detox your body using the tips in chapter 15 and then switch to a natural, water-based floor cleaning system such as the one outlined at BenGreenfieldFitness.com/rainbow.

6. Plastics

As you may remember from the last chapter, I go out of my way to avoid plastics by using Pyrex BPA-free containers and glass canning jars. I also use only BPA-free water bottles when hydrating during workouts. I prefer the Specialized Purist, which is infused with silicon dioxide. This forms a protective glasslike barrier inside the bottle and prevents odors, stains, and mold from attaching to the inner surface. It's the same type of technology used in the water bottles at BenGreenfieldFitness.com/gear.

I avoid heating or microwaving any plastic that contains anything I might eat or drink, especially foods with oils or fats, which tend to be excellent carriers for many of the chemicals in plastic. I don't even let plastic sit in a hot car.

Table 18-1 shows how plastics, even many deemed "safe" by the powers that be, are not really that safe at all.

Symbol	Abbre-viation	Polymer name	TABLE 18-1
(1)	PETE or PET	Polyethylene terephthalate (also known as polyester)	Suspected cancer-causing properties. Acetaldehyde was found to migrate into water. Does not clean well; do not reuse bottles.
(2)	HDPE or PE_HD	High-density polyethylene	Little research about these. No evidence of toxicity, endocrine disruption, or estrogen mimics. Migration occurs with high temps and especially with fats or oils. HDPE generally exhibits less migration. There is evidence of migration into food products, even dry foods.
(3)	PVC	Polyvinyl chloride (think plastic wrap)	Some but not all phthalates found in PVC (polyvinylchloride or vinyl) may be considered harmful to fetuses and young infants in any concentration. PVCs are suitable only for older children, if at all. May contain BPA.
(4)	LDPE or PE-LD	Low-density polyethylene	Few scholarly studies. No evidence of leaching.
(5)	PP	Polypropylene	Stabilizers used in polypropylene are biologically active (potentially affecting nerve transmission) and tend to leach from the plastic.
(6)	PS	Polystyrene (think convert store coffee and picnic plates)	Is a mutagen (carcinogenic or cancer-causing effects), neurotoxic, cytogenetic (chromosomal and lymphatic abnormalities)
(7)	OTHER or O	Other plastics, including acrylic, acrylonitrile, and polycarbonate	Polycarbonate (Lexan) is used extensively in food-contact utensils, including baby bottles, sports bottles, food containers, and tableware. Its basic monomer is bisphenol A (BPA), originally synthesized in the 1930s as an estrogen for pharmacological use. Some, like PLA, have no BPA and are considered safe.

In our super-space-age era, I realize that it may be nearly impossible to eliminate plastic from your life completely. So I recommend doing your best to limit your exposure to the worst offenders, which are typically the plastics numbered 3, 6, or 7, and then follow these simple rules:

1. **Limit your use of plastic bottles.** Bottled water is not extremely harmful in small amounts, but BPA exposure can be an issue with frequent or prolonged use. BPA, or bisphenol A, is linked to cancer and phthalates, both of which can cause hormonal and neural damage. One report from the Centers for Disease Control and Prevention found BPA present in 92.6 percent of adults[4], but the good news is that another study found that when you stop using BPA-containing items for just three days, you can reduce your BPA levels by about 66 percent. Use glass bottles, BPA-free bottles, or glass jars to transport and drink your water[21]. If your budget allows, try to drink water that comes in glass bottles, such as Perrier, Gerolsteiner, or Pellegrino, when you are traveling.

2. **Be aware of other common sources of BPA.** Besides plastic bottles, canned foods and shopping receipts are also significant sources of BPA. You should also avoid plastic food packaging and containers whenever you can—and never heat foods near these items. Choose baby bottles made from glass or BPA-free plastic. If you have children, avoid vinyl pacifiers for babies and stay away from children's toys marked with a 3 or "PVC."

3. **Replace your plastic shower curtains.** Use natural cotton, hemp, or nylon curtains, such as those by Bean Products or Ex-cell Living.

4. **Avoid nonstick pans, pots, bakeware, and utensils,** since the Teflon coating contains perfluorinated chemicals (PFCs) similar to the chemicals leached from plastic. Even if you're not scraping the pan with utensils, the chemicals can still leach into your food. Just remember: Whatever surface you cook on, you wind up eating. As you learned in the last chapter, we mostly use cast-iron cookware.

5. **Use wet cleaning rather than dry cleaning if it's a reasonable option.** If not, tell your dry cleaner not to use plastic wrap, or remove it as soon as possible after picking up your clean clothes, since the plastic traps the dry-cleaning chemicals on clothes and in your closet. Let your dry cleaning air out (preferably outside) before you put it away.

Once you become aware of the dangers of plastics, you'll begin to notice them all over your home. But through awareness and gradual removal, you can easily banish most of them from your life. Once again—if you have been exposed for a long time, do a detox.

7. Pesticides and Herbicides

I admit it: I don't eat organic, pesticide-free 100 percent of the time. Sometimes I mess up and eat one of the "Dirty Dozen" pesticide-laden produce items. (See Table 18-2, or go to ewg.org for a constantly updated list.) Usually it's when I'm at a backyard barbecue or a friend's home for dinner and that spinach salad or handful of cherries looks so good. In a situation like this, I simply pop some activated charcoal

TABLE 18-2

THE DIRTY DOZEN+ Buy these organic	
1.	Apples
2.	Peaches
3.	Nectarines
4.	Strawberries
5.	Grapes
6.	Celery
7.	Spinach
8.	Sweet bell peppers
9.	Cucumbers
10.	Cherry tomatoes
11.	Snap peas — imported
12.	Potatoes
+	Hot peppers
+	Kale/collard greens

TABLE 18-3

THE TERRIBLE 20 Always buy these organic (Listed from highest pesticide content.)		THE FAB 14 On a budget, choose these conventionally (Listed from lowest pesticide content.)	
1.	Apples*	1.	Avocado
2.	Peaches	2.	Pineapples
3.	Nectarines	3.	Cabbage
4.	Strawberries	4.	Sweet peas
5.	Grapes	5.	Onions
6.	Celery	6.	Asparagus
7.	Spinach	7.	Mango
8.	Bell peppers	8.	Kiwi
9.	Cucumbers	9.	Eggplant
10.	Cherry tomatoes	10.	Grapefruit
11.	Snap peas	11.	Cantaloupe
12.	Soybeans (edamame)*	12.	Cauliflower
13.	Potatoes*	13.	Sweet potatoes
14.	Hot peppers	14.	Mushrooms
15.	Kale/collard greens		
16.	Blueberries		* potential GMO
17.	Lettuce		
18.	Yellow squash/ Zucchini*		
19.	Hawaiian papaya*		
20.	Sweet corn*		

capsules and take liposomal glutathione when I get home. You can read about both of those supplements in chapter 15.

But the majority of the time, I buy organic produce, and when I don't, I use a simple vinegar-cleansing trick that I'll tell you about shortly.

Many people seem to feel fine when they eat pesticide-laden produce. This is because, unlike contact with, say, mold and off-gassing carpet, you won't necessarily feel like crap immediately after pesticide exposure. In fact, the biggest danger from pesticides is not from the immediate effects, but from the harm that comes long after exposure or from repeated, low-dose exposure.

The Environmental Protection Agency recently reported that, in the United States alone, approximately five billion pounds of active pesticide ingredients are applied to our foods annually. That's a tremendous amount of poison entering our bodies; sure enough, a 2002 University of Washington study found pesticides in the urine samples of 109 out of 110 urban and suburban children.

As you would probably guess, food grown on certified-organic farms contains significantly less pesticide residue than food grown with synthetic pesticides. That may seem obvious, but the evidence has been available only since 2002, when research proved that children fed organic food have lower residues of certain pesticides in their bodies than children fed conventionally grown food.

So buy certified-organic produce. And if you really want to make educated decisions and fill your body with the most nourishing and least damaging produce, I recommend the book *Rich Food, Poor Food.*

In this grocery-shopping guide, Jayson and Mira Calton include excellent lists of "The Fab 14" and "The Terrible 20"—which show which produce items tend to be the least or most laden not only with harmful pesticides, but also with GMOs, chemical fertilizers, various synthetic substances, sewage, and irradiation. There's also a handy wallet guide like the one pictured in Table 18-3, available on their website (www.caltonnutrition.com), that you can use to reduce your pesticide exposure by 80 percent and avoid GMO produce 100 percent of the time.

As for that simple vinegar trick I mentioned for nonorganic produce? Any white vinegar will do, and you already plan on having that around as a natural cleaning product, right? Simply mix a solution of 10 percent vinegar to 90 percent water as a bath in your kitchen sink, then briefly place nonorganic vegetables or fruit in the solution, swish them around, and rinse thoroughly in plain (filtered!) water.

Of course, you also need to watch out for the pesticides and herbicides hanging around in your yard. After all, the average suburban lawn soaks up ten times as much chemical pesticide per acre as conventional farmland, with more than seventy million tons of fertilizers and pesticides applied to residential lawns and gardens annually!

I'm not a huge fan of lawns. We just finished digging up nearly our entire 1.2-acre yard and replacing it with a muddy, dirty vegetable garden. But if you do want that grand estate–like expanse of green grass, the only way to reduce your dependence on chemical fertilizers is to develop a healthy lawn that is naturally resistant to weeds, insects, and disease. You can do so by:

1. **Improving the soil:** You can get a lawn pH tester for a few bucks on Amazon. When you test, it should read between 6.5 and 7.0, which is slightly acidic. Soil that is too acidic needs a sprinkling of lime, and soil that is not acidic enough needs a sprinkling of sulfur.

2. **Choosing a local grass:** Grasses vary in the type of climate they prefer, the amount of water and nutrients required, shade tolerance, and the degree of wear they can withstand. Ask your local garden center to recommend grass that is best adapted to your area.

3. **Mowing often, but not too short:** Giving your lawn a "marine cut" is not the best idea, because surface roots become exposed, the soil dries out faster, and surface aeration is reduced. As a general rule, don't cut off more than one-third of the grass at any time, and shoot for about 2.5 to 3.5 inches. In most growing

conditions, this means a weekly mow (yes, I hire a guy off Craigslist to mow, because I hate mowing). When your lawn is done growing for the season, cut it a bit shorter, to about 2 inches. This minimizes the risk of mold buildup during winter.

4. **Watering deeply, but not too often:** Regular watering encourages your lawn to develop a deep root system, which makes the grass hardier and more drought-resistant. But you need to let the lawn dry out between waterings. Most healthy lawns require only one inch of water per week, which is about fifteen to twenty minutes of sprinkling once a day, such as in the early morning, when less water will be lost to evaporation.

5. **Fertilizing naturally:** Finally, when you do fertilize, go natural. I recommend the Ringer brand, which is basically a mix of certified organic minerals. An excellent resource for chemical-free yard recommendations is *The Organic Lawn Care Manual: A Natural, Low-Maintenance System for a Beautiful, Safe Lawn,* by Paul Tukey.

8. Metals

In the podcast episode "How Hidden Sources of Heavy Metals Are Destroying Your Health, and What You Can Do about It," I talk to Dr. David Minkoff about how exposure to heavy metals such as lead, arsenic, or mercury can cause chronic fatigue, poor mood, disrupted sleep, headaches, a compromised immune system, low hormones, and brain fog.

The biggest culprit is modern dentistry. Even though about 50 percent of dentists in the United States are now mercury-free, only an estimated 10 percent of dentists fully understand the health risks associated with dental amalgam—which is toxic mercury, despite what the misleading term *silver filling* might lead you to believe[13].

If you decide to replace your silver fillings, you should know that the process of removing and replacing them puts you at risk of acute toxicity from the mercury released, and this can cause serious damage to organs such as your liver and kidneys.

Because of this, and other metals that float near and can be absorbed into your mouth when you're at the dentist, my family and I use a holistic dentist. Holistic dentists operate from the perspective that your teeth are an integral part of your body and overall health and take precautions such as using a cold-water spray to minimize mercury vapors, putting a dental dam in your mouth so you don't swallow or inhale any toxins, using a high-volume evacuator near the tooth at all times to evacuate the mercury vapor, washing your mouth out immediately after any fillings have been removed, and using powerful room air purifiers.

The following organizations can help you find a holistic dentist:

- Consumers for Dental Choice
- Dental Amalgam Mercury Solutions
- Holistic Dental Association
- Huggins Applied Healing
- International Academy of Biological Dentistry and Medicine

- International Association of Mercury Safe Dentists
- ToxicTeeth.org

For more on this topic, read the article titled "How to Find a Biological Dentist that Can Treat You Holistically" at Mercola.com.

Unfortunately, you can get heavy-metal exposure from all sorts of sources that go way beyond the fillings in your mouth, including:

- Smog
- Car keys
- Toys made in China
- Secondhand cigarette smoke
- Pesticides and herbicides
- Protein powders and dietary supplements
- "Pristine" water (like that from my local Lake Coeur d'Alene) that, in fact, has huge amounts of runoff from mining
- Food stored in metal containers
- Big fish like tuna and dolphin
- Nuclear runoff from the nuclear plant meltdown in Fukushima, Japan

The list goes on and on. You can get tested for heavy metals through a company like DirectLabs, but if you've been exposed to any of the above (and who hasn't been?), you can assume that you'd benefit from pulling metals out of your body.

The process of binding heavy metals and pulling them out of your body is called chelation, and many substances will do that[12]. The metals generally exit your body through your stool, urine, hair, breath, and sweat. Some forms of chelation use the drug DMPS, but if you go to dmpsbackfire.com, you'll discover some of the serious problems that can be caused by conventional chelating drugs.

Chelators use ionic bonds, which are the attractions between the positive charge of a heavy metal and the negative charge of a chelating molecule. Because of this, chelation also has the ability to extract precious minerals from your body, which is why I don't recommend chelation drugs or natural chelation. Instead, I recommend using natural compounds that can gently draw heavy metals out of your body.

For optimal protection from heavy-metal exposure, Dr. Minkoff recommends 6 milligrams of iodine a day, magnesium in supplemental form (about 400–600 milligrams a day, or until you get a loose stool), and a greens supplement such as chlorella. But these supplements won't pull the metals out of your body.

For removing metals from your body, I highly recommend Metal-Free Heavy Metal Detoxification Formula, which is a sublingual spray composed of a unique short-protein chain called a peptide. Peptides are very small and easily absorbed. They interact with a heavy metal by wrapping around it so that the heavy metal can't interfere with or block normal cellular processes[14]. This interaction is called cage binding. So, rather than chelating precious minerals from your body along with heavy metals, the spray imprisons the mercury, arsenic, lead, aluminum, uranium, or cadmium, and your body then excretes it in your stool.

I use Metal-Free about thirty consecutive days each year (usually at the beginning of the year, when I also implement an easier exercise protocol, more juicing, and less food overall) to ensure that I'm regularly removing metal buildup from my body. I've included a link to it on the resource web page for this chapter.

9. Radiation

From the Fukushima disaster in Japan to the average airport security line to the radioactive compounds ingested during medical scans, such as X-rays, we're constantly bombarded by radiation—and it's an unfortunate fact that a nuclear disaster thousands of miles away can have implications for you as you sit sipping iced tea in your backyard.

One problem with radiation is that certain glands and tissues with lots of iodine receptors, including the thyroid, prostate, and breast, are extremely sensitive to oxidation and cell damage from radiation, especially when these tissues are low in iodine[24]. When radioactive iodine (found in most forms of radiation, including all the stuff that gets blown into the atmosphere after a disaster like Fukushima) gets into an area of the body that has lots of iodine receptors and these receptors are lacking iodine, the radioactive iodine latches onto the receptors and begins ionizing, oxidizing, and harming the tissues. But if the receptors have had adequate dietary exposure to iodine, then they do not readily grab the radioactive version.

The other issue with radiation, as I alluded to above, is that it causes oxidation—much like eating large quantities of heated vegetable oils or sugars can cause free radical damage—but to a far greater extent.

Here's the bottom line: Contrary to popular belief, you simply cannot stop ionizing radiation from entering or passing through your body by taking a supplement or drug. Radiation exposure is like a bunch of tiny bullets passing through your tissues. To completely protect yourself from radiation, you would have to dig an underground bunker with lead or concrete walls to separate you from the source of radiation. Good luck with that.

Rather than running from radiation, I recommend that you intensify your body's ability to repair damaged tissues and organs and equip yourself with large amounts of the proper nutrients to counteract the effects of ionizing, oxidizing radiation.

As I discuss in the podcast episode "Natural Ways to Protect Yourself from Radiation" (BenGreenfieldFitness.com/radiation), different forms of antioxidants protect you in different ways, so you can't simply take, say, high-dose vitamin C or high-dose iodine and call it good. In that podcast, I answer a question from a Japanese caller who was concerned about radiation exposure from Fukushima, and I recommended a protocol to counteract the effects of radiation. (You'll notice that many of these suggestions overlap with my recommendations for a healthy detox.)

Here are suggestions for daily radiation protection (things you should be doing for general health anyway—see the links on the resource web page for this chapter):

- Oral magnesium in supplement form (about 400–600 milligrams a day, or until you get a loose stool). You can read more about magnesium's protective effects against small daily doses of radiation at BeyondTrainingBook.com/magrad.

- A high-quality greens supplement, especially one with chlorella. I recommend RECOVERYbits. Eat twenty to thirty in the morning and evening, or put them in your smoothie. Also include liberal amounts of sea vegetables in your diet.

- A full-spectrum antioxidant such as Life Shotz—all the ingredients are derived from wild plants, which are some of the most "stressed" biological compounds on the planet due to their exposure to sun, wind, bugs, and so on. When you consume the extract of those wild plants, they pass their natural antioxidant properties on to you.

- Additional antioxidants from a high-quality supplement that contains omega-3s, vitamin D, and vitamin A. I recommend SuperEssentials fish oil or Twinlab's cod liver oil.

- Daily use of a trace liquid minerals supplement that contains fulvic acid and humic acid, such as Black Water, which you can find at BeyondTrainingBook. com/blackwater.

- If acute radiation exposure occurs or you travel frequently:

  - Metal-Free Heavy Metal Detoxification Formula—several sprays into your mouth as directed on the bottle.

  - Six milligrams of nascent iodine per day in a glass of water.

  - One to two servings of edible clay per day. Clay can actually draw radioactive compounds out of your body. And yes, it's like eating dirt. I recommend Edible Earth as one of the more absorbable and clean sources of clay.

To learn more about naturally protecting yourself from radiation and the huge problem with radiation exposure, I highly recommend Dr. Mark Sircus's book *Nuclear Toxicity Syndrome*. You'll find links to it and all the resources above on the web page for this chapter.

10. Personal-Care Products

Ever heard of the "dirty dozen of cosmetics"?

That's right, just as with produce, a plethora of ingredients found in beauty products aren't exactly beautiful. Research in the United States has shown that a significant percentage of the 82,000 ingredients used in personal-care products are industrial chemicals, including carcinogens, pesticides, reproductive toxins, and hormone disrupters—including plasticizers, degreasers, and surfactants[10]. And many people are unwittingly slapping, slathering, rubbing, spraying, spritzing, and massaging these chemicals onto their skin and hair, which are like sponges for these harmful chemicals.

For more information about the dirty dozen of cosmetics, you can check out the cosmetic dirty dozen background report at BeyondTrainingBook.com/dirtydozenbg, but in the meantime, I recommend heading to your bathroom, inspecting the labels on your personal-care products, and tossing out anything that contains any of the following twelve ingredients:

1. **BHA or BHT:** Used mainly in moisturizers and makeup as preservatives. Both are suspected endocrine disrupters and may cause cancer.

2. **Coal-tar dyes:** Indicated by "p-phenylenediamine," colors listed as "CI" followed by a five-digit number, or colors like FD&C Blue No. 1 or Blue 1, these dyes have potential to cause cancer and may be contaminated with heavy metals that are toxic to the brain.

3. **DEA-, MEA-, or TEA-related ingredients:** Used in creamy and foaming products, such as moisturizers and shampoos, they can react to form nitrosamines, which may cause cancer.

4. **Dibutyl phthalate:** Used as a plasticizer in some nail-care products. It's a suspected endocrine disrupter and reproductive toxicant.

5. **Formaldehyde-releasing preservatives:** Look for DMDM hydantoin, diazolidinyl urea, imidazolidinyl urea, methenamine, and quarternium-15. Used in a variety of cosmetics, they slowly release small amounts of formaldehyde, which causes cancer.

6. **Parabens:** Used in a variety of cosmetics as preservatives, these are suspected endocrine disrupters and may interfere with male reproductive functions.

7. **Perfume (aka fragrance):** Any mixture of fragrance ingredients used in a variety of cosmetics—even in "unscented" products. Some fragrance ingredients can trigger allergies and asthma; some are linked to cancer and neurotoxicity.

8. **PEG compounds:** Used in many cosmetic cream bases, these may be contaminated with 1,4-dioxane, which may cause cancer. Also look for propylene glycol and other "-eth-" ingredients (for example, polyethylene glycol).

9. **Petrolatum:** Used in some hair products for shine and as a moisture barrier in some lip balms, lipsticks, and moisturizers. This is a petroleum product that may be contaminated with polycyclic aromatic hydrocarbons, which may cause cancer.

10. **Siloxanes:** Look for ingredients ending in "-siloxane" or "-methicone" (such as cyclotetrasiloxane). These are used in a variety of cosmetics to soften, smooth, and moisten and are suspected endocrine disrupters and reproductive toxins.

11. **Sodium laureth sulfate:** Used in foaming cosmetics, such as shampoos, cleansers, and bubble bath, these may be contaminated with 1,4-dioxane, which may cause cancer. Also look for the related sodium lauryl sulfate.

12. **Triclosan:** Used in antibacterial cosmetics, such as toothpastes, cleansers, and antiperspirants, triclosan is a suspected endocrine disrupter and may contribute to antibiotic resistance in bacteria.

Whew!

When I first heard about this dirty dozen, I was tempted to shrug and just make sure that I continued to do things like use natural deodorant, avoid fluoride in toothpaste, and not use sunscreen unless absolutely necessary. But last year, I read new research—specifically the first peer-reviewed assessment of a large number of hormone disrupters and dangerous chemicals in a variety of household products[20]. The research is shocking because it reveals that products commonly labeled "green," "nontoxic," and "healthy" are actually laden with dangerous chemicals. And these are products that health-conscious consumers commonly buy and bring into our homes, kitchens, bathrooms, beds, and bodies—including air fresheners, dryer sheets, shampoo, bar soap, floor cleaner, sunscreen, and toothpaste.

So I've switched to following a basic rule that may seem silly at first glance, but seems pretty safe to me: If you can't eat it without getting seriously sick, don't put it on your body.

That's right. Your skin is a mouth, and slathering chemicals on it is pretty dang close to swallowing the stuff. Sure, you might get a slight tummy ache if you do eat some of the natural products I'm about to list, but they're not going to kill you or give you cancer like some of the items that may be in your medicine cabinet right now.

Based on this rule, here's what I use in my personal grooming protocol:

- **Face and skin moisturizer:** Extra-virgin olive oil or coconut oil—both have very good topical antibacterial, antiviral, and antiodor properties. This is why I also use coconut oil as a deodorant. Look for products by Skin Care for Athletes, Weleda, Suki, Indigo Wild, Primal Life Organics, and Trillium Organics.

- **Deodorant:** Coconut oil because of its antiodor properties; also Primal Pit Paste and Thai Crystal.

- **Shampoo and hair styling:** Nature's Blessing Hair Pomade, made with nettle, rosemary, sage, peppermint, thyme, alfalfa, pure virgin olive oil, pure coconut oil, sage oil, rosemary oil, bergamot oil, chlorophyll (from nettle and spinach), and pure mineral jelly. Other good products for shampooing and styling are made by Acure Organics and Yarok.

- **Soap:** Dr. Bronner's Magic Soaps Pure-Castile Unscented Baby-Mild Soap, made with water, organic coconut oil, organic palm oil, organic olive oil, organic hemp oil, organic jojoba oil, citric acid, and tocopherol. Many of the skincare-product manufacturers above also make soap.

- **Toothpaste:** Dental Herb Company Tooth and Gums Paste, made with essential oils of red thyme, cinnamon bark, eucalyptus, lavender, and peppermint and extracts of echinacea, gotu kola, and green tea. I haven't found anything that holds a candle to this stuff, although I occasionally use activated charcoal tooth powder for whitening.

- **Shaving gel:** Dr. Bronner's Magic Organic Lemongrass Lime Shaving Gel, made with organic sucrose, organic white grape juice, organic coconut oil, potassium hydroxide, organic olive oil, organic shikakai powder, organic hemp oil, organic jojoba oil, organic cornstarch, organic lemongrass oil, organic lemon oil, organic lime oil, citric acid, and tocopherol. Other good brands include Pacific and Dr. Carver's.

- **Sunscreen:** Badger Balm (most are about 30 SPF), made with zinc oxide, organic sunflower oil, organic extra-virgin olive oil, organic beeswax, organic jojoba, organic shea butter, organic cocoa butter, natural vitamin E, and essential oils. Other good sunscreen brands include Raw Elements, Kabana, and Mexitan.

- **Cologne:** Zen for Men Cypress Yuzu Spray Cologne by Enchanted Meadow. There are other good scents out there, but Enchanted Meadow products are derived from safe ingredients and essential oils, such as vitamin E; sweet almond, avocado, and jojoba oil; and extracts of aloe vera, rosemary, and chamomile. This way, I don't always smell like a coconut- and olive-oil-slathered hippie.

Of course, I realize that the personal needs of ladies may go beyond the few items that I use. So I bugged my wife to suggest some personal-care products for women that are 100 percent natural and organic. Munch away.

- **Makeup:** 100% Pure, Bite Beauty, and Josie Maran. These companies use healthy food-based or plant-derived ingredients, like manuka honey and mango seed oil.

- **Nail polish:** Scotch Naturals—100 percent nontoxic nail polish.

- **Fragrance:** Lavanila and Pacifica. Similar to the men's cologne I use, the bases are all healthy essential oils.

Go ahead and compare the ingredients in any of the products above with those in the personal-care products you're now using. Notice any differences? At the same CreativeLive presentation at which my wife and I demonstrated how to make your own housecleaning products, we also demonstrated how to make your own versions of many of the personal-care products listed above (BenGreenfieldFitness.com/creative). Finally, at the time of this writing, at GreenfieldFitnessSystems.com I am putting the finishing touches on an antiaging skin serum I personally designed that contains ingredients such as olive oil, carrot oil, and oregano oil and can be used as a moisturizer, fragrance, and aftershave by both men and women.

Perhaps, your head is once again spinning with all the new information about how to maximize your health and your performance. But don't let that stress you out. Start with baby steps. Do little things like these:

- Replace your regular water bottles with PCB-free ones.

- Shift to more natural personal-care products as you use up the ones you've already got.

- Start to become aware of when you're exposing your body to EMF, and minimize exposure when you can.

- Listen to your body and start paying attention to anything that smells or tastes synthetic.

- Equip your body with what it needs internally to fight external stressors.

Ultimately, you should think about living as simply and ancestrally as possible while still taking advantage of postindustrial comforts such as computers, teeth whitening, and swimming pools. You're now well equipped with the knowledge to make the right decisions to achieve that goal.

Additional resources, websites, helpful links, scientific references and surprise bonuses for this chapter are available at BeyondTrainingBook.com/Chapter18. Enjoy.

CHAPTER 19
The Zen of Getting Über-Fit without Neglecting Your Friends, Family, and Career

A few years ago, there was an article in the *Wall Street Journal* titled "A Workout Ate My Marriage." It begins with the tale of Caren Waxman, the wife of an endurance athlete, who wakes up alone every morning, including holidays, because her husband leaves before dawn every day to work out for hours in preparation for a triathlon.

The article goes on to describe other exercise widows and widowers who often wake to an empty bed. Or their dinner plans are spoiled because their partner can't eat complex foods or big meals before an evening workout. And of course, forget about parties or other nighttime social events that even remotely threaten to sacrifice the quality of the almighty morning workout.

Regret grows as romance wanes, because the athlete in the relationship collapses like a sack of potatoes by 9 p.m. Intense commitment to a demanding training schedule for triathlons, marathons, CrossFit, or some other big physical goal leaves couples fighting about who does chores, who gets time alone, and who decides where and how the family plays together.

And while the effect of extreme exercise on divorce rates has never really been investigated, resentment on the part of friends, spouses, and other family members is an undeniable reality, with many lonely wives, husbands, and children wondering when the exercise insanity is going to end.

Of course, the consequences of extreme fitness pursuits may go beyond family disputes and may also include ruining other important relationships and friendships, loss of income or a stagnating career, and an inability to do anything well except lift a heavy weight; row 500 meters like a torpedo; or swim, bike, and run faster than everyone else on the block.

Let me ask you a question: You don't want to regret the finish line, do you?

Let me ask you another question: Are you missing the important things in life?

Let me ask you one more question: Is your tombstone or obituary simply going to say, "This Person Was Really Good at Exercising"?

The fact is, unless you're a professional athlete and your paycheck depends on your performance, the temporary glory of crossing the finish line of an Ironman triathlon or a marathon, winning CrossFit regionals, or riding your bike a hundred miles is simply not worth neglecting your friends, your family, your career, and all the other things in life you could be enjoying and will be there when your days of athletic prowess are over.

But the fact is, there's a way to become über-fit without creating exercise widows or exercise orphans, without giving up important advances in your career, without missing out on good friendships, and without feeling as if you never had a chance to indulge your interests in other pursuits—like music, theater, cooking, art, sports, or whatever else strikes your fancy.

So in this chapter and the next one, I'm going to fill you in on all the insider-training and time-saving secrets that allow me to be ranked among the fittest folks on the planet while still having time to write, play guitar, play tennis and noon basketball, learn new languages, travel, take my wife out on dates, throw dinner parties, and play for at least two hours every day with my twin boys.

You may find that this chapter is skewed toward endurance athletes—particularly Ironman triathletes. Not only is that my personal area of extreme expertise, but I also find that endurance athletes tend to feel more pressure to put in longer hours than CrossFitters, weight lifters, or recreational exercisers.

However, no matter who you are, you've got some serious exercise-time-management gems coming at you.

The Overexercising Ironman

As you learned in chapter 3, most endurance athletes—and especially Ironman triathletes—overdo exercise big-time. CrossFitters, obstacle racers, cyclists, marathoners, and swimmers aren't far behind. As you may recall, according to the Ironman website, the average number of hours per week devoted to training for the World Championships generally falls between 18 and 22, with an enormous training distance for each discipline.

So the majority of Ironman triathletes training for the World Championships in Kona put in close to three hours a day, and as an Ironman coach and competitor, I can tell you that the training programs of other Ironman triathletes aren't far behind. Yes, professional triathletes train up to four to six hours a day, but their job depends on it. Does yours?

Exceptions to the Rule

There are some exceptions to the rule. Take Sami Inkinen, for instance. Sami had an amateur Ironman winning time of 8:24 at Ironman Sweden in 2013, and the year before his finishes included:

- Overall amateur champion at Wildflower Triathlon Long Course
- Overall amateur champion at Hawaii 70.3 Ironman
- Age-group world champion at Ironman 70.3 in Las Vegas
- Age-group world champion runner-up at Ironman World Championships in Hawaii, with an 8:58:59 Kona performance

Yet despite kicking the butts of the athletes who trained twenty to thirty hours a week and beating many of the professional Ironman triathletes, Sami trains a maximum of about twelve hours a week using many of the methods you're going to learn about in this chapter.

At that same Ironman Hawaii (in 2012), I was about a half-hour behind Sami, completing the race in 9:36—but on a training schedule of ten hours a week (which I detail in the *LAVA* magazine article "Unconventional Triathlon Training" and in chapter 3 with the ancestral-athlete approach).

In the podcast episode "How to Maximize Triathlon Success with Minimal Training Time" (BenGreenfieldFitness.com/sami), Sami divulges the details of many of his personal strategies (including interesting practices such as using a swim snorkel and doing most of his bike training on a CompuTrainer). But I'm going to outline several important takeaways from that discussion, as well as the thirteen tips and tricks I've picked up over the years to spend no more time than I have to in the pursuit of über-fitness.

Thirteen Ways to Get More Fit in Less Time

Please revisit chapter 3, in which I outline much of the science behind these techniques and why they work so well.

1. Do Short Swims

To be a decent swimmer, you don't need to accumulate tons of yardage. You simply need frequent exposure to the water. Swimming requires much more efficiency, economy, and "feel for the water" than it does pure fitness (which is why a twelve-year-old girl can easily beat me in a 100-meter pool sprint). For this reason, frequency and consistency are more important than marathonesque swim workouts of sixty to ninety minutes, such as in a typical Masters swim class or classic swim workout.

Let's use Ironman swim training as an example. For Ironman, you need to swim "long" only once a week, and that swim shouldn't ever be longer than 4,000 meters. Rather than a steady, slow swim, you should structure this workout to include hard, race-pace intervals with short rests (such as a warm-up, 3 × 1,000 at race pace, and a cool-down). Then you can simply pepper additional, brief 15- to 30-minute swims, such as 20 × 50 or 10 × 100, throughout the week, preferably before a strength-training session, bike, or run so that you minimize prep time (goggles, swim cap, preshower, postshower, etc.).

2. Train Indoors

Outdoor bike rides and runs often involve getting into workout clothing, inflating tires, filling water bottles, scheduling, driving to and meeting with a group, and other preparatory activities that can take fifteen to twenty minutes before your training session even begins. And once you're finally out there, traffic lights and stop signs can significantly detract from the efficiency of your workout. For athletes who live where there is wintry weather, this process becomes even more laborious, what with all the layers of clothing, hats, gloves, and toe warmers and, of course, removing and washing all that gear once you're done with the workout.

Recently *LAVA* magazine did a story on the Ironman's current fastest cyclist, Jan Frodeno, who does 99 percent of his bicycle training indoors, only riding outdoors in the few days leading up to a race.

So if you want to get the most bang for your training buck, find a place in your house to be your "pain cave," set up an indoor trainer or treadmill, and do one or two short, intense indoor sessions a week. You'll stay focused and structured with this approach. If you need some ideas for killer indoor-training workouts, three of my favorites are MaccaX cycling and treadmill workouts, Sufferfest cycling workouts, and Runervals treadmill workouts. Links to all my favorite versions appear on the resource web page for this chapter.

To save commuting time, make sure you've got a good home gym, too. I wrote an entire article and recorded a podcast episode on putting together a home gym, but my personal setup cost less than $300 and includes a suspension strap, an indoor-sprinting device called a FIT10, a stability ball, a Gymstick, a door-frame pull-up bar, and some sandbags and kettlebells from Onnit.com/bengreenfield. Zero fancy machines required, and I save valuable time by heading out to the garage rather than dressing appropriately for the weather and fighting stop signs, stoplights, traffic, and grandmothers on inline skates with their eight grandchildren and two poodles.

And if you can't get to the pool, check out my "Official 'Baby It's Too Cold Outside to Drive to the Pool' Swim Workout" (BeyondTrainingBook.com/bgfcold-swim), which simply requires some elastic tubing or the slightly more pricey but more swim-appropriate StretchCordz.

3. Minimize Off-Season Training

In contrast to their peers, who are disappearing into the basement during the winter to do three- to four-hour indoor-trainer sessions followed by long jaunts on the treadmill, or heading outside to do four- to six-hour bike rides several months before their actual Ironman race, most of my athletes save all their "big training" for that final eight to twelve weeks before a big event. I encourage you to do this, too. When you really need mental and physical freshness and vigor, one of the biggest mistakes you can make is to beat yourself up all fall and winter in preparation for a spring or summer event.

After all, do you really think that a two-hour run in January is going to help you in an August marathon or obstacle race, or that watching back-to-back movies on your indoor trainer during the winter is going to create any kind of fitness that's going to still be "with you" in a summer Ironman?

4. Train Alone

Don't get me wrong—I completely understand the concept of "tribe," the importance of social interaction, and the motivation that comes from peer pressure and a friendly, competitive environment. If training is your only social outlet and it's not stealing time from your family or other things you want to do, then by all means join a Masters swim, running, cycling, or triathlon club or a CrossFit box.

But if you really want to maximize your time and workout efficacy, then train alone as much as possible, whether you're training indoors or outdoors. Here's why: Group training sessions not only suck up tons more time in terms of scheduling them, gathering the group (someone is always late, right?), and actually training, but these sessions rarely simulate what you're going to experience during an event. Think about it: How often during an Ironman, for example, are you drafting off a bike close to the front of you or beside you, socializing, or frequently fluctuating pace?

The gym can be another time-suck. With plush chairs and couches conveniently located near big-screen TVs; smoothie bars stocked with snacks; piles of magazines;

friends; workout buddies; and vibration platforms, scales, saunas, spas, flyers, articles, and fancy new workout contraptions, you can literally spend hours at the gym preparing to exercise, eating for exercise, learning about exercise, and talking about exercise—without actually doing much exercise.

Case in point: I recently went to the gym to take a metabolism-boosting class that was marketed to advanced exercisers. The class was scheduled to begin at 6:30. I left my house at 6 so I'd get there by 6:15. I waited around for fifteen minutes for the class to start, and then a few more minutes waiting for latecomers. I then wasted another ten minutes in the class warm-up, although I'd already warmed up while waiting. Each section of the class included demos and instructions from the teacher. By the time the class was over and we spent ten minutes doing a very easy cool-down and some stretches, I had devoted ninety minutes to "working out," but when I looked at my watch, I discovered that I engaged in significant fitness-boosting exercise for a total of only twenty-two minutes (although I guarantee that many class participants proudly checked off the class as being sixty minutes of exercise).

Had I stayed home and used my own inexpensive exercise equipment, I could have done three times as much exercise and still had plenty of time left over.

5. Do One Long Run

You heard me right. In your buildup to a marathon or an Ironman triathlon, you really need only one long run—typically three to four weeks before your event. Just the other day, during an Endurance Planet podcast (EndurancePlanet.com), the host, Tawnee Prazak, informed me that her coach advised twenty runs of up to twenty miles each before her actual marathon. I responded by pointing out that that strategy is all well and good if the race involves a paycheck for you, but if not, then you've suddenly spent nineteen weekends pounding the pavement when you could have been spending time with your family or pursuing a new hobby. And while you can recover relatively quickly from a long bike ride, a long run (two-plus hours) can significantly impact your joints and keep you inflamed and beat up for several weeks.

So what do you do instead of a long run? In the same way that anaerobic high-intensity interval sessions have been shown to significantly enhance aerobic fitness, short and intense runs of eighty to ninety minutes are all you really need to prepare for a marathon or an Ironman—and some of my best Ironman performances have come from running only once a week for eighty to ninety minutes (with elliptical training on my ElliptiGo or noon basketball or tennis for the other "run" sessions). Similarly, for longer obstacle course races such as a Spartan Beast (13 to 16 miles), I do almost no long running with very minimal run volume each week, and instead opt for more joint-friendly jaunts up a very steep incline treadmill set at up to a 40 percent incline. The trick is to make each of those runs or steep walks high-quality sessions, not long, slow death marches. Do the session on fresh legs, after a good night's rest, and you'll maximize the intensity and efficiency of your one key run session.

And for Pete's sake, whether it's your one long run or any of the eighty- to ninety-minute runs, make it a devoted practice of form, efficiency, economy, and turnover and not a mindless slog in which you mentally check out or forget about form.

6. Run on Short Courses

When you run, try to stay away from long courses—like three-plus-mile loops or lengthy trails—because the longer the course, the more likely it is that you'll take your time and run it slow. Instead, run on tracks, neighborhood blocks, or short loops, which are far more conducive to brief, high-quality, and intense intervals. It's a strange mental trick, but the closer you are to home or the shorter the loops that you're running, the faster you typically go. Perhaps your body simply knows that it's always relatively near a safe haven, food, and comfort, so it's OK to go hard.

For example, if I am running more than once a week, one of my key Ironman training sessions is 12 × 200-meter repeats—in the cul-de-sac outside my house. Including full recovery between repeats, this workout takes a maximum of thirty minutes, but if I perform it at maximum intensity, I feel as though I've run two hours by the time I finish. And my kids can join me on their bikes and "race Daddy."

7. Lift

I focused on this extensively in chapter 3, but several research studies have shown that strength training can improve endurance performance by increasing neuromuscular recruitment, efficiency, and economy—especially for cyclists and runners[1,2]. In other words, you can get fit without necessarily spinning or running for hours on end. Anecdotal evidence, particularly from many older endurance athletes, suggests that strength training also plays a significant role in injury prevention. And you can even get a serious cardiovascular boost from certain types of strength training, including the super-slow and isometric training discussed in chapter 4.

The nice part is that when you lift, it's easy to train at home, with your family. My twin boys often drag their kid-sized kettlebells and medicine balls into the backyard and join me for swings and slams. They also have miniature jump ropes, yoga mats, and their own stability ball. Sure, the workout is not quite as high-quality as if I had strapped on my earphones and headed to the squat rack at the gym, but once again, I want my tombstone to say more than "He Was a Good Exerciser." I'd rather my children have some fond memories of sweating with Dad. (More on training as a family later.)

8. Eat Lunch Fast

It's never a good idea to eat extremely fast meals in a stressed state—or, as my mother refers to it, "hoovering" your food like a vacuum cleaner.

At the same time, I've heard many people complain about not having enough time in the day for both exercise and the other things they want to enjoy while they spend an entire hour simply eating lunch.

In reality, you can get a healthy, solid lunch of real food into your system in ten to fifteen minutes—and much less time than that if it's in the form of a smoothie or shake. In other words, when lunch hour rolls around, you can head out for a thirty- to fifty-minute training session, get back, take a fast cold shower, and still have plenty of time for lunch.

So what kind of lunch takes a long time to eat? Salads, casseroles, dinner leftovers—and pretty much anything that requires cutlery or getting together with a group to eat. Choose these faster lunch alternatives instead: wraps, smoothies, shakes, or edible real food that you take out on your training session with you. Chapter 11 includes plenty of fast, easy, real meals, and chapter 16 cites plenty of foods that you can take with you on the go.

9. Commute

I own a Honda Ridgeline pickup, but I drive it barely once a week. Sometimes I worry that I'll forget how to drive. That's because I walk or bike nearly everywhere.

Self-propelled commuting is not only a great way to mimic an ancestral, hunter-gatherer life, but it can drastically cut down on training time. For example, you can skip all your bike workouts for the week and simply ride your bike to work. Put your clothes in a backpack and pack wipes to clean up afterward. If you're like me, you can even go so far as to wash your hair in the sink. For two years, I trained for the bike part of Ironman competitions just by commuting eight miles on my bike five days a week, then doing one tougher, slightly longer effort on the weekend.

If this doesn't work for your job location, training schedule, or life, you can also:

- Run or bike to the grocery store for small items. (I often do things like run hard to the store, then run easy back while I'm carrying bags of spinach or bananas.)
- Grab a backpack and run errands (post office, bank, etc.) on your bike, sprinting between stoplights and stop signs and recovering during your stops.
- Ride or run to social events like parties, carrying a backpack with a change of clothes or stashing it in your family's car, and then drive home with your friends or family.

There's a reason those Ethiopian boys who run to school every day grow up to be world-champion marathoners.

10. Include the Family

As soon as my wife and I found out that we were going to have twins, we bought a double bike trailer and a double jogger. The bike trailer always had two little bike helmets and a bunch of books and toys inside to keep the kids entertained during rides. And until the boys were too heavy to push around, we used the double jogger nearly every day for neighborhood jogs, 5Ks and 10Ks, nature field trips, running the kids to soccer-tots practice, running to the gym, and even running to the grocery store. In my book *10 Ways to Grow Tiny Superhumans,* available at GreenfieldFitnessSystems. com, I outline even more ways to include your children in your workouts, including hypoxic swim sets with a kid on your back, steep uphill run sprints with a kid piggy-backing on you, baby yoga, bear crawls, crab crawls, and more.

If you have younger children, try to join a gym or health club that is child-friendly with free kid care (such as the YMCA) so that you and your spouse can exercise together while your kids are safely supervised. And if you have older children, begin to include them in your workouts. Several times a week, my boys and I go Fitness Exploring, a fun workout that involves running through the neighborhood finding trees to climb, obstacles to jump from, curbs and fences to balance on, and other elements of play around us—a technique discussed in my phone app podcast episode with Darryl Edwards, who owns the fantastic FitnessExploring.com site. This type of play—also seen in movements such as Parkour or MovNat—is suggested in chapter 5 as a method for improving full-body balance and somatosensory input. I also highly recommend checking out the website My Kids' Adventures for even more fun physical activities that you can do with your family.

Once a month, I take the kids to the local sporting-goods store and let them choose a new piece of fitness equipment, such as a small kettlebell, medicine ball, or dumbbell, just to keep them excited about fitness and about joining me in my home workouts.

Some training schedules and coaches advise "invisible training," which means training only early in the morning or late at night when your training is "invisible" to your family, but I encourage the complete opposite: Make your family part of your training.

11. Communicate

You, your spouse, your family, your friends, your coworkers, and your boss should be aware of your training schedule when you have a five-hour bike ride planned for the weekend, or you decide to disappear to the gym for an extra hour on Wednesday morning. Trust me—it's better to be transparent about the huge amount of time you are devoting to fitness than to try to keep it secret.

We used to keep a giant calendar on the bulletin board by our front door, where we wrote down workouts, family events, races, and sometimes the ever-present reminder for me to "mow the lawn already" (which I never actually do anymore). Nowadays, we are slightly more geeky and use a shared Google calendar, which is synced to both of our computers. Jessa knows my training plans and I know hers, and whenever it becomes necessary, I can share the calendar with coworkers, employees, friends, and the like. Even though it's an extra step, I try to have a basic idea of where I'll be and when at least thirty to sixty days in advance so that there are no surprises. I don't lay things out too thoroughly—just enough that my family and friends have a general idea of what I'm up to.

Don't be embarrassed to wear your training schedule on your sleeve: Most people will respect you for being committed to fitness. Just make sure to give advance notice, and when the temptation arises to be rigid with your training schedule, remember to ask yourself whether fitness is your hobby or your job.

12. Cross-Train Socially

Even though I perform my triathlon training nearly 100 percent solo, many of my social relationships are formed from playing tennis with a group of guys in my local tennis league, smacking around a volleyball on Sunday afternoons with friends, and hopping into the occasional noon basketball game at the gym. For me, these are social outlets that keep me from being an isolated training geek who has lost the skill to communicate with the general public.

Of course, you're not "wasting precious fitness time" when you add cross-training to your training schedule. There is a wide world of sports just outside your front door—and many of these sports are not only entertaining and a fresh mental break from your normal training routine, but also a perfect way to address cardiovascular fitness deficiencies, train weak muscles, stimulate and grow the mind, and expand social circles.

While the social sports of bowling, softball, and baseball may not be the best cardiovascular cross-training activities, look into soccer, basketball, tennis, cricket, and, if you're willing to carry your own bag and forgo the cart, golf.

For more details and tips on how to socialize, get fit, and cross-train simultaneously, check out my two-part series on cross-training at EverymanTri.com (BeyondTrainingBook.com/trioffseason) and my Get-Fit Guy episode entitled "How to Get Fit While Playing Sports," which you can find at QuickAndDirtyTips.com.

13. Grease the Groove

As I explain back in chapter 4, the idea behind "greasing the groove" is that instead of doing a long workout at the gym, you spread your exercise out over the course of the day. Doing so not only allows you to become proficient at certain movements but also keeps your metabolism elevated throughout the day and gets you fit or maintains fitness without always having to set aside time for structured workouts. For example, I have a pull-up bar above the door of my office. Every time I walk under that bar, I do five pull-ups.

Other ways I grease the groove are:

- Beginning every day with ten minutes of yoga and calisthenics with deep nasal breathing.
- Doing twenty bodyweight squats every time I take a bathroom break (and of course, using the BenGreenfieldFitness.com/SquattyPotty).
- Doing twenty-five kettlebell swings at least once a day.
- Spending as much of the workday as possible at a standing workstation or treadmill workstation (full details on my current office setup are in the video at BeyondTrainingBook.com/standingoffice).
- Doing a hundred jumping jacks for every hour I sit. (I often sit when I write.)
- Taking an icy-cold shower two to three times each day (massive cardiovascular and mind/productivity-enhancing benefits).
- Consistently engaging in the deep, diaphragmatic breathing you learned about in chapter 9. For more on why this works, even for something like Ironman training, listen to the BenGreenfieldFitness.com podcast episode "How to Biohack Your Workouts, Your Diet, and Your Life to Get More Done in Less Time."

You get the idea. You don't have to "work out" to be working out. This is one of the biggest ways I trick my body into staying in fitness-gaining hunter-gatherer mode all day long, freeing up more time for family, friends, work, and play.

All the tips I've just shared with you are already included with or can be worked into the training plans that accompany this book, as well as my three existing "minimalist" endurance-training plans: Tri-Ripped (TriRipped.com), Triathlon Dominator (TriathlonDominator.com), Obstacle Dominator (ObstacleDominator.com), and Marathon Dominator (MarathonDominator.com).

Incidentally, I wrote this chapter while hooked up to a Compex electrostimulation device that was firing away on my quads and hamstrings—giving me a training and recovery effect while I sat on the couch writing and my kids played with Legos on either side of me. Had I wanted to burn fat at the same time, I could have worn my Cool Fat Burner vest as well. If you want to free up even more time and are willing to incorporate these time-saving, biohacking technologies, I highly recommend that you go back and review the section "Underground Training Tactics for Enhancing Endurance" in chapter 4.

Finally, you may also want to tune into my USA Triathlon webinar titled "Balancing Work, Life, and Triathlon," which I link to on the web page below.

Additional resources, helpful links, scientific references, websites, and surprise bonuses for this chapter are available at BeyondTrainingBook.com/Chapter19. Enjoy.

CHAPTER 20

My Top Ten Time-Saving and Productivity Tips— Including How to Quit Mowing Your Lawn

Now that you know how to spend less time working out, it's time to delve into other lifestyle hacks and habits that you can use to get even more done in less time. Whether you're a soccer mom, a blogger, a triathlete, a busy CEO, or a student, my top ten time-saving and productivity tips are going to instantly free up your most precious commodity—your time. Here they are, the strategies I personally use every day, including not mowing my own lawn.

1. Use Buckets

I used to keep a checklist. One really long, annoying list, filled with items like:

Write article about rehabilitating shoulder

Call Grandma

Arrange podcast interview with a sleep specialist

Clean garage

Watch iMovie tutorial online

I thought I was being clever and efficient by keeping one long tally of everything I needed to get done and checking it off as I went along. After all, if you want to get things done, you need to write them down, right? Each night, I'd a crumple into an exhausted heap, having checked off as many items as possible. Then I'd wake up the next day to begin checking off items again.

Bad move. The checklist is a cruel system—a never-ending loop with no start and no end.

I have a much smarter, cleaner system now—I use "buckets." I simply assign days to specific tasks, and I do only those tasks on those specific days. For example:

I do phone consults only on Tuesdays and Thursdays.

I shoot videos only on Tuesdays.

I record audio only on Wednesdays.

I write articles only on Fridays.

You get the idea. So if I get inspiration for, say, a video about how to make a low-carb kale smoothie, I don't add that task to a big list and get around to it when I get to that part of the list. Nor do I drop everything and go make the video. I simply open up my Tuesday Evernote document, write down "shoot low-carb kale smoothie video," and move on—forgetting about the smoothie video until Tuesday and moving that task off my plate into the Tuesday bucket.

So if I get through Tuesday's bucket at 6 p.m., great. The rest of the day is free to use as I please; I don't have to move on to the next item on an endless list. And yes, while major projects and recurring tasks generally are assigned to specific days, I do some things every day, such as work out for sixty minutes, write fiction for fifteen minutes, and play guitar for twenty minutes. But these are activities that I consider to be self-improvement and right up there with eating food or drinking water.

Let's just say that the bucket system will greatly simplify your life. More on Evernote later.

2. Eliminate Television

That's right. I'm bringing out the big guns. Painful, I know.

Here's the deal: I haven't watched commercial television in more than a decade. (I also don't read the newspaper or listen to the news, but eliminating those is optional.)

Allow me to clarify: I do own a TV. I watch about one movie a month. But I have no television reception. Here's why: Television pummels you with excessive information and distraction, even if your intention is to watch only one particular program.

I'd rather grab information when I need it. If there's a program I want to watch, I get it from Hulu or use the free open-source video player app Miro and move on, with minimal commercial breaks. The few times I've found myself getting sucked into Hulu (or any other website full of shiny distractions) too frequently, I prevent myself from accessing it by using tools like LeechBlock for Firefox and StayFocusd for Chrome (you can find links to these on the resource web page at the end of this chapter).

3. Eat Simply

You don't need to feel guilty about a lack of variety in your meals. You can definitely rotate through the forty easy meals in chapter 11, and between the Internet and books, you can go crazy with new recipes forever, but I purposely keep my food choices to a minimum.

My eating "system" is very simple: 99 percent of the time, I eat the same thing for breakfast (green smoothie), for lunch (sardine salad), and for an afternoon snack (coconut milk with protein powder)—which saves a lot of brain time pondering what to eat and saves a lot of prep time, because the more you do something, the faster you're able to do it. For dinner, we eat out, or I try a new recipe and include my children so it's a fun learning project, or Jessa cooks.

By following this approach, you'll know exactly how much of your staple meals you need to eat to keep you sated and productive and avoid getting stuck in a nutritional no man's land.

Just try it for a week: smoothie for breakfast, salad for lunch, quick snack in the afternoon, and something new for dinner.

4. Outsource

As you know, I don't mow my own lawn.

I also don't go to the bank. Or the post office. And I rarely go to the grocery store, unless I'm cycling or running there.

I also spend barely any time handling personal finances, dealing with computer malfunctions, ordering items from Amazon, or making phone calls I don't want to make.

See, my personal destiny in life is to shatter the conventional wisdom of what the accepted capabilities of our body and mind are—and to teach as many people as possible how to discover the delicate balance between achieving amazing feats of physical performance and staying healthy, living long, and looking good. And the simple fact is that I can't achieve that when I'm standing in line at the post office to buy stamps or putting lawn clippings in a garbage bag. I can do it when I'm creating content, writing, shooting videos, recording audio, or talking on the phone or Skype with clients.

So I outsource. Here are some of the key online resources you can use to do it, too:

- **Craigslist:** This is where I find people to do my housecleaning, local shopping, banking, Amazon ordering, post office runs, and, of course, mowing the lawn.

- **Fancy Hands:** Here you can hire a virtual assistant to plan personal travel—flights, hotels, airport shuttles, etc.—using miles from various airline rewards programs that you keep at AwardWallet.com. Of course, you could have that virtual assistant perform a huge variety of other tasks, too. A similar service, and the creation of your own virtual assistant "team," is offered by my friend Ari Meisel at LessDoing.com.

- **Elance (converting to the new name Upwork):** For finding a freelancer to fix a website, design a graphic, create spreadsheets, or do anything tech related that you don't want to learn how to do yourself.

- **TaskRabbit:** Where college students, recent retirees, stay-at-home moms, and young professionals seeking side gigs—literally the people in your neighborhood—are dying get your grocery shopping and other time-consuming to-dos done for you. (Yes, you can do background checks.)

- **GoDaddy:** Personal finances used to be a huge drag and time-suck for me, so until I recently decided my finances were so complex that I needed to hire a personal accountant to track everything in Quickbooks, I used GoDaddy Bookkeeping. It pulls all my small-business and personal finances into one place and takes care of all my bookkeeping so I can skip spreadsheets, data entry, and having piles of paper everywhere. Any purchase I make from a credit card or bank account goes straight into Outright, all by itself. And you can share your GoDaddy account with an accountant, so your taxes can be easily prepared. Another option is to use a virtual accountant from Bench.co.

- **HootSuite:** I have five Twitter accounts, more than a dozen Facebook pages, several Google+ pages, YouTube channels, Instagram, Pinterest, a LinkedIn account—you name the social media platform and I'm probably on it. HootSuite is a social media management system that allows me and a virtual assistant to manage most of these accounts with one interface on a single, easy-to-use dashboard.

- **FastCustomer:** Who likes waiting on hold? With FastCustomer, you log in, say whom you'd like to talk with (for example, your bank, your cell phone carrier, or your insurance company), and as soon as someone is available, a customer service agent from that company calls you. I don't know how the magic wheels work, and I haven't asked. All I know is that I rarely sit on hold anymore.

- **Fetch and Operator:** Fetch and Operator are just two examples of websites that do all your shopping for you. You simply download the free app, tell it what you want, and it finds the item for you at the lowest possible price.

I could go on and on, but you get the idea: Delegate the things you don't want to do or don't need to do, and you will free up tons of time.

5. Be Smart with E-mail

I receive more than a hundred e-mails an hour. No joke.

Aside from giving virtual assistants access to some of my e-mail addresses to manually filter them, unsubscribe from junk, and forward to me only what requires my personal attention, I follow several other rules with e-mail:

- All push notifications for e-mail are turned off on my phone and computer. This means I get e-mail only when I actually check my mail—no annoying rings or dings telling me that I have a life-altering offer from Groupon.

- I check e-mail only three times per day: 9 a.m., noon, and 7 p.m. If people have to send me something important enough to warrant my personal attention before then, they probably have my cell phone number and can call me. The only exceptions to this rule are two special e-mail folders that I set up for messages from my operations manager, my virtual assistants, and my private clients. I check those folders more frequently while blocking e-mail from other sources.

- I have more than thirty folders in Gmail, which is what I use for managing e-mail. Every message that comes in has a "rule" associated with it that sends it to its specific folder, based on either the sender or a keyword in the body of the message. Newsletters go to the Newsletter folder. Shopping deals go into the Deals folder. E-mails from QuickandDirtyTips.com go into the QAndD folder. E-mails from my operations manager, Matt, go into the Matt folder. So when I finally do get around to checking e-mail, I know which folders to prioritize and can quickly delete and empty others.

- I use two plug-ins: Inbox Pause and Boomerang. Inbox Pause allows me to pause my inbox so that I can't even see if new e-mails have come in until I decide to unpause. Boomerang allows me to avoid a hodgepodge of e-mails flying back and forth by giving me the option to write an e-mail but select a later time for it to be sent, such as four hours later, the next day, or the next week.

- I use Text Expander, which saves my fingers and keyboard by allowing me to associate custom keyboard shortcuts with sentences that I frequently type. For example, Alt+P automatically writes the sentence "Great question! I can answer in a future podcast if you ask your question via audio by going to Speakpipe. com/BenGreenfield."

- If you use Apple Mail, you can use a program called Mailhub to do most of these tasks. It allows you to file, create new mailboxes, and delete or assign actions to your e-mail effortlessly without interrupting your workflow. If you suffer from e-mail overload, I highly recommend using Mailhub or Gmail.

6. Eliminate Distractions

When I'm working, I'm like a horse wearing blinders. In other words:

- My phone is in airplane mode or silent mode, or, if I'm expecting an important call, push notifications are turned off so that nothing comes in from Facebook, Twitter, etc.

- As mentioned earlier, e-mails are in manual-retrieve mode only.

- Any browser windows that enable pop-up notifications, such as Facebook messages, are closed.

- I wear headphones. I find music or podcasts distracting while I'm working, but I wear headphones anyway—especially if I'm working in public. It makes people far less likely to interrupt you, and if they do interrupt, you can pretend that you don't hear them.

Be ruthless in guarding your time and eliminating distractions. Learn how to say no. Do high-intensity work intervals, then take a break when necessary or when you've run out of creative energy. Then recharge and return. That's the way I do it.

7. Avoid Snacking

As I point out in the article "Diet Myth News Flash: Snacking Will Not Boost Your Metabolism," it is a complete nutritional fallacy that frequent snacking keeps your metabolism elevated or is healthier than eating three square meals a day.

I used to be the guy who arrived at work toting a yogurt, some baby carrots and sugar snap peas, an apple, a bag of nuts, a salad, and a small sandwich. And then I realized that my entire day was focused on food and taking breaks to eat.

Frequently interrupting tasks to visit the vending machine, make yourself a smoothie, snag some trail mix, or make another cup of coffee or tea is distracting, and all those mini-breaks add up to a significant loss in productivity. Plus, your brain runs better on fatty-acid ketones than it does on frequent surges of glucose.

So ditch snacking. My standby is a glass of soda water and some gum to chomp on. With that strategy, combined with the fat adaptation tips outlined in the nutrition section of this book, I can pound away on a project for five or six hours without eating.

8. Aggregate Content

Have you ever found yourself trapped in the Internet quicksand of reading all the latest news, interesting articles, shocking stories, and anything else that happens to come through Twitter, Facebook, or your e-mail? Before long, an hour of burning your eyeballs with your browser has gone by, and you've achieved nothing at all.

So I aggregate content and ignore everything else. An aggregate is a collection of items that form a total quantity. This chapter is a perfect example. I've aggregated ten tips for you that work. You could read just this chapter and ignore everything else, and you'd literally double your productivity. Alternatively, you could go and Google "productivity tips," and you'd certainly find many, many more tips, but you'd also get sucked down a rabbit hole of reading, reading, reading. Make sense?

So think of aggregating like making your own newspaper or magazine with only the things that you want to see, and nothing else. Here's how I aggregate:

- I use Feedly, a news-aggregator application that works on your iPhone, Kindle, and pretty much any web browser and mobile device running iOS or Android. I plug the address of any blog I want to follow into Feedly, and my Feedly window shows up every morning with a list of the latest posts on the blogs I've selected— without my needing to visit those blogs or get distracted by going to a site that also aggregates content (such as Alltop) but doesn't feature content laser-targeted to what I personally want to see each day. Using Feedly, I subscribe to about thirty health, fitness, nutrition, technology, and marketing blogs and ignore everything else. For me, that's about forty-five minutes of reading each day.

- I also use Stone Hearth News, a news feed that goes straight to my e-mail and selectively tracks and reproduces fresh and reliable news and information about health, medicine, and science. And I rely on bloggers who surf the Internet and save me the work by finding cool, cutting-edge articles that appeal to me (kind of like I do on Twitter for my followers, but in more than 140 characters). This includes the Suppversity blog, Examine.com's *Research Digest,* Chris Kresser's *RoundUp,* Mark Sisson's *Weekend Link Love,* Alan Aragon's *Research Review,* and SaveYourself.ca's *Microblog.*

9. Start with the Hard Stuff

In the podcast episode titled "Is It OK to Be Addicted to Exercise?" (BenGreenfieldFitness.com/addict), Mishka Shubaly mentioned that he starts every day with his run because, for him, that is the most mentally difficult, physically draining, and stressful part of the day.

I'm the exact opposite of Mishka. For me, runs are liberating and stress-relieving, so I do them later in the day when I have slightly less energy and need a pick-me-up. However, what's hard for me or requires a great deal of my mental or physical willpower and energy includes:

- Taking my morning heart-rate-variability measurements
- Doing yoga and meditation
- Foam rolling and mobility work
- And (believe it or not) writing and creating content

So I do all these things the very first thing in the morning, before I even think about accomplishing any other tasks that I may find easier, more appealing, or less physically or mentally demanding, such as checking e-mail, doing social media work, cleaning my desk, or even eating breakfast.

If you really want to get scientific with this concept, you can even split tasks into "creative" tasks and "productive" tasks and do those tasks at the time of day that allows you to do them best. I explain exactly how to do this in "Four Steps to Getting More Done During Your Peak Time of Day" at BenGreenfieldFitness.com/4steps.

But for now, just think about what's hardest for you to do, and get it done first. Then move on to easier, less draining activities. There is one important caveat: If I'm about to sit down to write a monster article, I will quickly review any e-mails in important folders to ensure that I don't have any "fires" to put out. But I'm careful that this quick review doesn't turn into a Facebook or Twitter rabbit hole.

10. Keep a Clear Mind

Call me stupid or simple, but I have a hard time juggling multiple ideas, concepts, or reminders in my head at one time—such as "charge my bike battery," "remember to read the book about low-back pain," "check out the new website that scans your car keys," and so on.

Instead, I do my best work with a 100 percent clean and clear mind. So I write down everything (and put it in the appropriate bucket, of course), and then it's out of my mind and I can focus on the task at hand. To achieve this, I use the following tools:

- **Evernote:** Evernote is a suite of software and services designed for note-taking and archiving. A "note" can be a piece of formatted text, a full web page or a web page excerpt, a photo, a voice memo, or a handwritten "ink" note. Notes can also have file attachments. Notes can be sorted into folders, then tagged, annotated, edited, given comments, searched, and exported as part of a notebook. Since Evernote syncs to my iPhone, Kindle, MacBook, and any computer that I happen to use to access the Internet, it essentially functions as my second brain.

- **SendtoReader:** I use SendtoReader to deliver articles to my Kindle Fire so I can read them later, at my convenience, rather than dropping everything I'm doing and getting distracted by some brand-new article in the *New York Times* about fecal transplants for healing gut issues. It works like this: Say I come across an article on Feedly that is a bit too long and complex for me to read at the time. I use SendtoReader to send the article to my Kindle, then check it out later, like when I'm on an airplane or relaxing on the patio in the evening. (Reading articles on my bright laptop screen is typically the last thing I want to be doing at the end of a workday because I associate my laptop with "work," but my Kindle is for "leisure and learning.")

- **BusyCal:** BusyCal is the ultimate calendar app for Mac, packed with powerful time-saving tools in a friendly, easy-to-use package. It supports iCloud, Google Calendar, and other "CalDAV" servers, enabling you to sync and share your calendars with other computers running BusyCal or the built-in calendar app on Macs, iPhones, and iPads. It beats the pants off the basic iCal that comes with the Mac and allows me to quickly schedule meetings and events, then get them out of my mind as fast as possible. If you're not using a Mac, you should be, but in the meantime, you can find some BusyCal alternatives for Windows at BeyondTrainingBook.com/cals.

- **FollowUpThen.com:** I often used to send an e-mail to which I needed a timely reply and then spend the next few days wondering if the e-mail was delivered, if the recipient read it, if I needed to follow up, etc. When you have dozens of such e-mails rattling around in your head, it can become quite distracting. With

FollowUpThen, I cc an e-mail address such as 30days@followupthen.com or sep302015@followupthen.com. Then, on my specified date, FollowUpThen automatically sends a reminder to either me, the recipient, or both, depending on the setting I choose.

And of course, I keep a pen and pad at my bedside. If you're like me and occasionally wake up at 4:30 a.m. with random thoughts/ideas/brainstorms bouncing around in your head, you'd be surprised at how quickly you can get back to sleep if you simply jot them down and forget about them until later. I would use the notes function on my iPhone, but as you learned in chapter 10, that brief blast of blue light can disrupt your sleep cycle for hours, so paper and pen is best.

What I've just shared with you are my "biggest wins" when it comes to saving time and producing as much as possible in the least amount of time. If you are hungry for more, you may want to visit a few sites that I personally follow:

- **Lifehacker:** Tips, tricks, and downloads for getting things done. Warning: Don't get sucked into reading all the content—just find topics of interest to you.

- **Less Doing:** The blog of lifehacker Ari Meisel, who was a guest on my podcast episode "How to Biohack Your Workouts, Your Diet & Your Life to Get More Done in Less Time."

- **43 Folders:** A website devoted to helping you find the time and focus to do your best creative work.

- **Dumb Little Man:** Tips for life, including suggestions relating to money, happiness, and relationships.

- **The 4-Hour Life:** Even more ways to simplify and automate your life, built on concepts from Tim Ferriss's book *The 4-Hour Workweek*.

In the next and final section of this book, you're going to take everything you've learned until now and blow it out of the water by fixing, enhancing, and growing your brain. You're going to learn the two ways your brain malfunctions and exactly what you can do about it, and the best ways to protect your precious brain neurons, get rid of brain inflammation, become smarter, gain focus, and increase IQ as quickly as possible.

After all, if you're going to go beyond training and simply being a "good exerciser," you want to maximize the potential of your body's most amazing organ, right?

Additional resources, helpful links, scientific references, websites, and surprise bonuses for this chapter are available at BeyondTrainingBook.com/Chapter20. Enjoy.

5

THE BRAIN

CHAPTER 21
Two Ways Your Brain Breaks and Exactly What You Can Do About It: Fixing Neurotransmitter Dysfunction

Have you ever woken up and stumbled out of bed to your computer, or perhaps even pulled your laptop or smartphone out from beside the bed, and launched straight into work, even though you knew deep down that it would be healthier to take a moment to relax?

Have you ever opened the refrigerator, seen a dizzying array of fresh vegetables and healthy proteins that might require some labor to pull into a meal, and proceeded to grab a dark chocolate bar and a jar of nut butter instead?

Have you ever been in the middle of a race, such as a triathlon or marathon, and realized that you had absolutely no clue how much you'd eaten, how much you'd hydrated, or even what mile or kilometer marker you were at?

Have you ever been in the middle of a workout, like a long run, and suddenly started walking because your brain seemed to simply shut down?

Blame your busy life, blame your muscles, or blame your gut, but the stark truth is that each of those scenarios is a perfect example of what can happen when your mind is not properly tuned and your brain is out of order.

So now you're going to discover the two ways your brain malfunctions and exactly what you can do about it. Then you're going to get an amazing array of tools, tricks, and tips to tune your mind, hack your brain, boost your IQ, enhance your focus, and zoom into the coveted, effortless zone of peak performance.

The Central-Governor Model of Fatigue

When it comes to achieving peak physical performance or pushing yourself to the extreme limits of endurance exhaustion, what do you think is the most important part of your physiology? Your muscles? Your heart? Your lungs? The surprising answer is "None of the above."

The ultimate arbiter of fatigue is actually situated right between your ears. That's right: It's your brain.

That the brain is the main cause of fatigue is a theory I first encountered when I interviewed Dr. Timothy Noakes in the podcast episode "How You Can Use the 'Central Governor' to Tap into Your Muscle's Hidden Potential." In this episode, Dr. Noakes explained how being tired can be all in your mind, and that you can actually trick your body into exercising longer, going harder, or lifting heavier if you "distract" it with techniques like counting to 20, 50, or 100 over and over again; focusing on a small, intermediate goal like the next telephone pole, street sign, or repetition; listening to a repetitive music beat; engaging in repetitive self-talk; or even using visualization exercises before a big workout or event.

What Noakes calls the central-governor model of fatigue is based on the fact that if your brain or your heart runs out of oxygen or is subjected to sustained periods of hypoxia (low oxygen), you can die or suffer permanent damage to these organs. So your brain (the central governor) is wired to limit how hard, how heavy, or how long you can go by reducing your nervous system's recruitment of muscle fibers. And this reduced recruitment causes the sensation of fatigue. Your brain simply says, "Stop," and your body says, "OK."

It's possible that there's more to fatigue than low oxygen, and that it may depend on the amount of ketones (fatty acids) or trace amounts of glucose available to vital organs—so you can think of the central-governor model as a kind of survival mechanism in which your brain makes a conscious effort to limit energy expenditure in order to save fuel for other precious organs, such as your heart, your lungs, and your brain.

Figure 21-1 shows the vicious cycle that can ensue when your brain begins to shut down blood circulation to your heart and your muscles.

FIGURE 21-1

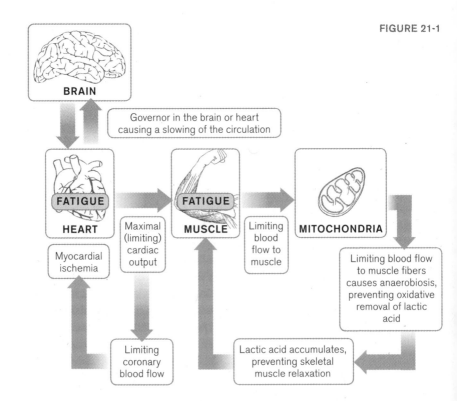

Decision-Making Fatigue

Interestingly, the fatigue brought on by your central governor can be compounded if you are distracted by other details, such as problem solving, the complexity of an exercise or movement, or anxiety about work, family, or life in general.

Dr. Samuele Marcora, a British sports scientist, says that for this reason, fatigue can be as much a perception of your mind as a physiological state. The anterior cingulate cortex in your brain is responsible for controlling your heart rate and breathing. But it's also involved in making complex decisions, paying attention to details, and doing things like figuring out whether you are supposed to be using your right leg or your left leg, deciphering a spreadsheet, or avoiding distractions from the commotion around you. In other words, the more you require your brain to do at any given time, the faster it's probably going to fatigue—regardless of how fit your muscles, lungs, or heart are.

Dr. Marcora argues that this kind of fatigue is a simple matter of conflict resolution—a struggle between the part of your brain that wants you to quit and the part that wants you to keep going—and that the more "decision-making" fatigue you're subjected to during exercise, the faster you're going to fail physically.

This notion that fatigue is more a state of mind than an actual physiological state makes perfect sense when you watch runners who seem to be on the brink of complete physical breakdown, who look as if they can't run another step, then suddenly sprint all-out for the last 200 to 300 yards of a 5K race.

Shocking the Brain into Submission

A 2012 study on cyclists adds even more credence to the idea that your brain is ultimately responsible for fatigue. In this study, Brazilian sports scientists used a noninvasive form of brain stimulation called transcranial direct-current stimulation to apply a tiny electrical current to the brain's cortex[6]. Remember, the cortex is the primary culprit when it comes to exercise fatigue[5]. The theory was that this stimulation would briefly interrupt the way neurons in the cortex communicate with one another and distract the brain from shutting down the body. Of course, there was also a control group of cyclists who had electrodes attached but didn't get any stimulation.

So what were the results of this brain tweaking? After twenty minutes of real or fake brain stimulation, the cyclists completed an all-out ride to exhaustion. Sure enough, the cyclists who got the electrical stimulation had significantly lower heart rates, lower perceived rates of exertion, and a 4 percent greater power output (that may sound small, but it's huge for a cyclist).

The researchers noted that increased performance may be caused by more than mere "distraction" of the brain, but rather by a mingling of pleasure and pain centers in the brain. This is because the right side of the cortex is strongly linked to feelings of pain and physical exertion, while the left side is linked to pleasant feelings and emotions that arise when you see someone smile or hear your favorite song or cuddle up with a loved one.

What Is the Zone?

Interestingly, this feeling of pleasure or happiness in the presence of physical exertion is very similar to what is often described as being "in the zone."

In psychology, being in the zone is a mental state in which someone performing an activity is fully immersed in a feeling of energized focus, complete involvement, and enjoyment in the process[7]. When athletes enter the zone during physical performance, they often achieve a personal best while describing their performance as effortless. And the zone is not just an "airy-fairy" state: In sports performance labs, the 8- to 12-hertz alpha brain waves you learned about in chapter 10 have been shown to be correlated with these zonelike states of relaxed alertness.

Ultimately, the takeaway from Dr. Noakes, Dr. Marcora, and those crazy Brazilian cyclist-electrocuting scientists is this: If your brain is healthy enough to optimally process information and communicate with your body, and trained enough to resist distractions, not only are you going to perform better, but you are also going to equip your brain to achieve that level of effortless performance called the zone.

Let's say you want to override your central governor, distract your brain, and enter the coveted zone so that you can push your body and mind beyond what you imagine you're capable of achieving. And let's say you want to do it without wearing a giant cap full of electrodes and undergoing mild shock therapy.

Well, in the same way that you must fix your gut before giving it the thousands of calories necessary for fueling huge amounts of physical activity, you must also fix your brain before asking it to allow your body to perform amazing physical feats. So let's dig into the two ways your brain breaks and exactly what you can do about it (see Figure 21-2).

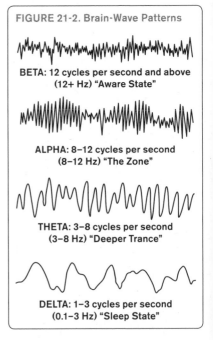

FIGURE 21-2. Brain-Wave Patterns

BETA: 12 cycles per second and above
(12+ Hz) "Aware State"

ALPHA: 8–12 cycles per second
(8–12 Hz) "The Zone"

THETA: 3–8 cycles per second
(3–8 Hz) "Deeper Trance"

DELTA: 1–3 cycles per second
(0.1–3 Hz) "Sleep State"

THE TWO WAYS
YOUR BRAIN BREAKS DOWN

As you now know, your brain is the primary determinant of where your true performance capabilities lie—not to mention that a well-functioning, optimally tuned brain is also pretty darn important when it comes to your quality of life, your work productivity, your communication skills, your problem-solving abilities, and much more.

Unfortunately, most of us walk around with damaged, inflamed, poorly functioning, and poorly trained brains. This is usually because of a combination of two factors:

1. Neurotransmitter problems

2. HPA-axis dysfunction

If you address both of these issues, your brain tissue, nerve cells, and neurons will be healthy enough to process information and seamlessly communicate with your body during a workout or race, healthy enough for you to train your brain to resist becoming distracted by random e-mails or tempting foods, and healthy enough for your mind to allow you to experience huge mental and physical performance breakthroughs.

So let's learn how to fix these issues.

How Nerves Communicate

Before you can understand neurotransmitter problems, you need to understand how your nerves communicate with one another. I'm not going to give you a comprehensive primer on the nervous system, but it's important for you to know why neurotransmitters are so dang important.

Like the wires in your home's electrical system, nerve cells make connections with one another in tiny circuits called neural pathways. But unlike the wires in your home, these nerve cells do not touch, but instead come very close together at a junction-like synapse (see Figure 21-3). At the synapse, the two nerve cells are separated by a small gap called a synaptic cleft. The sending neuron is called the presynaptic cell (in this case, an axon), while the receiving neuron is called the postsynaptic cell (in this case, a dendrite).

In a one-way direction across the synapse from the presynaptic cell to the postsynaptic cell, your body sends chemical messages using neurotransmitters (which you first learned about in chapter 4, when discovering how to enhance your power and speed). This is called synaptic transmission.

Let's look at an example of synaptic transmission that uses a neurotransmitter you may have heard of: serotonin.

In this case, the presynaptic cell makes serotonin from the amino acid tryptophan and then packages the serotonin into vesicles located in the end terminals. When a

FIGURE 21-3

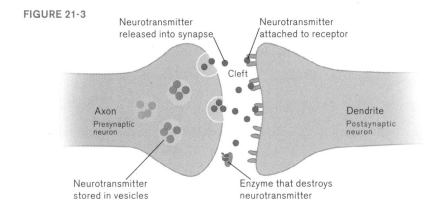

Neurotransmitter released into synapse

Neurotransmitter attached to receptor

Cleft

Axon
Presynaptic neuron

Dendrite
Postsynaptic neuron

Neurotransmitter stored in vesicles

Enzyme that destroys neurotransmitter

signal called an "action potential" arrives from your brain, that signal passes through presynaptic cells into the end terminals[3].

At this point, when the signal arrives, the serotonin is released and passes across the synaptic cleft, where it binds with special proteins called receptors on the outside of the postsynaptic cell. If enough serotonin binds to those receptors, a threshold level is reached, and the action potential is propagated in that cell and moves on to the next cell. In the case of something like your muscles moving, the action potential eventually reaches skeletal muscle fibers and causes a contraction.

So that the nerve doesn't stay in a constant "turned on" state, the remaining serotonin molecules in the synaptic cleft are destroyed by special enzymes in the cleft called monoamine oxidase and catechol-O-methyltransferase. Some serotonin also gets taken back up by specific transporters on the presynaptic cell (this is called "reuptake"). All this enables the nerve signal to be turned "off" and readies the synapse to receive another action potential. (See Figure 21-4.)

Of course, in addition to serotonin, there are many other types of neurotransmitters, including acetylcholine, norepinephrine, dopamine, and gamma-aminobutyric acid (GABA). But let's say you have a neurotransmitter deficit of serotonin, which would compromise synaptic transmission of any nerve signals in your body that are dependent on serotonin. Similar to a deficit of other neurotransmitters, such as norepinephrine, epinephrine, and dopamine, a serotonin deficit can result in depression, appetite cravings, brain fog, low IQ, anxiety, panic attacks, insomnia, eating disorders, migraines, and distractibility or ADD.

Millions of people walk around every day with some kind of neurotransmitter deficiency or suboptimal nerve-cell communication. You've probably experienced at least one of these issues, right? The good news is that you don't have to check yourself into a mental institution. Here are eight ways you can fix these kinds of neurotransmitter problems yourself.

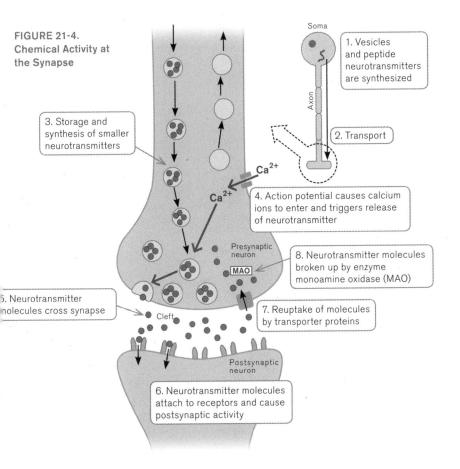

FIGURE 21-4.
Chemical Activity at the Synapse

1. Vesicles and peptide neurotransmitters are synthesized

2. Transport

3. Storage and synthesis of smaller neurotransmitters

4. Action potential causes calcium ions to enter and triggers release of neurotransmitter

5. Neurotransmitter molecules cross synapse

6. Neurotransmitter molecules attach to receptors and cause postsynaptic activity

7. Reuptake of molecules by transporter proteins

8. Neurotransmitter molecules broken up by enzyme monoamine oxidase (MAO)

Soma

Axon

Ca^{2+}

Ca^{2+}

Presynaptic neuron

MAO

Cleft

Postsynaptic neuron

1. Taper Off or Stop Taking Antidepressants

Prozac, Sarafem, Paxil, Zoloft, Celexa, Lexapro, Effexor, Cymbalta, Pristiq—the list of popular antidepressant drugs goes on and on, with hundreds of millions of prescriptions handed out and billions of dollars in sales each year.

I wouldn't even be talking about this issue if I hadn't done consults with many very active individuals who are either on antidepressants, depressed, or showing signs of depression. Perhaps it's the nature of the beast—as physically active people we tend to rely on exercise for a high, and when that high is missing or we're not fulfilled by it anymore, we tend to get down. And at that point, antidepressants may seem like an attractive solution.

Now, I'm not a doctor, and I'm not recommending that you quit cold turkey if you're on antidepressants, but if you want to gradually get off these medications, you should pay attention to the other seven ways to address neurotransmitter issues.

Here's why antidepressants are such a problem: They work either by increasing brain levels of serotonin or by blocking reuptake of serotonin. That's why most of them are called SSRIs, or selective serotonin reuptake inhibitors.

These SSRIs cause a short-term "flooding" of the brain with serotonin, as well as a very fast degrading or breaking down of serotonin as it is left to hang around in the synaptic cleft (see Figure 21-5).

As a result, not only is more and more serotonin eventually required as serotonin receptors become desensitized to the constant flow of neurotransmitters, but there is also less naturally available serotonin as your biology begins to rely on external sources[1]. When you do release your own serotonin, it winds up getting broken down far more quickly than normal, because the enzymes in the synaptic cleft have been "trained" to break down serotonin rapidly.

So not only do you need constantly greater dosages of antidepressants, but you also end up depleting 40 to 60 percent of the serotonin receptors in your brain! In addition, the serotonin receptors in your liver, kidneys, and colon can be damaged by antidepressants, which affects your delicate gut-brain balance and your regulation of appetite. It's a vicious cycle!

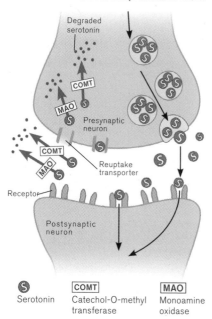

FIGURE 21-5.
How Antidepressants Work

Serotonin | COMT Catechol-O-methyl transferase | MAO Monoamine oxidase

There's a great deal of evidence that antidepressants do not really work well anyway. Meta-analyses of antidepressants have revealed that SSRIs have no clinically meaningful advantage over a placebo, and claims that antidepressants are more effective in more severe cases of depression have little evidence to support them. The few studies that have shown antidepressants to have a small degree of superiority over placebos were poorly designed. You can read more about the flaws in these studies in an excellent article I've linked to on the web page for this chapter.

Ultimately, antidepressants have not been convincingly shown to affect the long-term outcome of depression or suicide rates, and chronic exposure to SSRIs can actually make you feel apathetic or less engaged in life.

2. Use Moderate Stimulants

Low-dose caffeine can improve mental performance and protect against Alzheimer's, so you don't need to avoid caffeine entirely (unless you are in a state of adrenal fatigue). But like antidepressants, high doses of caffeine, ephedrine, ephedra, guarana, Ritalin, and other central nervous system stimulants can flood the brain with neurotransmitters, creating neurotransmitter resistance or long-term receptor damage[8].

There's a reason that I drink no more than eight to ten ounces of black coffee a day and switch to decaf for at least one week every couple months. People who frequently consume caffeinated coffee, tea, soda, or energy drinks actually change their brain's chemistry and physical characteristics over time. Because it is both water- and fat-soluble, caffeine can easily cross your blood-brain barrier, and as you dump more and more caffeine into your body, your brain cells grow more receptors for a neurotransmitter called adenosine.

Adenosine causes feelings of tiredness, but as you can see in Figure 21-6, the structure of caffeine closely resembles adenosine—so caffeine can easily fit into your brain cells' receptors for adenosine. With its receptors constantly plugged up by caffeine, adenosine can no longer bind to those receptors and cause the feeling of tiredness[9]. Unfortunately, your body's response is to create more and more adenosine receptors—so you eventually need more and more caffeine to block the feeling of tiredness—and over time, you build up a tolerance.

FIGURE 21-6

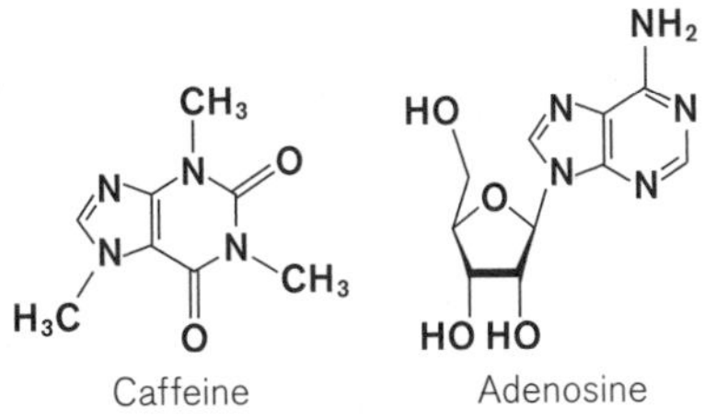

Caffeine

Adenosine

The good news is that to kick a caffeine habit and reset your adenosine receptors, you need to take only a seven- to twelve-day caffeine break, which is why I recommend taking a weeklong hiatus from coffee and similar stimulants every couple months.

3. Avoid Toxin Exposure

Whether it's mycotoxins from moldy coffee, the fragrance of your or your partner's cologne wafting into your nostrils, or the air freshener hanging in your car, toxins affect the production of neurotransmitters and sensitivity to neurotransmitters, causing brain damage, brain fog, and fuzzy thinking.

It's probably not necessary for me reiterate everything in chapter 18—just follow the rules there. But to refresh your mind, a few of the biggies are:

- Eat organic fruits and vegetables whenever possible (or wash them in a water-and-vinegar solution).
- Use natural cleaning products (lemon juice, vinegar, baking soda, etc.).
- Use natural personal-care products (avoid parabens, dyes, fragrances, etc.).
- Use home air and water filters.
- Go to a holistic dentist.
- Get a HEPA filter installed in your home.

Once you begin to make these changes, you'll find it interesting that when you do encounter an attack against your neurotransmitters, such as walking through the perfume section of a store at the mall, you'll be extremely sensitive and notice it almost immediately. It's important to pay attention to your body in these situations. If something looks, tastes, or smells synthetic, avoid it.

4. Avoid Sensory Overload

Twenty-first-century sensory overload—in the form of rapid visual and auditory effects from television, movies, computer games, electronic monitors flickering faster than the eye can detect, radio and electromagnetic field (EMF) waves, fluorescent lighting, a hurried lifestyle, and excessive work—requires your brain to constantly modulate these higher levels of sensory bombardment than it ever would have encountered in an ancestral setting.

Your brain has to calm itself down from all these stimuli using its own precious supply of calming, inhibitory neurotransmitters, such as serotonin and GABA. This overstimulation has a significant impact on neurotransmitters and neurotransmitter receptors. So consider the following:

- Do you listen to loud music while you're exercising?
- Do you constantly watch fast-moving, exciting, or violent movies or play violent video games, especially before bed?
- Do you play lots of computer games, often for long periods (several hours)?
- Do you spend much of your day staring at a computer monitor?
- Is music always playing in the background?
- Is your home or workplace illuminated with artificial, fluorescent lighting?

If so, go back and read the section in chapter 18 on mitigating the effects of this EMF. Do not be afraid of silence, quiet, and rest. Do not be afraid to unplug. Take time to breathe.

5. Fix Your Gut

As you learned in chapter 15, your gut is your second brain.

The enteric nervous system in your gut uses more than thirty neurotransmitters, just like your brain; in fact, 95 percent of the body's serotonin is in the gut. This makes sense when you consider that in the twenty-seven feet from your esophagus to your anus, there are about 100 million neurons, more than in either your spinal cord or your entire peripheral nervous system!

This also explains why irritable bowel syndrome, which afflicts nearly every active individual now and then, develops in part from too much serotonin in the gut—a neurotransmitter imbalance. (As you can probably imagine, this is why antidepressants can cause serious gut issues.)

Not only does your gut lining produce neurotransmitters, but the billions of bacteria living in your gut also churn out neurotransmitters. So if your gut lining is damaged or your gut flora is out of balance, you are at serious risk for neurotransmitter deficiencies and imbalances.

The best ways to address these gut-brain issues are spelled out in chapter 15: Listen to your body, test, and fix the problem.

6. Replace Building Blocks

Neurotransmitters are composed primarily of amino acids, B vitamins, and minerals. A deficiency of any of these three crucial compounds can leave you with inadequate neurotransmitter building blocks.

As you learned in chapter 5, some of the highest-quality amino acid sources are grass-fed beef, wild salmon, eggs from pastured chickens, raw organic dairy, almonds and almond butter, quinoa, and spirulina or chlorella. I've found that many people who struggle with poor sleep or lack of motivation tied to neurotransmitter issues benefit from the use of essential amino acids. When I'm about to do a workout that I know is going to tax my brain with intense focus or competition, I usually take five to ten grams of NatureAminos, which is an optimally balanced blend of all eight essential amino acids.

For the nervous system to synthesize and circulate the neurotransmitters formed by amino acid precursors, you need to have adequate B-complex vitamins: vitamins B_6, B_{12}, and folate are especially important in nerve metabolism. Excellent food sources of vitamin B_6 include bell peppers, turnip greens, and spinach; excellent sources of folate include spinach, parsley, broccoli, beets, turnip and mustard greens, asparagus, romaine lettuce, calf's liver, and lentils; excellent sources of B_{12} include calf's liver and red snapper. For vitamin B supplementation, I recommend either a liposomal vitamin B_{12} spray or an antioxidant–vitamin B powder blend.

You'll get very good doses of minerals from a well-balanced diet that includes a broad spectrum of the real, nutrient-dense foods listed in chapter 11. But if you sweat a lot or are under a lot of exercise or lifestyle stress (remember that adrenal stress depletes minerals), you should also consume a mineral-rich source of protein, such as a goat-milk-based protein powder (goat protein is higher in minerals) and a daily dose of either a trace-liquid-mineral supplement or liberal use of a high-quality salt, such as Himalayan sea salt.

7. Neurotransmitter Repletion

Often, simply eating adequate protein or taking essential-amino-acid supplements is not enough, such as in cases of depression, insomnia, or severe lack of motivation. In these situations, neurotransmitter repletion via amino acid therapy can be effective but ideally should be done under medical supervision, because if you don't use the proper ratios you can make neurotransmitter imbalances and your issues worse— even if you feel better temporarily.

One example of neurotransmitter repletion with an amino acid blend that can be helpful for insomnia, depression, or lack of motivation is taking 3,000 milligrams of tyrosine and 300 milligrams of 5-HTP, split into three daily doses. There are several supplements that contain tyrosine and 5-HTP in the exact ratios you need, including TravaCor by NeuroScience (my preferred blend), Neuro-5-HTP Plus by Biotics, and CraveArrest for Designs for Health.

Another protocol for neurotransmitter repletion is to use a supplement called NeuroReplete to balance catecholamines and increase serotonin, then CysReplete to increase catecholamine synthesis and D5 Mucuna to increase dopamine synthesis. This is a little more sophisticated than the previous options, so keep reading for a warning and disclaimer. Contrary to what you may think, you can find these products yourself and don't necessarily need a medical practitioner to order them for you. I've put helpful links on the web page for this chapter.

You shouldn't attempt repletion without knowing what you're doing. For example, taking only 5-HTP or improperly balanced 5-HTP can deplete dopamine. Taking only L-dopa (from something like D5 Mucuna) or improperly balanced L-dopa depletes serotonin, sulfur-based amino acids, L-tryptophan, and tyrosine. High doses of sulfur-based amino acids can deplete serotonin and dopamine.

Dr. Daniel Kalish is an expert when it comes to neurotransmitter-repletion therapy, and I highly recommend checking out the Kalish Institute website (kalishinstitute. com), reading *The Kalish Method,* or speaking with a licensed Kalish practitioner before experimenting with this stuff. Another very good resource for neurotransmit-. ter repletion can be found at neuroassist.com.

You can test your neurotransmitter levels to see where you might be deficient. I recommend the NeuroAdrenal Expanded test, available from DirectLabs. It is a salivary screen for the hormones DHEA and cortisol, along with the urinary neurotransmitters epinephrine, norepinephrine, dopamine, DOPAC, serotonin, 5HIAA, glycine, taurine, GABA, glutamate, PEA, and histamine.

Finally, if you are interested in how to combine a highly accurate, gold-standard form of urinary neurotransmitter testing with neurotransmitter repletion, check out DBS Labs (labdbs.com) or the neuroendocrine profile at BenGreenfieldFitness.com/ directlabs.

8. Lube Your Nerves with Fats

In chapter 4, you learned that one way to enhance the speed with which your brain communicates with your body is to care for the health of your nerves. Your nerves are wrapped in myelin sheaths, and a diet for a healthy nervous system should include the nutrients that support the formation of these sheaths as well as the health of the nervous system as a whole. After all, it doesn't matter how many neurotransmitters you produce if they can't get their messages across because your myelin sheaths are damaged (see Figure 21-7).

For this reason, I not only advise that you follow the fat-percentage-intake recommendations in chapter 13, but also recommend a high intake of omega-3 fatty acids, especially docosahexaenoic acid (DHA). DHA is particularly important in building the myelin sheath structure and preventing the degradation and breakdown of nerve cells.

Flax seeds, walnuts, kale, collard greens, and winter squash are excellent sources of omega-3 fatty acids, but the amount of DHA actually absorbed from seeds, nuts, and plants may be relatively low. Sources of more readily available omega-3 fatty acids and DHA include salmon, sardines, cloves, grass-fed beef, halibut, shrimp, cod, tuna (don't overdo this one, as it tends to be a source of heavy-metal contamination), and (especially for vegans or vegetarians) algae-based DHA supplements, such as EN-ERGYbits or marine phytoplankton. Other foods that support neuronal membranes and

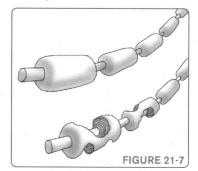

FIGURE 21-7

myelin sheaths, because they are high in oleic acids, include olive oil, almonds, pecans, macadamia nuts, and avocados. So there you have it: Avoid antidepressants, modulate stimulants, avoid toxins, avoid sensory overload, fix your gut, replace building blocks, eat healthy fats, and, if necessary, replete with neurotransmitter therapy. You now know how to make sure that your nerve cells are highly tuned communicators, ready to listen and respond appropriately to commands from your brain. Not surprisingly, many of the strategies in this chapter are similar to those in chapter 4 and can be used not just to increase focus, decrease distractions, and feel better but also to enhance power and speed, which are highly dependent on the nervous system.

Fixing HPA-Axis Dysfunction

As you learned earlier in this chapter, there are two ways your brain can break down: neurotransmitter imbalances and HPA-axis dysfunction.

You already learned how to fix neurotransmitter deficits and imbalances. Now you're going to learn how to fix HPA-axis dysfunction. If you pay attention to and implement all these fixes, your brain will be 100 percent "tuned"—and you'll be primed for mental and physical performance breakthroughs, not to mention enhanced motivation, decreased distractions, and a better mood.

What Is HPA-Axis Dysfunction?

The HPA axis includes three specific parts of your body (see Figure 21-8):

1. The hypothalamus (part of your forebrain)
2. The pituitary gland (just below the hypothalamus)
3. The adrenal glands (at the top of the kidneys)

These three parts work together to regulate functions such as stress response, mood, digestion, immune system, libido, metabolism, and energy levels. Before understanding how to fix your HPA axis, it's important to understand how the axis works in the first place, so let's talk about the chemicals that your HSA axis depends on.

1. **Corticotropin-releasing hormone (CRH):** Also referred to as corticotropin-releasing factor (CRF), this hormone is produced and secreted by the hypothalamus in response to stress, and it then stimulates the pituitary gland to secrete adrenocorticotropic hormone. The more stressed your body is (from diet, lifestyle, work, or anything else), the more CRH your hypothalamus churns out.

2. **Adrenocorticotropic hormone (ACTH):** ACTH is released by the pituitary gland and travels to your kidneys to stimulate the adrenal glands to increase production of glucocorticoids.

3. **Glucocorticoids:** The glucocorticoids produced in the adrenal glands are steroids that regulate metabolic rate, inflammation, and immune response. You've already learned about the most well-known glucocorticoid: cortisol.

FIGURE 21-8

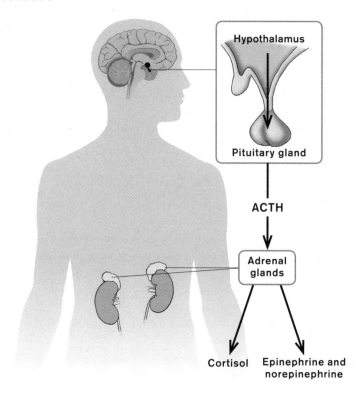

4. **Cortisol:** Cortisol is best known for activating your physical response to stress, including injury, lack of sleep, excessive exercise, anxiety, and depression. It prepares your body to withstand these triggers by stimulating norepinephrine (also known as noradrenaline) to activate your fight-or-flight response.

It's important to understand that the HPA axis operates on feedback loops. A feedback loop occurs when the output of a system in your body somehow loops back to that system as input and influences its functioning. A positive feedback loop increases that system's output; a negative feedback loop decreases it.

So let's look at how a feedback loop operates in the HPA axis—in this case with regard to cortisol. At the same time that cortisol activates your fight-or-flight stress response, it also sends a signal to your hypothalamus to inhibit CRH production and a signal to your pituitary gland to inhibit ACTH. In this feedback loop, cortisol is able to reduce norepinephrine activity, gradually calming you down—it's a well-functioning system of checks and balances[3].

In healthy people who don't have much stress, this entire HPA-axis feedback loop works in harmony. But when cortisol and norepinephrine are chronically overproduced, the HPA axis eventually becomes desensitized to the negative feedback telling it to "calm down," leading to chronic stress on the hypothalamus, pituitary gland, and adrenal glands (see Figure 21-9). Eventually, this leads to neural failure, which eventually causes the nasty adrenal fatigue issues discussed in chapters 6, 7, and 8. It is called HPA-axis dysregulation[5].

Interestingly, HPA-axis dysregulation is completely linked to neurotransmitter imbalance. For example, SSRIs can be very effective at treating panic issues because as serotonin levels rise, levels of norepinephrine fall. Of course, as you know, this is not the best way to treat stress, since you'll simply need higher and higher doses of antidepressants as time goes on and your body becomes desensitized to serotonin[2]. But it is a good way to point out the fact that you become better equipped to fix HPA-axis dysfunction as neurotransmitter production is enhanced.

FIGURE 21-9. HPA Axis

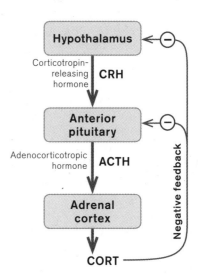

Four Ways to Fix HPA-Axis Dysfunction

Fortunately, you've already learned just about everything you need to know about how to address HPA-axis dysfunction, but I'm going to give you a quick review. If you address each of these components, your neural feedback loops will be balanced.

1. Destress

I like to think of myself as "stress selfish." In other words, I guard my brain like a mama bear guards her cub when it comes to shielding it from stress. I go to bed several minutes earlier than necessary so that when I wake up, I don't have to bolt upright out of bed and rush to my first task. If work gets extremely intense and I find myself breathing shallowly, I go for a walk or even lie down on the bed, the floor, or the couch and do several minutes of deep breathing. I purposefully avoid speaking with people from whom I get "negative energy." All these little steps add up to protecting my HPA axis.

What else can you do to destress?

Flip back to chapter 7. There you will find a big list of all the various daily stresses that can disrupt the HPA axis, from tight schedules to relationship conflicts to poorly designed training equipment or subpar training conditions.

In chapter 9, you learned that breathing, meditation, tai chi, yoga, coherence, a hobby, and high-quality sleep are all extremely effective ways to destress.

Go back and review those two chapters. Take stress seriously. Do not abuse your body, and your brain will thank you.

2. Avoid Excessive Exercise

Overtraining is one of the quickest paths to HPA-axis dysfunction, and it leads to many of the brain fog, mood, and irritability issues that many athletes, especially endurance athletes, complain about.

In my podcast interview "The Cost of Being a Bad-Ass—How to Cure Your Hormones with Dr. Sara Gottfried" (BenGreenfieldFitness.com/sara), Dr. Gottfried explains that overexercising chronically elevates cortisol levels and talks about what you can do about it. I spell this out in detail in chapters 6, 7, and 8.

If your cortisol levels are high from loads of exercise, revisit those chapters. Follow the recovery protocols, and consider supplementation with Chinese adaptogenic herbs such as TianChi or InnerPeace; plenty of electrolytes, preferably with liquid trace minerals or Himalayan sea salt; 2,000–5,000 milligrams of a whole-foods vitamin C source; and 4–6 grams a day of good fish oil that contains vitamin E with mixed tocopherols.

I also recommend that you check out the Greenfield Fitness Systems Hormone Pack (available at GreenfieldFitnessSystems.com), which I designed—putting together trace liquid minerals, fish oil, and TianChi—specifically to promote hormone stabilization and balance in a gentle and natural manner. If you've been overdoing it with exercise, this pack can help bring your HPA axis back into balance.

3. Shut Down Inflammation

When I wake up with a "fuzzy brain" (which can happen after a late night out, too much alcohol, or sleep disruption), one of the first things I do is pop 1,000 milligrams of EXOS curcumin, which is a highly absorbable form derived from curcumin phytosome and can rapidly shut down inflammation and mitigate the effect of a poor night's sleep on the HPA axis. Curcumin is a potent neural anti-inflammatory; you can even purchase it in powder form and add it to coffee or break open capsules to add to coffee.

Decreasing inflammation is a potent means of protecting and repairing the HPA axis. Using mice, researchers have experimented with a protein involved in inflammation in the hypothalamus called NF-kB. When NF-kB is switched off in the hypothalamus, the mice live about 20 percent longer[6]. On the flip side, increasing NF-kB not only accelerates aging but also decreases another important brain protein called GnRH. When less GnRH is present, fewer new brain cells are created, and aging is accelerated even more[1].

This is just one example of how inflammation can affect the HPA axis. Elevated cortisol levels can also cause systemic inflammation (and vice versa), which further aggravates the HPA axis.

As you learned in chapter 8, maximizing your intake of anti-inflammatory foods and minimizing pro-inflammatory foods is just one step toward controlling inflammation. From fish oil to cold thermogenesis to pulsed electromagnetic field therapy, there are a couple dozen other strategies in that chapter for decreasing inflammation. Most of those protocols work not only on the muscles but also on the HPA axis.

4. Sleep

In chapter 10, you learned that the only time your body repairs neurons and nerve cells is when you're sleeping—especially during deep-sleep stages between 2 a.m. and 6 a.m., when your body temperature decreases.

So if you're attempting to fix your HPA axis and you're not getting quality sleep, you're never going to be able to fully recover and repair. As a matter of fact, because of the crucial role that sleep plays in the health of your nervous system, getting adequate sleep is the single most important strategy you can employ to fix your brain and enhance your mental function.

Even if you incorporate all the biohacks I'm going to give you in the next chapter, you're never going to experience optimal nerve and brain performance if you aren't sleeping properly—and this is all the more true the night after a hard workout. In the same way that you need to be selfish with stress, you need to be selfish with sleep.

At this point, you shouldn't be surprised that the four best strategies to fix your HPA axis are to destress, avoid excessive exercise, shut down inflammation, and prioritize sleep. There's a reason these strategies appeared in the recovery chapter, too: The more you damage the body, the more fragile your brain becomes.

All four of the fixes you just learned about are interrelated and codependent, and if you get them all dialed in, your hypothalamic-pituitary-adrenal feedback loops will work with wonderful efficiency.

In the next chapter, you're going to get an amazing array of tools, tricks, and tips to tune your mind, hack your brain, boost your IQ, enhance your focus, and instantly get into the coveted, effortless zone of peak performance. I should also mention that if you really enjoyed the past two chapters, you should check out the excellent book *Why Isn't My Brain Working?* by Dr. Datis Kharrazian and some very good biohacking alternatives to antidepressants at BiohacksBlog.com.

Additional resources, websites, helpful links, scientific references, and surprise bonuses for this chapter are available at BeyondTrainingBook.com/Chapter21. Enjoy.

CHAPTER 22
Twenty-Eight Ways to Hack Your Brain: A Complete Guide to Enhancing Your Brainpower, Creativity, Focus, Motivation, and IQ

Let's say you've done a good job of fixing your brain. Your neurotransmitters are balanced, and your HPA axis is functioning properly. But now you want to take things to the next level. You want to experience better living through science. You want to be able to read books faster, converse with ease and intelligence, maximize your work productivity, and have laserlike focus and motivation during your workouts.

With the right combination of nutrients, supplements, smart drugs, gear, and even brain exercises, you can achieve this level of mental superiority. And it's not as hard as you might think—nor does it necessarily require expensive brain-hacking electronic equipment (although that option does exist).

Consider this chapter your how-to guide for hacking your brain and making yourself smarter. I realize that the information and choices may be overwhelming, so at the end of this chapter I'll cut to the chase and tell you exactly what I do to hack my own brain. And of course, there is also a resource web page jam-packed with links at the end of this chapter.

Nootropics

In the 2011 movie *Limitless,* Bradley Cooper's character gets his hands on a smart drug that enables him to become cognitively superhuman. The only known side effect is that his eyes change color while he is on the drug, but that changes over the course of the film. The side effects, including withdrawal symptoms, begin to get worse and worse. It's a sci-fi thriller with a not-so-feel-good message about addiction and performance-enhancing substances. And goons chasing you.

Makes smart drugs sound dangerous, right?

Like any good sci-fi film, this movie questions our assumptions about the limits of science. And some of what it is suggesting is not science fiction today. Smart drugs and nootropics are a current reality, being used more and more not to treat or remedy any active condition or complaint but to boost already typical or superior performance, in colleges, board rooms, and military theatres and by forward-thinking gerontologists.

With the wide variety of compounds available today that have some research support for cognitive effects, it is important to understand the risks and benefits associated with their use, or at least know how to choose smarter when choosing things that affect your brain.

For example, one of the most popular misconceptions about smart drugs is that they are the same as nootropics. This may be due to the fact that people use them for similar benefits, but ultimately they do not share the same range of effects, mechanisms of action, safety, or side effects.

The word *nootropics* refers to drugs, supplements, nutraceuticals, and functional foods that improve mental functions, such as cognition, memory, intelligence, motivation, attention, and concentration[4]. I get into the difference between the more natural nootropics and the less natural smart drugs in my podcast interview with Dr. Andrew Hill, which you can find at BenGreenfieldFitness.com/smartdrugvsnootropic.

In this section, I am purposefully not going to include any compounds that are potentially harmful or are unproven in long-term studies, that give you a biological free pass that you may regret in the future, or that are banned by sporting organizations because of their potential to overstimulate the cardiovascular system. This includes compounds such as modafinil, centrophenoxine, picamilon, and sulbutiamine. If you want to explore those nootropics, I highly recommend grabbing the free online manuals "The Limitless Pill" and "Do It Yourself Nanotech Nutrients Guide" (at BenGreenfieldFitness.com/nano). They are written by Mark Joyner, who was a guest on the podcast episode "Are Your Expensive Multivitamins Even Absorbed . . . or Are There Better Ways to Deliver Precious Nutrients to Your Body?" (BenGreenfieldFitness.com/absorb).

You'll notice that many of the nootropics listed below are either fat-soluble compounds or dependent on fat for their absorption or proper utilization. In other words, it doesn't matter how many brain-hacking nutrients you take if you're eating a low-fat diet or shooting for a low blood cholesterol value. So go back and read chapter 13 and adjust your diet accordingly, if necessary.

1. Alpha Lipoic Acid

Alpha lipoic acid (ALA) is a fatty acid that easily crosses the blood-brain barrier (a wall of tiny vessels and structural cells that protects your brain) and goes into the brain. There it prevents neurological decline with age and is effective against diabetic neuropathy[10].

ALA has been shown to reduce oxidative damage in neuronal cells, increase the release of the neurotransmitter glutamate in your synapses, and increase dopamine and acetylcholine availability. Brands vary, but the general dosage for a brain-boosting effect is 300–600 milligrams.

2. Carnitine

Carnitine is another precursor to acetylcholine. It performs a variety of functions in your brain, including synthesis and stabilization of cell membranes, regulation of neural genes and proteins, improvement in the working of mitochondria (the energy powerhouses of the cell), protection from free radical damage to the brain, better transmission of acetylcholine, and enhanced glucose uptake[13].

Carnitine has been shown to be very effective at alleviating certain side effects of aging, like neurological decline and chronic fatigue, and also improving insulin sensitivity and blood vessel health. It has beneficial effects on neurons, repairing them from damage caused by conditions such as a high amount of blood sugar fluctuations. As you learned in chapter 4, carnitine also increases fat burning and mitochondrial respiration, so you get a brain buzz along with more energy when you take it before a workout. Brands vary, but I recommend 750–2,000 milligrams a day, split into two doses. Both carnitine and creatine are helpful if you're doing lots of strength training or explosive exercise and want to kill two birds with one stone.

3. Caffeine

It has been proved that 100 milligrams of caffeine—about the amount in one cup of black coffee—improves memory recall[11]. This happens because caffeine blocks a receptor in the central nervous system that is responsible for binding a compound called adenosine. When adenosine is inhibited, the activity of dopamine and glutamate—two feel-good, alertness-increasing, brain-stimulating compounds—is increased.

However, as you learned in the previous chapter, more is not better when it comes to caffeine, because higher doses may decrease blood flow to the brain, and you can quickly build up a tolerance to caffeine's positive effects. Furthermore, caffeine is responsible for at least three disorders recognized by the American Psychiatric Association: caffeine intoxication, caffeine-induced sleep disorder, and caffeine-induced anxiety disorder. If you do indulge in coffee, make sure that it's fresh coffee from Arabica beans, not coffee from powders or substitutes, since low-quality coffee and coffee products are high in mycotoxins, which ironically give you fuzzy thinking.

If you want to combine caffeine's benefits with MCT oil and ketosis, go for Bulletproof Coffee (see the recipe in chapter 11), but at least once every few weeks, switch to decaf to avoid building up a caffeine tolerance. Another form of coffee that combines caffeine with other ingredients that you'll learn about in this chapter (such as Alpha-GPC, L-theanine, DMAE, and taurine) is Kimera Koffee, available at KimeraKoffee.com with 10 percent discount code BEN10.

4. Creatine

As I reported in my article "What Are the Best Biohacks of the World's Top Biohackers?" (BenGreenfieldFitness.com/biohack), I recently discovered that creatine not only has strength- and power-enhancing effects but can also be a very effective nootropic. Creatine may have a neuroprotective effect by slowing down neuronal cell death, and it may also increase levels of the neurotransmitter glutamate, improve memory and learning, counter depression, and suppress steep spikes in serotonin[1].

This news is especially important for vegans and vegetarians, who may find that by consuming adequate dietary fats combined with creatine, they can stave off much of the cognitive fuzziness that can accompany a plant-based diet.

Most studies on creatine use a "loading protocol" of 0.6 to 0.7 grams per pound of body weight for five to seven days, followed by 5 grams of creatine per day after that. However, if you're already eating meat, as little as 2 grams a day is enough supplementation to maintain average stores of creatine. I personally do not load at all, as studies on long-term use show that it's unnecessary. I simply take 5 grams of creatine per day, 365 days a year, varying between the highly absorbable tablet form of Cre-O2 from Millennium Sports and the powder form CreaPure by EXOS.

5. Fatty Acids

Arachidonic acid, one of the most abundant fatty acids in the brain, is crucial for neurological health because it helps build the cell membranes in the hippocampus, helps protect the brain from free radical damage, and activates proteins that are responsible for the growth and repair of neurons in the brain[5]. In one study, eighteen-month-olds given arachidonic acid supplements for seventeen weeks showed significant improvements in intelligence; in adults, impaired arachidonic acid metabolism or insufficient arachidonic acid intake is linked to brain defects such as Alzheimer's and bipolar disorder.

In my opinion, it's silly to supplement with arachidonic acid since it is readily available in food sources, including tilapia, catfish, yellowtail, mackerel (sushi, anyone?), fatty cuts of meat, duck, eggs, and dairy. If you want a better brain, make sure to get your chompers on fatty foods.

Incidentally, this highlights a reason why very active women need to be careful not to let their body fat levels fall too low if they plan on having children. Hip and butt fat are full of the specific omega-3 fatty acids and DHA necessary for major brain development during a baby's growth, and if a woman is low on body fat and low in DHA, the baby's intelligence may be severely compromised.

6. Fish Oil

As you learned in the last chapter, signals used in thought, memory, and processing bounce around in your brain and are transferred from one brain cell (neuron) to another through a synapse, the point at which the signals cross a physical channel before moving on to the next neuron. The walls through which these signals need to pass are composed of cell membranes that are about 20 percent essential fatty acids—like the omega-3 fatty acids in fish oil.

Specifically, these omega-3 fatty acids may make the membranes that form these walls more elastic, making it easier for signals to spread throughout the nervous system. With inadequate omega-3 fatty acids, these walls lose flexibility, and electrical impulses are impeded. Inadequate fatty acids may also harm the function of structures called G-proteins, which are inside the cell membrane and are vital to the transmission of signals between brain cells.

As little as two grams a day of omega-3 fatty acids like fish oil may reduce the severity of dyslexia and ADHD, Alzheimer's, brain atrophy, and cognitive decline while simultaneously improving mental function[17].

Don't waste your money on cheap, ethyl-ester forms of fish oil that are found in most supplements. Instead, pair one to two grams of a daily dose of triglyceride-based fish oil with regular intake of cold-water fish like mackerel, herring, anchovies, or sardines. It's also a good idea to consume a fish oil that includes antioxidants, such as astaxanthin, vitamin D, and vitamin E, and to step up the amount of dark leafy greens and dark fruit on your plate, or include a good antioxidant supplement. This is all the more important if you decide to "mega-dose" with eight to ten grams of fish oil a day (which I do on any day I'm not eating fish and often recommend for hard-charging athletes).

7. Huperzine A

I think Huperzine A has been flying off the shelves since Tim Ferriss mentioned it in his book *The 4-Hour Body*. Huperzine A is an acetylcholinesterase inhibitor, which means that more of the neurotransmitter acetylcholine is allowed to rush around in your brain. Acetylcholine is an important neurotransmitter found in many nootropics. The basic mechanism of action of many smart drugs is simply to halt the breakdown of acetylcholine or, put another way, to maximize the production of acetylcholine.

Studies have shown that Huperzine A has neuroprotective effects and enhances cognitive function in animals and humans[16]. But what most people don't know is that there are natural herbal sources of Huperzine A. For example, in Chinese herbal medicine, club moss is used to slow the progression of Alzheimer's. Guess what the active ingredient in club moss is? That's right—Huperzine A.

Be very careful if you order club moss, however. Most Chinese herbs sit in big bins in China for several years and get old, ineffective, and sprayed with toxic ethylene oxide. TianChi is the only Chinese adaptogenic herb complex that I've found that has effective doses of club moss, along with a cocktail of other brain-boosting ingredients—including citicholine, which is one of the best ways simulate the production of acetylcholine. It's pricey but, in my opinion, well worth it. I take one packet of TianChi on an empty stomach every morning. If you wanted to follow just one of my brain-boosting tips and instantly feel the difference, TianChi would be the best choice.

8. L-Phenylalanine

L-phenylalanine is an amino acid that is converted into L-tyrosine. L-tyrosine, in turn, is converted into L-dopa, which is further converted into dopamine, nor-epinephrine (noradrenaline), and epinephrine (adrenaline)—the primary neurotransmitters responsible for increasing alertness and focus[15]. The nice thing is that L-phenylalanine can achieve this effect without throwing your HPA axis off-kilter.

Earlier you learned about the performance-boosting effect of essential-amino-acid supplements. Most contain a good dose of L-phenylalanine in a balanced ratio to other amino acids. So their brain-boosting power is yet another good reason to have them around.

9. L-Theanine

L-theanine is one of the major amino acids in green tea and black tea, and it appears to play a role in reducing stress and anxiety. Specifically, it blocks glutamic acid's access to glutamate receptors in your brain and, in doing so, can increase alpha-brain-wave activity, boost cognitive ability, and provide a calming effect. So not only can L-theanine help you sleep, but it also promotes relaxed focus[18].

I like to mix L-theanine with caffeine for the sweet combination of pick-me-up and improved focus and mood. Four good sources of L-theanine are green tea (I prefer edible green tea), NeuroScience TravaCor (described in the previous chapter), Delta-E (a powdered supplement that can be added to water), and Smart Caffeine pills, which are a blend of theanine and caffeine. I put links to each of these products on the web page for this chapter.

10. MCTs

When your body burns fatty acids as fuel, it produces an end product called acetyl-CoA. Acetyl-CoA is then converted into ketones, which are a fuel that is preferentially used by your brain. At high enough levels of blood ketones, you begin to experience a significant cognitive boost and an increase in focus, which is one of the reasons I included ketosis as a dietary performance strategy in chapter 14.

One of the quickest ways to generate ketones from fatty acids is to use a special kind of fat called medium-chain triglycerides, or MCTs[9]. While you can get ample MCTs from coconut oil, you can get them in an even more purified and concentrated form from liquid MCT oil.

MCTs are easy to use. You can make Bulletproof Coffee (see the recipe in chapter 11) or swallow a couple tablespoons of coconut oil in the midmorning or midafternoon. Too many MCTs can easily cause an upset stomach, so start small, and increase your dosage gradually.

This just in: A special kind of ketone is sold in the form of beta-hydroxybutyrate (BHB) salts that can instantly increase blood ketone levels without your needing to consume any fat. Although it has yet to be approved by the FDA, it could be an interesting supplement to keep an eye on. For details, listen to my podcast episode with Dr. D'Agostino titled "A Deep Dive into Ketosis: How Navy SEALs, Extreme Athletes & Busy Executives Can Enhance Physical and Mental Performance with the Secret Weapon of Ketone Fuel." You can check it out at BenGreenfieldFitness.com/ketones (it includes links to the BHB, too).

11. Phosphatidylserine

Unlike similar triglycerides and dietary fats, phosphatidylserine is found in abundance in neural tissue, where it serves as a structural component of cell membranes and acts to increase available acetylcholine levels[12] (more on why that's a good thing later).

Phosphatidylserine has been shown to improve memory and spatial recognition in rats and may improve cognitive performance and memory in humans. However, the majority of studies on humans have been done on elderly individuals (in whom phosphatidylserine has been shown to be beneficial in slowing the progression of Alzheimer's disease and dementia).

Although you can find phosphatidylserine in supplement and pill forms (especially in the form of krill oil), it tends to be expensive, especially when you consider that you can get it in fairly high concentrations in seafood, particularly herring and mackerel. Perhaps you're beginning to realize that it might be a good idea to learn to love sushi and sashimi if you don't already—or at least to start putting some good-quality canned herring or mackerel on your salad every now and again.

12. Vitamin D

I've praised the efficacy of vitamin D for everything from boosting hormone levels to promoting bone health. But there are actually receptors for vitamin D in the central nervous system and in the hippocampus region of the brain (governing memory and spatial recognition). Vitamin D not only protects neurons but also regulates enzymes in the brain and cerebrospinal fluid that are involved in neurotransmitter synthesis and nerve growth[3].

One recent study investigating vitamin D and cognitive function found that the lower a person's vitamin D levels, the worse that person performed on mental tests. Another study found that people with lower vitamin D levels process information more slowly—with this effect being more pronounced in individuals older than sixty.

It's important to understand that none of the strategies I'm about to give you are better than daily exposure to sunlight combined with adequate fat intake. But to get the memory-enhancement effect of increased vitamin D (especially if you live in a northern climate or get limited sun exposure), include a few teaspoons of cod liver oil frequently in your diet, eat beef and butter, have calf's liver now and then, and take approximately 2,000–4,000 IU of vitamin D daily, preferably from a highly absorbable liquid source, such as a spray or an oil.

When it comes to vitamin D, there can be a law of diminishing returns, so I highly recommend keeping an eye on your vitamin D level by having it tested; your goal is a level between 40 and 80 ng/ml. Finally, if you're a vegetarian or vegan or you eat inadequate amounts of fat, do not just take a bunch of vitamin D by itself, because it can be toxic unless you pair it with vitamins A and K.

13. Vitamin K$_2$

Your brain contains one of the highest concentrations of vitamin K$_2$ in your entire body, and this is where vitamin K$_2$ prevents free radical damage to neurons and contributes to the production of the protective myelin sheaths around your brain cells.

I already discussed vitamin K$_2$ in chapter 14 as an important supplement for vegans and vegetarians. Vitamin K$_2$ is a relatively new darling on the supplement front, and many folks are rushing out to buy and use it for its bone-building, brain-building, and other remarkable benefits[2]. But unless you are vegan or vegetarian or you have a serious deficiency or disease that requires K$_2$ intake, you're better off getting your K$_2$ from natural sources, such as grass-fed beef, fermented dairy products (like kefir), and natto (a fermented soybean derivative). Reread chapter 14 if you want to learn more about K$_2$ supplements and dosage.

14. CBD

Due to their properties that help protect nerve cells, especially brain cells, cannabinoids—specifically the cannabidiols derived from CBD that I introduce in my BenGreenfieldFitness.com article "A 100% Legal Way to Get All the Benefits of Weed Without Actually Smoking Weed"—play a key role in slowing and preventing the damage to the brain found in patients with Alzheimer's disease, as well as other forms of dementia, depression, and neurodegeneration.

Components of CBD can inhibit the enzyme acetylcholinesterase, which plays a key role in inducing amyloid plaques that form in the brain to cause Alzheimer's and dementia. And finally, if you do happen to smoke weed and you're concerned about the potential memory-damaging effects of THC, then it's important to know that CBD can counteract these effects[19], especially when taken in conjunction with marijuana. You can learn more about CBD at BenGreenfieldFitness.com/CBD.

15. Tryptophan

You are probably familiar with this essential amino acid because it is present in turkey, and people (erroneously) believe that it makes them sleepy. However, tryptophan is also available in pill form, and it is most commonly taken as a non-prescription aid for depression. Tryptophan works by increasing the amount of serotonin in your brain. When used for this purpose, it is typically taken three or four times per day for a total of eight to twelve grams. Additionally, at least one study has linked this natural nootropic to a reduction in memory deficits[20].

16. Bacopa Monnieri

Bacopa monnieri[21] is an extract from the Brahmi plant. According to WebMD, Bacopa is used for a wide variety of purposes, including as a supplemental Alzheimer's treatment and a way to reduce anxiety. Evidence suggests that this natural nootropic is effective at improving memory and hand-eye coordination. There have also been some studies linking Bacopa with a reduction in anxiety, insomnia, and concentration issues. In one study, participants were given 300 milligrams a day for twelve weeks, and there were reported improvements in thinking ability and memory.

17. Lion's Mane

This edible mushroom can be found in gourmet food stores and is also available in supplement form. Like many other mushrooms, Lion's Mane is believed to offer benefits that go beyond nutrition. In fact, several studies[22] have been conducted in an attempt to discover the full potential of Lion's Mane, and the results are very promising. For example, a daily dose of 750 milligrams gave test subjects a significant boost in cognitive functionality. A small clinical study showcased the possibility that this nootropic can reduce anxiety and depression. I also discuss the potent Lion's Mane dual extracted mushroom tea in my podcast with foursigmafoods at BenGreenfieldFitness.com/foursigmapodcast.

18. Gingko Biloba

Leaves from the ginkgo biloba tree have been used in Chinese medicine for thousands of years. The Mayo Clinic did an analysis[23] of each of the medical purposes for which this nootropic is used and determined that there is a good amount of scientific evidence to suggest that ginkgo biloba is useful for improving cognitive performance and reducing anxiety.

19. Artichoke Extract

A popular ingredient in many nootropics is artichoke extract, which is made from the leaves of artichokes. A lot of evidence strongly suggests that artichoke extract supplements offer neural antioxidant properties. Additionally, several nootropic user reviews have mentioned enhanced memory in relation to taking this product. Tim Ferriss talked about this a bit in my most recent podcast with him, particularly referencing its presence in CILTEP.

20. Aniracetam

Aniracetam modulates excitatory receptors in the brain and decreases the rate of receptor desensitization, which results in the strengthening of neuron interconnections, allowing short-term memories to form. In other words, it can help you build better wiring between neurons. It also increases blood flow to the association cortex, the area of the brain known for higher-level processing and holistic thinking. One of my favorite sources of this compound is a pill called Nexus, which combines aniracetam (vital for short-term memory as well as brain speed and acceleration) with phosphatidylserine (which increases activation of receptors called AMPA receptors to strengthen neuron interconnections) and Pycnogenol, a French maritime pine bark extract, which is an antioxidant that modulates nNOS (an important neurotransmitter for mental performance). You can read more about this product at BenGreenfieldFitness.com/nexus.

I realize that this seems like an intimidating boatload of ingredients to choose from! But it is not always necessary to purchase each component of a nootropic stack separately. Instead, you can turn to combination pills that take away all the guesswork. One of the biggest perks associated with this approach is that you will not need to portion out the specific dosage of each supplement in your stack. It can also be more cost-effective to take advantage of this format. Here are a few of my favorite done-for-you options.

CILTEP

When it comes to natural stacking, CILTEP is by far one of the most frequently utilized and discussed options. Created in 2012 by a nootropic and neurochemistry enthusiast, this blend's popularity quickly soared after users, including Tim Ferriss, began reporting positive results. All the ingredients in the CILTEP pill are natural, so people who wish to steer clear of synthesized products can easily do so. The main base ingredients in this supplement are artichoke extracts and forskolin.

Each CILTEP pill also contains vitamin B_6, L-phenylalanine, and acetyl-L-carnitine. The manufacturer recommends taking two to three capsules at the beginning of each day. It has been suggested that skipping one or two days per week offers better results. Although CILTEP itself has not undergone medical testing, all the individual ingredients have been proven to be beneficial to the human body and brain. Therefore, it is not surprising that CILTEP has found a big audience. In fact, one of the biggest proponents of this natural nootropic blend is Martin Jacobson, who reportedly utilized CILTEP while winning the 2014 World Series of Poker. I interview

CILTEP creator Roy Krebs in the podcast episode at BenGreenfieldFitness.com/CILTEPpodcast.

Alpha Brain

This combination product is touted as containing all Earth-grown ingredients, which earns it a spot on the natural stack list. Just like CILTEP, Alpha Brain (created by the company Onnit) combines all the components into a single pill for easier use. According to a clinical trial that was conducted by the Boston Center for Memory, this product demonstrated a notable increase in cognitive performance in healthy individuals.

Alpha Brain contains Alpha-GPC, AC-11, Bacopa monnieri, and Huperzine A. Medical testing has shown that Alpha-GPC has the potential to boost memory and learning capacity. AC-11 is derived from a rain-forest herb, and studies have found that it may be able to help people in a variety of ways, such as by slowing the growth of cell cancers due to its reported DNA-repairing antioxidant properties.

Reviews of Alpha Brain suggest taking two or three capsules per day. It has also been pointed out that this supplement appears to work best when taken daily for at least two weeks. Most people indicate that the effects associated with Alpha Brain become more pronounced over time, so you need to let this nootropic blend build up in your system before you judge its overall effectiveness.

Earlier, I mentioned the aniracetam compound Nexus. The primary difference between Alpha Brain and Nexus is that Alpha Brain makes you feel like you think faster when it comes to word formation and recall, which comes in handy when, say, giving a speech, while Nexus improves overall productivity and wakefulness, which comes in handy when, say, you have a list of twenty-five tasks to complete for the day.

TianChi

The list of herbs and ingredients in TianChi is way too long to include here, but you can read them in full detail at GreenfieldFitnessSystems.com. Basically, TianChi contains nearly every herb or ingredient you've read about so far in this chapter.

Every herb used in TianChi is far more pure and potent than the typical old, ineffective, and often dangerous or nasty-ingredient-laced nootropic herbs on the market. Very few products contain 100 percent whole herb extracts. On average, the herbal extracts are at least 10:1 yields, meaning that it takes ten pounds of raw herb to produce one pound of pure extract. Most manufacturers start with pure yield and cut them to concentrations of 4:1 or 5:1 by adding filler, producing a cheaper but less effective extract. Imagine buying a 5:1 extract that originally was 45:1.

In contrast, the herbal extracts used in TianChi yield 12:1 or greater; there is even an herb in TianChi that is a 45:1 yield. In other words, you would have to take nine times as much herb from any other source to equal the potency in TianChi. And you would be getting mostly filler, harmful ingredients, and very few results. All the herbs in TianChi are non-GMO, kosher-certified, and non-irradiated. They are extracted in purified water and test free of heavy metals. The creator, a Chinese herbalist based out of Oregon, uses only herbs found in their natural state, free from pesticides and exposure to pollution. Strangely enough, I've found the effects of TianChi to be even more enhanced when consumed with beet juice or beet powder, probably due to the vasodilation effect of the beets.

When it comes to nootropics, the burning question I get most often is: "What do *you* use, Ben?"

To be honest, I fluctuate. I've used everything you just read about, from CILTEP to Alpha Brain to TianChi to mushroom extracts, and I've also made my own blends of L-theanine and caffeine and blends of piracetam, aniracetam, and Alpha-GPC.

When I travel (which is quite often), I tend to take something that is easily portable, usually capsules of CILTEP or Alpha Brain. I do not rely regularly on these, but I do use them prior to speaking on stage or heavy bouts of writing.

And when I'm at home, I tend to stick to a big cup of mold-free black coffee early in the morning, TianChi in the mid-morning on very cognitively demanding or sleep-deprived days, and mushroom blends like Lion's Mane in the afternoon. In the evening, it's usually cannabidiol via NatureCBD for relaxation, and occasionally, when I'm playing music, at a party, or writing, THC/CBD combinations either vaporized or in edible form (completely legal in my home state of Washington). To maintain my sensitivity and avoid building up tolerances, I switch to decaf coffee one week out of every three and cut out all smart drugs, nootropics, and cannabis-based products one week out of every three.

Finally, just prior to writing this chapter, I experimented twice with the following stack: three capsules of Alpha-Brain and two capsules of NatureCBD. Both times I used this stack I was short on sleep (operating on about five hours of sleep), and both times I was as productive as a madman from about 5 a.m. to 1 p.m. I fell asleep for about an hour, then woke up in a pile of my own drool, feeling incredibly refreshed and like a new man. So at this point, although I can't say that I'd recommend this stack unless you have the option of a nap, it is probably the most powerful blend I've experienced yet.

Brain-Enhancing Gear

21. Electrical Stimulation

In chapter 21, you saw how cyclists could be "tricked" into performing at a higher capacity when they were electrically stimulated before riding to exhaustion. Pulsed electrical currents across the head not only distract the cortex in a manner that can increase physical performance, but can also increase blood flow to the brain and production of neurotransmitters and alpha brain waves.

Devices available for electrical stimulation of the brain include:

- **Transcranial direct-current stimulation (tDCS),** which passes a current across your forehead and is being tested by the Air Force to promote cognitive enhancement. At foc.us, you can grab a smartphone-controlled tDCS device that looks like high-tech sunglasses for $249. Another popular device is the Fisher Wallace Stimulator, which employs a headband to secure electrodes that deliver mild electrical currents.

- **Cranial electrotherapy stimulation (CES),** which is similar to tDCS but applies a current to your earlobes rather than your forehead. Mind Alive also makes a CES device called the Oasis, as well as a device called the DAVID PAL 36, which combines light and sound with CES.
- **Pulsed electromagnetic frequencies (PEMFs).** A magnetic frequency in the 10-hertz range (completely safe and far lower than what a cell phone radiates) increases cell membrane potential in your brain and boosts alpha-brain-wave production. This can be useful for focus as well as sleep. You know that I use an EarthPulse under my mattress while sleeping, but I also place it on my desk when I'm working.

The field of neurofeedback is growing by leaps and bounds. By the time you read this, I'm sure that new devices will have hit the market. To stay on the cutting edge of brain-hacking gear, I recommend the website Quantified Self (quantifiedself. com).

22. Light Therapy

A dip in alertness and focus during the day is often due to excess melatonin, which can induce sleepiness. Unfortunately, the common "wisdom" is to expose the eyes to more light in the morning by using something like a light box, which produces blue light. The problem is that, while it suppresses melatonin production and can increase alertness, the wavelength of blue light can cause damage to your retina and eventually cause macular degeneration and loss of good vision.

It appears that the best way to increase mental acuity and focus during the day is to advance the melatonin cycle so that it is completed before you wake up. Basically, you do this by (1) limiting your exposure to blue light in the early evening; limiting the use of TVs, e-readers, smartphones, and computers; and using blue-light blocking glasses, software like f.lux, and computer-screen shields; (2) getting as much morning sun exposure as possible or, if that's not an option, waking with a "sunrise" clock or waking light in your bedroom.

23. Neurofeedback

Neurofeedback (aka biofeedback) devices—which I first introduced in chapter 8—do nothing to your brain. They simply show you what your brain is doing so that you can train it to focus, block pain, learn faster, and so on.

For example, one popular piece of neurofeedback gear is the Upgraded Focus Brain Trainer, which includes a headband with small red and infrared LED lights that "pierce" the skin and skull to assess the color of your brain tissue. This light is then reflected back to a camera that measures the exact color of oxygenated brain blood. Your brain's data is then sent to your computer so that you can correct what you're doing in real time (for example, think relaxing thoughts, focus better, or make a quicker decision)—and increase blood circulation to your brain.

In this case, the neurofeedback device is based on studies that show a direct relationship between an increase in brain performance and oxygenation of the blood supply. More blood flow also results in faster removal of waste metabolites from brain tissues and more capillaries and neuron connections within the trained area of the brain.

Another example of neurofeedback is the game Journey to the Wild Divine, which measures skin resistance and heart rate to detect your level of stress and then trains you to become more aware and less stressed.

Then there's the Muse headband, which uses biofeedback to give you real-time feedback that allows you to monitor what's happening in your brain while you meditate with a combination of the headband and the Muse app.

In chapter 9, you learned about coherence. This is a process whereby you train yourself to increase heart rate variability by using special software made by the Institute of HeartMath connected to an earlobe device called the emWave2 or the smartphone Inner Balance sensor. Based on the intimate connection between your heart and your brain, as your heart-rate-variability increases, you can increase both alpha-brain-wave production and neurotransmitter production. Amazingly, the heart's electrical field is up to sixty times greater than the brain's, and it can interact not only with your own brain, but also with the brains of others around you. So you may find that, as you teach yourself how to improve your heart rate variability, you may also enhance the mental focus and relaxation of coworkers, friends, and family.

Finally, if you're interested, you can find a licensed biofeedback practitioner at bcia.org. If you consult with one, you can expect to fill out a comprehensive questionnaire, then have an EEG. This results in a brain map that shows which areas of your brain are overactive and which are underactive. You then engage in feedback sessions that may involve a simple light or tone or game that responds when the system detects desired brain activity. For other brain activity, the rewarding tone, light, or game is taken away. Typically, it takes twenty to forty biofeedback visits for someone to overcome issues such as cravings, anxiety, or depression—so it is more commonly used for brain problems than for brain enhancement.

24. Sound Frequencies

As you learned in chapter 3, your brain waves respond quite readily to sound frequencies, beats, notes, and music. There's a direct correlation between specific brain-wave states and neurotransmitter production. I highly recommend going back and rereading pages 90–92, where I spotlight Dr. Jeffrey Thompson's neuroacoustics CDs, the Entrainer Acoustics downloadable MP3 audio tracks, and the wristband that emits specific frequencies to increase alpha-brain-wave production.

In that chapter, I also mention audiovisual entrainment, which takes the concept of sound one step further, using flashes of lights and pulses of tones to guide the brain into various states of brain-wave activity. There's an interesting device called the DAVID Delight Pro made by Mind Alive that does this. I do not personally use it, but many biohackers swear by it.

Brain-Enhancing Activities

25. Aerobic Exercise

Brain-derived neurotrophic factor (BDNF) is a protein that acts in your central nervous system and peripheral nervous system to help existing neurons survive and thrive and to encourage the growth of new neurons and neuronal connections (synapses).

Research has shown that exercise, and specifically aerobic exercise, can significantly enhance secretion of BDNF[6]. Why aerobic exercise? It appears that various growth factors must be carried from the periphery of your body into your brain to start a molecular cascade there to prompt BDNF creation. To bring this on, you need to increase your blood flow. You could make this happen with weight training, but unfortunately, weight training stimulates the production of growth factors in the muscles that stay in the muscles and aren't transported to the brain.

So how can you exercise to get smarter?

I recommend fitting in a twenty- to forty-five-minute run, bike ride, or other bout of cardio in the morning on any day that demands serious brainpower. It doesn't have to be hard or make your legs, arms, or lungs burn. Just get your heart beating and your blood flowing (a rate of perceived exertion of 4–6 on a scale of 1–10). In this case, harder is not better, and could leave you excessively fatigued. In addition, excess cortisol has actually been shown to reduce BDNF.

26. Brain Aerobics

There is continuing research that brain exercises (like Sudoku) can help "age-proof" your brain and help keep it functioning at peak capacity. A good brain-aerobics exercise must have novelty, variety, and challenge[8].

Going to work every day to your "mentally challenging" job does not qualify as novelty; doing the same brain exercise day after day does not qualify as variety; and engaging in brain activities that are familiar or easy (such as playing the same demanding computer game every day) eventually ceases to qualify as a challenge. In the same way that you should vary your physical exercises at the gym, you should vary your mental exercises, too. In other words, make your brain lift heavy stuff in a variety of different ways. One of my friends, Dr. Arlene Taylor, has a bunch of free brain-aerobic exercises on her website (BeyondTrainingBook.com/brainexrcse).

You can also do a search for "brain exercises" in the iTunes store or any other app store and find good apps to challenge your brain—Angry Birds probably doesn't count. Two of my favorites are Brainscape, which allows you to create flash cards and learning activities that you can easily access from your phone, and n-back training, which involves memorizing a progressively more difficult sequence of colored squares.

Incidentally, playing a sport that involves thinking ahead to solve problems as you go, like tennis or golf, counts—as do board games like chess and checkers.

27. Chewing Gum

Many people chew gum to relieve stress, and some believe that it helps them concentrate[14]. Neuroscience researchers have studied whether it improves attention, memory, and other aspects of cognition. Although the research is not entirely conclusive, chewing gum may increase blood flow to the brain, delivering not only nutrients but also additional oxygen.

In any event, I frequently chew gum when writing and engaging in mentally demanding or stressful tasks. Just make sure you chew a good brand that is free of artificial sweeteners, chemical colors, and sweeteners, like B-Fresh or Simply Gum.

28. Music

In addition to helping you exercise harder, music has been proved to assist with "dopaminergic neurotransmission," which basically means that—as with the use of binaural beats and sounds—it can cause a giant dopamine release in your brain and make you smarter and more mentally responsive. Music may also, through something called a "calmodulin pathway," cause a reduction in blood pressure and increased blood flow to the brain[7].

However, music can be distracting, so don't constantly pump it into your ears. The most powerful effects of music on brain development are through learning music. Yes, I am suggesting that you pick up a musical instrument, play Guitar Hero occasionally, or install that mini-piano app on your phone. Seriously.

As promised, I'm going to share with you a typical brain-hacking day in my life so you know how I personally take advantage of the tools in this chapter.

6:30 a.m.: Wake up. Five minutes of heart-rate-variability training with NatureBeat while lying in bed.

6:45 a.m.: One cup of coffee (occasionally substituting delta-E or green tea). Three capsules of Nexus, CILTEP, or Alpha Brain. Five grams of creatine.

7 a.m.: Ten to fifteen minutes of light aerobic exercise (yoga and calisthenics) in the morning sunshine.

9 a.m.: High-fat breakfast, including MCT oil.

10 a.m.: Work, chewing gum and keeping EarthPulse on if more focus is needed.

12 p.m.: High-fat lunch, usually sardines, eggs, herring, or mackerel.

1 p.m.: Nap on Biomat.

4 p.m.: Work out; includes learning at least one new exercise or movement. If a very busy day or anticipating a long night, one packet of TianChi in water pre-workout.

7 p.m.: High-fat dinner.

8 p.m.: Guitar or tennis practice.

9 p.m.: Reading book or Kindle with low-blue-light glasses.

10 p.m.: Bedtime in darkness. Sleep on EarthPulse if returning from travel or jet-lagged.

The two best brain-enhancing books I've read are both written by Dr. Eric Braverman, a true brain expert: *The Edge Effect,* which discusses how to reverse or prevent Alzheimer's, aging, memory loss, weight gain, and sexual dysfunction, and *Younger Brain, Sharper Mind,* which lays out a six-step plan for preserving and improving memory and attention at any age. As mentioned earlier, I also highly recommend the free e-manual *The Limitless Pill,* by Mark Joyner. Finally, the book *Why Isn't My Brain Working?* by Dr. Datis Kharrazian is a fantastic read, as are all the articles at BiohacksBlog.com and the smart drug resources at BeyondTrainingBook. com/nootropics. I've included other links and resources on the web page for this chapter. (You'll also find links to more of my favorite books at the bottom of the page at BenGreenfieldFitness.com/benrecommends.)

Additional resources, helpful links, scientific references, and surprise bonuses for this chapter are available at BeyondTrainingBook.com/Chapter22. Enjoy.

CHAPTER 23

Ten Rules for Becoming an Ancestral Athlete

If you were to take everything you've learned in this book and condense it into ten simple rules, they would look very similar to the official Ten Rules for Becoming an Ancestral Athlete that I'm about to lay on you.

1. Change Your Lens

2. Be Uncomfortable

3. Be Comfortable

4. Work

5. Optimize Fertility

6. Eat the Earth

7. Empty the Trash

8. Use Science

9. Keep a Clear Head

10. Don't Fret

1. Change Your Lens

If you're into fitness, diet, or healthy living, you're bombarded every day by new workouts, fat-loss methods, training templates, nutrition supplements, camps, clinics, diets, apps, biohacks, research studies, and a mind-boggling variety of other ways to enhance your body.

But to know if the latest fad is going to meld perfectly with your ancestral self, you must look at everything through the lens of health rather than performance. That is, you must question not only whether a particular method is efficacious in the short term, but also what its long-term effects on health or longevity will be. In other words, you need to think "beyond training."

Take fat loss, for example. You've probably seen the story on TV: An obese person, often weighing in excess of 400 pounds, is subjected to weeks of calorie restriction and intense physical activity for hours a day—and the fat melts off like magic. But if you want this *Biggest Loser*–style of weight loss, you need to be careful. With a combination of extreme calorie restriction and excessive exercise, you get long-lasting metabolic damage (a nearly 30 percent decrease in your metabolism), accompanied by damage to organs such as your heart and liver. Sure, there are performance benefits to fat loss, but the long-term health implications are dire and unnecessary. Slow, steady, patient weight loss is the way to go.

Or take the mind-set that a high-carbohydrate diet and carbohydrate loading result in superior performance in endurance athletes. As you've learned, yes, this is certainly true, but it applies only to in-the-moment performance and has significant long-term aftereffects, such as pancreatic failure, nerve damage, and chronic inflammation. If that damage is worth it to you, then you are either mildly masochistic or you value performance much more than health. If you desire a long, quality life, you may need to switch your lens.

On the flip side, a very-low-carbohydrate diet has been shown to improve metabolic efficiency, but in many people—especially women—chronic, excessive carbohydrate depletion can cause hypothyroidism and other hormone imbalances—so once again, you must value health over performance, listen to your body, and question the long-term health implications of any new regimen. (In this case, the consequences of low carbohydrate intake can be mitigated with sane amounts of carbohydrate intake, while avoiding excessive carbohydrate restriction, especially on higher-activity days.)

2. Be Uncomfortable

At a recent Ancestral Health Symposium (go to ancestryfoundation.org), I had the pleasure of attending a talk by Nassim Taleb, the author of the excellent book *Antifragile*. In the talk, Taleb illustrated how, just as bones and muscles become stronger when subjected to variety, stress, and tension, other things benefit from stress, disorder, volatility, and turmoil.

In other words, it's OK (and perfectly ancestral) not to always be in control or have everything dialed in—that is, to let randomness play a role in your life. Ancient humans did not have air-conditioning and central heating, so it's OK for your bedroom, your office, or your car to sometimes be too hot or too cold. Refrigerators are another relatively modern luxury, so it's OK to occasionally go hungry or fast or eat unusual meals (breakfast for dinner, anyone?). Sometimes lions and bears chase you, so it's OK to skip that aerobic bike ride and do a short, intense, four-minute Tabata set instead, and vice versa.

So be uncomfortable. Let yourself experience occasional, sane amounts of natural stress and disorder. This will be an antidote to fragility, keep you alive and vibrant, and allow your lungs, muscles, and heart to gradually adapt to the demands you place on them.

Incidentally, in addition to reading *Antifragile*, I highly recommend *The Paleo Manifesto*, by John Durant. While I personally am not a Paleo-diet adherent, the book is chock-full of inspiration for tapping into your "uncomfortable" ancestral side.

3. Be Comfortable

Yes, I've purposefully placed rule number 3 right after rule number 2. After all, constant discomfort is the equivalent of chronic stress.

Warriors do not fight constantly. They rest between battles. And the best athletes know that their biggest gains come during the days between tough sessions. By contrast, they feel the most worn down from endless hard workouts without breaks. This is the reason for splitting training years, months, and weeks into specific periods that include both work and rest.

Often we try to turn every workout into a deep dive into the pain cave that leaves us gasping for oxygen long afterward. Or we avoid that red-hot intensity and instead wear our bodies down with hours of deadening junk miles. Either way, we never quite feel satisfied unless we roll out of bed with some soreness or end the day having burned as many calories as possible.

Not allowing for breathing space happens elsewhere in life, too. For example, we set aside time to play with our children, but all the while our smartphone is in our pocket vibrating with notifications from work, Facebook, or Twitter. Or we go out to dinner to relax but place that same phone strategically next to our plate—just to satisfy our addiction to productivity or stimulation or ego.

Sometimes your body and mind simply need to be unstimulated, to be comfortable, to rest, to be lazy. I've written about how nerve cell repair, memory formation, recovery of the adrenal glands, muscle building, and removal of inflammation all occur when your body and mind are in a peaceful state. And yet many of us simply don't know how to stop working. The ability to relax and rest is a positive habit that must be acquired, so stop working and start working on it.

4. Work

My father-in-law is a skinny ex-Montana rancher who now manages a sheep farm at the University of Idaho. When our family visits him, I get to witness his daily routine: an early morning of feeding hungry sheep followed by a day of walking through pastures, lifting farm machinery, and fixing equipment. He doesn't ever step foot in a gym, yet he stays lean and strong year-round.

Perhaps this gene for getting your exercise from your work was passed on to his daughter, because during the spring and summer, my wife rarely exercises. Instead, she spends the day in our backyard garden, pushing a heavy wheelbarrow, digging holes, moving rocks, planting trees, and pulling weeds.

If you're lucky enough to be a farmer, gardener, builder, or personal trainer or to work in any other profession that involves daily moving, lifting, bending, rowing, pushing, pulling, lunging, or squatting, you know how your body feels at the end of the day—energized, awake, and alive. It's quite a contrast to the stale, burned-out, fried state that most people are in after long periods slouched in a chair staring at a computer screen or hunched over the steering wheel of a car or truck.

I'm not saying that you should quit your office job, but you do need to hack it to simulate the hunter-gatherer lifestyle as much as possible. Replace your traditional desk with a standing workstation or treadmill desk. Install a pull-up bar in the door of your office. If you work from home, keep something heavy in your garage, like a sandbag or barbell that you can lift every now and again. Never sit for longer than an hour without getting up and doing jumping jacks, bodyweight squats, or some hip opening stretches and leg swings.

After all, research has shown that when it comes to health and longevity, it doesn't matter how hard you exercise if you spend the rest of your day in a seated position. So think about how you can adjust your daily routine so that your body is constantly active.

5. Optimize Fertility

I believe it was Tim Ferriss whom I first heard say, "A fertile man is a healthy man." And this makes perfect sense.

Whether you're a man or a woman, the loss of your ability to reproduce is a sure sign that your body is falling apart and that you're running low on the hormones, vitamins, and minerals to sustain life. For example, because the femoral artery is relatively small compared with the larger arteries feeding the heart, poor circulation or blood vessel blockage from arginine deficiencies, low nitric oxide, or excessive plaque from mineral imbalances often manifest in erectile dysfunction or lack of blood flow to sexual organs long before an actual heart attack takes place. It is the "canary in the coal mine."

We're lucky enough to be able to test hormones such as testosterone, estrogens, progesterone, DHEA, and sex-hormone-binding globulin that, if low or imbalanced, result in impotence, infertility, a lack of sexual drive, and an inability to experience sexual pleasure. Even if you don't have access to fancy quantitative-testing protocols, you can still keep your finger on the qualitative pulse of your fertility by paying attention to your libido, your orgasms, your monthly cycles, your erections, and your fluid production.

As a man, I can personally attest to the fact that my best athletic performance comes during the same weeks that my sexual performance peaks. In my consults with many women, I've noticed that a loss of menstruation often comes several months before stress fractures, overtraining syndrome, and drops in athletic performance rear their heads. Of course, the exception to this rule is postmenopausal women—but even this population should not make it their goal to maintain rail-thin levels of leanness due to the potential degradation of neurons and damage to the neuromuscular system from inadequate calories and fat intake.

So make it your goal not simply to survive, but to thrive. And thriving means maintaining the ability to make babies, whether or not you actually do so.

6. Eat the Earth

To keep my body in a maximum state of fatty acid utilization, I use a combination of SuperStarch, d-ribose, nootropics, essential amino acids, wasp extract, and MCT oil when I'm competing in an Ironman triathlon. But the truth is that although this cocktail is relatively healthy compared with sugar-laden engineered beverages, gels, and bars, I use it only when I absolutely must.

Instead, I'm far happier eating food that comes straight from the earth in its whole, recognizable form. I head out for a bike ride with raw almonds in my jersey pocket, chomp on a sweet potato before a weight-training session, or simply let the real meals that I spread throughout the day fuel any physical activity I do. I don't pay much heed to advanced fueling science or lab-concocted pre- and postworkout "nutrition" unless aerodynamics, weight, or time spent consuming fuel becomes a performance consideration.

You can label this way of eating Primal, Paleo, Ancestral, Perfect, Just Eating Real Food, or whatever else you want to, but eating naturally should be the foundation of your fueling strategy. Grabbing a shake from your gym bag, unwrapping a factory-made energy bar, or dumping powder into a bike bottle should be rare, saved for the times when you're doing something relatively "unnatural," like rowing a half marathon at the CrossFit Games or toeing the line of a marathon or triathlon.

7. Empty the Trash

Many athletes and exercise enthusiasts go years without cleaning up their insides. But the thousands of calories you must consume to support consistent exercise or challenging physical feats significantly stresses the detox and waste-removal pathways in your liver, kidneys, pancreas, and gut. When you combine this with the inflammation, ammonia-based toxins, and metabolites that build up in your muscles and bloodstream from tough workouts and life stress, you must allow your organs the luxury of being cleaned and destressed at some point.

Our ancestors did not always have a steady influx of calories; they sometimes had to simply eat fewer calories and move less. In other words, training to eat and eating to train was not the 365-days-a-year routine that many of us practice today. A recent article I read in the newspaper reported that Americans eat an average of fifteen times per day. This doesn't even seem possible until you start to count that kombucha drink you slammed after breakfast, the handful of nuts before lunch, the piece of candy in the early afternoon, the pre-workout and/or post-workout meal, dinner, dessert, and any other beverages you might drink in between all that stuffing your face.

In chapter 8, I wrote about how fasting and detoxing are powerful strategies for taking out the trash that builds up in your vital organs and cells, but I've witnessed many athletes taking this information only halfway to heart and using the daily consumption of an antioxidant, gut-flush, or liver-cleansing supplement to justify continuing to eat as much as possible and exercise at maximum capacity each day.

The fact is that to truly empty your body's trash, you must combine detoxification nutrients with complete rest and a low calorie intake. So set aside one day a week or month, one week a season, or one month a year as a period in which you combine gentle restorative physical activity with a low calorie intake and a detoxification protocol.

You wouldn't let the trash accumulate, ferment, and rot in your kitchen, office, or bathroom for years on end, would you? Treat your body the same way.

8. Use Science

Some athletes take "living ancestrally" a bit too far. They never use supplements or high-power blenders, they avoid expensive recovery technology like electrostimulation and compression gear, and they never go near a heart-rate-variability monitor or self-quantification device.

They argue that unplugged living is natural.

But, paradoxically, these same athletes then expose their bodies to extremely unnatural situations, such as running for miles on hard pavement along diesel-truck-polluted roads, sitting their delicate reproductive-organ tissues on a hard bike saddle for hours on end, swimming in chlorinated water, pumping iron in a gym bombarded with EMF and cleaning chemicals, eating herbicide-tainted fruits and vegetables grown in mineral-depleted soil, and drinking gallons of fluoridated water from the municipal water supply.

Unless you're a monk ensconced on a pristine mountaintop in the Himalayas, you sometimes need to accept the fact that you live in a postindustrial era. So you are often exposed to relatively unnatural activities, foods, and environments, and you may actually benefit from a bit of better living through science.

Your ancestors weren't dummies. If they couldn't eat cold-water fish every day, I'll bet they would have popped the triglyceride-based fish-oil supplement that you have in your refrigerator. If their muscles were a wreck, sore and swollen from a day of hiking, hunting, or gathering, I'll bet they would have appreciated some compression gear, cold thermogenesis, electrostimulation, or other "unnatural" modern recovery protocol. If they were hurtling in a winged metal tube 40,000 feet above the ground to a destination six time zones away, I'll bet they would have considered using an earthing device or taking a melatonin supplement.

So be smart and use science when it makes sense. Modern technology, whether it's cars, smartphones, computers, Twitter, or the X-rays you get from medical diagnostic imaging, can help you be healthier and happier, so don't shun it altogether.

9. Keep a Clear Head

How many times have you found yourself eating lunch while simultaneously reading a blog post, listening to a podcast, and answering an e-mail? How many times have you been at the gym, riding your bike, or even taking a relaxing bath and found yourself texting, tweeting, or Facebooking? How many times have you found yourself listening to the radio, driving a car, and taking quick glances at the e-mails on your smartphone—all at the same time?

This kind of multitasking not only gives you fuzzy thinking, poor creative production, sensory overload, neurotransmitter depletion, and chronic stress, but it's also downright dangerous. If you've ever tried to build a fire while camping, gut a deer after a kill-shot, or fight off an assailant, then you know that these activities require intense concentration.

Yet we actually train our minds to constantly be distracted and full of fleeting, random thoughts, tasks, and ideas. There's new evidence suggesting that this is the equivalent of training ourselves to develop a unique kind of attention deficit disorder.

Multitasking also creates decision fatigue that prevents your brain's cortex from allowing you to tap into high levels of physical performance—thus causing you to fatigue faster.

You simply won't thrive and survive if you're always distracted, so focus on one task at a time, and be mentally and physically present, especially when it matters most—such as during a workout or when you're with your family. If you need to, keep a pen and pad handy, assign specific tasks to specific days, and use all the other productivity techniques I give you in chapter 20.

Plan wisely for the future, but live in the present with a clear head.

10. Don't Fret

I'm going to talk about my wife again. I'm jealous of her. She doesn't think about her carbohydrate, protein, and fat ratios. Ever. With an almost childlike innocence, she simply goes out to the garden or opens the refrigerator or a cupboard and eats real food when she's hungry. She wouldn't know what a gram of carbohydrate looked like if her life depended on it. By contrast, things like ketosis, protein toxicity, or oxidation are always lingering in the back of my mind.

Jessa doesn't plan her workouts or write things down in a calendar. When she feels the urge to exercise, she grabs our dog, Blitzen, and heads out on the trails. When she's sore or tired, she doesn't "push through." By contrast, I adhere to a rigid schedule that pressures me to complete the day's workout no matter how I feel or what signals my body is sending me.

She doesn't set an alarm, use a sleep mask, cover up ambient noise with an app, or take sleep supplements. She just goes to bed when she's tired and gets up when her body feels rested and refreshed. By contrast, I wear my nerdy blue-light-blocking glasses at night, feel guilty if I'm not in bed within several hours of sunset, and pop out of bed wide awake at the same time each morning.

Is this simply because we're hardwired differently? I doubt it. Watch children who haven't yet been tainted by life stress, by peer pressure to look better, or by diet brainwashing, and they're the same way—they eat, sleep, play, and exercise largely when they feel like it.

I'm not arguing against the value of self-control, knowledge, and self-discipline. But I do suspect that if we stay on the paths we're on, my wife will probably outlive me and have a higher quality of life in the process.

So my goal is to fret less and live more. This may not make me a better athlete per se, but being an athlete isn't how I pay the bills. As I've said before, the last thing I want written in my obituary or on my tombstone is, "He Was Really Good at Exercising."

What about you?

These rules are very similar to my friend Mark Sisson's Primal rules. They include:

- Avoid chronic cardio.
- Barefoot is best.
- Chronic stress is to be avoided.
- Ditch grains, refined sugar, and processed seed oils.

- Expose yourself to stressors.
- Fat is good for you.
- Get sun exposure.
- Hunger is normal.
- Train with intensity.
- Eat mostly plants and animals.
- Keep up with your social relationships.
- Lift heavy things.
- Mind your carb intake.
- Play more.
- Run really fast sometimes.
- Sit less.
- Challenge your mind.
- Walk a lot.
- Prioritize sleep.

You can read Mark's Primal rules in more detail at BeyondTrainingBook.com/AZGuide.

I wrote the draft of this chapter while speeding down a highway in the passenger seat of my Toyota on the way to compete in Ironman Canada, with an EMF-blocking pad under my MacBook, techno music pumping through my earbuds, and a Wi-Fi hotspot device just two feet from my head.

So I'm chuckling to myself as I reflect on the fact that I've penned a chapter on ancestral living while living quite un-ancestrally.

But we're about to pull into a truck stop for a break.

And when we do, I'll reach into a paper bag in the back of the car, grab a ripe, juicy tomato I plucked from our garden before we hit the road, and bite into its luscious flesh, wiping the juice from my chin as I step out of the car and into the warm sunshine. I'll grab my twin boys and go exploring in the lush trees behind the gas station. Maybe we'll chase a rabbit or quail. I'll take a long, lazy, lunging stretch. I'll kiss my wife. I'll take a few deep breaths of the fresh air being wind-whipped up the hills behind the highway.

Then we'll get back in the car and keep driving, but from those few fleeting moments, I'll feel my ancestral roots thriving for hours afterward. Will you?

Additional resources, helpful links, scientific references, and surprise bonuses for this chapter are available at BeyondTrainingBook.com/Chapter23. Enjoy.

CHAPTER 24

Closing Thoughts and Additional Resources

Closing Thoughts

Whether due to our innate pursuit of perfection, our constant quest to reach the next milestone, or our lofty aspirations to ascend our own personal Mount Everest, it is incredibly easy to develop a passion for extreme exercise and endurance sports that keeps drawing us into more and more training, WOD after WOD, obstacle after obstacle, race after race, month after month, and year after year.

That's part of the thrill of endurance competition—the chance to satisfy the thirst for battle, for conquest, for adventure, and for the thrill of the chase. But at some point, every endurance athlete has a "come to Jesus" moment when we realize that the sport we love can actually harm our bodies.

When that moment comes, you have two choices: either keep doing what you're doing until you self-combust, or move on to the next chapter in your life. Some very good endurance athletes, such as Mark Sisson, author of the *Mark's Daily Apple* website, who is respected for his wealth of knowledge on health, fitness, and nutrition, simply move on to the next chapter, forgoing hardcore, masochistic sports altogether.

Countless other individuals continue to push forward and punish themselves until they are forced to quit by heart attacks, hip replacements, or pure biological burnout.

But what if you had a third choice? The choice to defy the commonly accepted, orthodox methods of endurance training? The choice to stop throwing ourselves like eggs at a wall until we finally crack? The choice to pursue the ultimate combination of health and performance while continuing to participate in the sports we love?

Showing you that a viable third choice exists was my goal in writing this book. I wanted you to know that if you do things the right way, you can keep competing in the sport you love without completely destroying your body.

Now take a deep breath before you keep reading.

Notice that I said without *completely* destroying your body. Deep down, I doubt any of us thinks that a daily battle with the hot pavement, muggy gym, joint-crushing barbell, or thrashing waves is truly healthy. I doubt any of us thinks that puking into a garbage can bleary-eyed at 5 a.m. at the CrossFit box is truly healthy, or that "running from a bear" for twelve hours during an Ironman triathlon is truly healthy.

But discomfort, aging, illness, injury, and death are part of being human. Life includes significant doses of sickness, injury, suffering, and pain. Our short existence on this planet is a package deal that includes both good times and bad times—and we must embrace that reality in its entirety. You must accept the fact that you're not always going to feel good and that you're never going to be perfectly healthy if doing something like competing in Ironman triathlons truly makes you happy.

While it would be foolish to think that you can somehow biohack and pill-pop your way to immortality, you can still take small steps to mitigate the damage you're doing to your body. You have already started by reading this book. You can review the previous chapter, "Ten Rules for Becoming an Ancestral Athlete," and implement those rules to find a sane balance between achieving lofty physical performance goals, being healthy, enjoying life, and accepting the reality that you'll never completely insulate yourself from damage.*

After all, life is short. Use your body. Play hard. But play smart, too. Your heart, muscles, joints, skin, mind, and grandkids will thank you.

I want to thank you for joining me on this journey of discovery and for taking the deep dive into finding out what your body is truly capable of when you care for it properly.

Remember: You and I share a secret. It's not the insanity or the masochism that seduces us into pushing our bodies to the max. It's the adventure. The escape. The chance to be a superhero, even if just for a fleeting day. And that's what keeps us coming back, workout after workout, race after race, month after month, and year after year.

Let's just do it the right way, shall we? Let's think beyond training.

*Right now I am headed to the local heart clinic for a full cardiac stress test to see what ten years of extreme exercise has done to my heart. You can read the hidden chapter section of this book at BeyondTrainingBook.com/heart for the results.

Training Plans, Meal Plans, and Additional Resources

I've given a host of practical examples throughout the past several hundred pages, such as the Tale of Two Triathletes in chapter 1, the Forty Easy Meals for Busy Athletes in chapter 11, and the day of brain-hacking in chapter 21.

Initially, I thought it would be great to take all the concepts in this book and roll them into one easy daily training plan that you could simply tear out and stick on your refrigerator. But a detailed daily training plan with workouts, recovery protocols, biohacks, meals, and supplements would require hundreds of additional pages—and there just isn't enough space (or trees) for that. Furthermore, each of us has different goals, needs, fitness levels, and access to the many tools, resources, gear, foods, supplements, and activities I've highlighted in this book.

So instead I've opted to turn to technology to provide you with detailed, downloadable training plans, meal plans, and additional resources. On the resource web page at the end of this chapter, you will find the following training and meal plans:

- 24-Week Ancestral Athlete Ironman Triathlon Training Plan, based on HIIT training and quality over quantity

- 24-Week Polarized Ironman Triathlon Training Plan, based on smart aerobic training and high volume

- 20-Week Ancestral Athlete Marathon Training Plan, based on HIIT training and quality over quantity

- 20-Week Polarized Marathon Training Plan, based on smart aerobic training and high volume

- 12-Week Detox and Adrenal Reboot Plan, based on the concepts discussed in chapter 8

- 12-Week *Beyond Training* Meal Plan that uses the fueling concepts discussed in part 3

The plans are available in downloadable PDF format and on a slick, dynamic online TrainingPeaks platform. This platform allow your plans to be synced to your phone, computer, calendar, heart rate monitor, power meter, and any other devices you use. Incidentally, TrainingPeaks is the online platform that I use to coach all my clients and athletes.

Of course, as the proud owner of this book, you'll need a special coupon code in order to access these Training Plans for free. That code (drumroll, please) is BEYONDTRAININGVIP.

You'll find the full audio version of this book for your listening pleasure at BenGreenfieldFitness.com/btaudible.

Finally, you can get your bonus hidden chapters, bonus videos, and a constantly growing list of free extras for this book by visiting BeyondTrainingBook.com/HiddenChapters:

Username: BeyondTrainingVIP

Password: hiddenchapters

What's Next . . .

I've been asked what more I can do to help people once they've read this book. So allow me share what I call my "rebel yell." Ready? Here we go.

My name is Ben Greenfield.

I love getting fit, feeling good about the way my body looks, and fulfilling my deep-seated drive to live life to the fullest by achieving difficult feats of physical performance. But I was fed up with feeling like crap from all the extreme exercising, strange foods, constant stress and soreness, and worry about the toll my ridiculous lifestyle was taking on my body. So I created a way of training, eating, and living that is perfectly healthy and natural, but still allows me to look and feel my best and perform at my peak capabilities.

And then I wrote this book so that you could, too.

But what's next? What's Ben Greenfield going to be when he finally grows up?

Great question. (And by the way, I'll put a fantastic resource on this chapter's resource web page with a formula for creating your own "rebel yell.")

While I'll keep writing articles, keep my SuperhumanCoach.com mentorship program open, and hopefully even host more live events, I don't necessarily see this book as my "swan song," so to speak.

Instead, in my wildest dreams (on a perfectly average day), what I ultimately want to do is provide you with a single, convenient portal that gives you all the lifestyle solutions, coaching, consulting, foods, supplements, gear, technology, biohacks, knowledge, and education you need to live life to the fullest while pursuing the ultimate combination of health and performance, and I want to be able to offer you my expertise and support there inside that portal.

I want you to be able to live life at whatever screamingly fast pace makes you happy and fulfilled, and I want you to feel good the whole time you're doing it.

What is this feeling called, and how do you get it 24/7?

I simply call this feeling . . . Nature. And you can learn more about the Nature brand at GreenfieldFitnessSystems.com. I guarantee you'll like what you find there, and I guarantee I'll be there to help you every step of the way in your journey to go Beyond Training.

Additional resources, helpful links, scientific references, websites, and surprise bonuses for this chapter are available at BeyondTrainingBook.com/Chapter24. Enjoy.

FIGURE CREDITS

Figure 2-1. Adapted from *The Science of Sport*. Retrieved from www. sportsscientists.com

Figure 2-2. Adapted from *Journal of Nutrition and Metabolism* (2010), available at Open Beta, an Open Access Biomedical Image Search Engine. Retrieved from http://openi.nlm.nih.gov/detailedresult.php?img=3005844_JNUME2010-905612.009&query=atp turnover&fields=all&favor=none&it=none&sub=none&uniq=1&sp=none&coll=none&req=4&npos=17&prt=

Table 2-2. Adapted from "Intervals, Thresholds, and Long Slow Distance: the Role of Intensity and Duration in Endurance Training" in *Sportsci.org*. Retrieved from www.sportsci.org/2009/ss.htm

Figure 3-1. Adapted from "The Pareto Principle: 5 Ways to Have More Time and Be More Successful" in *Love My Life Right Now*. Retrieved from http://lmlrn.com/the-pareto-principle-have-more-time-and-be-more-successful/

Figure 3-2. Adapted from "HIIT vs. Continuous Endurance Training: Battle of the Aerobic Titans" in *Idea: Health & Fitness Organization*. Retrieved from www.ideafit.com/fitness-library/hiit-vs-continuous-endurance-training-battle-of-the-aerobic-titans

Figure 4-3. Adapted from "Scientific Research Validates Holosync's Benefits" in *Centerpointe Research Center*. Retrieved from www.centerpointe.com/articles/articles-research

Figure 4-4. Adapted from "Achieve Effortless Meditation with Binaural Beats" in *Clear Mind Meditation Techniques*. Retrieved from www.clear-mind-meditation-techniques.com/binaural-beats-for-meditation.html

Table 5-1. Adapted from "Comparison of Normalized Maximum Aerobic Capacity and Body Composition of Sumo Wrestlers to Athletes in Combat and Other Sports" in *Journal of Sports Science and Medicine*. Retrieved from www.jssm.org/combat/1/3/v5combat-3.pdf

Table 5-2. Adapted from *Weight Training for Triathlon: The Ultimate Guide*, by Ben Greenfield (Price World Publishing, 2012).

Figure 5-1. Adapted from "Stretching Makes You Weaker (Sometimes That's a Good Thing)" in *Wold Fitness Notebook*. Retrieved from http://woldfitness.com/2013/02/stretching-makes-you-weaker-sometimes-thats-a-good-thing/

Figure 5-2. Detail. Adapted from "Multiple Sclerosis" in *MedlinePlus*. Retrieved from www.nlm.nih.gov/medlineplus/multiplesclerosis.html

Figure 5-3. Adapted from *Weight Training for Triathlon: The Ultimate Guide*, by Ben Greenfield (Price World Publishing, 2012).

Figure 5-8. Adapted from "The Human Balance System" in *Vestibular Disorders Association*. Retrieved from http://vestibular.org/understanding-vestibular-disorder/human-balance-system

Figure 5-9. Adapted from "Approaching Epidemic: Brain Damage from Mobile Phone Radiation" in *Mercola*. Retrieved from http://articles.mercola.com/sites/articles/archive/2009/09/03/Brain-Damage-From-Mobile-Phone-Radiation.aspx

Figures 6-1–6-4. Adapted from "Recovery from Training: A Brief Review" in *The Association of Rowing Coaches, South Africa*. Retrieved from http://arcrsa.blogspot.com/2011/05/recovery-from-training.html

Figure 6-5. Adapted from "Satellite Cells in Skeletal Muscle Proliferate and Regeneration" in *Doctors Gates*. Retrieved from http://doctorsgates.blogspot.com/2011/02/satellite-cells-in-skeletal-muscle.html

Figure 6-6. Adapted from "A Plateau Is a High Form of Flattery" in *Daniel James Fitness Blog*. Retrieved from http://danieljamesfitnessblog.com/a-plateau-is-a-high-form-of-flattery/

Figures 7-3 and 7-4. Adapted from "Evidence of Parasympathetic Hyperactivity in Functionally Overreached Athletes" in *Medicine & Science in Sports & Exercise*. Retrieved from http://journals.lww.com/acsm-msse/pages/default.aspx

Figure 7-5. Adapted from "Help! I Want to Feel Better" in *Mind Body Spirit Center*. Retrieved from http://drsharonnorling.com/health-report/

Figure 7-7. Adapted from "The Profile of Mood States (POMS)" in *Measuremental*. Retrieved from http://measuremental.com/poms.html

Figure 7-10. Adapted from "Fatigue? Weight Gain? Depression? Maybe It's Your Thyroid" in *Vreeland Clinic: Science and Nature, Balanced for Health*. Retrieved from http://thevreelandclinic.wordpress.com/2011/01/14/fatigue-weight-gain-depression-maybe-its-your-thyroid/

Figure 7-12. Primary sources for data:

Shores, M. M., A. M. Matsumoto, K. L. Sloan, and D. R. Kivlahan. "Low Serum Testosterone and Mortality in Male Veterans." *Archives of Internal Medicine*. 2006 Aug 14;166(15):1660–5.

Laughlin G. A., E. Barrett-Connor, and J. Bergstrom. "Low Serum Testosterone and Mortality in Older Men." *Journal of Clinical Endocrinology & Metabolism*. 2008 Jan;93(1):68–75.

Shores, M. M., V. M. Moceri, D. A. Gruenwals, et al. "Low Testosterone Is Associated with Decreased Function and Increased Mortality Risk: A Preliminary Study of Men in a Geriatric Rehabilitation Unit." *Journal of the American Geriatrics Society*. 2004;52: 2077–81.

Figure 7-13. Adapted from "Female Salivary Testosterone: Measurement, Challenges and Applications" in *Intech*. Retrieved from www.intechopen.com/books/steroids-from-physiology-to-clinical-medicine/female-salivary-testosterone-measurement-challenges-and-applications

Figure 7-14. Adapted from "Bio-identical Hormones: What is Cortisol?" in *Amy Brenner, MD & Associates, LLC*. Retrieved from www.dramybrenner.com/bhrt_cortisol.htm

Figure 7-15. Adapted from "Heart Rate Variability Analysis Scientific Background" in *Biocom Technologies*. Retrieved from www.biocomtech.com/hrvscientific

Figure 9-1. Adapted from "The Mind Body Connection" in *My Holistic Healing*. Retrieved from www.my-holistic-healing.com/mind-body-connection.html. Originally published in *Ageless Body, Timeless Mind*, by Deepak Chopra.

Figure 9-2. Adapted from "Thinking from the Heart–Heart Brain Science" in *Applied Consciousness*. Retrieved from http://appliedconsciousnessintl.com/thinking-from-the-heart-heart-brain-science. Originally published in "Speaking from the Heart," *Edge Science* (No. 6/Jan/Mar 2011). Adaptation used with permission of the Institute of HeartMath, Boulder Creek, Calif.

Table 10-1. Source: National Sleep Foundation.

Figure 10-1. Adapted from "Human Body Temperature" in *Wikipedia*. Retrieved from http://en.wikipedia.org/wiki/Human_body_temperature

Figure 10-2. Adapted from "Achieve Effortless Meditation with Binaural Beats" in *Clear Mind Meditation Techniques*. Retrieved from www.clear-mind-meditation-techniques.com/binaural-beats-for-meditation.html

Figure 10-4. Adapted from "The Five Stages of Sleep & the Journey Through the Night" in *End Your Sleep Deprivation*. Retrieved from www.end-your-sleep-deprivation.com/stages-of-sleep.html

Figure 13-3. Adapted from "Fat Burning: Using Body Fat Instead of Carbohydrates as Fuel" in *Peak Performance*. Retrieved from www.pponline.co.uk/encyc/fat-burning-using-body-fat-instead-of-carbohydrates-as-fuel-40844

Figure 13-4. Adapted from infographic by Trish McAlaster in *How to Run Fast*. Originally accompanied Alex Hutchinson's article "Carbo-loading: Is it the key the day before the marathon?" in *The Globe and Mail*. Retrieved from http://how2runfast.com/post/16346068994/how-much-can-you-carbo-load-infographic-this

Figure 14-1. Adapted from *One2One Nutrition*. Retrieved from www.one2onenutrition.co.uk/Images/Newsletter-photos/Metabolic-Typing-Steroid-Hormone-Pathway.jpg

Figure 15-2. Adapted from *Windy City CrossFit*. Retrieved from www.windycitycrossfit.com/.a/6a00e39823747b88330134890332f5970c-800wi

Table 15-1. Adapted from "Fodmap Diet." Retrieved from www.docstoc.com/docs/124151863/Foods-suitable-on-low-fodmap-diet

Figure 15-3. Adapted from Feb/Mar 2013 *Townsend Letter*. Retrieved from www.townsendletter.com/FebMarch2013/Fig1ibs.jpg

Figure 15-4. Adapted from "The Hidden Causes of Heartburn and GERD" in *Chris Kresser: Health for the 21st Century*. Retrieved from http://chriskresser.com/the-hidden-causes-of-heartburn-and-gerd

Figure 15-6. Adapted from "Detoxification" in *Houston Health & Wellness Center*. Retrieved from www.healthandwellnessctr.com/detoxification/

Figure 18-1. Source: Geneva Associates.

Table 18-1. Adapted from *Nurse Jon's Glutathione Disease Cure*. Retrieved from www.glutathionediseasecure.com/images/plastic-coding-graphics-completed-PNG-1.jpg

Table 18-2. Source: www.ewg.org/foodnews/summary.php

Figure 18-2. Courtesy of Jayson Calton, PhD, and Mira Calton, CN, authors of *Rich Food Poor Food* (www.caltonnutrition.com/rich-food-poor-food/)

Figure 21-1. Adapted from "Fatigue Is a Brain-Derived Emotion That Regulates the Exercise Behavior to Ensure the Protection of Whole Body Homeostasis" in *Frontiers in Physiology*. Retrieved from www.frontiersin.org/Striated_Muscle_Physiology/10.3389/fphys.2012.00082/full

Figure 21-3. Adapted from http://25.media.tumblr.com/tumblr_matg3vsnVT1qmsda8o1_500.jpg

Figure 21-4. Adapted from "Chemical Synapse" in *Wikipedia*. Retrieved from http://en.wikipedia.org/wiki/Chemical_synapse

Figure 21-5. Adapted from "How Antidepressants Work" in *HowStuffWorks*. Retrieved from http://science.howstuffworks.com/life/antidepressant2.htm

Figure 21-7. Adapted from "Multiple Sclerosis" in *MedlinePlus*. Retrieved from www.nlm.nih.gov/medlineplus/multiplesclerosis.html

Figure 21-9. Adapted from "Hypothalamic-Pituitary-Adrenal Axis" in *Wikipedia*. Retrieved from http://en.wikipedia.org/wiki/Hpa_axis

INDEX